Joseph Augustus Seiss

The Evangelical Psalmist

A collection of tunes and hymns for use in congregational and social worship

Joseph Augustus Seiss

The Evangelical Psalmist
A collection of tunes and hymns for use in congregational and social worship

ISBN/EAN: 9783337290375

Printed in Europe, USA, Canada, Australia, Japan

Cover: Foto ©Lupo / pixelio.de

More available books at **www.hansebooks.com**

THE
Evangelical Psalmist:

A COLLECTION OF
TUNES AND HYMNS

FOR USE IN
CONGREGATIONAL AND SOCIAL WORSHIP.

Venite, Exultemus Domino.

PHILADELPHIA:
LINDSAY & BLAKISTON.
1860.

Entered according to act of Congress, in the year 1859, by
LINDSAY & BLAKISTON,
in the Clerk's Office of the District Court of the United States for the Eastern District of Pennsylvania.

STEREOTYPED BY L. JOHNSON & CO.
PHILADELPHIA.

TABLE OF CONTENTS.

	PAGES
PREFACE—Suggestions—Directions to Singers..	3–8
HYMNS FOR THE COMMENCEMENT OF WORSHIP	9–31
Adoration and Praise	9–17
Invocation	17–31
GOD—His Being, Attributes, Works, and Providence..	32–48
CHRIST—His Divine Glory and Incarnation	49–52
His Nativity (Christmas Hymns)	53–57
His Names, Life, Character, and Offices	58–64
His Sufferings, Death, and Resurrection	65–77
His Ascension, Exaltation, and Intercession	78–83
Redemption through Him	84–95
THE HOLY SPIRIT	96–98
INVITATIONS AND WARNINGS (Gospel Call)	99–123
CHRISTIAN EXPERIENCE—Penitential	124–145
Submission, Faith, Joy, and Hope	146–170
Trials and Temptations	171–183
Backslidings and Declensions	184–186
Holy Aspirations	187–200
Christian Fellowship and Love	201–205
Faith and Works—Love to Christ	206–210
Anticipations of Heaven	211–225
MEANS OF GRACE—The Word	226–230
Baptism—Lord's Supper	231–243
The Ministry—Church and Kingdom	244–266
The Lord's Day—Prayer—Angels	266–281
DEPRESSIONS AND REVIVALS	281–284
MISSIONS—CHARITIES AND REFORMS	284–293
SPECIAL OCCASIONS—Times and Seasons	294–306
Sickness—Death—Judgment—Eternity	307–325
DISMISSIONS AND DOXOLOGIES	326–332
CHANTS	334–379
ANTHEMS	380–318
INDEXES—Of Subjects	419–422
Of First Lines	423–431
Of Tunes (Alphabetical and Metrical)	432–435
Of Numbers to Hymns	436–438

PREFACE.

This Book is meant to be a *Manual of Sacred Music*, adapted to the hymns in use in Lutheran Churches. It is designed to meet the wants of choirs, choristers, families, and congregations, in the department of psalmody. It is a collection of tunes, printed with the hymns to which they may be appropriately sung. It is not designed to supersede the hymn-book, but to be used in connection with it. Changes have indeed been made. The necessities of the case required a new arrangement of the hymns. Some hymns have been omitted; others not in the hymn-book have been inserted; some have been slightly shortened, and others restored to their original forms. But these changes are not such as at all to prevent the joint use of the two books, or to render a separate hymn-book necessary where this is used. Each hymn is still accompanied with its number the same as in the hymn-book, and a table of these numbers, as compared with those of the new arrangement, is given among the indexes. By these means a hymn may be readily announced from this book to be turned to in the hymn-book, and one announced from the hymn-book easily found here, without referring to the list of first lines. There are therefore no practical difficulties of any serious moment to prevent the introduction of this book in connection with the hymn-book.

Choirs will here find more available music, and generally of a superior quality for church-purposes, than in any of the ordinary collections. The selections have been made with the aid of twenty or more choristers, organists, amateurs, and professors of music, in different sections of our Church, and embrace the best sacred melodies of practical value known to the compilers.

In adapting the tunes to the hymns, great respect has been paid to the common Christian sense, so far as it has assigned certain music to particular words and sentiments. Care, however, has been exercised to exclude non-churchly and effeminate tunes and mere quartette music, by which our psalmody has been quite too much enfeebled. Two tunes of the same metre, as far as practicable, have been placed on each opening of the book,—the one major and the other minor, or the one very plain and familiar and the other somewhat more elaborate and artistic,—in order to furnish a choice to the singer.

The book itself is meant to contribute to the important work of improving our worship in the department of holy song. That improvement in this direction is greatly needed, is too obvious to be questioned; and that a work of this sort, put into our choirs, families, and church-pews, would do much towards the desired amendment, is admitted by prominent denominations in this and other countries, and has been demonstrated in the experience of many congregations in which the expedient has been tried.

If only our choirs and the leaders of our church-music adopt this book, should they follow it no further than their own taste may dictate, the result will be decidedly beneficial. To such it is therefore very particularly commended.

In the family, also, it is expected that a good work will be done by the introduction of such a book. It will serve to connect the music of the Church with that of the Home. It will put the church-tunes in the hands of the young people, to be learned and sung in the family, and around the fireside, as now they seldom are, or can be. Multitudes of tongues now dumb in our sanctuaries will thus be loosed to join in singing praises to the God of all grace.

An important feature of the book is the appendage of a large collection of *Chants and Anthems*, accommodated to the Church seasons and all the necessities likely to arise where it is intended to serve. *Chanting* was the original form of Church song. The Savior himself engaged in it, when he sung with his disciples. It was doubtless in the eye of the apostles when they gave directions to Christians to sing psalms and to admonish one another in spiritual songs. It is the most ancient, the most scriptural, and the most churchly form of sacred music. It is best fitted for purposes of devotion. It is fully adapted to a clear enunciation of the words, and the subordination of music to thought. It precludes display. It leaves the mind free to the full impression of what is uttered, and is peculiarly favorable to an unconstrained outpouring of the heart. It is the most simple form in which many voices may unite in the simultaneous musical utterance of the same words. Children readily acquire it, and delight in it. Nor is there a more interesting part of worship, either for families, Sunday-schools, or Churches.

It is therefore thought to be a great recommendation of this work that it furnishes such ample facilities for a more general use of this form of devotional exercise. For a number of years have the editors been employed in its preparation. No pains have been spared to produce a book adapted to the need, and in all respects worthy of the favorable regard, of the Churches. It is the joint-product of three Lutheran clergymen, assisted by numerous ministers, laymen, musicians, and others, who have shown a deep interest in the enterprise, which is in no respect a matter of speculation or pecuniary profit. The low rate at which the book is sold (scarcely exceeding the cost of the flimsiest and most worthless of the ordinary music-books) will require large sales and a long time to repay what has been expended upon it.

As to the intrinsic merits of the book, the Church has had important testimony beyond the character and reputation of those concerned in its compilation. A special committee of the Lutheran Board of Publication examined it in manuscript, and officially reported it to be a book well prepared and in all respects such as ought to be given to our people. A large number of the proof-sheets were also submitted to the last General Synod, whose special committee on the subject reported favorably upon the work, and brought in resolutions for the sanction of the same; although, at the desire of some of the brethren, the final adoption of the report was postponed.

Of course, not all will be entirely satisfied with what has been done. It would be impossible to construct a book in which all could fully concur. A book of tunes and hymns for the Church is especially liable to exceptions and conflicting criticism. There is consequently no hope that this publication will please every one. But it is expected that, in its leading features, it will meet all reasonable demands. Though it may embrace defects,—which are always more easily detected than remedied,—yet, on the whole, it is a work which claims to be in advance of any collection of hymns or music yet offered to our Churches in this country.

With thanks to the friends who have aided in its preparation, the compilers now issue it, praying that God, whom it is meant to honor, may sanction it with his blessing, and direct its destiny for good.

SUGGESTIONS.

In the hope that our pastors and people will be disposed to co-operate in the effort to promote *congregational* as distinguished from mere *choir* singing, it may be important to submit a few suggestions as to the mode in which their aid can be most efficiently rendered.

The place at which to begin is, of course, the Family, which God has ordained to be the nursery of all that is good. Singing in the home, particularly in worship, is to be commended for its own sake, but still more in its relation to the singing in the sanctuary. If all devout people, possessing the necessary gifts, would employ them upon the songs of Zion in their families, they would need less prompting to lift up their voices in the house of God. Let there be sacred singing in the family; let the children be encouraged to learn the Church tunes and to become familiar with the principal chants: it will help to make the household blessed, and lay the foundation for a glorious improvement in the musical exercises of the public congregation.

The Sunday-school presents another important opening for effort in the same direction. In these gatherings of children, singing is necessarily one of the principal exercises,—at any rate, for the younger classes. They delight in it more than in any thing else. They are prepared to join in it from their early infancy; and, if rightly directed, nothing is more profitable. Here, then, let the songs of the Church be introduced and accurately taught. Many of the tunes in this book, and most of the chants may be quite as easily learned as the ditties which usually constitute the first lessons of our infant classes. They are, moreover, free from bad associations, much more effective for impressing devotional sentiment upon the young heart; and acquaintance with them will be a real preparation of the pupil for duties awaiting it in the great congregation. It would also be a valuable gain every way if our children, in learning the hymns of the Church, could at the same time be taught the tunes to which they are to be sung. A little attention in this particular would yield the happiest results. Let those, therefore, who have charge of our Sunday-schools, and of the music of those schools, lend their aid, and not withhold the vast influence which it is within their power to contribute in furthering the ends contemplated in this book.

An additional expedient, and more directly effective, is the calling of congregational meetings to practice the music of the Church. These may be held as often as once a week for most of the year, and should be under the supervision of the minister or a committee of the Church appointed for the purpose. The pastor should be present at such meetings, to give them the necessary encouragement and solemnity, and to prevent them from degenerating into mere giddy singing-schools. If he himself should be able to lead in the exercises, it would be all the better; if not, the leadership ought to be given to the chorister or organist of the church, or to some other competent person employed for the purpose. The choir should be especially invited to give their co-operation, and also all the singers of the congregation. Attention should at first be confined to but a few tunes, and those should be carefully practiced in connection with the hymns to be sung on the following Sunday. A plan similar to this has been tried in the Church of one of the compilers, with marked advantage. A large number of persons thus become well prepared to take part in the singing, and to give life and character to that delightful part of our public worship. Perhaps the most desirable and efficient organization of such efforts would be the formation of a general *choral society* in the congregation. Good congregational singing certainly deserves all that may thus be expended upon it. The great Luther says, "With those who neglect the music of the Church, as all fanatics do, I cannot be satisfied; for music is a gift of God, by which Satan may be repulsed and sorrow driven away. Next to theology, I give it the highest place and honor. The youth should be trained in the use of it; a schoolmaster is deficient without skill in it; and no young men should be ordained to the ministry without having been well exercised in the schools where it is taught."

Let the experiment, therefore, be earnestly made as here suggested. Success may be limited at first; but every good thing requires labor, and perseverance will soon overcome all obstacles.

DIRECTIONS TO SINGERS.

The music in this book is all harmonized for four parts, though printed in condensed score, on two staves.

The Treble Clef or Staff contains the *air* or *soprano* part, and the *alto*, which may easily be distinguished by the stems of the notes turning contrary ways; those of the *air* turning upwards, and those of the *alto* turning downwards. Where this is not the case, the lowest notes always contain the *alto* part.

The Bass Clef or Staff contains both the *bass* and *tenor* parts, the *bass* being the lowest notes, with the stems usually turned downwards, and the *tenor* in the upper notes, with the stems for the most part turned upwards.

But few marks or directions have been given for the rendering of the music. Dynamic variations should spring from the sentiment of the words, rather than be arbitrarily attached, as is usual, to the tunes. It is therefore left to singers to study and observe the hymns, that they may modulate the expression to the sense of what is to be sung. It was part of the original plan of the compilers to print dynamic characters with each line or stanza of the hymns; but it was found so to encumber and cramp the page, that they were compelled to abandon it. Only let singers and players enter into the spirit of the worship, and seek to render both the words and the music with the distinctness and animation of Christian men and women, and not as "a parcel of anchorites wailing in the tombs and catacombs," and very little else will be wanting. The remarks once made by Dr. Watts are still very appropriate:—

"It were to be wished that we might not dwell so long on every note, and produce the same syllables to such tiresome extent, with a constant uniformity of time; which disguises the music, and puts the congregation quite out of breath; whereas, if the method of singing were but reformed to a greater speed of pronunciation, we might often enjoy the pleasure of a longer psalm, with less expense of time and breath; and our psalmody would be more agreeable to that of the ancient Churches, more intelligible to others, and more delightful to ourselves."

Evangelical Psalmist

L. M. OLD HUNDREDTH.

1   *A Psalm of Praise.*   44

BEFORE Jehovah's awful throne,
  Ye nations bow with sacred joy:
Know that the Lord is God alone ;
  He can create, and he destroy.

2 His sov'reign pow'r, without our aid,
  Made us of clay, and form'd us men,
And when like wand'ring sheep we stray'd,
  He brought us to his fold again.

3 We are his people, we his care,
  Our souls and all our mortal frame :
What lasting honors shall we rear,
  Almighty Maker, to thy name !

4 We'll crowd thy gates with thankful songs,
  High as the heav'ns our voices raise ;
And earth, with her ten thousand tongues,
  Shall fill thy courts with sounding praise.

5 Wide as the world is thy command,
  Vast as eternity thy love ;
Firm as a rock thy truth must stand,
  When rolling years shall cease to move.

2   *Praise for Divine Blessings.*   598

GREAT God, at whose all-pow'rful call
  At first arose this beauteous frame !
By thee the seasons change, and all
  The changing seasons speak thy name.

2 Thy bounty bids the infant year
  From winter storms recover'd rise ;
When thousand grateful scenes appear,
  Fresh op'ning to our wond'ring eyes.

3 Oh, how delightful 'tis to see
  The earth in vernal beauty drest !
While in each herb, and flower, and tree,
  Thy blooming glories shine confest !

4 Aloft, full beaming, reigns the sun,
  And light and genial heat conveys ;
And, while he leads the seasons on,
  From thee derives his quick'ning rays.

5 Indulgent God ! from ev'ry part
  Thy plenteous blessings largely flow ;
We see, we taste ; let ev'ry heart
  With grateful love and duty glow.

ADORATION AND PRAISE.

C. M. ST. JOHN'S.

1. We sing th' almight-y pow'r of God, Who bade the moun-tains rise, Who spread the flow-ing seas a-broad, And built the lof-ty skies.

3 *Divine Glories.* **60**

WE sing th' almighty pow'r of God,
  Who bade the mountains rise,
Who spread the flowing seas abroad,
  And built the lofty skies.

2 We sing the wisdom that ordain'd
  The sun to rule the day;
The moon shines full at his command,
  And all the stars obey.

3 We sing the goodness of the Lord,
  Who fills the earth with food;
Who form'd his creatures by a word,
  And then pronounced them good.

4 Lord, how thy wonders are display'd,
  Where'er we turn our eyes;
Whether we view the ground we tread,
  Or gaze upon the skies!

5 There's not a plant nor flow'r below,
  But makes thy glories known:
And clouds arise, and tempests blow,
  By order from thy throne.

6 On thee each moment we depend;
  If thou withdraw, we die.
Oh, may we ne'er that God offend,
  Who is forever nigh!

4 *The Glory of God.* **56**

FATHER, how wide thy glory shines!
  How high thy wonders rise!
Known thro' the earth by thousand signs,
  By thousands through the skies.

2 Those mighty orbs proclaim thy power,
  Their motions speak thy skill,
And on the wings of every hour
  We read thy patience still.

3 But when we view thy strange design
  To save rebellious worms,
Our souls are fill'd with awe divine,
  To see what God performs.

4 When sinners break the Father's law,
  Thy dying Son atones;
Oh the dear mysteries of his cross!
  The triumphs of his groans!

5 Now the full glories of the Lamb
  Adorn the heavenly plains;
Sweet cherubs learn Immanuel's name,
  And try their choicest strains.

6 Oh, may I bear some humble part
  In that immortal song;
Wonder and joy shall tune my heart,
  And love command my tongue.

5 *Praise for Divine Goodness.* **45**

YE humble souls, approach your God
  With songs of sacred praise;
For he is good, immensely good,
  And kind are all his ways.

2 All nature owns his guardian care;
  In him we live and move;
But nobler benefits declare
  The wonders of his love.

3 He gave his Son, his only Son,
  To ransom rebel worms;
'Tis here he makes his goodness known
  In its diviner forms.

4 To this dear refuge, Lord, we come;
  On this our hope relies;
A safe defence, a peaceful home,
  When storms of trouble rise.

5 Thine eye beholds with kind regard
  The souls who trust in thee;
Their humble hope thou wilt reward
  With bliss divinely free.

6 Great God, to thine almighty love
  What honors shall we raise!
Not all the raptured songs above
  Can render equal praise.

6   *Father, Son, and Spirit.*   41

FATHER of glory! to thy name
  Immortal praise we give:
Who dost an act of grace proclaim,
  And bid us rebels live.

2 Immortal honor to the Son,
  Who makes thine anger cease:
Our lives he ransom'd with his own,
  And died to make our peace.

3 To thy Almighty Spirit be
  Immortal glory giv'n,
Whose influence brings us near to thee,
  And trains us up for heav'n.

4 Let men, with their united voice,
  Adore th' eternal God,
And spread his honors and their joys
  Through nations far abroad.

5 Let faith, and love, and duty join
  One general song to raise;
Let saints in earth and heaven combine
  In harmony and praise.

7   *Greatness of God.*   52

LONG as I live I'll bless thy name,
  God of eternal love!
My work and joy shall be the same
  In the bright world above.

2 Great is the Lord, his pow'r unknown,
  And let his praise be great;
I'll sing the honors of thy throne,
  Thy works of grace repeat.

3 Thy grace shall dwell upon my tongue;
  And while my lips rejoice,
The men that hear my sacred song
  Shall join their cheerful voice.

4 Fathers to sons shall teach thy name,
  And children learn thy ways;
Ages to come thy truth proclaim,
  And nations sound thy praise.

5 Thy glorious deeds of ancient date,
  Shall through the world be known:
Thine arm of pow'r, thy heav'nly state,
  With public splendor shown.

6 The world is managed by thy hands,
  Thy saints are ruled by love;
And thine eternal kingdom stands,
  Though rocks and hills remove.

8   *God in His Works.*   58

HAIL, great Creator, wise and good!
  To thee our songs we raise.
Nature, through all her various scenes,
  Invites us to thy praise.

2 At morning, noon, and ev'ning mild,
  Fresh wonders strike our view;
And while we gaze, our hearts exult
  With transports ever new.

3 Thy glory beams in ev'ry star
  Which gilds the gloom of night,
And decks the smiling face of morn
  With rays of cheerful light.

4 The lofty hill, the humble lawn,
  With countless beauties shine;
The silent grove, the awful shade,
  Proclaim thy power divine.

5 Great nature's God, still may these scenes
  Our serious hours engage!
Still may our grateful hearts consult
  Thy works' instructive page!

6 And while in all thy wondrous works
  Thy varied love we see,
Still may the contemplation lead
  Our hearts, O God, to thee!

9   *Divine Glories.*   51

INDULGENT Father! how divine,
  How bright thy bounties are!
Through nature's ample round they shine,
  Thy goodness to declare.

2 But in the nobler work of grace,
  What sweeter mercy smiles
In my benign Redeemer's face,
  And ev'ry fear beguiles.

3 Such wonders, Lord, while I survey,
  To thee my thanks shall rise,
When morning ushers in the day,
  Or ev'ning veils the skies.

4 When glimm'ring life resigns its flame,
  Thy praise shall tune my breath;
The sweet remembrance of thy name
  Shall gild the shades of death.

5 But, oh! how blest my song shall rise,
  When freed from feeble clay,
And all thy glories meet mine eyes
  In one eternal day.

6 Not seraphs, who resound thy name,
  Through you ethereal plains,
Shall glow with a diviner flame,
  Or raise sublimer strains.

ADORATION AND PRAISE.

C. M. P. MERIBAH.

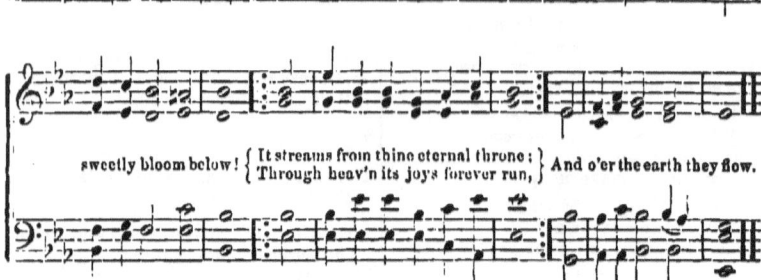

1. My God, thy boundless love I praise: How bright on high its glories blaze, How sweetly bloom below! { It streams from thine eternal throne; Through heav'n its joys forever run, } And o'er the earth they flow.

10 *Praise for Divine Love.* **33**

MY GOD, thy boundless love I praise:
  How bright on high its glories blaze,
    How sweetly bloom below!
It streams from thine eternal throne;
Through heav'n its joys forever run,
  And o'er the earth they flow.

2 'Tis love that paints the purple morn,
And bids the clouds, in air upborne,
  Their genial drops distil:
In ev'ry vernal beam it glows,
And breathes in ev'ry gale that blows,
  And glides in ev'ry rill.

3 It robes in cheerful green the ground,
And pours its flow'ry beauties round,
  Whose sweets perfume the gale:
Its bounties richly spread the plain,
The blushing fruit, the golden grain,
  And smile on ev'ry vale.

4 But in thy gospel see it shine,
With grace and glories more divine,
  Proclaiming sins forgiv'n.
There faith, bright cherub, points the way
To realms of everlasting day,
  And opens all her heav'n.

5 Then let the love, that makes me blest,
With cheerful praise inspire my breast,
  And ardent gratitude;

And all my thoughts and passions tend
To thee, my Father and my Friend,
  My soul's eternal good.

11 *God Exalted.* **57**

PARENT of good! thy works of might,
  I trace with wonder and delight;
    Thy name is all divine.
There's naught in earth or sea or air,
Or heav'n itself, that's good or fair,
  But what is wholly thine.

2 Immensely high thy glories rise;
They strike my soul with sweet surprise
  And sacred pleasure yield;
An ocean wide without a bound,
Where ev'ry noble wish is drown'd,
  And ev'ry want is fill'd.

3 To thee my warm affections move,
In sweet astonishment and love,
  While at thy feet I fall;
I pant for naught beneath the skies;
To thee my ardent wishes rise,
  O mine eternal All!

4 What shall I do to spread thy praise,
My God! through my remaining days,
  Or how thy name adore?
To thee I consecrate my breath;
Let me be thine in life and death,
  And thine for evermore.

ADORATION AND PRAISE.

6 Lines 8's. NEWCOURT.

12   *Praise.*   47

I'LL praise my Maker whilst I've breath;
   And, when my voice is lost in death,
   Praise shall employ my nobler pow'rs;
My days of praise shall ne'er be past
Whilst life and thought and being last,
   Or immortality endures.

2 Happy the man whose hopes rely
On Israel's God, who made the sky,
   And earth, and seas, with all their train.
His truth forever stands secure;
He saves th' oppress'd, he feeds the poor;
   And none shall find his promise vain.

3 The Lord pours eye-sight on the blind;
The Lord supports the fainting mind;
   He sends the lab'ring conscience peace;
He helps the stranger in distress,
The widow and the fatherless,
   And grants the pris'ner sweet release.

4 I'll praise him while he lends me breath,
And, when my voice is lost in death,
   Praise shall employ my nobler pow'rs;

My days of praise shall ne'er be past,
Whilst life and thought and being last,
   Or immortality endures.

13   *The Spirit.*   181

ETERNAL Spirit, source of light,
   Enliv'ning, consecrating fire,
Descend, and, with celestial heat,
   Our dull, our frozen hearts inspire;
Our souls refine, our dross consume;
Come, condescending Spirit, come!

2 In our cold breasts, oh strike a spark
   Of that pure flame which seraphs feel;
Nor let us wander in the dark,
   Nor lie benumb'd and stupid still.
Come, vivifying Spirit, come!
And make our hearts thy constant home.

3 Let pure devotion's fervors rise!
   Let ev'ry pious passion glow!
Oh, let the raptures of the skies
   Kindle in our cold hearts below.
Come, purifying Spirit, come,
And make our souls thy constant home!

ADORATION AND PRAISE.

S. M. SILVER STREET.

14   *Worship.*

COME, sound his praise abroad,
   And hymns of glory sing!
Jehovah is the sov'reign God,
   The universal King.

2 He form'd the deeps unknown;
   He gave the seas their bound;
The wat'ry worlds are all his own,
   And all the solid ground.

3 Come, worship at his throne;
   Come, bow before the Lord :
We are his works and not our own,
   He form'd us by his word.

4 To-day attend his voice,
   Nor dare provoke his rod ;
Come, like the people of his choice,
   And own your gracious God !

15   *God's Mercy.*

MY soul, repeat his praise
   Whose mercies are so great ;
Whose anger is so slow to rise,
   So ready to abate.

2 God will not always chide ;
   And, when his wrath is felt,
His strokes are fewer than our crimes,
   And lighter than our guilt.

3 High as the heav'ns are rais'd
   Above the ground we tread,
So far the riches of his grace
   Our highest thoughts exceed.

4 His grace subdues our sins,
   And his forgiving love
Far as the east is from the west
   Doth all our guilt remove.

5 The pity of the Lord,
   To those who fear his name,
Is such as tender parents feel ;
   He knows our feeble frame.

6 Our days are as the grass,
   Or like the morning flower ;
If one sharp blast sweep o'er the field,
   It withers in an hour.

7 But thy compassions, Lord,
   To endless years endure ;
And children's children ever find
   Thy words of promise sure.

16   *Father, Word, and Spirit.*   807

FATHER, in whom we live,
   In whom we are and move,
All glory, pow'r and praise, receive,
   For thy creating love.

2 O thou incarnate Word,
   Let all thy ransom'd race
Unite in thanks, with one accord,
   For thy redeeming grace.

3 Spirit of holiness,
   Let all thy saints adore
Thy sacred gifts, and join to bless
   Thy heart-renewing pow'r.

4 The grace on man bestow'd,
   Ye heav'nly choirs, proclaim,
And cry, " Salvation to our God !
   Salvation to the Lamb!"

ADORATION AND PRAISE.

S. M. SCHNEIDER.

1. Oh, bless the Lord, my soul! Let all with-in me join, And aid my tongue to bless his name Whose fa-vors are di-vine.

17   *Praise for Mercies.*   **53**

OH, bless the Lord, my soul!
  Let all within me join,
And aid my tongue to bless his name
  Whose favors are divine.

2 Oh, bless the Lord, my soul!
  Nor let his mercies lie
Forgotten in unthankfulness,
  And without praises die.

3 'Tis he forgives thy sins;
  'Tis he relieves thy pain;
'Tis he that heals thy sicknesses,
  And gives thee strength again.

4 He crowns thy life with love,
  When rescued from the grave,
He. that redeem'd our souls from death,
  Hath boundless pow'r to save.

5 He fills the poor with good;
  He gives the suff'rers rest.
The Lord hath justice for the proud,
  And mercy for th' oppress'd.

6 His wondrous works and ways
  He made by Moses known;
But sent the world his truth and grace
  By his beloved Son.

18   *Morning Worship.*   **622**

WE lift our hearts to thee,
  O Day-star from on high!
The sun itself is but thy shade,
  Yet cheers both earth and sky.

2 Oh, let thine orient beams
  The night of sin disperse,
The mists of error and of vice
  Which shade the universe!

3 How beauteous nature now!
  How dark and sad before!
With joy we view the pleasing change,
  And nature's God adore.

4 Oh, may no gloomy crime
  Pollute the rising day;
May Jesus' blood, like morning dew,
  Wash all our stains away.

5 May we this life improve,
  To mourn for errors past;
And live this short, revolving day,
  As if it were our last.

19   *Preserving Grace.*   **295**

TO God the only wise,
  Our Saviour and our King,
Let all the saints below the skies
  Their humble praises bring.

2 'Tis his almighty love,
  His counsel and his care,
Preserves us safe from sin and death,
  And ev'ry hurtful snare.

3 He will present our souls
  Unblemish'd and complete,
Before the glory of his face,
  With joys divinely great.

4 Then all his faithful sons
  Shall meet around the throne,
Shall bless the conduct of his grace,
  And make his wonders known.

5 To our Redeemer, God,
  Wisdom and pow'r belongs,
Immortal crowns of majesty,
  And everlasting songs.

ADORATION AND PRAISE.

L. M. DUKE STREET.

1. From all that dwell be-low the skies, Let the Cre-a-tor's praise a-rise;
Let the Re-deem-er's name be sung, Through every land, by every tongue.

20 *Exhortation to Praise.* **895**

FROM all that dwell below the skies,
  Let the Creator's praise arise;
Let the Redeemer's name be sung,
Through every land, by every tongue.

2 Eternal are thy mercies, Lord;
Eternal truth attend thy word:
Thy praise shall sound from shore to shore,
Till suns shall rise and set no more.

3 Your lofty themes, ye mortals, bring;
In songs of praise divinely sing;
The great salvation loud proclaim,
And shout for joy the Saviour's name.

4 In every land begin the song;
To every land the strains belong;
In cheerful sounds all voices raise,
And fill the world with loudest praise.

21 *A Song of Praise.* **39**

TO God, the universal King,
  Let all mankind their tribute bring;
All that have breath, your voices raise
In songs of never-ceasing praise.

2 The spacious earth on which we tread,
And wider heav'ns stretch'd o'er our head,
A large and solemn temple frame
To celebrate its Builder's fame.

3 Here the bright sun, that rules the day,
As through the sky he makes his way,
To all the world proclaims aloud
The boundless sov'reignty of God.

4 When from his courts the sun retires,
And with the day his voice expires,
The moon and stars adopt the song,
And through the night their praise prolong.

5 The list'ning earth with rapture hears
Th' harmonious music of the spheres,
And all her tribes the notes repeat,
That God is wise, and good, and great.

6 But man, endow'd with nobler powers,
His God in nobler strains adores;
His is the gift to know the song,
As well as sing with tuneful tongue.

22 *The Majesty of God.* **40**

ETERNAL and immortal King!
  Thy peerless splendors none can bear,
But darkness veils seraphic eyes,
When God with all his glory's there.

2 Yet faith can pierce the awful gloom,
The great Invisible can see;
And with its tremblings mingle joy,
In fix'd regards, great God! to thee.

3 Then ev'ry tempting form of sin,
Aw'd by thy presence, disappears;
And all the glowing, raptur'd soul
The likeness, it contemplates, wears.

4 Oh, ever present to my heart!
Witness to its extreme desire;
Behold it presses on to thee,
For it hath caught the heav'nly fire.

5 This one petition would I urge:
To have thee ever in my sight!
In life, in death, in worlds unknown,
My only portion and delight.

ADORATION AND PRAISE. 17

23   *Glory of God.*   37

YE sons of men, in sacred lays
    Attempt the great Creator's praise;
But who an equal song can frame?
What verse can reach the lofty theme?

2 He sits enthron'd amidst the spheres,
And glory like a garment wears;
While boundless wisdom, pow'r, and grace
Command our awe, transcend our praise.

3 Before his throne a shining band
Of cherubs and of seraphs stand;
Ethereal spirits, who in flight
Outstrip the rapid speed of light.

4 To God all nature owes its birth;
He form'd this pond'rous globe of earth,
He rais'd the glorious arch on high,
And measur'd out the azure sky.

5 In all our Maker's grand designs
Omnipotence with wisdom shines;
His works, through all this wondrous frame,
Bear the great impress of his name.

6 Rais'd on devotion's lofty wing,
Let us his high perfections sing:
Oh, let his praise employ our tongue,
Whilst list'ning worlds applaud the song!

24   *Divine Goodness.*   599

ETERNAL Source of ev'ry joy!
    Well may thy praise our lips employ,
While in thy temple we appear
To hail thee sov'reign of the year.

2 Wide as the wheels of nature roll,
Thy hand supports and guides the whole!
The sun is taught by thee to rise,
And darkness when to veil the skies.

3 The flow'ry spring, at thy command,
Perfumes the air and paints the land;
The summer rays with vigor shine
To raise the corn and load the vine.

4 Thy hand in autumn richly pours,
Through all our coast, redundant stores;
And winters, soften'd by thy care,
No more the face of horror wear.

5 Seasons and months, and weeks and days,
Demand successive songs of praise;
And be the grateful homage paid,
With morning light and ev'ning shade.

6 Here in thy house let incense rise,
And circling Sabbaths bless our eyes,
Till to those lofty heights we soar
Where days and years revolve no more.

25   *Praise for Divine Mercies.*   46

GIVE to our God immortal praise!
    Mercy and truth are all his ways.
Wonders of grace to God belong:
Repeat his mercies in your song.

2 Give to the Lord of lords renown,
The King of kings with glory crown.
His mercies ever shall endure,
When lords and kings are known no more:

3 He built the earth, he spread the sky,
And fix'd the starry lights on high.
Wonders of grace to God belong:
Repeat his mercies in your song.

4 He fills the sun with morning light;
He bids the moon direct the night.
His mercies ever shall endure,
When suns and moons shall shine no more.

5 He sent his Son with pow'r to save
From guilt, and darkness, and the grave.
Wonders of grace to God belong:
Repeat his mercies in your song.

6 Through this vain world he guides our feet,
And leads us to his heav'nly seat.
His mercies ever shall endure,
When this vain world shall be no more.

26   *Every Thing in God's Hand.*   67

GREATEST of beings, source of life,
    Sov'reign of air, and earth, and sea!
All nature feels thy pow'r; but man
A grateful tribute pays to thee.

2 Subject to wants, to thee he looks,
And from thy goodness seeks supplies;
And when, oppress'd with guilt, he mourns,
Thy mercy lifts him to the skies.

3 Children, whose little minds, unform'd,
Ne'er rais'd a tender thought to heav'n;
And men, whom reason lifts to God,
Though oft by passion downward driv'n;

4 All, great Creator! all are thine;
All feel thy providential care;
And, through each varying scene of life,
Alike thy constant pity share.

5 And, whether grief oppress the heart,
Or whether joy elate the breast,
Or life still keep its little course,
Or death invite the heart to rest;

6 All are thy messengers, and all
Thy sacred pleasure, Lord, obey;
And all are training man to dwell
Nearer to bliss and nearer thee.

ADORATION AND PRAISE.

L. M. WARD.

1. E-ter-nal God, al-migh-ty cause Of earth, and seas, and worlds unknown, All things are sub-ject to thy laws; All things de-pend on thee a-lone.

27   God Alone.   18

ETERNAL God, almighty cause
Of earth, of seas, and worlds unknown,
All things are subject to thy laws;
All things depend on thee alone.

2 Thy glorious being singly stands,
Of all within itself possest;
By none controll'd in thy commands,
And in thyself completely blest.

3 To thee alone ourselves we owe;
Let heav'n and earth due homage pay:
All other gods we disavow,
Deny their claims, renounce their sway.

4 In thee, O Lord, our hope shall rest,
Fountain of peace and joy and love!
Thy favor only makes us blest;
Without thee all would nothing prove.

5 Worship to thee alone belongs;
Worship to thee alone we give;
Thine be our hearts and thine our songs,
And to thy glory we would live.

6 Spread thy great name thro' heathen lands
Their idol-deities dethrone;
Subdue the world to thy commands,
And reign, as thou art, God alone.

28   God Incomprehensible.   19

GREAT God, in vain man's narrow view
Attempts to look thy nature through;
Our lab'ring pow'rs with rev'rence own
Thy glories never can be known.

2 Not the high seraph's mighty thought,
Who countless years his God has sought,
Such wondrous height or depth can find,
Or fully trace thy boundless mind.

3 Yet, Lord, thy kindness deigns to show
Enough for mortal men to know;
While wisdom, goodness, pow'r divine
Through all thy works and conduct shine.

4 Oh, may our souls with rapture trace
Thy works of nature and of grace,
Explore thy sacred truth, and still
Press on to know and do thy will!

29   Praise for Blessings.   969

ALMIGHTY Sov'reign of the skies,
To thee let songs of gladness rise,
Each grateful heart its tribute bring,
And ev'ry voice thy goodness sing.

2 From thee our choicest blessings flow,
Life, health, and strength thy hands bestow;
The daily good thy creatures share,
Springs from thy providential care.

3 The rich profusion nature yields,
The harvest waving o'er the fields,
The cheering light, refreshing shower,
Are gifts from thy exhaustless store.

4 At thy command the vernal bloom
Revives the world from winter's gloom;
The summer's heat the fruit matures,
And autumn all her treasures pours.

5 From thee proceed domestic ties,
Connubial bliss, parental joys;
On thy support the nations stand,
Obedient to thy high command.

6 Let ev'ry pow'r of heart and tongue
Unite to swell the grateful song;
While age and youth in chorus join,
And praise the majesty divine.

30 God Exalted. 13

ETERNAL Power! whose high abode
Becomes the grandeur of a God;
Infinite lengths beyond the bounds
Where stars revolve their little rounds!

2 Far in the depths of space, thy throne
Burns with a lustre all its own:
In shining ranks, beneath thy feet,
Angelic pow'rs and splendors meet.

3 Lord, what shall feeble mortals do?
We would adore our Maker too:
With lowly minds to thee we cry,
The Great, the Holy, and the High.

4 God is in heav'n, and man below;
Short be our tunes, our words be few:
Let sacred rev'rence check our songs,
And praise sit silent on our tongues.

31 Majesty of God. 771

COME, O my soul, in sacred lays
Attempt thy great Creator's praise:
But oh, what tongue can speak his fame?
What verse can reach the lofty theme?

2 Enthron'd amid the radiant spheres,
He glory like a garment wears;
To form a robe of light divine,
Ten thousand suns around him shine.

3 In all our Maker's grand designs
Almighty pow'r, with wisdom, shines;
His works, through all this wondrous frame,
Declare the glory of his name.

4 Rais'd on devotion's lofty wing,
Do thou, my soul, his glories sing;
And let his praise employ thy tongue
Till list'ning worlds shall join the song.

32 Majesty of God. 16

WHAT is our God, or what his name,
Nor men can learn, nor angels teach;
He dwells conceal'd in radiant flame,
Where neither eyes nor thoughts can reach.

2 The spacious worlds of heavenly light,
Compar'd with him, how short they fall!
How dark are they, and he how bright!
Nothing are they, and God is all.

3 He spoke the wondrous word, and lo!
Creation rose at his command;
Whirlwinds and seas their limits know,
Bound in the hollow of his hand.

4 Then fly, my song, an endless round,
The lofty tune let Gabriel raise;
All nature dwell upon the sound,
But we can ne'er fulfil the praise.

33 Father, Son, and Spirit. 42

BLESS'D be the Father and his love;
To whose celestial source we owe
Rivers of endless joy above,
And rills of comfort here below.

2 Glory to thee, great Son of God,
From whose dear wounded body rolls
A precious stream of vital blood,
Pardon and life for dying souls.

3 We give the sacred Spirit praise,
Who in our hearts of sin and woe
Makes living springs of grace arise,
And into boundless glory flow.

4 Thus God the Father, God the Son,
And God the Spirit, we adore,
That sea of life and love unknown,
Without a bottom or a shore.

34 God Eternal. 21

ALL-POW'RFUL, self-existent God,
Who all creation dost sustain!
Thou wast, and art, and art to come,
And everlasting is thy reign.

2 Fix'd and eternal as thy days,
Each glorious attribute divine,
Through ages infinite, shall still
With undiminish'd lustre shine.

3 Fountain of being! source of good!
Immutable dost thou remain;
Nor can the shadow of a change
Obscure the glories of thy reign.

4 Earth may with all her pow'rs dissolve,
If such the great Creator's will;
But thou forever art the same;
"I am," is thy memorial still.

35 Majesty of God. 22

GIVE to the Lord, ye sons of fame,
Give to the Lord renown and pow'r;
Ascribe due honors to his name,
And his eternal might adore.

2 The Lord proclaims his pow'r aloud,
O'er the vast ocean and the land;
His voice divides the wat'ry cloud,
And lightnings blaze at his command.

3 His thunders rend the vaulted skies,
And palaces and temples shake;
The mountains tremble at the noise,
The valleys roar, the deserts quake.

4 The Lord sits sov'reign o'er the flood;
Jehovah reigns forever king;
But makes his church his blest abode,
Where we his awful glories sing.

5 We see no terrors in his name,
But in our God a Father find:
The voice that shakes all nature's frame
Speaks comfort to the pious mind.

ADORATION AND PRAISE.

C. M. DEVIZES.

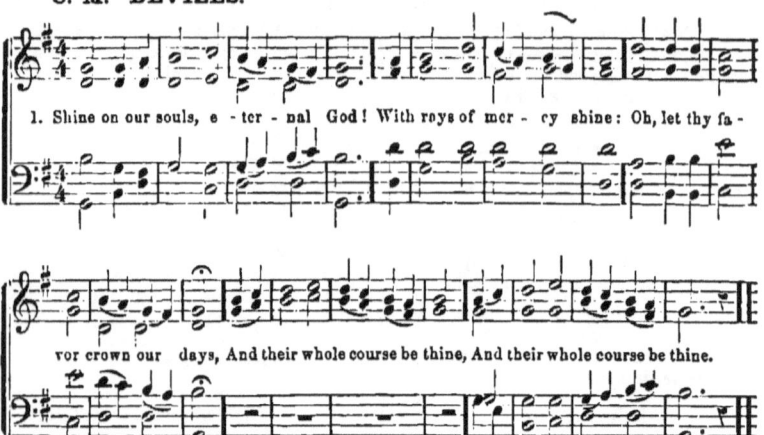

1. Shine on our souls, e-ter-nal God! With rays of mer-cy shine: Oh, let thy fa-vor crown our days, And their whole course be thine, And their whole course be thine.

36 *Prosperity from God.* **80**

SHINE on our souls, eternal God!
  With rays of mercy shine:
Oh, let thy favor crown our days,
  And their whole course be thine.

2 Did we not raise our hands to thee,
  Our hands might toil in vain:
Small joy success itself could give,
  If thou thy love restrain.

3 'Tis ours the furrows to prepare,
  And sow the precious grain:
'Tis thine to give the sun and air,
  And to command the rain.

4 With thee let ev'ry week begin,
  With thee each day be spent,
For thee each fleeting hour improv'd,
  Since each by thee is lent.

5 Thus cheer us through this toilsome road
  Till all our labors cease;
And thus prepare our weary souls
  For everlasting peace.

37 *Morning Hymn.* **620**

TO thee let my first off'rings rise,
  Whose sun creates my day;
Swift as the gladd'ning influence flies,
  And spotless as his ray.

2 This day thy fav'ring hand be nigh,
  So oft vouchsafed before!
Still may it lead, protect, supply,
  And I that hand adore.

3 If bliss thy Providence impart,
  For which, resign'd, I pray,
Give me to feel the grateful heart!
  And, without guilt, be gay!

4 Affliction should thy love intend,
  As vice or folly's cure,
Patient to gain that blessed end,
  May I the means endure.

5 Be this and ev'ry future day
  Still wiser than the past;
And, when I all my life survey,
  May grace sustain at last!

38 *God Omnipresent.* **773**

JEHOVAH God! thy gracious pow'r
  On ev'ry hand we see;
Oh, may the blessings of each hour
  Lead all our thoughts to thee.

2 If, on the wings of morn, we speed
  To earth's remotest bound,
Thy right hand will our footsteps lead,
  Thine arm our path surround.

3 Thy pow'r is in the ocean deeps,
  And reaches to the skies;
Thine eye of mercy never sleeps,
  Thy goodness never dies.

4 From morn till noon, till latest eve,
  The hand of God we see!
And all the blessings we receive,
  Ceaseless, proceed from thee.

5 In all the varying scenes of time,
  On thee our hopes depend;
In ev'ry age, in ev'ry clime,
  Our Father and our Friend.

ADORATION AND PRAISE.

C. M. LANESBORO'.

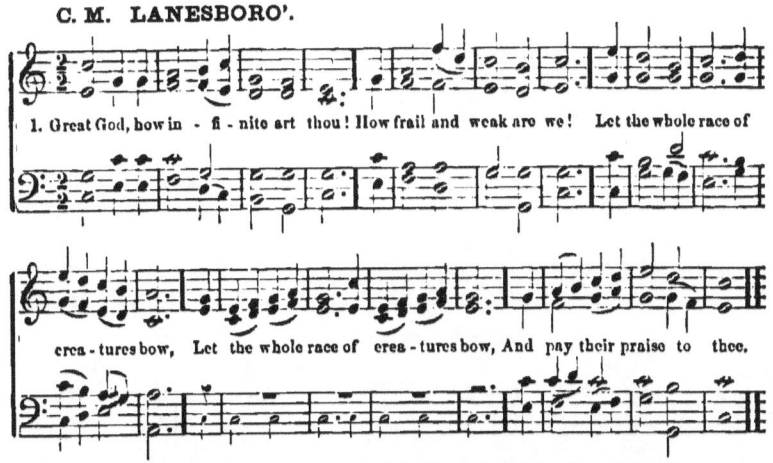

1. Great God, how in-fi-nite art thou! How frail and weak are we! Let the whole race of crea-tures bow, Let the whole race of crea-tures bow, And pay their praise to thee.

39 *God Infinite.* **20**

GREAT God, how infinite art thou!
 How frail and weak are we!
Let the whole race of creatures bow,
And pay their praise to thee.

2 Thy throne eternal ages stood,
 Ere earth or heav'n was made;
Thou art the ever-living God,
 Were all the nations dead.

3 Nature and time all open lie
 To thine immense survey,
From the formation of the sky
 To the last awful day.

4 Eternity, with all its years,
 Stands present to thy view;
To thee there's nothing old appears,
 To thee there's nothing new.

5 Our lives thro' various scenes are drawn,
 And vex'd with trifling cares;
While thine eternal thought moves on
 Thine undisturb'd affairs.

6 Great God, how infinite art thou!
 How frail and weak are we!
Let the whole race of creatures bow,
And pay their praise to thee.

40 *Morning Song.* **942**

LORD, in the morning thou shalt hear
 My voice ascending high;
To thee will I direct my pray'r,
 To thee lift up mine eye;—

2 Up to the hills where Christ has gone
 To plead for all his saints,
Presenting at his Father's throne
 Our songs and our complaints.

3 Thou art a God before whose sight
 The wicked shall not stand;
Sinners shall ne'er be thy delight,
 Nor dwell at thy right hand.

4 But to thy house will I resort,
 To taste thy mercies there;
I will frequent thy holy court
 And worship in thy fear.

5 Oh, may thy Spirit guide my feet
 In ways of righteousness;
Make ev'ry path of duty straight
 And plain before my face.

41 *God Holy and Just.* **28**

HOLY and rev'rend is the name
 Of our eternal King;
Thrice holy, Lord! the angels cry:
 Thrice holy let us sing.

2 Holy is he in all his works,
 And saints are his delight;
But sinners and their wicked ways
 Are hateful in his sight.

3 The deepest rev'rence, homage, love,
 Pay, O my soul, to God;
Lift with thy hands a holy heart
 To his sublime abode.

4 Thou, righteous God! preserve my mind
 From all pollution free;
Thine image form within my breast,
 That I thy face may see.

ADORATION AND PRAISE.

C. M. ZANESVILLE.

1. The Lord, how fear - ful is his name! How wide is his com-mand! Na - ture, with all her mov - ing frame, Rests on his might - y hand.

42   *Majesty and Grace of God.*   66

THE Lord, how fearful is his name!
  How wide is his command!
Nature, with all her moving frame,
  Rests on his mighty hand.

2 Immortal glory forms his throne,
  And light his awful robe,
Whilst, with a smile or with a frown,
  He manages the globe.

3 Adoring angels round him fall,
  In all their shining forms;
His sov'reign eye looks o'er them all,
  And pities mortal worms.

4 Now, let the Lord forever reign,
  And sway us as he will;
Sick or in health, in ease or pain,
  We are his fav'rites still.

43   *God Sought.*   767

COME, O thou King of all thy saints,
  Our humble tribute own,
While, with our praises and complaints,
  We bow before thy throne.

2 How should our songs, like those above,
  With warm devotion rise!
How should our souls, on wings of love,
  Mount upward to the skies!

3 But, ah, the song, how faint it flows!
  How languid our desire!
How dim the sacred passion glows
  Till thou the heart inspire!

4 Dear Saviour, let thy glory shine,
  And fill thy temples here,
Till life and love, and joy divine,
  A heaven on earth appear.

44   *God our Support.*   65

LET the whole race of creatures lie
  Abas'd before the Lord!
Whate'er his pow'rful hand has form'd,
  He governs with a word.

2 Ten thousand ages ere the skies
  Were into motion brought,
All the long years and worlds to come
  Stood present to his thought.

3 There's not a sparrow or a worm
  O'erlook'd in his decrees:
He raises monarchs to the throne,
  Or sinks, with equal ease.

4 If light attend the course I go,
  'Tis he provides the rays;
And 'tis his hand that hides my sun,
  If darkness clouds my days.

5 Trusting his wisdom and his love,
  I would not wish to know
What in the book of his decrees
  Awaits me here below.

45   *Spring.*   601

WHEN verdure clothes the fertile vale,
  And blossoms deck the spray,
And fragrance breathes in ev'ry gale,
  How sweet the vernal day!

2 O God of nature and of grace,
  Thy heav'nly gifts impart;
Then shall my meditation trace
  Spring, blooming in my heart.

3 Inspir'd to praise, I then shall join
  Glad nature's cheerful song,
And love and gratitude divine
  Attune my joyful tongue.

ADORATION AND PRAISE.

7's. HENDON.

46 *Praise to God.* **49**

GLORY be to God on high,
God, whose glory fills the sky;
Peace on earth to man forgiv'n,
Man, the well belov'd of heav'n.
          Glory be, &c.

2 Favor'd mortals, raise the song;
Endless thanks to God belong:
Hearts o'erflowing with his praise,
Join the hymns your voices raise:

3 Call the tribes of beings round,
From creation's utmost bound;
Where the Godhead shines confess'd,
There be solemn praise address'd.

4 Mark the wonders of his hand!
Power, no empire can withstand;
Wisdom, angels' glorious theme;
Goodness, one eternal stream.

5 Awful Being! from thy throne
Send the promis'd blessings down;
Let thy light, thy truth, thy peace,
Bid our raging passions cease.

47 *Songs of Praise.* **770**

SONGS of praise the angels sang,
Heav'n with hallelujahs rang,
When Jehovah's work begun,
When he spake and it was done.

2 Songs of praise awoke the morn
When the Prince of Peace was born;
Songs of praise arose when he
Captive led captivity.

3 Heav'n and earth must pass away;
Songs of praise shall crown that day:
God will make new heav'ns and earth;
Songs of praise shall hail their birth.

4 And shall man alone be dumb,
Till that glorious kingdom come?
No: the church delights to raise
Psalms, and hymns, and songs of praise.

5 Saints below, with heart and voice,
Still in songs of praise rejoice;
Learning here, by faith and love,
Songs of praise to sing above.

48 *Honor to Christ.* **776**

COME, thou Savior of our race,
Choicest gift of heav'nly grace:
O thou blessed Virgin's Son!
Be thy race on earth begun.

2 Not of mortal blood or birth,
He descends from heav'n to earth—
By the Holy Ghost conceiv'd,
Truly man, to be believ'd.

3 Wondrous birth! O wondrous child
Of the virgin undefil'd!
Though by all the world disown'd,
Still to be in heav'n enthron'd.

4 Equal to the Father now,
Though to dust thou once didst bow:
Boundless shall thy kingdom be—
When shall we its glories see?

5 Praise the Father on his throne;
Praise his co-eternal Son;
Praise the Holy Spirit, too;
Let each age the praise renew.

ADORATION AND PRAISE.

8's, 6 lines. ELIAS.

1. Searcher of hearts! to thee are known
 The inmost secrets of my breast;
 At home, abroad, in crowds, alone,
 Thou mark'st my rising and my rest,
 My thoughts far off, through ev'ry maze,
 Source, stream, and issue,—all my ways.

49. God the Searcher of Hearts.

SEARCHER of hearts! to thee are known
 The inmost secrets of my breast;
At home, abroad, in crowds, alone,
Thou mark'st my rising and my rest,
My thoughts far off, through ev'ry maze,
Source, stream, and issue,—all my ways.

2 No word that from my mouth proceeds,
Evil or good, escapes thine ear;
Witness thou art to all my deeds—
Before, behind, forever near.
Such knowledge is for me too high:
I live but in my Maker's eye.

3 How from thy presence should I go,
Or whither from thy spirit flee,
Since all above, around, below,
Exist in thine immensity?
If up to heaven I take my way,
I meet thee in eternal day.

4 If in the grave I make my bed
With worms and dust, lo! thou art there;
If on the wings of morning sped,
Beyond the ocean I repair,
I feel thine all-controlling will
And thy right hand upholds me still.

5 How precious are thy thoughts of peace,
O God, to me! How great the sum!
New ev'ry morn, they never cease;
They were, they are, and yet shall come,
In number and in compass more
Than all the sand on ocean's shore.

6 Search me, O God, and know my heart;
Try me, my secret soul survey;
And warn thy servant to depart
From every false and evil way;
And let thy truth my guidance be
To life and immortality.

50. God, Lord of the Sea.

LORD of the Sea! thy potent sway
 Old ocean's wildest waves obey;
The gale that whistles through the shrouds,
The storm that drives the freighted clouds,
If but thy whisper order peace,
How soon their rude commotions cease!

2 Lord of the Sea! the seaman keep
From all the dangers of the deep!
When high the white-capp'd billows rise,
When tempests roar along the skies,
When foes or shoals awaken fear,
Oh, be thou, in thy mercy, near!

3 Lord of the Sea! a sea is life,—
A sea of care, and woe, and strife.
With watchful pains we steer along,
Battling with winds and tempests strong.
And when our voyage here shall cease,
Oh, grant us everlasting peace.

INVOCATION.

L. M. LOUVAN.

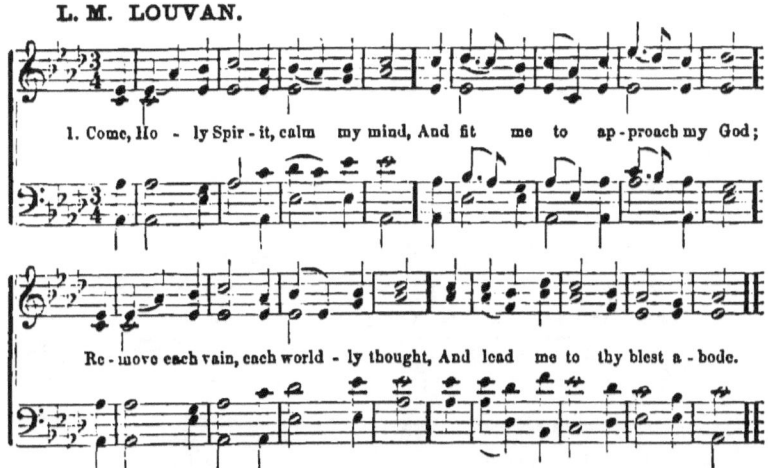

1. Come, Ho - ly Spir - it, calm my mind, And fit me to ap - proach my God; Re - move each vain, each world - ly thought, And lead me to thy blest a - bode.

57 *For the Spirit.* **797**

COME, Holy Spirit, calm my mind,
  And fit me to approach my God;
Remove each vain, each worldly thought,
And lead me to thy blest abode.

2 Hast thou imparted to my soul
A living spark of holy fire?
Oh, kindle now the sacred flame,
And make me burn with pure desire.

3 A brighter faith and hope impart,
And let me now my Savior see:
Oh, soothe and cheer my burden'd heart,
And bid my spirit rest in thee.

58 *For Grace and Life.* **805**

FATHER of heav'n, whose love profound,
  A ransom for our souls has found,
Before thy throne we sinners bend;
To us thy pard'ning love extend.

2 Almighty Son, incarnate Word,
Our Prophet, Priest, Redeemer, Lord,
Before thy throne we sinners bend;
To us thy saving grace extend.

3 Eternal Spirit, by whose breath,
The soul is rais'd from sin and death,
Before thy throne we sinners bend;
To us thy quick'ning pow'r extend.

4 Jehovah! Father, Spirit, Son!
Eternal Godhead, Three in One!
Before thy throne we sinners bend;
Grace, pardon, life, to us extend.

59 *For the Teachings of the Spirit.*

COME, blessèd Spirit! source of light,
  Whose power and grace are unconfined,
Dispel the gloomy shades of night,—
The thicker darkness of the mind.

2 To mine illumin'd eyes display
The glorious truth thy word reveals;
Cause me to run the heavenly way,
Thy book unfold and loose the seals.

3 Thine inward teachings make me know,
The mysteries of redeeming love,
The vanity of things below,
And excellence of things above.

4 While through this dubious maze I stray,
Spread like the sun thy beams abroad,
To show the dangers of the way,
And guide my feeble steps to God.

60 *Divine Grace Implored.*

OH, hear me, Lord! on thee I call,
  And prostrate at thy footstool fall;
Propitious in my cause appear,
And bow to my request thine ear.

2 Look down, my only hope! look down;
Behold me, but without a frown;
And ne'er to my desiring eye
Thy presence, heav'nly Lord! deny.

3 Oh, let me, on thine aid reclin'd,
Thee still my great salvation find;
Nor leave me helpless and forlorn,
The absence of thy grace to mourn.

4 Adopted by thy care, in thee
The Parent and the Friend I see;
And, nourish'd by thy fost'ring hand,
Within thy courts secure I stand.

INVOCATION.

7s. PLEYEL'S HYMN.

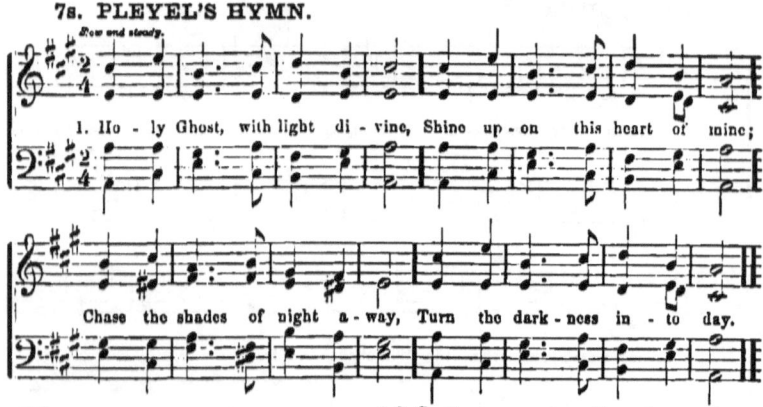

Slow and steady.

1. Ho-ly Ghost, with light di-vine, Shine up-on this heart of mine; Chase the shades of night a-way, Turn the dark-ness in-to day.

61   *For the Spirit's Influence.*   **795**

HOLY Ghost, with light divine,
   Shine upon this heart of mine;
Chase the shades of night away,
Turn the darkness into day.

2 Let me see my Savior's face,
Let me all his beauties trace;
Show those glorious truths to me,
Which are only known to thee.

3 Holy Ghost, with pow'r divine,
Cleanse this guilty heart of mine;
Long has sin, without control,
Held dominion o'er my soul.

4 Holy Ghost, with joy divine,
Cheer this sadden'd heart of mine;
Bid my many woes depart,
Heal my wounded, bleeding heart.

5 Bid my sin and sorrow cease;
Fill me with thy heav'nly peace;
Joy divine I then shall prove,
Light of truth—and fire of love.

6 Holy Spirit, all divine,
Dwell within this heart of mine;
Cast down ev'ry idol's throne,
Reign supreme—and reign alone.

62   *Humble Prayer.*   **497**

LORD, we come before thee now,
   At thy feet we humbly bow;
Oh, do not our suit disdain;
Shall we seek thee, Lord, in vain?

2 In thine own appointed way,
Now we seek thee, here we stay;
Lord, we cannot let thee go
Till a blessing thou bestow.

3 Send some message from thy word
That may joy and peace afford;
Let thy Spirit now impart
Full salvation to each heart.

4 Comfort those who weep and mourn,
Let the time of joy return;
Those who are cast down, lift up;
Make them strong in faith and hope.

5 Grant that all may seek and find
Thee a God supremely kind;
Heal the sick, the captive free,
Let us all rejoice in thee.

63   *For a Blessing in the Temple.*   **768**

TO thy temple we repair;
   Lord, we love to worship there;
There, within the veil, we meet
Christ upon the mercy-seat.

2 While thy glorious name is sung,
Tune our lips, inspire our tongue;
Then our joyful songs shall bless
Christ, the Lord, our Righteousness.

3 While to thee our prayers ascend,
Let thine ear in love attend;
Hear us when thy Spirit pleads,
Hear, for Jesus intercedes.

4 While thy word is heard with awe,
While we tremble at thy law,
Let thy gospel's wondrous love
Ev'ry doubt and fear remove.

5 From thy house, when we return,
Let our hearts within us burn;
Then, at ev'ning, we may say,
"We have walked with God to-day."

INVOCATION. 29

L. M. LUTON.

1. Thy pre-sence, gra-cious God, af-ford, Pre-pare us to re-ceive thy word; Now let thy voice en-gage our ear, And faith be mix'd with what I hear.

64 *Before Sermon.* **494**

THY presence, gracious God, afford,
  Prepare us to receive thy word;
Now let thy voice engage our ear,
And faith be mix'd with what we hear

2 Distracting thoughts and cares remove,
And fix our hearts and hopes above:
With food divine may we be fed,
And satisfied with living bread.

3 To us the sacred word apply,
With sov'reign pow'r and energy;
And may we, in thy faith and fear,
Reduce to practice what we hear.

4 Father, in us thy Son reveal;
Teach us to know and do thy will;
Thy saving pow'r and love display,
And guide us to the realms of day.

65 *For the Divine Blessing.*

JESUS, where'er thy people meet,
  They find an open mercy-seat;
Where'er they seek thee, thou art found,
And ev'ry place is holy ground.

2 Great Shepherd of thy chosen few!
To us thy mercies here renew;
Here to our waiting hearts proclaim
The sweetness of thy saving name.

66 *For Divine Presence.* **492**

WHERE two or three, with sweet accord,
  Obedient to their sovereign Lord,
Meet to recount his acts of grace,
And offer solemn pray'r and praise;

2 "There," says the Savior, "will I be,
Amid this little company;
To them unveil my smiling face,
And shed my glories round the place."

3 We meet at thy command, dear Lord,
Relying on thy faithful word:
Now send thy Spirit from above,
Now fill our hearts with heav'nly love.

67* *For the Spirit's Influence.* **798**

GRACIOUS Spirit—Love divine!
  Let thy light within me shine;
All my guilty fears remove;
  Fill me with thy heav'nly love.

2 Speak thy pard'ning grace to me;
  Set the burden'd sinner free;
Lead me to the lamb of God;
  Wash me in his precious blood.

3 Life and peace to me impart;
  Seal salvation on my heart;
Dwell thyself within my breast,
  Earnest of immortal rest.

4 Let me never from thee stray;
  Keep me in the narrow way;
Fill my soul with joy divine;
  Keep me, Lord, forever thine.

* Sung to *Pleyel's Hymn.*

INVOCATION.

C. M. EASTBURN.

1. In thy great name, O Lord, we come, To wor-ship at thy feet;
Oh, pour thy ho-ly Spir-it down On all that now shall meet.

68 *Prayer for the Spirit.* **496**

IN thy great name, O Lord, we come,
  To worship at thy feet;
Oh, pour thy holy Spirit down
  On all that now shall meet.

2 We come to hear Jehovah speak,
  To hear the Savior's voice:
Thy face and favor, Lord, we seek,
  Now make our hearts rejoice.

3 Teach us to pray and praise, and hear
  And understand thy word;
To feel thy blissful presence near,
  And trust our living Lord.

4 Here let thy pow'r and grace be felt;
  Thy love and mercy known;
Our icy hearts, dear Jesus, melt,
  And break this flinty stone.

5 Let sinners, Lord, thy goodness prove,
  And saints rejoice in thee;
Let rebels be subdued by love,
  And to the Savior flee.

6 This house with grace and glory fill,
  This congregation bless;
Thy great salvation now reveal,
  Thy glorious righteousness.

69 *Before Sermon.* **495**

JESUS, thou dear redeeming Lord,
  Thy blessing we implore!
Open the door to preach thy word,
  The great, effectual door.

2 Gather the outcasts in, and save
  From sin and Satan's power!
And let them now acceptance have,
  And know their gracious hour.

3 Lover of souls! thou know'st to prize
  What thou hast bought so dear;
Come, then, and in thy people's eyes
  With all thy wounds appear!

4 Appear, as when of old confest
  The suff'ring Son of God;
And let us see thee in thy vest
  But newly dipt in blood.

5 The hardness of our hearts remove,
  Thou who for sin hast died;
Show us the tokens of thy love,
  Thy feet, thy hands, thy side.

70 *For Divine Aid.* **175**

MY hope, my portion, and my God,
  How little art thou known
By all the judgments of thy rod,
  And blessings of thy throne!

2 How cold and feeble is my love!
  How negligent my fear!
How low my hope of joys above!
  How few affections there!

3 Great God! thy gracious aid impart,
  To give thy word success;
Write thy salvation in my heart,
  That I may learn thy grace.

4 Show my forgetful feet the way
  That leads to joys on high:
There knowledge grows without decay,
  And love shall never die.

71 *For Grace in Trial.* 974

FATHER of all our mercies, thou
  In whom we move and live,
Hear us in heaven, thy dwelling, now,
  And answer, and forgive.

2 When harass'd by ten thousand foes,
  Our helplessness we feel,
O give the weary soul repose,
  The wounded spirit heal.

3 When dire temptations gather round,
  And threaten or allure,
By storm or calm, in thee be found
  A refuge strong and sure.

4 From day to day, O may we grow
  In faith, in hope, and love,
And walk in holiness below
  To holiness above.

72 *The Spirit Desired.* 930

SPIRIT divine, attend our prayer,
  And make this house thy home;
Descend with all thy gracious power.
  O come, great Spirit, come!

2 Come as the light—to us reveal
  Our sinfulness and woe,
And lead us in the paths of life,
  Where all the righteous go.

3 Come as the fire, and purge our hearts,
  Like sacrificial flame;
Let ev'ry soul an off'ring be
  To our Redeemer's name.

4 Come as the dew, and sweetly bless
  This consecrated hour;
May souls unfaithful learn to know
  Thy fertilizing power.

5 Come as a dove, and spread thy wings,
  The wings of peaceful love,
And let the church on earth become
  Blest as the church above.

73 *A Solemn Invocation.*

BE thou, O God! by night and day
  My Guide, my Guard from sin,
My Life, my Trust, my Light divine,
  To keep me pure within;—

2 Pure as the air, when day's first light
  A cloudless sky illumes,
And active as the lark, that soars
  Till heav'n shines round its plumes.

3 So may my soul, upon the wings
  Of faith, unwearied rise,
Till at the gate of heaven it sings
  Midst light from paradise.

74 *For Divine Grace.* 910

RETIRE, vain world, a while retire,
  And leave us with the Lord;
Thy gifts ne'er fill one just desire,
  Nor lasting bliss afford.

2 Blest Jesus! come now gently down,
  And fill this hallow'd place;
O make thy glorious goings known,—
  Diffuse abroad thy grace.

3 Shine, dearest Lord, from realms of
  Disperse the gloom of night;   [day—
Chase all our clouds and doubts away,
  And turn the shades to light.

4 Behold, and pity, from above,
  Our cold and languid frame;
Oh, shed abroad thy quick'ning love,
  And we'll adore thy name.

5 Make known thy pow'r, victorious King,
  Subdue each stubborn will;
Then sov'reign grace we'll join to sing
  On Zion's sacred hill.

75 *At the Commencement of Worship.*

AGAIN we sinners come to thee,
  God of all might sublime;
Hear us, through Christ, our only plea,
  And save us now in him.

2 Possess and fill our wandering minds;
  Our hearts uplift and stay;
Fear scatter to the driving winds,
  And take our guilt away.

3 Give us on thy rich truth to feed,
  And on thy word to rest;—
Thy truth can make us free indeed,
  Thy word can make us blest.

4 Give us to feel thy pard'ning love,
  To taste thy joyous grace;
To sing, to pray, as those above
  Who see thy smiling face.

5 And thus, with holy angel throngs,
  Pure worship we will bring,
And in our everlasting songs,
  Our God and Savior sing.

76 *For Effective Salvation.*

COME, blessed Savior, from above,
  O'er all our hearts to reign;
Come, plant the kingdom of thy love
  In every heart of man.

2 All sin and sorrow then shall cease;—
  Thy Holy Spirit given,
Pure joy and everlasting peace,
  Shall turn our earth to heaven!

C. M. CLARENDON.

1. Some se-raph, lend your heav'nly tongue, Or harp of gold-en string, That I may raise a lof-ty song To our e-ter-nal King.

77   *God Incomprehensible.*   15

SOME seraph, lend your heav'nly tongue,
    Or harp of golden string,
That I may raise a lofty song
    To our eternal King.

2 Thy names, how infinite they be!
    Great EVERLASTING ONE!
Boundless thy might and majesty,
    And unconfined thy throne.

3 Thy glory shines immensely bright;
    Exhaustless is thy grace;
Immortal day breaks from thine eyes,
    And Gabriel veils his face.

4 Thine essence is a vast abyss,
    Which angels cannot sound;
An ocean of infinities,
    Where all our thoughts are drown'd.

5 The myst'ries of creation lie
    Beneath enlighten'd minds;
Thoughts can ascend above the sky
    And fly before the winds;

6 Reason may grasp the massy hills,
    And stretch from pole to pole;
But half thy name our spirit fills,
    And overloads our soul.

78   *God the Searcher of Hearts.*   29

GOD is a Spirit, just and wise;
    He sees our inmost mind;
In vain to heav'n we raise our cries,
    And leave our souls behind.

2 Nothing but truth before his throne
    With honor can appear.
The painted hypocrites are known
    Through the disguise they wear.

3 Their lifted eyes salute the skies,
    Their bended knees the ground:
But God abhors the sacrifice
    Where not the heart is found.

4 Lord, search my thoughts, & try my ways,
    And make my soul sincere:
Then shall I stand before thy face,
    And find acceptance there.

79   *God no Respecter of Persons.*   30

WITH eye impartial, heav'n's high King
    Surveys each human tribe;
No earthly pomp his eyes can charm,
    Nor wealth his favor bribe.

2 The rich and poor, of equal clay,
    His pow'rful hand did frame;
All souls are his, and him alike
    Their common Parent claim.

3 Ye sons of men of high degree,
    Your great Superior own;
Praise him for all his gifts, and pay
    Your homage at his throne.

4 Trust in the Lord, ye humble poor,
    And banish ev'ry fear:
The God you serve will ne'er forsake
    The man of heart sincere.

80 God Omniscient. 26

LORD, all I am is known to thee!
In vain my soul would try
To shun thy presence, or to flee
The notice of thine eye

2 Thine all-surrounding sight surveys
My rising and my rest,
My public walks, my private ways,
And secrets of my breast.

3 My thoughts lie open to thee, Lord,
Before they're form'd within;
And ere my lips pronounce the word,
Thou knowest the sense I mean.

4 Oh, wondrous knowledge, deep and high;
Where can a creature hide?
Within thy circling arms I lie,
Beset on ev'ry side.

81 God Gracious. 34

SWEET is the mem'ry of thy grace,
O God, my heav'nly King!
Let age to age thy righteousness
In songs of glory sing.

2 God reigns on high, but not confines
His goodness to the skies.
Through the whole earth his bounty shines,
And every want supplies.

3 With longing eyes thy creatures wait
On thee for daily food:
Thy lib'ral hand provides their meat,
And fills their mouths with good.

4 How kind and gracious is the Lord,
How slow his anger moves!
How soon he sends his pard'ning word
To cheer the souls he loves!

5 Creatures, with all their endless race,
Thy pow'r and praise proclaim;
But saints who taste thy richer grace
Delight to bless thy name.

82 Divine Omniscience. 774

ALMIGHTY God! thy piercing eye
Strikes through the shades of night,
And our most secret actions lie
All open to thy sight.

2 There's not a sin that we commit,
Nor wicked word we say,
But in thy dreadful book 'tis writ
Against the judgment day.

3 And must the crimes that I have done
Be read and publish'd there?
Be all expos'd before the sun,
While men and angels hear?

4 Lord, at thy foot ashamed I lie,
Upward I dare not look;
Pardon my sins before I die,
And blot them from thy book.

5 Remember all the dying pains
That my Redeemer felt,
And let his blood wash out my stains,
And answer for my guilt.

6 Oh, may I now forever fear
T' indulge a sinful thought,
Since the great God can see and hear,
And writes down ev'ry fault.

83 God is Love. 38

AMID the splendors of thy state,
My God, thy love appears
With the soft radiance of the moon
Among a thousand stars.

2 Nature through all her ample round
Thy boundless power proclaims,
And in melodious accents speaks
The goodness of thy names.

3 Thy justice, holiness, and truth,
Our solemn awe excite;
But the sweet charms of sov'reign grace
O'erwhelm us with delight.

4 Sinai, in clouds and smoke and fire,
Thunders thy dreadful name;
But Sion sings, in melting notes,
The honors of the Lamb.

5 In all thy doctrines and commands,
Thy counsels and designs,
In ev'ry work thy hands have fram'd,
Thy love supremely shines.

6 Angels and men the news proclaim
Through earth and heav'n above,
The joyful, the transporting news,
That God, the Lord, is love!

84 The Power of God.

THE Lord our God is full of might,
The winds obey his will;
He speaks, and in his heavenly height,
The rolling sun stands still.

2 Rebel, ye waves, and o'er the land
With threatening aspect roar:
The Lord uplifts his awful hand,
And chains you to the shore.

3 His voice sublime is heard afar,
In distant peals it dies;
He yokes the whirlwinds to his car,
And sweeps the howling skies.

4 Ye nations, bend—in reverence bend;
Ye monarchs, wait his nod;
And bid the choral song ascend
To celebrate your God.

BEING AND ATTRIBUTES OF GOD.

L. M. HAMBURG.

1. Thou art, O God! a spir-it pure, Un-seen, unknown to mor-tal eyes;
Th' im-mor-tal, th' e-ter-nal King, The great, the good, the on-ly wise.

85   *God a Spirit.*   14

THOU art, O God! a spirit pure,
    Unseen, unknown to mortal eyes;
Th' immortal, th' eternal King,
The great, the good, the only wise.

2 Whilst nature changes, and her works
Corrupt, decay, dissolve, and die,
Thine essence pure no change shall see,
Secure in immortality.

3 Thou great Invisible! what hand
Can draw thine image, spotless, fair!
To what in heaven, to what on earth,
Can men th' immortal King compare!

4 Let stupid heathens frame their gods
Of gold and silver, wood and stone;
Ours is the God that made the heav'ns;
Jehovah he, and God alone.

5 My soul, thy purest homage pay,
In truth and spirit him adore;
More shall this please than sacrifice,
Than outward forms delight him more.

86   *Omnipresence and Omniscience.*   25

LORD, thou hast search'd & seen me thro',
    Thine eye commands, with piercing view,
My rising and my resting hours,
My heart and flesh, with all their pow'rs.

2 Could I so false, so faithless, prove,
To quit thy service and thy love,
Where, Lord, could I thy presence shun,
Or from thy dreadful glory run?

3 If, mounted on a morning ray,
I fly beyond the western sea,
Thy swifter hand would first arrive,
And there arrest thy fugitive.

4 Or should I try to shun thy sight
Beneath the spreading veil of night,
One glance of thine, one piercing ray,
Would kindle darkness into day.

5 The veil of night is no disguise,
No screen from thine all-searching eyes;
Thy hand can seize thy foes as soon
Thro' midnight shades as blazing noon.

6 Oh, may these tho'ts possess my breast,
Where'er I rove, where'er I rest!
Nor let my weaker passions dare
Consent to sin, for God is there.

87   *Majesty of God.*   772

WHEN Israel forth from Egypt went,
    And Jacob left the stranger's land,
God's glory shadow'd Judah's tent,
And Israel own'd her Monarch's hand.

2 The sea beheld his pow'r and fled;
Back to her source was Jordan driv'n;
The trembling mountains shook for dread;
From their strong base the hills were riven.

3 O sea! what terrors urg'd thy flight?
Why, Jordan, did thy flood retreat?
Why mov'd the hills? And whence the fright
That shook the mountains from their seat?

4 Tremble, O earth, when God appears,—
Before the might of Jacob's God;
Whose pow'r the flinty rock declares,
And, melting, pours the gushing flood.

L. M. PARK STREET.

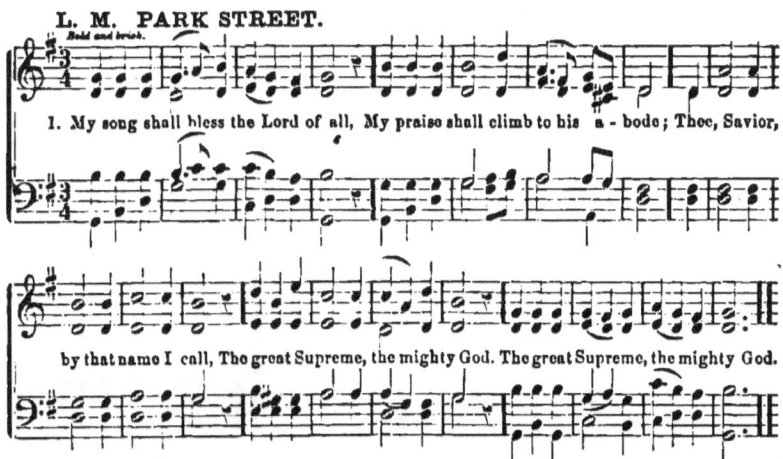

1. My song shall bless the Lord of all, My praise shall climb to his a-bode; Thee, Savior, by that name I call, The great Supreme, the mighty God. The great Supreme, the mighty God.

88   *God our Savior.*   111

MY song shall bless the Lord of all,
My praise shall climb to his abode;
Thee, Savior, by that name I call,
The great Supreme, the mighty God.

2 Without beginning or decline,
Object of faith, and not of sense;
Eternal ages saw him shine,
He shines eternal ages hence.

3 As much, when in the manger laid,
Almighty Ruler of the sky,
As when the six days' work he made
Fill'd all the morning-stars with joy

4 Of all the crowns Jehovah bears,
Salvation is his dearest claim:
That gracious sound well pleas'd he hears,
And owns Immanuel for his name.

5 A cheerful confidence I feel,
My well-plac'd hopes with joy I see:
My bosom glows with heav'nly zeal
To worship him who died for me.

89   *Riches of Divine Goodness.*   61

LET the high heav'ns your songs invite;
Those spacious fields of brilliant light,
Where sun, and moon, and planets roll,
And stars that glow from pole to pole.

2 Sing earth in verdant robes array'd,
Its herbs and flowers, its fruits and shade,
Peopled with life of various forms,
Of fish, and fowl, and beasts, and worms.

3 But oh, that brighter world above,
Where lives and reigns incarnate love;
God's only Son, in flesh array'd,
For man a bleeding victim made!

4 Thither, my soul, with rapture soar,
There in the land of praise adore;
The theme demands an angel's lay,
Demands an everlasting day.

90   *God Praised by His Works.*   59

THE spacious firmament on high,
With all the blue ethereal sky,
And spangled heav'ns, a shining frame,
Their great Original proclaim.

2 Th' unwearied sun, from day to day,
Does his Creator's pow'r display,
And publishes to ev'ry land
The work of an almighty hand.

3 Soon as the ev'ning shades prevail,
The moon takes up the wondrous tale,
And nightly to the list'ning earth
Repeats the story of her birth:

4 Whilst all the stars that round her burn,
And all the planets in their turn,
Confirm the tidings, as they roll,
And spread the truth from pole to pole.

5 What though in solemn silence all
Move round the dark terrestrial ball?
What though no real voice nor sound
Amidst their radiant orbs be found?

6 In reason's ear they all rejoice,
And utter forth a glorious voice,
Forever singing, as they shine—
The hand that made us is divine.

THE WORKS OF GOD.

C. M. WARWICK.

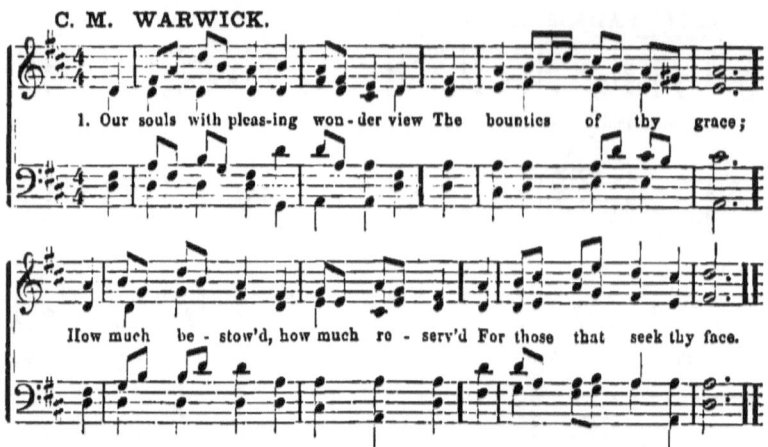

1. Our souls with pleas-ing won-der view The bounties of thy grace;
How much be-stow'd, how much re-serv'd For those that seek thy face.

91 *God's Goodness in His Works.* **35**

OUR souls with pleasing wonder view
 The bounties of thy grace;
How much bestow'd, how much reserv'd
 For those that seek thy face.

2 Thy lib'ral hand with worldly bliss
 Oft makes their cup run o'er;
And in the cov'nant of thy love
 They find diviner store.

3 Here mercy hides their num'rous sins;
 Here grace their souls renews;
Here hope, and love, and joy, and peace
 Their heav'nly beams diffuse.

4 But oh, what treasures yet unknown
 Are lodg'd in worlds to come!
If these th' enjoyments of the way,
 How happy is their home!

92 *The Soul.* **64**

WHAT is the thing of greatest price,
 The whole creation round?
That which was lost in Paradise,
 That which in Christ is found:

2 The soul of man—Jehovah's breath,
 That keeps two worlds at strife;
Hell moves beneath to work its death;
 Heaven stoops to give it life.

3 God, to redeem it, did not spare
 His well-beloved Son;
Jesus, to save it, deign'd to bear
 The sins of all in one.

4 And is this treasure borne below,
 In earthen vessels frail?
Can none its utmost value know,
 Till flesh and spirit fail?

5 Then let us gather round the cross,
 That knowledge to obtain;
Not by the soul's eternal loss,
 But everlasting gain.

93 *Wisdom of God in Nature.* **27**

SONGS of immortal praise belong
 To my almighty God:
He hath my heart, and he my tongue,
 To spread his name abroad.

2 How great the works his hand hath
 How glorious in our sight! [wrought!
And men in ev'ry age have sought
 His wonders with delight.

3 How most exact is nature's frame!
 How wise th' eternal mind!
His counsels never change the scheme
 That his first thoughts design'd.

4 When he redeem'd the sons of men,
 He fix'd his cov'nant sure:
The orders, that his lips pronounce,
 To endless years endure.

94 *God in Nature.* **23**

'TWAS God who hurl'd the rolling spheres
 And stretch'd the boundless skies;
Who form'd the plan of endless years,
 And bade the ages rise.

2 From everlasting is his might,
 Immense and unconfin'd:
He pierces through the realms of light,
 And rides upon the wind.

4 Ye worlds, with ev'ry living thing,
 Fulfill his high command;
Mortals, pay homage to your King,
 And own his ruling hand.

THE WORKS OF GOD.

8, 7, 8, 7, 8, 8, 7. LUTHER'S HYMN.

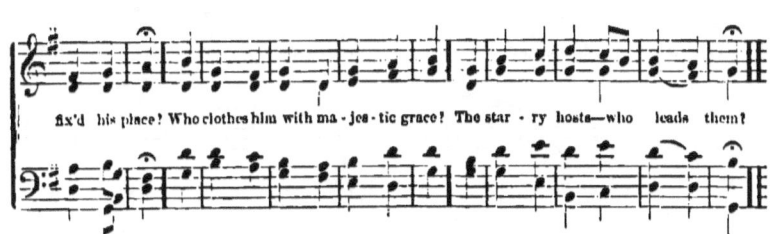

95   *Nature praises God.*   **62**

THE earth, where'er I turn mine eye,
  Reveals her Maker's glory;
Through day and night the shining sky
  Of praise repeats its story;
Who for the sun there fix'd his place?
Who clothes him with majestic grace?
  The starry hosts—who leads them?

2 Who rules the restless raging winds?
  The clouds, in rain distilling?
And who the lap of earth unbinds,
  Our stores with plenty filling?
Great God, thy praises shall abide,
And, with thy goodness, reach as wide
  As wide creation reaches.

3 But man,—a body, of thy hand
  The marvellous formation;
'Tis man,—a soul to understand
  Thy wonders of creation;
'Tis man,—who to himself supplies
Best proof that thou art good and wise,—
  Who best should sing thy praises.

4 Now pay thine honors to his name,
  My soul, his glories telling:
Thy Father and thy God proclaim,
  The world's glad anthem swelling:
Let all our race, with one accord,
Love, trust, and serve our common Lord:
  Who can refuse to serve him?

96   *The Judgment.*   **735**

GREAT God, what do I see and hear!
  The end of things created!
I see the Judge of man appear
  On clouds of glory seated:
The trumpet sounds; the graves restore
The dead which they contain'd before;
  Prepare, my soul, to meet him.

2 The dead in Christ shall first arise,
  At the last trumpet's sounding,
Caught up to meet him in the skies,
  With joy their Lord surrounding;
No gloomy fears their souls dismay,
His presence sheds eternal day
  On those prepar'd to meet him.

3 But sinners, fill'd with guilty fears,
  Behold his wrath prevailing,
For they shall rise, and find their tears
  And sighs are unavailing;
The day of grace is past and gone;
Trembling they stand before the throne,
  All unprepar'd to meet him.

4 Great God, what do I see and hear!
  The end of things created!
The Judge of man I see appear,
  On clouds of glory seated:
Beneath his cross I view the day
When heav'n and earth shall pass away,
  And thus prepare to meet him.

PROVIDENCE.

L. M. MENDON.

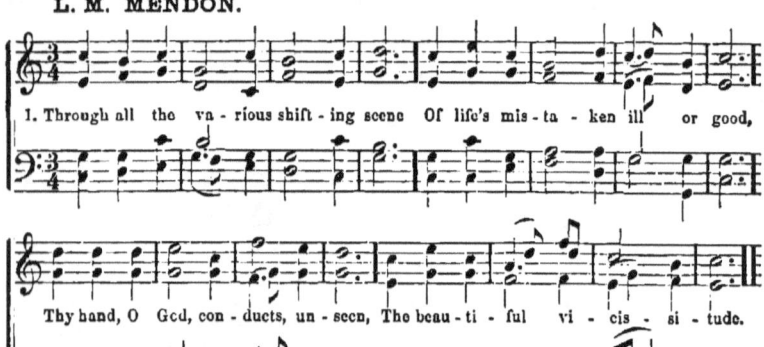

1. Through all the va-rious shift-ing scene Of life's mis-ta-ken ill or good, Thy hand, O God, con-ducts, un-seen, The beau-ti-ful vi-cis-si-tude.

97   *Goodness of Providence.*   **68**

THROUGH all the various shifting scene
Of life's mistaken ill or good,
Thy hand, O God, conducts, unseen,
The beautiful vicissitude.

2 Thou givest with paternal care,
Howe'er unjustly we complain,
To all their necessary share
Of joy and sorrow, health and pain.

3 Trust we to youth, or friends, or pow'r?
Fix we on this terrestrial ball?
When most secure, the coming hour,
If thou see fit, may blast them all.

4 Thy powerful consolations cheer;
Thy smiles suppress the deep-fetch'd sigh;
Thy hand can dry the trickling tear
That secret wets the widow's eye.

5 All things on earth, and all in heav'n,
On thine eternal will depend;
And all for greater good were giv'n,
Would man pursue th' appointed end.

6 Be this my care:—To all beside,
Indiff'rent let my wishes be.
Passion be calm, abas'd be pride,
And fix'd my soul, great God! on thee.

98   *God a Merciful Preserver.*   **609**

GOD of my life, to thee belong
The thankful heart, the grateful song;
Touch'd by thy love, each tuneful chord
Resounds the goodness of the Lord.

2 Thou hast preserv'd my fleeting breath,
And chas'd the gloomy shades of death;
The venom'd arrows vainly fly,
When God our great Deliv'rer's nigh.

3 Yet why, dear Lord, this tender care?
Why does thy hand so kindly rear
A useless cumb'rer of the ground,
On which no pleasant fruits are found?

4 Still may the barren fig-tree stand!
And, cultivated by thy hand,
Verdure, and bloom, and fruit afford,
Meet tribute to its bounteous Lord.

5 So shall thy praise employ my breath
Through life, and in the arms of death
My soul the pleasant theme prolong,
Then rise to aid th' angelic song.

99   *Providence.*   **84**

THY ways, O Lord! with wise design,
Are fram'd upon thy throne above;
And every dark and bending line
Meets in the centre of thy love.

2 With feeble light, and half obscure,
Poor mortals thine arrangements view;
Not knowing that the least are sure,
And the mysterious just and true.

3 Thy flock, thine own peculiar care,
Though now they seem to roam uney'd,
Are led or driven only where
They best and safest may abide.

4 They neither know nor trace the way:
But whilst they trust thy guardian eye,
Their feet shall ne'er to ruin stray,
Nor shall the weakest fail or die.

5 My favor'd soul shall meekly learn
To lay her reason at thy throne;
Too weak thy secrets to discern,
I'll trust thee for my guide alone.

PROVIDENCE.

L. M. ORLAND.

1. 'Tis wisdom, mer-cy, love di-vine, Which mingles blessings with our cares;
And shall our thankless heart re-pine That we ob-tain not all our pray'rs?

100   *Resignation to Providence.*   **86**

'TIS wisdom, mercy, love divine,
  Which mingles blessing with our cares;
And shall our thankless heart repine
That we obtain not all our prayers?

2 From want of faith our sorrows flow;
Short-sighted mortals, weak and blind,
Bend down their eyes to earth and woe,
And doubt if Providence be kind.

3 Should heaven with every wish comply,
Say, would the grant relieve the care?
Perhaps the good for which we sigh
Might change its name and prove a snare.

4 Were once our vain desires subdued,
The will resign'd, the heart at rest;
In every scene we should conclude
The will of heaven is right, is best.

101   *The Seasons.*   **605**

GREAT God, as seasons disappear,
  And changes mark the rolling year;
As time, with rapid pinions, flies,
May ev'ry season make us wise.

2 Long has thy favor crown'd our days,
And summer shed again its rays;
Our harvest months have o'er us roll'd,
And fill'd our fields with waving gold.

3 The solemn harvest comes apace,
The closing day of life and grace:
Time of decision, awful hour!
Around it let no tempests low'r!

4 Prepare us, Lord, by grace divine,
Like stars in heaven to rise and shine;
Then shall our happy souls above
Reap the full harvest of thy love!

102   *God our Refuge.*   **71**

GOD is the refuge of his saints,
  When storms of deep distress invade;
Ere we can offer our complaints,
Behold him present with his aid.

2 Let mountains from their seats be hurl'd
Down to the deep, and buried there;
Convulsions shake the solid world:
Our faith shall never yield to fear.

3 Loud may the troubled ocean roar,
In sacred peace our souls abide;
While ev'ry nation, ev'ry shore
Trembles and dreads the swelling tide.

4 'Mid storms and tempests, Lord, thy word
Does ev'ry rising fear control;
Sweet peace thy promises afford,
And well sustain the fainting soul.

103   *Elijah fed.*   **83**

WHEN God's own people stand in need,
  His goodness will provide supplies:
Thus, when Elijah faints for bread,
A raven to his succor flies.

2 This wonder oft has been renew'd,
And saints by sweet experience find
Their evil overrul'd for good,
Their foes to friendly deeds inclin'd.

3 Who can distrust that mighty hand
Which rules with universal sway,
Which nature's laws can countermand,
Or feed us by a bird of prey!

PROVIDENCE.

C. M. STEPHENS.

1. God moves in a mysterious way, His wonders to perform;
He plants his foot-steps in the sea, And rides up-on the storm.

104 *God's Ways mysterious.* **69**

GOD moves in a mysterious way,
  His wonders to perform;
He plants his footsteps in the sea,
  And rides upon the storm.

2 Deep in unfathomable mines
  Of never-failing skill,
He treasures up his bright designs,
  And works his sov'reign will.

3 Ye fearful saints! fresh courage take:
  The clouds ye so much dread
Are big with mercy, and will break
  In blessings on your head.

4 Judge not the Lord by feeble sense,
  But trust him for his grace;
Behind a frowning providence
  He hides a smiling face.

5 His purposes will ripen fast,
  Unfolding ev'ry hour:
The bud may have a bitter taste,
  But sweet will be the flow'r.

6 Blind unbelief is sure to err,
  And scan his work in vain:
God is his own interpreter,
  And he will make it plain

105 *God our Help.* **74**

TO calm the sorrows of the mind,
  Our heav'nly Friend is nigh,
To wipe the anxious tear that starts
  Or trembles in the eye.

2 Thou canst, when anguish rends the heart,
  The secret woe control;
The inward malady canst heal,
  The sickness of the soul.

3 Thou canst repress the rising sigh;
  Canst soothe each mortal care;
And ev'ry deep and heart-felt groan
  Is wafted to thine ear.

4 Thy gracious eye is watchful still;
  Thy potent arm can save
From threat'ning danger and disease,
  And the devouring grave.

5 When, pale and languid all the frame,
  The ruthless hand of pain
Arrests the feeble pow'rs of life,
  The help of man is vain.

6 'Tis thou, great God! alone canst check
  The progress of disease;
And sickness, aw'd by pow'r divine,
  The high command obeys.

7 Eternal source of life and health,
  And ev'ry bliss we feel!
In sorrow and in joy to thee,
  Our grateful hearts appeal.

106 *Dependence on God.* **75**

LET others boast how strong they be,
  Nor death nor danger fear;
While we confess, O Lord, to thee,
  What feeble things we are.

2 Fresh as the grass our bodies stand,
  And flourish bright and gay:
A blasting wind sweeps o'er the land,
  And fades the grass away.

3 Our life contains a thousand springs,
  And dies if one be gone:
Strange! that a harp of thousand strings
  Should keep in tune so long.

4 But 'tis our God supports our frame,
  The God that form'd us first:
Salvation to th' almighty name
  That rear'd us from the dust.

5 While we have breath, or life, or tongues,
  Our Maker we'll adore.
His spirit moves our heaving lungs,
  Or they would breathe no more.

107 Safety in God. 81

HOW are thy servants blest, O Lord!
  How sure is their defence!
Eternal Wisdom is their guide,
  Their help Omnipotence.

2 In foreign realms and lands remote,
  Supported by thy care,
They pass unhurt through burning climes,
  And breathe in tainted air.

3 Thy mercy gladdens ev'ry soil,
  Makes ev'ry region please;
The hoary frozen hills it warms,
  And smoothes the boist'rous seas.

4 Though by the dreadful tempest toss'd
  High on the broken wave,
They know thou art not slow to hear,
  Nor impotent to save.

5 The storm is laid, the winds retire,
  Obedient to thy will;
The sea, that roars at thy command,
  At thy command is still.

6 From all my griefs and straits, O Lord!
  Thy mercy sets me free;
Whilst in the confidence of prayer
  My heart takes hold on thee.

7 In midst of dangers, fears, and deaths,
  Thy goodness I'll adore;
And praise thee for thy mercies past,
  And humbly hope for more.

8 My life, while thou preserv'st my life,
  Thy sacrifice shall be;
And oh, may death, when death shall come,
  Unite my soul to thee!

108 Dark Providence. 82

THY way, O God, is in the sea,
  Thy paths I cannot trace,
Nor comprehend the mystery
  Of thine unbounded grace.

2 Here the dark veils of flesh and sense
  My captive soul surround;
Mysterious deeps of providence
  My wond'ring thoughts confound.

3 As through a glass, I dimly see
  The wonders of thy love,

How little do I know of thee,
  Or of the joys above!

4 'Tis but in part I know thy will:
  I bless thee for the sight;
When will thy love the rest reveal,
  In glory's clearer light?

5 With raptures shall I then survey
  Thy providence and grace;
And spend an everlasting day
  In wonder, love, and praise.

109 God our Help.

WHEN earthly joys glide swift away,
  When hopes and comforts flee,
When foes beset, and friends betray,
  I turn, my God, to thee.

2 Thy nature, Lord, no change can know,
  Thy promise still is sure;
And ills can ne'er so hopeless grow,
  But thou canst find a cure.

3 Deliverance comes, most bright and blest,
  At danger's darkest hour;
And man's extremity is best
  To prove Almighty power.

110 Praise for Providence. 87

ALMIGHTY Father! gracious Lord!
  Kind guardian of my days!
Thy mercies let my heart record
  In songs of grateful praise.

2 In life's first dawn, my tender frame
  Was thine indulgent care,
Long ere I could pronounce thy name,
  Or breathe the infant pray'r.

3 Around my path what dangers rose!
  What snares o'erspread my road!
No pow'r could guard me from my foes,
  But my preserver, God.

4 Yet I adore thee, gracious Lord!
  For favors more divine:
That I have known thy sacred word,
  Where all thy glories shine.

5 And may I hope that Christ is mine?
  That source of every bliss—
That noblest gift of love divine;
  What wondrous grace is this!

6 My highest praise, alas, how poor!
  How cold my highest love!
Dear Savior, teach me to adore
  As angels do above.

7 And as this mortal frame decays,
  And earthly comfort flies,
Complete the wonders of thy grace,
  And raise me to the skies.

PROVIDENCE.

C. M. GIVE.

1. And art thou with us, gra-cious Lord, To dis-si-pate our fear? Dost thou pro-claim thy-self our God, Our God for-ev-er near?

111 *Trust in God.* 78

AND art thou with us, gracious Lord,
   To dissipate our fear?
Dost thou proclaim thyself our God,
   Our God forever near?

2 Doth thy right hand, which form'd the
   And bears up all the skies,   [earth,
Stretch from on high its friendly aid,
   When dangers round us rise?

3 And wilt thou lead our weary souls
   To that delightful scene
Where rivers of salvation flow
   Through pastures ever green?

4 On thy support our souls shall lean,
   And banish ev'ry care;
The gloomy vale of death shall smile,
   If God be with us there.

5 While we his gracious succor prove,
   'Midst all our various ways,
The darkest shades through which we pass,
   Shall echo with his praise.

112 *Praise for Preservation.* 616

LORD of my life! oh, may thy praise
   Employ my noblest pow'rs,
Whose goodness lengthens out my days
   And fills the circling hours!

2 Preserv'd by thine Almighty arm,
   I pass the shades of night,
Serene and safe from ev'ry harm,
   And see returning light.

3 While many spent the night in sighs,
   And restless pains and woes,
In gentle sleep I clos'd mine eyes
   And undisturb'd repose.

4 When sleep, death's semblance, o'er me
   And I unconscious lay,   [spread,
Thy watchful care was round my bed
   To guard my feeble clay.

5 Oh, let the same almighty care
   My waking hours attend;
From ev'ry trespass, ev'ry snare,
   My heedless steps defend.

6 Smile on my minutes as they roll,
   And guide my future days;
And let thy goodness fill my soul
   With gratitude and praise.

113 *Harvest Hymn.* 933

FOUNTAIN of mercy, God of love,
   How rich thy bounties are!
The rolling seasons, as they move,
   Proclaim thy constant care.

2 When in the bosom of the earth
   The sower hid the grain,
Thy goodness mark'd its secret birth
   And sent the early rain.

3 The spring's sweet influence, Lord, was
   The plants in beauty grew;   [thine;
Thou mad'st refulgent suns to shine,
   And gav'st refreshing dew.

4 These various mercies from above
  Matur'd the swelling grain;
A kindly harvest crowns thy love,
  And plenty fills the plain.

5 We own and bless thy gracious sway;
  Thy hand all nature hails:
Seed-time nor harvest, night nor day,
  Summer nor winter, fails.

114   *Preservation.*   614

ONCE more, my soul, the rising day
  Salutes thy waking eyes,
Once more, my voice, thy tribute pay
  To him that rules the skies.

2 Night unto night his name repeats,
  The day renews the sound,
Wide as the heav'n on which he sits
  To turn the seasons round.

3 'Tis he supports my mortal frame,
  My tongue shall speak his praise:
My sins would rouse his wrath to flame,
  And yet his wrath delays.

4 A thousand wretched souls are fled
  Since the last setting sun,
And yet thou length'nest out my thread,
  And yet my moments run.

5 Great God, let all my hours be thine
  Whilst I enjoy the light,
Then shall my sun in smiles decline
  And bring a pleasant night.

115   *Goodness of Providence.*   619

GREAT God! my early vows to thee
  With gratitude I'll bring,
And at the rosy dawn of day,
  Thy lofty praises sing.

2 Thou round the heav'nly arch dost draw
  A dark and sable veil,
And all the beauties of the world
  From mortal eyes conceal.

3 Again the sky with golden beams
  Thy skillful hands adorn,
And paint with cheerful splendor gay
  The fair ascending morn.

4 And as the gloomy night returns,
  Or smiling day renews,
Thy constant goodness still my soul
  With benefits pursues.

5 For this will I my vows to thee
  With ev'ning incense bring;
And at the rosy dawn of day
  Thy lofty praises sing.

116   *The Sea Obedient.*   961

MAKER of all things, mighty Lord!
  We own thy power divine;
The winds and waves obey thy word,
  For all their strength is thine.

2 Wide as the wintry tempests sweep,
  They work thy sov'reign will;
Thy voice is heard upon the deep,
  And all its waves are still.

3 When dangers threat in ev'ry form
  And death itself is near;
O God! amidst the raging storm,
  We're safe beneath thy care.

4 With trembling hope on thee we stay
  To rescue from the grave:
Thou, whom the elements obey,
  Art ever near to save.

117   *Fear not.*   88

YE trembling souls! dismiss your fears,
  Be mercy all your theme;
Mercy, which like a river flows
  In one continued stream.

2 Fear not the pow'rs of earth and hell:
  God will these pow'rs restrain,
His mighty arm their rage repel,
  And make their efforts vain.

3 Fear not the want of outward good
  He still for his provides,
Grants them supplies of daily food,
  And gives them heav'n besides.

4 Fear not that he will e'er forsake,
  Or leave his work undone;
He's faithful to his promises,
  And faithful to his Son.

5 Fear not the terrors of the grave,
  Nor death's tremendous sting;
He will from endless wrath preserve,
  To endless glory bring.

6 You in his wisdom, pow'r, and grace,
  May confidently trust:
His wisdom guides, his pow'r protects,
  His grace rewards the just.

PROVIDENCE.

L. M. WARD.

118 *Afflictions from God.* **73**

NOT from relentless fate's dark womb,
Or from the dust, our troubles come;
No fickle chance presides o'er grief,
To cause the pain, or send relief.

2 Look up, and see, ye sorrowing saints!
The cause and cure of your complaints.
Know, 'tis your heav'nly Father's will:
Bid ev'ry murmur then be still.

3 He sees we need the painful yoke;
Yet love directs his heaviest stroke.
He takes no pleasure in our smart,
But wounds to heal and cheer the heart.

4 Blest trials those that cleanse from sin,
And make the soul all pure within,
Wean the fond mind from earthly toys,
To seek and taste celestial joys!

119 *Christ our Refuge.* **469**

GOD of my life, whose gracious pow'r
Thro' various deaths my soul hath led,
Or turn'd aside the fatal hour,
Or lifted up my sinking head!

2 In all my ways thy hand I own,
Thy ruling providence I see:
Assist me still my course to run,
And still direct my paths to thee.

3 Whither, oh, whither should I fly,
But to my loving Savior's breast;
Secure within thine arms to lie,
And safe beneath thy wings to rest?

4 I have no skill the snare to shun,
But thou, O Christ! my wisdom art:
I ever into ruin run,
But thou art greater than my heart.

5 Foolish, and impotent, and blind,
Lead me a way I have not known;
Bring me where I my heav'n may find,
The heav'n of loving thee alone.

6 Enlarge my heart to make thee room;
Enter, and in me ever stay:
The crooked then shall straight become,
The darkness shall be lost in day.

120 *Mercies Renewed.* **612**

MY God, how endless is thy love!
Thy gifts are ev'ry ev'ning new,
And morning mercies from above
Gently descend like early dew.

2 Thou spread'st the curtains of the night,
Great Guardian of my sleeping hours;
Thy sov'reign word restores the light,
And quickens all my drowsy pow'rs.

3 I yield myself to thy command,
To thee devote my nights and days;
Perpetual blessings from thy hand
Demand perpetual hymns of praise.

121 *God in Life and Death.* **673**

WHEN mortal man resigns his breath,
'Tis God directs the shafts of death;
Casual though the stroke appear,
He sends the fatal messenger.

2 All pow'r is in that hand divine;
That hand must first the warrant sign.
Who first inspir'd the breath of life,
Prolongs or ends the mortal strife.

3 If thou my body hence wilt raise,
I'll publish my Restorer's praise,
My life at thy dear hands receive,
And only for thy glory live.

PROVIDENCE. 45

122   *Trust in God.*   72

GIVE to the winds thy fears;
 Hope, and be undismay'd;
God hears thy sighs, and counts thy tears,
 And shall lift up thy head.

2 Through waves and clouds and storms,
 He gently clears thy way;
Wait thou his time, so shall this night
 Soon end in joyous day.

3 What though thou rulest not?
 Yet heav'n, and earth, and hell
Proclaim, God sitteth on the throne,
 And ruleth all things well.

4 Thine everlasting truth,
 Father, thy ceaseless love
Sees all thy children's wants, and knows
 What best for each will prove.

5 And whatsoe'er thou will'st,
 Thou dost, O King of kings;
What thine unerring wisdom chose,
 Thy power to being brings.

6 Let us in life, in death,
 Thy steadfast truth declare;
And publish, with our latest breath,
 Thy love and guardian care.

123   *God our Shepherd.*   855

THE Lord my Shepherd is;
 I shall be well supplied:
Since he is mine and I am his,
 What can I want beside?

2 He leads me to the place
 Where heav'nly pasture grows,
Where living waters gently pass,
 And full salvation flows.

3 If e'er I go astray,
 He doth my soul reclaim,
And guides me, in his own right way,
 For his most holy name.

4 While he affords his aid,
 I cannot yield to fear;
Tho' I should walk thro' death's dark shade,
 My Shepherd's with me there.

5 In sight of all my foes,
 Thou dost my table spread;
My cup with blessings overflows,
 And joy exalts my head.

6 The bounties of thy love
 Shall crown my future days;
Nor from thy house will I remove,
 Nor cease to speak thy praise.

124   *The Good Shepherd.*   783

WHILE my Redeemer's near,
 My Shepherd and my Guide,
I bid farewell to ev'ry fear;
 My wants are all supplied.

2 To ever-fragrant meads,
 Where rich abundance grows,
His gracious hands indulgent leads,
 And guards my sweet repose.

3 Dear Shepherd, if I stray,
 My wand'ring feet restore;
And guard me with thy watchful eye,
 And let me rove no more.

46 PROVIDENCE.

125 *Gracious Providence.* 615

HOSANNA with a cheerful sound
To God's upholding hand!
Ten thousand snares our path surround,
And yet secure we stand.

2 How wondrous is that mighty pow'r
Which form'd us with a word!
And ev'ry day, and ev'ry hour,
We lean upon the Lord.

3 The ev'ning rests our weary head,
And mercy guards the room;
We wake, and we admire the bed
That was not made our tomb.

4 The rising morn cannot assure
That we shall end the day;
For death stands ready at the door
To take our lives away.

5 God is our sun, whose daily light
Our joy and safety brings;
Our feeble frame lies safe at night
Beneath his shelt'ring wings.

126 *Harvest Hymn.* 603

TO praise the ever-bounteous Lord,
My soul, wake all thy pow'rs:
He calls, and at his voice come forth
The smiling harvest hours.

2 His cov'nant with the earth he keeps;
My tongue, his goodness sing;
Summer and winter know their time,
His harvest crowns the spring.

3 Well pleas'd, the toiling swains behold
The waving yellow crop:
With joy they bear the sheaves away
And sow again in hope.

4 Thus teach me, gracious God, to sow
The seeds of righteousness:
Smile on my soul, and with thy beams
The rip'ning harvest bless.

5 Then, in the last great harvest, I
Shall reap a glorious crop:
The harvest shall by far exceed
What I have shown in hope.

127 *God our Help.* 959

O GOD, our help in ages past,
Our hope for years to come,
Our shelter from the stormy blast
And our eternal home,—

2 Beneath the shadow of thy throne
Thy saints have dwelt secure;
Sufficient is thine arm alone,
And our defence is sure.

3 Before the hills in order stood,
Or earth receiv'd her frame,
From everlasting thou art God,
To endless years the same.

4 Thy word commands our flesh to dust,
"Return, ye sons of men;"
All nations rose from earth at first,
And turn to earth again.

PROVIDENCE. 47

8's, 6 lines. ELIAS.

1. Thus far on life's per-plex-ing path, Thus far thou, Lord, our steps hast led,
Snatch'd from the world's pursu-ing wrath, Un-harm'd, tho' floods hung o'er our head.
Like ran-som'd Is-rael on the shore, Here then we pause, look back, a-dore.

128 *God our Helper.*

THUS far on life's perplexing path,
Thus far thou, Lord, our steps hast led,
Snatch'd from the world's pursuing wrath,
Unharm'd, tho' floods hung o'er our head.
Like ransom'd Israel on the shore,
Here then we pause, look back, adore.

2 Strangers and pilgrims here below,
Like all our fathers in their day,
We to the land of promise go,
Lord, by thine own appointed way
Still guide, illumine, cheer our flight,
In cloud by day, in fire by night.

3 Protect us, through the wilderness,
From ev'ry peril, plague, and foe:
With bread from heav'n thy people bless,
And living streams, where'er we go:
Nor let our rebel hearts repine,
Or follow any voice but thine.

4 Thy holy law to us proclaim,
But not from Sinai's top alone:
Hid in the rock-cleft, be thy name
And all thy goodness to us shown:
And may we never bow the knee
Or worship any God but thee.

5 When we have number'd all our years,
And stand at length on Jordan's brink,
Though the flesh fail with mortal fears,
Oh, let not then the spirit sink:
But strong in faith, and hope, and love,
Plunge through the stream, to rise above.

129 *God our Shepherd.* **79**

THE Lord my pasture shall prepare,
And feed me with a shepherd's care;
His presence shall my wants supply,
And guard me with a watchful eye:
My noonday walks he shall attend,
And all my midnight hours defend.

2 When in the sultry glebe I faint,
Or on the thirsty mountains pant,
To fertile vales and dewy meads
My weary, wandering steps he leads,
Where peaceful rivers, soft and slow,
Amid the verdant landscape flow.

3 Though in a bare and rugged way,
Through devious, lonely wilds I stray,
His bounty shall my pains beguile;
The barren wilderness shall smile,
With lively greens and herbage crown'd,
And streams shall murmur all around.

4 Though in the paths of death I tread,
With gloomy horrors overspread,
My steadfast heart shall fear no ill,
For thou, O Lord! art with me still;
Thy friendly crook shall give me aid,
And guide me through the dismal shade.

PROVIDENCE.

8, 7, 7, 8, 7, 7. MELANCTHON.

1. As the eagle fondly hovers O'er its young defenseless brood, So my God from danger covers, Granting me all needed good. With a father's love he eyed me, When began mine infant days; Ere my heart could mean his praise, He with watchful care supplied me. All things else their time will last, But his love, when time is past.

130 *God our Help.* **85**

AS the eagle fondly hovers
  O'er its young defenseless brood,
So my God from danger covers,
  Granting me all needed good.
With a father's love he eyed me,
  When began mine infant days ;
Ere my heart could mean his praise,
He with watchful care supplied me.
All things else their time will last,
But his love, when time is past.

2 For me, wretched—hopeless lying,—
  Worthy of his wrath alone,
He to shame, and griefs, and dying,
  Gave his well-beloved Son.
Who the love of God can measure?
  None of all our feeble race,—
While, on ev'ry side, we trace
Proofs that mercy is his pleasure.
Great my sins, but high above
Reaches his unbounded love.

3 As my teacher, to direct me,
  He has sent his Spirit too ;
Who, to comfort and protect me,
  Should his scheme of love pursue ;
And, while I am sin bewailing,
  Give me hope ;—in weakness, strength,
  Light in darkness ;—till, at length,
I might sing his grace unfailing,
  And, though earthly griefs annoy,
  Triumph still with holy joy.

4 Shall I, weary of confiding,
  Fear what may the future be ?
Since on earth I've been residing,
  God has daily cared for me.
When I think what he has sent me,—
  Comforts for my earthly home,
  Pledges for the life to come,—
What more need I to content me ?
  Shall I mine own weakness fear ?
  He, my confidence, is near.

5 Oh, how many springs of sadness
  Has my God in mercy dried !
And how many streams of gladness
  To my soul has he supplied !
When his purpose he's concealing,
  On his wisdom I will rest,—
  Still he's doing what is best,
All my ills and anguish healing :
  His, a father's love to me
  Has been, and will ever be.

CHRIST'S DIVINE GLORY AND INCARNATION.

L. M. CHEMNITZ.

1. Bright King of glo-ry, dread-ful God! Our spi-rits bow be-fore thy seat; To thee we lift an hum-ble thought, And wor-ship at thine aw-ful feet.

131 *Christ's Divine Glory.* **100**

BRIGHT King of glory, dreadful God!
Our spirits bow before thy seat;
To thee we lift an humble thought,
And worship at thine awful feet.

2 A thousand seraphs, strong and bright,
Stand round the glorious Deity;
But who amongst the sons of light
Pretends comparison with thee!

3 Yet there is one of human frame,
Jesus, array'd in flesh and blood,
Thinks it no robbery to claim
A full equality with God.

4 Their glory shines with equal beams;
Their essence is forever one;
Though they are known by different names,
The Father God, and God the Son.

5 Then let the name of Christ our King
With equal honors be ador'd;
His praise let ev'ry angel sing,
And all the nations own their Lord.

132 *Christ's Glory and Incarnation.* **99**

ERE the blue heav'ns were stretch'd abroad,
From everlasting was the Word;
With God he was; the Word was God,
And must divinely be ador'd.

2 By his own power were all things made;
By him supported all things stand:
He is the whole creation's Head,
And angels fly at his command.

3 Ere sin was born, or Satan fell,
He led the host of morning stars;
(Thy generation who can tell,
Or count the number of thy years?)

4 But lo, he leaves those heav'nly forms,
The Word descends and dwells in clay,
That he may converse hold with worms,
Drest in such feeble flesh as they.

5 Mortals with joy beheld his face,
Th' eternal Father's only Son;
How full of truth! how full of grace!
When through his form the Godhead shone.

6 Archangels leave their high abode,
To learn new myst'ries here, and tell
The love of our descending God,
The glories of Immanuel.

133 *Christ's Worshiped in Glory.*

AROUND the Savior's lofty throne,
Ten thousand times ten thousand sing;
They worship him as God alone,
And crown him—everlasting King!

2 Approach, ye saints! this God is yours;
'Tis Jesus fills the throne above:
Ye cannot want, while God endures;
Ye cannot fail, while God is love.

3 Jesus, thou everlasting King!
To Thee the praise of heaven belongs;
Yet, smile on us, who fain would bring
The tribute of our humble songs.

4 Though sin defile our worship here,
We hope, ere long, Thy face to view;
And, when our souls in heaven appear,
We'll praise Thy name as angels do.

CHRIST'S GLORY AND INCARNATION.

C. M. ST. ANN'S.

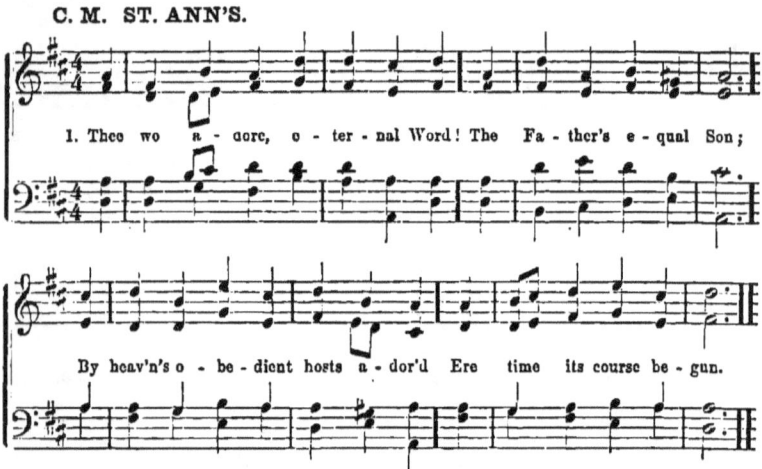

134 *Deity of Christ.*   101

THEE we adore, eternal Word!
  The Father's equal Son;
By heav'n's obedient hosts ador'd
  Ere time its course begun.

2 The first creation has display'd
    Thine energy divine;
  For not a single thing was made
    By other hands than thine.

3 But ransom'd sinners, with delight,
    Sublimer facts survey,—
  The all-creating Word unites
    Himself to dust and clay.

4 Creation's Author now assumes
    A Creature's humble form ;
  A man of grief and woe becomes,
    Is trod on like a worm.

5 The Lord of glory bears the shame
    To vile transgressors due ;
  Justice the Prince of life condemns
    To die in anguish too.

6 God over all, forever blest,
    The righteous curse endures ;
  And thus, to souls with sin distrest,
    Eternal bliss insures.

7 What wonders in thy person meet,
    My Savior, all divine!
  I fall with rapture at thy feet,
    And would be wholly thine.

135 *The Name of Jesus.*   330

JESUS, in thy transporting name
  What glories meet our eyes!

Thou art the seraphs' lofty theme,
  The wonder of the skies.

2 Well might the heav'ns with wonder view
    A love so strange as thine ;
  No thought of angels ever knew
    Compassion so divine.

3 And didst thou, Savior, leave the sky,
    To sink beneath our woes?
  Didst thou descend to bleed and die
    For thy rebellious foes?

4 Oh, may our willing hearts confess
    Thy sweet, thy gentle sway ;
  Glad captives of thy matchless grace,
    Thy righteous rule obey.

136 *The Savior's Glory.*

JESUS, my Lord, my life, my light!
  Oh, come with blissful ray ;
Break radiant through the shades of night,
  And chase my fears away.

2 Then shall my soul with rapture trace
    The wonders of thy love ;
  But the full glories of thy face
    Are only known above.

137 *Honors to Christ.*   347

HOSANNA to the royal Son
  Of David's ancient line,
His natures two, his person one,
  Mysterious and divine.

2 The root of David here we find,
    And offspring is the same ;
  Eternity and time are join'd
    In our Immanuel's name.

CHRIST'S GLORY AND INCARNATION. 51

Blest he that comes to wretched men
With peaceful news from heav'n;
Iosannas of the highest strain
To Christ the Lord be giv'n.

Let mortals ne'er refuse to take
Th' hosanna on their tongues,
Lest rocks and stones should rise, and break
Their silence into songs.

138   *Praise to Christ.*   **353**

O our Redeemer's glorious name
  Awake the sacred song!
Oh, may his love (immortal flame!)
Tune ev'ry heart and tongue.

2 His love what mortal thought can reach!
  What mortal tongue display!
Imagination's utmost stretch
  In wonder dies away.

3 He left his radiant throne on high,
  Left the bright realms of bliss,
And came to earth to bleed and die!
  Was ever love like this?

4 Dear Lord, while we adoring pay
  Our humble thanks to thee,
May ev'ry heart with rapture say,
  "The Savior died for me."

S. M. ST. THOMAS.

1. Raise your triumphant songs To an immortal tune;
Let the wide earth resound the deeds Celestial grace has done.

139   *The Messenger of Love.*   **106**

RAISE your triumphant songs
   To an immortal tune;
Let the wide earth resound the deeds
Celestial grace has done.

2 Sing how eternal love
  Its chief Beloved chose,
And bade him raise our wretched race
  From their abyss of woes.

3 His hand no thunder bears,
  No terror clothes his brow;
No bolts to drive our guilty souls
  To fiercer flames below.

4 'Twas mercy fill'd the throne,
  When wrath stood silent by,
When Christ was sent with pardon down
  To rebels doom'd to die.

5 Now, sinners, dry your tears;
  Let hopeless sorrow cease;
Bow to the sceptre of his love,
  And take the offer'd peace.

140   *Christ's Incarnation.*   **112**

YE saints, proclaim abroad
   The honors of your King;
To Jesus, your incarnate God,
   Your songs of praises sing.

2 Not angels round the throne
  Of majesty above,
Are half so much oblig'd as we
  To our Immanuel's love.

3 They never sunk so low,
  They are not rais'd so high;
They never knew such depths of woe,
  Such heights of majesty.

4 The Savior did not join
  Their nature to his own;
For them he shed no blood divine,
  Nor breath'd a single groan.

5 May we with angels vie
  The Savior to adore;
Our debts are greater far than theirs,
  Oh, be our praises more!

CHRIST'S GLORY AND INCARNATION.

141 *Jesus above all Praise.* **332.**

JOIN all the glorious names
  Of wisdom, love, and pow'r,
That ever mortals knew,
  That angels ever bore:
All are too mean
  To speak his worth:
Too mean to set
  My Savior forth.

2 But, oh, what gentle terms,
    What condescending ways,
  Doth our Redeemer use
    To teach his heav'nly grace!
  Mine eyes with joy
    And wonder see
  What forms of love
    He bears for me.

3 Array'd in mortal flesh,
    He like an angel stands,
  And holds the promises
    And pardons in his hands;
  Commission'd from
    His Father's throne,
  To make his grace
    To mortals known.

4 Great Prophet of my God!
    My tongue would bless thy name:
  By thee the joyful news
    Of our salvation came,
  The joyful news
    Of sins forgiv'n,
  Of hell subdu'd,
    And peace with heav'n.

142 *Mission of Christ.*

COME, every pious heart,
  That loves the Savior's name!
Your noblest powers exert,
  To celebrate his fame;
Tell all above,
  And all below,
The debt of love
  To him you owe.

2 He left his starry crown,
    And laid his robes aside;
  On wings of love, came down,
    And wept, and bled, and died;
  What he endured,
    No tongue can tell,
  To save our souls
    From death and hell.

3 From the dark grave he rose,—
    The mansion of the dead;
  And thence his mighty foes
    In glorious triumph led;
  Up through the sky
    The conqu'ror rode,
  And reigns on high,
    The Savior God.

4 From thence he'll quickly come,—
    His chariot will not stay,—
  And bear our spirits home
    To realms of endless day:
  There shall we see
    His lovely face,
  And ever be
    In his embrace.

143 *Praise for Christ.* 110

GIVE thanks to God most high,
  The universal Lord,
The sov'reign King of kings;
  And be his grace ador'd.
    His pow'r and grace
    Are still the same;
    And let his name
    Have endless praise.

2 He saw the nations lie
  All perishing in sin,
And pitied the sad state
  The ruin'd world was in.
    Thy mercy, Lord,
    Shall still endure,
    And ever sure
    Abides thy word.

3 He sent his only Son
  To save us from our woe,
From Satan, sin, and death,
  And ev'ry hurtful foe.
    His pow'r and grace
    Are still the same;
    And let his name
    Have endless praise.

4 Give thanks aloud to God,
  To God the heav'nly King;
And let the spacious earth
  His works and glories sing.
    Thy mercy, Lord,
    Shall still endure;
    And ever sure
    Abides thy word.

144 *Advent.* 104

HARK! what celestial notes,
  What melody we hear!
Soft on the morn it floats,
  And fills the ravish'd ear!
    The tuneful shell,
    The golden lyre,
    And vocal choir,
    The concert swell.

2 Th' angelic hosts descend,
  With harmony divine;
See how from heav'n they bend,
  And in full chorus join.
    Fear not, say they;
    Great joy we bring:
    Jesus, your King,
    Is born to-day.

3 He comes, from error's night
  Your wand'ring feet to save;
To realms of bliss and light
  He lifts you from the grave.
    This glorious morn,
    (Let all attend!)
    Your matchless friend,
    Your Savior's born.

4 Glory to God on high!
  Ye mortals, spread the sound,
And let your raptures fly
  To earth's remotest bound:
    For peace on earth,
    From God in heav'n,
    To man was giv'n,
    At Jesus' birth.

THE SAVIOR'S NATIVITY.

C. M. HENRY.
With spirit.

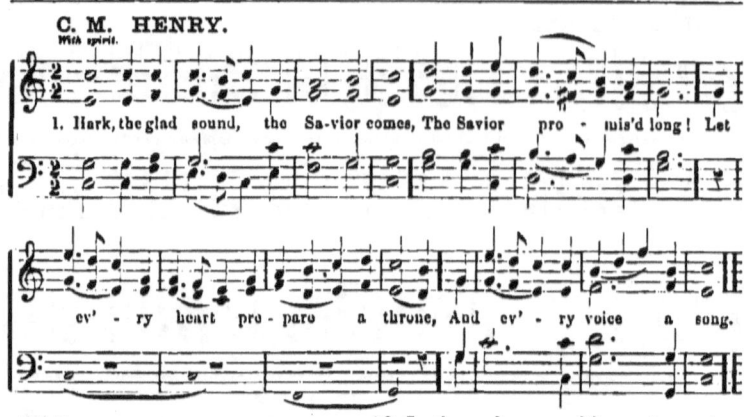

1. Hark, the glad sound, the Sa-vior comes, The Savior pro-mis'd long! Let ev'-ry heart pre-pare a throne, And ev'-ry voice a song.

145   *The Nativity.*   105

HARK, the glad sound, the Savior comes,
  The Savior promis'd long!
Let ev'ry heart prepare a throne,
  And ev'ry voice a song.

2 On him the Spirit, largely pour'd,
  Exerts his sacred fire ;
Wisdom, and might, and zeal, and love,
  His holy breast inspire.

3 He comes, the pris'ners to release,
  In Satan's bondage held :
The gates of brass before him burst,
  The iron fetters yield.

4 He comes, from thickest films of vice
  To clear the mental ray ;
And on the eyes, oppress'd with night,
  To pour celestial day.

5 He comes, the broken heart to bind,
  The bleeding soul to cure,
And with the treasures of his grace,
  T' enrich the humble poor.

6 Our glad hosannas, Prince of peace!
  Thy welcome shall proclaim ;
And heaven's eternal arches ring
  With thy beloved name.

146   *Joy at the Birth of Christ.*   108

HIGH let us swell our tuneful notes
  And join th' angelic throng ;
For angels no such love have known,
  T' awake a cheerful song.

2 Good will to guilty men is shown,
  And peace on earth is giv'n ;
For lo! the incarnate Savior comes,
  A messenger from heav'n.

3 Justice and grace, with sweet accord,
  His rising beams adorn :
Let heav'n and earth in concert join,
  Now such a child is born.

4 Glory to God, in highest strains,
  In highest worlds be paid !
His glory by our lips proclaim'd,
  And by our lives display'd !

5 When shall we reach those blissful realms
  Where Christ exalted reigns,
And learn of yon celestial choir
  Their own immortal strains ?

147   *The Advent.*

WHILE shepherds watch'd their flocks by
  All seated on the ground,   [night,
The angel of the Lord came down,
  And glory shone around.

2 "Fear not," said he,—for mighty dread
  Had seized their troubled mind ;—
"Glad tidings of great joy I bring,
  To you and all mankind.

3 "To you, in David's town, this day,
  Is born of David's line
The Savior, who is Christ the Lord ;
  And this shall be the sign :

4 "The heav'nly babe you there shall find,
  To human view display'd,
All meanly wrapt in swathing bands,
  And in a manger laid.

5 All glory be to God on high,
  And to the earth be peace ;
Good will henceforth from heav'n to man,
  Begin and never cease.

THE SAVIOR'S NATIVITY.

C. M. CHRISTMAS.

1. Joy to the world! the Lord is come! Let earth re-ceive her King: Let ev'-ry heart pre-pare him room, And heav'n and na-ture sing, And heav'n and na-ture sing.

148 *The Advent.* **107**

JOY to the world! the Lord is come!
Let earth receive her King:
Let ev'ry heart prepare him room,
And heav'n and nature sing.

2 Joy to the earth! the Savior reigns!
Let men their songs employ;
While fields & floods, rocks, hills, & plains
Repeat the sounding joy.

3 No more let sins and sorrows grow,
Nor thorns infest the ground;
He comes to make his blessings flow
Far as the curse is found.

4 He rules the world with truth and grace,
And makes the nations prove
The glories of his righteousness,
And wonders of his love.

149 *Glory to God at the Birth of Jesus.*

CALM on the list'ning ear of night
Come heav'n's melodious strains,
Where wild Judea stretches far
Her silver-mantled plains.

2 Celestial choirs, from courts above,
Shed sacred glories there,
And angels, with their sparkling lyres,
Make music on the air.

3 The joyous hills of Palestine
Send back the glad reply,
And greet, from all their holy heights,
The Day-spring from on high.

4 O'er the blue depths of Galilee
There comes a holier calm,
And Sharon waves, in solemn praise,
Her silent groves of palm.

5 "Glory to God!" the sounding skies
Aloud with anthems ring;
"Peace to the earth, good will to men,
From heav'n's eternal King!"

150 *The Incarnation.*

MORTALS awake, with angels join,
And chant the solemn lay:
Joy, love, and gratitude combine
To hail th' auspicious day.

2 In heav'n the rapt'rous song began,
And sweet seraphic fire
Through all the shining legions ran,
And strung and tuned the lyre.

3 Down through the portals of the sky,
The heav'nly tidings ran;
And angels flew, with eager joy,
To bear the news to man.

4 With joy the chorus we'll repeat—
"Glory to God on high;
Good will and peace to men complete:
Jesus is born to die."

5 Hail, Prince of life! forever hail,
Redeemer, Brother, Friend!
Tho' earth, and time, and life should fail,
Thy praise shall never end.

THE SAVIOR'S NATIVITY.

L. M. CREATION.

1. Praise ye the Lord, who reigns a-bove, Fix'd on his throne of truth and love: Be-hold the fin-ger of his pow'r; Con-tem-plate, won-der, and a-dore.

---

151 *Mercy in Christ.* **109**

PRAISE ye the Lord, who reigns above,
  Fix'd on his throne of truth and love:
Behold the finger of his pow'r;
Contemplate, wonder, and adore.

2 When man, debas'd and guilty man,
From crime to crime with madness ran,
Well might his arm its thunders launch,
And blast th' ungrateful, root and branch.

3 But clemency with justice strove,
To save the people of his love:
"Go, my beloved Son!" he cried,
"Be thou their Savior, thou their guide."

4 The eastern star with glory streams,
It comes, with healing on its beams;
Dark mists of error fly away,
And Judah hails the rising day.

5 His sacred memory we bless
Whose holy gospel we profess;
And praise his great almighty name
From whom such light and favor came.

152 *Messiah.* **102**

GLORY to God! who reigns above,
  Who dwells in light, whose name is love;
Ye saints and angels, if ye can,
Declare the love of God to man.

2 Oh, what can more his love commend!
His dear, his only Son to send,
That man, condemn'd to die, might live,
And God be glorious to forgive!

3 Messiah's come—with joy behold
The days by prophets long foretold:
Judah, thy royal sceptre's broke;
And time still proves what Jacob spoke.

4 Daniel, thy weeks are all expir'd,—
The time prophetic seals requir'd;
Cut off for sins, but not his own,
The Prince, Messiah, doth atone.

5 We see the prophecies fulfill'd
In Jesus, that most wondrous child:
His birth, his life, his death, combine
To prove his character divine.

153 *Nativity of Christ.*

WAKE, O my soul, and hail the morn,
  For unto us a Savior's born;
See how the angels wing their way,
To usher in the glorious day!

2 Hark! what sweet music, what a song,
Sounds from the bright, celestial throng!
Sweet song! whose melting sounds impart
Joy to each raptur'd, listening heart.

3 Come, join the angels in the sky:
Glory to God who reigns on high;
Let peace and love on earth abound,
While time revolves and years roll round.

THE SAVIOR'S NATIVITY.

L. M. PARK STREET.

1. Welcome the hope of Israel's race, The messenger of truth and grace! Your hearts in righteousness prepare; Behold your wish'd redemption near! Behold your wish'd redemption near!

---

154. *The Savior's Advent.*

WELCOME the hope of Israel's race,
  The messenger of truth and grace!
Your hearts in righteousness prepare;
Behold your wish'd redemption near!

2 See glory bursting from the skies,
O'er Judah's land effulgent rise;
And fix amidst her coasts its seat,
Where justice, truth, and mercy meet.

3 While faith and hope, their offspring dear,
Attendant on their steps appear;
And join'd in friendly compact move,
Bless'd with philanthropy and love.

4 Truth in thy lands, O Earth! shall spring;
And righteousness, her healing wing
Expanding, downward cast her eye;
While heav'n's great Monarch, from on high,

5 The heathen gloom shall chase away,
And usher in a glorious day;
And from his own propitious will
The promis'd grace to man fulfill.

155. *Hallelujah to the Lord.*

LOUD hallelujahs to the Lord,
  From distant worlds where creatures dwell,
Let heav'n begin the solemn word,
And sound it far o'er earth and hell.

2 High on a throne his glories dwell,
An awful throne of shining bliss:
Fly through the world, O sun! and tell
How dark thy bliss compar'd to his.

3 Jehovah—'tis a glorious word!
Oh, may it dwell on every tongue!

But saints, who best have known the Lord
Are bound to raise the noblest song.

4 Speak of the wonders of that love
Which Gabriel plays on every chord;
From all below, and all above,
Loud hallelujahs to the Lord!

156. *The Star of Bethlehem.* 161

WHEN marshall'd on the nightly plain,
  The glitt'ring hosts bestud the sky;
One star alone, of all the train,
Can fix the sinner's wand'ring eye.

2 Hark! hark! to God the chorus breaks,
From every host, from every gem;
But one alone the Savior speaks,
It is the star of Bethlehem.

3 Once on the raging seas I rode,
The storm was loud,—the night was dark,
The ocean yawn'd,—and rudely blow'd
The wind that toss'd my found'ring bark.

4 Deep horror then my vitals froze,
Death-struck, I ceas'd the tide to stem;
When suddenly a star arose,
It was the star of Bethlehem.

5 It was my guide, my light, my all,
It bade my dark forebodings cease;
And through the storm and danger's thrall,
It led me to the port of peace.

6 Now safely moor'd—my perils o'er,
I'll sing, first in night's diadem,
Forever and forever more,
The star!—the star of Bethlehem!

CHRIST'S LIFE AND CHARACTER.

C. M. DORCHESTER.

1. Behold, where in a mortal form Appears each grace divine! The virtues, all in Jesus met, With mildest radiance shine.

157 *Goodness of Jesus.* **115**

BEHOLD, where in a mortal form
Appears each grace divine!
The virtues, all in Jesus met,
With mildest radiance shine.

2 To spread the rays of heav'nly light,
To give the mourner joy;
To preach glad tidings to the poor,
Was his divine employ.

3 Lowly in heart, to all his friends
A friend and servant found;
He wash'd their feet, he wip'd their tears,
And heal'd each bleeding wound.

4 Midst keen reproach and cruel scorn,
Patient and meek he stood;
His foes, ungrateful, sought his life;
He labor'd for their good.

5 To God he left his righteous cause,
And still his task pursued;
While humble pray'r and holy faith
His fainting strength renew'd.

6 In the last hours of deep distress,
Before his Father's throne,
With soul resign'd he bow'd, and said,
" Thy will, not mine, be done !"

7 Be Christ our pattern and our guide !
His image may we bear !
Oh, may we tread his holy steps,
His joy and glory share!

158 *Forbearance.* **116**

GOD of my mercy and my praise!
Thy glory is my song;

Though sinners speak against thy grace
With a blaspheming tongue.

2 When in the form of mortal man
Thy Son on earth was found,
With cruel slanders, false and vain,
They compass'd him around.

3 Their mis'ries his compassion mov'd;
Their peace he still pursued:
They render'd hatred for his love,
And evil for his good.

4 Their malice rag'd without a cause;
Yet with his dying breath
He pray'd for murd'rers on his cross,
And bless'd his foes in death.

5 Lord, shall thy bright example shine
In vain before mine eyes?
Give me a soul akin to thine,
To love mine enemies.

159 *Excellence of Christ's Example.*

IN duties and in sufferings too,
Thy path, my Lord, I'd trace;
As thou hast done, so would I do,
Depending on thy grace.

2 Inflamed with zeal, 'twas thy delight
To do thy Father's will;
Oh, may that zeal my soul excite
Thy precepts to fulfill!

3 Unsullied meekness, truth, and love,
Through all thy conduct shine;
Oh, may my whole deportment prove
A copy, Lord, of thine!

CHRIST'S LIFE AND CHARACTER.

8s, 7s. HOLLAZ.

1. One there is, a-bove all o-thers, Well de-serves the name of Friend; His is love, be-yond a bro-ther's, Cost-ly, free, and knows no end.

160 *Christ a Friend.* 165

ONE there is, above all others,
  Well deserves the name of Friend;
His is love, beyond a brother's,
  Costly, free, and knows no end.

2 Which of all our friends, to save us,
  Could or would have shed his blood!
But this Savior died to have us
  Reconcil'd in him to God.

3 When he liv'd on earth abaséd,
  Friend of sinners was his name;
Now, above all glory raiséd,
  He rejoices in the same.

4 Oh, for grace our hearts to soften!
  Teach us, Lord, at length to love;
We, alas! forget too often
  What a Friend we have above.

161 *Christ victorious.*

WHO is this that comes from Edom,
  All his raiment stain'd with blood,
To the captive speaking freedom,
  Bringing and restoring good?

2 'Tis the Savior, now victorious,
  Trav'ling onward in his might.
'Tis the Savior. Oh, how glorious
  To his people is the sight!

3 Why that blood his raiment staining?
  'Tis the blood of many slain:
Of his foes there's none remaining,
  None the contest to maintain.

4 Mighty Victor, reign forever!
  Wear the crown so dearly won!
Never shall thy people, never,
  Cease to sing what thou hast done!

162 *The Precious Word.* 7

BY the thoughtless world derided,
  Still I love the Word of God:
'Tis the crook by which I'm guided,
  Often 'tis a chast'ning rod.

2 'Tis a sword that cuts asunder
  All my pride and vanity,
When abased I lie, and wonder
  That he spares a wretch like me.

3 This confirms me when I waver,
  Sets my trembling judgment right;
When I stray, how much soever,
  This is my restoring light.

4 Satan oft, and sin, assail me
  With temptations ever new;
Then there's nothing can avail me,
  Till my bleeding Lord I view.

5 Faith I need: O Lord, bestow it;
  Give my lab'ring mind relief;
Oft, alas! I doubt, I know it,
  Help, oh, help my unbelief.

6 Dearest Savior, by thy merit
  May I gain a future crown;
Guide, oh, guide me by thy Spirit,
  Till these storms are overblown.

CHRIST'S LIFE AND CHARACTER.

L. M. COMMUNION.

1. My dear Redeemer, and my Lord! I read my duty in thy word:
But in thy life the law appears Drawn out in living characters.

163 *Jesus our Pattern.* **114**

MY dear Redeemer, and my Lord!
  I read my duty in thy word:
But in thy life the law appears
Drawn out in living characters.

2 Such was thy truth, and such thy zeal,
Such def'rence to thy Father's will,
Thy love and meekness so divine,
I would transcribe and make them mine.

3 Cold mountains and the midnight air
Witness'd the fervor of thy pray'r:
The desert thy temptations knew,
Thy conflict and thy vict'ry too!

4 Be thou my pattern; make me bear
More of thy gracious image here;
Then God the Judge shall own my name
Among the foll'wers of the Lamb.

164 *Jesus our Pattern.* **117**

"FATHER divine," the Savior cried,
  While horrors press'd on ev'ry side,
And prostrate on the ground he lay,
"Remove this bitter cup away.

2 " But if these pangs must still be borne,
Or helpless man be left forlorn,
I bow my soul before thy throne,
And say, Thy will, not mine, be done."

3 Thus our submissive souls would bow,
And, taught by Jesus, lie as low:
Our *hearts*, and not our lips alone,
Would say, "Thy will, not ours, be done."

4 Then, though like him in dust we lie,
We'll view the blissful moment nigh,
Which, from our portion in his pains,
Calls to the joy in which he reigns.

165 *Jesus our Pattern.* **120**

AND is the gospel peace and love?
  Such let our conversation be;
The serpent blended with the dove,
Wisdom and meek simplicity.

2 Whene'er the angry passions rise,
And tempt our thoughts or tongues to strife,
On Jesus let us fix our eyes,
Bright pattern of the Christian life.

3 Oh, how benevolent and kind!
How mild, how ready to forgive!
Be this the temper of our mind,
And these the rules by which we live.

4 To do his heav'nly Father's will,
Was his employment and delight;
Humility and holy zeal
Shone through his life divinely bright.

5 Dispensing good where'er he came,
The labors of his life were love;
If then we love the Savior's name,
Let his divine example move!

6 But, oh, how blind, how weak we are!
How frail! how apt to turn aside!
Lord, we depend upon thy care,
And ask thy Spirit for our guide.

7 Thy fair example may we trace,
To teach us what we ought to be!
Make us, by thy transforming grace,
Dear Savior, daily more like thee.

166   Teachings of Jesus.   780

HOW sweetly flow'd the gospel sound
   From lips of gentleness and grace,
When list'ning thousands gather'd round,
And joy and gladness fill'd the place!

2 From heav'n he came, of heav'n he spoke,
To heav'n he led his foll'wers' way;
Dark clouds of gloomy night he broke,
Unveiling an immortal day.

3 "Come, wand'rers, to my Father's home
Come, all ye weary ones, and rest;"
Yes, sacred Teacher, we will come,
Obey thee, love thee, and be blest.

4 Decay, then, tenements of dust;
Pillars of earthly pride, decay:
A nobler mansion waits the just,
And Jesus has prepar'd the way.

167   The Transfiguration.   118

WHEN at a distance, Lord, we trace
   The various glories of thy face,
What transport glows in ev'ry breast,
And charms our cares and woes to rest!

2 Alone with thee, in darkest cell,
On some bleak mountain would I dwell,
Rather than pompous courts behold,
And share their grandeur and their gold.

3 Away, ye dreams of mortal joy;
Raptures divine my thoughts employ;
I see the King of glory shine,
And feel his love, and call him mine.

4 On Tabor thus his servants view'd
His lustre, when transform'd he stood;
And, bidding earthly scenes farewell,
Cried, "Lord, 'tis pleasant here to dwell."

5 Yet still our elevated eyes
To nobler visions long to rise;
That grand assembly would we join,
Where all thy saints around thee shine.

6 That mount, how bright! those forms, how fair!
'Tis good to dwell forever there!
Come, death, dear envoy of my God,
And bear me to that blest abode.

168   Miracles of Christ.   119

BEHOLD, the blind their sight receive!
   Behold, the dead awake and live!
The dumb speak wonders, and the lame
Leap like the hart, and bless his name.

2 Thus doth th' eternal Spirit own
And seal the mission of the Son;
The Father vindicates his cause,
While he hangs bleeding on the cross.

3 He dies; the heav'ns in mourning stood;
He rises, and appears a God.
Behold the Lord ascending high,
No more to bleed, no more to die.

4 Hence, and forever, from my heart
I bid my doubts and fears depart;
And to those hands my soul resign,
Which bear credentials so divine.

169   The Transfiguration.   784

ON Tabor's top the Savior stands,
   His alter'd face resplendent shines,
And while he elevates his hands,
What glory marks its gentle lines!

2 Two heav'nly forms descend to wait
Upon their suff'ring Prince below;
But while they worship at his feet,
They talk of fast approaching woe.

3 Amid the lustre of the scene,
To Calvary he turns his eyes,
And with submission, all serene
He marks the future tempest rise.

4 Oh let us climb the mount of pray'r,
Where all his beaming glories shine,
And, gazing on his brightness there,
Our woes forget in joys divine.

170   Characters of Christ.   782

WHAT various, lovely characters
   The condescending Savior bears!
All human virtues, all divine,
In him unite—in splendor shine.

2 The Corner-stone on which we build;
The Balm by which our souls are heal'd;
The Morning Star, whose cheering ray
Dispels the shades, and brings the day.

3 He is the burden'd sinner's Rest;
Our Prophet and atoning Priest;
Our Advocate before the throne,
Who with our pray'rs presents his own.

4 He is our Captain and our Guide;
The Friend, the Husband of the Bride;
The Counselor, the Prince of Peace;
The Lord our Strength and Righteousness;

5 The Fountain whence our blessings flow;
A Lamb, and yet a Lion too;
The Sun for light and guidance giv'n;
The Door which opens into heav'n.

6 He is the Shepherd of the sheep,
Who does his flock in safety keep;
The Conqu'ror he, the Judge of men;
The Faithful Witness, the Amen!

CHRIST'S NAMES.

L. M. IOSCO.

1. O thou, whose beams se-rene-ly bright Can chase the dark-ness of my soul, And pour a flood of pu-rest light Where now the shades of mid-night roll:

171   Christ the Morning Star.   162

1 O THOU, whose beams serenely bright
  Can chase the darkness of my soul,
And pour a flood of purest light
Where now the shades of midnight roll:

2 Ah! why so long should horror shroud
This mourning breast with deep despair?
Break through the dark and envious cloud,
Arise, arise, O Morning Star.

3 Through a long night of griefs and fears,
With gloom and sorrow compass'd round,
I drop my uncomplaining tears,
Nor yet the radiant dawn have found;

4 Still towards the chambers of the day,
With eyes intent, expecting there,
With patient hope, thy promis'd ray,
I long for thee, sweet Morning Star.

5 Increasing clouds announce thee nigh,
Slumber my weary eyes invades;
Death spreads his horrors o'er the sky,
And thickens all the gather'd shades.

6 I yield, I bow my drooping head,
Resign, at length, my anxious care;
I sink a while among the dead,
To wake and hail my Morning Star.

172   Christ the Morning Star.   163

1 YE worlds of light that roll so near
  The Savior's throne of shining bliss,
Oh, tell how mean your glories are,
How faint and few, compar'd with his!

2 We sing the bright and Morning Star
Jesus, the spring of light and love:

See, how its rays, diffus'd from far,
Conduct us to the realms above!

3 Its cheering beams spread wide abroad,
Point out the doubtful Christian's way:
Still, as he goes, he finds the road
Enlighten'd with a constant day.

4 When shall we reach the heav'nly place
Where this bright Star shall brightest shine?
Leave far behind these scenes of night,
And view a lustre so divine?

173   Physician of Souls.   168

1 DEEP are the wounds which sin has made;
  Where shall the sinner find a cure?
In vain, alas, is Nature's aid;
The work exceeds all Nature's pow'r.

2 Sin, like a raging fever, reigns
With fatal strength in ev'ry part;
The dire contagion fills the veins,
And spreads its poison to the heart.

3 And can no sov'reign balm be found?
And is no kind physician nigh,
To ease the pain and heal the wound,
Ere life and hope forever fly?

4 There is a great Physician near:
Look up, O fainting soul, and live;
See, in his heav'nly smiles appear
Such ease as Nature cannot give!

5 See, in the Savior's dying blood,
Life, health, and bliss abundant flow;
'Tis only this dear, sacred flood
Can ease thy pain and heal thy woe.

CHRIST'S NAMES.

7s. HOTHAM.

174   *The Rock of Ages.*   **164**

ROCK of Ages, cleft for me,
  Let me hide myself in thee!
Let the water and the blood,
From thy wounded side which flow'd,
Be of sin the perfect cure,
Save me, Lord! and make me pure.

2 Not the labors of my hands
Can fulfill thy law's demands:
Could my zeal no respite know,
Could my tears forever flow,
All for sin could not atone!
Thou must save, and thou alone!

3 Nothing in my hand I bring;
Simply to thy cross I cling!
Naked, come to thee for dress;
Helpless, look to thee for grace;
Foul, I to thy fountain fly;
Wash me, Savior, or I die!

4 While I draw this fleeting breath,
When my eyelids close in death,
When I soar to worlds unknown,
See thee on thy judgment-throne,

Rock of Ages, cleft for me,
Let me hide myself in thee.

175   *The Bread and Wine.*   **880**

BREAD of heav'n! on thee I feed,
  For thy flesh is meat indeed:
Ever may my soul be fed,
With this true and living bread;
Day by day with strength supplied,
Through the life of him who died.

2 Vine of heav'n! thy blood supplies
This blest cup of sacrifice:
'Tis thy wounds my healing give,
To thy cross I look, and live.
Thou my life! Oh, let me be
Rooted, grounded, built on thee.

Doxology.

PRAISE the Name of God most high;
  Praise him, all below the sky;
Praise him, all ye heavenly host—
Father, Son, and Holy Ghost:
As through countless ages past,
Evermore his praise shall last.

CHRIST'S NAMES.

7s & 6s. MISSIONARY HYMN.

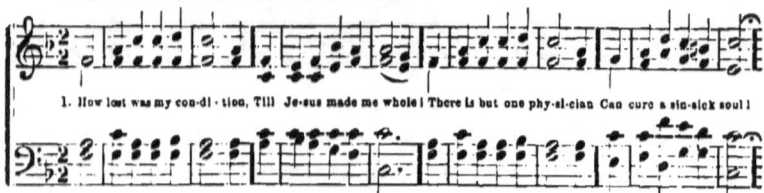

1. How lost was my con-di-tion, Till Jesus made me whole! There is but one phy-si-cian Can cure a sin-sick soul!

The worst of all dis-eas-es Is light, compared with sin; On ev'-ry part it sei-zes, But rages most with-in.

---

176   *The Great Physician.*   **169**

HOW lost was my condition,
  Till JESUS made me whole!
There is but one physician
  Can cure a sin-sick soul!
The worst of all diseases
  Is light, compared with sin;
On ev'ry part it seizes,
  But rages most within.

2 From men great skill professing
  I thought a cure to gain;
But this prov'd more distressing,
  And added to my pain:
Some said that nothing ail'd me,
  Some gave me up for lost;
Thus ev'ry refuge fail'd me,
  And all my hopes were cross'd.

3 At length this great Physician—
  How matchless is his grace!—
Accepted my petition,
  And undertook my case:
Next door to death he found me,
  And snatch'd me from the grave,
To tell to all around me
  His wondrous power to save.

4 A dying, risen Jesus,
  Seen by the eye of faith,
At once from danger frees us,
  And saves the soul from death.
Come, then, to this Physician,
  His help he'll freely give;
He makes no hard condition:
  'Tis only—look—and live.

---

177   *The Lord's Anointed.*   **777**

HAIL to the Lord's Anointed,
  Great David's greater Son!
Hail, in the time appointed,
  His reign on earth begun!
He comes to break oppression,
  To set the captive free,
To take away transgression
  And rule in equity.

2 He comes, with succor speedy,
  To those who suffer wrong;
To help the poor and needy,
  And bid the weak be strong;
To give them songs for sighing,
  Their darkness turn to light,
Whose souls condemn'd and dying
  Were precious in his sight.

3 He shall come down like showers,
  Upon the fruitful earth,
And love, joy, hope, like flowers,
  Spring, in his path, to birth;
Before him, on the mountains,
  Shall peace, the herald, go;
And righteousness, in fountains,
  From hill to valley flow.

4 Kings shall fall down before him,
  And gold and incense bring;
All nations shall adore him,
  His praise all people sing.
The tide of time shall never
  His covenant remove;
His name shall stand forever,
  That name to us is love.

CHRIST'S SUFFERINGS AND DEATH.

11s. CANA.

1. Thou sweet glid-ing Ke-dron, by thy sil-ver streams,
Our Sa-viour at mid-night, when moon-light's pale beams
D.C. And lose in thy mur-murs the toils of the day.

Shone bright on the wa-ters, would fre-quent-ly stray,

178 *Kedron and the Garden of Olives.* **785**

THOU sweet gliding Kedron, by thy silver streams,
   Our Savior at midnight, when moonlight's pale beams
Shone bright on the waters, would frequently stray,
And lose in thy murmurs the toils of the day.

2 How damp were the vapors that fell on his head!
How hard was his pillow, how humble his bed!
The angels, astonish'd, grew sad at the sight,
And follow'd their Master with solemn delight.

3 O garden of Olives, thou dear honor'd spot,
The fame of thy wonders shall ne'er be forgot;
The theme most transporting to seraphs above;
The triumph of sorrow,—the triumph of love.

4 Come, saints, and adore him; come bow at his feet!
Oh, give him the glory, the praise that is meet;
Let joyful hosannas unceasing arise,
And join the full chorus that gladdens the skies.

179 *The Savior's Sufferings.*

O CHRISTIAN, remember the blood that was shed,
   When Calvary's victim to slaughter was led,
When, sad and forsaken, the garden alone
Gave ear to his sorrow, and echoed his moan.

2 Remember the conflict with insult and scorn,
The robe of derision, the chaplet of thorn,
The sin-cleansing fountain that stream'd from his side,
When, "Father, forgive them," he utter'd and died.

Doxology.

O FATHER Almighty, to thee be address'd,
   With Christ and the Spirit, one God ever bless'd,
All glory and worship from earth and from heaven,
As was, and is now, and shall ever be given.

CHRIST'S SUFFERINGS AND DEATH.

L. M. ELPARAN.

1. 'Tis mid-night—and on O-live's brow The star is dimm'd that late-ly shone;
'Tis mid-night—in the gar-den now The suff'ring Sa-vior prays a-lone.

180 Gethsemane. 122

1 'TIS midnight—and on Olive's brow
The star is dimm'd that lately shone;
'Tis midnight—in the garden now
The suff'ring Savior prays alone.

2 'Tis midnight—and from all remov'd,
Immanuel wrestles lone, with fears;
E'en the disciple that he lov'd
Heeds not his Master's griefs and tears.

3 'Tis midnight—and for others' guilt
The man of sorrows weeps in blood;
Yet he that hath in anguish knelt
Is not forsaken by his God.

4 'Tis midnight—and from other plains
Is borne the song that angels know:
Unheard by mortals are the strains
That sweetly soothe the Savior's woe.

181 'Tis Finished. 138

1 "'TIS finish'd!"—so the Savior cried,
And meekly bow'd his head and died;
"'Tis finish'd—yes, the race is run,
The battle fought, the vict'ry won.

2 "'Tis finish'd!—all that heav'n decreed,
And all the ancient prophets said,
Is now fulfill'd, as was design'd,
In me, the Savior of mankind.

3 "'Tis finish'd!—Aaron now no more
Must stain his robes with purple gore;
The sacred veil is rent in twain,
And Jewish rites no more remain.

4 "'Tis finish'd!—this my dying groan
Shall sins of ev'ry kind atone:

Millions shall be redeem'd from death,
By this my last expiring breath.

5 "'Tis finish'd!—Heav'n is reconcil'd,
And all the pow'rs of darkness spoil'd;
Peace, love, and happiness again
Return and dwell with sinful man."

6 'Tis finish'd!—let the joyful sound
Be heard through all the nations round;
'Tis finish'd!—let the echo fly
Thro' heav'n and hell, thro' earth and sky.

182 Savior Dying. 125

1 STRETCH'D on the cross, the Savior dies:
Hark! his expiring groans arise!
See, from his hands, his feet, his side,
Runs down the sacred crimson tide!

2 But life attends the dreadful sound,
And flows from ev'ry bleeding wound;
The vital stream, how free it flows
To save and cleanse his rebel foes!

3 To suffer in the traitor's place,
To die for man,—surprising grace!
Yet pass rebellious angels by—
Oh, why for man, dear Savior, why?

4 Can I survey this scene of woe,
Where mingling grief and wonder flow,
And yet my heart unmov'd remain,
Insensible to love or pain?

5 Come, dearest Lord! thy grace impart,
To warm this cold, this stupid heart;
Till all its pow'rs and passions move
In melting grief and ardent love.

CHRIST'S SUFFERINGS AND DEATH.

L. M. MUNICH.

1. Come, let our mournful songs re-cord The dy-ing sor-rows of our Lord, When he ex-pir'd in shame and blood, Like one for-sa-ken of his God.

183 *Sufferings of Christ.* **123**

COME, let our mournful songs record
   The dying sorrows of our Lord,
When he expir'd in shame and blood,
Like one forsaken of his God.

2 The Jews beheld him thus forlorn,
And shook their heads, & laugh'd in scorn:
"He rescued others from the grave,
Now let him try himself to save."

3 O harden'd people! cruel priests!
How they stood round like savage beasts!
Like lions ready to devour,
When God had left him in their pow'r!

4 They wound his head, his hands, his feet,
Till streams of blood each other meet;
By lot his garments they divide,
And mock the pangs in which he died.

5 But, gracious God, thy pow'r and love
Have made his death a blessing prove ;
Though once upon the cross he bled,
Immortal honors crown his head.

6 Through Christ the Son our guilt forgive,
And let the mourning sinner live !
The Lord will hear us in his name,
Nor shall our hope be turn'd to shame.

184 *Our Savior.* **846**

COME, guilty sinners, come and see
   Your great atoning Sacrifice:
Behold, on yonder gory tree,
The King of kings for rebels dies.

2 How gracious, how severe thou art,
Just God, in thy redeeming plan !

The spear that pierc'd Immanuel's heart
Reveal'd the fount of life for man.

3 Hail, hallow'd cross, accurs'd no more;
Rich tree of life to all our race ;
Blest tree of Paradise, which bore
The choicest fruit—the gift of grace.

4 Lord, shall our grief or joy prevail ?
Our heart is rent amidst their strife ;
Shall we the Victim's death bewail,
Or hail it as our way to life ?

5 Thy dying, living, boundless love,
While here below shall tune our tongue,
And, when we join the choir above,
Thy love be our triumphant song.

185 *Crucifixion to the World.* **129**

WHEN I survey the wondrous cross
   On which the Prince of glory died,
My richest gain I count but loss,
And pour contempt on all my pride.

2 Forbid it, Lord, that I should boast,
Save in the death of Christ my God ;
All the vain things that charm me most,
I sacrifice them to his blood.

3 See from his head, his hands, his feet,
Sorrow and love flow mingled down :
Did e'er such love and sorrow meet ?
Or thorns compose so rich a crown ?

4 Were the whole realm of nature mine,
That were a present far too small ;
Love so amazing, so divine,
Demands my soul, my life, my all.

CHRIST'S SUFFERINGS AND DEATH.

L. M. GERHARD.

1. He dies, the Friend of sinners dies! Lo! Salem's daughters weep around; A solemn darkness veils the skies, A sudden trembling shakes the ground.

186   *Christ Dying and Living.*   144

HE dies, the Friend of sinners dies!
   Lo! Salem's daughters weep around;
A solemn darkness veils the skies,
A sudden trembling shakes the ground.

2 Come, saints, and drop a tear or two
For him who groan'd beneath your load;
He shed a thousand drops for you,
A thousand drops of richer blood!

3 Here's love and grief beyond degree:
The Lord of glory dies for men!
But lo!—what sudden joys we see!
Jesus, the dead, revives again.

4 The rising God forsakes the tomb,
In vain the tomb forbids his rise:
Cherubic legions guard him home,
And shout him welcome to the skies.

5 Break off your tears, ye saints, and tell
How high our great Deliv'rer reigns;
Sing how he spoil'd the hosts of hell,
And led the monster Death in chains.

6 Say, "Live forever, wondrous King!
Born to redeem, and strong to save!"
Then ask the monster, "Where's thy sting?
And where's thy vict'ry, boasting Grave?"

187   *Viewing the Cross.*   142

NOW be that sacrifice survey'd
   Which for our souls the Savior made,
While love to sinners fir'd his heart,
And conquer'd all the killing smart.

2 Blest Jesus, while thy grace I sing,
What grateful tribute shall I bring,

That earth and heav'n and all may see
My love to him who died for me?

3 That off'ring, Lord, thy word hath taught;
Nor be thy new command forgot,
That, if their Master's death can move,
Thy servants should each other love.

4 When on the cross I fix mine eye,
Let ev'ry sinful passion die;
And may I ever ready be
To serve, forgive, and love like thee.

188   *Salvation in the Cross.*   132

HERE at thy cross, my dying Lord,
   I lay my soul beneath thy love,
Beneath the droppings of thy blood,
Jesus, nor shall it e'er remove.

2 Not all that tyrants think or say,
With rage and lightning in their eyes,
Nor hell shall fright my heart away,
Should hell with all its legions rise.

3 Should worlds conspire to drive me thence,
Moveless and firm this heart should lie;
Resolv'd (for that's my last defense)
If I must perish, there to die.

4 But speak, my Lord, and calm my fear;
Am I not safe beneath thy shade?
Thy vengeance will not strike me here,
Nor Satan dare my soul invade.

5 Yes, I'm secure beneath thy blood,
And all my foes shall lose their aim,
Hosanna to my dying Lord,
And my best honors to his name.

CHRIST'S SUFFERINGS AND DEATH.

C. M. NAOMI.

1. Be-hold the Sa - vior of mankind Nail'd to the shameful tree!

How vast the love that him inclin'd To bleed and die for thee!

189 *Christ's Dying Love.* **124**

BEHOLD the Savior of mankind
  Nail'd to the shameful tree!
How vast the love that him inclin'd
  To bleed and die for me!

2 "My God!" he cries; all nature shakes,
  And earth's strong pillars bend!
The gate of death in sunder breaks,
  The solid marbles rend.

3 'Tis done! the precious ransom's paid:
  "Receive my soul!" he cries:
Behold, he bows his sacred head!
  He bows his head and dies!

4 But soon he'll break death's tyrant chain,
  And in full glory shine;
O Lamb of God! was ever pain,
  Was ever love, like thine!

190 *The Suffering Savior.* **133**

ALAS! and did my Savior bleed,
  And did my Sov'reign die?
Would he devote that sacred head
  For such a worm as I?

2 Was it for crimes that I had done
  He groan'd upon the tree?
Amazing pity! grace unknown!
  And love beyond degree!

3 Well might the sun in darkness hide,
  And shut his glories in,
When Christ the mighty Savior died
  For man the creature's sin!

4 Thus might I hide my blushing face,
  While his dear cross appears:
Dissolve my heart in thankfulness,
  And melt my eyes to tears.

5 But drops of grief can ne'er repay
  The debt of love I owe;
Here, Lord, I give myself away,
  'Tis all that I can do.

191 *Salvation by Grace.* **338**

LORD, we confess our num'rous faults,
  How great our guilt has been!
Foolish and vain were all our thoughts,
  And all our lives were sin.

2 But, O my soul, forever praise,
  Forever love His name
Who turns thy feet from dang'rous ways
  Of folly, sin, and shame.

3 'Tis not by works of righteousness
  Which our own hands have done,
But we are sav'd by sov'reign grace
  Abounding through his Son.

4 'Tis from the mercy of our God
  That all our hopes begin;
'Tis by the water and the blood
  Our souls are wash'd from sin.

5 'Tis through the purchase of His death,
  Who hung upon the tree,
The Spirit is sent down to breathe
  On such dry bones as we.

6 Rais'd from the dead, we live anew;
  And justified by grace,
We shall appear in glory too,
  And see our Father's face.

CHRIST'S SUFFERINGS AND DEATH.

8s, 7s. BAVARIA.

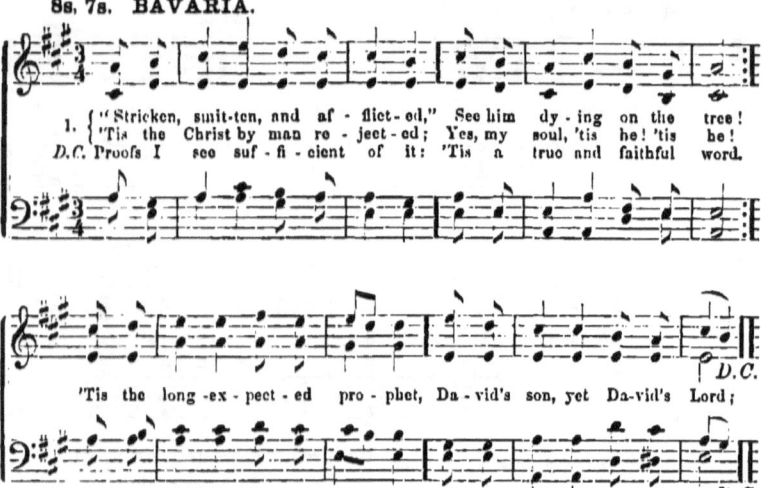

192   *Suffering Savior.*   126

"STRICKEN, smitten, and afflicted,"
   See him dying on the tree!
'Tis the Christ by man rejected:
   Yes, my soul, 'tis he! 'tis he!
'Tis the long-expected prophet,
   David's son, yet David's Lord;
Proofs I see sufficient of it:
   'Tis a true and faithful word.

2 Tell me, ye who hear him groaning,
   Was there ever grief like his?
Friends through fear his cause disowning,
   Foes insulting his distress:
Many hands were rais'd to wound him,
   None would interpose to save;
But the deepest stroke that pierc'd him
   Was the stroke that justice gave.

3 Ye who think of sin but lightly,
   Nor suppose the evil great,
Here may view its nature rightly,
   Here its guilt may estimate.
Mark the sacrifice appointed!
   See who bears the awful load;
'Tis the WORD, the LORD'S ANOINTED,
   Son of man, and Son of God.

4 Here we have a firm foundation;
   Here's the refuge of the lost:
Christ's the rock of our salvation:
   His the name of which we boast:

Lamb of God for sinners wounded!
   Sacrifice to cancel guilt!
None shall ever be confounded
   Who on him their hope have built.

193   *It is Finished.*   139

HARK! the voice of love and mercy
   Sounds aloud from Calvary!
See! it rends the rocks asunder,
   Shakes the earth, and veils the sky!
   "It is finish'd!"
Hear the dying Savior cry!

2 It is finish'd!—Oh, what pleasure
   Do these charming words afford!
Heavenly blessings, without measure,
   Flow to us from Christ the Lord,
   It is finish'd!—
Saints, the dying words record.

3 Finish'd all the types and shadows
   Of the ceremonial law!
Finish'd all that God had promis'd;
   Death and hell no more shall awe.
   It is finish'd!—
Saints, from hence your comfort draw.

4 Tune your harps anew, ye seraphs,
   Join to sing the pleasing theme;
All in earth, and all in heaven,
   Join to praise Immanuel's name,
   Hallelujah!
Glory to the bleeding Lamb!

CHRIST'S SUFFERINGS AND DEATH.

7s & 6s. CRUCIFIX.

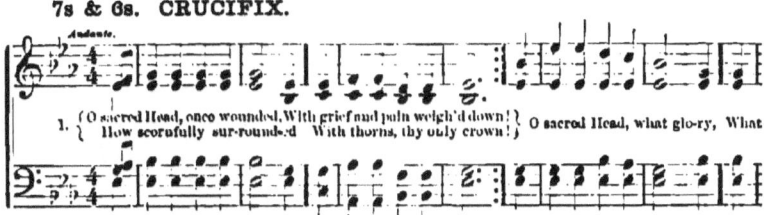

194 *Suffering Savior.* **788**

O SACRED Head, once wounded,
  With grief and pain weigh'd down!
How scornfully surrounded
  With thorns, thy only crown!
O sacred Head, what glory,
  What bliss, till now was thine!
Yet, though despis'd and gory,
  I joy to call thee mine.

2 How art thou pale with anguish,
  With sore abuse and scorn!
How does that visage languish,
  Which once was bright as morn!
Thy grief and thy compassion
  Were all for sinners' gain;
Mine, *mine* was the transgression,
  But thine the deadly pain.

3 What language shall I borrow
  To praise thee, dearest Friend,
For this thy dying sorrow,—
  Thy pity without end!
Lord, make me thine forever,
  Nor let me faithless prove;
Oh, let me never, never
  Abuse such dying love!

4 Forbid that I should leave thee;
  O Jesus, leave not me;
By faith I would receive thee;
  Thy blood can make me free,
When strength and comfort languish,
  And I must hence depart;
Release me then from anguish,
  By thine own wounded heart.

5 Be near when I am dying,
  Oh, show thy cross to me!
And for my succor flying,
  Come, Lord, to set me free.
These eyes new faith receiving,
  From Jesus shall not move;
For he who dies believing,
  Dies safely—through thy love.

195 *Christ our Substitute.*

I LAY my sins on Jesus,
  The spotless Lamb of God;
He bears them all and frees us
  From the accursed load.
I bring my guilt to Jesus,
  To wash my crimson stains
White, in his blood most precious,
  Till not a spot remains.

2 I lay my wants on Jesus;
  All fullness dwells in him;
He heals all my diseases,
  He doth my soul redeem.
I lay my griefs on Jesus,
  My burdens and my cares;
He from them all releases,
  He all my sorrow shares.

3 I long to be like Jesus,
  Meek, loving, lovely, mild,
I long to be like Jesus,
  The Father's holy Child.
I long to be with Jesus,
  Amid the heav'nly throng,
To sing with saints his praises,
  To learn the angels' song.

CHRIST'S SUFFERINGS AND DEATH.

7s. MARTYN.

196 *A Litany.* **792**

SAVIOR, when in dust to thee
  Low we bow th' adoring knee;
When, repentant, to the skies
Scarce we lift our streaming eyes;
Oh, by all thy pains and woe,
Suffer'd once for man below,
Bending from thy throne on high,
Hear our solemn litany.

2 By thy birth and early years,
By thy human griefs and fears,
By thy fasting and distress
In the lonely wilderness;
By the vict'ry in the hour
Of the subtle tempter's pow'r;
Jesus, look with pitying eye;
Hear our solemn litany.

3 By thine hour of dark despair,
By thine agony of pray'r,
By the purple robe of scorn,
By thy wounds—the crown of thorn—
By thy cross—thy pangs and cries,
By thy perfect sacrifice,
Jesus, look with pitying eye;
Hear our solemn litany.

4 By thy deep expiring groan,
By thy seal'd sepulchral stone,
By thy triumphs o'er the grave,
By thy power from death to save,
Mighty God, ascended Lord,
To thy throne in heaven restor'd—
Prince and Savior, hear our cry,
Hear our solemn litany.

197 *Three Mounts.* **861**

WHEN on Sinai's top I see
  God descend in majesty,
To proclaim his holy law,
All my spirit sinks with awe.
When, in ecstasy sublime,
Tabor's glorious steep I climb,
At the too-transporting light,
Darkness rushes o'er my sight.

2 When on Calvary I rest,
God in flesh made manifest,
Shines in my Redeemer's face,
Full of beauty, truth, and grace.
Here I could forever stay,
Weep and gaze my soul away;
Thou art heav'n on earth to me,
Lovely, mournful Calvary.

198 *How to win Souls.* **558**

WOULD you win a soul to God?
  Tell him of a Savior's blood,
Once for dying sinners spilt,
To atone for all their guilt.

2 Tell him how the streams did glide
From his hands, his feet, his side;
How his head with thorns was crown'd,
And his heart in sorrow drown'd;—

3 How he yielded up his breath;
How he agoniz'd in death;
How he lives to intercede—
Christ our Advocate and Head.

4 Tell him of that liberty
Wherewith Jesus makes us free;
Sweetly speak of sins forgiv'n,—
Earnest of the joys of heav'n.

CHRIST'S SUFFERINGS AND DEATH.

7s. 6 lines. CALVARY.

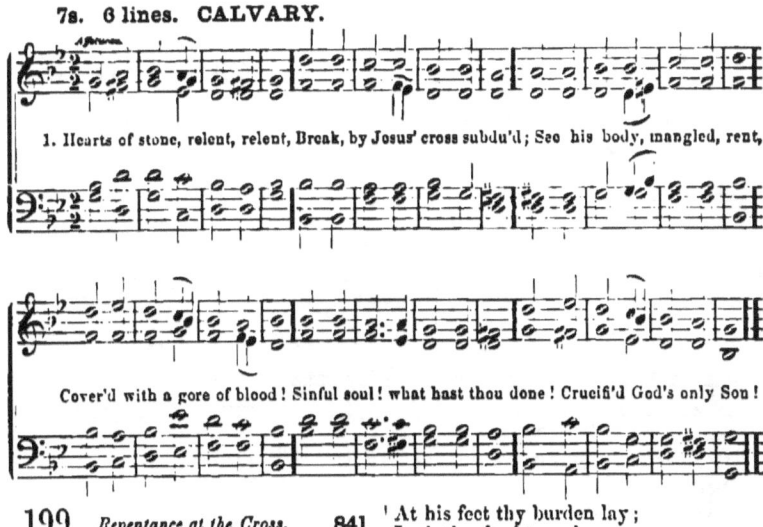

1. Hearts of stone, relent, relent, Break, by Jesus' cross subdu'd; See his body, mangled, rent, Cover'd with a gore of blood! Sinful soul! what hast thou done! Crucifi'd God's only Son!

199 *Repentance at the Cross.* **841**

HEARTS of stone, relent, relent,
  Break, by Jesus' cross subdu'd;
See his body, mangled, rent,
  Cover'd with a gore of blood!
Sinful soul! what hast thou done!
Crucifi'd God's only Son!

2 Yes, thy sins have done the deed,
  Driven the nails that fix'd him there,
Crown'd with thorns his sacred head,
  Pierc'd him with the bloody spear,
Made his soul a sacrifice,—
While for sinful man he dies.

3 Wilt thou let him bleed in vain,—
  Still to death thy Lord pursue?
Open all his wounds again,—
  And the shameful cross renew?
No: with all my sins I'll part,
Break, oh, break, my bleeding heart!

200   *Look to Jesus.*   **822**

WEARY sinner, keep thine eyes,
  On th' atoning Sacrifice;
View him bleeding on the tree,
Pouring out his life for thee;
There the dreadful curse he bore:
Weeping soul, lament no more.

2 Cast thy guilty soul on him;
Find him mighty to redeem;
At his feet thy burden lay;
Look thy doubts and care away;
Now by faith the Son embrace,
Plead his promise, trust his grace.

201   *Suffering Savior.*   **860**

GO to dark Gethsemane,
  Ye that feel the tempter's pow'r,
Your Redeemer's conflict see,
  Watch with him one bitter hour;
Turn not from his griefs away,
Learn of Jesus Christ to pray.

2 Follow to the judgment-hall,
  View the Lord of life arraign'd;
Oh, the wormwood and the gall!
  Oh, the pangs his soul sustain'd!
Shun not suff'ring, shame, or loss;
Learn of him to bear the cross.

3 Calv'ry's mournful mountain climb:
  There, adoring at his feet,
Mark that miracle of time,
  God's own sacrifice complete:
"It is finish'd!" hear him cry:
Learn of Jesus Christ to die.

4 Early hasten to the tomb,
  Where they laid his breathless clay,—
All is solitude and gloom,—
  Who hath taken him away?
Christ is ris'n; he meets our eyes!
Savior, teach us so to rise.

CHRIST'S DEATH AND RESURRECTION.

S. M. WATCHMAN.

1. Be-hold th' a-ma-zing sight, The Sa-vior lift-ed high! Be-hold the Son of God's de-light Ex-pire in ag-o-ny.

202 *Dying Love of Christ.* **141**

BEHOLD th' amazing sight,
 The Savior lifted high!
Behold the Son of God's delight
 Expire in agony.

2 For whom, for whom, my heart,
 Were all these sorrows borne?
Why did he feel that piercing smart?
 And meet that various scorn?

3 For love of us he bled,
 And all in torture died;
'Twas love that bow'd his fainting head,
 And op'd his gushing side.

4 I see, and I adore,
 In sympathy of love;
I feel the strong, attractive pow'r
 To lift my soul above.

5 Drawn by such cords as these,
 Let all the earth combine
With cheerful ardor to confess
 The energy divine.

6 In thee our hearts unite,
 Nor share thy griefs alone,
But from thy cross pursue their flight
 To thy triumphant throne.

203 *Christ's Resurrection.* **148**

SEE what a living stone
 The builders did refuse!
Yet God hath built his church thereon,
 In spite of envious Jews.

2 The work, O Lord, is thine,
 And wondrous in our eyes;
This day declares it all divine,
 This day did Jesus rise.

3 This is the glorious day
 That our Redeemer made;
Let us rejoice, and sing, and pray;
 Let all the church be glad.

4 Hosanna to the King
 Of David's royal blood!
Bless him, ye saints; he comes to bring
 Salvation from your God.

5 We bless thy holy word
 Which all this grace displays;
And offer on thine altar, Lord,
 Our sacrifice of praise.

204 *The Risen Savior.* **150**

"THE Lord is ris'n indeed,"
 And are the tidings true?
Yes, we beheld the Savior bleed,
 And saw him living, too.

2 "The Lord is ris'n indeed,"
 Then Justice asks no more;
Mercy and Truth are now agreed,
 Who stood oppos'd before.

3 "The Lord is ris'n indeed,"
 Then is his work perform'd;
The captive surely now is freed,
 And death, our foe, disarm'd.

4 "The Lord is ris'n indeed,"
 Attending angels, hear;
Up to the courts of heav'n, with speed,
 The joyful tidings bear.

5 Then take your golden lyres,
 And strike each cheerful chord,
Join all the bright, celestial choirs
 To sing our risen Lord.

CHRIST'S RESURRECTION. 75

7's. HENDON.

1. "Christ, the Lord, is ris'n to-day," Sons of men and an-gels say, Raise your joys and triumphs high; Sing, ye heav'ns, and earth re-ply. Sing, ye heav'ns, and earth reply.

205   *Christ Risen.*   147

"CHRIST, the Lord, is ris'n to-day,"
   Sons of men and angels say,
Raise your joys and triumphs high;
Sing, ye heav'ns, and earth reply.

2 Love's redeeming work is done;
Fought the fight, the battle won:
Lo! our sun's eclipse is o'er,
Lo! he sets in blood no more.

3 Vain the stone, the watch, the seal;
Christ has burst the gates of hell.
Death in vain forbids his rise;
Christ has open'd Paradise.

4 Lives again our glorious King:
Where, O Death, is now thy sting?
Once he died our souls to save:
Where's thy victory, boasting grave?

5 Hail, the Lord of earth and heav'n!
Praise to thee by both be given!
Thee we greet triumphant now;
Hail the Resurrection—thou.

206   *The Risen Savior.*   152

JESUS, our triumphant Head,
   Ris'n victorious from the dead,
To the realms of glory's gone,
To ascend his rightful throne.

2 Cherubs on the Conqu'ror gaze,
Seraphs glow with brighter blaze;
Each bright order of the sky
Hails him as he passes by.

3 Heav'n its King congratulates,
Opens wide her golden gates;
Angels songs of vict'ry bring;
All the blissful regions ring.

4 Sinners, join the heav'nly pow'rs,
For redemption all is ours;
Humble penitents shall prove
Blood-bought pardon, dying love.

5 Hail, thou dear, thou worthy Lord!
Holy Lamb! incarnate word!
Hail, thou suff'ring Son of God!
Take the trophies of thy blood.

207   *Christ Risen.*   145

ANGELS, roll the rock away;
   Death, yield up thy mighty prey:
See, he rises from the tomb,
Glowing in immortal bloom.

2 'Tis the Savior! angels, raise
Fame's eternal trump of praise;
Let the world's remotest bound
Hear the joy-inspiring sound.

3 Heav'n unfolds her portals wide;
Glorious hero! through them ride:
King of glory! mount the throne;
Thy great Father's and thy own.

4 Hosts of heav'n, seraphic choirs!
Tune and sweep your sounding lyres;
Shout, O Earth! in rapt'rous songs
With ten thousand thousand tongues.

5 Ev'ry note with wonder swell;
Sin o'erthrown, and captiv'd hell!
Where is now, O Death! thy sting?
Where thy terrors, vanquish'd king?

CHRIST'S RESURRECTION.

C. M. PHUVAH.

1. Ye humble souls that seek the Lord, Cast all your fears away; Draw near, and with delight behold The place where Jesus lay.

208 *The Savior's Resurrection.* **146**

YE humble souls that seek the Lord,
  Cast all your fears away,
Draw near, and with delight behold
  The place where Jesus lay.

2 Thus low the Lord of life was brought,
  Such wonders love can do!
Thus low in death the Savior lay,
  Who liv'd and bled for you!

3 If ye have wept at yonder cross,
  And still your sorrows rise,
Stoop down and view the vanquish'd Grave,
  And wipe your weeping eyes.

4 Your Savior lives, forever lives,
  Raise a triumphant strain;
No pow'rs of hell, nor bars of Death
  The Conqu'ror could detain.

5 O'er heaven and earth he now presides,
  Though once among the dead;
And to eternity shall reign,
  Creation's glorious Head.

6 With joy like his shall ev'ry saint
  His empty tomb survey;
And rise with his ascending Lord
  To realms of endless day.

209 *The Resurrection of Christ.*

BLEST morning, whose first op'ning rays
  Beheld our rising God;
That saw him triumph o'er the dust,
  And leave his last abode.

2 In the cold prison of a tomb
  The great Redeemer lay,
Till the revolving skies had brought
  The third, th' appointed day.

3 Hell and the Grave their forces joined
  To hold our Lord in vain;
The sleeping Conqueror arose,
  And burst their feeble chain.

4 To thy great name, almighty Lord,
  These sacred hours we pay;
And loud hosannas shall proclaim
  The triumph of the day.

5 Salvation and immortal praise
  To our victorious King!
Let heav'n and earth, and rocks and seas
  With glad hosannas ring.

210 *The Risen Christ.*

SEARCH not in yonder narrow tomb
  For Him who lives on high:
Heav'n spreads her gates to make him room,
  His glory fills the sky.

2 Lift up your hearts, lift up your eyes,
  The Savior is not here:
In triumph did the Conqu'ror rise
  To grace a brighter sphere.

3 Angels, with loud, exulting songs,
  Welcome their Lord again:
To us the victory belongs,
  For he for us was slain.

CHRIST'S RESURRECTION. 77

C. L. M. HOW CALM AND BEAUTIFUL.

1. How calm and beau-ti-ful the morn That gilds the sacred tomb, Where once the Cru-ci-fied was borne, And veil'd in mid-night gloom! Oh, weep no more the Sa-vior slain; The Lord is risen—He lives a-gain.

211 *Easter Morning.*

HOW calm and beautiful the morn
 That gilds the sacred tomb,
Where once the Crucified was borne,
 And veil'd in midnight gloom!
Oh, weep no more the Savior slain;
The Lord is risen—He lives again.

2 Ye mourning saints! dry ev'ry tear
 For your departed Lord;
"Behold the place—He is not there,"
 The tomb is all unbarr'd:
The gates of death were clos'd in vain:
The Lord is risen—He lives again.

3 Now cheerful to the house of prayer
 Your early footsteps bend,
The Savior will Himself be there,
 Your advocate and friend:
Once by the law your hopes were slain,
But now in Christ ye live again.

4 How tranquil now the rising day!
 'Tis Jesus still appears,
A risen Lord to chase away
 Your unbelieving fears:
Oh, weep no more your comforts slain,
The Lord is risen—He lives again.

5 And when the shades of evening fall,
 When life's last hour draws nigh,
If Jesus shine upon the soul,
 How blissful then to die!
Since He has risen who once was slain,
Ye die in Christ to live again.

212 *Trusting under Darkness.* **816**

OH, let my trembling soul be still,
 While darkness veils the sky;
And wait thy wise, thy holy will,
 Wrapp'd yet in mystery:
I cannot, Lord, thy purpose see;
But all is well—since rul'd by thee.

2 Thus, trusting in thy love, I tread
 The path of duty on;
What though some cherish'd joys are fled
 Some flatt'ring dreams are gone?
Yet purer, brighter joys remain:
Why should my spirit then complain?

CHRIST'S ASCENSION AND EXALTATION.

L. M. DUKE STREET.

1. Rejoice, ye shining worlds on high; Behold the king of glory nigh! Who can this King of glory be? The mighty Lord, the Savior he.

213   *Ascension.*   151

REJOICE, ye shining worlds on high;
   Behold the King of glory nigh!
Who can this King of glory be?
The mighty Lord, the Savior he.

2 Ye heav'nly gates, your leaves display,
To make the Lord, the Savior, way:
Laden with spoils from earth and hell,
The Conqu'ror comes, with God to dwell.

3 Rais'd from the dead, he goes before,
He opens heav'n's eternal door,
To give his saints a blest abode
Near their Redeemer and their God.

214   *Christ's Sufferings and Glory.*   154

WHAT equal honors shall we bring
   To thee, O Lord our God, the Lamb,
When all the notes that angels sing
Are far inferior to thy name?

2 Worthy is he that once was slain,
The Prince of peace that groan'd and died,
Worthy to rise, and live, and reign
At his Almighty Father's side.

3 Pow'r and dominion are his due,
Who stood condemn'd at Pilate's bar:
Wisdom belongs to Jesus too,
Though he was charg'd with madness here.

4 All riches are his native right,
Yet he sustain'd amazing loss:
To him ascribe eternal night,
Who nail'd his weakness to the cross.

5 Honor immortal must be paid,
Instead of scandal and of scorn;
While glory shines around his head,
And a bright crown without a thorn.

6 Blessings forever on the Lamb,
Who bore the curse for wretched men;
Let angels sound his sacred name,
And ev'ry creature say, Amen.

215   *Ascension.*   155

OUR Lord has risen from the dead;
   Our Jesus has gone up on high;
The pow'rs of hell are captive led—
Dragg'd to the portals of the sky.

2 There his triumphal chariot waits,
And angels chant the solemn lay:
"Lift up your heads, ye heav'nly gates!
Ye everlasting doors, give way!"

3 Loose all your bars of massy light,
And wide unfold the radiant scene;
He claims these mansions as his right:
Receive the King of glory in.

4 "Who is the King of glory, who?"
The Lord that all his foes o'ercame,
The world, sin, death, and hell o'erthrew;
And Jesus is the Conq'ror's name.

5 "Who is the King of glory, who?"
The Lord of boundless pow'r possess'd,
The King of saints and angels too,
God over all, forever blest.

CHRIST'S ASCENSION AND EXALTATION.

L. M. MIGDOL.

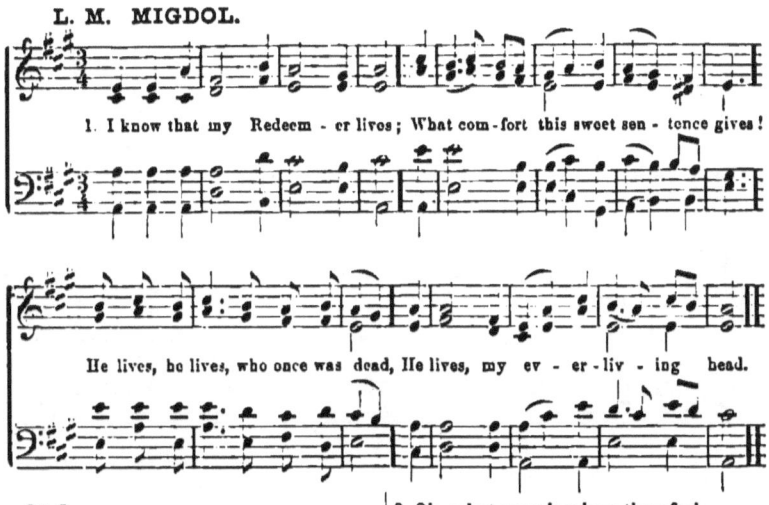

1. I know that my Redeem-er lives; What com-fort this sweet sen-tence gives! He lives, he lives, who once was dead, He lives, my ev-er-liv-ing head.

216 *The Redeemer Lives.* **158**

I KNOW that my Redeemer lives;
 What comfort this sweet sentence gives!
He lives, he lives, who once was dead,
He lives, my ever-living head.

2 He lives to bless me with his love,
He lives to plead for me above,
He lives my hungry soul to feed,
He lives to help in time of need.

3 He lives to grant me rich supply,
He lives to guide me with his eye,
He lives to comfort me when faint,
He lives to hear my soul's complaint.

4 He lives to silence all my fears,
He lives to stop and wipe my tears,
He lives to calm my troubled heart,
He lives, all blessings to impart.

5 He lives, all glory to his name!
He lives, my Jesus, still the same;
Oh, the sweet joy this sentence gives,
I know that my Redeemer lives!

217 *Christ in Glory.*

OH for a sight, a blissful sight
 Of our almighty Father's throne!
There sits the Savior crown'd with light,
Clothed in a body like our own.

2 Adoring saints around him stand,
While thrones and pow'rs before him fall;
The God shines gracious through the man,
And sheds sweet glories on them all.

3 Oh, what amazing joys they feel,
While to their golden harps they sing,
And sit on every heavenly hill,
And spread the triumphs of their King!

218 *Christ Exalted.* **159**

NOW let us raise our cheerful strains,
 And join the blissful choir above;
There our exalted Savior reigns,
And there they sing his wondrous love.

2 While seraphs tune th' immortal song,
Oh, may we feel the sacred flame;
And every heart and every tongue
Adore the Savior's glorious name.

3 Jesus, who once upon the tree
In agonizing pains expir'd:
Who died for rebels,—yes, 'tis he!
How bright, how lovely, how admir'd!

4 Jesus, who died that we might live,
Died in the wretched traitor's place,
Oh, what returns can mortals give
For such immeasurable grace!

5 Were universal nature ours,
And art with all her boasted store;
Nature and art, with all their pow'rs,
Would still confess the off'rer poor.

6 Yet, though for bounty so divine
We ne'er can equal honors raise,
Jesus! may all our hearts be thine,
And all our tongues proclaim thy praise.

CHRIST'S ASCENSION AND EXALTATION.

C. M. WARWICK.

1. Come, let us lift our voices high, High as our joys arise; And join the songs above the sky, Where pleasure never dies.

219 *The Triumph.* **140**

COME, let us lift our voices high,
 High as our joys arise;
And join the songs above the sky,
 Where pleasure never dies.

2 Jesus, the Lord that fought and bled
 How kind his smiles appear!
What melting, soothing words he says
 To ev'ry humble ear!

3 "For you, the objects of my love,
 It was for you I died:
Behold my hands, behold my feet,
 And look into my side.

4 "These are the wounds for you I bore,
 The tokens of my pains,
When I came down to free your souls
 From misery and chains."

5 We give thee, Lord, our highest praise
 For goodness so divine;
Oh, may we ever feel thy grace,
 And die to ev'ry sin!

220 *Christ Adored.* **160**

OH, the delights, the heav'nly joys,
 The glories of the place,
Where Jesus sheds the brightest beams
 Of his o'erflowing grace!

2 Sweet majesty and awful love
 Sit smiling on his brow;
And all the glorious ranks above
 At humble distance bow.

3 Archangels sound his lofty praise
 Through ev'ry heav'nly street;

And lay their highest honors down,
 Submissive at his feet.

4 This is the man, th' exalted man,
 Whom we, unseen, adore:
But when our eyes behold his face,
 Our hearts shall love him more.

5 Now to the Lamb, that once was slain,
 Be endless blessings paid;
Salvation, glory, joy, remain
 Forever on thy head!

221 *Tribute to the Lamb.* **136**

COME, let us join our cheerful songs
 With angels round the throne;
Ten thousand are their tongues,
 But all their joys are one.

2 "Worthy the Lamb that died," they cry,
 To be exalted thus;
"Worthy the Lamb," our lips reply,
 For he was slain for us.

3 Jesus is worthy to receive
 Honor and pow'r divine;
And blessings more than we can give,
 Be, Lord, forever thine.

4 Let all that dwell above the sky,
 And air and earth and seas,
Conspire to lift thy glories high,
 And speak thine endless praise!

5 The whole creation join in one,
 To bless the sacred name
Of Him that sits upon the throne,
 And to adore the Lamb.

CHRIST'S ASCENSION AND EXALTATION.

C. M. CORONATION.

1. All hail the pow'r of Jesus' name! Let angels prostrate fall; Bring forth the royal diadem, And crown him—Lord of all; Bring forth the royal diadem, And crown him—Lord of all.

222 *Coronation of Christ.* **845**

ALL hail the power of Jesus' name!
Let angels prostrate fall;
Bring forth the royal diadem,
And crown him—Lord of all.

2 Crown him—ye martyrs of our God,
Who from his altar call:
Extol the strength of Israel's might,
And crown him—Lord of all.

3 Hail him, ye heirs of David's line,
Whom David, Lord, did call—
The God incarnate—man divine,
And crown him—Lord of all.

4 Let every kindred, every tribe,
On this terrestrial ball,
To him all majesty ascribe,
And crown him—Lord of all.

223 *The Joyful Triumph.*

ARISE, ye people, and adore:
Exulting, strike the chord!
Let all the earth, from shore to shore,
Confess th' Almighty Lord.

2 Glad shouts aloud, wide echoing round,
Th' ascending God proclaim;
Th' angelic choir respond the sound,
And shake creation's frame.

3 They sing of death and hell o'erthrown
In that triumphant hour;
And God exalts his conqu'ring Son
To his right hand of power.

4 Oh, shout, ye people, and adore;
Exulting strike the chord!
Let all the earth, from shore to shore,
Confess th' almighty Lord!

224 *Christ in Heaven.* **153**

THE Lord of life, with glory crown'd,
On heav'n's exalted throne,
Forgets not those for whom on earth
He heav'd his dying groan.

2 His greatness now no tongue of man
Or seraph bright can tell ;
Yet still the chief of all his joys,
That souls are sav'd from hell.

3 For this he taught, and toil'd, and bled;
For this his life was giv'n ;
For this he fought, and vanquish'd death;
For this he reigns in heav'n.

4 Join, all ye saints beneath the sky,
Your grateful praise to give ;
Sing loud hosannas to his name,
With whom you too shall live.

CHRIST'S INTERCESSION.

H. M. LENOX.

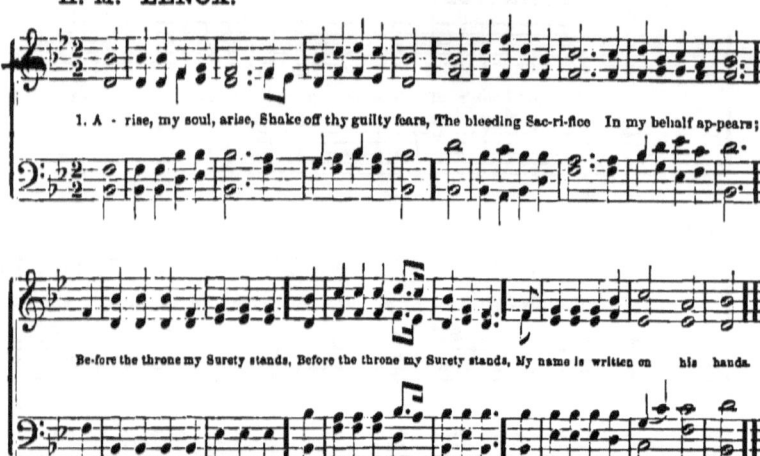

1. A-rise, my soul, arise, Shake off thy guilty fears, The bleeding Sac-ri-fice In my behalf ap-pears;
Be-fore the throne my Surety stands, Before the throne my Surety stands, My name is written on his hands.

225   *Christ's Intercession.*   **157**

ARISE, my soul, arise,
  Shake off thy guilty fears,
The bleeding Sacrifice
  In my behalf appears;
Before the throne my Surety stands,
My name is written on his hands.

2 He ever lives above,
  For me to intercede;
His all-redeeming love,
  His precious blood to plead;
His blood aton'd for all our race,
And sprinkles now the throne of grace.

3 Five bleeding wounds he bears,
  Receiv'd on Calvary;
They pour effectual prayers,
  They strongly speak for me;
Forgive him, oh, forgive, they cry,
Nor let that ransom'd sinner die.

4 The Father hears him pray,
  His dear anointed One;
He cannot turn away,
  Cannot refuse his Son;
His Spirit answers to the blood,
And tells me I am born of God.

5 My God is reconcil'd,
  His pard'ning voice I hear:
He owns me for his child,
  I can no longer fear;
With confidence I now draw nigh,
And Father, Abba Father! cry.

226   *Christ Precious.*   **329**

LET earth and heaven agree,
  Angels and men be join'd,
To celebrate with me
  The Savior of mankind;
T' adore the all-atoning Lamb,
And bless the sound of Jesus' name.

2 Jesus! harmonious name!
  It charms the host above;
They evermore proclaim,
  And wonder at his love;
'Tis all their happiness to gaze,
'Tis heaven to see our Jesus' face.

3 Stung by the scorpion sin,
  My poor expiring soul
The balmy sound drinks in,
  And is at once made whole:
See there my Lord upon the tree!
I know, I feel he died for me.

4 Oh, unexampled love!
  Oh, all-redeeming grace!
How swiftly didst thou move
  To save a fallen race!
What shall I do to make it known,
What thou for all mankind hast done?

5 Oh for a trumpet voice,
  On all the world to call;
To bid their hearts rejoice
  In him who died for all!
For all, my Lord was crucified;
For all, for all, my Savior died.

CHRIST'S INTERCESSION.

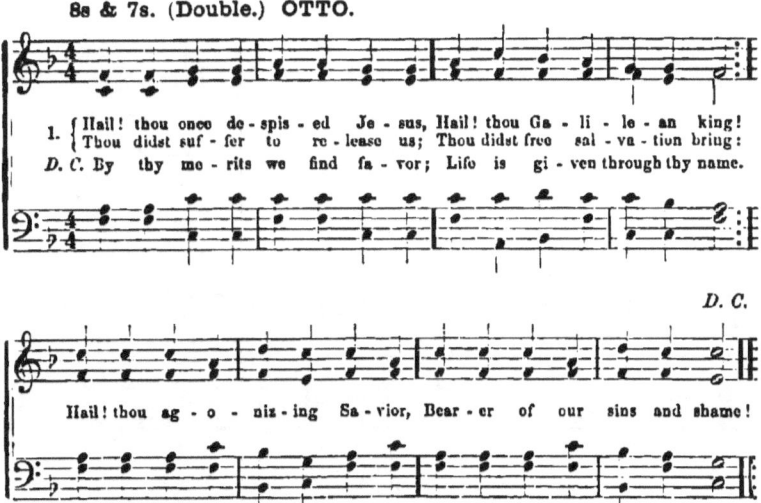

8s & 7s. (Double.) OTTO.

1. Hail! thou once de-spis-ed Je-sus, Hail! thou Ga-li-le-an king!
   Thou didst suf-fer to re-lease us; Thou didst free sal-va-tion bring:
D. C. By thy me-rits we find fa-vor; Life is gi-ven through thy name.

Hail! thou ag-o-niz-ing Sa-vior, Bear-er of our sins and shame!

227 *Christ our Mediator.* **346**

HAIL! thou once despised Jesus,
  Hail! thou Galilean king!
Thou didst suffer to release us;
  Thou didst free salvation bring:
Hail! thou agonizing Savior,
  Bearer of our sins and shame!
By thy merits we find favor;
  Life is given through thy name.

2 Paschal Lamb, by God appointed,
  All our sins on thee were laid;
By almighty love anointed,
  Thou hast full atonement made:
All thy people are forgiven
  Through the virtue of thy blood;
Open'd is the gate of heaven;
  Peace is made 'twixt man and God.

3 Jesus, hail! enthron'd in glory,
  There forever to abide!
All the heav'nly hosts adore thee,
  Seated at thy Father's side:
There for sinners thou art pleading;
  There thou dost our place prepare;
Ever for us interceding,
  Till in glory we appear.

4 Worship, honor, pow'r, and blessing,
  Thou art worthy to receive;
Loudest praises, without ceasing,
  Meet it is for us to give;

Help, ye bright angelic spirits!
  Bring your sweetest, noblest lays!
Help to sing our Savior's merits;
  Help to chant Immanuel's praise.

228 *Christ, the Savior.*

HAIL, thou long-expected Jesus!
  Born to set thy people free;
From our sins and fears release us,
  Let us find our rest in thee.
Israel's strength and consolation,
  Hope of all the saints thou art;
Long-desir'd of ev'ry nation,
  Joy of ev'ry waiting heart.

2 Born, thy people to deliver—
  Born a child, yet God our King—
Born to reign in us forever—
  Now thy gracious kingdom bring.
By thine own eternal Spirit,
  Rule in all our hearts alone;
By thine all-sufficient merit,
  Raise us to thy glorious throne.

229 *Aid Implored.*

BE thou near us, blessed Savior,
  Still at morn and eve the same;
Give us faith that cannot waver,—
  Kindle in us heav'n's own flame.

2 When the fervent pray'r is glowing,
  Graciously sustain that pray'r:—
When the song of praise is flowing,
  Let that song thine impress bear.

REDEMPTION THROUGH CHRIST.

S. M. LABAN.

1. Well, the Redeemer's gone T' appear before our God, To sprinkle o'er the flaming throne With his atoning blood.

230 *Intercession of Christ.* **156**

WELL, the Redeemer's gone
  T' appear before our God,
To sprinkle o'er the flaming throne
  With his atoning blood.

2 No fiery vengeance now,
  Nor burning wrath, comes down;
If justice call for sinners' blood,
  The Savior shows his own.

3 Before his Father's eye
  Our humble suit he moves;
The Father lays his thunder by,
  And looks, and smiles, and loves.

4 Now may our joyful tongues
  Our Maker's honor sing,
Jesus the priest receives our songs,
  And bears them to the King.

5 On earth his mercy reigns,
  And triumphs all above;
But, Lord, how weak are mortal strains
  To speak immortal love!

231 *Praise for Redemption.* **137**

AUTHOR of life and bliss!
  Thy goodness I adore;
Oh, give me strength to speak thy praise,
  And grace to love thee more!

2 First for this world, so fair,
  My daily thanks shall rise;
For ev'ry comfort, ev'ry joy,
  Thy bounteous hand supplies.

3 But yet a nobler cause
  Demands my warmest love—
Can words describe the wondrous gift
  Descending from above?

4 The Savior dwelt on earth,
  He died, that we might live;
Endur'd the sorrows of the cross,
  Immortal hope to give.

5 Ah, who can tell the scorn
  The dear Redeemer bore?
Or who describe the heavy grief
  Which the blest bosom tore?

6 Low in the grave he lay,
  While darkness veil'd the skies:
But lo! he bursts the bands of death;
  To glory see him rise!

7 Father! this work is thine;
  For us thou gav'st thy Son:
Oh, may we all devoted be,
  And live to thee alone!

232 *Christ our Sacrifice.* **320**

NOT all the blood of beasts,
  On Jewish altars slain,
Could give the guilty conscience peace,
  Or wash away the stain.

2 But Christ, the heav'nly Lamb,
  Takes all our sins away;
A sacrifice of nobler name
  And richer blood than they.

3 My faith would lay her hand
  On that dear head of thine;
While as a penitent I stand,
  And there confess my sin.

REDEMPTION THROUGH CHRIST. 85

4 My soul looks back to see
   The burden thou didst bear
When hanging on the cursed tree,
   And hopes her guilt was there.

5 Believing, we rejoice
   To see the curse remove;
We bless the Lamb with cheerful voice,
   And sing his bleeding love.

233 *Praise for Redemption.* 135

HOSANNA to the Son
   Of David and of God,
Who brought the news of pardon down,
   And bought it with his blood!

2 To Christ th' anointed King
   Be endless blessings giv'n!
Let the whole earth his glory sing,
   Who made our peace with heav'n.

8's, 6 Lines. NEWCOURT.

1. We sing the wise, the gracious plan, Which God devis'd ere time be-gan, At length dis-clos'd in all its light; We bless the won-drous birth of love, Which beams around us from a-bove, With grace so free and hopes so bright.

234 *Salvation in Christ for all.* 339

WE sing the wise, the gracious plan,
   Which God devis'd ere time began,
At length disclos'd in all its light;
We bless the wondrous birth of love,
Which beams around us from above,
With grace so free and hopes so bright.

2 Here has the wise eternal mind
In Christ, their common head, conjoin'd
   Gentiles and Jews, and earth and heav'n.
Thro' him, from the great Father's throne,
Rivers of bliss come rolling down,
   And endless peace and life are giv'n.

3 No more the awful cherubs guard
The tree of life with flaming sword,
   To drive afar man's trembling race.
At Salem's pearly gates they stand,
And, smiling, wait, a friendly band,
   To welcome strangers to the place.

4 While we expect that glorious sight,
Love shall our hearts with theirs unite,
   And ardent hope our bosoms raise.
From earth's low cottages of clay,
To those resplendent realms of day,
   We'll try to send the sounding praise.

REDEMPTION THROUGH CHRIST.

L. M. ROTHWELL.

1. He lives, the great Redeemer lives, (What joy the blest assurance gives!) And now, before his Father, God, Pleads the full merit of his blood, Pleads the full merit of his blood.

235   *Christ our Advocate.*   **789**

HE lives, the great Redeemer lives,
   (What joy the blest assurance gives!)
And now, before his Father, God,
Pleads the full merit of his blood.

2 Repeated crimes awake our fears,
And justice arm'd with frowns appears ;
But in the Savior's lovely face
Sweet mercy smiles, and all is peace.

3 Hence, then, ye black, despairing tho'ts !
Above our fears, above our faults,
His pow'rful intercessions rise,
And guilt recedes and terror dies.

4 In ev'ry dark, distressful hour,
When sin and Satan join their pow'r,
Let this dear hope repel the dart,
That Jesus bears us on his heart.

5 Great Advocate, Almighty Friend—
On him our humble hopes depend :
Our cause can never, never fail,
For Jesus pleads and must prevail.

236   *Salvation only in Jesus.*   **315**

IN vain would boasting reason find
   The path to happiness and God ;
Her weak directions leave the mind
Bewilder'd in a doubtful road.

2 Jesus, thy words alone impart
Eternal life ; on these I live ;
Diviner comforts cheer my heart
Than all the pow'rs of nature give.

3 Here let my constant feet abide ;
Thou art the true, the living way :
Let thy good Spirit be my guide
To the bright realms of endless day.

4 The various forms that men devise,
To shake my faith with treach'rous art,
I scorn as vanity and lies,
And bind thy gospel to my heart.

237   *Redemption in Christ alone.*   **322**

ENSLAV'D by sin, and bound in chains,
   Beneath its dreadful tyrant sway,
And doom'd to everlasting pains,
We wretched guilty captives lay.

2 Nor gold nor gems could buy our peace ;
Nor the whole world's collected store
Suffice to purchase our release ;
A thousand worlds were all too poor.

3 Jesus, the Lord, the mighty God,
An all-sufficient ransom paid :
O matchless price ! his precious blood
For vile, rebellious traitors shed !

4 Jesus the sacrifice became
To rescue guilty souls from hell ;
The spotless, bleeding, dying Lamb
Beneath avenging justice fell.

5 Amazing goodness ! love divine !
Oh, may our grateful hearts adore
The matchless grace ; nor yield to sin,
Nor wear its cruel fetters more !

REDEMPTION THROUGH CHRIST.

L. M. FEDERAL STREET.

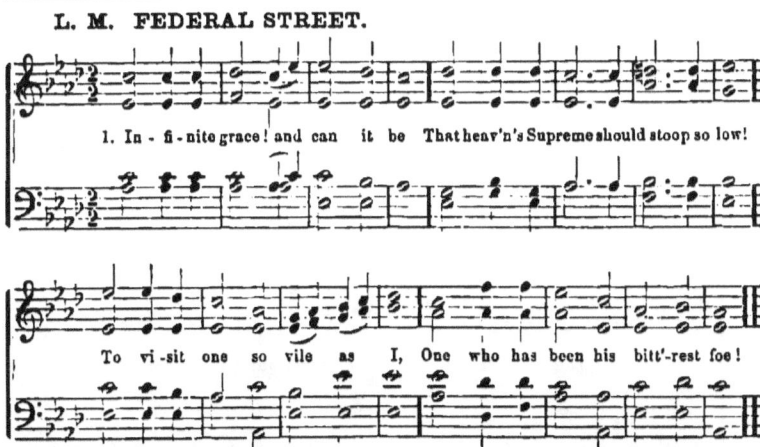

1. In-fi-nite grace! and can it be That heav'n's Supreme should stoop so low! To vi-sit one so vile as I, One who has been his bitt'-rest foe!

238 *Wonders of Redemption.* **333**

INFINITE grace! and can it be
That heav'n's Supreme should stoop so
To visit one so vile as I, [low!
One who has been his bitt'rest foe!

2 Can holiness and wisdom join,
With truth, with justice, and with grace,
To make eternal blessing mine,
And sin, with all its guilt, erase?

3 Oh love! beyond conception great,
That form'd the vast, stupendous plan!
Where all divine perfections meet
To reconcile rebellious man!

4 There wisdom shines in fullest blaze,
And justice all her rights maintains!
Astonish'd angels stoop to gaze,
While mercy o'er the guilty reigns.

5 Yes, mercy reigns, and justice too—
In Christ, harmoniously they meet:
He paid to justice all her due,
And now he fills the mercy-seat.

6 With grateful songs then let our souls
Surround our gracious Father's throne;
And all between the distant poles
His truth and mercy ever own.

239 *Praise for Redemption.* **340**

OH that I had a seraph's fire,
His rapt'rous song and golden lyre,
To chant the love and grace supreme,
Reveal'd as in the gospel scheme.

2 Here's pardon for transgressions past—
It matters not how black their cast;
And, O my soul, with wonder view,
For sins to come, here's pardon too.

3 When Jesus died, our debts were paid;
Our sins, laid on this Scape-Goat's head
Were to the trackless desert driv'n,
And, by his boundless love, forgiv'n.

4 In this abyss of love profound,
When sought for they shall not be found;
Hid from Jehovah's piercing eye,
There, in oblivion's shades, they lie.

240 *Salvation in Christ.* **345**

OF him who did salvation bring
I could forever think and sing;
Arise, ye guilty, he'll forgive;
Arise, ye needy, he'll relieve.

2 Ask but his grace, and lo! 'tis giv'n;
Ask, and he turns your hell to heav'n;
Though sin and sorrow wound my soul,
Jesus, thy balm will make it whole.

3 To shame our sins he blush'd in blood,
He clos'd his eyes to show us God;
Let all the world fall down and know
That none but God such love can show.

4 'Tis thee I love, for thee alone
I shed my tears and make my moan!
Where'er I am, where'er I move,
I meet the object of my love.

5 Insatiate to this spring I fly;
I drink, and yet am ever dry;
Ah! who against thy charms is proof?
Ah! who that loves can love enough?

REDEMPTION THROUGH CHRIST.

C. M. COWPER.

1. There is a foun-tain fill'd with blood Drawn from Im-man-uel's veins; And sinners, plung'd beneath that flood, Lose all their guilty stains, Lose all their guilty stains.

241   *Christ the Fountain.*   327

THERE is a fountain fill'd with blood
   Drawn from Immanuel's veins;
And sinners, plung'd beneath that flood,
   Lose all their guilty stains.

2 The dying thief rejoic'd to see
   That fountain in his day;
Oh, there may I, though vile as he,
   Wash all my sins away!

3 Dear dying Lamb, thy precious blood
   Shall never lose its pow'r,
Till all the ransom'd church of God
   Be sav'd, to sin no more.

4 E'er since, by faith, I saw the stream
   Thy flowing wounds supply,
Redeeming love has been my theme,
   And shall be till I die.

5 Then, in a nobler, sweeter song,
   I'll sing thy pow'r to save;
When this poor lisping, stamm'ring tongue
   Lies silent in the grave.

242   *Reconciliation.*   348

DEAREST of all the names above,
   My Jesus, and my God,
Who can resist thy heav'nly love,
   Or trifle with thy blood?

2 'Tis by the merits of thy death
   The Father smiles again;
'Tis by thine interceding breath
   The Spirit dwells with men.

3 Till God in human flesh I see,
   My thoughts no comfort find;
The holy, just, and sacred Three
   Are terrors to my mind.

4 But if Immanuel's face appear,
   My hope, my joy begins;
His name forbids my slavish fear,
   His grace removes my sins.

5 While Jews on their own law rely,
   And Greeks of wisdom boast,
I love th' incarnate mystery,
   And there I fix my trust.

243   *Redeeming Grace.*   349

PLUNG'D in a gulf of dark despair
   We wretched sinners lay,
Without one cheerful beam of hope,
   Or spark of glimm'ring day.

2 With pitying eyes, the Prince of Grace
   Beheld our helpless grief,
He saw, and (oh, amazing love!)
   He ran to our relief.

3 Down from the shining seats above
   With joyful haste he fled,
Enter'd the grave in mortal flesh,
   And dwelt among the dead.

4 He spoil'd the pow'rs of darkness thus,
   And brake our iron chains;
Jesus has freed our captive souls
   From everlasting pains.

5 Oh, for this love let rocks and hills
   Their lasting silence break,
And all harmonious human tongues
   The Savior's praises speak.

REDEMPTION THROUGH CHRIST.

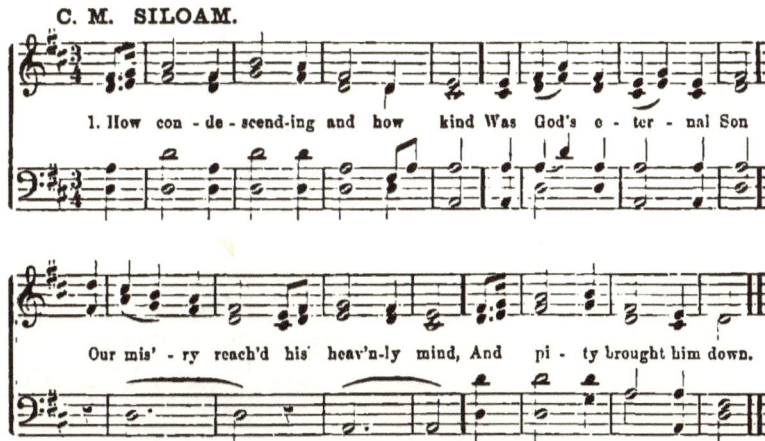

C. M. SILOAM.

1. How con-de-scend-ing and how kind Was God's e-ter-nal Son
Our mis'-ry reach'd his heav'n-ly mind, And pi-ty brought him down.

244 *Redeeming Love.* **131**

HOW condescending and how kind
 Was God's eternal Son!
Our mis'ry reach'd his heav'nly mind,
 And pity brought him down.

2 This was compassion like a God,
 That when the Savior knew
The price of pardon was his blood,
 His pity ne'er withdrew.

3 Now, though he reigns exalted high,
 His love is still as great:
Well he remembers Calvary,
 Nor should his saints forget.

4 Here we receive repeated seals
 Of Jesus' dying love:
Hard is the heart that never feels
 One soft affection move.

245 *God's Grace.* **32**

THY ceaseless, unexhausted love,
 Unmerited and free,
Delights our evil to remove,
 And help our misery.

2 Thou waitest to be gracious still;
 Thou dost with sinners bear;
That, sav'd, we may thy goodness feel,
 And all thy grace declare.

3 Thy goodness and thy truth to me,
 To ev'ry soul abound;
A vast unfathomable sea
 Where all our thoughts are drown'd.

4 Its streams the whole creation reach,
 So plenteous is the store;
Enough for all, enough for each,
 Enough for evermore.

5 Faithful, O Lord, thy mercies are;
 A rock which cannot move:
A thousand promises declare
 Thy constancy of love.

6 Throughout the universe it reigns,
 Unalterably sure;
And, while the truth of God remains,
 His goodness must endure.

246 *The Cross no Offense.* **12**

SHALL atheists dare insult the cross
 Of our Redeemer God?
Shall infidels reproach his laws,
 Or trample on his blood?

2 What if he chose mysterious ways
 To cleanse us from our faults?
May not the works of sov'reign grace
 Transcend our feeble thoughts?

3 What if the gospel bids us fight
 With flesh, and self, and sin?
The prize is most divinely bright,
 Which we are call'd to win.

4 What if the foolish and the poor
 His glorious grace partake?
This but confirms his truth the more,
 For so the prophets spake.

5 Then let our faith grow firm and strong,
 Our lips profess his word;
Nor blush, nor fear to walk among
 The men that love the Lord.

REDEMPTION THROUGH CHRIST.

C. M. ORTONVILLE.

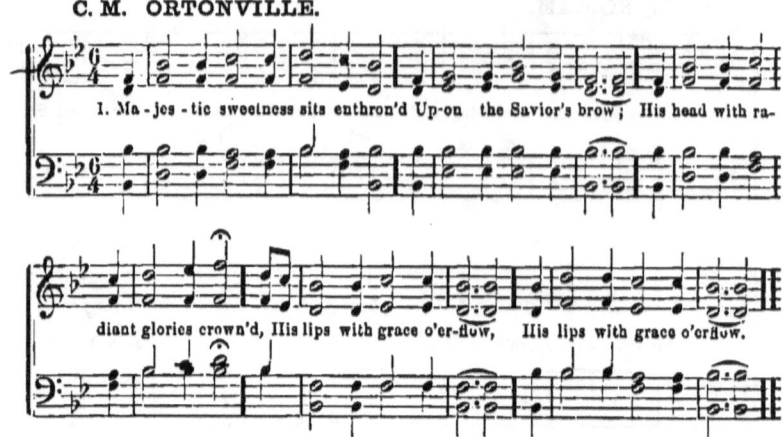

1. Ma-jes-tic sweetness sits enthron'd Up-on the Savior's brow; His head with ra-diant glories crown'd, His lips with grace o'er-flow, His lips with grace o'erflow.

247   *The Dear Redeemer.*   **791**

MAJESTIC sweetness sits enthron'd
　Upon the Savior's brow;
His head with radiant glories crown'd,
　His lips with grace o'erflow.

2 No mortal can with him compare
　Among the sons of men;
Fairer is he than all the fair
　Who fill the heav'nly train.

3 He saw me plung'd in deep distress,
　And flew to my relief;
For me he bore the shameful cross,
　And carried all my grief.

4 To him I owe my life and breath,
　And all the joys I have;
He makes me triumph over death,
　And saves me from the grave.

5 To heav'n, the place of his abode,
　He brings my weary feet,
Shows me the glories of my God,
　And makes my joys complete.

6 Since from his bounty I receive
　Such proofs of love divine,
Had I a thousand hearts to give,
　Lord, they should all be thine.

248   *Christ Precious.*   **373**

HOW sweet the name of Jesus sounds
　In a believer's ear!
It soothes his sorrows, heals his wounds,
　And drives away his fear.

2 It makes the wounded spirit whole,
　And calms the troubled breast;

'Tis manna to the hungry soul,
　And to the weary, rest.

3 By him my pray'rs acceptance gain,
　Although with sin defil'd;
Satan accuses me in vain,
　And I am own'd a child.

4 Weak is the effort of my heart,
　And cold my warmest thought;
But when I see thee as thou art,
　I'll praise thee as I ought.

5 Till then, I would thy love proclaim
　With ev'ry fleeting breath;
And may the music of thy name
　Refresh my soul in death.

249   *Way, Truth, and Life.*   **121**

THOU art the way; to thee alone
　From sin and death we flee;
And he who would the Father seek,
　Must seek him, Lord, through thee.

2 Thou art the truth; thy word alone
　True wisdom can impart;
Thou only canst instruct the mind,
　And purify the heart.

3 Thou art the life; the rending tomb
　Proclaims thy conqu'ring arm;
And those who put their trust in thee,
　Nor death nor hell shall harm.

4 Thou art the way, the truth, the life;
　Grant us to know that way,
That truth to keep, that life to win,
　Which lead to endless day.

REDEMPTION THROUGH CHRIST.

C. M. WOODSTOCK.

1. Oh for a thou-sand tongues to sing My dear Re-deem-er's praise, The glo-ries of my God and King, The tri-umphs of his grace.

250 *The Grace of Christ.* **337**

OH for a thousand tongues to sing
  My dear Redeemer's praise;
The glories of my God and King,
  The triumphs of his grace!

2 My gracious Master and my God,
  Assist me to proclaim,
To spread through all the earth abroad,
  The honors of thy name.

3 Jesus, the name that calms our fears,
  That bids our sorrows cease;
'Tis music in the sinner's ears;
  'Tis life, and health, and peace.

4 He breaks the pow'r of reigning sin,
  He sets the pris'ner free;
His blood can make the foulest clean,
  His blood avail'd for me.

5 Let us obey—we then shall know,
  Shall feel our sins forgiv'n
Anticipate our heav'n below,
  And own that love is heav'n.

251 *Inexhaustible Grace.* **189**

JEHOVAH'S grace, how full, how free:
  His language how divine!
"My Son, thou ever art with me,
  And all I have is thine.

2 "My saints shall each a portion share,
  That's worthy of a God;
They are my chief, my constant care—
  The purchase of my blood.

3 "Both grace and glory I will give,
  And nothing good deny;
With me my saints shall ever live,
  And reign with me on high.

4 "And should a hundred thousand more
  Accept the proffer'd grace,
I have a heav'n prepar'd—for all;
  Nor shall you have the less."

5 Then, dearest Lord, let millions come,
  And feast on pard'ning grace;
Bring prodigals, bring exiles home,
  And we will sing thy praise.

252 *Salvation.* **362**

SALVATION, O, the joyful sound!
  Glad tidings to our ears;
A sov'reign balm for ev'ry wound,
  A cordial for our fears.

2 Buried in sorrow and in sin,
  At hell's dark door we lay:
But we arise by grace divine,
  To see a heav'nly day.

3 Salvation! let the echo fly
  The spacious earth around;
While all the armies of the sky
  Conspire to raise the sound.

4 Salvation! O thou bleeding Lamb,
  To thee the praise belongs;
Our hearts shall kindle at thy name
  Thy name inspire our songs.

REDEMPTION THROUGH CHRIST.

L. M. STONEFIELD.

Where shall the tribes of Ad-am find The sov'-reign good to fill the mind?
Ye sons of mo-ral wis-dom, show The spring whence living wa-ters flow.

253 *Christ the Life.* **335**

WHERE shall the tribes of Adam find
The sov'reign good to fill the mind?
Ye sons of moral wisdom, show
The spring whence living waters flow.

2 In vain I ask—for Nature's pow'r
Extends but to this mortal hour;
'Twas but a poor relief she gave
Against the terrors of the grave.

3 Jesus, our kinsman and our God,
Array'd in majesty and blood,
Thou art our Life! our souls in thee
Possess a full felicity.

4 All our immortal hopes are laid
In thee, our Surety and our Head;
Thy cross, thy cradle, and thy throne,
Are fraught with glories yet unknown.

5 Here let my soul forever lie,
Beneath the blessings of thine eye;
'Tis heav'n on earth, 'tis heav'n above,
To see thy face, to taste thy love.

254 *Christ our Hiding-Place.* **334**

HAIL, boundless love, that first began
The scheme to rescue fallen man!
Hail, matchless, free, eternal grace,
That gave my soul a hiding-place.

2 Against the God that rules the sky
I fought with hands uplifted high;
Despis'd his rich, abounding grace,
Too proud to seek a hiding-place.

3 Indignant Justice stood in view;
To Sinai's fiery mount I flew;

I felt the arrows of distress,
But found I had no hiding-place.

4 Ere long a heav'nly voice I heard,
And Mercy's angel form appear'd;
Conducted me to rest and peace
In Jesus Christ, my Hiding-Place.

255 *Christ our Help.* **311**

BY various maxims, forms, and rules,
That pass for wisdom in the schools,
I strove my passions to restrain;
But all my efforts prov'd in vain.

2 But since the Savior I have known,
My rules are all reduc'd to one—
To keep my Lord, by faith, in view;
This strength supplies and motives too.

3 I see him lead a suff'ring life,
Patient amidst reproach and strife;
And from this pattern courage take
To bear and suffer for his sake.

4 Upon the cross I see him bleed,
And by the sight from guilt am freed;
This sight destroys the life of sin,
And quickens heav'nly life within.

5 To look to Jesus as he rose,
Confirms my faith, disarms my foes:
Satan I shame and overcome
By pointing to my Savior's tomb.

6 I see him look with pity down
And hold in view the conqu'ror's crown.
If press'd with griefs and cares before,
My soul revives, and asks no more.

L. M. HINGHAM.

1. Lord, what was man when made at first, A-dam, the offspring of the dust, That thou sh'dst set him and his race But just be-low an an-gel's place, But just be-low an an-gel's place.

256   *Adam and Christ.*   92

LORD, what was man when made at first,
Adam, the offspring of the dust,
That thou shouldst set him and his race
But just below an angel's place?

2 That thou shouldst raise his nature so,
And make him lord of all below;
Make every beast and bird submit,
And lay the fishes at his feet?

3 But, oh, what brighter glories wait
To crown the second Adam's state!
What honors shall thy Son adorn,
Who condescended to be born!

4 See him below his angels made,
See him in dust amongst the dead,
To save a ruin'd world from sin:
But he shall reign with pow'r divine.

5 The world to come, redeem'd from all
The mis'ries that attend the fall,
New-made, and glorious, shall submit
At our exalted Savior's feet.

257   *Christ our Substitute.*   127

'TWAS for our sake, eternal God,
Thy Son sustain'd that heavy load
Of base reproach and sore disgrace,
And shame defil'd his sacred face.

2 The Jews, his brethren and his kin,
Abus'd him, when he check'd their sin;
While he fulfill'd thy holy laws,
They hated him without a cause.

3 Zeal for the temple of his God
Consum'd his life, expos'd his blood;
Reproaches at thy glory thrown
He felt, and mourn'd them as his own,

4 His friends forsook, his foll'wers fled,
While foes and arms surround his head:
They nail him to the shameful tree;
There hung my Lord, who died for me.

5 But God his Father heard his cry,
Rais'd from the dead, he reigns on high;
The nations learn his righteousness,
And humble sinners taste his grace.

258   *Salvation by Grace.*   317

SELF-righteous souls on works rely,
And boast their moral dignity;
But if I lisp a song of praise,
Grace is the note my soul shall raise.

2 'Twas grace that quicken'd me when dead,
And grace my soul to Jesus led;
Grace brings me pardon for my sin—
'Tis grace subdues my lusts within.

3 'Tis grace that sweetens ev'ry cross,
'Tis grace supports in ev'ry loss;
In Jesus' grace my soul is strong—
Grace is my hope and Christ my song.

4 'Tis grace defends when danger's near;
And 'tis by grace I persevere;
'Tis grace constrains my soul to love—
Free grace is all they sing above.

5 Thro' endless years, of grace I'll sing,
Adore and bless my heav'nly King;
I'll cast my crown before his throne,
Sav'd by his sov'reign grace alone.

REDEMPTION THROUGH CHRIST.

8s, 7s, & 4s.   OLIPHANT.

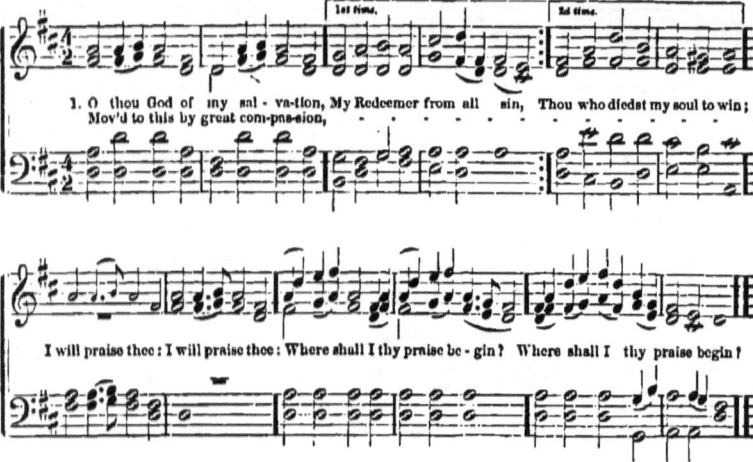

259   *Praise for Redemption.*   **344**

O THOU God of my salvation,
  My Redeemer from all sin,
Mov'd to this by great compassion,
  Thou who diedst my soul to win;
    I will praise thee:
  Where shall I thy praise begin?

2 While the angel-choirs are crying
  Glory to the great I AM,
I with them would still be vying,
  Glory, glory to the Lamb!
    Oh, how precious
  Is the sound of Jesus' name!

3 Now I see, with joy and wonder,
  Whence the healing streams arose;
Angel-minds are lost to ponder
  Dying love's mysterious cause;
    Yet the blessing
  Down to all, to me it flows.

4 Though unseen, I love the Savior,
  He almighty grace hath shown;
Pardon'd guilt and purchas'd favor,
  This he makes to mortals known,
    Give him glory,
  Glory, glory is his own.

5 Angels now are hov'ring round us,
  Unperceiv'd, they mix the throng,
Wond'ring at the love that crown'd us,
  Glad to join the holy song:
    Hallelujah,
  Love and praise to Christ belong.

260   *Salvation by Grace.*   **321**

EVERY fallen soul by sinning
  Merits everlasting pain;
But thy love, without beginning,
  Has redeem'd the world again.
    Countless millions
  Shall in life through Jesus reign.

2 Pause, my soul, adore and wonder!
  Ask, "Oh, why such love to me?"
Grace hath put me in the number
  Of the Savior's family:
    Hallelujah!
  Thanks, eternal thanks, to thee!

3 Since that love had no beginning,
  And shall never, never cease;
Keep, O keep me, Lord, from sinning!
  Guide me in the way of peace!
    Make me walk in
  All the paths of holiness.

4 When I quit this feeble mansion,
  And my soul returns to thee;
Let the pow'r of thy ascension
  Manifest itself in me;
    Through thy Spirit,
  Give the final victory!

5 When the angel sounds the trumpet;
  When my soul and body join;
When my Savior comes to judgment,
  Bright in majesty divine;
    Let me triumph
  In thy righteousness as mine.

REDEMPTION THROUGH CHRIST.

261 *Full Redemption anticipated.* **475**

EVERY moment brings me nearer
 To my long-sought rest above ;
Higher mounts my soul, and higher—
 Oh, how happy to remove;
  Then, forever,
 Shall I sing redeeming love.

2 Soon shall I be gone to glory—
 Join the bright, angelic race,
There repeat the pleasing story—
 I was sav'd by sov'reign grace ;
  And for ever
 View my loving Savior's face.

3 Though my burden sore oppress me,
 And I shrink beneath my pain,
Jesus Christ will soon release me,
 And your loss will be my gain :
  Precious Saviour,
 With my Lord I shall remain.

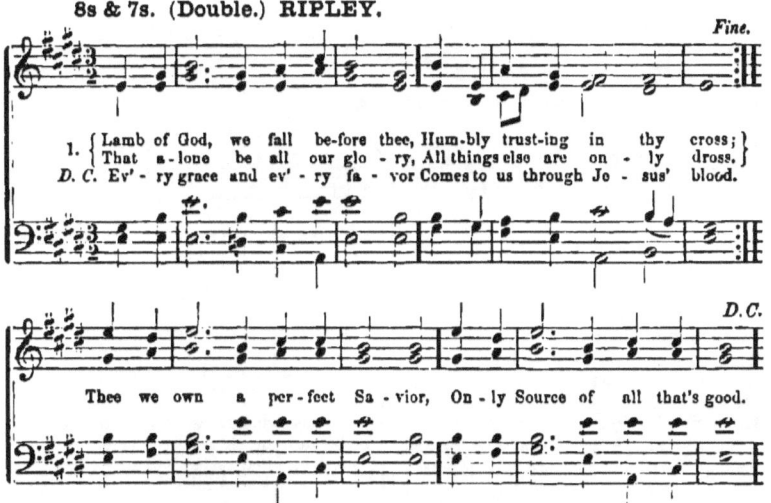

8s & 7s. (Double.) RIPLEY.

1. Lamb of God, we fall before thee, Humbly trusting in thy cross;
   That alone be all our glo-ry, All things else are on-ly dross.
D. C. Ev'-ry grace and ev'-ry fa-vor Comes to us through Je-sus' blood.

Thee we own a per-fect Sa-vior, On-ly Source of all that's good.

262 *Christ our All.* **336**

LAMB of God, we fall before thee,
 Humbly trusting in thy cross;
That alone be all our glory,
 All things else are only dross.
Thee we own a perfect Savior,
 Only Source of all that's good.
Ev'ry grace and ev'ry favor
 Comes to us through Jesus' blood.

2 Jesus gives us true repentance,
 By his Spirit sent from heav'n ;
Whispers this transporting sentence,
 "Son, thy sins are all forgiv'n."
Faith he grants us to believe it,
 Grateful hearts his love to prize:
Want we wisdom ? he must give it;
 Hearing ears and seeing eyes.

3 Jesus gives us pure affections,
 Wills to do what he requires ;
Makes us follow his directions,
 And what he commands—inspires.
All our prayers, and all our praises,
 Rightly offer'd in his name,
He that dictates them is Jesus;
 He that answers is the same.

263 *Rest in Jesus.*

EARTHLY joys no longer please us,
 Here would we present them all,
Seek our only rest in Jesus—
 Him our Lord and Master call.
Faith, our languid spirits cheering,
 Points to brighter worlds above,
Bids us look for his appearing—
 Bids us triumph in his love.

2 May our lights be always burning,
 And our loins be girded round,
Waiting for the Lord's returning—
 Longing for the welcome sound !
Thus, the Christian life adoring,
 Never will we be afraid,
Should he come at night or morning—
 Early dawn or evening shade.

THE HOLY SPIRIT.

L. M. CREATION.

1. A-wake, my soul, in joy-ful lays, And sing thy great Re-deem-er's praise; He just-ly claims a song from me, His lov-ing-kind-ness, oh, how free!

264 *Loving-Kindness.* **328**

AWAKE, my soul, in joyful lays,
And sing thy great Redeemer's praise;
He justly claims a song from me,
His loving-kindness, oh, how free!

2 He saw me ruin'd in the fall,
Yet lov'd me notwithstanding all;
He sav'd me from my lost estate,
His loving-kindness, oh, how great!

3 Though num'rous hosts of mighty foes,
Though earth and hell my way oppose,
He safely leads my soul along,
His loving-kindness, oh, how strong!

4 When trouble, like a gloomy cloud,
Has gather'd thick and thunder'd loud,
He near my soul has always stood,
His loving-kindness, oh, how good!

5 Often I feel my sinful heart
Prone from my Jesus to depart;
But though I have him oft forgot,
His loving-kindness changes not.

6 Soon shall I pass the gloomy vale,
Soon all my mortal pow'rs must fail;
Oh, may my last expiring breath
His loving-kindness sing in death!

7 Then let me mount and soar away
To the bright world of endless day;
And sing, with raptures and surprise,
His loving-kindness in the skies.

265 *Wonders in the Cross.* **833**

BLEST Jesus! when thy cross I view,—
That myst'ry to th' angelic host,—
I gaze with grief and rapture too,
And all my soul's in wonder lost.

2 What strange compassion fill'd thy breast,
That brought thee from thy throne on high,
To woes that cannot be express'd,
To be despis'd, to groan, and die?

3 Was it for man, rebellious man,
Sunk by his crimes below the grave,
Who, justly doom'd to endless pain,
Found none to pity or to save?

4 For man didst thou forsake the sky,
To bleed upon th' accursed tree?
And didst thou taste of death to buy
Immortal life and bliss for me?

5 Had I a voice to praise thy name,
Loud as the trump that wakes the dead,
Had I the raptur'd seraph's flame,
My debt of love could ne'er be paid.

266 *Pentecost.* **528**

GREAT was the day, the joy was great,
When the divine disciples met;
While on their heads the Spirit came,
And sat like tongues of cloven flame.

2 What gifts, what miracles he gave!
And pow'r to give and pow'r to save! [words,
Furnish'd their tongues with wondrous
Instead of shields and spears and swords.

3 Nations, the learned and the rude,
Are by those heav'nly arms subdu'd;
While Satan rages at his loss
And hates the doctrine of the cross.

4 Great King of grace, my heart subdue,
I would be led in triumph too—
A willing captive to my Lord—
And sing the vict'ries of his word.

THE HOLY SPIRIT. 97

L. M. LOUVAN.

1. E-ter-nal Spi-rit! we con-fess And sing the won-ders of thy grace:
Thy pow'r con-veys our bless-ings down From God the Fa-ther and the Son.

267 *Work of the Spirit.* **172**

ETERNAL Spirit! we confess
And sing the wonders of thy grace:
Thy pow'r conveys our blessings down
From God the Father and the Son.

2 Enlighten'd by thy heav'nly ray,
Our shades and darkness turn to day:
Thine inward teachings make us know,
Our danger and our refuge too.

3 Thy power and glory work within,
And break the chains of reigning sin,
Do our imperious lusts subdue,
And form our wretched hearts anew.

4 The troubled conscience knows thy voice,
Thy cheering words awake our joys;
Thy words allay the stormy wind,
And calm the surges of the mind.

268 *The Spirit invoked.* **173**

COME, gracious Spirit, heav'nly Dove,
With light and comfort from above,
Be thou our guardian, thou our guide;
O'er ev'ry thought and step preside.

2 Conduct us safe, conduct us far
From ev'ry sin and hurtful snare:
Lead to thy word, that rules must give,
And teach us lessons how to live.

3 The light of truth to us display,
That we may know and love thy way:
Plant holy fear in ev'ry heart,
That we from thee may ne'er depart.

4 Lead us to righteousness, the road
That we must take, to dwell with God;
Lead us to Christ,—the living way;
Nor let us from his pasture stray.

5 Lead us to God, our final rest,
In his enjoyment to be blest;
Lead us to heaven, the seat of bliss,
Where pleasure in perfection is.

269 *The Comforter.* **177**

SURE the blest Comforter is nigh,
'Tis he sustains my fainting heart;
Else would my hope forever die,
And ev'ry cheering ray depart.

2 When some kind promise glads my soul,
Do I not find his healing voice
The tempest of my fears control,
And bid my drooping pow'rs rejoice?

3 What less than thine almighty word
Can raise my heart from earth and dust!
And bid me cleave to thee, my Lord,
My life, my treasure, and my trust!

4 And when my cheerful hope can say,
"I love my God, and taste his grace;"
Lord, is it not thy blissful ray,
Which brings this dawn of sacred peace?

5 Let thy kind Spirit in my heart
Forever dwell, O God of love;
And light and heav'nly peace impart,
Sweet earnest of the joys above.

THE HOLY SPIRIT.

C. M. PARKER.

1. For-ev-er bless-ed be the Lord, My Sa-vior and my shield! He sends his Spi-rit with his word, To arm me for the field.

270. Aid of the Spirit. 176

FOREVER blessed be the Lord,
  My Savior and my shield!
He sends his Spirit with his word,
  To arm me for the field.

2 When sin and hell their force unite,
  He makes my soul his care;
Instructs me in the heav'nly fight,
  And guards me through the war.

3 A friend and helper so divine
  My fainting hope shall raise:
He makes the glorious vict'ry mine,
  And his shall be the praise.

271. Quench not the Spirit. 801

QUENCH not the Spirit of the Lord,
  The Holy One from heav'n;
The Comforter, belov'd, ador'd,
  To man in mercy giv'n.

2 Quench not the Spirit of the Lord:
  He will not always strive:
O tremble at that awful word;
  Sinner! awake and live.

3 Quench not the Spirit of the Lord,
  It is thine only hope:
O let his aid be now implor'd;
  Let pray'r be lifted up.

4 Grieve not the Spirit of the Lord,
  Heirs of redeeming grace;
With grateful hearts his love record,
  Whose presence fills the place.

272. All may be Saved. 201

JESUS, thy blessings are not few,
  Nor is thy gospel weak;
Thy grace can melt the stubborn Jew,
  And heal the dying Greek.

2 Wide as the reach of Satan's rage
  Does thy salvation flow;
'Tis not confin'd to sex or age,
  The lofty or the low.

3 While grace is offer'd to the prince,
  The poor may take their share;
No mortal has a just pretence
  To perish in despair.

4 Come, all ye wretched sinners, come,
  He'll form your souls anew;
His gospel and his heart have room
  For rebels such as you.

273. Presence of the Spirit.

THE Holy Comforter has come—
  We feel his presence here—
Our hearts would now no longer roam,
  But bow in filial fear.

2 This breathing tenderness of love,
  This hush of solemn power;
'Tis heaven descending from above,
  To fill this favor'd hour.

3 How excellent the truth appears,
  How sweet the song we raise!
E'en grief sits smiling in her tears,
  And lifts her soul in praise.

4 No more let sin our hearts deceive,
  Nor earthly cares betray,
Oh, let us never, never grieve
  The Comforter away.

INVITATIONS AND WARNINGS.

C. M. HENRY.

1. What language now salutes the ear, And 'tis our Father's voice! Let all the world attentive hear, And ev'ry soul rejoice.

274 *Give God thy Heart.* **190**

WHAT language now salutes the ear,
 And 'tis our Father's voice!
Let all the world attentive hear,
 And ev'ry soul rejoice.

2 Sinner, he kindly speaks to thee,
 However vile thou art;
Here's grace and pardon, rich and free—
 My son, give me thy heart.

3 Tho' thou hast long my grace withstood,
 And said to me, "Depart,"
I claim the purchase of my blood—
 My son, give me thy heart.

4 I'll form thee for myself alone,
 And ev'ry good impart;
I'll make my great salvation known—
 My son, give me thy heart.

5 Come, Lord, and conquer now my heart,
 Set up in me thy throne;
Bid sin and Satan hence depart,
 And claim me as thine own.

275 *Yet there is Room.* **184**

COME, sinners, to the gospel feast;
 Oh, come without delay;
For there is room in Jesus' breast
 For all who will obey.

2 There's room in God's eternal love
 To save thy precious soul,
Room in the Spirit's grace above
 To heal and make thee whole.

3 There's room within the church, redeem'd
 With blood of Christ divine;
Room in the white-robed throng conven'd,
 For that dear soul of thine.

4 There's room in heaven among the choir,
 And harps and crowns of gold,
And glorious palms of vict'ry there,
 And joys that ne'er were told.

5 There's room around thy Father's board,
 For thee and thousands more:
Oh, come and welcome to the Lord:
 Yea, come this very hour.

276 *Living Waters.* **191**

OH, what amazing words of grace
 Are in the gospel found!
Suited to ev'ry sinner's case,
 Who hears the joyful sound.

2 Poor, sinful, thirsty, fainting souls
 Are freely welcome here;
Salvation, like a river, rolls,
 Abundant, free, and clear.

3 Come then, with all your wants & wounds,
 Your ev'ry burden bring!
Here love, unchanging love, abounds,
 A deep celestial spring!

4 Whoever will (oh, gracious word!)
 Shall of this stream partake:
Come, thirsty souls, and bless the Lord,
 And drink for Jesus' sake!

5 Millions of sinners, vile as you,
 Have here found life and peace;
Come, then, and prove its virtues too,
 And drink, adore, and bless.

INVITATIONS AND WARNINGS.

S. M. SHIRLAND.

1. Let ev'-ry ear at-tend, And ev'-ry heart re-joice; The trum-pet of the gos-pel sounds With an in-vit-ing voice.

277 *Gospel Invitation.* **188**

LET ev'ry ear attend,
  And ev'ry heart rejoice;
The trumpet of the gospel sounds
  With an inviting voice.

2 Ho! all ye starving souls,
  That feed upon the wind,
And vainly strive with earthly toys
  To fill an empty mind:

3 Here wisdom has prepar'd
  A soul-reviving feast,
And bids your longing appetites
  The rich provision taste.

4 Ho! ye that pant for streams,
  And pine away and die,
Here you may quench your raging thirst
  With springs that never dry.

5 Rivers of mercy here
  In a rich ocean join;
Salvation in abundance flows,
  Like floods of milk and wine.

6 The gates of gospel grace
  Stand open night and day;
Lord! we are come to seek supplies,
  And drive our wants away.

278 *Be Free.* **130**

AND shall we still be slaves,
  And in our fetters lie,
When summon'd by a voice divine
  T' assert our liberty?

2 Did the great Savior bleed,
  Our freedom to obtain?
And shall we trample on his blood,
  And glory in our chain?

3 Shall we go on in sin,
  Because thy grace abounds;
Or crucify the Lord again,
  And open all his wounds?

4 Forbid it, mighty God!
  Nor let it e'er be said
That those, for whom thy Son has died,
  In vice are lost and dead.

5 The man that durst despise
  The law that Moses brought,
Behold! how terribly he dies
  For his presumptuous fault.

6 But sorer vengeance falls
  On that rebellious race,
Who hate to hear when Jesus calls,
  And dare resist his grace.

279 *Gospel Invitation.* **226**

THE Spirit in our hearts
  Is whisp'ring, "Sinner, come;"
The Bride, the church of Christ, proclaims
  To all his children, "Come!"

2 Let him that heareth say
  To all about him, "Come;"
Let him that thirsts for righteousness,
  To Christ the fountain come.

3 Yes, whosoever will,
  Oh, let him freely come,
And freely drink the stream of life;
  'Tis Jesus bids him come.

INVITATIONS AND WARNINGS.

S. M. INVERNESS.

1. Now is th' ac-cept-ed time, Now is the day of grace;
Now, sin-ners, come with-out de-lay, And seek the Sa-vior's face.

280 Now the Time. 182
NOW is th' accepted time,
   Now is the day of grace;
Now, sinners, come without delay,
   And seek the Savior's face.

2 Now is th' accepted time,
   The Savior calls to-day;
To-morrow it may be too late,
   Then why should you delay?

3 Now is th' accepted time,
   The gospel bids you come:
And ev'ry promise in his word
   Declares there yet is room.

4 Lord, draw reluctant souls,
   And feast them with thy love;
Then will the angels clap their wings,
   And bear the news above.

281 The Day is Declining. 827
THE swift-declining day,
   How fast its moments fly,
While ev'ning's broad and gloomy shade
   Gains on the western sky!

2 Ye mortals, mark its pace,
   And use the hours of light;
For, know, its Maker can command
   An instant, endless night.

3 Give glory to the Lord
   Who rules the rolling sphere;
Submissive, at his footstool bow,
   And seek salvation there.

4 Then shall new lustre break
   Through all the heavy gloom.
And lead you to unchanging light
   In your celestial home.

282 The Harvest Ending. 237
I SAW, beyond the tomb,
   The awful Judge appear,
Prepar'd to scan with strict account
   My blessings wasted here.

2 His wrath, like flaming fire,
   Burn'd to the lowest hell—
And in that hopeless world of woe
   He bade my spirit dwell.

3 Ye sinners, fear the Lord,
   While yet 'tis call'd to-day;
Soon will the awful voice of death
   Command your souls away.

4 Soon may the harvest close,—
   The summer soon be o'er,—
And then your injur'd, angry God
   Will hear your pray'rs no more.

283 Now, the Day of Grace. 826
NOW is the day of grace;
   Now to the Savior come;
The Lord is calling, "Seek my face,
   And I will guide you home."

2 A Father bids you speed;
   Oh, wherefore then delay?
He calls in love; he sees your need;
   He bids you come to-day.

3 To-day the prize is won;
   The promise is to save;
Then, oh, be wise; to-morrow's sun
   May shine upon your grave.

INVITATIONS AND WARNINGS.

L. M. WELLS.

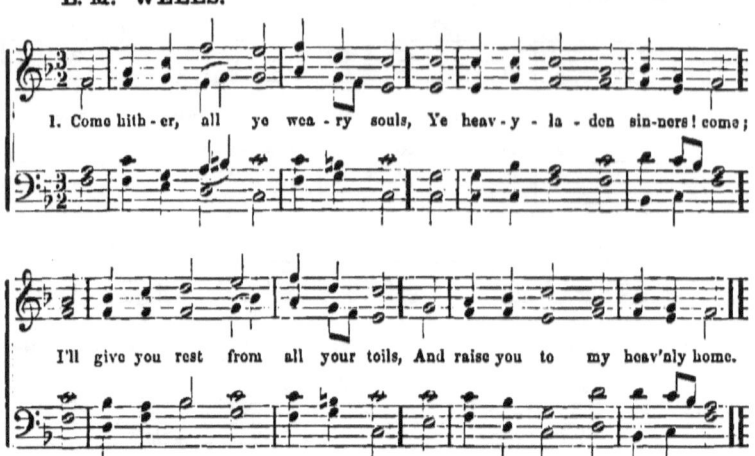

1. Come hith-er, all ye wea-ry souls, Ye heav-y-la-den sin-ners! come; I'll give you rest from all your toils, And raise you to my heav'nly home.

284   *Christ's Invitation.*   193

"COME hither, all ye weary souls,
   Ye heavy-laden sinners! come;
I'll give you rest from all your toils,
And raise you to my heav'nly home.

2 "They shall find rest that learn of me;
I'm of a meek and lowly mind;
But passion rages like the sea,
And pride is restless as the wind.

3 "Bless'd is the man whose shoulders take
My yoke and bear it with delight!
My yoke is easy to his neck;
My grace shall make the burden light."

4 Jesus! we come at thy command,
With faith, and hope, and humble zeal;
Resign our spirits to thy hand,
To mould and guide us at thy will.

285   *The Sinner Warned.*   218

HASTEN, O sinner, to be wise,
   And stay not for the morrow's sun;
The longer wisdom you despise,
The harder is she to be won.

2 Oh, hasten, mercy to implore,
And stay not for the morrow's sun,
For fear thy season should be o'er
Before this ev'ning's course be run.

3 Hasten, O sinner, to return,
And stay not for the morrow's sun,
For fear thy lamp should fail to burn
Before the needful work is done.

4 Hasten, O sinner, to be blest,
And stay not for the morrow's sun,
For fear the curse should thee arrest
Before the morrow is begun.

286   *The Sinner Welcome.*   192

HARK! 'tis the Savior's voice I hear,
   Come, trembling soul, dispel thy fear!
He saith, and who his word can doubt?
He will in no wise cast you out!

2 Doth Satan fill you with dismay,
And tell you, Christ will cast away?
It is a truth, why should you doubt?
He will in no wise cast you out!

3 Doth sin appear before your view,
Of scarlet or of crimson hue?
If black as hell, why should you doubt?
He will in no wise cast you out!

4 The publican and dying thief
Applied to Christ, and found relief;
Nor need you entertain a doubt:
He will in no wise cast you out!

5 Approach your God, make no delay,
He waits to welcome you to-day;
His mercy try, nor longer doubt:
He will in no wise cast you out!

INVITATIONS AND WARNINGS.

287 *Expostulation.* **244**

WHY will ye lavish out your years
    Amidst a thousand trifling cares,
While, in the various range of thought
The one thing needful is forgot?

2 Why will ye chase the fleeting wind
And famish an immortal mind,
While angels with regret look down
To see you spurn a heav'nly crown?

3 Th' eternal God calls from above,
And Jesus pleads his dying love;
Awaken'd conscience gives you pain;
And shall they join their pleas in vain?

4 Almighty God! thine aid impart,
To fix conviction on the heart:
Thy pow'r can clear the darkest eyes,
And make the haughtiest scorner wise.

288 *Rest for the Penitent.* **912**

COME, weary souls, with sin distress'd,
    Come, and accept the promis'd rest;
The Savior's gracious call obey,
And cast your gloomy fears away.

2 Here mercy's boundless ocean flows,
To cleanse your guilt and heal your woes;
Pardon and life and endless peace;
How rich the gift, how free the grace!

3 Lord, we accept, with thankful heart,
The hope thy gracious words impart;
We come with trembling, yet rejoice,
And bless the kind, inviting voice.

4 Dear Savior, let thy wondrous love
Confirm our faith, our fears remove;
Oh, sweetly influence ev'ry breast,
And guide us to eternal rest.

7s & 6s. PASSAIC.

1. Re-mem-ber thy Creator While youth's fair spring is bright, Be-fore thy cares are great-er, Before comes age's night;
While yet the sun shines o'er thee, While stars the darkness cheer, While life is all before thee, Thy great Cre-a-tor fear.

289 *Remembering thy Creator.* **954**

REMEMBER thy Creator
    While youth's fair spring is bright,
Before thy cares are greater,
    Before comes age's night;
While yet the sun shines o'er thee,
    While stars the darkness cheer,
While life is all before thee,
    Thy great Creator fear.

2 Remember thy Creator
    Ere life resigns its trust,
Ere sinks dissolving nature,
    And dust returns to dust;
Before with God who gave it,
    The spirit shall appear:
He cries, who died to save it,
    "Thy great Creator fear."

290 *Confidence in God.* **856**

GOD is my strong salvation;
    What foe have I to fear?
In darkness and temptation,
    My light, my help, is near;
Though hosts encamp around me,
    Firm in the fight I stand;
What terror can confound me,
    With God at my right hand?

2 Place on the Lord reliance;
    My soul, with courage wait;
His truth be thine affiance,
    When faint and desolate;
His might thy heart shall strengthen,
    His love thy joy increase;
Mercy thy days shall lengthen;
    The Lord will give thee peace.

INVITATIONS AND WARNINGS.

7s. ESHTAMOA.

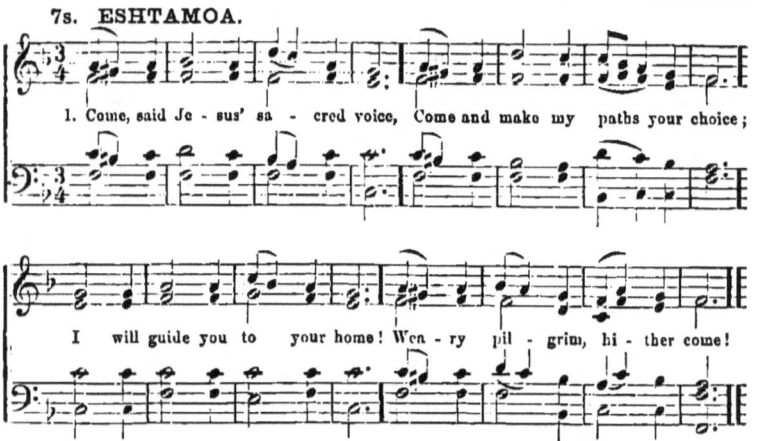

1. Come, said Jesus' sacred voice, Come and make my paths your choice; I will guide you to your home! Weary pilgrim, hither come!

291 *The weary Sinner called.* **221**

COME, said Jesus' sacred voice,
  Come and make my paths your choice;
I will guide you to your home!
Weary pilgrim, hither come!

2 Thou who, houseless, sole, forlorn,
Long hast borne the proud world's scorn,
Long hast roam'd the barren waste;
Weary pilgrim, hither haste!

3 Ye who, toss'd on beds of pain,
Seek for ease, but seek in vain;
Ye, whose swoll'n and sleepless eyes
Watch to see the morning rise;

4 Ye, by fiercer anguish torn,
Guilt, in strong remorse, who mourn,
Here repose your heavy care;
Conscience wounded who can bear?

5 Sinner, come! for here is found
Balm that flows for ev'ry wound;
Peace that ever shall endure;
Rest eternal, sacred, sure.

292 *Why will ye Die?* **185**

WHAT could your Redeemer do
  More than he hath done for you?
To procure your peace with God,
Could he more than shed his blood?

2 After all his proofs of love,
All his drawings from above,
Why will ye your Lord deny?
Why will ye resolve to die?

3 Turn, he cries, ye sinners, turn:
By his life your God hath sworn;

He would have you turn and live,
He would all the world receive.

4 If your death were his delight,
Would he you to life invite?
Would he ask, beseech, and cry,
Why will ye resolve to die?

5 Sinners, turn, while God is near!
Dare not think him insincere:
Now, e'en now, your Savior stands,
All day long he spreads his hands!

6 See, the suff'ring God appears,
Jesus weeps, believe his tears!
Mingled with his blood they cry,
"Why will ye resolve to die?"

293 *Expostulation.* **820**

SINNER, is thy heart at rest?
  Is thy bosom void of fear?
Art thou not by guilt oppress'd?
Speaks not conscience in thine ear?

2 Can this world afford thee bliss?
Can it chase away thy gloom?
Flatt'ring, false, and vain it is:—
Tremble at the worldling's doom.

3 Think, O sinner, on thine end;
See the judgment-day appear!
Thither must thy spirit wend:
There thy righteous sentence hear.

4 Wretched, ruin'd, helpless soul,
To a Savior's blood apply;
He alone can make thee whole;
Fly to Jesus,—sinner, fly.

INVITATIONS AND WARNINGS.

7s. BENEVENTO.

294 *Sinners, Turn.* **824**

SINNERS, turn, why will ye die?
  God, your Maker, asks you why:
God, who did your being give,
Made you with himself to live;
He the fatal cause demands,
Asks the work of his own hands,
Why, ye thankless creatures, why
Will ye slight his love, and die?

2 Sinners, turn, why will ye die?
God, your Savior, asks you why;
He, who did your souls retrieve,
Died himself that you might live!
Will ye let him die in vain?
Crucify your Lord again?
Why, ye ransom'd sinners, why
Will ye slight his grace, and die?

3 Sinners, turn, why will ye die?
God, the Spirit, asks you why:
He who all your lives hath strove,
Woo'd you to embrace his love:
Will ye not his grace receive?
Will ye still refuse to live?
Why, ye long-sought sinners, why
Will ye grieve your God, and die?

295 *Redeeming Love.* **350**

NOW begin the heav'nly theme,
  Sing aloud in Jesus' name!
Ye, who his salvation prove,
Triumph in redeeming love.

2 Ye who see the Father's grace
Beaming in the Savior's face,
As to heav'n ye onward move,
Bless and praise redeeming love.

3 Mourning souls! dry up your tears,
Banish all your guilty fears;
See your guilt and curse remove,
Cancell'd by redeeming love.

4 Ye, alas! who long have been
Willing slaves of death and sin,
Now from bliss no longer rove;
Stop, and taste redeeming love.

5 Welcome all, by sin opprest,
Welcome to his sacred rest;
Nothing brought him from above,
Nothing but redeeming love.

6 When his Spirit leads us home,
When we to his glory come,
We shall the fullness prove
Of our Lord's redeeming love.

7 He subdu'd th' infernal pow'rs;
Those tremendous foes of ours,
From their cursed empire drove,
Mighty in redeeming love.

8 Hither, then, your music bring;
Strike aloud the joyful string!
Mortals! join the host above,
Join to praise redeeming love.

INVITATIONS AND WARNINGS.

C. M. HEBER.

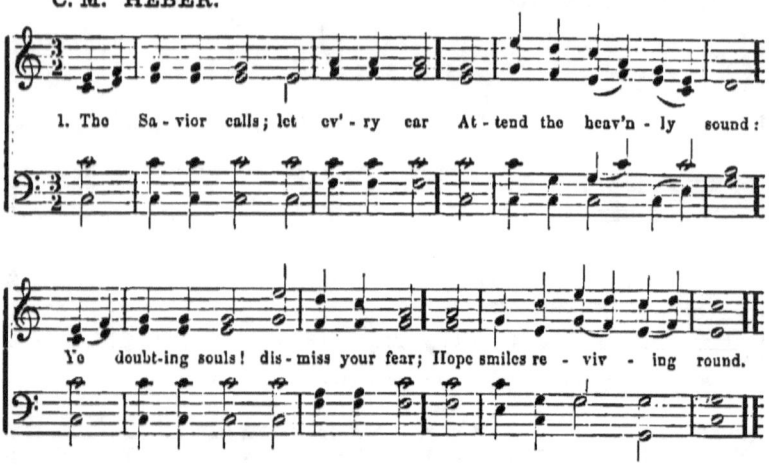

1. The Savior calls; let ev'ry ear Attend the heav'nly sound: Ye doubting souls! dismiss your fear; Hope smiles reviving round.

296 *The Savior Calls.* **194**

THE Savior calls; let ev'ry ear
   Attend the heav'nly sound:
Ye doubting souls! dismiss your fear;
   Hope smiles reviving round.

2 For ev'ry thirsty, longing heart,
   Here streams of bounty flow;
And life, and health, and bliss impart,
   To banish mortal woe.

3 Here springs of sacred pleasure rise,
   To ease your ev'ry pain:
Immortal fountain! full supplies!
   Nor shall you thirst in vain.

4 Ye sinners! come, 'tis mercy's voice;
   The gracious call obey;
Mercy invites to heav'nly joys:—
   And can you yet delay?

5 Dear Savior! draw reluctant hearts;
   To thee let sinners fly,
And take the bliss thy love imparts,
   And drink, and never die.

297 *The Gospel Feast.* **198**

YE wretched, hungry, starving poor,
   Behold a royal feast!
Where mercy spreads her bounteous store
   For ev'ry humble guest.

2 See, Jesus stands with open arms;
   He calls, he bids you come!
Guilt holds you back, and fear alarms:
   But see, there yet is room!

3 Room in the Savior's bleeding heart;
   There love and pity meet:
Nor will he bid the soul depart
   That trembles at his feet.

4 In him the Father, reconcil'd,
   Invites your souls to come:
The rebel shall be call'd a child,
   And kindly welcom'd home.

5 Oh, come, and with his children taste
   The blessings of his love:
While hope attends the sweet repast
   Of nobler joys above.

298 *Gospel Feast.* **195**

THE King of heav'n his table spreads,
   And dainties crown the board:
Not all the boasted joys of earth
   Could such delight afford.

2 Pardon and peace to dying men,
   And endless life, are giv'n,
Thro' the rich blood which Jesus shed,
   To raise the soul to heav'n.

3 Ye hungry poor, who long have stray'd
   In sin's dark mazes, come;
Come from your most obscure retreats,
   And grace will find you room.

4 Millions of souls, in glory now,
   Were fed and feasted here,
And millions more, still on the way,
   Around the board appear.

5 Yet is his house and heart so large,
   That millions more may come;
Nor could the whole assembled world
   O'erfill the spacious room.

6 All things are ready: enter in,
   Nor weak excuses frame:
Come, take your places at the feast,
   And bless the Founder's name.

INVITATIONS AND WARNINGS.

C. M. STEPHENS.

1. A-maz-ing sight, the Sa-vior stands And knocks at ev'-ry door! Ten thou-sand bless-ings in his hands To sat-is-fy the poor.

299 *The Savior's Call.* **200**

AMAZING sight, the Savior stands
And knocks at ev'ry door!
Ten thousand blessings in his hands
To satisfy the poor.

2 "Behold," he saith, "I bleed and die
To bring you to my rest:—
Hear, sinners, while I'm passing by,
And be forever blest.

3 "Will you despise my bleeding love,
And choose the way to hell?
Or in the glorious realms above,
With me forever dwell?

4 "Not to condemn your wretched race
Have I in judgment come;
But to display unbounded grace,
And bring lost sinners home.

5 "Say—will you hear my gracious voice,
And have your sins forgiv'n?
Or will you make that wretched choice,
And bar yourselves from heav'n?"

300 *Now is the Time.* **230**

NOW is the time, th' accepted hour,
O sinners, come away;
The Savior's knocking at your door,
Arise without delay.

2 Oh! don't refuse to give him room,
Lest mercy should withdraw;
He'll then in robes of vengeance come
To execute his law.

3 Then where, poor mortals, will you be,
If destitute of grace,
When you your injur'd Judge shall see,
And stand before his face?

4 Oh! could you shun that dreadful sight,
How would you wish to fly
To the dark shades of endless night,
From that all-searching eye!

5 The dead awak'd must all appear,
And you among them stand,
Before the great impartial bar,
Arraign'd at Christ's left hand.

6 Let not these warnings be in vain;
But lend a list'ning ear;
Lest you should meet them all again,
When wrapt in keen despair.

301 *The Young Exhorted.* **199**

YE hearts with youthful vigor warm,
In smiling crowds draw near;
And turn from ev'ry mortal charm,
A Savior's voice to hear.

2 He, Lord of all the worlds on high,
Stoops to converse with you;
And lays his radiant glories by,
Your friendship to pursue.

3 "The soul that longs to see my face,
Is sure my love to gain;
And those that early seek my grace
Shall never seek in vain."

4 What object, Lord, my soul should move,
If once compar'd with thee?
What beauty should command my love,
Like that in Christ I see?

5 Away, ye false, delusive toys,
Vain tempters of the mind!
'Tis here I fix my lasting choice,
And here true bliss I find.

INVITATIONS AND WARNINGS.

L. M. UXBRIDGE.

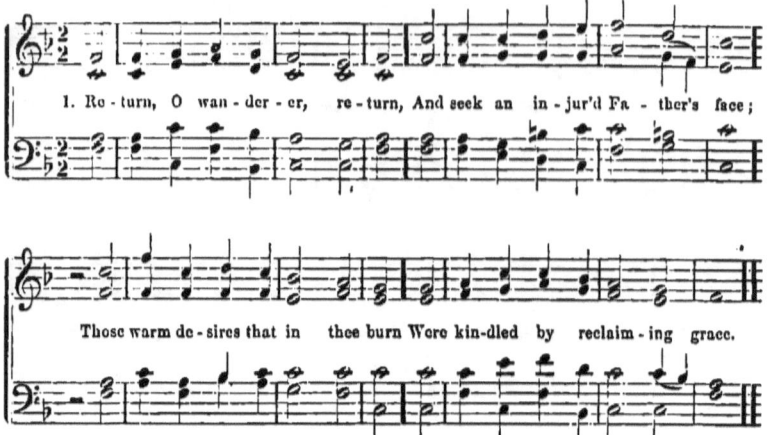

1. Re-turn, O wan-der-er, re-turn, And seek an in-jur'd Fa-ther's face; Those warm de-sires that in thee burn Were kin-dled by reclaim-ing grace.

302   *The Wanderer Called.*   203

RETURN; O wanderer, return,
   And seek an injur'd Father's face;
Those warm desires that in thee burn
Were kindled by reclaiming grace.

2 Return, O wanderer, return,
And seek a Father's melting heart;
His pitying eyes thy grief discern,
His hand shall heal thy inward smart.

3 Return, O wanderer, return,
Thy Savior bids thy spirit live;
Go to his bleeding feet, and learn
How freely Jesus can forgive.

4 Return, O wanderer, return,
And wipe away the falling tear:
'Tis God who says, "No longer mourn,"
'Tis mercy's voice invites thee near.

303   *Life is the Time.*   217

LIFE is the time to serve the Lord,
   The time t' insure the great reward;
And while the lamp holds out to burn,
The vilest sinner may return.

2 Life is the hour that God has given
To 'scape from hell, and fly to heaven;
The day of grace; and mortals may
Secure the blessings of the day.

3 The living know that they must die,
But all the dead forgotten lie:
They have no share in all that's done
Beneath the circuit of the sun.

4 Then what my thoughts design to do,
My hands, with all your might pursue,
Since no device nor work is found,
Nor faith, nor hope, beneath the ground.

5 There are no acts of pardon past
In the cold grave to which we haste,
But darkness, death, and long despair
Reign in eternal silence there.

304   *The Savior knocking.*   204

BEHOLD a stranger at the door
   He gently knocks—has knock'd before,
Hath waited long—is waiting still
You treat no other friend so ill.

2 Oh, lovely attitude! he stands
With melting heart and loaded hands!
Oh, matchless kindness! and he shows
This matchless kindness to his foes!

3 But will he prove a friend indeed?
He will,—the very friend you need;
The friend of sinners—yes, 'tis He,
With garments dy'd on Calvary.

4 Rise, touch'd with gratitude divine;
Turn out his enemy and thine,—
That soul-destroying monster sin,
And let the heav'nly stranger in.

5 Admit him, ere his anger burn;
His feet departed ne'er return;
Admit him, or the hour's at hand
You'll at his door rejected stand.

INVITATIONS AND WARNINGS.

L. M. HAMBURG.

1. Say, sinner, hath a voice within Oft whisper'd to thy secret soul, Urg'd thee to leave the ways of sin, And yield thy heart to God's control?

305 *Strivings of the Spirit.* **229**

SAY, sinner, hath a voice within
Oft whisper'd to thy secret soul,
Urg'd thee to leave the ways of sin,
And yield thy heart to God's control?

2 Hath something met thee in the path
Of worldliness and vanity,
And pointed to the coming wrath,
And warn'd thee from that wrath to flee?

3 Sinner, it was a heav'nly voice,—
It was the Spirit's gracious call;
It bade thee make the better choice,
And haste to seek in Christ thine all.

4 Spurn not the call to life and light;
Regard in time the warning kind;
That call thou mayst not always slight,
And yet the gate of mercy find.

5 God's Spirit will not always strive
With harden'd self-destroying man;
Ye, who persist his love to grieve,
May never hear his voice again.

6 Sinner! perhaps this very day
Thy last accepted time may be:
Oh! shouldst thou grieve him now away,
Then hope may never beam on thee.

306 *Time to Awake.* **234**

AWAKE, awake, O sluggish soul,
Awake and view thy setting sun;
See how the shades of death advance,
Ere half the task of life is done.

2 Death!—'tis an awful, solemn sound;
Oh! let it wake the slumb'ring ear!
Apace the dreadful conqu'ror comes,
With all his pale companions near.

3 Thy drowsy eyes will soon be clos'd—
These friendly warnings heard no more;
Soon will the mighty Judge approach,
E'en now he stands before the door.

4 To-day attend his gracious voice;
This is the summons that he sends:
"Awake,—for on this transient hour
Thy long eternity depends."

307 *The Balance of Justice.* **235**

RAISE, tho'tless sinner, raise thine eye;
Behold God's balance lifted high!
There shall his justice be display'd,
And there thy hope and life be weigh'd.

2 See in one scale his perfect law;
Mark with what force its precepts draw:
Wouldst thou the awful test sustain?—
Thy works how light! thy tho'ts how vain!

3 Behold, the hand of God appears
To trace in dreadful characters;
"Sinner—thy soul is wanting found,
And wrath shall smite thee to the ground."

4 One only hope may yet prevail—
Christ hath a weight to turn the scale;
Still doth the gospel publish peace,
And show a Savior's righteousness.

5 Jesus, exert thy power to save,
Deep on this heart thy truth engrave;
Great God, the load of guilt remove,
That trembling lips may sing thy love.

INVITATIONS AND WARNINGS.

C. M. EASTBURN.

1. Sin-ners! the voice of God re-gard: 'Tis mer-cy speaks to-day; He calls you by his gra-cious word From sin's de-struc-tive way.

308   *Expostulation.*   243

SINNERS! the voice of God regard:
'Tis mercy speaks to-day;
He calls you by his gracious word
From sin's destructive way.

2 Like the rough sea that cannot rest,
You live devoid of peace;
A thousand stings within your breast
Deprive your souls of ease.

3 Your way is dark, and leads to hell:
Why will you persevere?
Can you in endless torments dwell,
Shut up in black despair?

4 Bow to the sceptre of his word,
Renouncing ev'ry sin;
Submit to him, your sov'reign Lord,
And learn his will divine.

5 His love exceeds your highest thoughts;
He pardons like a God;
He will forgive your num'rous faults,
Through the Redeemer's blood.

309   *Backsliders exhorted.*   407

BACKSLIDERS, who your mis'ry feel,
Attend your Savior's call;
Return, he'll your backslidings heal;
O crown him Lord of all.

2 Though crimson sin increase your guilt,
And painful is your thrall,
For broken hearts his blood was spilt;
O crown him Lord of all.

3 Take with you words, approach his throne,
And low before him fall;
He understands the spirit's groan;
O crown him Lord of all.

4 Whoever comes he'll not cast out,
Although your faith be small:
His faithfulness you cannot doubt;
O crown him Lord of all.

310   *The Scoffer.*   236

ALL ye who laugh and sport with death,
And say there is no hell,
The gasp of your expiring breath
Will send you there to dwell.

2 When iron slumbers bind your flesh,
With strange surprise you'll find
Immortal vigor springs afresh,
And tortures wake the mind!

3 Then you'll confess the frightful names
Of plagues you scorn'd before,
No more shall sound like idle dreams,
Like foolish tales no more.

311   *Deceit of Sin.*   91

SIN has a thousand treach'rous arts
To practice on the mind;
With flatt'ring looks she tempts our hearts,
But leaves a sting behind.

2 With names of virtue she deceives
The aged and the young;
And while the heedless wretch believes,
She makes his fetters strong.

3 She pleads for all the joy she brings,
And gives a fair pretence;
But cheats the soul of heav'nly things
And chains it down to sense.

4 So on a tree divinely fair
Grew the forbidden food;
Our mother took the poison there,
And tainted all her blood.

INVITATIONS AND WARNINGS.

C. M. CLARENDON.

1. Sin-ners, this so-lemn truth re-gard! Hear, all ye sons of men; For Christ, the Sa-vior, hath de-clar'd, "Ye must be born a-gain."

312 *New Birth Required.* **215**

SINNERS, this solemn truth regard!
  Hear, all ye sons of men;
For Christ, the Savior, hath declar'd,
  "Ye must be born again."

2 Whate'er might be your birth or blood,
  The sinner's boast is vain;
Thus saith the glorious Son of God,
  "Ye must be born again."

3 Our nature's totally deprav'd—
  The heart a sink of sin;
Without a change we can't be sav'd;
  "Ye must be born again."

4 Spirit of life, thy grace impart,
  And breathe on sinners slain;
Bear witness, Lord, in ev'ry heart,
  That we are born again.

5 Dear Savior, let us now begin
  To trust and love thy word;
And, by forsaking ev'ry sin,
  Prove we are born of God.

313 *Self-Examination.* **864**

STRIVE first of all thyself to know,
  To feel the plague of sin,
Expos'd to everlasting woe,
  And nothing good within.

2 To know thy wretched, sinful state,
  Averse to all that's good;
To feel thy guilt exceeding great,
  Thy heart opposed to God.

3 To know thy law-condemned case,
  And own thy sentence just;

Thy heart subdu'd by sov'reign grace,
  And humbled in the dust.

4 To know the pangs of pious grief,
  For sins against the Lord;
To know that naught can give relief,
  But trusting in his word.

5 To know that thou art born of God,
  Thy num'rous sins forgiv'n,
Thy soul redeem'd by Jesus' blood,
  And thou an heir of heav'n.

314 *The Leper Healed.* **207**

WHEN the poor leper's case I read,
  My own describ'd I feel;
Sin is a leprosy indeed,
  Which none but Christ can heal.

2 What anguish did my soul endure,
  Till hope and patience ceas'd!
The more I strove myself to cure,
  The more the plague increas'd.

3 While thus I lay distress'd, I saw
  The Savior passing by;
To him, though fill'd with shame and awe,
  I rais'd my mournful cry.

4 He heard, and with a gracious look
  Pronounc'd the healing word;
"I will—be clean," and while he spoke
  I felt my health restor'd.

5 Come, sinners, seize the present hour,
  The Savior's grace to prove:
He can relieve, for he is pow'r—
  He will, for he is love.

INVITATIONS AND WARNINGS.

8s, 7s, & 4s.　OLIPHANT.

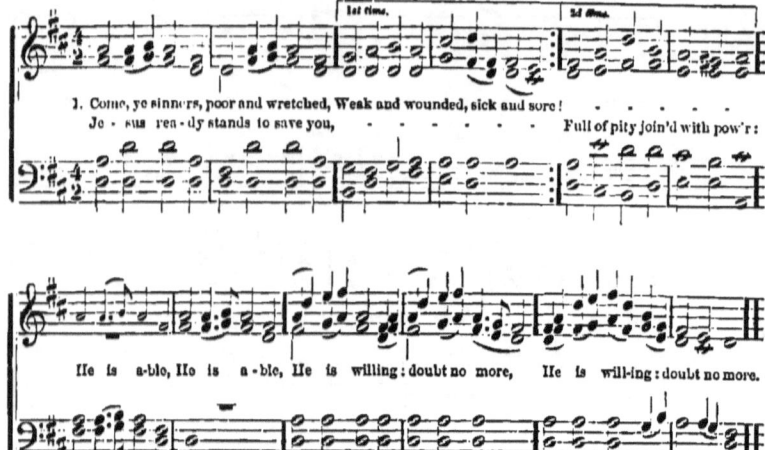

1. Come, ye sinners, poor and wretched, Weak and wounded, sick and sore! Je-sus rea-dy stands to save you, Full of pity join'd with pow'r: He is a-ble, He is a-ble, He is willing: doubt no more, He is will-ing: doubt no more.

315   *Sinners invited.*   183

COME, ye sinners, poor and wretched,
  Weak and wounded, sick and sore!
Jesus ready stands to save you,
  Full of pity join'd with pow'r:
    He is able,
He is willing: doubt no more.

2 Come, ye thirsty! come and welcome;
  God's free bounty glorify:
True belief, and true repentance,—
  Ev'ry grace that brings us nigh,—
    Without money,
Come to Jesus Christ, and buy.

3 Let not conscience make you linger,
  Nor of fitness fondly dream;
All the *fitness* he requireth
  Is to feel your need of him;
    This he gives you;
'Tis his Spirit's rising beam.

4 Come, ye weary, heavy laden,
  Lost and ruin'd by the fall!
If you tarry till you're better,
  You will never come at all:
    Not the righteous—
Sinners Jesus came to call.

5 Lo! th' incarnate God ascended,
  Pleads the merit of his blood:
Venture to him, venture wholly,
  Let no other trust intrude;
    None but Jesus
Can do helpless sinners good.

316   *The Glad Message.*   187

SINNERS, will you scorn the message,
  Sent in mercy from above,
Every sentence—oh, how tender!
  Ev'ry line is full of love:
    Listen to it,
Ev'ry line is full of love.

2 Hear the heralds of the gospel
  News from Zion's King proclaim,
To each rebel sinner—"Pardon,
  Free forgiveness in his name."
    How important!
Free forgiveness in his name!

3 Tempted souls, they bring you succor;
  Fearful hearts, they quell your fears,
And with news of consolation,
  Chase away the falling tears:
    Tender heralds—
Chase away the falling tears.

4 False professors, grov'ling worldlings,
  Callous hearers of the word,
While the messengers address you,
  Take the warnings they afford;
    We entreat you,
Take the warnings they afford.

5 O ye angels, hov'ring round us,
  Waiting spirits, speed your way,
Hasten to the courts of heaven,
  Tidings bear without delay:
    Rebel sinners
Glad the message will obey.

INVITATIONS AND WARNINGS. 113

8s, 7s, 4s. OSGOOD.

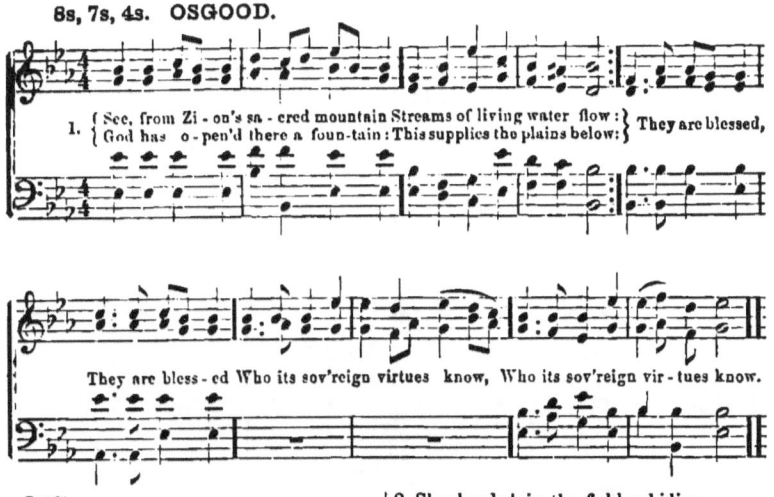

See, from Zi-on's sa-cred mountain Streams of living water flow:
God has o-pen'd there a foun-tain: This supplies the plains below:
They are blessed,
They are bless-ed Who its sov'reign virtues know, Who its sov'reign vir-tues know.

317 *The Fountain Opened.* **196**

SEE, from Zion's sacred mountain
  Streams of living water flow:
God has open'd there a fountain:
  This supplies the plains below;
    They are blessed
  Who its sov'reign virtues know.

2 Through ten thousand channels flowing,
    Streams of mercy find their way;
  Life, and health, and joy bestowing,
    Making all around look gay:
      O ye nations!
    Hail the long-expected day.

3 Gladden'd by the flowing treasure,
    All enriching as it goes,
  Lo, the desert smiles with pleasure,
    Buds and blossoms as the rose,
      Ev'ry object
    Sings for joy where'er it flows.

4 Trees of life, the banks adorning,
    Yield their fruit to all around;
  Those who eat are sav'd from mourning,
    Pleasure comes and hopes abound:
      Fair their portion!
    Endless life with glory crown'd.

318 *Call to Worship Jesus.* **778**

ANGELS! from the realms of glory,
  Wing your flight o'er all the earth;
Ye, who sang creation's story,
  Now proclaim Messiah's birth:
    Come and worship—
  Worship Christ the new-born King.

2 Shepherds! in the fields abiding,
    Watching o'er your flocks by night;
  God with man is now residing,
    Yonder shines the heav'nly light.
      Come and worship—
    Worship Christ, the new-born King.

3 Sages! leave your contemplations;
    Brighter visions beam afar:
  Seek the great Desire of nations,
    Ye have seen his natal star:
      Come and worship—
    Worship Christ, the new-born King.

4 Saints! before the altar bending,
    Watching long in hope and fear,
  Suddenly the Lord, descending,
    In his temple shall appear:
      Come and worship—
    Worship Christ, the new-born King.

319 *The Voice of Mercy.*

HEAR, O sinner, mercy hails you;
  Now with sweetest voice she calls;
Bids you haste to Christ thy Savior,
  Ere the stroke of Justice falls:
    Hear, O sinner!
  'Tis the voice of mercy calls.

2 Haste, O sinner, to the Savior;
  Seek his mercy while you may;
Soon the day of grace will leave you;
  Soon your life will pass away.
    Haste, O sinner!
  You may perish by delay.

INVITATIONS AND WARNINGS.

S. M. THATCHER.

1. The man is ev-er blest Who shuns the sinners' ways; Amongst their coun-sels nev-er stands, Nor takes the scorn-er's place:

320 *The Righteous and the Wicked.* 212

THE man is ever blest
　Who shuns the sinners' ways;
Amongst their councils never stands,
　Nor takes the scorner's place:

2 But makes the law of God
　His study and delight,
Amidst the labors of the day
　And watches of the night.

3 He like a tree shall thrive,
　With waters near the root;
Fresh as the leaf his name shall live,
　His works are heav'nly fruit.

4 Not so th' ungodly race,
　They no such blessings find;
Their hopes shall flee like empty chaff
　Before the driving wind.

5 How will they bear to stand
　Before that judgment-seat
Where all the saints at Christ's right hand
　In full assembly meet?

6 He knows and he approves
　The way the righteous go:
But sinners and their works shall meet
　A dreadful overthrow.

321 *Admonition from the Judgment.* 751

AND will the Judge descend?
　And must the dead arise?
And not a single soul escape
　His all-discerning eyes!

2 How will my heart endure
　The terrors of that day,

When earth and heav'n, before his face,
　Astonish'd, shrink away?

3 But ere that trumpet shakes
　The mansions of the dead,
Hark, from the gospel's cheering sound
　What joyful tidings spread!

4 Ye sinners, seek his grace
　Whose wrath ye cannot bear;
Fly to the shelter of his cross,
　And find salvation there.

5 So shall that curse remove,
　By which the Savior bled;
And the last awful day shall pour
　His blessings on your head.

322 *Trust in God.* 852

COMMIT thou all thy griefs
　And ways into his hands,
To his sure truth and tender care,
　Who earth and heav'n commands,—

2 Who points the clouds their course,
　Whom winds and seas obey;
He shall direct thy wand'ring feet;
　He shall prepare thy way.

3 Put thou thy trust in God;
　In duty's path go on;
Fix on his word thy stedfast eye;
　So shall thy work be done.

4 No profit canst thou gain
　By self-consuming care;
To him commend thy cause; his ear
　Attends thy softest pray'r.

INVITATIONS AND WARNINGS. 115

7s. **EDYFIELD.**

1. Sinner, what has earth to show
Like the joys believers know?
Is thy path of fading flowers
Half so bright, so sweet as ours?

323 *Expostulation.* **98**

SINNER, what has earth to show
Like the joys believers know?
Is thy path of fading flowers
Half so bright, so sweet as ours?

2 Doth a skilful, healing friend
On thy daily path attend,
And, where thorns and stings abound,
Shed a balm on ev'ry wound?

3 When the tempest rolls on high,
Hast thou still a refuge nigh?
Can, oh, can thy dying breath
Summon one more strong than death?

4 Canst thou, in that awful day,
Fearless tread the gloomy way,
Plead a glorious ransom giv'n,
Burst from earth, and soar to heav'n?

324 *The Sinner Entreated.* **828**

SINNER, rouse thee from thy sleep;
Wake, and o'er thy folly weep;
Raise thy spirit, dark and dead;
Jesus waits his light to shed.

2 Awake from sleep; arise from death;
See the bright and living path;
Watchful, tread that path; be wise;
Leave thy folly; seek the skies.

3 Leave thy folly; cease from crime;
From this hour redeem thy time;
Life secure without delay;
Evil is thy mortal day.

4 Oh, then, rouse thee from thy sleep;
Wake, and o'er thy folly weep;
Jesus calls from death and night;
Jesus waits to shed his light.

325 *Prepare to meet thy God.* **239**

SINNER, art thou still secure?
Wilt thou still refuse to pray?
Can thy heart or hands endure
In the Lord's avenging day?

2 See, his mighty arm is bared!
Awful terrors clothe his brow!
For his judgment stand prepared,
Thou must either break or bow.

3 At his presence nature shakes,
Earth, affrighted, hastes to flee;
Solid mountains melt like wax
What will then become of thee?

4 Who his advent may abide?
You that glory in your shame,
Will you find a place to hide
When the world is wrapt in flame?

5 Lord, prepare us by thy grace:
Soon we must resign our breath,
And our souls be call'd to pass
Through the iron gate of death.

6 Let us now our day improve,
Listen to the gospel voice:
Seek the things that are above:
Scorn the world's pretended joys.

INVITATIONS AND WARNINGS.

L. M. WARD.

1. Now, in the heat of youth-ful blood, Re-mem-ber your Cre-a-tor, God: Be-hold, the months come hast'ning on, When you shall say, "My joys are gone."

326 *A Call to Youth.* **653**

NOW, in the heat of youthful blood,
   Remember your Creator, God:
Behold, the months come hast'ning on,
When you shall say, "My joys are gone."

2 Behold, the aged sinner goes,
Laden with guilt and heavy woes,
Down to the regions of the dead,
With endless curses on his head.

3 The dust returns to dust again;
The soul, in agonies of pain,
Ascends to God, not there to dwell,
But hears her doom, and sinks to hell.

4 God of the young! turn off their eyes,
From earth's alluring vanities;
And let the warnings of thy word
Awake their souls to fear the Lord!

327 *Nearness of Eternity.* **242**

ETERNITY is just at hand!
   And shall I waste my ebbing sand,
And careless view departing day,
And throw my inch of time away?

2 Yes, an eternity there is
Of endless woe, or endless bliss;
And swift as time fulfills its round,
We to eternity are bound.

3 What countless millions of mankind
Have left this fleeting world behind!
They're gone! but where?—ah, pause & see,
Gone to a long eternity.

4 Sinner! canst thou forever dwell
In all the fiery deeps of hell?
And is death nothing, then, to thee,
Death, and a dread eternity?

328 *The Broad Road.* **817**

BROAD is the road that leads to death,
   And thousands walk together there;
But wisdom shows a narrow path,
With here and there a traveler.

2 "Deny thyself, and take thy cross,"
Is the Redeemer's great command;
Nature must count her gold but dross,
If she would gain this heav'nly land.

3 The fearful soul that tires and faints,
And walks the ways of God no more,
Is but esteem'd almost a saint,
And makes his own destruction sure.

4 Lord, let not all my hopes be vain;
Create my heart entirely new;
Which hypocrites could ne'er attain,
Which false apostates never knew.

329 *The Sinner's Prosperity Cursed.* **94**

LORD, what a thoughtless wretch was I,
   To mourn, and murmur, and repine
To see the wicked plac'd on high,
In pride and robes of honor shine!

2 But, oh, their end, their dreadful end!
Thy sanctuary taught me so:
On slipp'ry rocks I see them stand,
And fiery billows roll below.

3 Their fancied joys, how fast they flee!
Like dreams as fleeting and as vain,
Their songs of softest harmony
Are but a prelude to their pain.

4 Now I esteem their mirth and wine
Too dear to purchase with my blood;
Lord, 'tis enough that thou art mine,
My life, my portion, and my God.

330 *Vanity of Earthly Things.* 97

WHAT are possessions, fame, and pow'r,
  The boasted splendor of the great?
What gold, which dazzled eyes adore,
And seek with endless toils and sweat?

2 Express their charms, declare their use,
That we their merits may descry;
Tell us what good they can produce,
Or what important wants supply.

3 If, wounded with the sense of sin,
To them for pardon we should pray,
Will they restore our peace within,
And wash our guilty stains away?

4 Can they celestial life inspire,
Nature with pow'r divine renew,

With pure and sacred transports fire
Our bosom, and our lusts subdue?

5 When with the pangs of death we strive,
And yield all comforts here for lost,
Will they support us, will they give
Kind succor, when we need it most?

6 When at th' Almighty's awful bar,
To hear our final doom, we stand,
Can they incline the Judge to spare,
Or wrest the vengeance from his hand?

7 Sinners, your idols we despise,
If these reliefs they cannot grant;
Why should we such delusions prize,
And pine in everlasting want?

11s & 10s. COME, YE DISCONSOLATE.

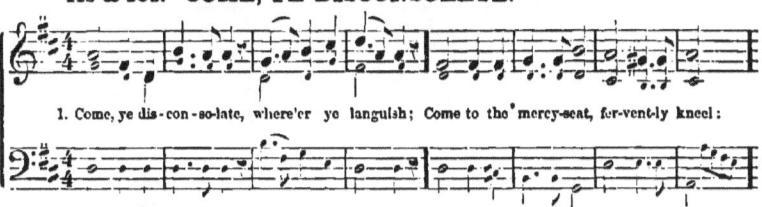

1. Come, ye dis-con-so-late, where'er ye languish; Come to the mercy-seat, fer-vent-ly kneel:

First time, Duet; second time, Chorus.

Here bring your wounded hearts, here tell your anguish; Earth has no sorrows that heav'n cannot heal.

331 *The Mercy-Seat.* 814

COME, ye disconsolate, where'er ye languish,
  Come, at the mercy-seat fervently kneel:
Here bring your wounded hearts, here tell your anguish;
  Earth has no sorrows that heav'n cannot heal.

2 Joy of the desolate, light of the straying,
  Hope of the penitent, fadeless and pure,
Here speaks the Comforter, in mercy saying,
  Earth has no sorrows that heav'n cannot cure.

3 Here see the bread of life; see waters flowing
  Forth from the throne of God, boundless in love:
Come to the feast prepared; come, ever knowing
  Earth has no sorrows but heav'n can remove.

INVITATIONS AND WARNINGS.

C. M. AVON.

1. Come, hum-ble sin-ner, in whose breast A thou-sand thoughts re-volve, Come, with your guilt and fear op-prest, And make this last re-solve.

332 *The Resolve.* 216

COME, humble sinner, in whose breast
A thousand thoughts revolve,
Come with your guilt and fear opprest,
And make this last resolve:—

2 "I'll go to Jesus, though my sin
Hath like a mountain rose;
I know his courts, I'll enter in,
Whatever may oppose.

3 "Prostrate I'll lie before his throne,
And there my guilt confess;
I'll tell him I'm a wretch undone,
Without his sov'reign grace.

4 "Perhaps he will admit my plea,
Perhaps will hear my pray'r;
But if I perish, I will pray,
And perish only there.

5 "I can but perish if I go:
I am resolv'd to try;
For if I stay away, I know
I must forever die.

6 "But if I die with mercy sought,
When I the King have tried,
That were to die (delightful thought!)
As sinner never died."

333 *Warning from the Grave.* 726

BENEATH our feet and o'er our head
Is equal warning giv'n;
Beneath us lie the countless dead,
And far above is heav'n.

2 Death rides on ev'ry passing breeze,
And lurks in ev'ry flower;
Each season has its own disease,
Its peril ev'ry hour.

3 Turn, mortal, turn: thy danger know;
Where'er thy foot can tread,
The earth rings hollow from below,
And warns thee of her dead.

4 Turn, sinner, turn: thy soul apply
To truths divinely given;
The forms which underneath thee lie
Shall live for hell or heaven.

334 *Time is Short.* 227

THE time is short! the season near
When death will us remove;
To leave our friends, however dear,
And all we fondly love.

2 The time is short! sinners, beware,
Nor trifle time away;
The word of great salvation hear,
While it is call'd to-day.

3 The time is short! ye rebels, now,
To Christ the Lord submit;
To mercy's golden scepter bow,
And fall at Jesus' feet.

4 The time is short! ye saints, rejoice—
The Lord will quickly come:
Soon shall you hear the Bridegroom's voice,
To call you to your home.

5 The time is short! it swiftly flies—
The hour is just at hand,
When we shall mount above the skies,
And reach the wish'd-for land.

6 The time is short! the moment near
When we shall dwell above,
And be forever happy there
With Jesus, whom we love.

INVITATIONS AND WARNINGS.

11s. HINTON.

335 *Delay not.* 825

DELAY not, delay not, O sinner, draw near;
The waters of life are now flowing for thee!
No price is demanded, the Savior is here,
Redemption is purchas'd, salvation is free.

2 Delay not, delay not; why longer abuse
The love and compassion of Jesus, thy God?
A fountain is open'd, how canst thou refuse
To wash and be cleans'd in his pardoning blood?

3 Delay not, delay not, O sinner, to come,
For mercy still lingers, and calls thee to-day;
Her voice is not heard in the vale of the tomb;
Her message, unheeded, will soon pass away.

4 Delay not, delay not! the Spirit of grace,
Long griev'd and resisted, may take its sad flight,
And leave thee in darkness to finish thy race,
To sink in the gloom of eternity's night.

336 *Acquaint thyself with God.* 823

ACQUAINT thyself quickly, O sinner, with God,
And joy, like the sunshine, shall beam on thy road,
And peace, like the dew-drop, shall fall on thy head,
And sleep, like an angel, shall visit thy bed.

2 Acquaint thyself quickly, O sinner, with God,
And he shall be with thee, when fears are abroad:
Thy safeguard in dangers that threaten thy path;
Thy joy in the valley and shadow of death.

INVITATIONS AND WARNINGS.

7s & 6s. AMSTERDAM.

1. Stop, poor sin-ner, stop and think, Be-fore you fur-ther go:
Will you sport up-on the brink Of ev-er-last-ing woe? On the verge of ru-in, stop; Now the friendly warning take; Stay your footsteps, ere you drop In-to the burning lake.

337 *The Alarm.* **240**

STOP, poor sinner, stop and think,
  Before you further go:
Will you sport upon the brink
  Of everlasting woe?
On the verge of ruin, stop;
  Now the friendly warning take;
Stay your footsteps, ere you drop
  Into the burning lake.

2 Say, have you an arm like God,
  That you his will oppose?
Fear you not that iron rod
  With which he breaks his foes?
Can you stand in that dread day,
  Which his justice shall proclaim,
When the earth shall melt away
  Like wax before the flame?

3 But there yet remains a hope;
  His mercy you may know;
Though his arm is lifted up,
  He still suspends the blow.
'Twas for sinners Jesus died;
  Sinners he invites to come;
None who seek shall be denied;
  There still—there still is room.

338 *The Pilgrim's Song.* **854**

RISE, my soul, and stretch thy wings,
  Thy better portion trace;
Rise from transitory things
  Toward heav'n, thy native place:
Sun and moon and stars decay,
  Time shall soon this earth remove;
Rise, my soul, and haste away,
  To seats prepar'd above.

2 Rivers to the ocean run,
  Nor stay in all their course:
Fire, ascending, seeks the sun;
  Both speed them to their source:
So a soul that's born of God
  Pants to view his glorious face,
Upward tends to his abode
  To rest in his embrace.

3 Cease, ye pilgrims, cease to mourn,
  Press onward to the prize;
Soon your Savior will return,
  Triumphant in the skies:
Yet a season, and you know
  Happy entrance will be giv'n;
All your sorrows left below,
  And earth exchang'd for heav'n.

339 *Flight of Time.*

TIME is winging us away
  To our eternal home:
Life is but a winter's day,
  A journey to the tomb;
Youth and vigor soon will flee,
  Blooming beauty lose its charms;
All that's mortal soon will be
  Enclos'd in death's cold arms.

2 Time is winging us away
  To our eternal home:
Life is but a winter's day,
  A journey to the tomb:
But the Christian shall enjoy
  Health and beauty soon above;
Far beyond the world's alloy,
  Secure in Jesus' love.

340   *The Warning Voice.*   830

THAT warning voice, O sinner, hear,
  And while salvation lingers near,
The heav'nly call obey;
Flee from destruction's downward path,
Flee from the threat'ning storm of wrath
  That rises o'er thy way.

2 Soon night comes on with thick'ning shade,
The tempest hovers o'er thy head,
  The winds their fury pour;
The lightnings rend the earth and skies,
The thunders roar, the flames arise:
  What terrors fill that hour!

3 That warning voice, O sinner, hear,
Whose accents linger on thine ear;
  Thy footsteps now retrace;
Renounce thy sins, and be forgiv'n,
Believe, become an heir of heav'n,
  And sing redeeming grace.

4 Then, while a voice of pardon speaks,
The storm is hush'd, the morning breaks,
  The heav'ns are all serene;
Fresh verdure clothes the beauteous fields,
Joy echoes on the distant hills,
  New wonders fill the scene.

341   *An Awakening Thought.*   248

THOU God of glorious majesty,
  To thee, against myself, to thee,
    A worm of earth, I cry;
A half-awaken'd child of man,
An heir of endless bliss or pain,
    A sinner born to die!

2 Lo! on a narrow neck of land,
'Twixt two unbounded seas I stand,
    Secure, insensible:
A point of time, a moment's space,
Removes me to that heav'nly place,
    Or shuts me up in hell.

3 O God, mine inmost soul convert!
And deeply on my thoughtful heart
    Eternal things impress:
Give me to feel the solemn weight,
And tremble on the brink of fate,
    And wake to righteousness.

4 Before me place in dread array
The pomp of that tremendous day
    When thou with clouds shalt come
To judge the nations at thy bar;
And tell me, Lord, shall I be there
    To meet a joyful doom?

5 Be this my one great bus'ness here,
With serious industry and fear
    Eternal bliss t' insure:
Thine utmost counsel to fulfill,
And suffer all thy righteous will,
    And to the end endure.

6 Then Savior, then, my soul receive,
Transported from this vale to live
    And reign with thee above,
Where faith is sweetly lost in sight,
And hope in full supreme delight
    And everlasting love.

INVITATIONS AND WARNINGS.

C. L. M. HOW CALM AND BEAUTIFUL.

1. Go watch and pray; thou canst not tell How near thine hour may be; Thou canst not know how soon the bell May toll its notes for thee: Death's countless snares be-set thy way: Frail child of dust, go watch and pray.

342 *Watch and Pray.* **815**

GO watch and pray; thou canst not tell
How near thine hour may be;
Thou canst not know how soon the bell
May toll its notes for thee:
Death's countless snares beset thy way:
Frail child of dust, go watch and pray.

2 Fond youth, while free from blighting care,
Does thy firm pulse beat high?
Do hope's glad visions bright and fair,
Dilate before thine eye?
Soon these must change—must pass away,
Frail child of dust, go watch and pray.

3 Thou aged man! life's wintry storm
Hath sear'd thy vernal bloom;
With trembling limbs and wasting form,
Thou'rt bending o'er the tomb:
And can vain hope lead thee astray?
Go, weary pilgrim! watch and pray.

4 Ambition, stop thy panting breath!
Pride, sink thy lifted eye!
Behold! the caverns, dark with death,
Before you open lie:

The heav'nly warning now obey;
Ye sons of pride, go watch and pray.

343 *Forget Thyself and Come.*

FORGET thyself, Christ bade thee come
To think upon his love,
Which could reverse the sinner's doom
And write his name above;
Bid the returning rebel live,
And freely all his sins forgive.

2 Forget thyself, and think what pain,
What agony, he bore,
To wash away each guilty stain,
To bless thee evermore,
To fit thee for his high abode,
The temple of the living God.

3 Forget thyself, but let thy soul
With mem'ries overflow,
Rejoice in his supreme control,
And seek his will to know.
With thankful heart approach the feast,
And thou wilt be a welcome guest.

INVITATIONS AND WARNINGS.

8, 8, 7, 8, 8. ETERNITY.
With vigor and expression.

1. E-ter-ni-ty! ter-ri-fic word, With-in the heart a piercing sword! Beginning without ending! { E-ter-ni-ty! un-mea-sur'd time! / I sink beneath the thought sublime } That I to thee am tend-ing: Deep hor-ror fills my quak-ing heart, My lips in speech re-fuse to part.

344 *Terrors of Eternity.* 245

ETERNITY! terrific word,
  Within the heart a piercing sword!
 Beginning without ending!
Eternity! unmeasur'd time!
I sink beneath the thought sublime
  That I to thee am tending:
Deep horror fills my quaking heart,
My lips in speech refuse to part.

2 Eternity! Oh, what a pang!
Eternity! no serpent's fang
  Could send that thrill of terror.
When I revolve thy clanking chains,
Thy dark abyss of deathless pains,
  My soul is fill'd with horror.
Oh, search the universe around,
No equal terror can be found!

3 Awake, O man, from sinful sleep;
Bethink thyself, thou straying sheep,
  Seek God by true repentance!
Awake, behold thy wasting sand,
Eternity is just at hand,
  And brings thine awful sentence.
This is, perchance, thy final day:
Who knows how soon he's snatch'd away?

4 Eternity! terrific word,
Within the heart a piercing sword!
  Beginning without ending!
Eternity! unmeasur'd time!
I sink beneath the thought sublime
  That I to thee am tending:
Lord Jesus, when it pleaseth thee,
Grant me thy blest eternity!

CHRISTIAN EXPERIENCE—PENITENTIAL.

C. M. HEATH.

1. There is a voice of sov'reign grace Sounds from the sacred word:
"Ho! ye despairing sinners, come, And trust upon the Lord."

345 *The Penitent's Surrender.* **241**

THERE is a voice of sov'reign grace
  Sounds from the sacred word:
"Ho! ye despairing sinners, come,
  And trust upon the Lord."

2 My soul obeys th' Almighty call,
  And runs to this relief:
I would believe thy promise, Lord,
  Oh, help my unbelief.

3 To the dear fountain of thy blood,
  Incarnate God, I fly;
Here let me wash my spotted soul
  From crimes of deepest dye.

4 A guilty, weak, and helpless worm,
  On thy kind arms I fall;
Be thou my strength and righteousness,
  My Jesus and my all!

346 *The Contrite Heart.* **255**

THE Lord will happiness divine
  On contrite hearts bestow;
Then tell me, gracious God! is mine
  A contrite heart or no?

2 I hear, but seem to hear in vain,
  Insensible as steel;
If aught is felt, 'tis only pain
  To find I cannot feel.

3 I sometimes think myself inclin'd
  To love thee, if I could;
But often feel another mind,
  Averse to all that's good.

4 My best desires are faint and few,
  I fain would strive for more;
But when I cry, "My strength renew,"
  Seem weaker than before.

5 Thy saints are comforted, I know,
  And love thy house of pray'r;
I therefore go where others go,
  But find no comfort there.

6 Oh, make this heart rejoice or ache;
  Decide this doubt for me;
And, if it be not broken, break—
  And heal it, if it be.

347 *The Penitent.* **257**

DEAR Jesus! prostrate at thy feet
  A guilty rebel lies,
And upward to the mercy-seat
  Presumes to lift his eyes.

2 Oh, let not justice frown me hence;
  Stay, stay the vengeful storm:
Forbid it that Omnipotence
  Should crush a feeble worm.

3 If tears of sorrow would suffice
  To pay the debt I owe,
Tears should flow from both my weeping eyes
  In ceaseless torrents flow.

4 But no such sacrifice I plead
  To expiate my guilt;
No tears, but those which thou hast shed,—
  No blood, but thou hast spilt.

5 Think of thy sorrows, dearest Lord!
  And all my sins forgive:
Justice will well approve the word
  That bids the sinner live.

CHRISTIAN EXPERIENCE—PENITENTIAL.

C. M. ARLINGTON.

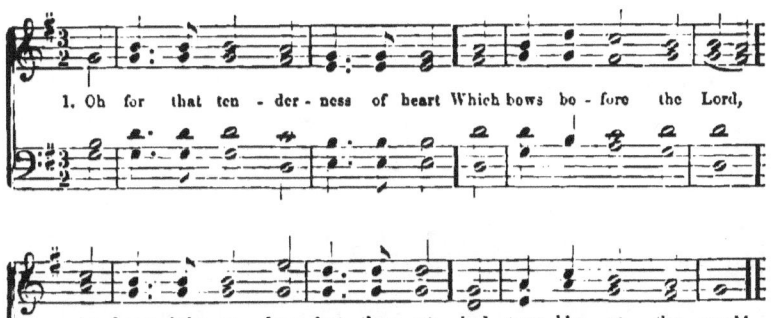

1. Oh for that tenderness of heart Which bows before the Lord, Acknowledges how just thou art, And trembles at thy word!

348 *For a Tender Heart.* **250**

OH for that tenderness of heart
 Which bows before the Lord,
Acknowledges how just thou art,
 And trembles at thy word!

2 Oh for those humble contrite tears
 Which from repentance flow,
That consciousness of guilt which fears
 The long-suspended blow!

3 Savior, to me in pity give
 The sensible distress,
The pledge thou wilt at last receive,
 And bid me die in peace;

4 Wilt from the dreadful day remove
 Before the evil come,
My spirit hide with saints above,
 My body in the tomb.

349 *For a New Heart.* **251**

OH for a heart to praise my God,
 A heart from sin set free!
A heart that always feels thy blood
 So freely spilt for me!

2 A heart resign'd, submissive, meek,
 My great Redeemer's throne;
Where only Christ is heard to speak,
 Where Jesus reigns alone.

3 Oh for a lowly, contrite heart,
 Believing, true, and clean;
Which neither life nor death can part
 From him that dwells within!

4 A heart in ev'ry thought renew'd,
 And full of love divine;
Perfect, and right, and pure, and good,
 A copy, Lord, of thine!

5 Thy nature, gracious Lord, impart,
 Come quickly from above;
Write thy new name upon my heart,
 Thy new, best name of love.

350 *Sin Bewailed.* **259**

WITH tears of anguish I lament,
 Here at thy feet, my God,
My passion, pride, and discontent,
 And vile ingratitude.

2 Sure there was ne'er a heart so base,
 So false, as mine has been,
So faithless to its promises,
 So prone to ev'ry sin!

3 My reason tells me thy commands
 Are holy, just, and true;
Tells me whate'er my God demands
 Is his most righteous due.

4 Reason I hear, her counsels weigh,
 And all her words approve;
But still I find it hard t' obey,
 And harder yet to love.

5 How long, dear Savior, shall I feel
 These strugglings in my breast?
When wilt thou bow my stubborn will
 And give my conscience rest?

6 Break, sov'reign grace, O break the charm,
 And set the captive free;
Reveal, Almighty God, thine arm,
 And haste to rescue me.

CHRISTIAN EXPERIENCE—PENITENTIAL.

C. M. TRIAS.

1. Source of e-ter-nal joys di-vine, To thee my soul as-pires;
Oh, could I say, "The Lord is mine," 'Tis all my soul de-sires.

351 *Seeking All in Christ.* **281**

SOURCE of eternal joys divine,
  To thee my soul aspires;
Oh, could I say, "The Lord is mine,"
  'Tis all my soul desires.

2 My hope, my trust, my life, my Lord,
  Assure me of thy love;
Oh, speak the kind, transporting word,
  And bid my fears remove.

3 Then shall my thankful pow'rs rejoice,
  And triumph in my God,
Till heav'nly rapture tune my voice
  To spread thy praise abroad.

352 *Sin Bewailed.* **267**

OH, if my soul were form'd for woe,
  How would I vent my sighs!
Repentance should like rivers flow
  From both my streaming eyes.

2 'Twas for my sins my dearest Lord
  Hung on the cursed tree,
And groan'd away a dying life
  For thee, my soul, for thee.

3 Oh, how I hate those lusts of mine
  That crucified my Lord,
Those sins that pierc'd and nail'd his flesh
  Fast to the fatal wood!

4 Yes, my Redeemer, they shall die,
  My heart has so decreed,
Nor will I spare the guilty things
  That made my Savior bleed.

5 Whilst with a melting, broken heart
  My murder'd Lord I view,
I'll raise revenge against my sins,
  And slay the murd'rers too.

353 *Longing for Renewal.* **277**

JESUS, if still thou art to-day
  As yesterday the same,
Present to heal, in me display
  The virtue of thy name.

2 Loathsome, and foul, and self-abhorr'd,
  I sink beneath my sin:
But if thou wilt, a gracious word
  Of thine can make me clean.

3 Thou seest me deaf to thy commands,
  Open, O Lord, my ear;
Bid me stretch out my wither'd hands
  And lift them up in prayer.

4 Silent, (alas! thou know'st how long,)
  My voice I cannot raise;
But oh! when thou shalt loose my tongue,
  The dumb shall sing thy praise.

5 Lame at the pool I still am found:
  Give, and my strength employ;
Light as a hart I then shall bound,
  The lame shall leap for joy.

6 Blind from my birth to guilt and thee,
  And dark I am within;
The love of God I cannot see,—
  The sinfulness of sin.

7 But thou, they say, art passing by,
  Oh, let me find thee near!
Jesus, in mercy, hear my cry,
  Thou Son of David, hear!

8 Long have I waited in the way
  For thee, the heav'nly light;
Command me to be brought, and say,
  "Sinner, receive thy sight."

C. M. CHESTNUT STREET.

1. Smote by the law, I'm just-ly slain; Great God, be-hold my case; Pi-ty a sin-ner fill'd with pain, Nor drive me from thy face.

354 *Terror turned to Joy.* **268**

SMOTE by the law, I'm justly slain;
  Great God, behold my case;
Pity a sinner fill'd with pain,
  Nor drive me from thy face.

2 Dread terrors fright my guilty soul—
  Thy justice, all in flames,
Gives sentence to this heart so foul,
  So hard, so full of crimes.

3 'Tis trembling hardness that I feel;
  I fear, but don't relent,—
Perhaps of endless death the seal;
  Oh that I could repent!

4 My pray'rs, my tears, my vows are vile;
  My duties black with guilt;
On such a wretch can mercy smile,
  Though Jesus' blood was spilt?

5 Speechless I sink to endless night,
  I see an op'ning hell:
But lo! what glory strikes my sight!
  Such glory who can tell?

6 Enwrapt in these bright beams of peace,
  I feel a gracious God:
Swell, swell the note—oh tell his grace;
  Sound his high praise abroad!

355 *Prayer for Pardon.* **288**

THOU hidden God, for whom I groan,
  Till thou thyself declare,
God inaccessible, unknown,
  Regard a sinner's pray'r.

2 A sinner welt'ring in his blood;
  Unpurg'd and unforgiv'n;
Far distant from the living God,
  As far as hell from heav'n,—

3 An unregen'rate child of man,
  To thee for faith I call;
Pity thy fallen creature's pain,
  And raise me from my fall.

4 The darkness which, thro' thee, I feel,
  Thou only canst remove:
Thine own eternal power reveal,
  The Deity of love.

5 Show me the blood that bought my peace,
  The cov'nant blood apply,
And all my griefs at once shall cease,
  And all my sins shall die.

356 *Penitential Regrets.* **262**

AH, what can I, a sinner, do,
  With all my guilt opprest?
I feel the hardness of my heart,
  And conscience knows no rest.

2 Great God, thy good and perfect law
  Does all my life condemn;
The secret evils of my soul
  Fill me with fear and shame.

3 How many precious Sabbaths gone,
  I never can recall;
And, oh, what cause have I to mourn,
  Who misimprov'd them all!

4 How long, how often have I heard
  Of Jesus, and of heav'n;
Yet scarcely listen'd to his word,
  Or pray'd to be forgiv'n!

5 Constrain me, Lord, to turn to thee,
  And grant renewing grace;
For thou this flinty heart canst break,
  And thine shall be the praise.

CHRISTIAN EXPERIENCE—PENITENTIAL.

L. M. ORFORD.

1. Oh for a glance of heav'n-ly day, To take this stubborn heart a-way, And thaw with beams of love di-vine This heart, this fro-zen heart of mine.

357 *Hardness of Heart Lamented.* **253**

OH for a glance of heav'nly day,
 To take this stubborn heart away,
And thaw with beams of love divine
This heart, this frozen heart of mine!

2 The rocks can rend: the earth can quake;
The seas can roar; the mountains shake;
Of feeling all things show some sign,
But this unfeeling heart of mine.

3 To hear the sorrows thou hast felt,
O Lord, an adamant might melt;
But I can read each moving line,
And nothing moves this heart of mine.

4 Thy judgments too, which devils fear,
(Amazing thought!) unmov'd I hear;
Goodness and wrath in vain combine
To stir this stupid heart of mine.

5 Eternal Spirit! mighty God!
Apply to me the Savior's blood;
'Tis his rich blood, and his alone,
Can move and melt this heart of stone.

358 *Conflict with Sin.* **260**

HOW sad and awful is my state!
 The very thing I do I hate!
When I to God draw near in pray'r,
I feel the conflict even there!

2 I mourn, because I cannot mourn;
I hate my sin, yet cannot turn;
I grieve, because I cannot grieve;
I hear the truth, but can't believe.

3 Where shall so great a sinner run?
I see I'm ruin'd and undone;
Dear Lord, in pity now draw near,
And banish ev'ry rising fear.

4 Thy blood, dear Lord, which thou hast
Can make this rocky heart to melt; [spilt,
Thy blood can make me clean within—
Thy blood can pardon all my sin.

5 'Tis on th' atonement of that blood,
I now approach to thee, my God;
This is my hope, this is my claim—
Jesus has died to hide my sin.

359 *Awaking.* **261**

ALAS, alas, how blind I've been,
 How little of myself I've seen!
Sportive I sail'd the sensual tide,
Thoughtless of God, whom I defied.

2 Oft have I heard of heav'n, and hell,
Where bliss and woe eternal dwell;
But mock'd the threats of truth divine,
And scorn'd the place where angels shine.

3 My heart has long refus'd the blood
Of Jesus, the descending God;
And guilty passion boldly broke
The holy law which heav'n had spoke.

4 Th' alluring world controll'd my choice;
When conscience spake, I hush'd its voice;
Securely laugh'd along the road
Which hapless millions first had trod.

5 But now th' Almighty God comes near
And fills my soul with awful fear—
Perhaps I sink to endless pain,
Nor hear the voice of joy again.

360 *Penitence.* 266

O LORD, my God, in mercy turn,
  In mercy hear a sinner mourn!
To thee I call, to thee I cry,
Oh, leave me, leave me not to die!

2 O pleasures past, what are ye now
But thorns about my bleeding brow?
Spectres that hover round my brain,
And aggravate and mock my pain.

3 For pleasure I have giv'n my soul;
Now, justice, let thy thunders roll!
Now, vengeance, smile—and with a blow
Lay the rebellious ingrate low.

4 Yet, Jesus, Jesus! there I'll cling;
I'll crowd beneath his shelt'ring wing;
I'll clasp the cross, and, holding there,
E'en me, oh bliss!—his wrath may spare.

361 *Seeking Pardon.* 271

LORD, at thy feet I prostrate fall,
  Opprest with fears, to thee I call:
Reveal thy pard'ning love to me,
And set my captive spirit free.

2 Hast thou not said, "Seek ye my face"?
The invitation I embrace;
I'll seek thy face; thy Spirit give!
Oh, let me see thy face, and live.

3 I'll wait, perhaps my Lord may come;
If I turn back, hell is my doom;
And, begging, in his way I'll lie
Till the dear Savior passes by.

4 I'll seek his face with cries and tears,
With secret sighs and fervent prayers;
And, if not heard, I'll waiting sit,
And perish at my Savior's feet.

5 But canst thou, Lord, see all my pain,
And bid me seek thy face in vain?
No! Jesus will not, can't deceive:
The soul that seeks his face shall live.

362 *Depravity Confessed.* 254

LORD, I am vile, conceiv'd in sin,
  And born unholy and unclean;
Sprung from the man whose guilty fall
Corrupts the race and taints us all.

2 Soon as we draw our infant breath,
The seeds of sin grow up for death;
Thy law demands a perfect heart,
But we're defil'd in ev'ry part.

3 Great God, create my heart anew,
And form my spirit pure and true;
Oh, make me wise betimes to spy
My danger and my remedy.

4 Behold, I fall before thy face;
My only refuge is thy grace:
No outward forms can make me clean;
The leprosy lies deep within.

5 No bleeding bird, nor bleeding beast,
Nor hyssop-branch, nor sprinkling priest,
Nor running brook, nor flood, nor sea,
Can wash the dismal stain away.

6 Jesus, my God, thy blood alone
Hath pow'r sufficient to atone;
Thy blood can make me white as snow;
No Jewish types could cleanse me so.

363 *Awaking.* 272

WITH melting heart and weeping eyes,
  My guilty soul for mercy cries;
What shall I do, or whither flee,
T' escape that vengeance due to me?

2 Till now, I saw no danger nigh;
I liv'd at ease, nor fear'd to die;
Wrapt up in self-deceit and pride,
"I shall have peace at last," I cried.

3 But when, great God! thy light divine
Had shone on this dark soul of mine,
Then I beheld, with trembling awe,
The terrors of thy holy law.

4 How dreadful now my guilt appears,
In childhood, youth, and growing years!
Before thy pure discerning eye,
Lord, what a filthy wretch am I!

5 Should vengeance still my soul pursue,
Death and destruction are my due;
Yet mercy can my guilt forgive,
And bid a dying sinner live.

364 *Undone without Christ.*

BEFORE thy high and holy throne
  I stand convicted and undone;
Yet in thy plenitude of grace
Thou bid'st me come and seek thy face.

2 And come I will to Jesus' feet,
And low before the mercy-seat
Acknowledge all my guilt and shame,
And trust forever in his name.

3 Enough for me that Christ hath died:
Justice Divine is satisfied;
This, this is now my only plea,
That Jesus shed his blood for me.

4 And dost thou, Lord, my sins forgive,
Bid the returning ingrate live?
Never from thee will I depart:
Take full possession of my heart.

CHRISTIAN EXPERIENCE—PENITENTIAL.

S. M. DOVER.

1. O let me now re-pent! With all my i-dols part; And to thy gra-cious eye pre-sent An hum-ble, con-trite heart!

365 *For True Repentance.* 249

O LET me now repent!
  With all my idols part;
And to thy gracious eye present
  An humble, contrite heart!

2 A heart with grief opprest,
  For having griev'd my God;
A troubled heart, that cannot rest
  Till sprinkled with thy blood!

3 Jesus, on me bestow
  The penitent desire;
With true sincerity of woe
  My aching breast inspire;

4 With soft'ning pity look,
  And melt my hardness down;
Strike with thy love's resistless stroke,
  And break this heart of stone!

366 *Conviction.* 264

MY former hopes are fled,
  My terror now begins;
I feel, alas! that I am dead
  In trespasses and sins.

2 Ah, whither shall I fly?
  I hear the thunder roar;
The law proclaims destruction nigh,
  And vengeance at the door.

3 When I review my ways,
  I dread impending doom;
But sure a friendly whisper says,
  "Flee from the wrath to come."

4 I see, or think I see,
  A glimm'ring from afar;
A beam of day that shines for me,
  To save me from despair.

5 Forerunner of the sun,
  It marks the pilgrim's way;
I'll gaze upon it while I run,
  And watch the rising day.

367 *Difficulties Lamented.* 291

I WOULD, but cannot sing,
  I would, but cannot pray;
For Satan meets me when I try,
  And frights my soul away.

2 I would, but can't repent,
  Though I endeavor oft;
This stony heart can ne'er relent,
  Till Jesus makes it soft.

3 I would, but cannot love,
  Though woo'd by love divine;
No arguments have pow'r to move
  A soul so base as mine.

4 I would, but cannot rest
  In God's most holy will;
I know what he appoints is best,
  Yet murmur at it still.

5 O could I but believe!
  Then all would easy be;
I would, but cannot—Lord, relieve;
  My help must come from thee!

368 *Waiting at Bethesda.* 292

BESIDE the gospel pool,
  Appointed for the poor,
From year to year my helpless soul
  Has waited for a cure.

2 How often have I seen
  The healing waters move,
And others round me, stepping in,
  Their efficacy prove!

3 But my complaints remain;
  I feel the very same,
As full of guilt, and fear, and pain,
  As when at first I came.

4 Oh, would the Lord appear,
  My malady to heal!
He knows how long I've languish'd here,
  And what distress I feel.

5 Yet here, from day to day,
  I'll wait, and hope, and try:
Can Jesus hear a sinner pray,
  And suffer him to die?

6 No—he is full of grace;
  He never will permit
A soul, that fain would see his face,
  To perish at his feet.

369 *For Mercy.* 278

MY gracious, loving Lord,
  To thee what shall I say?
Well may I tremble at thy word,
  And scarce presume to pray.

2 Ten thousand wants have I;
  Alas! I all things want!
But thou hast bid me always pray,
  And never, never faint.

3 Yet, Lord, well might I fear,
  Fear e'en to ask thy grace,
So oft have I, alas! drawn near,
  And mock'd thee to thy face.

4 Nigh with my lips I drew—
  My lips were all unclean;
Thee with my heart I never knew—
  My heart was full of sin.

370 *For Light and Pardon.* 796

COME, Holy Spirit, come;
  Let thy bright beams arise:
Dispel the sorrow from our minds,
  The darkness from our eyes.

2 Convince us all of sin,
  Then lead to Jesus' blood,
And to our wond'ring view reveal
  The mercies of our God.

3 Revive our drooping faith,
  Our doubts and fears remove,
And kindle in our breasts the flame
  Of never-dying love.

4 'Tis thine to cleanse the heart,
  To sanctify the soul,
To pour fresh life in ev'ry part,
  And new-create the whole.

5 Dwell, Spirit, in our hearts;
  Our minds from bondage free;
Then shall we know, and praise, and love
  The Father, Son, and Thee.

371 *Inward Conflict.* 838

AND wilt thou yet be found,
  And may I still draw near?
Then listen to the plaintive sound
  Of a poor sinner's pray'r.

2 Jesus, thine aid afford,
  If still the same thou art,
To thee I look, to thee, my Lord!
  Lift up a fainting heart.

3 Thou seest my troubled breast,
  The struggles of my will,
The foes that interrupt my rest,
  The agonies I feel.

4 O my offended Lord,
  Restore my inward peace,
I know thou canst; pronounce the word,
  And bid the tempest cease!

5 I long to see thy face,
  Thy Spirit I implore,
The living water of thy grace,
  That I may thirst no more.

372 *The Burden of Sin.* 836

AH! whither should I go,
  Burden'd, and sick, and faint!
To whom should I my troubles show,
  And pour out my complaint?

2 What is it keeps me back,
  From which I cannot part?
Which will not let the Savior take
  Possession of my heart?

3 Jesus, the hind'rance show,
  Which I have fear'd to see;
And let me now consent to know
  What keeps me back from thee.

4 Searcher of hearts, in mine
  Thy trying pow'r display;
Into its darkest corners shine,
  And take the vail away.

5 I now believe in thee
  Compassion reigns alone;
According to my faith, to me
  Oh let it, Lord, be done!

CHRISTIAN EXPERIENCE—PENITENTIAL.

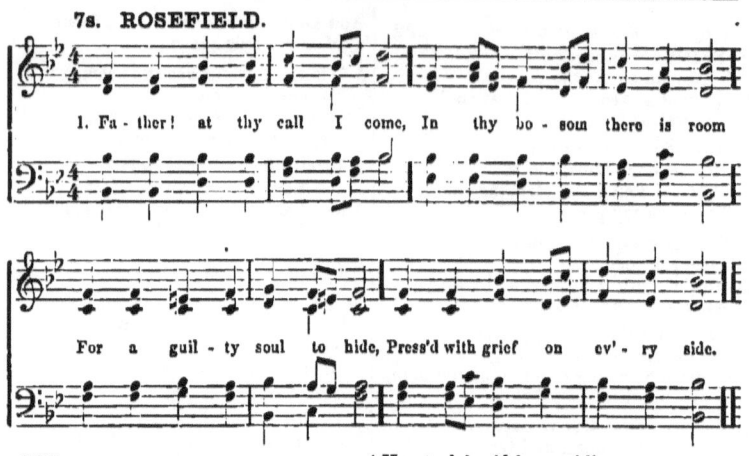

7s. ROSEFIELD.

1. Father! at thy call I come, In thy bosom there is room For a guilty soul to hide, Press'd with grief on ev'ry side.

373 *Penitential Sighs.* 256

FATHER! at thy call I come,
In thy bosom there is room
For a guilty soul to hide,
Press'd with grief on ev'ry side.

2 Darkness fills my trembling soul,
Floods of sorrow o'er me roll;
Pity, Father! pity me,
All my hope is placed in thee.

3 But may such a wretch as I—
Self-condemn'd, and doom'd to die,
Ever hope to be forgiv'n,
And be smil'd upon by heav'n?

4 Yes, I may! for I espy
Pity trickling from thine eye;
'Tis a Father's heart that moves,
Moves with pardon and with love.

5 Well I do remember, too,
What his love hath deign'd to do;
How he sent a Savior down,
All my follies to atone.

6 Has my elder brother died?
And is justice satisfied?
Why,—oh, why should I despair
Of my Father's tender care?

374 *Confession.* 258

GOD of mercy! God of grace!
Hear our penitential songs;
Oh, restore thy suppliant race,
Thou to whom our praise belongs!

2 Deep regret for follies past,
Talents wasted, time misspent;
Hearts debas'd by worldly cares,
Thankless for the blessings lent;

3 Foolish fears and fond desires
Vain regrets for things as vain;
Lips too seldom taught to praise,
Oft to murmur and complain;

4 These, and ev'ry secret fault,
Fill'd with grief and shame we own;
Humbled at thy feet we lie,
Seeking pardon from thy throne.

375 *The Sinner's Plea.* 294

WILL the pard'ning God despise
A poor mourner's sacrifice,
One who brings his all to thee,
All his sin and misery?

2 Savior, see my troubled breast,
Heaving, panting after rest;
Jesus, mark my swollen eye,
Seldom clos'd and never dry.

3 Listen to my plaintive moans,
And my deep repentant groans,
Keep not silence at my tears,
Quiet all my griefs and fears.

4 Good Physician, show thine art,
Bind thou up my broken heart;
Aches it not for thee, my God,
Panting for thy healing blood?

5 Jesus, answer all thy name,
Save me from my fear and shame;
Sunk in desp'rate misery,
Sinners' Friend, remember me!

376 Pardon. 283

SOV'REIGN Ruler, Lord of all,
  Prostrate at thy feet I fall:
Hear, oh, hear my ardent cry,
Frown not, lest I faint and die!

2 Vilest of the sons of men,
Worst of rebels, I have been:
Oft abus'd thee to thy face,
Trampled on thy richest grace.

3 Justly might thy vengeful dart
Pierce this broken, bleeding heart;
Justly might thy kindled ire
Blast me in eternal fire.

4 But with thee there's mercy found,
Balm to heal my ev'ry wound;
Thou canst soothe the troubled breast,
Give the weary wand'rer rest.

5 Then my humble pray'r attend,
Show thyself the sinner's Friend;
Bid the suff'rer cease to mourn,
Bid the prodigal return.

377 Sin bewailed. 265

COME, my soul, thy suit prepare,
  Jesus loves to answer pray'r;
He himself has bid thee pray,
Rise and ask without delay.

2 Thou art coming to a King,
Large petitions with thee bring,
For his grace and pow'r are such,
None can ever ask too much.

3 With my burden I begin:
Lord, remove this load of sin!
Let thy blood, for sinners spilt,
Set my conscience free from guilt.

4 Lord, I come to thee for rest,
Take possession of my breast;
There thy blood-bought right maintain,
And without a rival reign.

5 Show me what I have to do,
Ev'ry hour my strength renew,
Let me live a life of faith,
Let me die thy people's death.

378 Longing for the Redeemer.

GRACIOUS Lord, incline thine ear;
  My request vouchsafe to hear;
Hear my never-ceasing cry;
Give me Christ, or else I die.

2 All unholy and unclean,
I am nothing else but sin:
On thy mercy I rely;
Give me Christ, or else I die.

3 Thou dost promise to forgive
All who in thy Son believe:
Lord, I know thou canst not lie;
Give me Christ, or else I die.

4 Father, dost thou seem to frown?
Let me shelter in thy Son!
Jesus, to thine arms I fly:
Come and save me, or I die.

379 Deep Contrition. 835

JESUS, save my dying soul,
  Make the broken spirit whole;
Humbled in the dust I lie;
Savior, leave me not to die.

2 Jesus, full of ev'ry grace,
Now reveal thy smiling face;
Grant the joy of sin forgiv'n,
Foretaste of the bliss of heav'n.

3 All my guilt to thee is known—
Thou art righteous, thou alone:
All my help is from thy cross;
All besides I count but loss.

4 Lord, in thee I now believe;
Wilt thou—wilt thou not forgive?
Helpless at thy feet I lie;
Savior, leave me not to die.

380 Sinners, Come. 840

COME, ye weary sinners, come,
  All, who feel your heavy load:
Jesus calls the wand'rers home;
Hasten to your pard'ning God.

2 Come, ye guilty souls opprest,
Answer to the Savior's call:—
"Come, and I will give you rest;
Come, and I will save you all."

3 Jesus, full of truth and love,
We thy gracious call obey;
Faithful let thy mercies prove,
Take our load of guilt away.

4 Weary of this war within,
Weary of this endless strife,
Weary of ourselves and sin,
Weary of a wretched life;

5 Burden'd with a world of grief,
Burden'd with our sinful load,
Burden'd with this unbelief,
Burden'd with the wrath of God:

6 Lo, we come to thee for ease,
True and gracious as thou art;
Now our weary souls release,
Write forgiveness on our heart.

CHRISTIAN EXPERIENCE—PENITENTIAL.

C. M. PHUVAH.

1. Lord, at thy feet in dust I lie, And knock at mer-cy's door; With hum-ble heart and weep-ing eye, Thy fa-vor I im-plore.

---

381 *Imploring Mercy.* **290**

LORD, at thy feet in dust I lie,
  And knock at mercy's door;
With humble heart and weeping eye,
  Thy favor I implore.

2 On me, O Lord, do thou display
  Thy rich, forgiving love;
Oh, take my heinous guilt away,
  This heavy load remove.

3 Without thy grace, I sink opprest
  Down to the gates of hell;
Oh, give my troubled spirit rest,
  And all my fears dispel.

4 'Tis mercy, mercy I implore,
  Oh, may thy goodness move;
Thy grace is an exhaustless store,
  And thou thyself art love.

5 Should I at last in heav'n appear,
  To join thy saints above,
I'll tell that mercy brought me there
  And sing thy bleeding love.

382 *Imploring Mercy.* **298**

WHEN, rising from the bed of death,
  O'erwhelm'd with guilt and fear,
I see my Maker face to face,
  Oh, how shall I appear!

2 If now, while pardon may be found
  And mercy may be sought,
My heart with inward horror shrinks,
  And trembles at the thought;—

3 When thou, O Lord, shalt stand disclos'd
  In majesty severe,

And sit in judgment on my soul,
  Oh, how shall I appear!

4 But thou hast told the troubled mind
  Which does its sins lament,
That faith in Christ's atoning blood
  Shall endless woe prevent.

5 Then never shall my soul despair
  Her pardon to procure,
Who knows thine only Son has died
  To make that pardon sure.

6 And may I taste thy richer grace
  In that decisive hour,
When Christ to judgment shall descend,
  And time shall be no more.

383 *Contrition.* **299**

O THOU, whose tender mercy hears
  Contrition's humble sigh;
Whose hand, indulgent, wipes the tears
  From sorrow's weeping eye!

2 See! low before thy throne of grace,
  A wretched wand'rer mourn;
Hast thou not bid me seek thy face?
  Hast thou not said, Return?

3 Absent from thee, my Guide, my Light,
  Without one cheering ray,
Through dangers, fears, and gloomy night,
  How desolate my way!

4 Oh, shine on this benighted heart,
  With beams of mercy shine;
And let thy healing voice impart
  A taste of joys divine.

384. Deliverance from Sin. 301

1. OH, when wilt thou my Savior be?
Oh, when shall I be clean,
The true eternal Sabbath see,
A perfect rest from sin?

2. Jesus! the sinner's rest thou art
From guilt and fear and pain;
While thou art absent from my heart,
I look for rest in vain!

3. The consolations of thy word
My soul have long upheld:
The faithful promise of the Lord
Shall surely be fulfill'd.

4. Joining thy sheep in yonder fold,
Like them I shall rejoice;
Like them thy glory shall behold,
And hear my Shepherd's voice.

5. Oh that I now the voice might hear
That speaks my sins forgiven:
Thy word is pass'd to give me here
The inward pledge of heaven.

385. At the Mercy-Seat. 831

1. GREAT God, before thy mercy-seat,
Abas'd, in dust I fall;
My crimes of complicated guilt
Aloud for judgment call.

2. I own my ways to be corrupt,
My service stain'd with sin;
Make thou my broken spirit whole
My burden'd conscience clean.

3. Lord, send thy Spirit from above,
Implant a holy fear;
And through thine all-abounding grace
Bring thy salvation near.

4. On my distress'd, benighted soul,
Oh, cause thy face to shine:
Make me to hear thy pard'ning voice,
And tell me I am thine.

386. Burdened with Sin. 839

1. WITH guilt oppress'd, bow'd down with
Beneath its load I groan; [sin,
Give me, O Lord, a heart of flesh;
Remove this heart of stone,

2. A burden'd sinner, lo! I come,
In dread of death and hell:
Oh, seal my pardon with thy blood,
And all my fears dispel.

3. Nor peace, nor rest, my soul can find,
Till thy dear cross I see;
Till there in humble faith I cry,
"The Savior died for me."

4. Oh, give this true and living faith,
This soul-supporting view;
Till old things be forever past,
And all within be new.

387. Sin deplored. 90

1. LORD, I would spread my sore distress
And guilt before thine eyes;
Against thy laws, against thy grace,
How high my crimes arise!

2. I from the stock of Adam came,
Unholy and unclean;
All my original is shame,
And all my nature sin.

3. Born in a world of guilt, I drew
Contagion with my breath;
And as my days advanced, I grew
A juster prey for death.

4. Cleanse me, O Lord, and cheer my soul
With thy forgiving love;
Oh, make my broken spirit whole,
And bid my pains remove.

5. Let not thy Spirit e'er depart,
Nor drive me from thy face;
Create anew my sinful heart,
And fill it with thy grace.

388. Penitence.

1. PROSTRATE, dear Jesus, at thy feet,
A guilty rebel lies,
And upwards to thy mercy-seat
Presumes to lift his eyes.

2. Let not thy justice frown me hence:
Oh, stay the vengeful storm:
Forbid it, that Omnipotence
Should crush a feeble worm.

3. If tears of sorrow could suffice
To pay the debt I owe,
Tears should from both my weeping eyes
In ceaseless currents flow.

4. But no such sacrifice I plead
To expiate my guilt;
No tears, but those which thou hast shed,
No blood, but thou hast spilt.

5. Think of thy sorrows, dearest Lord,
And all my sins forgive;
Then Justice will approve the word
That bids the sinner live.

CHRISTIAN EXPERIENCE—PENITENTIAL.

L. M. AVERNO.

1. Show pi-ty, Lord! O Lord, for-give! Let a re-pent-ing sin-ner live:
Are not thy mer-cies large and free? May not the con-trite trust in thee?

389 *Pleading for Pardon.* **274**

SHOW pity, Lord! O Lord, forgive!
  Let a repenting sinner live:
Are not thy mercies large and free?
May not the contrite trust in thee?

2 With shame my num'rous sins I trace
Against thy law, against thy grace;
And, tho' my pray'r thou shouldst not hear,
My doom is just and thou art clear.

3 Yet save a penitent, O Lord!
Whose hope, still hov'ring round thy word,
Seeks for some precious promise there,
Some sure support against despair.

4 My sins are great, but don't surpass
The riches of eternal grace;
Great God, thy nature hath no bound,
So let thy pard'ning love be found.

5 Oh, wash my soul from ev'ry stain,
Nor let the guilt I mourn remain;
Give me to hear thy pard'ning voice,
And bid my bleeding heart rejoice.

6 Then shall thy love inspire my tongue,
Salvation shall be all my song;
And ev'ry pow'r shall join to bless
The Lord, my strength and righteousness.

390 *Imploring Mercy.* **273**

THOU Man of griefs, remember me,
  Thou surely never canst forget
Thy last mysterious agony,
Thy fainting pangs and bloody sweat!

2 When, wrestling in the strength of prayer,
Thy spirit sunk beneath its load!
Thy feeble flesh afraid to bear
The wrath of an almighty God!

3 Father, if I may call thee so,
Regard my fearful heart's desire,
Remove this load of guilty woe,
Nor let me in my sins expire!

4 I tremble lest the wrath divine,
Which bruises now my sinful soul,
Should bruise this wretched soul of mine
Long as eternal ages roll!

5 I deprecate that death alone,
That endless banishment from thee!
Oh, save me, through thine only Son,
Who trembled, wept, and bled for me!

391 *The Penitential Prayer.* **302**

OH that the Lord would hear my cry,
  And stay his anger, lest I die!
Thy wrath is just; yet, oh, forgive,
And let a mourning sinner live.

2 In all my frame, without, within,
I feel the sad effects of sin;
How long, my God, must I complain,
And deprecate thy wrath in vain?

3 Oh, should I die depriv'd of thee,
What being else can succor me?
Thy frowns would rend my soul in death,
And sink it to the depths beneath.

4 Ye darling sins that plague me so,
The greatest enemies I know,
Depart, for God has heard my pray'r,
And will not let me long despair.

5 No—I shall yet his goodness bless;
And when this transient life shall pass,
Then full of glory, I shall prove
He can be just, and sinners love.

CHRISTIAN EXPERIENCE—PENITENTIAL.

L. M. ORLAND.

1. O thou that dost in se-cret see, Re-gard a dy-ing sin-ner's pray'r; Out of the deep I cry to thee—Save, or I per-ish in de-spair.

392 *The Sinner's Prayer.* **284**

O THOU that dost in secret see,
  Regard a dying sinner's pray'r;
Out of the deep I cry to thee—
Save, or I perish in despair.

2 Weeping, to thee I lift mine eyes,
Mine eyes which fail with looking up:
For thee my heart laments and sighs—
Sick with desire and ling'ring hope.

3 Oh that I could but surely know
If I at last shall mercy find;
For what am I reserv'd below?
Tell me, thou Savior of mankind.

4 Let others walk with thee in light,
But bless me with one parting ray,
And ere I close mine eyes in night,
Give me to see thy perfect day.

393 *For a New Heart.* **275**

O THOU that hear'st when sinners cry!
  Though all my crimes before thee lie,
Behold them not with angry look,
But blot their mem'ry from thy book.

2 Create my nature pure within,
And form my soul averse to sin;
Let thy good Spirit ne'er depart,
Nor hide thy presence from my heart.

3 I cannot live without thy light,
Cast out and banish'd from thy sight;
Thy holy joys, O God, restore,
And guard me that I fall no more.

4 A broken heart, my God, my King,
Is all the sacrifice I bring:
The God of grace will ne'er despise
A broken heart for sacrifice.

5 My soul lies humbled in the dust,
And owns thy dreadful sentence just:
Look down, O Lord, with pitying eye,
And save the soul condemn'd to die.

394 *Pleading the Promises.* **276**

JESUS, if still the same thou art,
  If all thy promises are sure,
Set up thy kingdom in my heart,
And make me rich, for I am poor.

2 Thou hast pronounc'd the mourner blest,
And lo! for thee I ever mourn;
I cannot, no, I will not rest
Till thou, my only rest, return.

3 Where is the blessedness bestow'd
On all that hunger after thee?
I hunger now, I thirst, for God!
See the poor fainting sinner, see.

4 Ah, Lord! if thou art in that sigh,
Then hear thyself within me pray,
Hear in my heart thy Spirit's cry,
Mark what my lab'ring soul would say.

5 Shine on thy work, disperse the gloom;
Light in thy light I then shall see:
Say to my soul, "Thy light is come,
Glory divine is ris'n on thee."

6 Lord, I believe thy promise sure,
And trust thou wilt not long delay
Hungry, and sorrowful, and poor,
Upon thy word myself I stay.

CHRISTIAN EXPERIENCE—PENITENTIAL.

8s, 7s. HOLLAZ.

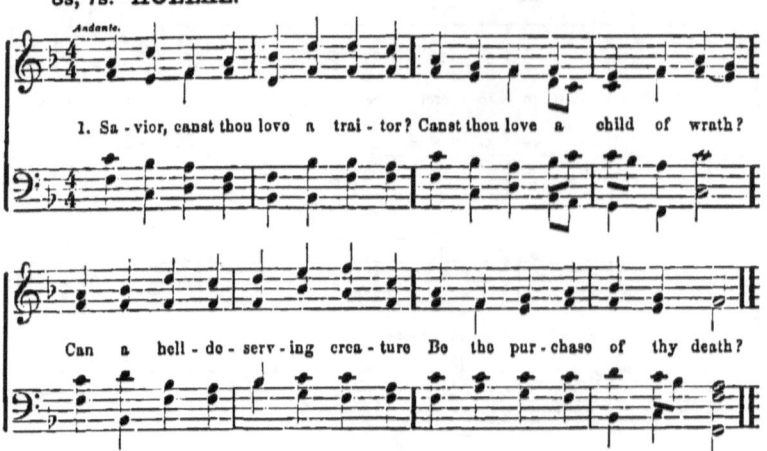

1. Sa-vior, canst thou love a trai-tor? Canst thou love a child of wrath? Can a hell-de-serv-ing crea-ture Be the pur-chase of thy death?

395 *Suing for Pardon.* **270**

SAVIOR, canst thou love a traitor?
  Canst thou love a child of wrath?
Can a hell-deserving creature
  Be the purchase of thy death?

2 Is thy blood so efficacious
  As to make my nature clean?
Is thy sacrifice so precious
  As to free my soul from sin?

3 Sin on ev'ry side surrounds me,
  I can hear of no relief;
Pangs of unbelief confound me,
  Help me, Lord, to bear my grief.

4 This is now my resolution,
  At thy dearest feet to fall;
Here I'll meet my condemnation,
  Or a freedom from my thrall.

5 If I meet with condemnation,
  Justly I deserve the same;
If I meet with free salvation,
  I will magnify thy name.

396 *Pleading for Mercy.* **280**

JESUS, full of all compassion,
  Hear thy humble suppliant's cry;
Let me know thy great salvation;
  See, I languish, faint, and die.

2 Guilty, but with heart relenting,
  Overwhelm'd with helpless grief,
Prostrate at thy feet repenting,
  Send, oh, send me quick relief!

3 Whither should a wretch be flying,
  But to him who comfort gives?
Whither, from the dread of dying,
  But to him who ever lives?

4 While I view thee, wounded, grieving,
  Breathless, on the cursed tree,
Fain I'd feel my heart believing
  That thou suffer'dst thus for me.

5 Hear, O blessed Savior, hear me!
  My soul cleaveth to the dust;
Send the Comforter to cheer me;
  Lo! in thee I put my trust.

397 *Bartimeus' Prayer.* **208**

"MERCY, O thou son of David!"
  Thus the blind Bartimeus pray'd;
"Others by thy word are saved,
  Now to me afford thine aid."

2 Money was not what he wanted,
  Though by begging us'd to live.
But he ask'd, and Jesus granted
  Alms which none but he could give.

3 "Lord, remove this grievous blindness,
  Let mine eyes behold the day!"
Straight he saw, and, won by kindness,
  Follow'd Jesus in the way.

4 Oh! methinks I hear him praising,
  Publishing to all around:
"Friends, is not my case amazing?
  What a Savior I have found!

5 "Oh! that all the blind but knew him,
  And would be advis'd by me!
Surely they would hasten to him,
  He would cause them all to see."

CHRISTIAN EXPERIENCE—PENITENTIAL

7s. HOTHAM.

1. Jesus, lover of my soul, Let me to thy bosom fly While the billows near me roll, While the tempest still is high; Hide me, O my Savior, hide, Till the storm of life be past, Safe into the haven guide, Oh, receive, Oh, receive, Oh, receive my soul at last!

398 *Christ our Refuge.* **167**

JESUS, lover of my soul,
 Let me to thy bosom fly
While the billows near me roll,
 While the tempest still is high;
Hide me, O my Savior, hide,
 Till the storm of life be past,
Safe into the haven guide,
 Oh, receive my soul at last!

2 Other refuge have I none,
 Lo! I, helpless, hang on thee:
Leave, oh, leave me not alone,
 Lest I basely shrink and flee:
Thou art all my trust and aid,
 All my help from thee I bring:
Cover my defenceless head
 With the shadow of thy wing!

3 Thou, O Christ, art all I want;
 Boundless love in thee I find:
Raise the fallen, cheer the faint,
 Heal the sick, and lead the blind.
Just and holy is thy name;
 I am all unrighteousness,
Vile and full of sin I am:
 Thou art full of truth and grace.

4 Plenteous grace with thee is found,
 Grace to pardon all my sin;
Let the healing streams abound,
 Make and keep me pure within.
Thou of life the fountain art,
 Freely let me take of thee:
Reign, O Lord, within my heart,
 Reign to all eternity.

399 *Reconciliation through Christ.* **413**

DEPTH of mercy! can there be
 Mercy still reserv'd for me?
Can my God his wrath forbear?
 Me, the chief of sinners, spare?
Long have I withstood his grace.
 Long provok'd him to his face;
Would not hearken to his calls,
 Griev'd him by a thousand falls.

2 Yet for me the Savior stands
 Shows his wounds and spreads his hands:
God is love! I know, I feel!
 Jesus weeps, and loves me still!
Savior, help me to repent!
 Let me now my fall lament!
Now my foul revolt deplore!
 Weep, believe, and sin no more.

CHRISTIAN EXPERIENCE—PENITENTIAL.

C. M. ST. MARTINS.

1. Dear Je-sus, let thy pity-ing eye Call back a wand'r-ing sheep: False to my vows, like Pe-ter, I Would fain, like Pe-ter, weep.

401 *Prayer for a New Heart.* **417**

DEAR Jesus, let thy pitying eye
  Call back a wand'ring sheep:
False to my vows, like Peter, I
Would fain, like Peter, weep.

2 Now let me be by grace restor'd,
  To me be mercy shown;
Oh, turn and look upon me, Lord,
And break my heart of stone.

3 Almighty Prince, enthron'd above,
  Repentance to impart,
Grant, through the greatness of thy love,
The humble, contrite heart.

4 Give, what I should have long implor'd,
  A taste of love unknown;
Oh, turn and look upon me, Lord,
And break my heart of stone.

5 Behold me, Savior, from above,
  Nor suffer me to die;
For life, and happiness, and love,
  Smile in thy gracious eye.

6 Speak but the reconciling word;
  Let mercy melt me down:
Oh, turn and look upon me, Lord,
And break my heart of stone.

402 *Hardness Lamented.* **202**

AND will the Lord thus condescend
  To visit sinful worms?
Thus at the door shall mercy stand
In all her winning forms?

2 Surprising grace!—and shall my heart
  Unmov'd and cold remain?
Has this hard rock no tender part?
Must mercy plead in vain?

3 Shall Jesus for admission sue—
  His charming voice unheard?
And this vile heart, his rightful due,
Remain forever barr'd?

4 'Tis sin, alas, with tyrant pow'r
  The lodging has possess'd;
And crowds of traitors bar the door
Against the heav'nly Guest.

5 Ye dang'rous inmates, hence depart:
  Dear Savior, enter in,
And guard the passage to my heart,
And keep out ev'ry sin.

403 *Returning Prodigal.* **205**

THE Prodigal, with streaming eyes,
  From folly just awake,
Reviews his wand'rings with surprise;
His heart begins to break.

2 "I starve," he cries, "nor can I bear
  The famine in this land;
While servants of my Father share
The bounty of his hand.

3 "With deep repentance I'll return
  And seek my Father's face;
Unworthy to be call'd a son,
I'll ask a servant's place."

4 Far off he saw him slowly move,
  In pensive silence mourn;
The Father ran with arms of love
  To welcome his return.

5 Through all the courts the tidings flew,
  And spread the joy around;
The angels tun'd their harps anew;
  The Prodigal is found!

404 *The Penitent Thief.* 206

AS on the cross the Savior hung,
  And wept, and bled, and died,
He pour'd salvation on a wretch
That languish'd at his side.

2 His crimes, with inward grief and shame
  The penitent confess'd;
Then turn'd his dying eyes to Christ,
  And thus his pray'r address'd:

3 "Jesus, thou Son and heir of heav'n!
  Thou spotless Lamb of God!
I see thee bath'd in sweat and tears,
  And welt'ring in thy blood.

4 "Yet quickly from these scenes of woe
  In triumph thou shalt rise,
Burst through the gloomy shades of death,
  And shine above the skies.

5 "Amid the glories of that world,
  Dear Savior, think on me,
And in the vict'ries of thy death
  Let me a sharer be."

6 His pray'r the dying Jesus hears,
  And instantly replies,
"To-day thy parting soul shall be
  With me in Paradise."

405 *Penitence and Hope.* 214

DEAR Savior, when my thoughts recall
  The wonders of thy grace,
Low, at thy feet, asham'd, I fall,
  And hide this wretched face.

2 Shall love like thine be thus repaid?
  Ah, vile, ungrateful heart!
By earth's low cares detain'd, betray'd
  From Jesus to depart;—

3 From Jesus, who alone can give
  True pleasure, peace, and rest;—
When absent from my Lord, I live
  Unsatisfied, unblest.

4 But he, for his own mercy's sake,
  My wand'ring soul restores;
He bids the mourning heart partake
  The pardon it implores.

5 Oh, while I breathe to thee, my Lord,
  The penitential sigh,
Confirm the kind, forgiving word,
  With pity in thine eye.

6 Then shall the mourner, at thy feet,
  Rejoice to seek thy face;
And, grateful, own how kind, how sweet,
  Is thy forgiving grace.

406 *Prayer for Christ's Help.* 781

AND didst thou, Jesus, condescend,
  When vail'd in human clay,
To heal the sick, the lame, the blind,
  And drive disease away?

2 Didst thou regard the beggar's cry,
  And cause the blind to see?
Thou Son of David, hear—oh, hear—
  Have mercy, too, on me.

3 And didst thou pity mortal woe,
  And sight and health restore?
Oh, pity, Lord, and save my soul;
  Which needs thy mercy more.

4 Didst thou thy trembling servant raise,
  When sinking in the wave?
I perish, Lord: oh, save my soul;
  For thou alone canst save.

407 *Flying to God.* 308

DEAR Refuge of my weary soul,
  On thee, when sorrows rise,
On thee, when waves of trouble roll,
  My fainting hope relies.

2 To thee I tell each rising grief,
  For thou alone canst heal;
Thy word can bring a sweet relief
  For ev'ry pain I feel.

3 But, oh, when gloomy doubts prevail,
  I fear to call thee mine;
The springs of comfort seem to fail,
  And all my hopes decline.

4 Yet, gracious God, where shall I flee?
  Thou art my only trust;
And still my soul would cleave to thee,
  Though prostrate in the dust.

CHRISTIAN EXPERIENCE—PENITENTIAL.

L. M. WINDHAM.

1. Stay, thou in-sult-ed Spi-rit, stay, Though I have done thee such de-spite; Nor cast the sin-ner quite a-way, Nor take thine ev-er-last-ing flight.

408 *The Spirit Grieved.* **228**

STAY, thou insulted Spirit, stay,
  Though I have done thee such despite;
Nor cast the sinner quite away,
Nor take thine everlasting flight.

2 Though I have steel'd my stubborn heart,
Oft shaken off my guilty fears,
And vex'd and urg'd thee to depart,
For many long, rebellious years;

3 Though I have most unfaithful been
Of all who e'er thy grace receiv'd,
Ten thousand times thy goodness seen,
Ten thousand times thy goodness griev'd;

4 Yet oh, the chief of sinners spare
In honor of my great High-Priest;
Nor in thy righteous anger swear
T' exclude me from thy people's rest.

5 This only woe I deprecate,
This only plague I pray remove,
Nor leave me in my lost estate,
Nor curse me with this want of love.

6 E'en now my weary soul release,
Upraise me with thy gracious hand
And guide into thy perfect peace,
And bring me to the promis'd land.

409 *Penitence.* **263**

O TURN, great Ruler of the skies,
  Turn from my sin thy searching eyes,
Nor let th' offenses of my hand
Within thy book recorded stand.

2 Give me a will to thine subdu'd,
A conscience pure, a soul renew'd;
Nor let me, wrapt in endless gloom,
An outcast from thy presence roam.

3 Oh, let thy Spirit to my heart
Once more his quick'ning aid impart,
My mind from ev'ry fear release,
And soothe my troubled thoughts to peace.

410 *Mourning Ingratitude.* **166**

POOR, weak, and worthless though I am,
  I have a rich, almighty Friend;
Jesus, the Savior, is his name,
He freely loves, and without end.

2 He ransom'd me from hell with blood,
And, by his pow'r, my foes controll'd,
He found me wand'ring far from God,
And brought me to his chosen fold.

3 But, ah! my inmost spirit mourns;
And well my eyes with tears may swim,
To think of my perverse returns;
I've been a faithless friend to him.

4 Often my gracious Friend I grieve,
Neglect, distrust, and disobey;
And often Satan's lies believe
Rather than all my Friend can say.

5 He bids me always freely come,
And promises whate'er I ask:
But I am languid, cold, and dumb,
And count my privilege a task.

6 Sure, were I not most vile and base,
I could not thus my Friend requite!
And were not he the God of grace,
He'd frown and spurn me from his sight.

CHRISTIAN EXPERIENCE—PENITENTIAL.

S. M. McEVERS.

411 *Prayer for Penitence.* **252**

OH, let me now repent!
  Oh, let me now believe!
Thou by whose voice the marble rent,
  The rock in sunder cleave!

2 Thou, by thy two-edg'd sword,
    My soul and spirit part;
  Strike with the hammer of thy word,
    And break my stubborn heart.

3 Savior and Prince of peace,
    The double grace bestow:
  Unloose the bands of wickedness,
    And let the captive go.

4 Grant me my sins to feel,
    And then the load remove:—
  Wound, and pour in, my wounds to heal,
    The balm of pard'ning love.

5 For thine own mercy's sake,
    The hinderance now remove,
  And into thy protection take
    The pris'ner of thy love.

6 Oh, may I now embrace
    Thine all-sufficient pow'r!
  And never more to sin give place,
    And never grieve thee more.

412 *Confession.* **908**

ONCE more we meet to pray,
  Once more our guilt confess;
Turn not, O Lord, thine ear away
  From creatures in distress.

2 Our sins to heav'n ascend,
    And there for vengeance cry;

O God, behold the sinner's Friend,
  Who intercedes on high.

3 Though we are vile indeed,
    And well deserve thy curse,
  The merits of thy Son we plead,
    Who lived and died for us.

4 Now let thy bosom yearn,
    As it hath done before;
  Return to us, O God, return,
    And ne'er forsake us more.

413 *Mercy Implored.* **412**

THOU Lord of all above
    And all below the sky,
  Before thy feet I prostrate fall,
    And for thy mercy cry.

2 Forgive my follies past,
    The crimes which I have done;
  Oh, bid a contrite sinner live,
    Through thine incarnate Son.

3 Guilt, like a heavy load,
    Upon my conscience lies;
  To thee I make my sorrows known,
    And lift my weeping eyes.

4 The burden which I feel,
    Thou only canst remove;
  Display, O Lord, thy pard'ning grace,
    And thine unbounded love.

5 One gracious look of thine
    Will ease my troubled breast;
  Oh, let me know my sins forgiv'n,
    And I shall then be blest.

CHRISTIAN EXPERIENCE—PENITENTIAL.

8s. 6 lines. BRIGHTON.

1. Dear Friend of friendless sin-ners, hear, And mag-ni-fy thy grace di-vine; Par-don a worm that would draw near, That would his heart to thee re-sign; A worm, by self and sin op-prest That pants to reach thy pro-mis'd rest.

414 *Prayer for Rest.* **296**

DEAR Friend of friendless sinners, hear,
And magnify thy grace divine;
Pardon a worm that would draw near,
That would his heart to thee resign;
A worm, by self and sin opprest
That pants to reach thy promis'd rest.

2 With holy fear and rev'rent love,
I long to lie beneath thy throne;
I long in thee to live, and move,
And stay myself on thee alone:
Teach me to lean upon thy breast,
To find in thee the promis'd rest.

3 Thou say'st thou wilt thy servants keep
In perfect peace, whose minds shall be
Like new-born babes, or helpless sheep,
Completely stay'd, dear Lord! on thee.
How calm their state, how truly blest,
Who trust on thee, the promis'd rest!

4 Take me, my Savior, as thine own,
And vindicate my righteous cause;
Be thou my portion, Lord, alone,
Incline me to obey thy laws:
In thy dear arms of love caress'd,
Give me to find thy promis'd rest.

5 Bid the tempestuous rage of sin,
With all its wrathful fury, die;
Let the Redeemer dwell within,
And turn my sorrows into joy:
Oh, may my heart, by thee possess'd,
Know thee to be my promis'd rest.

415 *The Penitent's Prayer.* **282**

FATHER of mercies. God of love!
Oh, hear an humble suppliant's cry:
Bend from thy lofty seat above,
Thy throne of glorious majesty:
Oh, deign to listen to my voice,
And bid this drooping heart rejoice.

2 I urge no merits of my own,
For I, alas! am all that's vile:
No—when I bow before thy throne,
Dare to converse with God a while,
Thy name, blest Jesus, is my plea,
That dearest, sweetest name to me!

3 Within this heart of mine I feel
The weight of sin's oppressive load:
Oh, help! or else I sink to hell,
Crush'd by thine arm, avenging God!
Entomb'd within that dread abyss,
And exil'd from the realms of bliss!

CHRISTIAN EXPERIENCE—PENITENTIAL.

7s. 6 lines. NUREMBURG.

1. Fa-ther, God, who se'st in me Only sin and mi-se-ry,
   Turn to thine A-noint-ed One, Look on thy be-lov-ed Son;

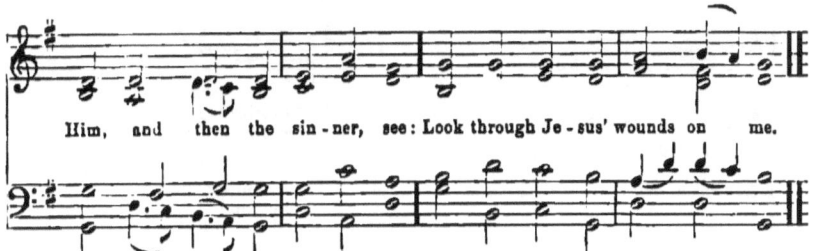

Him, and then the sin-ner, see: Look through Je-sus' wounds on me.

416 *Pleading the Atonement.* 297

FATHER, God, who se'st in me,
  Only sin and misery,
Turn to thine Anointed One,
Look on thy beloved Son;
Him, and then the sinner, see:
Look through Jesus' wounds on me.

2 Heav'nly Father, Lord of all,
Fear and shame thou bear'st my call!
Bow thine ear, in mercy bow,
Smile on me, a sinner, now!
Vow the stone to flesh convert,
Cast a look, and melt my heart.

3 Lord, I cannot let thee go
Till a blessing thou bestow;
Hear my Advocate divine,
Lo! to his, my suit I join;
Join'd with his, it cannot fail:
Let me now with thee prevail!

4 Jesus, answer from above,
Is not all thy nature love?
Pity from thine eye let fall;
Bless me whilst on thee I call:
Am I thine, thou Son of God?
Take the purchase of thy blood.

417 *The Call accepted.* 832

AM I call'd? and can it be!
  Has my Savior chosen me?
Guilty, wretched as I am,
Has he nam'd my worthless name?
Vilest of the vile am I,
Dare I raise my hopes so high?

2 Am I call'd? I dare not stay,
May not, must not, disobey;
Here, I lay me at thy feet,
Clinging to thy mercy-seat;
Thine I am and thine alone;
Lord, with me thy will be done.

3 Am I call'd? what shall I bring
As an off'ring to my King?
Poor, and blind, and naked, I
Trembling at thy footstool lie;
Naught but sin I call mine own,
Nor for sin can sin atone.

4 Am I call'd? an heir of God!
Wash'd, redeem'd by precious blood!
Father, lead me in thy hand,
Guide me to that better land,
Where my soul shall be at rest,
Pillow'd on my Savior's breast.

CHRISTIAN EXPERIENCE—SUBMISSION.

C. M. WOODSTOCK.

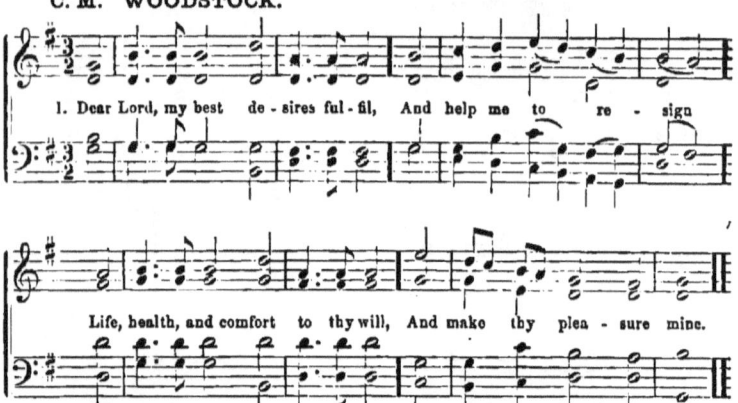

1. Dear Lord, my best de-sires ful-fil, And help me to re-sign Life, health, and comfort to thy will, And make thy plea-sure mine.

418 *Submission.* **435**

DEAR Lord, my best desires fulfil,
And help me to resign
Life, health, and comfort to thy will,
And make thy pleasure mine.

2 Why should I shrink at thy command,
Whose love forbids my fears?
Or tremble at the gracious hand
That wipes away my tears?

3 No: let me rather freely yield
What most I prize to thee,
Who never hast a good withheld,
Nor wilt withhold from me.

4 Thy favor, all my journey through,
Thou art engag'd to grant:
What else I want, or think I do,
'Tis better still to want.

5 Wisdom and mercy guide my way
Shall I resist them both?
A poor blind creature of a day,
And crush'd before the moth!

6 But ah! my inmost spirit cries,
Still bind me to thy sway;
Else the next cloud that veils my skies
Drives all these thoughts away.

419 *God the Soul's Portion.* **95**

WHEN in the light of faith divine
We look on things below,
Honor, and gold, and sensual joy,
How vain and dang'rous too!

2 Honor's a puff of noisy breath;
Yet men expose their blood,
And venture everlasting death
To gain that airy good.

3 Whilst others starve the nobler mind,
And feed on shining dust,
They sacrifice eternal bliss
To mean and sordid lust.

4 The pleasures that allure our sense
Are dang'rous snares to souls;
There's but a drop of flatt'ring sweet,
And dash'd with bitter bowls.

5 God is mine all-sufficient good,
My portion and my choice;
In him my vast desires are fill'd,
And all my pow'rs rejoice.

420 *The Christian's Choice.* **392**

THOU art my portion, O my God!
Soon as I know thy way,
My heart makes haste t' obey thy word,
And suffers no delay.

2 I choose the path of heav'nly truth,
And glory in my choice;
Not all the riches of the earth
Could make me so rejoice.

3 The testimonies of thy grace
I set before mine eyes;
Thence I derive my daily strength,
And there my comfort lies.

4 If e'er I wander from thy path,
I think upon my ways;
Then turn my feet to thy commands,
And trust thy pard'ning grace.

CHRISTIAN EXPERIENCE—SUBMISSION.

5 Now I am thine, forever thine;
  Oh, save thy servant, Lord!
Thou art my shield, my hiding-place;
  My hope is in thy word.
6 Thou hast inclin'd this heart of mine
  Thy statutes to fulfill;
And thus till mortal life shall end
  Would I perform thy will.

421 *Leaning upon God.* **437**

O GOD of Jacob, by whose hand
  Thy people still are fed;
Who, through this weary pilgrimage,
  Hast all our fathers led!
2 To thee our humble vows we raise,
  To thee address our prayer;

And in thy kind and faithful breast
  Deposit all our care.
3 Through each perplexing path of life
  Our wand'ring footsteps guide,
Give us each day our daily bread,
  And raiment fit provide.
4 Oh, spread thy cov'ring wings around,
  Till all our wand'rings cease,
And at our Father's lov'd abode
  Our souls arrive in peace!
5 To thee, as to our cov'nant God,
  We'll our whole selves resign;
And thankful own that all we are,
  And all we have, is thine.

7s, 6s, 8s. ENDOR. *Fine.*

1. { Lamb of God, for sinners slain, To thee I humbly pray:
   { Heal me of my grief and pain, Oh, take my sins away!
D.C. Je-sus, Mas-ter, seal my peace, And take me to thy breast!

From this bond-age, Lord, re-lease; No long-er let me be op-prest:
D.C.

422 *Peace in Jesus.* **279**

LAMB of God, for sinners slain,
  To thee I humbly pray;
Heal me of my grief and pain,
  Oh, take my sins away!
From this bondage, Lord, release;
  No longer let me be opprest:
Jesus, Master, seal my peace,
  And take me to thy breast.

2 Wilt thou cast a sinner out,
  Who humbly comes to thee?
No, my God, I cannot doubt:
  Thy mercy is for me:
Let me, then, obtain the grace,
  And be of paradise possest:
Jesus, Master, seal my peace,
  And take me to thy breast!

3 Worldly good I do not want,
  Be that to others giv'n;
Only for thy love I pant,
  My all in earth and heav'n;
This the crown I fain would seize,
  The good wherewith I would be blest;
Jesus, Master, seal my peace,
  And take me to thy breast.

4 This delight I fain would prove,
  And then resign my breath!
Join the happy few whose love
  Was mightier than death!
Let it not my Lord displease
  That I would die to be thy guest!
Jesus, Master, seal my peace,
  And take me to thy breast!

CHRISTIAN EXPERIENCE—SUBMISSION.

L. M. BLENDON.

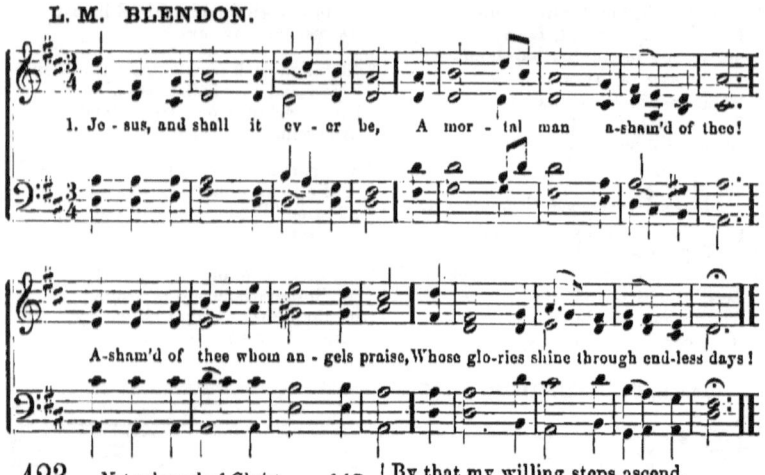

1. Je-sus, and shall it ev-er be, A mor-tal man a-sham'd of thee! A-sham'd of thee whom an-gels praise, Whose glo-ries shine through end-less days!

423   *Not ashamed of Christ.*   442

JESUS, and shall it ever be,
  A mortal man asham'd of thee!
Asham'd of thee, whom angels praise,
Whose glories shine through endless days!

2 Asham'd of Jesus! sooner far
Let ev'ning blush to own a star;
He sheds the beams of light divine
O'er this benighted soul of mine.

3 Asham'd of Jesus! just as soon
Let midnight be asham'd of noon:
'Tis midnight with my soul till he
Bright Morning Star! bid darkness flee.

4 Asham'd of Jesus! that dear Friend
On whom my hopes of heav'n depend!
No: when I blush be this my shame,
That I no more revere his name.

5 Asham'd of Jesus! yes, I may
When I've no guilt to wash away,
No tear to wipe, no good to crave,
No fears to quell, no soul to save.

6 Till then—nor is my boasting vain—
Till then I boast a Savior slain!
And, oh, may this my glory be,
That Christ is not asham'd of me!

424   *Choosing Heaven.*   450

WHAT thousands never knew the road!
  What thousands hate it when 'tis
None but the upright and sincere [known!
Will seek or choose it for their own.

2 A thousand ways in ruin end,
One only leads to joy on high;

By that my willing steps ascend,
Pleas'd with a journey to the sky.

3 No more I ask, or hope to find,
Delight or happiness below;
Sorrow may well possess the mind
That feeds where thorns and thistles grow.

4 The joy that fades is not for me,
I seek immortal joys above;
There glory without end shall be
The bright reward of faith and love.

425   *Coming to Christ.*

JUST as I am, without one plea,
  Save that thy blood was shed for me,
And that thou bid'st me come to thee,
O Lamb of God, I come! I come!

2 Just as I am, and waiting not,
To rid my soul of one dark blot,
To thee, whose blood can cleanse each spot,
O Lamb of God, I come! I come!

3 Just as I am, though toss'd about
With many a conflict, many a doubt,
With fears within and foes without,
O Lamb of God, I come! I come!

4 Just as I am—thou wilt receive,
Wilt welcome, pardon, cleanse, relieve,
Because thy promise I believe—
O Lamb of God, I come! I come!

5 Just as I am—thy love unknown
Has broken ev'ry barrier down;
Now to be thine, yea, thine alone—
O Lamb of God, I come! I come!

CHRISTIAN EXPERIENCE—SUBMISSION.

7s. Double. (6 lines, omitting repeat.) TELEMAN.

1. Father, Son, and Holy Ghost, One in Three, and Three in One, As by the celestial host, Let thy will on earth be done: Praise by all to thee be giv'n, Glorious Lord of earth and heav'n.

426 *Consecration to God.* **441**

FATHER, Son, and Holy Ghost,
  One in Three, and Three in One,
As by the celestial host,
  Let thy will on earth be done:
Praise by all to thee be giv'n,
Glorious Lord of earth and heav'n.

2 If so poor a worm as I
  May to thy great glory live,
All my actions sanctify,
  All my words and thoughts receive;
Claim me, for thy service claim,
All I have and all I am.

3 Take my soul and body's pow'rs!
  Take my mem'ry, mind, and will,
All my goods and all my hours,
  All I know and all I feel;
All I think, or speak, or do;
Take my heart, but make it new!

4 Now, O God, thine own I am;
  Now I give thee back thine own;
Freedom, friends, and health, and fame,
  Consecrate to thee alone:
Thine I live, thrice happy I;
Happier still if thine I die.

427 *Trusting in Divine Goodness.*

FATHER! thy paternal care
  Has my guardian been, my guide;
Ev'ry hallow'd wish and pray'r
  Has thy hand of love supplied.
Thine is ev'ry thought of bliss,
  Left by hours and days gone by:
Ev'ry hope thine offspring is,
  Beaming from futurity.

2 Ev'ry sun of splendid ray;
  Ev'ry moon that shines serene;
Ev'ry morn that welcomes day;
  Ev'ry evening's twilight scene;
Ev'ry hour which wisdom brings;
  Ev'ry incense at thy shrine;
These—and all life's holiest things
  And its fairest—all are thine.

3 And for all, my hymns shall rise
  Daily to thy gracious throne:
Thither let mine asking eyes
  Turn unwearied—righteous One!
Through life's strange vicissitude
  There reposing all my care;
Trusting still, through ill and good,
  Fix'd, and cheer'd, and counsell'd there.

CHRISTIAN EXPERIENCE—BELIEVING.

L. M. UXBRIDGE.

1. Lord, didst thou die, and not for me? Am I for-bid to trust thy blood?
Hast thou not par-don, rich and free, And grace, an o-verwhelm-ing flood?

428 *Humble Trust.* **303**

LORD, didst thou die, and not for me?
  Am I forbid to trust thy blood?
Hast thou not pardon, rich and free,
And grace, an overwhelming flood?

2 Presumptuous thought! to fix the bound,
To limit mercy's sov'reign reign:
What other happy souls have found,
I'll seek; nor shall I seek in vain.

3 I own my guilt, my sins confess;
Can men or devils make them more?
Of crimes, already numberless,
Vain the attempt to swell the score.

4 Were the black list before my sight,
While I remember thou hast died,
'Twould only urge my speedier flight
To seek salvation at thy side.

5 Low at thy feet I'll cast me down,
To thee reveal my guilt and fear;
And—if thou spurn me from thy throne,
I'll be the *first* who perish'd there.

429 *God the Portion of the Soul.* **304**

FAR from thy fold, O God, my feet
  Once moved in error's devious maze,
Nor found religious duties sweet,
Nor sought thy face, nor lov'd thy ways.

2 With tend'rest voice thou bad'st me flee
The paths which thou couldst ne'er approve;
Didst gently draw my soul to thee,
With cords of sweet, eternal love.

3 Now to thy footstool, Lord, I fly,
And low in self-abasement fall;
A vile, a helpless worm, I lie,
And thou, my God, art all in all.

4 Dearer, far dearer to my heart
Than all the joys that earth can give;
From fame, from wealth, & friends I'd part,
Beneath thy countenance to live.

5 And when, in smiling friendship drest,
Death bids me quit this mortal frame,
Gently reclin'd on Jesus' breast,
My latest breath shall bless his name.

6 Then my unfetter'd soul shall rise
And soar above yon starry spheres,
Join the full chorus of the skies,
And sing thy praise through endless years.

430 *Trusting Christ.* **306**

THOU only Sov'reign of my heart,
  My refuge, my almighty Friend,
And can my soul from thee depart
On whom alone my hopes depend?

2 Whither, ah, whither shall I go,
A wretched wand'rer from my Lord?
Can this dark world of sin and woe
One glimpse of happiness afford?

3 Eternal life thy words impart;
On these my fainting spirit lives;
Here sweeter comforts cheer my heart
Than all the round of nature gives.

4 Let earth's alluring joys combine;
While thou art near, in vain they call;
One smile, one blissful smile, of thine,
My gracious Lord, outweighs them all.

5 Low at thy feet my soul would lie;
Here safety dwells, and peace divine;
Still let me live beneath thine eye,
For life, eternal life, is thine.

431   *Trusting in God.*   309

WHAT mean these jealousies and fears?
    As if the Lord was loath to save,
Or lov'd to see us drench'd in tears,
Or sink with sorrow to the grave.

2 Does he want slaves to grace his throne?
Or rules he by an iron rod?
Loves he the deep despairing groan?
Is he a tyrant, or a God?

3 Not all the sins which we have wrought,
So much his tender mercy grieve
As this unkind, injurious thought,
That he's unwilling to forgive.

4 What tho' our crimes are black as night,
Or glowing like the crimson morn?
Immanuel's blood will make them white
As snow through the pure ether borne.

5 Lord, 'tis amazing grace we own,
And well may rebel worms surprise;
But was not thine incarnate Son
A most amazing sacrifice?

6 "I've found a ransom," saith the Lord,
    "No humble penitent shall die:"
Lord, we would now believe thy word,
And thine unbounded mercies try!

432   *Parting with Carnal Joys.*   310

I SEND the joys of earth away;
    Away, ye tempters of the mind,
False as the smooth, deceitful sea,
And empty as the whistling wind.

2 Your streams were floating me along
Down to the gulf of black despair,
And whilst I listen'd to your song,
Your streams had e'en convey'd me there.

3 Lord, I adore thy matchless grace,
That warn'd me of that dark abyss,
That drew me from those treach'rous seas,
And bade me seek superior bliss.

4 Now to the shining realms above
I stretch my hands and glance mine eyes;
Oh for the pinions of a dove,
To bear me to the upper skies;

5 There, from the bosom of my God,
Oceans of endless pleasure roll;
There would I fix my last abode,
And drown the sorrows of my soul.

433   *Trusting in God.*   312

SING to the Lord, who loud proclaims
    His various and his saving names:
Oh, may they not be heard alone,
But by our sure experience known.

2 Awake, our noblest pow'rs, to bless
The God of Abra'm, God of peace;
Now by a dearer title known,
Father and God of Christ, his Son.

3 Through ev'ry age his gracious ear
Is open to his servants' pray'r;
Nor can one humble soul complain
That it hath sought its God in vain.

4 What unbelieving heart shall dare
In whispers to suggest a fear,
While still he owns his ancient name,
The same his pow'r, his love the same!

5 To thee our souls in faith arise;
To thee we lift expecting eyes,
And boldly through the desert tread;
For God will guard, where God shall lead.

434   *Believing.*   318

NOT by the law of innocence
    Can Adam's sons arrive at heav'n;
New works can give us no pretense
To have our former sins forgiv'n:

2 Not the best deeds that we have done
Can make a wounded conscience whole!
Faith is the grace,—and faith alone,
That flies to Christ, and saves the soul.

3 Lord, I believe thy heav'nly word!
Fain would I have my soul renew'd:
I mourn for sin, and trust the Lord
To have it pardon'd and subdu'd.

4 Oh may thy grace its pow'r display!
Let guilt and death no longer reign;
Save me in thine appointed way,
Nor let my humble faith be vain!

435   *Meekly Trusting in God's Grace.*

GREAT God! and wilt thou condescend
    To be my Father and my Friend?
Wilt thou accept the songs of praise
Which such a feeble one can raise?

2 Art thou my Father? let me be
A meek, obedient child to thee,
And try, in word, and deed, and thought,
To serve and please thee as I ought.

3 Art thou my Father? I'll depend
Upon the care of such a Friend,
And ever strive to do and be
Whatever seemeth good to thee.

4 Art thou my Father? then, at last,
When all my days on earth are past,
Send down and take me in thy love,
To join the church and choir above.

CHRISTIAN EXPERIENCE—BELIEVING.

C. M. TRIAS.

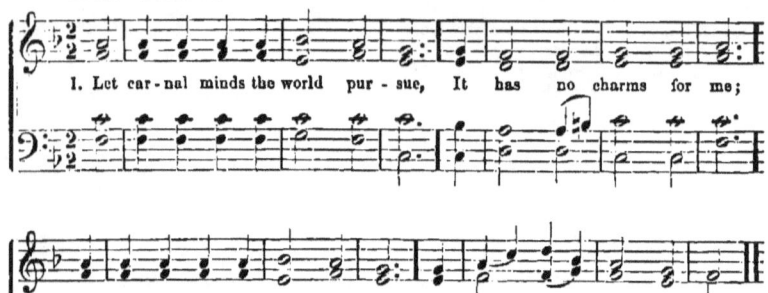

1. Let car-nal minds the world pur-sue, It has no charms for me;

Once I ad-mir'd its tri-fles too, But grace has set me free.

436 *Old Things passed away.* **307**

LET carnal minds the world pursue,
  It has no charms for me ;
Once I admir'd its trifles too,
  But grace has set me free.

2 Its fading charms no longer please,
  No more content afford ;
Far from my heart be joys like these,
  Now I have seen the Lord.

3 As by the light of op'ning day,
  The stars are all conceal'd ;
So earthly pleasures fade away,
  When Jesus is reveal'd.

4 Creatures no more divide my choice—
  I bid them all depart ;
His name, and love, and gracious voice,
  Have fix'd my roving heart.

5 Now, Lord, I would be thine alone,
  And wholly live to thee ;
But may I hope that thou wilt own
  A worthless worm like me ?

437 *The Power of Faith.* **313**

FAITH adds new charms to earthly bliss
  And saves me from its snares ;
Its aid in ev'ry duty brings,
  And softens all my cares ;

2 Extinguishes the thirst of sin,
  And lights the sacred fire
Of love to God and heav'nly things,
  And feeds the pure desire.

3 The wounded conscience knows its pow'r
  The healing balm to give ;
That balm the saddest heart can cheer,
  And make the dying live.

4 Wide it unvails celestial worlds,
  Where deathless pleasures reign ;
And bids me seek my portion there,
  Nor bids me seek in vain ;

5 Shows me the precious promise seal'd
  With my Redeemer's blood ;
And helps my feeble hope to rest
  Upon a faithful God.

6 There, there, unshaken, would I rest,
  Till this vile body dies,
And then on faith's triumphant wings
  At once to glory rise.

438 *A Living Faith.* **323**

MISTAKEN souls, that dream of heav'n,
  And make their empty boast
Of inward joys and sins forgiv'n,
  While they are slaves to lust !

2 Vain are our fancies, airy flights,
  If faith be cold and dead ;
None but a living pow'r unites
  To Christ, the living Head :—

3 A faith that changes all the heart ;
  A faith that works by love ;
That bids all sinful joys depart,
  And lifts the thoughts above.

4 Faith must obey our Father's will,
  As well as trust his grace ;
A pard'ning God is jealous still
  For his own holiness.

5 When from the curse he sets us free,
  He makes our natures clean ;
Nor would he send his Son to be
  The minister of sin.

439 For Strong Faith. 866

OH for a faith that will not shrink,
  Though press'd by ev'ry foe,
That will not tremble on the brink
Of any earthly woe!—

2 That will not murmur nor complain
Beneath the chast'ning rod,
But, in the hour of grief or pain,
Will lean upon its God;—

3 A faith that shines more bright and clear
When tempests rage without;
That when in danger knows no fear,
In darkness feels no doubt;

4 That bears, unmov'd, the world's dread frown,
Nor heeds its scornful smile;
That seas of trouble cannot drown,
Nor Satan's arts beguile;

5 A faith that keeps the narrow way
Till life's last hour is fled,
And with a pure and heav'nly ray
Lights up a dying bed.

6 Lord, give us such a faith as this,
And then, whate'er may come,
We'll taste, e'en here, the hallow'd bliss
Of an eternal home.

440 Refuge in Christ. 834

WHERE shall we sinners hide our heads?
  Can rocks or mountains save?
Or shall we wrap us in the shades
Of midnight and the grave?

2 Is there no shelter from the eye
Of an avenging God?
Jesus, to thy dear wounds we fly:
Bedew us with thy blood.

3 Those guardian drops our souls secure,
And wash away our sins;
Eternal justice frowns no more,
And conscience smiles within.

4 We bless that wondrous purple stream
That cleanses ev'ry stain;
Our souls are yet but half redeem'd,
If sin the tyrant reign.

441 Lord, remember me. 849

O THOU from whom all goodness flows,
  I lift my soul to thee;
In all my sorrows, conflicts, woes,
Dear Lord, remember me!

2 When on my aching, burden'd heart
My sins lie heavily,
Thy pardon grant, new peace impart:
Dear Lord, remember me!

3 When trials sore obstruct my way,
And ills I cannot flee,
Oh, let my strength be as my day:
Dear Lord, remember me!

4 When worn with pain, disease, and grief,
This feeble frame shall be,
Grant patience, rest, and kind relief:
Dear Lord, remember me!

5 When in the solemn hour of death
I wait thy just decree,
And when I draw my parting breath,
Savior, remember me!

6 And when before thy throne I stand
And lift my soul to thee,
Then, with the saints at thy right hand,
Dear Lord, remember me!

442 Not Ashamed of Jesus. 923

I'M not asham'd to own my Lord,
  Or to defend his cause,
Maintain the honor of his word,
The glory of his cross.

2 Jesus, my God!—I know his name—
His name is all my trust;
Nor will he put my soul to shame,
Nor let my hope be lost.

3 Firm as his throne his promise stands,
And he can well secure
What I've committed to his hands,
Till the decisive hour.

4 Then will he own my worthless name
Before his Father's face,
And in the new Jerusalem
Appoint my soul a place.

443 Taking Refuge at the Mercy-Seat.

DEAR Father! to thy mercy-seat
  My soul for shelter flies:
'Tis here I find a safe retreat,
When storms and tempests rise.

2 My cheerful hope can never die
If thou, my God! art near;
Thy grace can raise my comforts high,
And banish every fear.

3 My great Protector, and my Lord!
Thy constant aid impart;
Oh, let thy kind, thy gracious word
Sustain my trembling heart.

4 Oh, never let my soul remove
From this divine retreat;
Still let me trust thy pow'r and love
And dwell beneath thy feet.

CHRISTIAN EXPERIENCE—BELIEVING.

L. M. ILLA.
Moderato.

1. Come, Sa-vior Je - sus, from a - bove, As - sist me with thy heav'n-ly grace; Emp - ty my heart of earth - ly love, And for thy-self pre - pare the place.

444 *Christ the Believer's Portion.* **342**

COME, Savior Jesus, from above,
  Assist me with thy heav'nly grace;
Empty my heart of earthly love,
And for thyself prepare the place.

2 O let thy sacred presence fill,
And set my longing spirit free,
Which pants to have no other will
But night and day to feast on thee.

3 While in this region here below,
No other good will I pursue;
I'll bid this world of noise and show,
With all its glitt'ring snares, adieu.

4 That path, with humble speed, I'll seek,
In which my Savior's footsteps shine;
Nor will I hear, nor will I speak,
Of any other love than thine.

5 Henceforth may no profane delight
Divide this consecrated soul;
Possess it Thou, who hast the right,
As Lord and Master of the whole.

6 Nothing on earth do I desire,
But thy pure love within my breast:
This, only this, will I require,
And freely give up all the rest.

445 *Heavenly Grace.* **865**

O COME, thou great and gracious Pow'r,
  Accept a home within my breast;
My spirit cheer in ev'ry hour,
In ev'ry season give me rest.

2 Oh, teach me well to know my heart,
My folly and my sin to see;
On earth to bear a lowly part,
And give myself, my all, to thee.

3 Teach me to trust a Savior's name,
To feel a Savior's dying love;
To be redeem'd—be that my fame;—
My honors let me seek above.

4 When pleasure cheers & friendship smiles,
And smoothly sweeps my bark along,
Then save me from the tempter's wiles;
Be thou my joy, be thou my song.

5 And when affliction's gloomy pow'r
Shall shroud my soul in sad dismay,
Rise thou, a star to cheer that hour,
And lead me through the darken'd way.

6 And at the last, when ghastly death
This life's short, brittle thread shall break,
Do thou attend my latest breath,
Thy Spirit clothe me when I wake.

446 *Faith our Guide.* **314**

'TIS by the faith of joys to come
  We walk through deserts dark as night;
Till we arrive at heav'n our home,
Faith is our guide, and faith our light.

2 The want of sight she well supplies;
She makes the pearly gates appear;
Far into distant worlds she pries,
And brings eternal glories near.

3 Cheerful we tread the desert through,
While faith inspires a heav'nly ray,
Though lions roar, and tempests blow,
And rocks and dangers fill the way.

4 So Abra'm, by divine command,
Left his own house to walk with God;
His faith beheld the promis'd land,
And cheer'd him on his toilsome road.

CHRISTIAN EXPERIENCE—JOY AND HOPE.

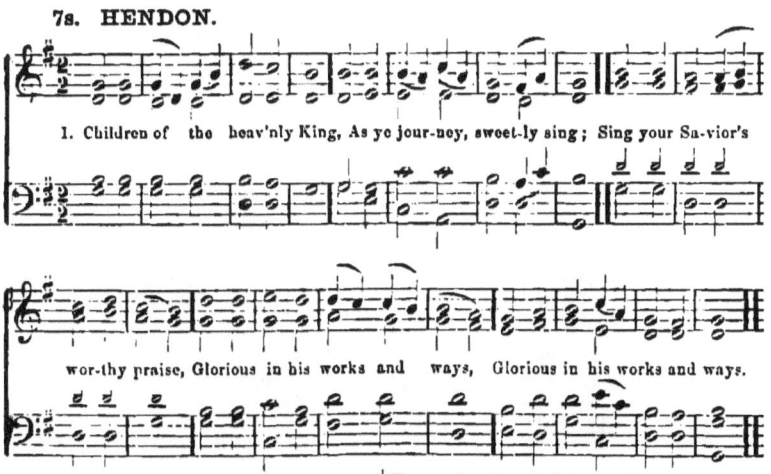

7s. HENDON.

1. Children of the heav'nly King, As ye journey, sweetly sing; Sing your Savior's worthy praise, Glorious in his works and ways, Glorious in his works and ways.

447 *Rejoicing in Hope.* **453**

CHILDREN of the heav'nly King,
As ye journey, sweetly sing;
Sing your Savior's worthy praise,
Glorious in his works and ways.

2 Ye are trav'ling home to God,
In the way the fathers trod;
They are happy now, and ye
Soon their happiness shall see.

3 Oh, ye banish'd seed, be glad!
Christ our advocate is made;
Us to save, our flesh assumes—
Brother to our souls becomes.

4 Shout, ye little flock, and blest;
You on Jesus' throne shall rest;
There your seat is now prepar'd—
There your kingdom and reward.

5 Lord, submissive make us go,
Gladly leaving all below;
Only thou our leader be,
And we still will follow thee.

448 *Love of Jesus.* **391**

LOVE divine, how sweet the sound!
May the theme on earth abound:
May the hearts of saints below
With the sacred rapture glow.

2 Love amazing, large and free,
Love unknown, to think on me!
Let that love upon me shine,
Savior, with its beams divine.

3 Better than earth's gilded toys,
Or an age of carnal joys;

Better far than Ophir's gold,
Love that never can be told;

4 Better than this life of mine,
Savior, is thy love divine:
Drop the veil, and let me see
Rivers of this love in thee.

5 While upon the earth I stay,
Love divine shall tune my lay;
When I soar to bliss above,
Still I'll praise a Savior's love.

449 *Trust in God.* **429**

SOV'REIGN Ruler of the skies,
Ever gracious, ever wise!
All my times are in thy hand,
All events at thy command.

2 Thou didst form me by thy pow'r;
Thou wilt guide me, hour by hour:
All my times shall ever be
Order'd by thy wise decree:

3 Times of sickness, times of health;
Times of penury and wealth;
Times of trial and of grief;
Times of triumph and relief.

4 O thou gracious, wise, and just!
In thy hands my life I trust:
Have I somewhat dearer still?
I resign it to thy will.

5 May I always own thy hand;
Still to thee submissive stand:
Know that thou art God alone;
I and mine are all thine own.

CHRISTIAN EXPERIENCE—JOY AND HOPE.

C. M. SWANWICK.

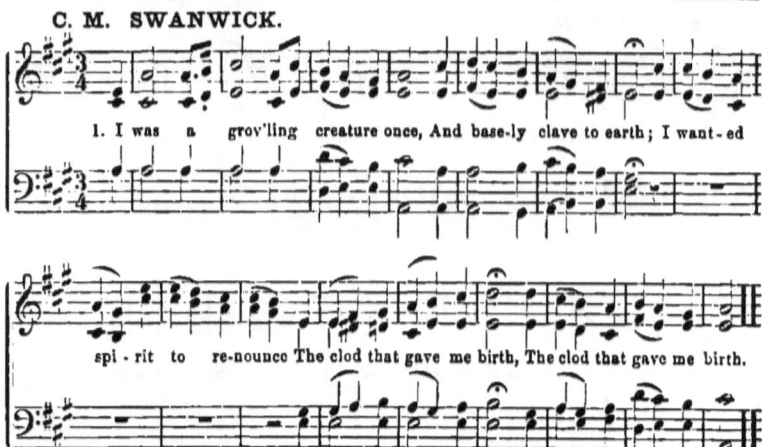

1. I was a grov'ling creature once, And base-ly clave to earth; I want-ed spi-rit to re-nounce The clod that gave me birth, The clod that gave me birth.

450 Lively Hope and Gracious Fear. 355

I WAS a grov'ling creature once,
  And basely clave to earth;
I wanted spirit to renounce
  The clod that gave me birth.

2 But God has breath'd upon a worm
  And sent me, from above,
Wings, such as clothe an angel's form,
  The wings of joy and love.

3 With these to Pisgah's top I fly,
  And there delighted stand,
To view beneath a shining sky
  The spacious promis'd land.

4 The Lord of all that vast domain
  Has promis'd it to me;
The length and breadth of all the plain,
  As far as faith can see.

5 How glorious is my privilege!
  Savior for help I call;
I stand upon a mountain's edge!
  Oh, keep me, lest I fall!

451 Desiring Assurance. 356

THOU Lord of all the worlds on high,
  Allow my humble claim;
Nor, while a child would raise its cry,
  Disdain a Father's name.

2 My Father, God, how sweet the sound!
  How tender and how dear!
Not all the melody of heav'n
  Could so delight the ear.

3 Come, sacred Spirit, seal the name
  On my believing heart,

And show that in Jehovah's grace
  I share a filial part.

4 By such a heav'nly signal cheer'd,
  Unwav'ring, I believe,
And Abba, Father, humbly cry;
  Nor can the sound deceive.

5 On wings of everlasting love
  The Comforter has come;
All terrors at his voice disperse,
  And endless pleasures bloom.

452 Changed by Grace. 360

WHEN God reveal'd his gracious name,
  And chang'd my mournful state,
My rapture seem'd a pleasing dream,
  The grace appear'd so great.

2 The world beheld the glorious change,
  And did thy hand confess;
My tongue broke out in unknown strains,
  And sung surprising grace.

3 "Great is the work," my neighbors cried,
  And own'd thy pow'r divine;
"Great is the work," my heart replied,
  "And be the glory thine."

4 The Lord can clear the darkest skies,
  Can give us day for night;
Make drops of sacred sorrow rise
  To rivers of delight.

5 Let those that sow in sadness wait
  Till the fair harvest come;
They shall confess their sheaves are great,
  And bring rich blessings home.

453   *Joy in God.*   363

MY soul doth magnify the Lord,
   My spirit doth rejoice
In God, my Savior, and *my* God;
   I hear his joyful voice.

2 I need not go abroad for joy,
   Who have a feast at home;
My sighs are now turn'd into songs—
   The Comforter is come.

3 Down from on high, the blessed Dove
   Is come into my breast,
To witness God's eternal love;
   This is my heav'nly feast.

4 There is a stream that issues forth
   From God's eternal throne,
And from the Lamb, a living stream,
   Clear as the crystal stone.

5 That stream doth water paradise;
   It makes the angels sing;
One cordial drop revives my heart;
   Hence all my joys do spring.

454   *Joys of Piety.*   369

OH, happy soul that lives on high!
   While men lie grov'ling here,
His hopes are fix'd above the sky,
   And faith forbids his fear.

2 His conscience knows no secret stings,
   While grace and joy combine
To form a life whose holy springs
   Are hidden and divine.

3 He waits in secret on his God;
   His God in secret sees;
Let earth be all in arms abroad,
   He dwells in heav'nly peace.

4 His pleasures rise from things unseen,
   Beyond this world and time,
Where neither eyes nor ears have been,
   Nor thoughts of mortals climb.

5 He looks to heav'n's eternal hill,
   To meet that glorious day:
But patient waits his Savior's will
   To fetch his soul away.

455   *Living by Faith.*   372

HAPPY the man whose wishes climb
   To mansions in the skies!
He looks on all the joys of time
   With undesiring eyes.

2 In vain soft pleasure spreads her charms,
   And throws her silken chain;
And wealth and fame invite his arms
   And tempt his ear in vain.

3 He knows that all these glitt'ring things
   Must yield to sure decay;
And sees on time's extended wings
   How swift they flee away.

4 To things unseen by mortal eyes,
   A beam of sacred light
Directs his view; his prospects rise
   All permanent and bright.

5 His hopes are fix'd on joys to come:
   Those blissful scenes on high
Shall flourish in immortal bloom
   When time and nature die.

456   *Joy in God.*   425

ARISE, my soul, my joyful powers,
   And triumph in my God;
Awake, my voice, and loud proclaim
   His glorious grace abroad.

2 The arms of everlasting love
   Beneath my soul he plac'd,
And on the Rock of ages set
   My slipp'ry footsteps fast.

3 The city of my blest abode
   Is wall'd around with grace;
Salvation for a bulwark stands
   To shield the sacred place.

4 Arise, my soul; awake, my voice,
   And tunes of pleasure sing;
Loud hallelujahs shall address
   My Savior and my King.

457   *Peace Returning.*

OH, speak that gracious word again,
   And cheer my drooping heart!
No voice but thine can soothe my pain,
   And bid my fears depart.

2 And canst thou still vouchsafe to own
   A worm so vile as I?
And may I still approach thy throne,
   And Abba, Father, cry?

3 My Savior, by his powerful word,
   Hath turn'd my night to day;
And all those heavenly joys restor'd,
   Which I had sinn'd away.

4 Dear Lord! I wonder and adore;
   Thy grace is all divine:
Oh, keep me, that I sin no more
   Against such love as thine.

CHRISTIAN EXPERIENCE—JOY AND HOPE.

C. M. BARBY.

1. Blest are the un-de-fil'd in heart, Whose ways are right and clean, Who nev-er from thy law de-part, But fly from ev'-ry sin.

458 *Blessedness of Saints.* **210**

BLEST are the undefil'd in heart,
 Whose ways are right and clean,
Who never from thy law depart,
 But fly from ev'ry sin.

2 Blest are the men that keep thy word,
 And practice thy commands;
With their whole hearts they seek the Lord
 And serve thee with their hands.

3 Great is their peace who love thy law;
 How firm their souls abide!
Nor can a bold temptation draw
 Their steady feet aside.

4 Then shall my heart have inward joy
 And keep my face from shame,
When all thy statutes I obey,
 And honor all thy name.

459 *God's Presence is Light.* **472**

MY God, the spring of all my joys,
 The life of my delights,
The glory of my brightest days,
 And comfort of my nights.

2 In darkest shades if he appear,
 My dawning is begun;
He is my soul's sweet morning star,
 And he my rising sun.

3 The op'ning heav'ns around me shine
 With beams of sacred bliss,
While Jesus shows his heart is mine,
 And whispers I am his!

4 My soul would leave this heavy clay
 At that transporting word,
Run up with joy the shining way
 T' embrace my dearest Lord.

5 Fearless of hell and ghastly death,
 I'd break through every foe;
The wings of love, and arms of faith
 Should bear me conq'ror through.

460 *Jesus Precious.* **386**

BLEST Jesus, when my soaring tho'ts
 O'er all thy graces rove,
Now is my soul in transport lost—
 In wonder, joy, and love!

2 Not softest strains can charm mine ears,
 Like thy beloved name;
Nor aught beneath the skies inspire
 My heart with equal flame.

3 Where'er I look, my wond'ring eyes
 Unnumber'd blessings see:
But what is life, with all its bliss,
 If once compar'd to thee?

4 Hast thou a rival in my breast?
 Search, Lord, for thou canst tell;
If aught can raise my passions thus,
 Or please my soul so well.

5 No, thou art precious to my heart,
 My portion and my joy;
Forever let thy boundless grace
 My sweetest thoughts employ.

6 When nature faints, around my bed
 Let thy bright glories shine;
And death shall all his terrors lose,
 In raptures so divine.

CHRISTIAN EXPERIENCE—JOY AND HOPE.

C. M. ST. ANN'S.

1. My God, my portion and my love! My ev-er-last-ing all! I've none but thee in heav'n a-bove, Or on this earth-ly ball.

461 *God the Portion of the Soul.* **286**

MY God, my portion and my love!
   My everlasting all!
I've none but thee in heav'n above,
   Or on this earthly ball.

2 In vain the bright meridian sun
   Scatters his feeble light:
Thy brighter beams create my noon;
   If thou withdraw, 'tis night.

3 And while upon my restless bed,
   Amongst the shades I roll,
If Christ his light around me shed,
   'Tis morning with my soul.

4 To thee I owe my wealth and friends,
   And health, and safe abode:
Thanks to thy name for meaner things;
   But they are not my God.

5 If I possess'd the spacious earth,
   And call'd the stars my own,
Without thy mercy and thyself,
   I were a wretch undone.

6 Let others stretch their arms like seas,
   And grasp in all the shore;
Grant me to see thy blissful face,
   And I desire no more!

462 *Following Christ.* **454**

OUR country is Immanuel's ground,
   We seek that promis'd soil:
The songs of Zion cheer our hearts,
   While strangers here we toil.

2 Oft do our eyes with joy o'erflow,
   And oft are bath'd in tears;
Yet naught but heav'n our hopes can raise,
   And naught but sin our fears.

3 The flow'rs, that spring along the road,
   We scarcely stoop to pluck;
We walk o'er beds of shining ore,
   Nor waste one anxious look.

4 We tread the path our Master trod;
   We bear the cross he bore;
And ev'ry thorn, that wounds our feet,
   His temples pierc'd before.

5 Our pow'rs are oft dissolv'd away
   In ecstasies of love;
And while our bodies wander here,
   Our souls are fix'd above.

463 *Parting with all for Christ.* **269**

YE glitt'ring toys of earth, adieu;
   A nobler choice be mine:
A heav'nly prize attracts my view,
   A treasure all divine.

2 Jesus, to multitudes unknown,—
   O name divinely sweet!—
Jesus, in thee, in thee alone,
   True wealth and honor meet.

3 Should earth's vain treasures all depart,
   Of this dear gift possest,
I'd clasp it to my joyful heart,
   And be forever blest.

4 Dear portion of my soul's desires,
   Thy love is bliss divine;
Accept the wish that love inspires,
   And let me call thee mine.

CHRISTIAN EXPERIENCE—JOY AND HOPE.

L. M. LURMAN.

1. I hear a voice that comes from far, From Calvary it sounds abroad; It soothes my soul, and calms my fear; It speaks of pardon bought with blood.

464   *Joy in the Gospel.*   359

I HEAR a voice that comes from far,
   From Calvary it sounds abroad;
It soothes my soul, and calms my fear;
It speaks of pardon bought with blood.

2 And is it true that many fly
The sound that bids my soul rejoice,
And rather choose in sin to die,
Than turn an ear to mercy's voice?

3 Alas for those!—the day is near
When mercy will be heard no more;
Then will they ask, in vain, to hear
The voice they would not hear before.

4 With such, I own, I once appear'd,
But now I know how great their loss;
For sweeter sounds were never heard
Than mercy utters from the cross.

465   *The Prospects of Faith.*   371

THERE is a glorious world on high,
   Resplendent with eternal day;
Faith views the blissful prospects nigh,
While God's own word reveals the way.

2 There shall the fav'rites of the Lord
With never-fading luster shine,
Surprising honor! vast reward!
Conferr'd on man by love divine.

3 How blest are those, how truly wise,
Who learn and keep the sacred road!
Happy the men, whom heav'n employs
To turn rebellious hearts to God!

4 To win them from the fatal way
Where erring folly thoughtless roves;

And that blest righteousness display,
Which Jesus wrought and God approves.

5 The shining firmament shall fade,
And sparkling stars resign their light:
But these shall know nor change nor shade,
Forever fair, forever bright.

6 On wings of faith and strong desire,
Oh, may our spirits daily rise;
And reach at last the shining choir,
In the bright mansions of the skies!

466   *Bliss of Salvation.*   365

INDULGENT God! to thee I raise
   My spirit fraught with joy and praise:
Grateful I bow before thy throne,
My debt of mercy there to own.

2 Rivers descending, Lord! from thee,
Perpetual glide to solace me:
Their varied virtues to rehearse,
Demands an everlasting verse.

3 And yet there is, beyond the rest,
One stream—the widest and the best—
Salvation! Lo, the purple flood
Rolls rich with my Redeemer's blood.

4 I taste—delight succeeds to woe;
I bathe—no waters cleanse me so:
Such joy and purity to share,
I would remain enraptur'd there.

5 My soul—with such a scene in view—
Bids mortal joys a glad adieu;
Nor dreads a few chastising woes
Sent with such love—so soon to close.

CHRISTIAN EXPERIENCE—JOY AND HOPE.

M. IOSCO.

1. Not all the no-bles of the earth, Who boast the ho-nors of their birth, Such re-al dig-ni-ty can claim, As those who bear the Chris-tian name.

Privileges of Believers. **368**

[N]ll the nobles of the earth,
[W]ho boast the honors of their birth,
[Re]al dignity can claim,
[A]s who bear the Christian name.

[Th]em the privilege is giv'n
[Th]e sons and heirs of heav'n;
[In] the God who reigns on high,
[He]irs of joy beyond the sky.

[T]ill he makes them early know,
[T]eaches their young feet to go;
[Gi]ves instruction to their minds,
[As] their hearts his precepts binds.

[Their] daily wants his hands supply;
[Their st]eps he guards with watchful eye;
[Leads] them from earth to heav'n above,
[And cr]owns them with eternal love.

[For] the honor, Lord, to be
[Of t]his num'rous family,
[On t]he gracious gift bestow,
[Call] thee Abba, Father, too.

[Ma]y my conduct ever prove
[Fill]'d piety and love!
[In] all my brethren clearly trace
[My F]ather's likeness in my face.

Christ our Righteousness. **867**

[JESUS], thy blood and righteousness
[My] beauty are, my glorious dress:
['Mid] flaming worlds, in these array'd,
[With jo]y shall I lift up my head.

[When] from the dust of death I rise,
[To claim] my mansion in the skies,

E'en then shall this be all my plea—
"Jesus hath liv'd, hath died for me."

3 Bold shall I stand in that great day,
For who aught to my charge shall lay?
Fully, through thee, absolv'd I am
From sin and fear, from guilt and shame.

4 This spotless robe the same appears
When ruin'd nature sinks in years;
No age can change its glorious hue,
The robe of Christ is ever new.

5 And when the dead shall hear thy voice,
Thy banish'd children shall rejoice;
Their beauty this, their glorious dress,
Jesus, the Lord our righteousness.

469 *Blessedness of Salvation.* **364**

BLEST is the man, forever blest,
Whose guilt is pardon'd by his God,
Whose sins with sorrow are confess'd,
And cover'd with his Savior's blood.

2 Blest is the man to whom the Lord
Imputes not his iniquities,
He pleads no merit of reward,
And not on works, but grace, relies.

3 From guile his heart and lips are free;
His humble joy, his holy fear,
With deep repentance well agree,
And join to prove his faith sincere.

4 How glorious is that righteousness
That hides and cancels all his sins!
While a bright evidence of grace
Through his whole life appears and shines.

CHRISTIAN EXPERIENCE—JOY AND HOPE.

S. M. LABAN.

1. How various and how new Are thy compassions, Lord! Each morning shall thy mercies show, Each night thy love record.

470 *Joy in the Lord.* **361**

HOW various and how new
  Are thy compassions, Lord!
Each morning shall thy mercies show,
  Each night thy love record.

2 Thy goodness, like the sun,
  Dawn'd on our early days,
Ere infant reason had begun
  To form our lips to praise.

3 Each object we beheld
  Gave pleasure to our eyes,
And nature all our senses held
  In bands of sweet surprise.

4 But pleasures more refin'd
  Awaited that blest day,
When light arose upon our mind
  To chase our sins away.

5 How new thy mercies then!
  How sov'reign and how free!
Our souls that had been dead in sin
  Were made alive to thee.

471 *Heavenly Joy on Earth.* **367**

COME, ye that love the Lord,
  And let your joys be known;
Join in a song with sweet accord,
  Whilst ye surround the throne.

2 Let those refuse to sing
  Who never knew our God;
But servants of the heav'nly King
  May speak their joys abroad.

3 The God who rules on high,
  Who all the earth surveys,
Who rides upon the stormy sky
  And calms the roaring seas:

4 This awful God is ours,
  Our Father and our love;
He will send down his heav'nly pow'rs
  To carry us above.

5 There we shall see his face,
  And never, never sin!
There, from the rivers of his grace,
  Drink endless pleasures in.

6 Yea, and before we rise
  To that immortal state,
The thoughts of such amazing bliss
  Should constant joys create.

7 The men of grace have found
  Glory begun below:
Celestial fruit on earthly ground
  From faith and hope may grow.

8 Then let our songs abound,
  And ev'ry tear be dry:
We're marching thro' Immanuel's ground
  To fairer worlds on high.

472 *Joys of Religion.* **370**

WHEN gloomy thoughts and fears
  The trembling heart invade,
And all the face of nature wears
  A universal shade;

2 Religion can assuage
  The tempest of the soul;
And ev'ry fear shall lose its rage
  At her divine control.

3 Through life's bewilder'd way,
  Her hand unerring leads;
And o'er the path her heav'nly ray
  A cheering lustre sheds.

CHRISTIAN EXPERIENCE—JOY AND HOPE.

4 When reason, tir'd and blind,
  Sinks helpless and afraid,
Thou blest supporter of the mind,
  How pow'rful is thine aid!

5 Oh, let me feel thy pow'r,
  And find thy sweet relief,
To brighten ev'ry gloomy hour,
  And soften ev'ry grief.

473 *It is well.* 468

WHAT cheering words are these!
    Their sweetness who can tell?
In time and to eternity,
  'Tis with the righteous well.

2 In ev'ry state secure,
  Kept by Jehovah's eye,
'Tis well with them while life endures,
  And well when call'd to die.

3 'Tis well when joys arise,
  'Tis well when sorrows flow;
'Tis well when darkness veils the skies,
  And strong temptations blow.

4 'Tis well when on the mount
  They feast on dying love;
And 'tis as well, in God's account,
  When they the furnace prove.

5 'Tis well when at his throne
  They wrestle, weep, and pray;
'Tis well when at his feet they groan,
  Yet bring their wants away.

6 'Tis well when Jesus calls,
  From earth and sin, arise,
Join with the hosts of blood-bought souls,
  Made to salvation wise.

474 *Abba, Father.* 428

MY Father! cheering name!
    Oh, may I call thee mine!
Give me with humble hope to claim
  A portion so divine.

2 This can my fears control,
  And bid my sorrows fly;
What real harm can reach my soul
  Beneath my Father's eye?

3 Whate'er thy will denies,
  I calmly would resign;
For thou art just, and good, and wise:
  Oh, bend my will to thine!

4 Whate'er thy will ordains,
  Oh, give me strength to bear;
Still let me know a Father reigns,
  And trust a Father's care.

5 Thy ways are little known
  To my weak, erring sight;

Yet shall my soul, believing, own
  That all thy ways are right.

6 My Father! blissful name!
  Beyond expression dear:
If thou admit my humble claim,
  I bid adieu to fear.

475 *Saved by Grace.* 316

GRACE! 'tis a charming sound!
    Harmonious to the ear!
Hear'n with the echo shall resound,
  And all the earth shall hear.

2 Grace first contriv'd the way
  To save rebellious man;
And all the steps *that* grace display
  Which drew the wondrous plan.

3 Grace led my roving feet
  To tread the heav'nly road;
And new supplies, each hour, I meet,
  While pressing on to God.

4 Grace taught my soul to pray,
  And made my eyes o'erflow:
'Twas grace which kept me to this day,
  And will not let me go.

5 Grace all the work shall crown,
  Through everlasting days;
It lays in heav'n the topmost stone,
  And well deserves the praise.

476 *The Joyful Song.* 914

AWAKE, and sing the song
    Of Moses and the Lamb;
Wake, ev'ry heart, and ev'ry tongue,
  To praise the Savior's name.

2 Sing of his dying love;
  Sing of his rising power;
Sing how he intercedes, above,
  For us, whose sins he bore.

3 Sing, till we feel our heart
  Ascending with our tongue;
Sing, till the love of sin depart,
  And grace inspire our song.

4 Sing on your heav'nly way,
  Ye ransom'd sinners, sing;
Sing on, rejoicing ev'ry day
  In Christ, th' eternal King.

5 Soon shall we hear him say,
  "Ye blessed children, come!"
Soon will he call us hence away
  To our eternal home.

6 There shall our raptur'd tongue
  His endless praise proclaim,
And sweeter voices tune the song
  Of Moses and the Lamb.

C. M. DEVIZES.

1. God, my support-er and my hope, My help for-ev - er near! Thine arm of mer-cy holds me up, And saves me from de - spair. And saves me from de - spair.

477 *God our Portion.* **287**

GOD, my supporter and my hope,
  My help forever near !
Thine arm of mercy holds me up,
And saves me from despair.

2 Thy counsels, Lord ! shall guide my feet
  Through this dark wilderness ;
Thy hand conduct me near thy seat,
  To dwell before thy face.

3 Were I in heav'n without my God,
  'Twould be no joy to me ;
And whilst this earth is my abode,
  I long for none but thee.

4 What if the springs of life were broke,
  And flesh and heart should faint ?
God is my soul's eternal rock,
  The strength of ev'ry saint.

5 Behold, the sinners, that remove
  Far from thy presence, die ;
Not all the idol-gods they love
  Can save them when they cry.

478 *Humble Joy.* **489**

FAIN would my soul with wonder trace
  Thy mercies, O my God !
And tell the riches of thy grace—
  The merits of thy blood.

2 With Israel's King, my heart would cry,
  While I review thy ways,
Tell me, my Savior, who am I,
  That I should see thy face ?

3 Form'd by thy hand, and form'd for thee,
  I would be ever thine:

My Savior, make my spirit free,
  With beams of mercy shine.

4 Fain would my soul with rapture dwell
  On thy redeeming grace ;
Oh, for a thousand tongues to tell
  My dear Redeemer's praise.

479 *Desiring Assurance.* **799**

WHY should the children of a King
  Go mourning all their days ?
Great Comforter, descend and bring
  Some tokens of thy grace.

2 Dost thou not dwell in all thy saints,
  And seal them, heirs of heav'n ?
When wilt thou banish my complaints,
  And show my sins forgiv'n ?

3 Assure my conscience of her part
  In my Redeemer's blood,
And bear thy witness, with my heart,
  That I am born of God.

4 Thou art the earnest of his love,
  The pledge of joys to come ;
And thy soft wings, celestial Dove,
  Will safely bear me home.

480 *Mourning and Rejoicing at the Cross.*

PREPARE us, Lord, to view thy cross,
  Who all our griefs hast borne ;
To look on thee, whom we have pierc'd,
  To look on thee, and mourn.

2 While thus we mourn, we would rejoice ;
  And, as thy cross we see,
Let each exclaim, in faith and hope,
  "The Savior died for me !"

CHRISTIAN EXPERIENCE—JOY AND HOPE.

C. M. ARLINGTON.

1. A-maz-ing grace!—how sweet the sound, That sav'd a wretch like me!
I once was lost, but now am found, Was blind, but now I see.

481 *Saving Grace.* **848**

AMAZING grace! how sweet the sound,
That sav'd a wretch like me!
I once was lost, but now am found,
Was blind, but now I see.

2 'Twas grace that taught my heart to fear,
'Twas grace my fears reliev'd;
How precious did that grace appear,
The hour I first believ'd!

3 Thro' many dangers, toils, and snares,
I have already come;
'Tis grace has brought me safe thus far,
And grace will lead me home.

4 Yes, when this flesh and heart shall fail,
And mortal life shall cease,
I shall possess within the vail
A life of joy and peace.

482 *Thanks for God's Mercies.* **851**

WHEN all thy mercies, O my God,
My rising soul surveys,
Transported with the view, I'm lost
In wonder, love, and praise.

2 Unnumber'd comforts on my soul
Thy tender care bestow'd,
Before my infant heart conceiv'd
From whom those comforts flow'd.

3 When in the slipp'ry paths of youth
With heedless steps I ran,
Thine arm, unseen, convey'd me safe,
And led me up to man.

4 Ten thousand thousand precious gifts
My daily thanks employ;
Nor is the least a cheerful heart,
That tastes those gifts with joy.

5 Through ev'ry period of my life
Thy goodness I'll pursue;
And after death, in distant worlds,
The glorious theme renew.

6 Through all eternity, to thee
A grateful song I'll raise;
But, oh, eternity's too short
To utter all thy praise.

483 *Encouragement from Christ.* **143**

HARK! 'tis our heav'nly Leader's voice
From the bright realms above;
Amidst the war's tumultuous rage,
A voice of pow'r and love.

2 "Fight on, my faithful band," he cries,
"Nor fear the mortal blow;
Who first in such a warfare dies
Shall speediest vict'ry know.

3 "I have my days of combat known,
And in the dust was laid;
But thence I mounted to my throne,
And glory crowns my head.

4 "This throne and glory you shall share;
My hands the crown shall give:
And you the sparkling honors wear,
While God himself shall live."

5 Lord! 'tis enough: our souls are fir'd
With courage and with love;
Vain are th' assaults of earth and hell;
Our hopes are fix'd above.

6 We'll trace the footsteps thou hast drawn
To triumph and renown;
Nor shun thy combat and thy cross,
May we but share thy crown.

CHRISTIAN EXPERIENCE—JOY AND HOPE.

8s & 7s. OTTO.

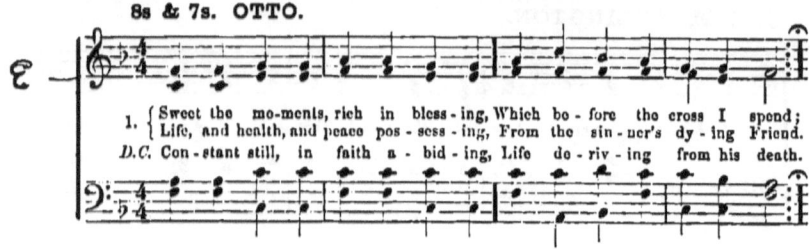

1. Sweet the moments, rich in blessing, Which before the cross I spend;
   Life, and health, and peace possessing, From the sinner's dying Friend.
   D.C. Constant still, in faith abiding, Life deriving from his death.

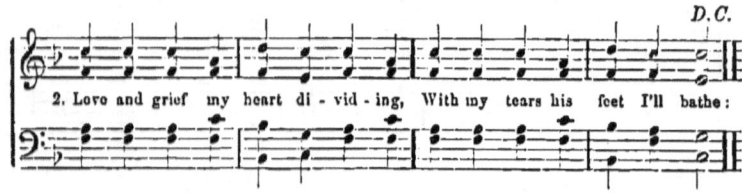

2. Love and grief my heart dividing, With my tears his feet I'll bathe:

---

484 *Sitting at Jesus' Feet.* **374**

SWEET the moments, rich in blessing,
Which before the cross I spend;
Life, and health, and peace possessing,
From the sinner's dying Friend.

2 Love and grief my heart dividing,
With my tears his feet I'll bathe:
Constant still, in faith abiding,
Life deriving from his death.

3 Truly blessed is this station—
Low before his cross I'll lie;
While I see divine compassion
Floating in his languid eye;

4 Here I'll sit—forever viewing
Mercy streaming in his blood:
Precious drops, my soul bedewing,
Plead and claim my peace with God.

485 *Joy in Divine Mercy.*

GOD is love; his mercy brightens
All the path in which we rove;
Bliss he wakes, and woe he lightens;
God is wisdom, God is love.

2 Chance and change are busy ever;
Man decays, and ages move;
But his mercy waneth never;
God is wisdom, God is love.

3 E'en the hour that darkest seemeth
Will his changeless goodness prove;
From the gloom his brightness streameth;
God is wisdom, God is love.

4 He with earthly cares entwineth
Hope and comfort from above;
Ev'rywhere his glory shineth;
God is wisdom, God is love.

486 *A Miracle of Grace.* **325**

HAIL! my ever-blessed Jesus,
Only thee I wish to sing;
To my soul thy name is precious,
Thou my prophet, priest, and king.

2 Oh, what mercy flows from heav'n,
Oh, what joy and happiness!
Love I much? I've much forgiv'n,
I'm a miracle of grace.

3 Once with Adam's race in ruin,
Unconcern'd in sin I lay;
Swift destruction still pursuing,
Till my Savior pass'd this way.

4 Witness, all ye hosts of heaven,
My Redeemer's tenderness;
Love I much? I've much forgiven,
I'm a miracle of grace.

5 Sing, ye bright angelic choir,
Praise the Lamb enthron'd above:
Whilst, astonish'd, I admire
God's free grace and boundless love.

6 That blest moment I receiv'd him,
Fill'd my soul with joy and peace;
Love I much? I've much forgiv'n,
I'm a miracle of grace.

CHRISTIAN EXPERIENCE—JOY AND HOPE. 167

487 *Grateful Recollections.* **452**

COME, thou fount of ev'ry blessing,
  Tune my heart to sing thy grace;
Streams of mercy, never ceasing,
  Call for songs of loudest praise:
Teach me some melodious sonnet
  Sung by flaming tongues above;
Praise the mount, oh, fix me on it!
  Mount of God's unchanging love.

2 Here I raise mine Ebenezer,
  Hither by thy help I've come,
And I hope, by thy good pleasure,
  Safely to arrive at home:
Jesus sought me when a stranger,
  Wand'ring from the fold of God;
He, to save my soul from danger,
  Interpos'd his precious blood.

3 Oh, to grace how great a debtor
  Daily I'm constrain'd to be!
Let that grace, Lord, like a fetter,
  Bind my wand'ring heart to thee!
Prone to wander, Lord, I feel it;
  Prone to leave the God I love—
Here's my heart, Lord, take and seal it,
  Seal it from thy courts above.

8s, 7s. SICILIAN HYMN.

1. Wel-come, wel-come, dear Re-deem-er, Wel-come to this heart of mine;
   Lord, I make a full sur-ren-der, Ev'-ry pow'r and thought be thine,

Thine en-tire-ly, Thine en-tire-ly, Through e-ter-nal a-ges thine.

488 *Joyful Surrender.* **305**

WELCOME, welcome, dear Redeemer,
  Welcome to this heart of mine;
Lord, I make a full surrender,
  Ev'ry pow'r and thought be thine,
Thine entirely,
  Through eternal ages thine.

2 Known to all to be thy mansion,
  Earth and hell will disappear,
Or in vain attempt possession,
  When they find the Lord is near—
Shout, O Zion!
  Shout, ye saints, the Lord is here!

489 *Joy of Conversion.* **358**

ON the brink of fiery ruin,
  Justice, with a flaming sword,
Was my guilty soul pursuing,
  When I first beheld my Lord.

2 Terrified with Sinai's thunder,
  Straight I flew to Calvary,
Where, by faith, with love and wonder,
  Him I saw who died for me.

3 "Sinner," he exclaim'd, "I've lov'd thee
  With an everlasting love:
Justice has in me approv'd thee;
  Thou shalt dwell with me above."

4 Sweet as angels' notes in heaven,
  When to golden harps they sound,
Is the voice of sins forgiven,
  To the soul by Satan bound.

5 Sweet as angels' harps in glory
  Was that heav'nly voice to me,
When I saw my Lord before me
  Bleed and die to set me free!

6 Saints, attend with holy wonder!
  Sinners, hear and sing his praise!
'Tis the God that holds the thunder
  Shows himself the God of grace!

CHRISTIAN EXPERIENCE—JOY AND HOPE.

C. M. P. ARIEL.

1. How happy is the pilgrim's lot, How free from ev'ry anxious thought, From worldly hope and fear!

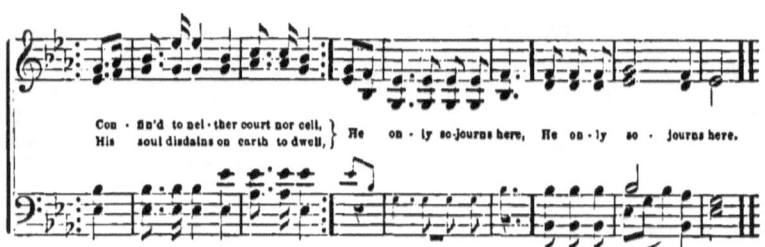

Confin'd to neither court nor cell, His soul disdains on earth to dwell, He on-ly so-journs here, He on-ly so-journs here.

490   *The Happy Lot.*   451

HOW happy is the pilgrim's lot,
  How free from ev'ry anxious thought,
From worldly hope and fear!
Confin'd to neither court nor cell,
His soul disdains on earth to dwell,
  He only sojourns here.

2 Though I no foot of land possess,
Nor cottage in this wilderness,
  A poor wayfaring man,
I lodge a while in tents below,
Or gladly wander to and fro
  Till I my Canaan gain.

3 Nothing on earth I call my own;
A stranger to the world unknown,
  I all their goods despise;
I trample on their whole delight,
And seek a city out of sight—
  A city in the skies.

4 There is my house and portion fair,
My treasure and my heart are there,
  And my abiding home;
For me my elder brethren stay,
And angels beckon me away,
  And Jesus bids me come!

5 I come, thy servant, Lord, replies,
I come, to meet thee in the skies
  And claim my heav'nly rest!

Now let the pilgrim's journey end;
Now, O my Savior, brother, friend,
  Receive me to thy breast!

491   *Joy in God's Service.*   382

HOW happy, gracious Lord, are we!
  Divinely drawn to follow thee;
Whose hours divided are
Betwixt the mount and multitude:
Our day is spent in doing good,
  Our night in praise and pray'r.

2 With us, no melancholy void;
No moments linger unemploy'd,
  Or unimprov'd below;
Our weariness of life is gone,
Who live to serve our God alone
  And only thee to know.

3 The winter's night and summer's day
Glide imperceptibly away,
  Too short to sing thy praise;
Too few we find the happy hours,
And haste to join those heav'nly pow'rs
  In everlasting lays.

4 With all who chant thy name on high,
And "Holy, holy, holy!" cry,
  A bright, harmonious throng,
We long thy praises to repeat,
And ceaseless sing around thy seat
  The new eternal song.

CHRISTIAN EXPERIENCE—JOY AND HOPE. 109

ELIAS. 6 lines, 8s.

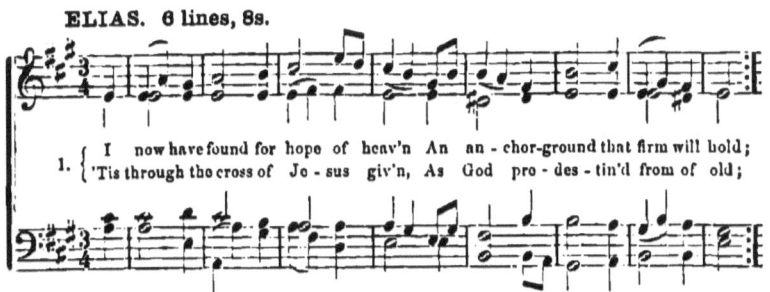

1. I now have found for hope of heav'n An an-chor-ground that firm will hold;
'Tis through the cross of Je-sus giv'n, As God pre-des-tin'd from of old;

The ground which shall en-dur-ing stay When earth and skies have pass'd a-way.

---

492 *Christ the Anchor of the Soul.* **357**

I NOW have found for hope of heav'n
   An anchor-ground that firm will hold;
'Tis through the cross of Jesus giv'n,
As God predestin'd from of old;
The ground which shall enduring stay
When earth and skies have pass'd away.

2 'Tis mercy—mercy without end,
Whose measure all our thoughts excels;
'Tis pity's arms, which wide extend,
Proving how God for sinners feels;
'Tis sweet compassion as it flows
To save us from eternal woes.

3 Were I depriv'd of all beside,
That could my soul or body cheer;
Should every grief of earth betide,
And not a friend be left me here;
I still have peace 'mid all my pains,
While pard'ning love my joy remains.

4 Upon this rock my soul shall stay
As long as on the earth I roam:
Here will I hope, and work, and pray,
Till God shall send to call me home.
On joyous wings I then shall rise,
And sing his mercy in the skies.

493 *The Joys of Pardon.*

GREAT God of wonders! all thy ways
   Are matchless, heav'nly, and divine:
But the bright glories of thy grace
More godlike and unrival'd shine;
Who is a pard'ning God like thee?
Or who has grace so rich and free?

2 Sins of such horror to forgive,
Such guilty, daring worms to spare—
This is thy grand prerogative,
And none shall in thine honor share.
Who is a pard'ning God like thee?
Or who has grace so rich and free?

3 Oh, may this vast, this matchless grace,
This godlike miracle of love,
Fill the wide earth with grateful praise,
And all the angelic choirs above.
Who is a pard'ning God like thee?
Or who has grace so rich and free?

4 In wonder lost, with trembling joy
We take the pardon of our God—
Pardon for sins of deepest dye,
A pardon giv'n through Jesus' blood.
Who is a pard'ning God like thee?
Or who has grace so rich and free?

CHRISTIAN EXPERIENCE—JOY AND HOPE.

L. M. BROWER.

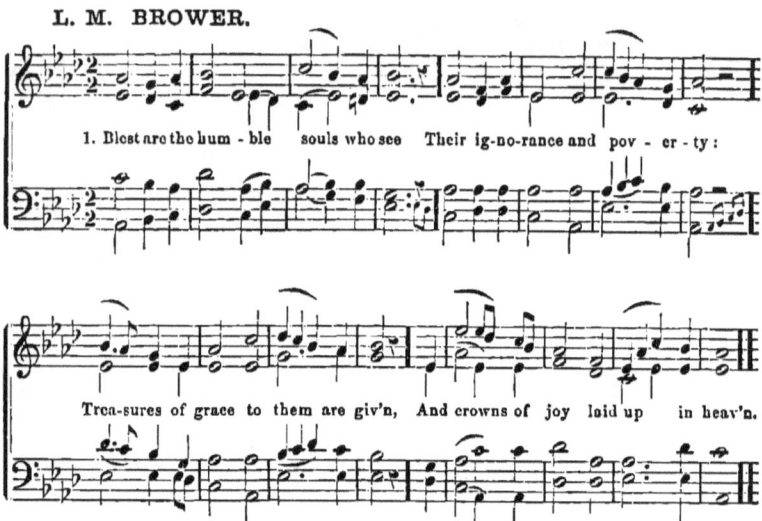

1. Blest are the humble souls who see Their ig-no-rance and pov-er-ty: Trea-sures of grace to them are giv'n, And crowns of joy laid up in heav'n.

494   *The Blessed.*   209

BLEST are the humble souls who see
Their emptiness and poverty :
Treasures of grace to them are giv'n,
And crowns of joy laid up in heav'n.

2 Blest are the men of broken heart,
Who mourn for sin with inward smart;
The blood of Christ divinely flows,
A healing balm for all their woes.

3 Blest are the meek, who stand afar
From rage and passion, noise and war;
God will secure their happy state,
And plead their cause against the great.

4 Blest are the souls who thirst for grace,
Hunger and long for righteousness :
They shall be well supplied and fed
With living streams and living bread.

5 Blest are the men whose hearts still move
And melt with sympathy and love :
From Christ the Lord they shall obtain
Like sympathy and love again.

6 Blest are the pure, whose hearts are clean
From the defiling power of sin :
With endless pleasure they shall see
A God of spotless purity.

7 Blest are the men of peaceful life,
Who quench the coals of growing strife ;
They shall be call'd the heirs of bliss,
The sons of God, the God of peace.

8 Blest are the suff'rers who partake
Of pain and shame for Jesus' sake :
Their souls shall triumph in the Lord,
Glory and joy are their reward.

495   *Blessedness of Religion.*   211

THROUGH shades and solitudes profound
The fainting trav'ler wends his way;
Bewild'ring meteors glare around,
And tempt his wand'ring feet astray,

2 Till mild religion from above
Descends, a sweet, engaging form,
The messenger of heav'nly love,
The bow of promise 'mid the storm.

3 Beyond the narrow vale of time,
Where bright celestial ages roll,
To scenes eternal, scenes sublime,
She points the way and leads the soul.

4 At her approach the grave appears
The gate of Paradise restor'd ;
Her voice the watching cherub hears,
And drops the double-flaming sword.

5 Baptiz'd with her renewing fire,
May we the crown of glory gain,
Rise when the hosts of heav'n expire,
And reign with God, forever reign !

CHRISTIAN EXPERIENCE—TRIALS AND TEMPTATIONS.

S. M. McEVERS.

1. When, o-ver-whelm'd with grief, My heart with-in me dies, Help-less, and far from all re-lief, To heav'n I lift mine eyes, To heav'n I lift mine eyes.

496   *Comfort in God.*   958

WHEN, overwhelm'd with grief,
  My heart within me dies,
Helpless, and far from all relief,
To heav'n I lift mine eyes.

2 Oh, lead me to the Rock
  That's high above my head,
And make the covert of thy wings
  My shelter and my shade.

3 Within thy presence, Lord,
  Forever I'll abide;
Thou art the tow'r of my defense,
  The refuge where I hide.

4 Thou givest me the lot
  Of those that fear thy name;
If endless life be their reward,
  I shall possess the same.

497   *Fight the Good Fight.*   415

SOLDIERS of Christ, arise,
  And gird your armor on,
Strong in the strength which God supplies
  Through his eternal Son.

2 Strong in the Lord of hosts,
  And in his mighty power,
The man who in the Savior trusts
  Is more than conqueror.

3 Stand, then, in his great might,
  With all his strength endued,
And take, to arm you for the fight,
  The panoply of God;—

4 That, having all things done,
  And all your conflicts past,
You may o'ercome through Christ alone,
  And stand complete at last.

5 From strength to strength go on;
  Wrestle, and fight, and pray;
Tread all the powers of darkness down,
  And win the well-fought day.

6 Still let the Spirit cry,
  In all his soldiers, "Come,"
Till Christ the Lord descends from high,
  And takes the conqu'rors home.

498   *Watch and Pray.*   463

MY soul, be on thy guard;
  Ten thousand foes arise;
The hosts of sin are pressing hard
  To draw thee from the skies.

2 Oh, watch, and fight, and pray;
  The battle ne'er give o'er;
Renew it boldly ev'ry day,
  And help divine implore.

3 Ne'er think the vict'ry won,
  Nor lay thine armor down:
Thine arduous work will not be done
  Till thou obtain thy crown.

4 Fight on, my soul, till death
  Shall bring thee to thy God;
He'll take thee, at thy parting breath,
  To his divine abode.

172 CHRISTIAN EXPERIENCE—TRIALS.

C. M. EASTBURN.

1. Sweet was the time when first I felt The Sa-vior's pard'- ning blood Ap-plied to cleanse my soul from guilt, And bring me home to God.

499 *Spiritual Declension.* **396**

SWEET was the time when first I felt
  The Savior's pard'ning blood
Applied to cleanse my soul from guilt,
  And bring me home to God.

2 Soon as the morn the light reveal'd,
  His praises tun'd my tongue;
And, when the ev'ning shades prevail'd,
  His love was all my song.

3 In vain the tempter spread his wiles,
  The world no more could charm;
I liv'd upon my Savior's smiles,
  And lean'd upon his arm.

4 In prayer, my soul drew near the Lord,
  And saw his glory shine;
And, when I read his holy word,
  I call'd each promise mine.

5 Now when the ev'ning shade prevails,
  My soul in darkness mourns;
And when the morn the light reveals,
  No light to me returns.

6 Now Satan threatens to prevail,
  And make my soul his prey;
Yet, Lord, thy mercies cannot fail,
  Oh, come without delay!

500 *Under Darkness.* **398**

REJOICE in God, the word commands,
  And fain would I obey;
Yet still my spirit, ling'ring, stands,
  While doubts impede my way.

2 How can my soul exult for joy,
  Which feels this load of sin,
And how can praise my tongue employ,
  While darkness reigns within?

3 If falling tears and rising sighs
  In triumph share a part,
Then, Lord, behold these streaming eyes,
  And search this bleeding heart!

4 My soul forgets to use her wings;
  My harp neglected lies;
For sin has broken all its strings,
  And guilt shuts out my joys.

5 The power, the sweetness of thy voice,
  Alone my heart can move;
Make me in Christ my Lord rejoice,
  And melt my soul to love.

501 *Holy Fortitude.* **462**

AM I a soldier of the cross,
  A follower of the Lamb?
And shall I fear to own his cause,
  Or blush to speak his name?

2 Must I be carried to the skies
  On flow'ry beds of ease,
While others fought to win the prize,
  And sail'd through bloody seas?

3 Are there no foes for me to face?
  Must I not stem the flood?
Is this vile world a friend to grace,
  To help me on to God?

4 Sure I must fight, if I would reign;
  Increase my courage, Lord!
I'll bear the toil, endure the pain,
  Supported by thy word.

5 Thy saints in all this glorious war
  Shall conquer though they die;
They see the triumph from afar,
  And seize it with their eye.

CHRISTIAN EXPERIENCE—TRIALS. 173

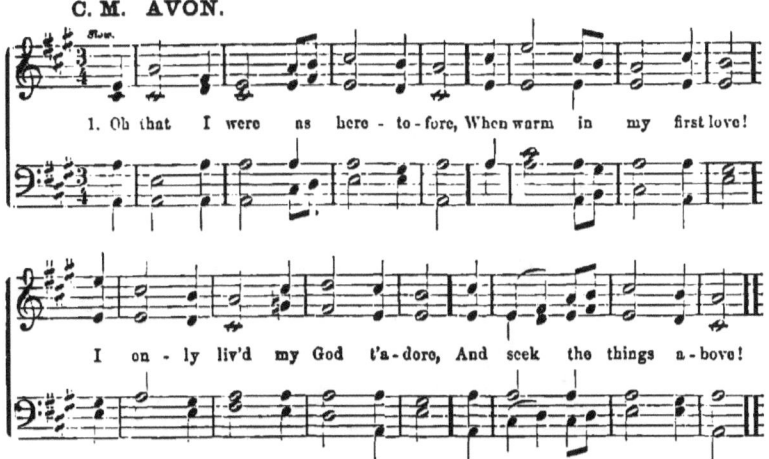

C. M. AVON.

1. Oh that I were as here-to-fore, When warm in my first love!
I on-ly liv'd my God t'a-dore, And seek the things a-bove!

502 *Under Depression.* **418**

OH that I were as heretofore,
   When warm in my first love!
I only liv'd my God t' adore,
And seek the things above!

2 Upon this head his candle shone,
   And, lavish of his grace,
With cords of love he drew me on,
And half unvail'd his face.

3 Far, far above all earthly things
   Triumphantly I rode;
I soar'd to heaven on eagles' wings,
And found and talk'd with God.

4 Where am I now! from what a height
Of happiness cast down!
The glory swallow'd up in night,
And faded is the crown.

5 O God, thou art my home, my rest,
For which I sigh in pain!
How shall I 'scape into thy breast,
My Eden how regain?

503 *Under Darkness.*

HEAR, gracious God! my humble moan,
   To thee I breathe my sighs;
When will this mournful night be gone,
And when my joys arise!

2 By every name of power and love,
   I would thy grace entreat;
Let not my humble hopes remove,
Nor leave thy mercy-seat.

3 Though now my soul in darkness mourns,
   Thy word is all my stay;
Here I would rest till light returns;—
Thy presence makes my day.

4 Speak, Lord! and bid celestial peace
Relieve my aching heart;
Oh, smile, and bid my sorrows cease,
And all the gloom depart.

5 Then shall my drooping spirits rise,
And bless thy healing rays
And change these deep, complaining sighs
To songs of sacred praise.

504 *God in Afflictions.* **458**

NOT from the dust affliction grows,
   Nor troubles rise by chance;
Yet we are born to care and woes,
A sad inheritance.

2 As sparks break out from burning coals
   And still are upwards borne,
So grief is rooted in our souls,
And man grows up to mourn.

3 Yet with my God I leave my cause,
   And trust his promis'd grace;
He rules me by his well-known laws
Of love and righteousness.

4 Not all the pains that e'er I bore
Shall spoil my future peace;
For death and hell can do no more
Than what my Father please.

CHRISTIAN EXPERIENCE—TRIALS.

L. M. GLASGOW.

1. Oh, could I find some peaceful bow'r, Where sin has nei-ther place nor pow'r; This trai-tor vile, I fain would shun, But can-not from his pre-sence run.

505 *Lamenting over Adhering Sin.* 401

OH, could I find some peaceful bow'r,
Where sin has neither place nor pow'r,
This traitor vile, I fain would shun,
But cannot from his presence run.

2 When to the throne of grace I flee,
He stands between my God and me,
Where'er I rove, where'er I rest,
I feel him working in my breast.

3 When I attempt to soar above,
To view the heights of Jesus' love,
This monster seems to mount the skies,
And vails his glory from mine eyes.

4 Lord, free me from this deadly foe,
Which keeps my faith and hope so low ;
I long to dwell in heaven, my home,
Where not one sinful thought can come.

506 *Wandering Thoughts.* 408

I LOVE the Lord ; but ah ! how far
My thoughts from the dear object are !
This wanton heart, how wide it roves !
And fancy meets a thousand loves.

2 If my soul burn to see my God,
I tread the courts of his abode ;
But troops of rivals throng the place,
And tempt me oft before his face.

3 Would I enjoy my Lord alone,
I bid my passions all begone,
All but my love ; and charge my will
To bar the door and guard it still.

4 But cares or trifles make or find
Still new approaches to the mind ;

Till I with grief and wonder see
Huge crowds betwixt the Lord and me.

5 This foolish heart can leave its God,
And shadows tempt its thoughts abroad,
How shall I fix this wand'ring mind ?
Or throw my fetters on the wind ?

6 Look gently down, almighty grace,
Prison me round in thine embrace ;
Pity the soul that would be thine,
And let thy pow'r my love confine.

507 *Afflictions Good.* 459

FATHER ! I bless thy gentle hand ;
How kind was thy chastising rod,
That forc'd my conscience to a stand,
And brought my wand'ring soul to God !

2 Foolish and vain, I went astray,
Before I felt thy scourging, Lord !
I left my guide and lost my way ;
But now I love and keep thy word.

3 'Tis good for me to wear the yoke,
For pride is apt to rise and swell ;
'Tis good to bear my Father's stroke,
That I may learn his statutes well.

4 Thy hands have made my mortal frame,
Thy spirit form'd my soul within ;
Teach me to know thy wondrous name,
And guard me safe from death and sin.

5 Then all that love and fear the Lord,
At my salvation shall rejoice ;
For I have trusted in thy word,
And made thy grace my only choice.

CHRISTIAN EXPERIENCE—TRIALS. 175

L. M. ROSEDALE.

1. The dark-en'd sky, how thick it low'rs! Troubled with storms and big with show'rs,
No cheerful gleam of light appears, But nature pours forth all her tears.

508 *Sowing in Tears.* **460**

THE darken'd sky, how thick it low'rs!
Troubled with storms & big with show'rs,
No cheerful gleam of light appears,
But nature pours forth all her tears.

2 Yet let the sons of grace revive:
God bids the soul that seeks him, live,
And, from the gloomiest shade of night,
Calls forth a morning of delight.

3 The seeds of ecstasy unknown
Are in these water'd furrows sown:
See the green blades, how thick they rise
And with fresh verdure bless our eyes!

4 In secret foldings they contain
Unnumber'd ears of golden grain;
And heav'n shall pour its beams around,
Till the ripe harvest load the ground.

5 Then shall the trembling mourner come,
And find his sheaves, & bring them home;
The voice, long broke with sighs, shall sing
Till heav'n with hallelujahs ring.

509 *Prayer answered by Crosses.* **445**

I ASK'D the Lord that I might grow
In faith, and love, and ev'ry grace,
Might more of his salvation know,
And seek more earnestly his face.

2 'Twas he who taught me thus to pray,
And he, I trust, has answer'd pray'r:
But it has been in such a way
As almost drove me to despair.

3 I hop'd that in some favor'd hour
At once he'd answer my request,
And by his love's constraining pow'r
Subdue my sins and give me rest.

4 Instead of this, he made me feel
The hidden evils of my heart,
And let the angry pow'rs of hell
Assault my soul in ev'ry part.

5 "Lord, why is this?" I, trembling, cried;
"Wilt thou pursue thy worm to death?"
"'Tis in this way," the Lord replied,
"I answer pray'r for grace and faith!

6 "These inward trials I employ,
From self and pride to set thee free,
And break thy schemes of earthly joy,
That thou may'st seek thine all in me."

510 *Hidings of God's Face.* **395**

HAPPY the hours, the golden days,
When I could call my Jesus mine,
And sit, and view his smiling face,
Enjoying pleasures all divine!

2 But now he's gone! (oh, mighty woe!)
Gone from my soul, and hides his love!
I hate the sins that griev'd him so,
The sins that forc'd him to remove!

3 Yet let my hope look through my tears,
And spy afar his glorious throne;
His chariot through the cleaving spheres
Shall bring the bright Beloved down.

4 Swift as a roe flies o'er the hills,
My soul springs out to meet him high:
Then shall the conqu'ror turn his wheels
And climb the mansions of the sky.

CHRISTIAN EXPERIENCE—TRIALS.

L. M. ALL-SAINTS.

1. My spirit looks to God alone; My rock and refuge is his throne: In all my fears, in all my straits, My soul on his salvation waits.

511 God our Only Trust. 473

MY spirit looks to God alone;
  My rock and refuge is his throne:
In all my fears, in all my straits,
My soul on his salvation waits.

2 Trust him, ye saints, in all your ways,
Pour out your hearts before his face:
When helpers fail, and foes invade,
God is our all-sufficient aid.

3 False are the men of high degree;
The baser sort are vanity:
Laid in the balance, both appear
Light as a puff of empty air.

4 Make not increasing gold your trust,
Nor set your heart on glitt'ring dust;
Why will you grasp the fleeting smoke
And not believe what God hath spoke?

5 Once has his awful voice declar'd,
Once and again my ears have heard,
"All power is his eternal due:
He must be fear'd and trusted too."

6 For sov'reign pow'r reigns not alone;
Grace is a partner of the throne:
Thy grace and justice, mighty Lord,
Shall well divide our last reward.

512 Thirst for God. 422

AS pants the hart for cooling springs,
  So longs my soul, O King of kings,
Thy face in near approach to see,
So thirsts, great Source of life, for thee.

2 With ardent zeal, with strong desires,
To thee, to thee, my soul aspires;

When shall I reach thy blest abode?
When meet the presence of my God?

3 God of my strength, attend my cry,
Say why, my great Preserver, why
Excluded from thy sight I go,
And bend beneath a weight of woe.

4 Why thus my soul with care opprest?
And whence the woes that fill my breast?
In all thy cares, in all thy woes,
On God thy steadfast hope repose.

5 To Him my thanks shall still be paid,
My sure defense, my constant aid;
His name my zeal shall ever raise,
And dictate to my lips his praise.

513 Safety in God. 471

COURAGE, my soul! while God is near,
  What enemy hast thou to fear?
How canst thou want a sure defense,
Whose refuge is Omnipotence?

2 Though thickest dangers crowd my way,
My God can chase my fears away;
My steadfast heart on him relies,
And all those dangers still defies.

3 Though billows after billows roll,
To overwhelm my sinking soul,
Firm as a rock my faith shall stand,
Upheld by God's almighty hand.

4 In life, his presence is my aid;
In death, 'twill guide me through the shade,
Chase all my rising fears away,
And turn my darkness into day.

514 *Courage required.* 411

STAND up, my soul, shake off thy fears,
 And gird the gospel armor on;
March to the gates of endless joy,
Where Jesus thy great Captain's gone.

2 Hell and thy sins resist thy course;
But hell and sin are vanquish'd foes;
Thy Savior nail'd them to the cross,
And sung the triumph when he rose.

3 Then let my soul march boldly on,
Press forward to the heav'nly gate;
There peace and joy eternal reign,
And glitt'ring robes for conqu'rors wait.

4 There shall I wear a starry crown,
And triumph in almighty grace
While all the armies of the skie
Join in my glorious Leader's praise.

515 *Hope encouraged.* 403

WHY sinks my weak, desponding mind?
 Why heaves my heart the anxious
Can sov'reign goodness be unkind? [sigh?
Am I not safe if God is nigh?

2 'Tis he supports this fainting frame;
On him alone my hopes recline:
The wondrous glories of his name, [shine!
How wide they spread! how bright they

3 Infinite wisdom! boundless pow'r!
Unchanging faithfulness and love!
Here let me trust, while I adore,
Nor from my Refuge e'er remove.

4 My God, if thou art mine indeed,
Then I have all my heart can crave;
A present help in times of need;
Still kind to hear, and strong to save.

5 Forgive my doubts, O gracious Lord!
And ease the sorrows of my breast:
Speak to my heart the healing word,
That thou art mine—and I am blest.

516 *Christian Life a Voyage.* 457

THE Christian navigates a sea
 Where various forms of death appear;
Nor skill, alas! nor pow'r has he
Aright his dang'rous course to steer.

2 Sometimes there lies a treach'rous rock
Beneath the surface of the wave!
He strikes, but yet survives the shock,
For Jesus is at hand to save.

3 But hark, the midnight tempest roars!
He seems forsaken and alone;
But Jesus, whom he then implores,
Unseen, preserves and leads him on.

4 His destin'd land he sometimes sees,
And thinks his toils will soon be o'er;
Expects some favorable breeze
Will waft him quickly to the shore.

5 But sudden clouds obstruct his view,
And he enjoys the sight no more;
Nor does he now believe it true
That he had even seen the shore.

6 Though fear his heart should overwhelm,
He'll reach the port for which he's bound,
For Jesus holds and guides the helm,
And safety is where he is found.

517 *In Times of Despondency.*

MY spirit sinks within me, Lord;
 But I will call thy grace to mind,
And times of past distress record,
When I have found my God was kind.

2 Yet will the Lord command his love,
When I address his throne by day,
Nor in the night his grace remove;
The night shall hear me sing and pray.

3 I'll chide my heart, that sinks so low;
Why should my soul indulge in grief?
Hope in the Lord, and praise him too;
He is my rest, my sure relief.

4 O God, thou art my hope, my joy;
Thy light and truth shall guide me still:
Thy word shall my best thoughts employ,
And lead me to thy heav'nly hill.

518 *The New Convert.* 366

THE new-born child of gospel grace,
 Like some fair tree when summer's nigh,
Beneath Immanuel's shining face,
Lifts up his blooming branch on high.

2 No fear he feels, he sees no foes,
No conflict yet his faith employs;
Nor has he learnt to whom he owes
The strength and peace his soul enjoys.

3 But sin soon darts its cruel sting,
And comforts sinking day by day;
What seem'd his own, a self-fed spring,
Proves but a brook that glides away.

4 When Gideon arm'd his num'rous host,
The Lord soon made his numbers less:
And said, lest Israel vainly boast,
"My arm procur'd me this success."

5 Thus will he bring our spirits down,
And draw our ebbing comforts low,
That sav'd by grace, but not our own,
We may not claim the praise we owe.

CHRISTIAN EXPERIENCE—TRIALS.

C. M. BALERMA.

1. Oh that I knew the se-cret place Where I might find my God!
I'd spread my wants be-fore his face, And pour my woes a-broad.

519 *Groanings after God.* **378**

OH that I knew the secret place
 Where I might find my God!
I'd spread my wants before his face,
 And pour my woes abroad.

2 I'd tell him how my sins arise,
 What sorrows I sustain;
How grace decays, and comfort dies,
 And leaves my heart in pain.

3 He knows what arguments I'd take
 To wrestle with my God;
I'd plead for his own mercy's sake,
 And for my Savior's blood.

4 My God will pity my complaints,
 And heal my broken bones,
He takes the meaning of his saints,
 The language of their groans.

5 Arise, my soul, from deep distress,
 And banish ev'ry fear;
He calls thee to his throne of grace,
 To spread thy sorrows there.

520 *Under Afflictions.* **464**

WHY should a living man complain
 Of deep distress within,
Since ev'ry sigh and ev'ry pain
 Is but the fruit of sin?

2 No, Lord, I'll patiently submit,
 Nor ever dare rebel;
And yet I may, here at thy feet,
 My painful feelings tell.

3 Thou seest what floods of sorrow rise,
 And beat upon my soul;
One trouble to another cries,
 Billows on billows roll.

4 From fear to hope, from hope to fear,
 My sinking soul is tost,
Till I am tempted in despair
 To give up all for lost.

5 Yet through the stormy clouds I look
 Once more to thee, my God:
Oh, fix my feet upon a rock
 Beyond the raging flood!

6 One look of mercy from thy face
 Will set my heart at ease;
One all-commanding word of grace
 Will make the tempest cease.

521 *Trust in Affliction.* **461**

AFFLICTION is a stormy deep,
 Where wave resounds to wave:
Though o'er my head the billows roll,
 I know the Lord can save.

2 The hand that now withholds my joys
 Can reinstate my peace;
And he who bade the tempest roar
 Can bid that tempest cease.

3 In the dark watches of the night,
 I'll count his mercies o'er;
I'll praise him for ten thousand past,
 And humbly sue for more.

4 When darkness and when sorrows rose
 And press'd on ev'ry side,
The Lord has still sustain'd my steps,
 And still has been my Guide.

5 Here will I rest, and build my hopes,
 Nor murmur at his rod;
He's more than all the world to me,
 My Health, my Life, my God.

CHRISTIAN EXPERIENCE—TRIALS.

C. M. STEPHENS.

1. Alas! what hourly dangers rise! What snares beset my way! To heav'n, oh, let me lift mine eyes, And hourly watch and pray.

522 *Succor implored in Conflicts.* **975**

ALAS! what hourly dangers rise!
  What snares beset my way!
To heaven, oh, let me lift mine eyes,
  And hourly watch and pray.

2 How oft my mournful thoughts complain,
  And melt in flowing tears!
My weak resistance, ah, how vain!
  How strong my foes and fears!

3 O gracious God, in whom I live,
  My feeble efforts aid;
Help me to watch, and pray, and strive,
  Though trembling and afraid.

4 Increase my faith, increase my hope,
  When foes and fears prevail;
Oh, bear my fainting spirit up,
  Or soon my strength will fail.

5 Whene'er temptations lure my heart,
  Or draw my feet aside,
My God, thy powerful aid impart,
  My Guardian and my Guide.

6 Oh, keep me in thy heavenly way,
  And bid the tempter flee;
And let me never, never stray
  From happiness and thee.

523 *A Prayer in Trials.*

BE merciful to me, O God!
  Be merciful to me,
For though I sink beneath thy rod,
  Yet do I trust in thee.

2 Thou art my refuge, and I know
  My burden thou dost bear,
And I would seek, where'er I go,
  To cast on thee my care.

3 Thou knowest, Lord, my flesh how frail,
  Strong though my spirit be;
Oh, then assist, when foes assail,
  The soul that clings to thee.

4 And, gracious Lord, whate'er befall,
  A thankful heart be mine—
A heart that answers to thy call,
  One that is wholly thine.

5 And may I ne'er forget that thou
  Wilt soon return again,
And those who love thy coming now
  Shall shine in glory then.

524 *Cross and Crown.*

MUST Jesus bear the cross alone,
  And all the world go free?
No, there's a cross for every one,
  And there's a cross for me.

2 How happy are the saints above,
  Who once were sorrowing here!
But now they taste unmingled love,
  And joy without a tear.

3 The consecrated cross I'll bear,
  Till death shall set me free;
And then go home, my crown to wear,
  For there's a crown for me.

CHRISTIAN EXPERIENCE—TRIALS.

8s, 7s, 4s. OSGOOD.

1. O my soul, what means this sadness? Wherefore art thou thus cast down?
Let thy griefs be turn'd to gladness, Bid thy restless fears be gone: Look to Jesus,
Look to Jesus, And rejoice in his dear name, And rejoice in his dear name.

525 *Cast Down yet Hoping.* **399**

O MY soul, what means this sadness?
  Wherefore art thou thus cast down?
Let thy griefs be turn'd to gladness,
  Bid thy restless fears be gone;
    Look to Jesus,
And rejoice in his dear name.

2 What though Satan's strong temptations
  Vex and grieve thee day by day,
And thy sinful inclinations
  Often fill thee with dismay?
    Thou shalt conquer,
Through the Lamb's redeeming blood.

3 Though ten thousand ills beset thee,
  From without and from within,
Jesus saith, he'll ne'er forget thee,
  But will save from hell and sin:
    He is faithful
To perform his gracious word.

4 Though distresses now attend thee,
  And thou tread'st the thorny road,
His right hand shall still defend thee;
  Soon he'll bring thee home to God!
    Therefore praise him—
Praise the great Redeemer's name.

5 Oh that I could now adore him
  Like the heav'nly host above,
Who forever bow before him,
  And unceasing sing his love!
    Happy songsters!
When shall I your chorus join?

526 *Christ our Guide.* **455**

GUIDE me, O thou great Jehovah!
  Pilgrim through this barren land;

I am weak, but thou art mighty,
  Hold me with thy powerful hand:
    Bread of heaven,
Feed me till I want no more.

2 Open thou the crystal fountain,
  Whence the healing streams do flow,
Let the fiery, cloudy pillar
  Lead me all my journey through:
    Strong Deliv'rer,
Be thou still my strength and shield.

3 When I tread the verge of Jordan,
  Bid my anxious fears subside;
Death of death, and hell's destruction,
  Land me safe on Canaan's side:
    Songs of praises
I will ever give to thee.

527* *Taking up the Cross.* **925**

JESUS, I my cross have taken,
  All to leave and follow thee;
Naked, poor, despis'd, forsaken,
  Thou, from hence, my all shalt be;

2 Perish ev'ry fond ambition,
  All I've sought, or hop'd, or known,
Yet how rich is my condition,
  God and heav'n are still mine own!

3 Let the world despise and leave me;
  They have left my Savior too;
Human hearts and looks deceive me—
  Thou art not, like them, untrue;

4 And whilst thou shalt smile upon me,
  God of wisdom, love and might,
Foes may hate and friends disown me,
  Show thy face and all is bright.

* For this hymn omit repeat in music.

CHRISTIAN EXPERIENCE—TRIALS.

8, 8, 7, 4, 8. SCHIRMER.

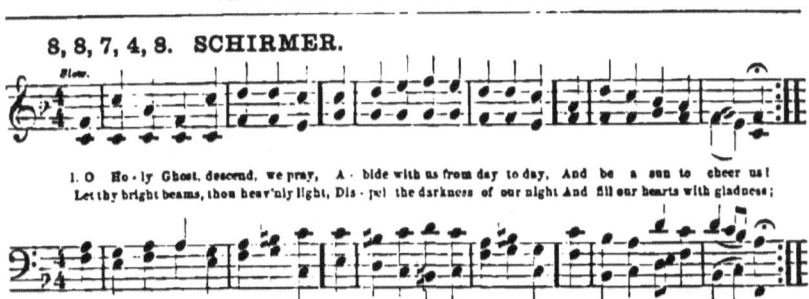

1. O Holy Ghost, descend, we pray, Abide with us from day to day, And be a sun to cheer us! Let thy bright beams, thou heav'nly light, Dispel the darkness of our night And fill our hearts with gladness;

That we To thee Truly living, To thee giving Pray'r unceas-ing, Still may be in love in-creas-ing.

528 *The Spirit our Helper.* 794

O HOLY Ghost, descend, we pray,
  Abide with us from day to day,
And be a sun to cheer us!
Let thy bright beams, thou heav'nly light,
Dispel the darkness of our night
And fill our hearts with gladness;
    That we
    To thee
    Truly living,
    To thee giving
    Pray'r unceasing,
Still may be in love increasing.

2 Give to thy word impressive pow'r
That in our hearts, from this good hour,
  As fire it may be burning;
That thee, the Father, and the Son,
And Spirit, on one common throne,
  We may as God acknowledge!
    Oh, stay
    And sway
    Our souls ever,
    That they never
    May forsake thee,
But by faith their refuge make thee.

3 Thou fountain whence all wisdom flows
Which God on pious hearts bestows,
  Grant us thy consolation,
That, in our pure faith's unity,
Our Christian brethren all may see
    Thy witness truly given.

    Hear us,
    Cheer us
    By thy teaching,
    That our preaching
    Thy salvation
Soon may tell to ev'ry nation.

4 Direct us by thy counsel still,
That we may understand thy will:
  Our ignorance enlighten.
Oh! grant us constancy, that we
May ever faithful prove to thee,
  How much soe'er we suffer.
    Descend,
    Defend
    From all errors
    And earth's terrors;
    Be our healing,
Jesus' love and peace revealing.

Doxology.

COME, let us now our honors bring,
  To Father, Son, and Spirit sing,—
The song of angels raising!
Let all below, and all above,
Unite in holy joy and love,
  Our God Jehovah praising!
    Adore,—
    Adore,—
    Praise the Father,
    And Redeemer,
    Without ending;
And the Spirit of Their sending.

CHRISTIAN EXPERIENCE—TRIALS.

10, 6, 9, 9, 4. HEYL.

529 *God our Light, Trust, and Shield.* **858**

GOD is my light! Never, my soul, despair
  In hours of thy distress!
The sun withdraws, & earth is dark & drear:
  My light will never cease;
On days of joy with splendor beaming—
Thro' nights of grief its rays are gleaming,
  God is my light!

2 God is my trust!—My soul, be not afraid!
  Thy helper will abide:
"I'll not forsake thee!" he has kindly said,—
  He's ever at thy side;
In feeble age will yet stand by thee;
No real good will he deny thee:
  God is my trust!

3 God is my shield!—Of me he taketh care,
  As none beside could do:
He guards my head, he watches ev'ry hair,
  All dangers brings me through:
While thousands, to vain helpers calling,
On right and left are near me falling,—
  He is my shield!

4 God's my reward!—Well pleas'd, I for-
  The path that he has shown: [ward go
It has no trials but my God will know
  When he allots my crown.

I'll gladly strive, the fight sustaining,
Until in death the vict'ry gaining,—
  God's my reward!

530 *Trust in God's Faithfulness.* **352**

OUR God is true! Then he will ne'er forsake
  For whom his love he shows;
Our God is true! We shall his care partake
  In all our joys and woes:
His wings will spread their shelter o'er us:
Tho' mountains quake, earth yawn before
  Our God is true! [us,

2 Our God is true!—He is a faithful friend,
  We from experience know;
And, rest assur'd, he will our souls defend
  From ev'ry watchful foe.
His cov'nant love gives no denial
To humble faith in hours of trial:
  Our God is true!

3 Our God is true!—Never forget, my soul,
  How kind and true he is!
Be true to God! Let this thy life control,
  And be devoutly his!
From loving him let nothing drive thee!
And of this stay let none deprive thee:—
  "Our God is true!"

CHRISTIAN EXPERIENCE—TRIALS.

7s. MARTYN.

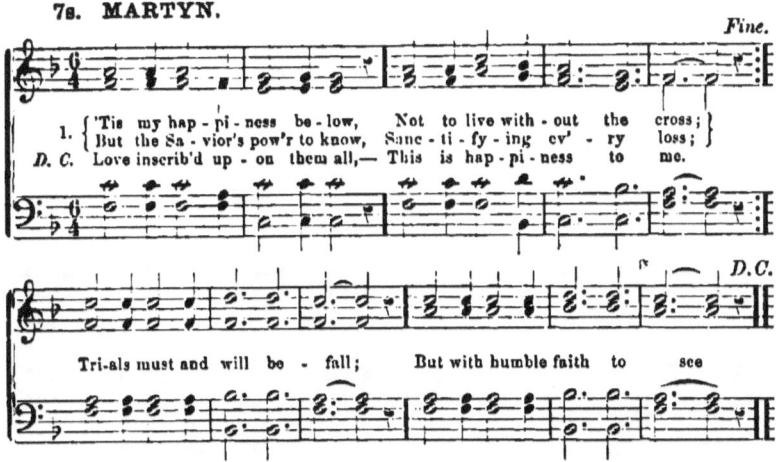

1. 'Tis my happiness below, Not to live without the cross;
But the Savior's pow'r to know, Sanctifying ev'ry loss;
D.C. Love inscrib'd upon them all,— This is happiness to me.

Trials must and will befall; But with humble faith to see

---

531 *Welcoming the Cross.* **444**

'TIS my happiness below,
  Not to live without the cross;
But the Savior's pow'r to know,
  Sanctifying ev'ry loss;
Trials must and will befall;
  But, with humble faith to see
Love inscrib'd upon them all,—
  This is happiness to me.

2 God, in Israel, sows the seeds
  Of affliction, pain, and toil;
These spring up, and choke the weeds
  Which would else o'erspread the soil.
Trials make the promise sweet;
  Trials give new life to pray'r;
Trials bring me to his feet,—
  Lay me low and keep me there.

532 *Onward, Christians.* **924**

OFT in danger, oft in woe,
  Onward, Christians, onward go;
Bear the toil, maintain the strife,
  Strengthen'd with the bread of life.
Let your drooping hearts be glad;
  March in heav'nly armor clad;
Fight, nor think the battle long;
  Soon shall vict'ry wake your song.

2 Let not sorrow dim your eye;
  Soon shall ev'ry tear be dry;
Let not fear your course impede;
  Great your strength if great your need.
Onward, then, to glory move;
  More than conqu'rors ye shall prove;
Though oppos'd by many a foe,
  Christian soldiers, onward go!

533 *"Lovest thou me?"* **397**

'TIS a point I long to know,
  Oft it causes anxious thought,
Do I love the Lord, or no?
  Am I his, or am I not?
If I love, why am I thus?
  Why this dull, this lifeless frame?
Hardly, sure, can they be worse,
  Who have never heard his name!

2 Could my heart so hard remain,
  Pray'r a task and burden prove,
Ev'ry trifle give me pain,
  If I knew a Savior's love?
When I turn mine eyes within,
  All is dark, and vain, and wild:
Fill'd with unbelief and sin,
  Can I deem myself a child?

3 If I pray, or hear, or read,
  Sin is mix'd with all I do;
You that love the Lord indeed,
  Tell me, is it thus with you?
Yet I mourn my stubborn will,
  Find my sin a grief and thrall;
Should I grieve for what I feel
  If I did not love at all?

4 Lord, decide the doubtful case!
  Thou who art thy people's Sun,
Shine upon thy work of grace,
  If it be indeed begun.
Let me love thee more and more,
  If I love at all, I pray;
If I have not lov'd before,
  Help me to begin to-day.

CHRISTIAN EXPERIENCE—BACKSLIDINGS.

C. M. ORTONVILLE.

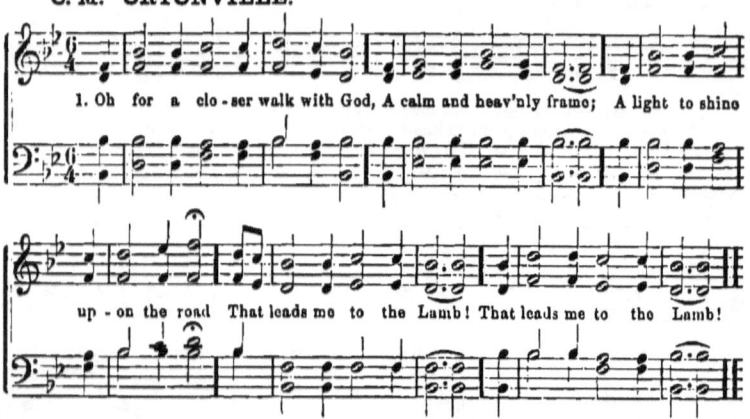

1. Oh for a clo-ser walk with God, A calm and heav'nly frame; A light to shine up-on the road That leads me to the Lamb! That leads me to the Lamb!

534 *For Nearness to God.* **416**

OH for a closer walk with God,
A calm and heavenly frame;
A light to shine upon the road
That leads me to the Lamb!

2 Where is the blessedness I knew
When first I saw the Lord?
Where is the soul-refreshing view
Of Jesus and his word?

3 What peaceful hours I once enjoy'd!
How sweet their mem'ry still!
But they have left an aching void
The world can never fill.

4 Return, O holy Dove, return!
Sweet messenger of rest;
I hate the sins that made thee mourn,
And drove thee from my breast:

5 The dearest idol I have known,
Whate'er that idol be,
Help me to tear it from thy throne,
And worship only thee.

6 So shall my walk be close with God,
Calm and serene my frame;
So purer light shall mark the road
That leads me to the Lamb.

535 *Confession and Pardon.* **414**

HOW oft, alas! this wretched heart
Has wander'd from the Lord!
How oft my roving thoughts depart,
Forgetful of his word!

2 Yet sov'reign mercy calls, "Return:"
Dear Lord, and may I come?
My vile ingratitude I mourn;
Oh, take the wand'rer home.

3 And canst thou, wilt thou yet forgive,
And bid my crimes remove?
And shall a pardon'd rebel live
To speak thy wondrous love?

4 Almighty grace, thy healing pow'r
How glorious, how divine!
That can to bliss and life restore
So vile a heart as mine.

5 Thy pard'ning love, so free, so sweet,
Dear Savior, I adore;
Oh, keep me at thy sacred feet,
And let me rove no more.

536 *Will ye also go away?* **405**

WHEN any turn from Zion's way,
(As numbers often do,)
Methinks I hear my Savior say,
"Wilt thou forsake me too?"

2 Ah, Lord! with such a heart as mine,
Unless thou hold me fast,
My faith will fail, I shall decline,
And prove like them at last.

3 'Tis thou alone hast power and grace
To save a wretch like me;
To whom, then, shall I turn my face
If I depart from thee?

4 Beyond a doubt, I rest assur'd,
Thou art the CHRIST of God;
Who hath eternal life secur'd,
By promise and by blood.

5 The help of men and angels join'd,
Could never reach my case!
Nor can I hope relief to find
But in thy boundless grace.

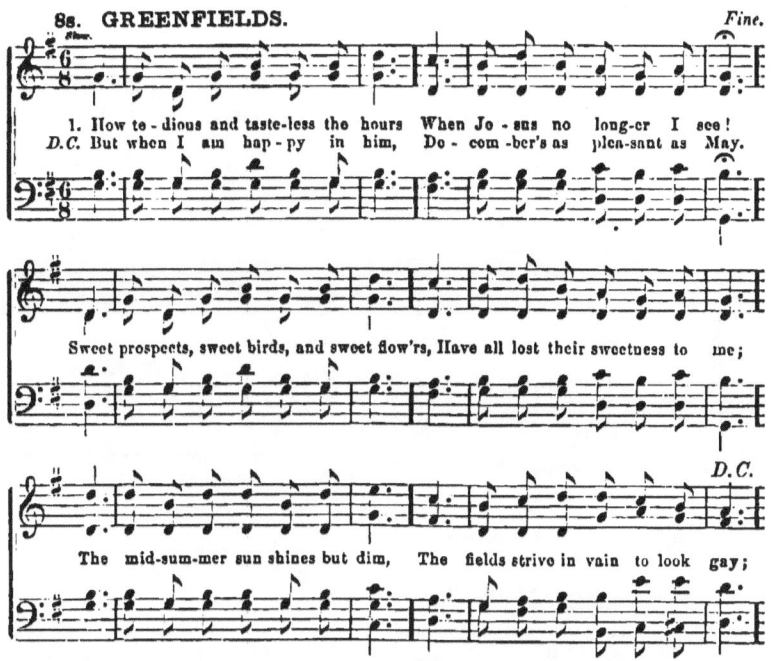

537 *All-Sufficiency of Jesus.* **380**

HOW tedious and tasteless the hours
When Jesus no longer I see !
Sweet prospects, sweet birds, and sweet
Have all lost their sweetness to me; [flow'rs,
The midsummer sun shines but dim,
The fields strive in vain to look gay ;
But when I am happy in him,
December's as pleasant as May.

2 His Name yields the richest perfume,
And sweeter than music his voice ;
His presence disperses my gloom,
And makes all within me rejoice ;
I should, were he always thus nigh,
Have nothing to wish or to fear ;
No mortal so happy as I,—
My summer would last all the year.

3 Content with beholding his face,
My all to his pleasure resign'd,
No changes of season or place
Would make any change in my mind :
Whilst blest with a sense of his love,
A palace a toy would appear ;
And prisons would palaces prove,
If Jesus would dwell with me there.

4 Dear Lord, if indeed I am thine,
If thou art my sun and my song,
Say, why do I languish and pine?
And why are my winters so long?
Oh, drive these dark clouds from my sky;
Thy soul-cheering presence restore ;
Or take me up to thee on high,
Where winter and clouds are no more.

538 *Longing to be with Jesus.*

MY Savior, whom absent I love,
Whom not having seen I adore,
Whose name is exalted above
All glory, dominion, and power !
Dissolve thou these bonds that detain
My soul from her portion in thee :
Oh, strike off this adamant chain,
And make me eternally free.

2 When that happy era begins,
When drest in thy glories I shine,
Nor grieve any more by my sins
The bosom on which I recline :
Oh, then shall the veil be removed,
And round me thy brightness be poured,
I'll meet him whom absent I loved,
Whom not having seen I adored.

CHRISTIAN EXPERIENCE—DECLENSIONS.

L. M. LANESVILLE.

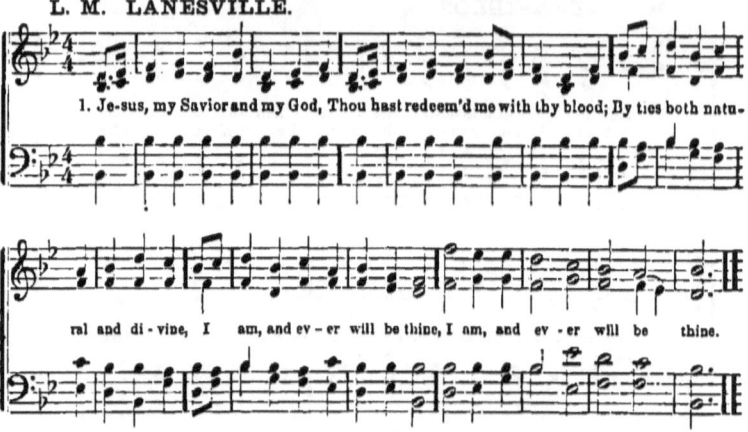

1. Je-sus, my Savior and my God, Thou hast redeem'd me with thy blood; By ties both natural and di-vine, I am, and ev-er will be thine, I am, and ev-er will be thine.

539 *Perseverance Desired.* **419**

JESUS, my Savior and my God,
   Thou hast redeem'd me with thy blood ;
By ties both natural and divine,
I am, and ever will be thine.

2 But ah! should this inconstant heart,
Ere I'm aware, from thee depart,
What dire reproach would fall on me
For such ingratitude to thee!

3 The thought I dread, the crime I hate;
The guilt, the shame, I deprecate,
And yet so mighty are my foes,
I dare not trust my warmest vows.

4 Pity my frailty, dearest Lord!
Grace in the needful hour afford :
Oh, steel this tim'rous heart of mine
With fortitude and love divine.

5 So shall I triumph o'er my fears,
And gather joy from all my tears ;
So shall I to the world proclaim
The honors of the Christian name.

540 *Inconstancy Lamented.* **409**

THE wand'ring star and fleeting wind
   Both represent th' unstable mind :
The morning cloud and early dew
Bring our inconstancy to view.

2 But cloud and wind, and dew and star,
Faint and imperfect emblems are ;
Nor can there aught in nature be
So fickle and so false as we.

3 Our outward walk, and inward frame,
Scarce through a single hour the same ;
We vow, and straight our vows forget,
And then these very vows repeat.

5 With flowing tears, Lord, we confess
Our folly and unsteadfastness :
When shall these hearts more fixed be,
Fix'd by thy grace, and fix'd for thee?

541 *For more Grace.* **420**

I THIRST, but not as once I did,
   The vain delights of earth to share :
Thy wounds, Immanuel, all forbid
That I should seek my pleasure there.

2 It was the sight of thy dear cross
First wean'd my soul from earthly things,
And taught me to esteem as dross
The mirth of fools and pomp of kings.

3 I want that grace that springs from thee,
That quickens all things where it flows,
And makes a wretched thorn like me
Bloom as the myrtle or the rose.

542 *Return of Joy.* **404**

WHEN darkness long has veil'd my mind,
   And smiling day once more appears,
Then, my Redeemer! then I find
The folly of my doubts and fears.

2 I chide my unbelieving heart,
And blush that I should ever be
Thus prone to act so base a part,
Or harbor one hard thought of thee.

3 Oh, let me then at length be taught
(What I am still so slow to learn)
That God is love, and changes not,—
Nor knows the shadow of a turn.

CHRISTIAN EXPERIENCE—ASPIRATIONS.

8s. PORTLAND.

1. Thou Shepherd of Is-r'el di-vine, The joy and de-sire of my heart,
For clo-ser com-mu-nion I pine, I long to re-side where thou art:
The pas-ture I lan-guish to find, Where all, who their Shep-herd o-bey,
Are fed, on thy bo-som re-clin'd, And screen'd from the heat of the day.

543 *For Closer Communion.* **377**

THOU Shepherd of Isr'el divine,
  The joy and desire of my heart,
For closer communion I pine,
  I long to reside where thou art:
The pasture I languish to find,
  Where all, who their Shepherd obey,
Are fed, on thy bosom reclin'd,
  And screen'd from the heat of the day.

2 Ah! show me that happiest place,
  The place of thy people's abode,
Where saints in an ecstasy gaze,
  And hang on a crucified God!
Thy love for a sinner declare,
  Thy passion and death on the tree;
My spirit to Calvary bear,
  To suffer and triumph with thee.

3 'Tis there, with the lambs of thy flock,
  There only I covet to rest,
To lie at the foot of the Rock,
  Or rise to be hid in thy breast;
'Tis there I would always abide,
  And never a moment depart;
Conceal'd in the cleft of thy side,
  Eternally held in thy heart.

CHRISTIAN EXPERIENCE—ASPIRATIONS.

L. M. AVERNO.

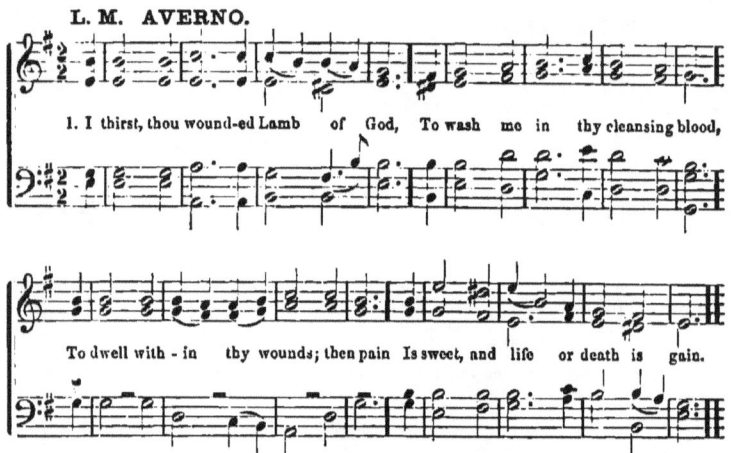

1. I thirst, thou wound-ed Lamb of God, To wash me in thy cleansing blood, To dwell with-in thy wounds; then pain Is sweet, and life or death is gain.

544 *Union with Christ.* **384**

I THIRST, thou wounded Lamb of God,
  To wash me in thy cleansing blood,
To dwell within thy wounds; then pain
Is sweet, and life or death is gain.

2 Take my poor heart, and let it be
Forever clos'd to all but thee!
Seal thou my breast, and let me wear
That pledge of love forever there.

3 How blest are they who still abide
Close shelter'd in thy bleeding side!
Who thence their life and strength derive,
And by thee move, and in thee live.

4 What are our works but sin and death,
Till thou thy quick'ning Spirit breathe?
Thou giv'st the pow'r, the grace to move:
Oh, wondrous grace! Oh, boundless love!

5 How can it be, thou heav'nly King,
That thou shouldst us to glory bring,
Make slaves the partners of thy throne,
Deck'd with a never-fading-crown?

6 Ah! Lord, enlarge our scanty thought,
To know the wonders thou hast wrought;
Unloose our stamm'ring tongues to tell
Thy love immense, unsearchable!

545 *For Deliverance from Sin.* **424**

OH that my load of sin were gone!
  Oh that I could at last submit
At Jesus' feet to lay it down,
To lay my soul at Jesus' feet!

2 Rest for my soul I long to find:
Savior, if mine indeed thou art,
Give me thy meek and lowly mind,
And stamp thine image on my heart.

3 Break off the yoke of inbred sin,
And fully set my spirit free;
I cannot rest till pure within,
Till I am wholly lost in thee.

4 Fain would I learn of thee, my God,
Thy light and easy burden prove,
The cross, all stain'd with hallow'd blood,
The labor of thy dying love.

5 I would, but thou must give the pow'r;
My heart from every sin release;
Bring near, bring near the joyful hour,
And fill me with thy perfect peace.

6 Come, Lord, the drooping sinner cheer,
Nor let thy chariot-wheels delay;
Appear in my poor heart, appear;
My God, my Savior, come away!

546 *Thirsting for God.* **383**

MY rising soul, with strong desires,
  To perfect happiness aspires,
With steady steps would tread the road
That leads to heaven—that leads to God.

2 I thirst to drink unmingled love
From the pure fountain-head above;
My dearest Lord, I long to be
Emptied of sin, and full of thee.

3 For thee I pant, for thee I burn;
Art thou withdrawn? again return,
Nor let me be the first to say,
Thou wilt not hear when sinners pray.

CHRISTIAN EXPERIENCE—ASPIRATIONS.

L. M. EFFINGHAM.

1. My God! permit me not to be A stranger to my-self and thee; A-midst a thousand tho'ts I rove, For-get-ful of my high-est love.

547 *For Spiritual-Mindedness.* **426**

MY God! permit me not to be
A stranger to myself and thee;
Amidst a thousand thoughts I rove,
Forgetful of my highest love.

2 Why should my passions mix with earth,
And thus debase my heav'nly birth?
Why should I cleave to things below,
And let my God, my Savior, go?

3 Call me away from flesh and sense;
Thy sov'reign word can draw me thence;
I would obey the voice divine,
And all inferior joys resign.

4 Be earth, with all her cares, withdrawn;
Let noise and vanity begone;
In secret silence of the mind,
My heav'n, and there my God, I find.

548 *For All-Needful Grace.* **331**

MY hope, my all, my Savior thou,
To thee, lo! now my soul I bow;
I feel the bliss thy wounds impart,
I find thee, Savior, in my heart.

2 Be thou my strength, be thou my way,
Protect me through my life's short day:
In all my acts may wisdom guide,
And keep me, Savior, near thy side.

3 Correct, reprove, and comfort me;
As I have need, my Savior be:
And if I would from thee depart,
Then clasp me, Savior, to thy heart.

4 In fierce temptation's darkest hour,
Save me from sin and Satan's pow'r;
Tear ev'ry idol from thy throne,
And reign, my Savior, reign alone.

5 My suff'ring time shall soon be o'er,
Then shall I sigh and weep no more,
My ransom'd soul shall soar away,
To sing thy praise in endless day.

549 *For Complete Sanctification.* **427**

RETURN, my roving heart, return,
And chase those shadowy forms no
Seek out some solitude to mourn, [more;
And thy forsaken God implore.

2 Wisdom and pleasure dwell at home:
Retir'd and silent, seek them there;
This is the way to overcome,
The way to break the tempter's snare.

3 O thou, great God, whose piercing eye
Distinctly marks each deep recess,
In these sequester'd hours, draw nigh,
And with thy presence fill the place.

4 Through all the windings of my heart,
My search let heav'nly wisdom guide;
And still its radiant beams impart,
Till all be search'd and purified.

5 Then with the visits of thy love
Vouchsafe my inmost soul to cheer;
Till ev'ry grace shall join to prove
That God has fix'd his dwelling there.

CHRISTIAN EXPERIENCE—ASPIRATIONS.

L. M. LUTON.

1. Great God, in-dulge my hum-ble claim: Be thou my hope, my joy, my rest! The glo-ries that com-pose thy name Stand all en-gag'd to make me blest.

550   *Panting for God.*   389

GREAT God, indulge my humble claim:
   Thou art my hope, my joy, my rest!
The glories that compose thy name
Stand all engag'd to make me blest.

2 Thou great and good, thou just and wise,
Thou art my Father and my God!
And I am thine, by sacred ties,
Thy child and servant, bought with blood.

3 With heart and eyes, and lifted hands,
For thee I long, for thee I look,
As travelers in thirsty lands
Pant for the cooling water-brook.

4 My life itself, without thy love,
No lasting pleasure can afford;
Yea, 'twould a tiresome burden prove,
If I were banish'd from the Lord.

5 I'll lift my hands, I'll raise my voice,
While I have breath to pray or praise,
This work shall make my heart rejoice
Throughout the remnant of my days.

551   *Hatred of Sin.*   421

THRICE holy Lord! I love thy truth,
   Nor dare thy least commandment slight:
Yet pierc'd by sin, the serpent's tooth,
I mourn the anguish of the bite.

2 But though the poison lurks within,
Hope bids me still with patience wait
Till death shall set me free from sin,
Free from the only thing I hate.

3 Had I a throne above the rest,
Where angels and archangels dwell,
One sin unslain within my breast
Would make that heav'n as dark as hell.

4 The pris'ner, sent to breathe fresh air,
And bless'd with liberty again,
Would mourn were he condemn'd to wear
One link of all his former chain.

5 But oh, no foe invades the bliss,
When glory crowns the Christian's head;
One view of Jesus, as he is,
Will strike all sin forever dead.

552   *For the Spirit's Guidance.*   178

AMIDST a world of hopes and fears,
   A world of cares, and toils, and tears,
Where foes alarm, and dangers threat,
And pleasures kill, and glories cheat:

2 Send down, O Lord! a heav'nly ray,
To guide me in the doubtful way;
And o'er me hold thy shield of pow'r,
To guard me in the dang'rous hour.

3 Teach me the flatt'ring paths to shun,
In which the thoughtless many run,
Who for a shade the substance miss,
And grasp their ruin in their bliss.

4 May never pleasure, wealth, or pride,
Allure my wand'ring soul aside;
But through this maze of mortal ill,
Safe lead me to thy heav'nly hill.

5 There glories shine, and pleasures roll,
That charm, delight, transport the soul,
And every longing wish shall be
Possess'd of boundless bliss in thee.

CHRISTIAN EXPERIENCE—ASPIRATIONS.

L. M. ALWAY.

1. What strange perplex-i-ties a-rise! What anxious fears and jea-lou-sies! What crowds in doubtful light ap-pear! How few, a-las, ap-prov'd and clear!

553   *For Self-Knowledge.*   **402**

WHAT strange perplexities arise!
    What anxious fears and jealousies!
What crowds in doubtful light appear!
How few, alas, approv'd and clear!

2 And what am I?—My soul, awake,
And an impartial survey take,
Does no dark sign, no ground of fear,
In practice or in heart appear?

3 What image does my spirit bear?
Is Jesus form'd and living there?
Say, do his lineaments divine
In thought, and word, and action shine?

4 Searcher of hearts, oh, search me still:
The secrets of my soul reveal;
My fears remove; let me appear
To God and mine own conscience clear!

554   *For Assurance.*   **93**

IN vain the world's alluring smile
    Would my unwary heart beguile;
Deluding world! its brightest day—
Dream of a moment—flits away.

2 To nobler bliss my soul aspires;
Come, Lord, and fill these large desires
With pow'r, and light, and love divine;
Oh, speak, and tell me thou art mine.

3 The blissful word, with joy replete,
Shall bid my gloomy fears retreat;
And heav'nly hope, serenely bright,
Illume and cheer my darkest night.

4 So shall my joyful spirit rise,
On wings of faith, above the skies,
Then dwell forever near thy throne,
In joys to mortal thought unknown.

555   *Living to Christ.*   **388**

LET tho'tless thousands choose the road
    That leads the soul away from God;
This happiness, dear Lord, be mine,
To live and die entirely thine.

2 On Christ, by faith, my soul would live,
From him, my life, my all receive;
To him devote my fleeting hours,
Serve him alone with all my pow'rs.

3 Christ is my everlasting All;
To him I look, on him I call;
He will my ev'ry want supply,
In time, and through eternity.

4 Soon will the Lord, my Life, appear;
Soon shall I end my trials here,
Leave sin and sorrow, death and pain;
To live is Christ—to die is gain.

5 Soon will the saints in glory meet,
Soon walk through ev'ry golden street,
And sing on ev'ry blissful plain,—
To live is Christ, to die is gain.

CHRISTIAN EXPERIENCE—ASPIRATIONS.

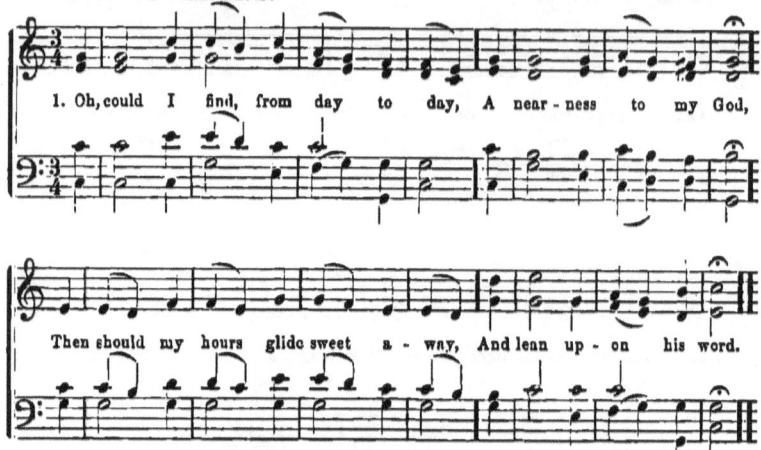

C. M. COVENTRY.

1. Oh, could I find, from day to day, A nearness to my God, Then should my hours glide sweet away, And lean upon his word.

556 *For Nearness to God.* **379**

OH, could I find, from day to day,
  A nearness to my God,
Then should my hours glide sweet away,
  And lean upon his word.

2 Lord, I desire with thee to live
  Anew from day to day;
In joys the world can never give,
  Nor ever take away.

3 O Jesus, come and rule my heart,
  And make me wholly thine,
That I may never more depart,
  Nor grieve thy love divine;

4 Thus, till my last expiring breath,
  Thy goodness I'll adore;
And when my flesh dissolves in death,
  My soul shall love thee more.

557 *For God's Grace.* **285**

TO thee, O God, my pray'r ascends,
  But not for golden stores;
Nor covet I the brightest gems
  On the rich Eastern shores:

2 Nor that deluding, empty joy
  Men call a mighty name,
Nor greatness with its pride and state,
  My restless thoughts inflame:—

3 Nor pleasure's fascinating charms
  My fond desires allure:
But nobler things than these from thee
  My wishes would secure.

4 The faith and hope of joys to come,
  My best affections move;

Thy light, thy favor, and thy smiles,
  Thine everlasting love.

5 These are the blessings I desire;
  Lord, be these blessings mine,
And all the glories of the world
  I cheerfully resign.

558 *For a New Nature.* **300**

SUPREME High-Priest, the pilgrim's Light,
  My heart for thee prepare;
Thine image stamp, and deeply write
  Thy superscription there.

2 Ah, let my forehead bear thy seal,
  My arm thy badge retain,
My heart the inward witness feel
  That I am born again.

3 Into thy humble mansion come,
  Set up thy dwelling here:
Possess my heart, and leave no room
  For sin to harbor there.

4 Ah, give me, Lord, the single eye,
  Which aims at naught but thee:
I fain would live, and yet not I—
  Let Jesus live in me.

5 Oh that the penetrating sight
  And eagle's eye were mine!
Undazzled at the boundless light
  Of Majesty divine;

6 That with the armies of the sky
  I too may sit and sing,
Add, Savior, to the eagle's eye,
  The dove's aspiring wing.

C. M. CLARENDON.

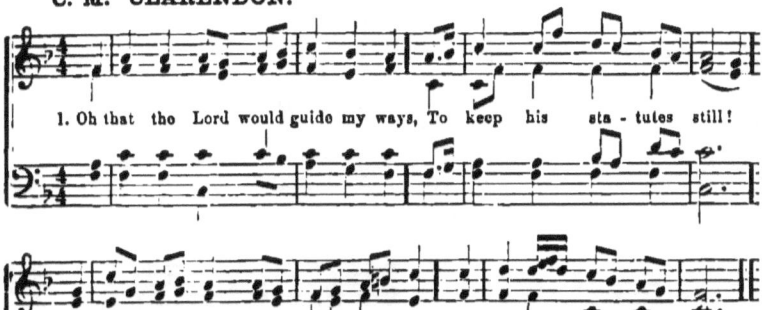

1. Oh that the Lord would guide my ways, To keep his statutes still!

Oh that my God would grant me grace, To know and do his will!

559 *Breathing after Holiness.* **179**

OH that the Lord would guide my ways,
  To keep his statutes still!
Oh that my God would grant me grace,
  To know and do his will!

2 Order my footsteps by thy word,
  And make my heart sincere;
Let sin have no dominion, Lord,
  But keep my conscience clear.

3 Assist my soul, too apt to stray,
  A stricter watch to keep;
And, should I e'er forget thy way,
  Restore thy wand'ring sheep.

4 Make me to walk in thy commands;
  'Tis a delightful road;
Nor let my head, or heart, or hands,
  Offend against my God.

560 *Spiritual Sloth deprecated.* **410**

MY drowsy powers, why sleep ye so?
  Awake, my sluggish soul!
Nothing has half thy work to do,
  Yet nothing's half so dull.

2 The little ants, for one poor grain,
  Labor, and toil, and strive;
Yet we, who have a heav'n t' obtain,
  How negligent we live!

3 We, for whose sake all nature stands,
  And stars their courses move;
We, for whose guard the angel bands
  Come flying from above;

4 We, for whom God the Son came down,
  And labor'd for our good,
How careless to secure that crown
  He purchas'd with his blood!

5 Lord, shall we lie so sluggish still!
  And never act our parts?
Come, holy Dove, from th' heav'nly hill,
  Renew and warm our hearts.

6 Then shall our active spirits move,
  Upward our souls shall rise;
With hands of faith and wings of love
  We'll fly and take the prize.

561 *Love to Christ.* **385**

DO not I love thee, O my Lord?
  Behold my heart, and see;
And turn each hateful idol out
  That dares to rival thee.

2 Do not I love thee from my soul?
  Then let me nothing love:
Dead be my heart to ev'ry joy
  Which thou dost not approve.

3 Is not thy name melodious still
  To mine attentive ear?
Doth not each pulse with pleasure beat,
  My Savior's voice to hear?

4 Hast thou a lamb in all thy flock
  I would disdain to feed?
Hast thou a foe before whose face
  I fear thy cause to plead?

5 Thou know'st I love thee, dearest Lord,
  But, oh, I long to soar
Far from the sphere of mortal joys,
  That I may love thee more.

CHRISTIAN EXPERIENCE—ASPIRATIONS.

L. M. STERLING.

1. Je-sus, my Sa-vior, Brother, Friend, On whom I cast my ev'-ry care, On whom for all things I de-pend, In-spire, and then ac-cept my pray'r.

562 *For Divine Help.* **343**

JESUS, my Savior, Brother, Friend,
 On whom I cast my ev'ry care,
On whom for all things I depend,
 Inspire, and then accept my prayer.

2 If I have tasted of thy grace,
 The grace that sure salvation brings,
If with me now thy Spirit stays,
 And, hov'ring, hides me in his wings;—

3 Still let him with my weakness stay,
 Nor for a moment's space depart;
Evil and danger turn away,
 And keep till he renews my heart.

4 When to the right or left I stray,
 His voice behind me may I hear,
"Return, and walk in Christ thy way,
 Fly back to Christ, for sin is near."

5 Jesus, I fain would walk in thee,
 From nature's ev'ry path retreat:
Thou art my way, my leader be,
 And set upon the rock my feet.

6 Uphold me, Savior, or I fall;
 Oh, reach to me thy gracious hand:
Only on thee for help I call;
 Only by faith in thee I stand.

563 *The Love of Christ.* **381**

JESUS, thy boundless love to me
 No thought can reach, no tongue declare;
Oh, knit my thankful heart to thee,
 And reign without a rival there.

2 Oh, grant that nothing in my soul
 May dwell, but thy pure love alone!

Oh, may thy love possess me whole!
 My joy, my treasure, and my crown.

3 Unwearied, may I this pursue,
 Dauntless to this high prize aspire;
Hourly within my soul renew
 This holy flame, this heav'nly fire.

4 Still let thy love point out my way;
 How wondrous things thy love has wrought!
Still lead me, lest I go astray;
 Direct my word, inspire my thought.

5 In suff'ring, be thy love my peace,
 In weakness, be thy love my pow'r,
And when the storms of life shall cease,
 Receive me in the trying hour.

564 *Vanity of Creatures.* **225**

MAN has a soul of vast desires;
 He burns within with restless fires;
Tost to and fro, his passions fly
 From vanity to vanity.

2 In vain on earth we hope to find
 Some solid good to fill the mind;
We try new pleasures, but we feel
 The inward thirst and torment still.

3 So, when a raging fever burns,
 We change from side to side by turns;
And 'tis a poor relief we gain,
 To change the place, but keep the pain.

4 Great God! subdue this vicious thirst,
 This love to vanity and dust;
Cure the vile fever of the mind,
 And feed our souls with joys refin'd.

CHRISTIAN EXPERIENCE—ASPIRATIONS.

S. M. THATCHER.

1. As-ton-ish'd and dis-tress'd, I turn mine eyes within;— My heart with hea-vy guilt oppress'd, The seat of ev'-ry sin.

565 *The Evil Heart.* **213**

ASTONISH'D and distress'd,
  I turn mine eyes within ;—
My heart with heavy guilt oppress'd,
  The seat of ev'ry sin.

2 What crowds of evil thoughts,
  What vile affections there !
Distrust, presumption, artful guile,
  Pride, envy, slavish fear !

3 Almighty King of saints !
  These hateful sins subdue ;
Dispel the darkness from my mind,
  And all my pow'rs renew.

4 Then shall my cheerful voice
  To thee hosannas raise ;
My soul shall glow with gratitude,—
  My lips pronounce thy praise.

566 *For Christian Graces.* **289**

JESUS, my strength, my hope,
  On thee I cast my care,
With humble confidence look up,
  And know thou hear'st my prayer.

2 I want a sober mind,
  A self-renouncing will,
That tramples on and casts behind
  The baits of pleasing ill.

3 A soul inur'd to pain,
  To hardship, grief, and loss ;
Bold to take up, firm to sustain,
  The consecrated cross.

4 I want a godly fear,
  A quick discerning eye,

That looks to thee when sin is near,
  And sees the tempter fly.

5 I want a heart to pray,
  To pray and never cease,
Never to murmur at thy stay
  Or wish my suff'rings less.

6 I want a true regard,
  A single, steady aim,
Unmov'd by threat'ning or reward,
  To thee and thy great name.

7 A jealous, deep concern
  For thine immortal praise ;
A pure desire that all may learn,
  And glorify thy grace.

567 *For Courage and Holiness.* **562**

EQUIP me for the war,
  And teach my hands to fight ;
My simple, upright heart prepare,
  And guide my words aright.

2 Control my ev'ry thought ;
  And all my sins remove ;
Let all my works in thee be wrought,
  Let all be wrought in love.

3 Oh, arm me with the mind,
  Meek Lamb, that was in thee !
And let enlighten'd zeal be join'd
  With perfect charity.

4 Oh, may I love like thee !
  In all thy footsteps tread ;
Thou hatest all iniquity,
  But nothing thou hast made.

CHRISTIAN EXPERIENCE—ASPIRATIONS.

C. M. HOWARD.

1. Spi-rit of ho-li-ness, look down, Our faint-ing hearts to cheer; And, when we trem-ble at thy frown, Oh, bring thy com-forts near.

568 *For the Spirit.* **800**

SPIRIT of holiness, look down,
 Our fainting hearts to cheer;
And, when we tremble at thy frown,
 Oh, bring thy comforts near.

2 The fear which thy convictions wrought,
 Oh, let thy grace remove;
And may the souls which thou hast taught
 To weep, now learn to love.

3 Now let thy saving mercy heal
 The wounds it made before;
Now on our hearts impress thy seal,
 That we may doubt no more.

4 Complete the work thou hast begun,
 And make our darkness light,
That we a glorious race may run,
 Till faith be lost in sight.

5 Then, as our wond'ring eyes discern
 The Lord's unclouded face,
In fitter language we shall learn
 To sing triumphant grace.

569 *Worldly Vanities Abjured.* **829**

BE thou, O Lord, my treasure here,
 And fix my thoughts above;
Unveil thy glories to my view,
 And bid me taste thy love.

2 The world how mean, with all its store,
 Compar'd with thee, my Lord!
Its vain and fleeting joys how few!
 How little they afford!

3 The goods of earth are empty things,
 And pleasures soon decay;
Its honors are but noisy breath,
 And scepters pass away.

4 Ye vain and glitt'ring toys, begone;
 Ye false delights, adieu;
My glorious Lord fills all the space,
 And leaves no room for you.

570 *For Help amid our Frailty.* **224**

HOW short and hasty is our life!
 How vast our souls' affairs!
Yet senseless mortals vainly strive
 To lavish out their years.

2 Our days run thoughtlessly along,
 Without a moment's stay;
Just like a story, or a song,
 We pass our lives away.

3 God from on high invites us home,
 But we march heedless on,
And ever hast'ning to the tomb,
 Stoop downwards as we run.

4 How we deserve the deepest hell,
 That slight the joys above!
What chains of vengeance should we feel,
 That break such cords of love!

5 Draw us, O Savior, with thy grace,
 And lift our thoughts on high,
That we may end this mortal race,
 And see salvation nigh.

CHRISTIAN EXPERIENCE—ASPIRATIONS.

C. M. HEATH.

1. My soul lies cleaving to the dust; Lord, give me life divine; From vain desires, and ev'ry lust, Turn off these eyes of mine.

571 *For Quickening Grace.* **973**

MY soul lies cleaving to the dust;
 Lord, give me life divine;
From vain desires, and ev'ry lust,
 Turn off these eyes of mine.

2 I need the influence of thy grace
 To speed me in thy way,
Lest I should loiter in my race
 Or turn my feet astray.

3 Are not thy mercies sov'reign still,
 And thou a faithful God?
Wilt thou not grant me warmer zeal
 To run the heav'nly road?

4 Does not my heart thy precepts love,
 And long to see thy face?
And yet how slow my spirits move
 Without enliv'ning grace!

5 Then shall I love thy gospel more,
 And ne'er forget thy word,
When I have felt its quick'ning power
 To draw me near the Lord.

572 *For True Piety.* **813**

RELIGION is the chief concern
 Of mortals here below;
May I its great importance learn,
 Its sov'reign virtue know!

2 More needful this, than glitt'ring wealth,
 Or aught the world bestows;
Nor reputation, food, or health,
 Can give us such repose.

3 Religion should our thoughts engage,
 Amidst our youthful bloom;
'Twill fit us for declining age,
 And for the awful tomb.

4 Oh, may my heart, by grace renew'd,
 Be my Redeemer's throne;
And be my stubborn will subdu'd,
 His government to own.

5 Let deep repentance, faith, and love
 Be join'd with godly fear,
And all my conversation prove
 My heart to be sincere.

573 *Danger of Love to Creatures.* **222**

HOW vain are all things here below!
 How false, and yet how fair!
Each pleasure hath its poison too,
 And ev'ry sweet a snare.

2 The brightest things below the sky
 Give but a flatt'ring light;
We should suspect some danger nigh
 Where we possess delight.

3 Our dearest joys and nearest friends,
 The partners of our blood,
How they divide our wav'ring minds,
 And leave but half for God!

4 Dear Savior, let thy beauties be
 My soul's eternal food;
And grace command my heart away
 From all created good.

8s & 7s. (Double.) RIPLEY.

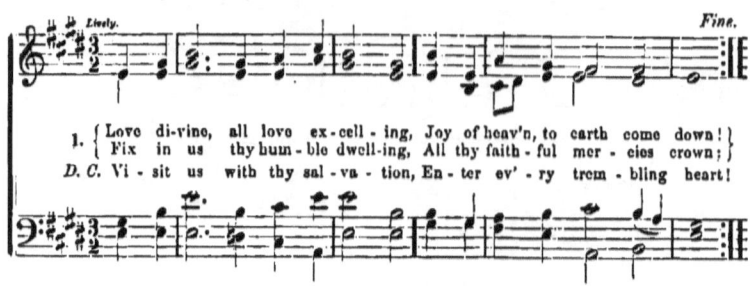

574 *Breathing after Holiness.* **423**

LOVE divine, all love excelling,
  Joy of heav'n, to earth come down!
Fix in us thy humble dwelling,
  All thy faithful mercies crown ;
Jesus, thou art all compassion,
  Pure, unbounded love thou art;
Visit us with thy salvation,
  Enter ev'ry trembling heart!

2 Breathe, oh, breathe thy lovely spirit
  Into ev'ry troubled breast!
Let us all in thee inherit,
  Let us find thy promis'd rest;
Take away the love of sinning,
  Alpha and Omega be,
End of faith, as its beginning,
  Set our hearts at liberty.

3 Come! almighty to deliver,
  Let us all thy life receive!
Suddenly return, and never,
  Never more thy temples leave!
Thee we would be always blessing,
  Serve thee as thy hosts above ;
Pray, and praise thee without ceasing,
  Glory in thy precious love.

4 Carry on thy new creation :
  Pure and holy may we be ;
Let us see our whole salvation
  Perfectly secur'd by thee ;
Chang'd from glory unto glory,
  Till in heav'n we take our place,
Till we cast our crowns before thee,
  Lost in wonder, love, and praise.

575 *Heavenly Aspirations.*

KNOW, my soul! thy full salvation ;
  Rise o'er sin, and fear, and care,
Joy to find in ev'ry station
  Something still to do and bear:
Think what Spirit dwells within thee ;
  Think what Father's smiles are thine ;
Think what Jesus did to win thee ;—
  Child of heaven! canst thou repine?

2 Haste thee on from grace to glory,
  Armed with faith, & wing'd with pray'r;
Heaven's eternal day's before thee,
  God's own hand shall guide thee there:
Soon shall close thine earthly mission,
  Soon shall pass thy pilgrim days ;
Hope shall change to glad fruition,
  Faith to sight, and pray'r to praise.

CHRISTIAN EXPERIENCE—ASPIRATIONS.

8s. 6 lines. BRIGHTON.

1. Oh that the Comforter would come! Nor visit as a transient guest, But fix in me his constant home, And keep possession of my breast, And make my soul his lov'd abode, The temple of the living God!

576 *For Holiness.* **803**

OH that the Comforter would come!
 Nor visit as a transient guest,
But fix in me his constant home,
And keep possession of my breast,
And make my soul his lov'd abode,
The temple of the living God!

2 Come, Holy Ghost, my heart inspire!
 Attest that I am born again;
Come, and baptize me now with fire,
Nor let thy former gifts be vain:
I cannot rest till I'm forgiv'n;
And find the earnest of my heav'n!

3 O love, I languish at thy stay!
I pine for thee with ling'ring smart!
Weary and faint through long delay:
When wilt thou come into my heart?
From sin and sorrow set me free,
And swallow up my soul in thee!

577 *For Light and Grace.* **941**

WHEN, streaming from the eastern skies,
 The morning light salutes mine eyes,
O Sun of righteousness divine!
On me, with beams of mercy, shine;
Chase the dark clouds of guilt away,
And turn my darkness into day.

2 When each day's scenes and labors close,
And wearied nature seeks repose,
With pard'ning mercy richly blest,
Guard me, my Savior, while I rest;
And, as each morning-sun shall rise,
Oh, lead me onward to the skies.

3 And, at my life's last setting sun,
My conflicts o'er, my labors done,
Jesus, thy heav'nly radiance shed,
To cheer and bless my dying-bed;
And from death's gloom my spirit raise,
To see thy face, and sing thy praise.

CHRISTIAN EXPERIENCE—ASPIRATIONS.

C. M. P. MERIBAH.

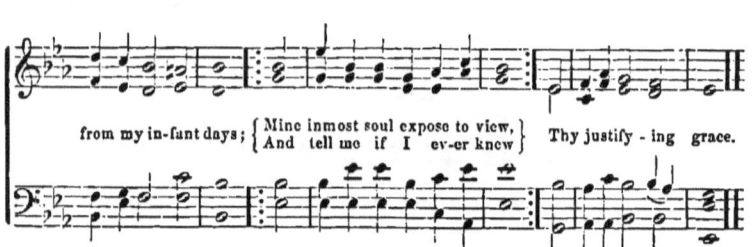

1. Thou great, mysterious, God unknown, Whose love hath gently led me on E'en from my infant days; { Mine inmost soul expose to view, And tell me if I ev-er knew } Thy justify-ing grace.

---

578 *For the Spirit's Witness.* **293**

THOU great, mysterious, God unknown,
   Whose love hath gently led me on
E'en from my infant days;
Mine inmost soul expose to view,
And tell me if I ever knew
   Thy justifying grace.

2 If I have only known thy fear,
And follow'd with a heart sincere
   Thy drawing from above,
Now, now the further grace bestow,
And let my sprinkled conscience know
   Thy sweet forgiving love.

3 Short of thy love I would not stop,
A stranger to the gospel hope,
   The sense of sin forgiv'n;
I would not, Lord, my soul deceive,
Without thine inward witness live,
   That antepast of heav'n.

4 If now the witness were in me,
Would he not testify of thee,
   In Jesus reconcil'd?
And should I not with faith draw nigh,
And boldly, Abba, Father, cry,
   I know myself thy child?

5 Ah! never let thy servant rest,
Till of my part in Christ possess'd,
   I on thy mercy feed:
Unworthy of the crumbs that fall,
Yet rais'd by him who died for all,
   To eat the children's bread.

6 Whate'er obstructs thy pard'ning love,
Or sin, or righteousness, remove,
   Thy glory to display;
My heart of unbelief convince,
And now absolve me from my sins,
   And take them all away.

579 *Longing to Forsake the World.*

THE mind was form'd to mount sublime
   Beyond the narrow bounds of time,
To everlasting things:
But earthly vapors dim her sight,
And hang with cold, oppressive weight
   Upon her drooping wings.

2 Bright scene of bliss, unclouded skies,
Invite my soul: oh, could I rise,
   Nor leave a thought below,
I'd bid farewell to anxious care,
And say to every tempting snare,
   Heaven calls, and I must go.

3 Heaven calls, and can I yet delay?
Can aught on earth engage my stay?
   Ah, wretched, lingering heart!
Come, Lord, with strength, and life, & light,
Assist and guard my upward flight,
   And bid the world depart.

Doxology.

TO Father, Son, and Holy Ghost,
   Be praise amid the heavenly host,
And in the church below;
From whom all creatures draw their breath,
By whom redemption blessed the earth,
   From whom all comforts flow.

CHRISTIAN EXPERIENCE—FELLOWSHIP. 201

L. M. WELLS.

1. How blest the sacred tie that binds, In union sweet, according minds! How swift the heav'n-ly course they run, Whose hearts, and faith, and hopes are one!

580   *Blessedness of Unity.*   433

HOW blest the sacred tie that binds,
   In union sweet, according minds!
How swift the heav'nly course they run,
Whose hearts, and faith, and hopes are one.

2 To each, the soul of each how dear!
What watchful love, what holy fear!
How doth the gen'rous flame within
Refine from earth and cleanse from sin!

3 Their streaming eyes together flow
For human guilt and mortal woe;
Their ardent prayers together rise,
Like mingling flames in sacrifice.

4 Together both they seek the place
Where God reveals his awful face;
How high, how strong their raptures swell,
There's none but kindred souls can tell.

5 Nor shall the glowing flame expire
'Midst nature's drooping, sick'ning fire:
Soon shall they meet in realms above,
A heav'n of joy, because of love.

581   *Joyous Fellowship.*   647

KINDRED in Christ, for his dear sake,
   A hearty welcome here receive:
May we together now partake
The joys which only he can give.

2 To you and us by grace 'tis giv'n
To know the Savior's precious name;
And shortly we shall meet in heav'n,
Our hope, our way, our end the same.

3 May he, by whose kind care we meet,
Send his good Spirit from above—

Make our communications sweet,
And cause our hearts to burn with love.

4 Forgotten be each worldly theme,
When Christians see each other thus;
We only wish to speak of him
Who liv'd, and died, and reigns for us.

5 We'll talk of all he did, and said,
And suffer'd for us here below;
The path he mark'd for us to tread,
And what he's doing for us now.

6 Thus, as the moments pass away,
We'll love and wonder and adore;
And hasten on the glorious day
When we shall meet to part no more.

582   *Welcome to Fellowship.*   920

COME in, thou blessed of the Lord!
   Oh! come in Jesus' precious name;
We welcome thee, with one accord,
And trust the Savior does the same.

2 Those joys which earth cannot afford,
We'll seek in fellowship to prove,
Join'd in one spirit to our Lord,
Together bound by mutual love.

3 And, while we pass this vale of tears,
We'll make our joys and sorrows known;
We'll share each other's hopes and fears,
And count a brother's cares our own.

4 Once more our welcome we repeat;
Receive assurance of our love;
Oh! may we all together meet
Around the throne of God above.

CHRISTIAN EXPERIENCE—FELLOWSHIP.

S. M. INVERNESS.

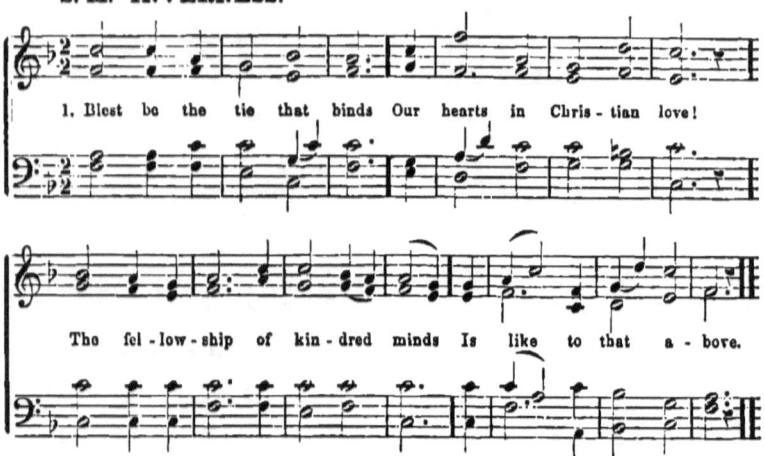

1. Blest be the tie that binds Our hearts in Christian love! The fellowship of kindred minds Is like to that above.

583 *Christian Union.* **432**

BLEST be the tie that binds
  Our hearts in Christian love!
The fellowship of kindred minds
  Is like to that above.

2 Before our Father's throne
  We pour our ardent pray'rs:
Our fears, our hopes, our aims are one,
  Our comforts and our cares.

3 We share our mutual woes,
  Our mutual burdens bear;
And often for each other flows
  The sympathizing tear.

4 When we asunder part,
  It gives us inward pain,
But we shall still be join'd in heart,
  And hope to meet again.

5 From sorrow, toil, and pain,
  And sin, we shall be free;
And perfect love and friendship reign
  Through all eternity.

584 *Brotherly Love.* **434**

LO, what a pleasing sight
  Are brethren that agree!
How blest are all whose hearts unite
  In bonds of piety!

2 From those celestial springs,
  Such streams of comfort flow,
As no increase of riches brings,
  Nor honors can bestow.

3 All in their stations move,
  And each performs his part,
In all the cares of life and love,
  With sympathizing heart.

4 Form'd for the purest joys,
  By one desire possest,
One aim the zeal of all employs,
  To make each other blest.

5 No bliss can equal theirs,
  Where such affections meet;
While praise devout, and mingled pray'rs,
  Make their communion sweet.

6 'Tis the same pleasure fills
  The breast in worlds above,
Where joy, like morning-dew, distils,
  And all the air is love.

585 *Meeting of Brethren.* **899**

AND are we yet alive,
  And see each others' face?
Glory and praise to Jesus give
  For his redeeming grace!

2 Preserv'd by pow'r divine
  To full salvation here,
Again in Jesus' praise we join,
  And in his sight appear.

3 What troubles have we seen!
  What conflicts have we pass'd!
Fightings without, and fears within,
  Since we assembled last!

4 But out of all the Lord
  Hath brought us by his love;
And still he does his help afford,
  And hides our life above.

CHRISTIAN EXPERIENCE—FELLOWSHIP.   203

5 Then let us make our boast
   Of his redeeming pow'r,
Which saves us to the uttermost,
   Till we can sin no more:

6 Let us take up the cross,
   Till we the crown obtain;
And gladly reckon all things loss,
   So we may Jesus gain.

586   *Parting of Brethren.*   649

AND let our bodies part,
   To diff'rent climes repair;
Inseparably join'd in heart
The friends of Jesus are.

2 Jesus, the corner-stone,
   Did first our hearts unite!
And still he keeps our spirits one,
   Who walk with him in white.

3 Oh, let us still proceed
   In Jesus' work below;
And following our triumphant Head,
   Onward to conquest go.

4 The vineyard of the Lord
   Before his lab'rers lies;
And lo! we see the vast reward
   Which waits us in the skies!

5 Oh, let our heart and mind
   Continually ascend,
That heaven of repose to find
   Where all our labors end.

6 Where all our toils are o'er,
   Our suff'rings and our pain;
Who meet on that eternal shore
   Shall never part again.

7 Oh, happy, happy place,
   Where saints and angels meet;
There we shall see each others' face,
   And all our brethren greet.

7s. EDYFIELD.

1. People of the living God, I have sought the world around,
Paths of sin and sorrow trod, Peace and comfort nowhere found.

587   *Cleaving to the Saints.*   919

PEOPLE of the living God,
   I have sought the world around,
Paths of sin and sorrow trod,
Peace and comfort nowhere found.

2 Now to you my spirit turns,
Turns a fugitive unblest;
Brethren, where your altar burns,
Oh, receive me into rest!

3 Lonely I no longer roam,
Like the cloud, the wind, the wave;
Where you dwell shall be my home,
Where you die shall be my grave.

4 Mine the God whom you adore;
Your Redeemer shall be mine;
Earth can fill my soul no more,
Ev'ry idol I resign.

5 Tell me not of gain and loss,
Ease, enjoyment, pomp, and pow'r;
Welcome, poverty and cross,
Shame, reproach, affliction's pow'r.

6 "Follow me!" I know thy voice;
Jesus, Lord, thy steps I see:
Now I take thy yoke by choice,
Light's thy burden now to me.

204 CHRISTIAN EXPERIENCE—FELLOWSHIP.

C. M. SILOAM.

1. Our souls by love to-geth-er knit, Ce-ment-ed, mix'd in one,
One hope, one heart, one mind, one voice, 'Tis heav'n on earth be-gun.

588 *Christian Fellowship.* **887**

OUR souls by love together knit,
   Cemented, mix'd in one,
One hope, one heart, one mind, one voice,
   'Tis heav'n on earth begun.

2 Our hearts have often burn'd within,
   And glow'd with sacred fire,
While Jesus spoke, and fed and bless'd,
   And fill'd th' enlarg'd desire.

3 The little cloud increases still,
   The heav'ns are big with rain;
We haste to catch the teeming shower,
   And all its moisture drain.

4 A rill, a stream, a torrent flows;
   But pour a mighty flood;
Oh, sweep the nations, shake the earth,
   Till all proclaim thee God.

5 And when thou mak'st thy jewels up,
   And sett'st thy starry crown;
When all thy sparkling gems shall shine,
   Proclaim'd by thee thine own;

6 May we, a little band of love,
   We sinners, sav'd by grace,
From glory unto glory chang'd,
   Behold thee face to face.

589 *At Parting.* **650**

LORD, when together here we meet,
   And taste thy heav'nly grace,
Thy smiles are so divinely sweet,
   We're loath to leave the place.

2 But, Father, since it is thy will
   That we must part again,

Oh, may thy special presence still
   With each of us remain!

3 And let us all in Christ be one,
   Bound with the chords of love,
Till we before thy glorious throne
   Shall joyful meet above.

4 All sin and sorrow from each heart
   Shall then forever fly;
Nor shall a thought that we must part
   Once interrupt our joy.

590 *Communion of Saints.* **896**

THE saints on earth, and those above,
   But one communion make;
Join'd to their Lord, in bonds of love,
   All of his grace partake.

2 One family, we dwell in him,
   One church above, beneath;
Though now divided by the stream,
   The narrow stream of death.

3 One army of the living God,
   To his commands we bow;
Part of the host have cross'd the flood,
   And part are crossing now.

4 Lo! thousands to their endless home
   Are swiftly born away;
And we are to the margin come,
   And soon must launch as they.

5 Lord Jesus! be our constant guide!
   Then, when the word is giv'n,
Bid death's cold flood its waves divide,
   And land us safe in heav'n.

CHRISTIAN EXPERIENCE—FELLOWSHIP.

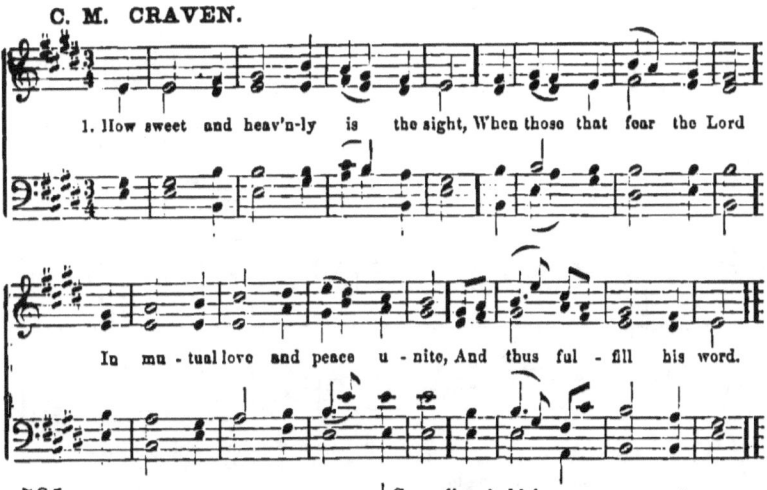

C. M. CRAVEN.

1. How sweet and heav'nly is the sight, When those that fear the Lord In mu-tual love and peace u-nite, And thus ful-fill his word.

591 *Holy Love.*

HOW sweet and heav'nly is the sight,
  When those that fear the Lord
In mutual love and peace unite,
  And thus fulfill his word.

2 When each can feel his brother's sigh,
  And with him bear a part;
When sorrow flows from eye to eye,
  And joy from heart to heart.

3 When love in one delightful stream
  Through every bosom flows,
And union sweet, with fond esteem,
  In every action glows.

4 Love is the golden chain that binds
  The happy souls above;
And he's an heir of heav'n that finds
  His bosom fill'd with love.

592 *Brotherly Love.*

LO! what an entertaining sight
  Are brethren who agree;—
Brethren whose cheerful hearts unite
  In bands of piety!

2 'Tis like the oil, divinely sweet,
  On Aaron's rev'rend head;
Which trickled down his holy face,
  And o'er his garments spread.

3 'Tis pleasant as the morning dews
  That fall on Zion's hill,
Where God his genial glory shows
  And makes his grace distill.

593 *Fellowship of Saints.*

OH, it is joy in one to meet
  Whom one communion blends,
Council to hold in converse sweet,
  And talk as Christian friends.

2 'Tis joy to think the angel train,
  Who 'mid heav'n's temple shine,
To seek our earthly temples deign,
  And in our anthems join.

3 But chief 'tis joy to think that He,
  To whom his church is dear,
Delights her gather'd flocks to see,
  Her joint devotions hear.

4 Then who would choose to walk abroad,
  While here such joys are given?
"This is indeed the house of God,
  And this the gate of heaven!"

594 *Holy Love.* 438

HAPPY the heart where graces reign,
  Where love inspires the breast:
Love is the brightest of the train,
  And strengthens all the rest.

2 Knowledge, alas! 'tis all in vain,
  And all in vain our fear:
Our stubborn sins will fight and reign,
  If love be absent there.

3 'Tis love that makes our cheerful feet
  In swift obedience move:
The devils know, and tremble too;
  But devils do not love.

4 This is the grace that lives and sings
  When faith and hope shall cease;
'Tis this shall strike our joyful strings
  In the sweet realms of bliss.

CHRISTIAN EXPERIENCE—FAITH AND WORKS.

C. M. CHESTNUT STREET.

1. Bright Source of ev-er-last-ing love! To thee our souls we raise; And to thy match-less boun-ty rear A mon-u-ment of praise.

595 *Faith and Works.* **354**

BRIGHT Source of everlasting love!
   To thee our souls we raise;
And to thy sov'reign bounty rear
   A monument of praise.

2 Thy mercy gilds the path of life
   With ev'ry cheering ray;
Kindly restrains the rising tear,
   Or wipes that tear away.

3 When, sunk in guilt, our race approach'd
   The borders of despair,
Thy grace thro' Jesus' blood proclaim'd
   A free salvation near.

4 What shall we render, bounteous Lord,
   For all the grace we see?
Alas! the goodness worms can yield
   Extendeth not to thee.

5 To scenes of woe, to beds of pain,
   We'll cheerfully repair;
And, with the gifts thy hand bestows,
   Relieve the mourners there.

6 The widow's heart shall sing for joy;
   The orphan shall be glad;
And hung'ring souls we'll gladly point
   To Christ the living bread.

7 Thus, what our heav'nly Father gave,
   Shall we as freely give;
Thus copy Him who lived to save,
   And died that we might live.

596 *Fruits of Love.* **431**

LET Pharisees of high esteem
   Their faith and zeal declare;
All their religion is a dream,
   If love be wanting there.

2 Love suffers long with patient eye,
   Nor is provok'd in haste:
She lets the present inj'ry die,
   And soon forget the past.

3 Malice and rage, those fires of hell,
   She quenches with her tongue;
Hopes and believes, and thinks no ill,
   Though she endures the wrong.

4 She ne'er desires nor seeks to know
   The scandals of the time;
Nor looks with pride on those below,
   Nor envies those that climb.

5 She lays her own advantage by,
   To seek her neighbor's good;
So God's own Son came down to die,
   And save us by his blood.

6 Love is the grace that keeps her pow'r
   In all the realms above;
There faith and hope are known no more,
   But saints forever love.

597 *Good Works Rewarded.* **662**

YES, there are joys that cannot die,
   With God laid up in store;
Treasure, beyond the changing sky,
   Brighter than golden ore.

2 The seeds which piety and love
   Have scatter'd here below,
In the fair, fertile fields above
   To ample harvests grow.

3 The mite my willing hands can give,
   At Jesus' feet I lay;
Grace shall the humble gift receive,
   And grace at large repay.

L. M. COMMUNION.

1. So let our lips and lives express The holy gospel we profess;
So let our works and virtues shine, To prove the doctrine all divine.

598 Grace and Holiness. 446

SO let our lips and lives express
The holy gospel we profess;
So let our works and virtues shine,
To prove the doctrine all divine!

2 Thus shall we best proclaim abroad
The honors of our Savior God,
When the salvation reigns within,
And grace subdues the pow'r of sin.

3 Our flesh and sense must be denied,
Passion and envy, lust and pride;
While justice, temp'rance, truth, and love
Our inward piety approve.

4 Religion bears our spirits up,
While we expect that blessed hope,
The bright appearance of the Lord,
And faith stands leaning on his word.

599 Love Demanded. 436

HAD I the tongues of Greeks and Jews,
And nobler speech than angels use,
If love be absent, I am found,
Like tinkling brass, an empty sound.

2 Were I inspir'd to preach and tell
All that is done in heav'n and hell,
Or could my faith the world remove,
Still, I am nothing without love.

3 Should I distribute all my store
To feed the hungry, clothe the poor,
Or give my body to the flame,
To gain a martyr's glorious name:

4 If love to God and love to men
Be absent, all my hopes are vain;
Nor tongues, nor gifts, nor fiery zeal
The work of love can e'er fulfill.

600* True Zeal. 863

ZEAL is that pure and heav'nly flame
The fire of love supplies;
While that which often bears the name
Is self in a disguise.

2 True zeal is merciful and mild,
Can pity and forbear;
The false is headstrong, fierce, and wild,
And breathes revenge and war.

3 While zeal for truth the Christian warms,
He knows the worth of peace;
But self contends for names and forms,
Its party to increase.

4 Self may its poor reward obtain,
And be applauded here;
But zeal the best applause will gain,
When Jesus shall appear.

5 Dear Lord, the idol self dethrone,
And from our hearts remove;
And let no zeal by us be shown,
But that which springs from love.

* To be sung to the tune on previous page.

CHRISTIAN EXPERIENCE—FAITH AND WORKS.

L. M. FEDERAL STREET.

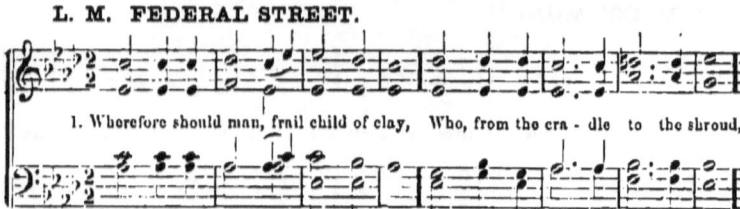

1. Wherefore should man, frail child of clay, Who, from the cra-dle to the shroud,

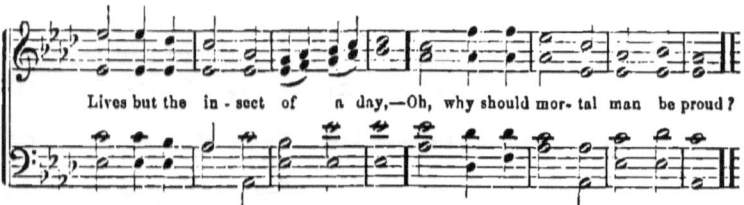

Lives but the in-sect of a day,—Oh, why should mor-tal man be proud?

601 *Pride Mortified.* **430**

Wherefore should man, frail child of clay,
Who, from the cradle to the shroud,
Lives but the insect of a day,—
Oh, why should mortal man be proud?

2 His brightest visions just appear,
Then vanish, and no more are found:
The stateliest pile his pride can rear,
A breath may level with the ground.

3 By doubts perplex'd, in error lost,
With trembling step he seeks his way:
How vain of wisdom's gift the boast!
Of reason's lamp how faint the ray!

4 Follies and crimes, a countless sum,
Are crowded in life's little span:
How ill, alas, does pride become
That erring, guilty creature, man!

5 God of my life! Father divine!
Give me a meek and lowly mind:
In modest worth oh let me shine,
And peace in humble virtue find.

602 *Love to Christ.* **390**

OF all the joys we mortals know,
Jesus, thy love exceeds the rest;
Love, the best blessing here below,
The highest rapture of the blest.

2 When round thy courts by day we rove,
Or ask the watchmen of the night
For some kind tidings from above,
Thy very name creates delight.

3 Jesus, our God, descend and come;
Our eyes would dwell upon thy face;

'Tis heav'n to see our Lord at home,
And feel the presence of his grace.

603 *Benevolence.* **661**

OH, what stupendous mercy shines
Around the majesty of heav'n!
Rebels he deigns to call his sons,
Their souls renew'd, their sins forgiv'n.

2 Go imitate the grace divine,—
The grace that blazes like a sun;
Hold forth your fair though feeble light,
Through all your lives let mercy run.

3 Upon your bounty's willing wings
Swift let the great salvation fly;
The hungry feed, the naked clothe;
To pain and sickness help apply.

4 When all is done, renounce your deeds—
Renounce self-righteousness with scorn:
Thus will you glorify your God,
And thus the Christian name adorn.

604 *"Labor on."*

GO, labor on, spend, and be spent—
Thy joy to do the Father's will,
It is the way the Master went,
Should not the servant tread it still?

2 Go, labor on, while it is day,
The world's dark night is hastening on;
Speed, speed thy work, cast sloth away:
It is not thus that souls are won.

3 Toil on, and in thy toil rejoice;
For toil comes rest, for exile, home;
Soon shalt thou hear the Bridegroom's
The midnight peal, Behold, I come! [voice,

CHRISTIAN EXPERIENCE—LOVE TO CHRIST.

C. M. P. ARIEL.

605 *Excellency of Christ.* **326**

OH, could I speak the matchless worth,
  Oh, could I sound the glories forth
Which in my Savior shine,
I'd soar and touch the heav'nly strings,
And vie with Gabriel, while he sings,
  In notes almost divine.

2 I'd sing the precious blood he spilt,
My ransom from the dreadful guilt
  Of sin and wrath divine;
I'd sing his glorious righteousness,
In which all-perfect heav'nly dress
  My soul shall ever shine.

3 I'd sing the characters he bears,
And all the forms of love he wears,
  Exalted on his throne:
In loftiest songs of sweetest praise,
I would to everlasting days
  Make all his glories known.

4 Well, the delightful day will come
When my dear Lord will bring me home,
  And I shall see his face;
Then, with my Savior, brother, friend,
A blest eternity I'll spend
  Triumphant in his grace.

606 *Unsearchable Love of Christ.* **324**

O LOVE divine, how sweet thou art!
  When shall I find my willing heart
All taken up by thee?
I long, and thirst, and faint to prove
The greatness of redeeming love,
  The love of Christ to me.

2 Stronger his love than death or hell;
Its riches are unsearchable.
  The first-born sons of light
Desire, in vain, its depth to see;
They cannot reach the mystery,
  The length, and breadth, and height.

3 Oh that I could forever sit,
With Mary, at the Master's feet!
  Be this my happy choice,
My only care, delight, and bliss,
My joy, my heaven on earth, be this,
  To hear the Bridegroom's voice.

4 Oh that I could, with favor'd John,
Recline my weary head upon
  The dear Redeemer's breast!
From care, and sin, and sorrow free,
Give me, O Lord, to find in thee
  My everlasting rest.

CHRISTIAN EXPERIENCE—LOVE TO CHRIST.

7s. ROSEFIELD.

1. Hark, my soul, it is the Lord; 'Tis thy Sa-vior, hear his word:

Je-sus speaks, and speaks to thee: "Say, poor sin-ner, lov'st thou me?"

---

607 *Lovest thou me?* **387**

HARK, my soul, it is the Lord;
  'Tis thy Savior, hear his word:
Jesus speaks, and speaks to thee:
"Say, poor sinner, lov'st thou me?

2 "I deliver'd thee when bound,
And, when bleeding, heal'd thy wound,
Sought thee wand'ring, set thee right,
Turn'd thy darkness into light.

3 "Can a woman's tender care
Cease towards the child she bare?
Yes, she may forgetful be,
Yet will I remember thee.

4 "Mine is an unchanging love,
Higher than the heights above,
Deeper than the depths beneath—
Free and faithful—strong as death.

5 "Thou shalt see my glory soon,
When the work of grace is done;
Partner of my throne shalt be:
Say, poor sinner, lov'st thou me?"

6 Lord, it is my chief complaint,
That my love is weak and faint:
Yet I love thee, and adore:
Oh for grace to love thee more!

608 *Jesus ever Precious.*

SWEET the time, exceeding sweet,
  When the saints together meet,—
When the Savior is the theme,—
When they join to sing of him!

2 Sing we then eternal love,
That which did the Father move;
He beheld the world undone,
Loved the world, and gave his Son.

3 Sweet the place, exceeding sweet,
Where the saints in glory meet,—
Where the Savior's still the theme,—
Where they see and sing of him!

609 *Prayer and Prospects of the Righteous.*

TO thy pastures fair and large,
  Heavenly Shepherd, lead thy charge,
And my couch with tenderest care
Midst the springing grass prepare.

2 When I faint with summer heat,
Thou shalt guide my weary feet
To the streams that, still and slow,
Through the verdant meadows flow.

3 Safe the dreary vale I tread,
By the shades of death o'erspread;
With thy rod and staff supplied,
This my guard, and that my guide.

4 Constant to my latest end,
Thou my footsteps shalt attend,
And shalt bid thy hallow'd dome
Yield me an eternal home.

ANTICIPATIONS OF HEAVEN.

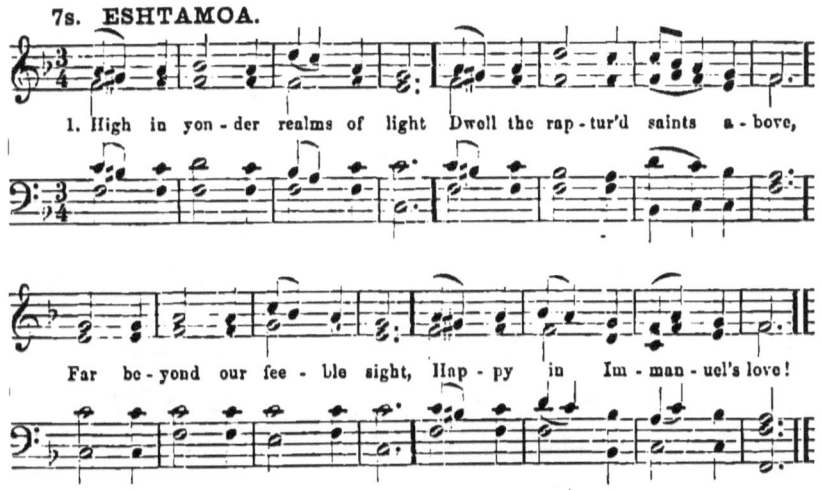

7s. ESHTAMOA.

1. High in yonder realms of light
Dwell the rap-tur'd saints a-bove,
Far be-yond our fee-ble sight,
Hap-py in Im-man-uel's love!

610 *Heaven.* **748**

HIGH in yonder realms of light
 Dwell the raptur'd saints above,
Far beyond our feeble sight,
Happy in Immanuel's love!

Pilgrims in this vale of tears,
Once they knew, like us below,
Gloomy doubts, distressing fears,
Torturing pain, and heavy woe.

But, these days of weeping o'er,
Past this scene of toil and pain,
They shall feel distress no more,
Never—never weep again.

'Mid the chorus of the skies,
Mid th' angelic lyres above,
Hark—their songs melodious rise,
Songs of praise to Jesus' love!

Happy spirits! ye are fled
Where no grief can entrance find:
Lull'd to rest the aching head,
Sooth'd the anguish of the mind!

Ev'ry tear is wip'd away—
Sighs no more shall heave the breast;
Night is lost in endless day—
Sorrow—in eternal rest!

611 *The Saints in Heaven.* **1002**

WHO are these in bright array,
 This innumerable throng,
Round the altar night and day,
Hymning their triumphant song?

"Worthy is the Lamb, once slain,
Blessing, honor, glory, pow'r,
Wisdom, riches, to obtain,
New dominion ev'ry hour."

3 These through fiery trials trod;
These from great affliction came;
Now, before the throne of God,
Seal'd with his eternal name.

4 Clad in raiment pure and white,
Victor palms in ev'ry hand,
Through their great Redeemer's might,
More than conquerors they stand.

5 Hunger, thirst, disease unknown,
On immortal fruits they feed:
Them the Lamb amidst the throne
Shall to living fountains lead.

6 Joy and gladness banish sighs;
Perfect love dispels their fears;
And forever from their eyes
God shall wipe away their tears.

612 *Heaven Open.*

WIDE, ye heavenly gates, unfold,
 Closed no more by death and sin:
Now the conqu'ring Lord behold,
Let the King of glory in.

2 Who shall to this blest abode
Follow in the Savior's train?
They who in his cleansing blood
Wash away each guilty stain.

3 They whose daily actions prove
Steadfast faith, and holy fear,
Fervent zeal, and grateful love,
They shall dwell forever here.

ANTICIPATIONS OF HEAVEN.

C. M. DORCHESTER.

1. Earth has engross'd my love too long! 'Tis time to lift mine eyes Upward, dear Father, to thy throne, And to my native skies.

613 *The Everlasting Song.* **739**

EARTH has engross'd my love too long!
'Tis time I lift mine eyes
Upward, dear Father, to thy throne,
And to my native skies.

2 There the blest man, my Savior, sits;
The God! how bright he shines!
And scatters infinite delights
On all the happy minds.

3 Seraphs, with elevated strains,
Circle the throne around;
And move and charm the starry plains
With an immortal sound.

4 Jesus, the Lord, their harps employ:
Jesus, my love, they sing!
Jesus, the life of all our joys,
Sounds sweet from ev'ry string.

5 Now let me mount and join their song,
And be an angel too;
My heart, my hand, my ear, my tongue,—
Here's joyful work for you.

6 I would begin the music here,
And so my soul should rise:
Oh for some heav'nly notes to bear
My passions to the skies!

614 *The Heavenly Canaan.* **738**

THERE is a land of pure delight,
Where saints immortal reign;
Infinite day excludes the night,
And pleasures banish pain.

2 There everlasting spring abides,
And never-with'ring flow'rs:

Death, like a narrow sea, divides
This heav'nly land from ours.

3 Sweet fields, beyond the swelling flood,
Stand dress'd in living green:
So to the Jews old Canaan stood,
While Jordan roll'd between.

4 But tim'rous mortals start and shrink,
To cross this narrow sea;
And linger, shiv'ring, on the brink,
And fear to launch away.

5 Oh, could we make our doubts remove,
Those gloomy doubts that rise,
And view the Canaan that we love
With unbeclouded eyes!

6 Could we but climb where Moses stood,
And view the landscape o'er,
Not Jordan's stream, nor death's cold flood,
Should fright us from the shore.

615 *Thoughts of Heaven.*

WHEN musing sorrow weeps the past,
And mourns the present pain;
How sweet to think of peace at last,
And feel that death is gain!

2 'Tis not that murm'ring thoughts arise,
And dread a Father's will;
'Tis not that meek submission flies,
And would not suffer still.

3 It is that heaven-taught faith surveys
The path to realms of light;
And longs her eagle plumes to raise,
And lose herself in sight.

ANTICIPATIONS OF HEAVEN. 213

4 It is that hope with ardor glows
To see him face to face.
Whose dying love no language knows
Sufficient art to trace.

5 It is that harass'd conscience feels
The pangs of struggling sin;
Sees, though afar, the hand that heals,
And ends her war within.

6 Oh! let me wing my hallow'd flight
From earth-born woe and care,
And soar above these clouds of night,
My Savior's bliss to share!

616 *The Joys unseen.* **742**

NOR eye hath seen, nor ear hath heard,
Nor sense nor reason known,
What joys the Father has prepar'd
For those that love the Son.

2 But the good Spirit of the Lord
Reveals a heav'n to come;
The beams of glory in his word
Allure and guide us home.

3 Pure are the joys above the sky,
And all the region peace;
No wanton lips, nor envious eye,
Can see or taste the bliss.

4 Those holy gates forever bar
Pollution, sin, and shame;
None shall obtain admittance there,
But foll'wers of the Lamb.

C. M. JERUSALEM.

1. Je-ru-salem! my hap-py home! Name ever dear to me! When shall my la-bors have an end, When shall my la-bors have an end, In joy and peace and thee?

617 *The Heavenly Jerusalem.* **749**

JERUSALEM! my happy home!
Name ever dear to me!
When shall my labors have an end,
In joy and peace and thee?

2 When shall these eyes thy heav'n-built [walls
And pearly gates behold?
Thy bulwarks with salvation strong,
And streets of shining gold?

3 Oh, when, thou city of my God,
Shall I thy courts ascend,
Where congregations ne'er break up,
And Sabbaths have no end?

4 There happier bow'rs than Eden's bloom,
Nor sin nor sorrow know:
Blest seats! through rude and stormy scenes
I onward press to you.

5 Why should I shrink at pain and woe,
Or feel at death dismay?
I've Canaan's goodly land in view,
And realms of endless day.

6 Apostles, martyrs, prophets, there,
Around my Savior stand;
And soon my friends in Christ below
Will join the glorious band.

7 Jerusalem! my happy home!
My soul still pants for thee;
Then shall my labors have an end,
When I thy joys shall see.

C. M. CHRISTMAS.

With animation.

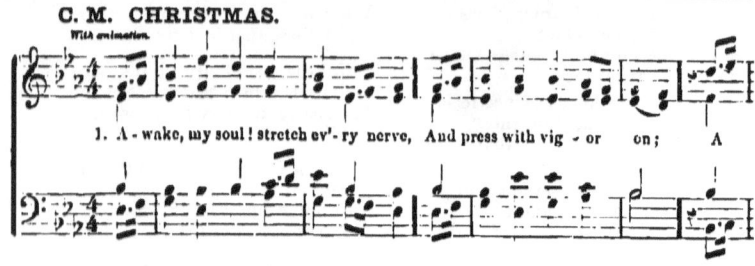

1. A-wake, my soul! stretch ev'-ry nerve, And press with vig-or on; A

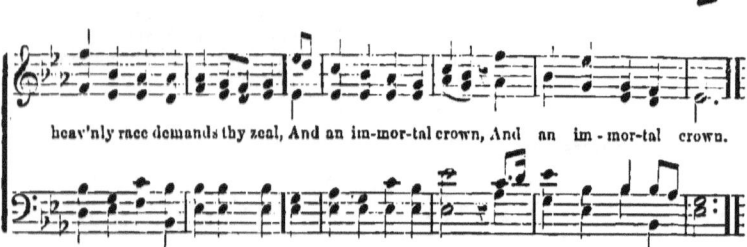

heav'nly race demands thy zeal, And an im-mor-tal crown, And an im-mor-tal crown.

618 *The Prize.* **857**

AWAKE, my soul! stretch ev'ry nerve,
  And press with vigor on;
A heav'nly race demands thy zeal,
  And an immortal crown.

2 A cloud of witnesses around
  Hold thee in full survey;
Forget the steps already trod,
  And onward urge thy way.

3 'Tis God's all-animating voice
  That calls thee from on high;
'Tis his own hand presents the prize
  To thine uplifted eye;—

4 That prize, with peerless glories bright,
  Which shall new lustre boast
When victors' wreaths and monarchs' gems
  Shall blend in common dust.

5 Bless'd Savior! introduced by thee,
  Have we our race begun;
And, crown'd with vict'ry, at thy feet
  We'll lay our laurels down.

619 *Following the Saved.* **870**

RISE, O my soul, pursue the path
  By ancient worthies trod;
Aspiring, view those holy men
  Who liv'd and walk'd with God.

2 Though dead, they speak in reason's ear,
  And in example live;
Their faith, and hope, and mighty deeds,
  Still fresh instruction give.

3 'Twas thro' the Lamb's most precious blood
  They conquer'd ev'ry foe;
To his almighty power and grace
  Their crowns of life they owe.

4 Lord, may I ever keep in view
  The patterns thou hast given,
And ne'er forsake the blessed road
  That led them safe to heaven!

620 *The Victory.* **869**

GIVE me the wings of faith, to rise
  Within the veil, and see
The saints above, how great their joys,
  How bright their glories be.

2 Once they were mourning here below,
  And bath'd their couch with tears:
They wrestled hard, as we do now,
  With sins, and doubts, and fears.

3 I ask'd them whence their vict'ry came:
  They, with united breath,
Ascribe their conquest to the Lamb,
  Their triumph to his death.

4 They mark'd the footsteps that he trod;
  His zeal inspir'd their breast;
And, following their incarnate God,
  Possess'd the promis'd rest.

5 Our glorious Leader claims our praise,
  For his own pattern given;
While the long cloud of witnesses
  Show the same path to heaven.

ANTICIPATIONS OF HEAVEN.

C. M. COVENTRY.

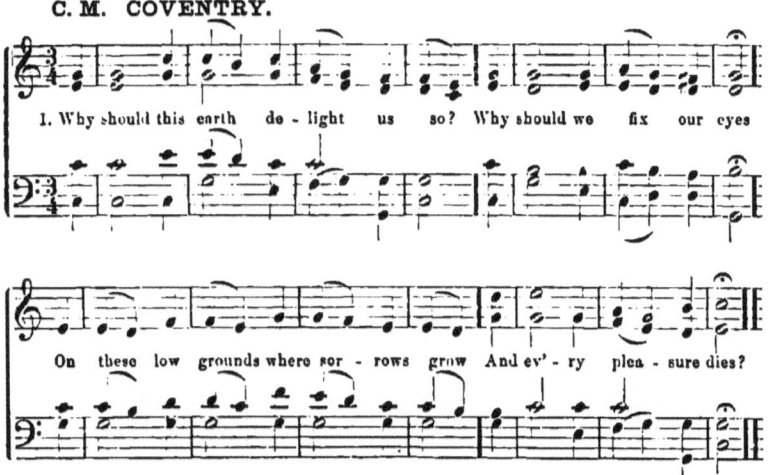

1. Why should this earth delight us so? Why should we fix our eyes
On these low grounds where sorrows grow And ev'ry pleasure dies?

621 *The Enduring World.* **96**

WHY should this earth delight us so?
  Why should we fix our eyes
On these low grounds where sorrows grow
  And ev'ry pleasure dies.

2 While Time his sharpest teeth prepares
  Our comforts to devour,
There is a land above the stars,
  And joys above his pow'r.

3 Nature shall be dissolv'd, and die,
  The sun must end his race,
The earth and sea away shall fly
  Before my Savior's face.

4 When will that glorious morning rise?
  When the last trumpet sound,
And call the nations to the skies,
  From underneath the ground?

622 *Unseen Joys.* **993**

OH, let our thoughts and wishes fly,
  Above these gloomy shades,
To those bright worlds beyond the sky,
  Which sorrow ne'er invades!

2 There joys unseen by mortal eyes,
  Or reason's feeble ray,
In ever-blooming prospect rise,
  Expos'd to no decay.

3 Lord, send a beam of light divine
  To guide our upward aim;
With one reviving look of thine,
  Our languid hearts inflame.

4 Oh, then on faith's sublimest wing,
  Our ardent souls shall rise
To those bright scenes where pleasures
  Immortal in the skies! [spring

623 *Earth receding.*

EARTH'S stormy night will soon be o'er,
  The raging wind shall cease—
The Christian's bark will reach the shore
  Of heav'n's eternal peace.

2 E'en now the distant rays appear
  To chase the gloom of night;
The Sun of righteousness is near,
  And terrors take their flight.

624 *Heaven.*

HOW glorious is the land we seek,
  A land without a tomb,
An everlasting resting-place,
  A sure and quiet home!

2 Far sunnier than the hills of time
  Are its eternal hills;
Far fresher than the rills of earth
  Are its eternal rills.

3 No blight can fall upon its flowers,
  No darkness fill its air,
It has a day forever bright,
  For Christ, its Sun, is there.

4 O Sun of love and peace, arise,
  Thy light upon us beam;
For all this life is but a sleep,
  And all this world a dream.

ANTICIPATIONS OF HEAVEN.

C. M. (Double.) BRATTLE STREET.

1. When I can read my ti-tle clear To man-sions in the skies, I bid fare-well to ev'-ry fear, And wipe my weep-ing eyes. Should earth a-gainst my soul en-gage, And hell-ish darts be hurl'd, Then I can smile at Sa-tan's rage And face a frown-ing world.

625 *The Hope of Heaven.* 466

WHEN I can read my title clear
To mansions in the skies,
I bid farewell to ev'ry fear,
And wipe my weeping eyes.

2 Should earth against my soul engage,
And hellish darts be hurl'd,
Then I can smile at Satan's rage
And face a frowning world.

3 Let cares like a wild deluge come,
And storms of sorrow fall,
May I but safely reach my home,
My God, my heav'n, my all.

4 There shall I bathe my weary soul
In seas of heav'nly rest,
And not a wave of trouble roll
Across my peaceful breast.

626 *Looking Heavenward.* 223

OUR days, alas! our mortal days,
Are short and wretched too:
"Evil and few," the patriarch says,
And well the patriarch knew.

2 'Tis but at best a narrow bound
That Heav'n allows to men,
And pains and sins run through the round
Of threescore years and ten.

ANTICIPATIONS OF HEAVEN. 217

3 Well, if ye must be sad and few,
  Run on, my days, in haste;
Moments of sin, and months of woe,
  Ye cannot fly too fast.

4 Let heav'nly love prepare my soul,
  And call her to the skies,
Where years of long salvation roll,
  And glory never dies.

627 *Anticipating Heaven.* **470**

AND let this feeble body fail
  And let it faint or die;
My soul shall quit the mournful vale
  And soar to worlds on high:
Shall join the disembodied saints,
  And find its long-sought rest,
That only bliss for which it pants,
  In the Redeemer's breast.

2 Oh, what hath Jesus bought for me!
  Before my ravish'd eyes
Rivers of life divine I see,
  And trees of Paradise!
I see a world of spirits bright,
  Who taste the pleasures there!
They all are rob'd in spotless white,
  And conqu'ring palms they bear.

3 Oh, what are all my suff'rings here,
  If, Lord, thou count me meet
With that enraptur'd host t' appear,
  And worship at thy feet!
Give joy or grief, give ease or pain,
  Take life or friends away,
But let me find them all again
  In that eternal day.

628 *Meditations on Future Glory.* **474**

'TIS sweet to rest in lively hope
  That, when my change shall come,
Angels will hover round my bed,
  And waft my spirit home!
There shall my disimprison'd soul
  Behold him and adore;
Be with his likeness satisfied,
  And grieve and sin no more.

2 Shall see him wear that very flesh
  On which my guilt was lain;
His love intense, his merit fresh,
  As though but newly slain.
Soon, too, my slumb'ring dust shall hear
  The trumpet's quick'ning sound;
And by my Savior's pow'r rebuilt,
  At his right hand be found.

3 These eyes shall see him in that day,
  The God that died for me!
And all my rising bones shall say,
  Lord, who is like to thee!

If such the views which grace unfolds,
  Weak as it is below,
What raptures must the church above,
  In Jesus' presence, know.

629 *Reunion in Heaven.* **1003**

BLEST hour, when virtuous friends shall
  Their early sorrows o'er; [meet,
And with celestial welcome greet,
  On an immortal shore.
The parent finds his long-lost child;
  Brothers on brothers gaze:
The tear of resignation mild,
  Is chang'd to joy and praise.

2 Each tender tie, dissolv'd with pain,
  With endless bliss is crown'd:
All that was dead revives again,
  All that was lost is found.
And while remembrance, ling'ring still,
  Draws joy from sorrowing hours,
New prospects rise, new pleasures fill
  The soul's expanding pow'rs.

630 *The Father's House.* **1000**

THERE is a place of sacred rest,
  Far, far beyond the skies,
Where beauty smiles eternally,
  And pleasure never dies;—
My Father's house, my heav'nly home,
  Where "many mansions" stand,
Prepar'd by hands divine for all
  Who seek the better land.

2 When toss'd upon the waves of life,
  With fear on ev'ry side,—
When fiercely howls the gath'ring storm,
  And foams the angry tide,—
Beyond the storm, beyond the gloom,
  Breaks forth the light of morn,
Bright beaming from my Father's house,
  To cheer the soul forlorn.

3 Yes, even at that fearful hour,
  When death shall seize his prey,
And from the place that knows us now,
  Shall hurry us away,—
The vision of that heav'nly home
  Shall cheer the parting soul,
And o'er it, mounting to the skies,
  A tide of rapture roll.

4 In that pure home of tearless joy
  Earth's parted friends shall meet,
With smiles of love that never fade,
  And blessedness complete:
There, there adieus are sounds unknown;
  Death frowns not on that scene,
But life and glorious beauty shine,
  Untroubled and serene.

ANTICIPATIONS OF HEAVEN.

L. M. STONEFIELD.

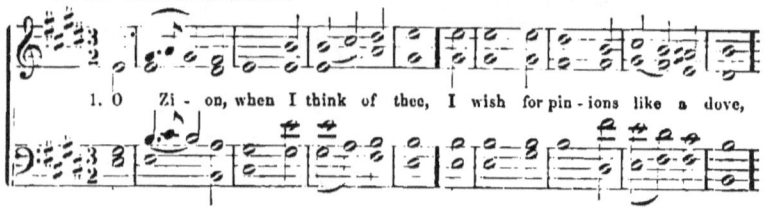

1. O Zi-on, when I think of thee, I wish for pin-ions like a dove,

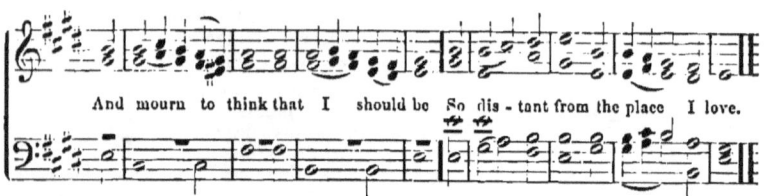

And mourn to think that I should be So dis-tant from the place I love.

631 *Longing for Heaven.* **448**

O ZION, when I think of thee,
  I wish for pinions like a dove,
And mourn to think that I should be
So distant from the place I love.

2 An exile here, and far from home,
  For Zion's sacred walls I sigh;
Thither the ransom'd nations come,
  And see the Savior eye to eye.

3 While here I walk on hostile ground,
  The few that I can call my friends,
Are, like myself, with fetters bound,
  And weariness our steps attends.

4 But yet we shall behold the day
  When Zion's children shall return,
Our sorrows then shall flee away,
  And we shall never, never mourn.

5 The hope that such a day will come
  Makes e'en the exile's portion sweet;
Though now we wander far from home,
  In Zion soon we all shall meet.

632 *We seek a City to come.* **447**

"WE'VE no abiding city here."
  This may distress the worldly mind;
But should not cost the saint a tear,
Who hopes a better rest to find.

2 "We've no abiding city here,"
  Sad truth, were this to be our home;
But let this thought our spirits cheer,
"We seek a city yet to come."

3 "We've no abiding city here,"
  Then let us live as pilgrims do;

Let not the world our rest appear,
But let us haste from all below.

4 "We've no abiding city here,"
We seek a city out of sight,
Zion its name,—the Lord is there,
It shines with everlasting light.

5 Oh, sweet abode of peace and love,
Where pilgrims freed from toil are blest!
Had I the pinions of the dove,
I'd flee to thee, and be at rest.

6 But hush, my soul, nor dare repine!
The time my God appoints is best:
While here, to do his will be *mine,*
And *his* to fix my time of rest.

633 *Prospects of the Righteous.* **728**

WHAT sinners value, I resign:
  Lord, 'tis enough that thou art mine!
I shall behold thy blissful face,
And stand complete in righteousness.

2 This life's a dream, an empty show;
But the bright world to which I go
Hath joys substantial and sincere;
When shall I wake and find me there?

3 Oh, glorious hour! oh, blest abode!
I shall be near and like my God;
And flesh and sin no more control
The sacred pleasures of the soul.

4 My flesh shall slumber in the ground
Till the last trumpet's joyful sound;
Then burst the chains with sweet surprise,
And in my Savior's image rise.

ANTICIPATIONS OF HEAVEN.

L. M. BLENDON.

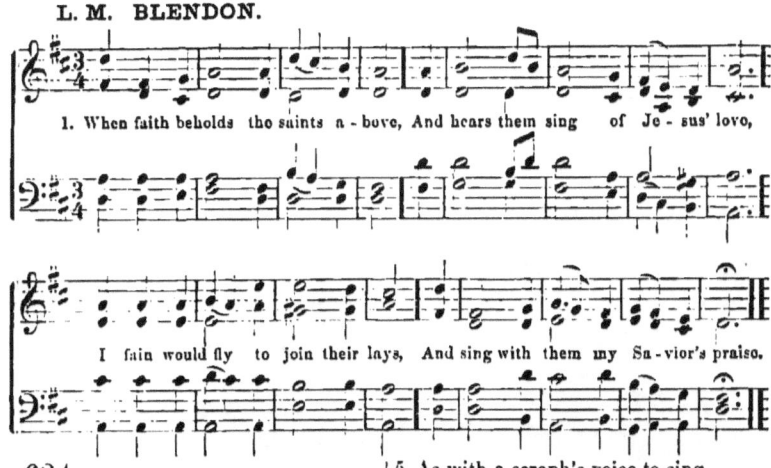

1. When faith beholds the saints above, And hears them sing of Jesus' love, I fain would fly to join their lays, And sing with them my Savior's praise.

634   *View of Heaven.*   **741**

WHEN faith beholds the saints above,
  And hears them sing of Jesus' love,
I fain would fly to join their lays,
And sing with them my Savior's praise.

2 But can my soul such bliss obtain,
Whose guilt deserves eternal pain?
Can I expect his face to see
Throughout a vast eternity?

3 If heav'n be mine, 'tis all of grace,
I'll praise him for the lowest place;
May I but reach within the door,
My anxious soul desires no more.

4 There, ye that love my Savior, sit,
There I with you would fain have place,
Among your thrones or at your feet,
So I might see his lovely face.

635   *Desiring to depart.*   **479**

WHILE on the verge of life I stand,
  And view the scene on either hand,
My spirit struggles with my clay,
And longs to wing its flight away.

2 Where Jesus dwells my soul would be,
And faints my much-lov'd Lord to see:
Earth, twine no more about my heart,
For 'tis far better to depart.

3 Come, ye angelic envoys, come,
And lead the willing pilgrim home;
Ye know the way to Jesus' throne,—
Source of my joys, and of your own.

4 That blissful interview, how sweet!
To fall transported at his feet!
Rais'd in his arms, to view his face,
Through the full beamings of his grace!

5 As with a seraph's voice to sing,
To fly as on a cherub's wing!
Performing, with unwearied hands,
The present Savior's high commands.

6 Yet, with these prospects full in sight,
We'll wait thy signal for the flight,
For, while thy service we pursue,
We find a heav'n in all we do.

636   *Mansions in Heaven.*   **467**

HOW do thy mercies close me round!
  Forever be thy name ador'd;
I blush in all things to abound—
The servant is above his Lord!

2 Inur'd to poverty and pain,
A suff'ring life my Master led:
The Son of God, the Son of man,
He had not where to lay his head.

3 But lo! a place he hath prepar'd
For me, whom watchful angels keep;
Yea, he himself becomes my guard;
He smooths my bed and gives me sleep

4 Jesus protects; my fears, begone!
What can the Rock of ages move!
Safe in thine arms I lay me down,
Thine everlasting arms of love.

5 I rest beneath th' Almighty's shade,
My griefs expire, my troubles cease;
Thou, Lord, on whom my soul is stay'd,
Wilt keep me still in perfect peace.

6 Me for thine own thou lov'st to take
In time and in eternity;
Thou never, never wilt forsake
A helpless worm that trusts in thee.

ANTICIPATIONS OF HEAVEN.

L. M. ROTHWELL.

1. There is a pure and peaceful wave, That rolls a-round the throne of love, Whose waters gladden as they lave The bright and heav'nly shores a-bove, The bright and heav'nly shores a-bove.

637 *The River of God.* **998**

THERE is a pure and peaceful wave,
   That rolls around the throne of love,
Whose waters gladden as they lave
   The bright and heav'nly shores above.

2 While streams which on that tide depend,
   Steal from those heav'nly shores away,
And on this desert world descend,
   Over our barren land to stray ;

  The pilgrim, faint and near to sink
   'neath his load of earthly woe,
Refresh'd beneath its verdant brink,
   Rejoices in its gentle flow.

4 There, O my soul, do thou repose,
   And hover o'er the hallow'd spring,
To drink the crystal wave, and there
   To lave thy wounded, weary wing

5 It may be that the waft of love
Some leaves on that pure tide hath driven ;
Which, passing from the shores above,
Have floated down to us from heaven.

6 So shall thy wants and woes be heal'd,
   By the blest influence they bring :
So thy parch'd lips shall be unseal'd,
   Thy Savior's worthy name to sing.

638 *Race for Heaven.* **859**

AWAKE, our souls, away, our fears,
   Let ev'ry trembling tho't be gone ;
Awake and run the heav'nly race,
   And put a cheerful courage on.

2 True, 'tis a strait and thorny road,
   And mortal spirits tire and faint ;

But they forget the mighty God,
Who feeds the strength of ev'ry saint.

3 The mighty God, whose matchless pow'r
   Is ever new and ever young,
Shall firm endure while endless years
   Their everlasting circles run.

4 From thee, the ever-flowing spring,
   Our souls shall drink a fresh supply ;
While such as trust their native strength
   Shall melt away, and droop and die.

5 Swift as an eagle cuts the air,
   We'll mount aloft to thine abode ;
On wings of love our souls shall fly,
   Nor tire amid the heav'nly road.

639 *Heaven the Soul's Portion.* **747**

FROM this world's joys and senseless
   Oh, come, my soul ! in haste retire ; [mirth
Assume the grandeur of thy birth,
   And to thy native heav'n aspire.

2 'Tis heav'n alone can make thee blest,
   Can ev'ry wish and want supply ;
Thy joy, thy crown, thine endless rest,
   Are all above the lofty sky.

3 Eternal mansions ! bright array !
   Oh, blest exchange ! transporting tho't !
Free from th' approaches of decay,
   Or the least shadow of a spot.

4 There shall mortality no more
   Its wide-extended empire boast,
Forgotten all its dreadful pow'r,
   In life's unbounded ocean lost.

ANTICIPATIONS OF HEAVEN.

8s. 6 lines. PALESTRINA.

1. Sweet is the tho't, the promise sweet, That friends, long se-ver'd friends, shall meet; That kindred souls, on earth disjoin'd, Shall meet, from earth-ly dross re-fin'd, Their mor-tal cares and sor-rows o'er, And min-gle hearts to part no more.

640 *Reunion in Heaven.* **872**
(Stanza 1 in Music.)

2 BUT for this hope, this blessed stay
When earthly comforts all decay,
Oh, who could view th' expiring eye,
Nor wish, with those they love, to die?
Who could receive their parting breath,
Nor long to follow them in death?

3 But we have brighter hopes: we know
Short is this pilgrimage of woe;
We know that our Redeemer lives;
We trust the promises he gives;
And part in hope to meet above,
Where all is joy, and all is love.

641 *Our Rest in Heaven.*

PEACE, troubled soul, whose plaintive moan
Hath taught the rocks the notes of woe;
Cease thy complaint, suppress thy groan,
And let thy tears forget to flow;
Behold, the precious balm is found,
To lull thy pain, to heal thy wound.

2 Though sorely now with sin oppress'd,
And burden'd with thy weighty load,

Yet there shall come relief and rest
By trusting in the Savior's blood;
Heav'n is our home—oh, glorious word!
Forever blessed be the Lord.

642 *Longing for Heaven.* **477**

TO languish for his native air
Can the poor wand'ring exile cease?
The tired, his wish of rest forbear?
The tortur'd, help desiring ease?
The slave, no more for freedom sigh?
Or I no longer pine to die?

2 As shipwreck'd mariners desire,
With eager grasp, to reach the shore;
As hirelings long t' obtain their hire,
And vet'rans wish their warfare o'er;
I languish from this earth to flee,
And grasp for—*immortality.*

3 To heav'n I lift my mournful eyes,
And all within me groans, " how long ?"
Oh, were I landed in the skies!
The bitter loss, the cruel wrong,
Should there no more my soul molest,
Or break my everlasting rest.

ANTICIPATIONS OF HEAVEN.

11s. HINTON.

1. I would not live al-way: I ask not to stay Where storm af-ter
storm ri-ses dark o'er the way: The few lu-cid mornings that dawn on us here,
A.S. Are enough for life's woes, full e-nough for its cheer.

643 *Longing for Heaven.* **873**

1 I WOULD not live alway: I ask not to stay
Where storm after storm rises dark o'er the way:
The few lucid mornings that dawn on us here,
Are enough for life's woes, full enough for its cheer.

2 I would not live alway thus fetter'd by sin,
Temptation without and corruption within:
E'en th' rapture of pardon is mingled with fears,
And th' cup of thanksgiving with penitent tears.

3 I would not live alway: no—welcome the tomb!
Since Jesus hath lain there, I dread not its gloom:
There sweet be my rest, till he bid me arise
To hail him in triumph descending the skies.

4 Who, who would live alway, away from his God;
Away from yon heav'n, that blissful abode,
Where rivers of pleasure flow o'er the bright plains,
And th' noontide of glory eternally reigns?

5 There the saints of all ages in harmony meet
Their Savior and brethren, transported to greet;
While anthems of rapture unceasingly roll,
And th' smile of the Lord is the feast of the soul.

644 *Hoping through the Promises.* **874**

1 HOW firm a foundation, ye saints of the Lord,
Is laid for your faith in his excellent word!
What more can he say than to you he has said?
You who unto Jesus for refuge have fled.

2 In ev'ry condition—in sickness, in health,
In poverty's vale, or abounding in wealth,
At home and abroad, on the land, on the sea,
As thy days may demand, so thy succor shall be.

ANTICIPATIONS OF HEAVEN.

3 The soul that on Jesus hath lean'd for repose,
He will not, he cannot desert to its foes;
That soul, though all hell should endeavor to shake,
He'll never—no, never—no, never forsake.

C. M. ST. MARTINS.

1. Far from these nar-row scenes of night Un-bound-ed glo-ries rise,
And realms of joy and pure de-light, Un-known to mor-tal eyes.

645 *The Glories of Heaven.* **999**

FAR from these narrow scenes of night
  Unbounded glories rise,
And realms of joy and pure delight,
  Unknown to mortal eyes.

2 Fair, distant land!—could mortal eyes
  But half its charms explore,
How would our spirits long to rise,
  And dwell on earth no more!

3 No cloud those blissful regions know—
  Realms ever bright and fair;
For sin, the source of mortal woe,
  Can never enter there.

4 Oh, may the heav'nly prospect fire
  Our hearts with ardent love,
Till wings of faith, and strong desire,
  Bear ev'ry thought above.

5 Prepare us, Lord, by grace divine,
  For thy bright courts on high:
Then bid our spirits rise and join
  The chorus of the sky.

646 *Heaven in Prospect.* **476**

ON Jordan's stormy banks I stand,
  And cast a wishful eye
To Canaan's fair and happy land,
  Where my possessions lie.

2 Oh, the transporting, rapt'rous scene,
  That rises to my sight!
Sweet fields array'd in living green,
  And rivers of delight!

3 There gen'rous fruits, that never fail,
  On trees immortal grow;
There rocks and hills, and brooks and vales,
  With milk and honey flow.

4 All o'er those wide-extended plains,
  Shines one eternal day;
There God the Son forever reigns,
  And scatters night away.

5 No chilling winds nor pois'nous breath
  Can reach that healthful shore;
Sickness and sorrow, pain and death,
  Are felt and fear'd no more.

6 When shall I reach that happy place,
  And be forever blest?
When shall I see my Father's face,
  And in his bosom rest?

7 Fill'd with delight, my raptur'd soul
  Would here no longer stay;
Though Jordan's waves around me roll,
  Fearless I'd launch away.

ANTICIPATIONS OF HEAVEN.

11s. HOME.

647 *The Saints' Sweet Home.* 997

'MID scenes of confusion and creature complaints,
How sweet to my soul is communion with saints!
To find at the banquet of mercy there's room,
And feel in the presence of Jesus at home!
    Home! home! sweet, sweet home!
Prepare me, dear Savior, for glory, my home.

2 Sweet bonds, that unite all the children of peace!
And thrice-precious Jesus, whose love cannot cease!
Though oft from thy presence in sadness I roam,
I long to behold thee in glory at home.
    Home, &c.

3 I sigh from this body of sin to be free,
Which hinders my joy and communion with thee;
Though now my temptations like billows may foam,
All, all will be peace when I'm with thee at home.
    Home, &c.

4 While here in the valley of conflict I stay,
Oh, give me submission and strength as my day!
In all my afflictions to thee would I come,
Rejoicing in hope of my glorious home.
    Home, &c.

5 Whate'er thou deniest, oh, give me thy grace,
The Spirit's sure witness, and smiles of thy face;
Indulge me with patience to wait at thy throne,
And find even now a sweet foretaste of home.
    Home, &c.

6 I long, dearest Lord, in thy beauties to shine,
No more as an exile in sorrow to pine,
And in thy dear image arise from the tomb,
With glorified millions to praise thee at home.
    Home, &c.

ANTICIPATIONS OF HEAVEN.

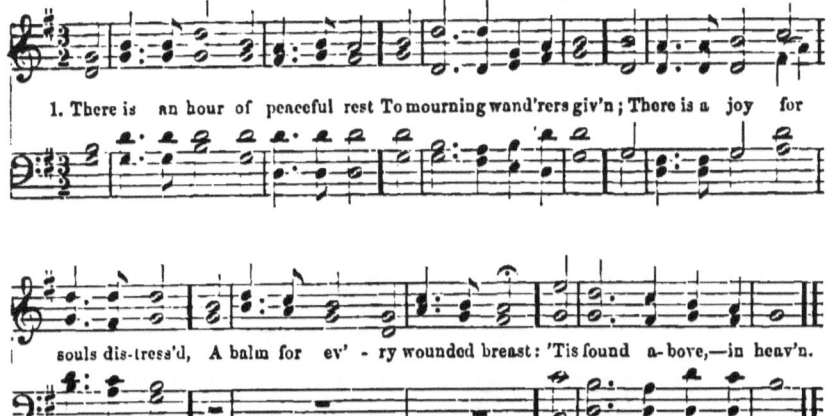

8, 6, 8, 8, 6. WOODLAND.

1. There is an hour of peaceful rest To mourning wand'rers giv'n; There is a joy for souls dis-tress'd, A balm for ev'-ry wounded breast: 'Tis found a-bove,—in heav'n.

648 *Heavenly Rest.* **994**

THERE is an hour of peaceful rest,
  To mourning wand'rers giv'n ;
There is a joy for souls distress'd,
A balm for ev'ry wounded breast:
  'Tis found above,—in heav'n.

2 There is a soft, a downy bed,
  'Tis fair as breath of ev'n ;
A couch for weary mortals spread,
Where they may rest the aching head,
  And find repose—in heav'n.

3 There is a home for weary souls,
  By sin and sorrow driv'n ;
When toss'd on life's tempestuous shoals,
Where storms arise and ocean rolls,
  And all is drear—but heav'n.

4 There faith lifts up her cheerful eye,
  To brighter prospects giv'n ;
And views the tempest passing by,
The ev'ning shadows quickly fly,
  And all serene—in heav'n.

5 There fragrant flow'rs immortal bloom,
  And joys supreme are giv'n ;
There joys divine disperse the gloom:—
Beyond the confines of the tomb
  Appears the dawn of heav'n.

649 *Heavenly Joys on Earth.*

OH, say no more there's nothing true
  But the bright scenes of heav'n !

There's truth in mercy's cheering page ;
  Directing youth, consoling age,
  Declaring sins forgiv'n.

2 Oh, say no more there's naught but heav'n
  That's calm, or true, or bright ;
Bright are the beams the Savior sheds,
The radiance that the gospel spreads,
  Amid this realm of night.

3 Tho' loud the blast, tho' dark the day,
  We oft have peace at ev'n :
And if we *here* have such delight,
In objects not unknown to sight,
  How calm, how bright is heav'n !

650 *The Hour of Peace.* **995**

THERE is an hour of hallow'd peace
  For those with care oppress'd,
When sighs & sorrowing tears shall cease,
  And all be hush'd to rest :

2 'Tis then the soul is freed from fears,
  And doubts that here annoy :
Then they that oft had sown in tears
  Shall reap again in joy.

3 There is a home of sweet repose,
  Where storms assail no more :
The stream of endless pleasure flows
  On that celestial shore :

4 There purity with love appears,
  And bliss without alloy ;
There they that oft had sown in tears
  Shall reap eternal joy.

MEANS OF GRACE—THE WORD.

L. M. DUKE STREET.

1. Eternal Spirit! 'twas thy breath The oracles of truth inspir'd;
And kings and holy seers of old With strong prophetic impulse fired.

651 *The Bible Inspired.* 1

ETERNAL Spirit! 'twas thy breath
The oracles of truth inspir'd;
And kings and holy seers of old
With strong prophetic impulse fired.

2 Mov'd by thy great almighty pow'r,
Their lips with heavenly wisdom flow'd;
Their hands a thousand wonders wrought,
Which bore the signature of God.

3 With gladsome hearts they spread the news
Of pardon, through a Savior's blood;
And to a num'rous seeking crowd
Mark'd out the path to his abode.

4 The pow'rs of earth and hell in vain
Against the sacred word combine;
Thy providence through ev'ry age
Securely guards the work divine.

5 Thee, its great author, source of light,
Thee, its preserver, we adore;
And humbly ask a ray from thee
Its hidden wonders to explore.

652 *The Bible a Pillar of Fire.* 8

WHEN Israel through the desert pass'd,
A fiery pillar went before,
To guide them through the dreary waste,
And lessen the fatigues they bore.

2 Such is thy glorious word, O God!
'Tis for our light and guidance given;
It sheds a lustre all abroad,
And points the path to bliss and heav'n.

3 It fills the soul with sweet delight,
And quickens its inactive powers;
It sets our wandering footsteps right;
Displays thy love, and kindles ours.

4 Its promises rejoice our hearts;
Its doctrines are divinely true;
Knowledge and pleasure it imparts;
It comforts and instructs us too.

5 Ye favor'd lands, who have this word,
Ye saints, who feel its saving power,
Unite your tongues to praise the Lord,
And his distinguish'd grace adore.

653 *Sacred Scripture.* 2

'TWAS by an order from the Lord,
The ancient prophets spoke his word;
His Spirit did their tongues inspire,
And warm'd their hearts with heav'nly fire.

2 The works & wonders which they wrought
Confirm'd the messages they brought;
The prophet's pen succeeds his breath,
To save the holy words from death.

3 Great God! mine eyes with pleasure look
On the dear volume of thy book;
There my Redeemer's face I see,
And read his name who died for me.

4 Let the false raptures of the mind
Be lost, and vanish in the wind;
Here I can fix my hope secure:
This is thy word, and must endure.

MEANS OF GRACE—THE WORD. 227

L. M. BROWER.

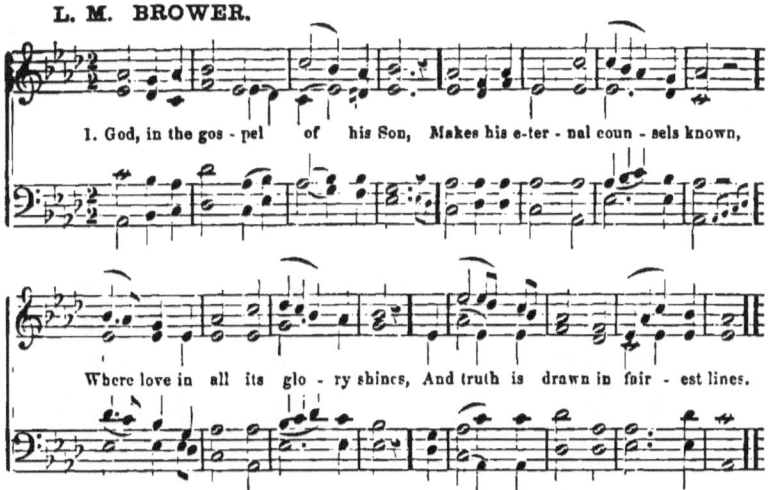

1. God, in the gos-pel of his Son, Makes his e-ter-nal coun-sels known,
Where love in all its glo-ry shines, And truth is drawn in fair-est lines.

654 *The Gospel Word.*

GOD, in the gospel of his Son,
    Makes his eternal counsels known,
Where love in all its glory shines,
And truth is drawn in fairest lines.

2 Here sinners of an humble frame
May taste his grace and learn his name;
May read, in characters of blood,
The wisdom, power, and grace of God.

3 Here faith reveals, to mortal eyes,
A brighter world beyond the skies;
Here shines the light which guides our way
From earth to realms of endless day.

4 Oh, grant us grace, almighty Lord!
To read and mark thy holy word,
Its truths with meekness to receive,
And by its holy precepts live.

5 May this blest volume ever lie
Close to my heart, and mine mine eye,—
Till life's last hour, my soul engage,
And be my chosen heritage.

655 *Destiny of the Bible.* 978

GO, Holy Book! thou word divine
    Of him who spake as man ne'er spake;
Go, for Omnipotence is thine,
And to thy truths the nations wake.

2 Go—and wherever man has trod,
Where there is one for whom Christ died,
Open the treasures of our God,
And tell them of the Crucified.

3 Fly—fly on wing of angel speed,
And bear the news of dying grace,
Say, Jesus is the Christ indeed,
And ransom'd ALL the human race.

4 The veil of ignorance shall rend,
And light shall pass through error's night,
And idols of the earth shall bend
Beneath the glory of thy might.

5 Onward in thy triumphant way,
Thou message of the Holy One,
Thy truth shall usher in the day,
The reign of God's beloved Son.

656 *The Scriptures Substantial.* 980

THIS world that we so highly prize,
    And seek so eagerly its smile—
What is it?—vanity and lies—
A broken cistern all the while.

2 Pleasure, with her delightful song,
That charms the unwary to beguile—
What is it?—the deceiver's tongue—
A broken cistern all the while.

3 Riches, that so absorb the mind
In anxious care and ceaseless toil—
What are they?—faithless as the wind—
A broken cistern all the while.

4 Yes—all are broken cisterns, Lord!
To those that wander far from thee:
The living stream is in thy word,
Thou Fount of immortality.

MEANS OF GRACE—THE WORD.

C. M. DEVIZES.

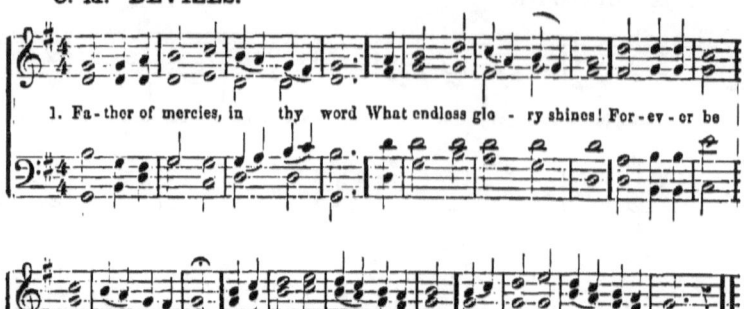

1. Fa-ther of mercies, in thy word What endless glo - ry shines! For-ev-er be thy name a - dor'd For those ce - les - tial lines, For those ce - les - tial lines.

657 *The Scriptures Suitable.*

FATHER of mercies, in thy word
  What endless glory shines!
Forever be thy name ador'd
  For these celestial lines.

2 Here may the wretched sons of want
  Exhaustless riches find;
Riches above what earth can grant,
  And lasting as the mind.

3 Here the fair tree of knowledge grows,
  And yields a free repast;
Sublimer sweets than nature knows
  Invite the longing taste.

4 Here the Redeemer's welcome voice
  Spreads heavenly peace around;
And life and everlasting joys
  Attend the blissful sound.

5 Oh, may these heav'nly pages be
  My ever dear delight;
And still new beauties may I see,
  And still increasing light!

6 Divine Instructor, gracious Lord!
  Be thou forever near;
Teach me to love thy sacred word,
  And view my Savior there.

658 *The Scriptures Excellent.*

LET all the heathen writers join
  To form one perfect book:
Great God! if once compar'd with thine,
  How mean their writings look!

2 Not the most perfect rules they gave
  Could show one sin forgiv'r,

Nor lead a step beyond the grave:
  But thine conduct to heav'n.

3 Lord, I have made thy word my choice,
  My lasting heritage;
There shall my noblest pow'rs rejoice,
  My warmest thoughts engage.

4 I'll read the hist'ries of thy love,
  And keep thy laws in sight,
While through thy promises I rove
  With ever fresh delight.

5 'Tis a broad land of wealth unknown,
  Where springs of life arise,
Seeds of immortal bliss are sown,
  And hidden glory lies.

659 *Glory of the Word.*

THE Spirit breathes upon the word,
  And brings the truth to sight;
Precepts and promises afford
  A sanctifying light.

2 A glory gilds the sacred page,
  Majestic like the sun;
It gives a light to every age,
  It gives—but borrows none.

3 The hand that gave it still supplies
  The gracious light and heat:
His truths upon the nations rise,
  They rise, but never set.

4 Let everlasting thanks be thine,
  For such a bright display,
As makes a world of darkness shine
  With beams of heav'nly day.

MEANS OF GRACE—THE WORD.

C. M. HEBER.

1. How shall the young secure their hearts, And guard their lives from sin?
Thy word the choicest rules imparts To keep the conscience clean.

660 *The Bible our Instructor.* 9

HOW shall the young secure their hearts,
And guard their lives from sin?
Thy word the choicest rules imparts
To keep the conscience clean.

2 When once it ent'reth to the mind,
It spreads such light abroad,
The meanest souls instruction find,
And raise their thoughts to God.

3 'Tis like the sun, a heav'nly light
That guides us all the day;
And through the dangers of the night
A lamp to lead our way.

4 The men that keep thy law with care,
And meditate thy word,
Grow wiser than their teachers are,
And better know the Lord.

5 Thy precepts make me truly wise:
I hate the sinner's road;
I hate mine own vain thoughts that rise,
But love thy law, my God.

6 Thy word is everlasting truth;
How pure is ev'ry page!
That holy book shall guide our youth,
And well support our age.

661 *Value of Religious Instruction.* 950

HOW happy are the young who hear
Instruction's warning voice,
And who celestial wisdom make
Their early—only choice!

2 For she has treasures greater far
Than east or west unfold;
And her rewards more precious are
Than all their stores of gold.

3 She guides the young with innocence
In pleasure's path to tread;
A crown of glory she bestows
Upon the aged head.

4 According as her labors rise,
So her rewards increase;
Her ways are ways of pleasantness,
And all her paths are peace.

662 *The Bible a Treasure.* 4

LET av'rice, borne from shore to shore,
Her chosen good pursue:
Thy word, O Lord, we value more
Than India or Peru.

2 Here mines of knowledge, love, and joy
Are open'd to our sight;
The purest gold without alloy,
And gems divinely bright.

3 The counsels of redeeming grace
These sacred leaves unfold;
And here the Savior's lovely face
Our raptur'd eyes behold.

4 Here light, descending from above,
Directs our doubtful feet;
Here promises of heav'nly love
Our ardent wishes meet.

5 Our num'rous griefs are here redrest,
And all our wants supplied;
Naught we can ask to make us blest
Is in this book denied.

MEANS OF GRACE—THE WORD.

C. M. ZANESVILLE.

1. La-den with guilt, and full of fears, I fly to thee, my Lord; And not a ray of hope ap-pears, But in thy writ-ten word.

663 *Consolation from the Bible.* 11

LADEN with guilt, and full of fears,
 I fly to thee, my Lord ;
And not a ray of hope appears,
 But in thy written word.

2 The volume of my Father's grace
 Does all my grief assuage ;
Here I behold my Savior's face
 In almost ev'ry page.

3 This is the field where hidden lies
 The pearl of price unknown ;
That merchant is divinely wise
 Who makes the pearl his own.

4 This is the Judge that ends the strife,
 Where wit and reason fail ;
My guide to everlasting life
 Through all this gloomy vale.

5 Oh, may thy counsels, mighty God !
 My roving feet command ;
Nor I forsake the happy road
 That leads to thy right hand.

664 *The Bible.*

LAMP of our feet ! whereby we trace
 Our path, when wont to stray ;
Stream from the Fount of heav'nly grace !
 Brook by the traveler's way !

2 Bread of our souls ! whereon we feed ;
 True manna from on high !
Our guide, our chart ! wherein we read
 Of realms beyond the sky.

3 Pillar of fire, through watches dark !
 Or radiant cloud by day !
When waves would whelm our tossing bark,
 Our anchor and our stay !

4 Childhood's preceptor ! manhood's trust !
 Old age's firm ally !
Our hope, when we go down to dust,
 Of immortality !

665 *Prayer for the Word's Success.* 560

ALMIGHTY God, thy word is cast
 Like seed upon the ground ;
Oh, let the dew of heav'n descend,
 And shed its influence round.

2 Let not the foe of Christ and man
 This holy seed remove ;
May it take root in ev'ry heart,
 And grow in faith and love !

3 Let not this life's deceitful cares,
 Nor worldly wealth and joy,
Nor scorching beam, nor stormy blast,
 The rising plant destroy.

4 Where'er the word of life is sown,
 A large increase bestow,
That all who hear thy message, Lord,
 Its saving pow'r may know.

666 *Walking in Light.*

WALK in the light ! so shalt thou know
 That fellowship of love
His Spirit only can bestow,
 Who reigns in light above.

2 Walk in the light !—and sin, abhorr'd,
 Shall ne'er defile again ;
The blood of Jesus Christ the Lord
 Shall cleanse from every stain.

MEANS OF GRACE—BAPTISM, ETC.   231

3 Walk in the light!—and thou shalt find
  Thy heart made truly His,
Who dwells in cloudless light enshrin'd,
  In whom no darkness is.

4 Walk in the light!—and thou shalt own
  Thy darkness pass'd away,
Because that light hath on thee shone
  In which is perfect day.

5 Walk in the light!—and e'en the tomb
  No fearful shade shall wear:
Glory shall chase away its gloom,
  For Christ has conquer'd there.

6 Walk in the light!—and life shall be
  A path, though stormy, bright;
For God by grace shall dwell in thee,
  And God himself is light.

7s. PLEYEL'S HYMN.

1. God of mer-cy, hear our pray'r For the chil-dren thou hast giv'n;
Let them all thy bless-ings share, Grace on earth and bliss in heav'n.

667 *For a Blessing on Children.* **949**

GOD of mercy, hear our pray'r
  For the children thou hast giv'n;
Let them all thy blessings share,
Grace on earth and bliss in heav'n.

2 Cleanse their souls from ev'ry stain,
  Through the Savior's precious blood;
Let them all be born again,
And be reconcil'd to God.

3 For this mercy, Lord, we cry;
  Bend thine ever-gracious ear:
While on thee our souls rely,
Hear our pray'r, in mercy hear.

668 *Holy Dedication.* **512**

PARDON'D through redeeming grace,
  In thy blessed Son reveal'd;
Worshiping before thy face,
Lord, to thee ourselves we yield.

2 Thou the sacrifice receive,
  Humbly offer'd through thy Son;
Quicken us in him to live;
Lord, in us thy will be done.

3 By the hallow'd outward sign,
  By the cleansing grace within,
Seal, and make us wholly thine;
Wash, and keep us pure from sin.

4 Call'd to bear the Christian name,
  May our vows and life accord;
And our ev'ry deed proclaim,
  "Holiness unto the Lord!"

669 *At the Baptism of a Child.* **876**

SAVIOR, Father, Brother, Friend,
  (Ev'ry tender name in one,)
Holy Jesus, now descend,
  Perfect what thou hast begun:

2 Whom we now devote to God,
  At a parent's hand receive;
With the purifying flood
  Now the Holy Spirit give.

3 While on this dear infant's head
  Pour we this translucid stream,
On the rite thy blessing shed,
  With thy blood the soul redeem.

4 Seal the grace upon the heart,
  By baptismal water shown;
While the symbol we impart,
  May the saving work be done.

MEANS OF GRACE—BAPTISM.

L. M. MIGDOL.

670 *At the Baptism of a Child.* **877**

UNITED pray'rs ascend to thee,
  Eternal Parent of mankind ;
Smile on this waiting family,
Thy blessing let thy servants find.

2 The father of the household bless,
The priest, the patriarch, let him move
That all his family may trace
In him thy law, in lines of love.

3 Regard the mother's anxious tears,
Her heart's desire, her earnest pray'rs,
And while her infant charge she rears,
Crown with success her pious cares.

4 Let the dear pledges of their love
Like tender plants around them grow,
Thy present grace, and joys above,
Upon their little ones bestow.

5 Receive at their believing hand
The babe whom they devote as thine,
Obedient to their Lord's command—
And seal with pow'r the rite divine.

6 To ev'ry member of their house
Thy grace impart, thy love extend ;
Grant ev'ry good that time allows,
With heav'nly joys that never end.

671 *Prayer for Children.* **654**

DEAR Savior, if these lambs should stray
  From thy secure enclosure's bound,
And, lur'd by worldly joys away,
Among the thoughtless crowd be found ;

2 Remember still that they are thine,
That thy dear sacred name they bear,

Think that the seal of love divine,—
The sign of cov'nant grace they wear.

3 In all their erring, sinful years,
Oh, let them ne'er forgotten be ;
Remember all the pray'rs and tears
Which made them consecrate to thee.

4 And when these lips no more can pray,
These eyes can weep for them no more,
Turn thou their feet from folly's way,
The wand'rers to thy fold restore.

672 *Prayer for Children.* **659**

NOW, Father, Son, and Holy Ghost,
  To whom we for our children cry !
The good desir'd and wanted most,
Out of thy richest grace supply.

2 Error and ignorance remove,
The blindness of their hearts and mind ;
Give them the wisdom from above,
Spotless and peaceable and kind.

3 Answer on them the end of all
Our cares and pains and studies here !
On them, recover'd from their fall,
Stamp'd with the humble character.

4 Unite what long has been disjoin'd,
Knowledge and vital piety ;
Learning and holiness combin'd,
And truth and love let all men see.

5 Father, accept them through thy Son,
And ever by thy Spirit guide !
Thy wisdom in their lives be shown,
Thy name confess'd and glorified.

MEANS OF GRACE—BAPTISM, ETC. 233

L. M. ILLA. *Moderato.*

1. Bro-ther in Christ, and well be-lov'd, To Jesus and his ser-vants dear, En-ter, and show thy-self ap-prov'd; En-ter, and find that God is here.

673 *Admitting a Member.* **589**

BROTHER in Christ, and well belov'd,
  To Jesus and his servants dear,
Enter, and show thyself approv'd;
Enter, and find that God is here.

2 Welcome from earth!—lo, the right hand
Of fellowship to thee we give!
With open arms and hearts we stand,
And thee in Jesus' name receive.

3 Say, is thy heart resolv'd as ours?
Then let it burn with sacred love,
Then let it taste the heav'nly pow'rs,
Partaker of the joys above.

4 Jesus, attend, thyself reveal,—
Are we not met in thy great name?
Thee in our midst we wait to feel,
We wait to catch the heav'nly flame.

674 *Dedication to God.* **590**

LORD, I am thine, entirely thine,
  Purchas'd and sav'd by blood divine;
With full consent thine I would be,
And own thy sov'reign right in me.

2 Here, Lord, my life, my soul, my all,
I yield to thee beyond recall;
Accept thine own, so long withheld—
Accept what I so freely yield!

3 Grant one poor sinner more a place
Among the children of thy grace;
A wretched sinner, lost to God,
But ransom'd by Immanuel's blood.

4 Thine would I live—thine would I die—
Be thine through all eternity;

The vow is past beyond repeal;
Now will I set the solemn seal.

5 Here at thy cross, where flows the blood
That bought my guilty soul for God,
Thee my new Master now I call,
And consecrate to thee my all.

6 Do thou assist a feeble worm
The great engagement to perform:
Thy grace assistance can extend,
And on that grace I will depend.

675 *Welcome at Confirmation.* **591**

WELCOME, thou well-belov'd of God,
  Thou heir of grace, redeem'd by blood;
Welcome with us thy hand to join
As partner of our lot divine.

2 With us the pilgrim's state embrace:
We're trav'ling to a blissful place;
The Holy Ghost, who knows the way,
Conduct thee on from day to day.

3 Take up thy cross and patient bear,
It shall be light and easy here:
Soon shalt thou sit with Jesus down,
And wear an everlasting crown.

676 *Baptism of the Spirit.* **878**

COME, Holy Ghost! come from on high,
  Baptizer of our spirits thou!
The sacramental seal apply,
And witness with the water now.

2 Exert thy gracious pow'r divine,
And sprinkle thou th' atoning blood;
May Father, Son, and Spirit join
To seal this child a child of God.

MEANS OF GRACE, BAPTISM, ETC.

L. M. CHEMNITZ.

1. O happy day, that stays my choice On thee, my Savior, and my God! Well may this glowing heart rejoice, And tell its raptures all abroad.

677 *Entering into Covenant.* **922**

O HAPPY day, that stays my choice
  On thee, my Savior, and my God!
Well may this glowing heart rejoice,
And tell its raptures all abroad.

2 O happy bond, that seals my vows
To him who merits all my love!
Let cheerful anthems fill his house,
While to that sacred shrine I move.

3 'Tis done:—the great transaction's done,
I am my Lord's, and he is mine:
He drew me—and I follow'd on—
Charm'd to confess the voice divine.

4 Now rest, my long-divided heart,
Fix'd on this blissful centre, rest;
With ashes who would grudge to part,
When call'd on angels' bread to feast?

5 High heav'n, that heard the solemn vow,
That vow renew'd shall daily hear:
Till in life's latest hour I bow,
And bless in death a bond so dear.

678 *Entire Consecration.* **917**

NOW I resolve, with all my heart,
  With all my power, to serve the Lord;
Nor from his ways will I depart,
Whose service is a rich reward.

2 Oh, be this service all my joy!
Around let my example shine,
Till others love the blest employ,
And join in labors so divine.

3 Be this the purpose of my soul,
My solemn, my determin'd choice,
To yield to his supreme control,
And in his kind commands rejoice.

4 Oh, may I never faint nor tire,
Nor, wand'ring, leave his sacred ways;
Great God! accept my soul's desire,
And give me strength to live thy praise.

679 *Devoted to God.* **927**

O LORD, thy heav'nly grace impart,
  And fix my frail, inconstant heart;
Henceforth my chief desire shall be
To dedicate myself to thee.

2 Whate'er pursuits my time employ,
One thought shall fill my soul with joy;
That silent, secret thought shall be,
That all my hopes are fix'd on thee.

3 Thy glorious eye pervadeth space;
Thy presence, Lord, fills ev'ry place;
And, wheresoe'er my lot may be,
Still shall my spirit cleave to thee.

4 Renouncing ev'ry worldly thing,
And safe beneath thy spreading wing,
My sweetest thought henceforth shall be,
That all I want I find in thee.

C. M. ORTONVILLE.

1. "Proclaim," said Christ, "my wondrous grace To all the sons of men; He who believes and is bap-tiz'd, Sal-va-tion shall ob-tain, Sal-va-tion shall ob-tain."

680 *Adult Baptism.* **511**

"PROCLAIM," said Christ, "my won-
    To all the sons of men; [drous grace
He who believes and is baptiz'd,
    Salvation shall obtain."

2 Let plenteous grace descend on those
    Who, hoping in thy word,
This day have publicly declar'd
    That Jesus is their Lord.

3 With cheerful feet may they go on,
    And run the Christian race;
And in the troubles of the way
    Find all-sufficient grace.

4 And when the awful message comes
    To call their souls away,
May they be found prepar'd to live
    In realms of endless day.

681 *Entering into Covenant.* **926**

COME, let us join our souls to God,
    In everlasting bands;
And seize the blessings he bestows,
    With eager hearts and hands.

2 Come, let us to his temple haste,
    And seek his favor there,
Before his footstool humbly bow,
    And pour our fervent pray'r.

3 Come, let us seal, without delay,
    The cov'nant of his grace;
Nor shall the years of distant life
    Its mem'ry e'er efface.

4 Thus in our youthful days we'll haste
    To seek our fathers' God,
And may we ne'er forsake the path
    Their blessed feet have trod.

682 *Self-Dedication.* **921**

WHAT shall I render to my God
    For all his kindness shown?
My feet shall visit thine abode,
    My songs address thy throne.

2 Among the saints that fill thy house,
    My off'rings shall be paid;
There shall my zeal perform the vows
    My soul in anguish made.

3 How much is mercy thy delight,
    Thou ever-blessed God!
How dear thy servants in thy sight—
    How precious is their blood!

4 How happy all thy servants are!
    How great thy grace to me!
My life, which thou hast made thy care,
    Lord! I devote to thee.

5 Now I am thine,—forever thine;
    Nor shall my purpose move;
Thy hand hath loosed my bonds of pain,
    And bound me with thy love.

6 Here, in thy courts, I leave my vow,
    And thy rich grace record;
Witness, ye saints! who hear me now
    If I forsake the Lord.

MEANS OF GRACE—BAPTISM.

C. M. PARKER.

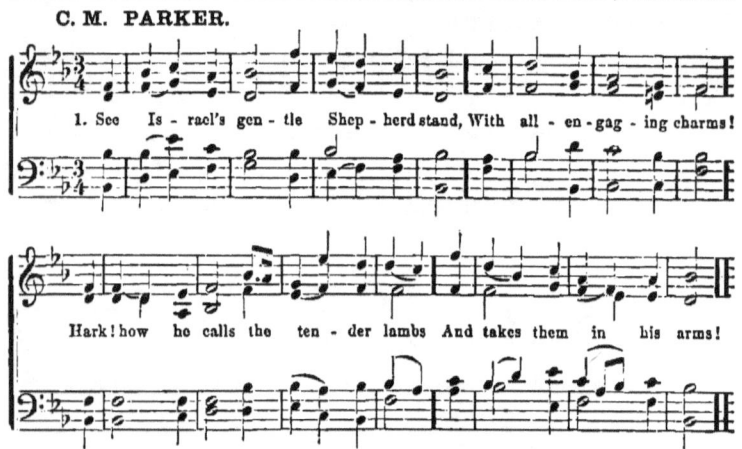

1. See Is-rael's gen-tle Shep-herd stand, With all-en-gag-ing charms! Hark! how he calls the ten-der lambs And takes them in his arms!

683 *Let them come.* **509**

SEE Israel's gentle Shepherd stand,
 With all-engaging charms!
Hark! how he calls the tender lambs
 And takes them in his arms!

2 "Permit them to approach," he cries,
 "Nor scorn their humble name;
It was to bless such souls as these,
 The Lord of angels came."

3 We bring them, Lord, with grateful hearts,
 And yield them up to thee;
Joyful that we ourselves are thine,
 Thine let our offspring be!

4 If orphans they are left behind,
 Thy guardian care we trust;
That care shall heal our bleeding hearts,
 If weeping o'er their dust.

684 *Joy over the New Convert.* **583**

OH, how divine, how sweet the joy,
 When but one sinner turns,
And, with an humble, broken heart,
 His sins and errors mourns!

2 Pleas'd with the news, the saints below,
 In songs their tongues employ;
Beyond the skies the tidings go,
 And heav'n is fill'd with joy.

3 Well pleas'd, the Father sees and hears
 The conscious sinner's moan;
Jesus receives him in his arms,
 And claims him for his own.

4 Nor angels can their joy contain,
 But kindle with new fire:
"The sinner lost is found," they sing,
 And strike the sounding lyre.

685 *Christ's Condescension to Infants.* **510**

BEHOLD, what condescending love
 Jesus on earth displays!
To babes and sucklings he extends
 The riches of his grace.

2 He still the ancient promise keeps,
 To our forefathers giv'n:
Young children in his arms he takes,
 And calls them heirs of heav'n.

3 Savior, receive this tender branch,
 And form his soul for God:
Baptize him with thy Spirit, Lord,
 And wash him with thy blood.

686 *Advantages of Early Piety.* **652**

HAPPY is he whose early years
 Receive instruction well;
Who hates the sinner's path, and fears
 The road that leads to hell.

2 'Tis easier work if we begin
 To serve the Lord betimes;
While sinners who grow old in sin
 Are harden'd by their crimes.

3 It saves us from a thousand snares
 To mind religion young;
With joy it crowns succeeding years,
 And makes our virtues strong.

MEANS OF GRACE—BAPTISM.

S. M. SILVER STREET.

1. Great God, now con-de-scend To bless our ris-ing race; Soon may their will-ing spir-its bend To thy vic-to-rious grace.

687 *Prayer for Children.* **658**

GREAT God, now condescend
  To bless our rising race;
Soon may their willing spirits bend
  To thy victorious grace.

2 Oh, what a vast delight
  Their happiness to see!
Our warmest wishes all unite
  To lead their souls to thee.

3 Dear Lord, thy Spirit pour
  Upon our infant seed;
Oh, bring the long'd-for happy hour
  That makes them thine indeed.

4 Thus let our favor'd race
  Surround thy sacred board,
There to adore thy sov'reign grace
  And sing their dying Lord.

688 *The Same.* **657**

THOU God of sov'reign grace,
  In mercy now appear;
We long to see thy smiling face,
  And feel that thou art near.

2 Receive these lambs to-day,
  O Shepherd of the flock,
And wash the stains of guilt away
  Beside the smitten Rock.

3 Thy saving health impart,
  O Comforter divine!
Now make these children pure in heart,
  Make them entirely thine.

4 To-day in love descend;
  Oh, come this precious hour;
In mercy now their spirits bend
  By thy resistless power.

5 Low bending at thy feet,
  Our offspring we resign;
Thine arm is strong, thy love is great,
  And high thy glories shine.

689 *Baptism of Infants.* **508**

LORD! what our ears have heard,
  Our eyes delighted trace,
Thy love in long succession shown
  To ev'ry virtuous race.

2 Our children thou dost claim,
  And mark them out for thine:
Ten thousand blessings to thy name
  For goodness so divine!

3 Thy cov'nant may they keep,
  And bless the happy bands
Which closer still engage our hearts
  To honor thy commands.

4 How great thy mercies, Lord!
  How plenteous is thy grace,
Which, in the promise of thy love,
  Includes our rising race.

5 Our offspring, still thy care,
  Shall own their fathers' God,
To latest times thy blessings share,
  And sound thy praise abroad.

MEANS OF GRACE—LORD'S SUPPER.

C. M. DUNDEE.

1. This is the feast of heav'n-ly wine, And God in-vites to sup:
The jui-ces of the liv-ing vine Were press'd to fill this cup.

690 *Welcome to the Lord's Table.* **515**

THIS is the feast of heav'nly wine,
  And God invites to sup:
The juices of the living vine
  Were press'd to fill this cup.

2 Oh, bless the Savior, ye that eat,
  With royal dainties fed;
Not heav'n affords a costlier treat,
  For Jesus is the bread.

3 The vile, the lost, he calls to them,
  Ye trembling souls, appear!
The righteous in their own esteem
  Have no acceptance here.

4 Approach, ye poor, nor dare refuse
  The banquet spread for you;
Dear Savior, this is welcome news,
  Then I may venture too.

5 If guilt and sin afford a plea,
  And may obtain a place,
Surely the Lord will welcome me,
  And I shall see his face.

691 *Christ in the Breaking of Bread.* **519**

O THOU who this mysterious bread
  Didst in Emmaus break,
Return herewith our souls to feed;
  And to thy foll'wers speak.

2 Unseal the volume of thy grace,
  Apply the gospel word;
Open our eyes to see thy face,
  Our hearts to know thee, Lord.

3 Of thee we still commune and mourn
  Till thou the veil remove:

Talk with us, and our hearts shall burn
  With flames of perfect love.

4 Enkindle now the heav'nly zeal,
  And make thy mercy known,
And give our pardon'd souls to feel
  That God and love are one.

692 *Remembering Christ.* **513**

ACCORDING to thy gracious word,
  In meek humility,
This will I do, my dying Lord,
  I will remember thee.

2 Thy body, broken for my sake,
  My bread from heav'n shall be;
Thy testamental cup I take,
  And thus remember thee.

3 Gethsemane can I forget,
  Or there thy conflict see,
Thine agony and bloody sweat,
  And not remember thee?

4 When to the cross I turn mine eyes,
  And rest on Calvary,
O Lamb of God, my sacrifice!
  I must remember thee.

5 Remember thee, and all thy pains,
  And all thy love to me;
Yea, while a breath, a pulse remains,
  Will I remember thee.

6 And when these failing lips grow dumb,
  And mind and mem'ry flee,
When thou shalt in thy kingdom come,
  Jesus, remember me.

MEANS OF GRACE—LORD'S SUPPER.

C. M. NAOMI.

1. Lord, at thy ta-ble I be-hold The wonders of thy grace;

But most of all ad-mire that I Should find a wel-come place:

693 *Sacramental Hymn.* **524**

LORD, at thy table I behold
  The wonders of thy grace;
But most of all admire that I
  Should find a welcome place:

2 I that am all defil'd with sin,
  A rebel to my God;
I that have crucified his Son,
  And trampled on his blood.

3 What strange, surprising grace is this,
  That such a soul has room!
My Savior takes me by the hand,
  My Jesus bids me come.

4 "Eat, O my friend," the Savior cries,
  "The feast was made for you;
For you I groan'd, and bled, and died,
  And rose, and triumph'd too."

5 With trembling faith, and bleeding hearts,
  Lord, we accept thy love:
'Tis a rich banquet we have had,
  What will it be above!

6 Had I ten thousand hearts, dear Lord,
  I'd give them all to thee;
Had I ten thousand tongues, they all
  Should join the harmony.

694 *Love to Christ and one another.* **522**

YE foll'wers of the Prince of peace,
  Who round his table draw,
Remember what his spirit was,
  What his peculiar law.

2 The love, which all his bosom fill'd,
  Did all his actions guide:
Inspir'd by love, he liv'd and taught;
  Inspir'd by love, he died.

3 And do you love him? do you feel
  Your warm affections move?
This is the proof which he demands,
  That you each other love.

4 Let each the sacred law fulfill;
  Like his be ev'ry mind;
Be ev'ry temper form'd by love,
  And ev'ry action kind.

5 Let none who call themselves his friends
  Disgrace the honor'd name;
But by a near resemblance prove
  The title which they claim.

695 *The Heavenly Food.* **525**

HERE at thy table, Lord, we meet
  To feed on food divine:
Thy body is the bread we eat,
  Thy precious blood the wine.

2 He that prepares this rich repast,
  Himself comes down and dies;
And then invites us thus to feast
  Upon the sacrifice.

3 Sure there was never love so free,
  Dear Savior, so divine!
Well thou mayst claim that heart of me
  Which owes so much to thine.

4 Yes, thou shalt surely have my heart,
  My soul, my strength, my all;
With life itself I'll freely part,
  My Jesus, at thy call.

MEANS OF GRACE—LORD'S SUPPER.

L. M. OLD HUNDREDTH.

1. 'Twas on that dreadful, doleful night, When pow'rs of earth and hell a-rose A-gainst the Son of God's de-light, And friends betray'd him to his foes.

696 *Institution of the Supper.* **514**

'TWAS on that dreadful, doleful night,
When pow'rs of earth and hell arose
Against the Son of God's delight,
And friends betray'd him to his foes.

2 Before the mournful scene began,
He took the bread, and bless'd, and brake;
What love through all his actions ran!
What wondrous words of grace he spake!

3 "This is my body broke for sin ;
Receive and eat the living food:"
Then took the cup and bless'd the wine :
"'Tis the new cov'nant in my blood."

4 "Do this (he cried) till time shall end,
In memory of your dying friend ;
Meet at my table and record
The love of your departed Lord."

5 Jesus, thy feast we celebrate,
We show thy death, we sing thy name,
Till thou return, and we shall eat
The marriage supper of the Lamb.

697 *The Lord's Table.* **526**

MY God! and is thy table spread?
And does thy cup with love o'erflow?
Thither be all thy children led,
And let them all its sweetness know.

2 Oh, let thy table honor'd be,
And furnish'd well with joyful guests;
And may each soul salvation see,
That here its sacred pledges tastes.

3 Let crowds approach ; with hearts pre-
With warm desire, let all attend ; [par'd
Nor, when we leave our Father's board,
The pleasure or the profit end.

4 Revive thy dying churches, Lord !
And bid our drooping graces live ;
And more that energy afford,
A Savior's death alone can give.

5 Nor let thy spreading gospel rest,
Till through the world thy truth has run,
Till with this bread all men be blest
Who sees the light or feel the sun.

698 *Commemorating the Savior's love.* **520**

"EAT, drink, in mem'ry of your friend!"
Such was our Master's last request;
Who all the pangs of death endur'd,
That we might live forever blest.

2 Yes, we'll record thy matchless grace,
Thou dearest, tend'rest, best of friends !
Thy dying love the noblest praise
Of long eternity transcends.

3 'Tis pleasure more than earth can give,
Thy goodness through those veils to see :
Thy table food celestial yields ;
And happy they who sit with thee.

4 But oh, what vast transporting joys
Shall fill our breasts, our tongues inspire,
When join'd with yon celestial train,
Our grateful souls thy love admire !

MEANS OF GRACE—LORD'S SUPPER.

L. M. COMMUNION.

1. Jesus is gone above the skies, Where our weak senses reach him not; And carnal objects court our eyes, To thrust our Savior from our thought.

699 *Memorials of the Savior's Grace.* **517**

JESUS is gone above the skies,
 Where our weak senses reach him not;
And carnal objects court our eyes,
To thrust our Savior from our thought.

2 He knows what wand'ring hearts we have,
 Apt to forget his lovely face;
And, to refresh our minds, he gave
 These kind memorials of his grace.

3 The Lord of life this table spread
 With his own flesh and dying blood;
We on the rich provision feed,
 And taste the wine and bless the God.

4 Let sinful sweets be all forgot,
 And earth grow less in our esteem;
Christ and his love fill ev'ry thought,
 And faith and hope be fix'd on him.

5 While he is absent from our sight,
 'Tis to prepare our souls a place;
That we may dwell in heav'nly light,
 And live forever near his face.

6 Our eyes look upward to the hills
 Whence our returning Lord shall come;
We wait thy chariot's awful wheels,
 To take us to our final home.

700 *Meditations on the Cross.* **523**

COME, see on bloody Calvary,
 Suspended on th' accursed tree,
A harmless suff'rer, cover'd o'er
With shame, and welt'ring in his gore.

2 Is this the Savior, long foretold,
To usher in the age of gold?
To make the reign of sorrow cease,
And bind the jarring world in peace?

3 'Tis He, 'tis He!—he kindly shrouds
His glories in a night of clouds,
That souls might from their ruin rise
And heir th' imperishable skies.

4 See, to their refuge and their rest,
From all the bonds of guilt releas'd,
Transgressors to his cross repair
And find a full redemption there.

5 Jesus, what millions of our race
Have been the triumphs of thy grace!
And millions more to thee shall fly,
And on thy sacrifice rely.

701 *Welcome to New Communicants.* **592**

WELCOME, ye hopeful heirs of heav'n,
 To this rich gospel feast of love—
This pledge is but the prelude giv'n
 To that immortal feast above.

2 How great the blessing, thus to meet
 Around the sacramental board,
And hold, by faith, communion sweet
 With Christ, our dear and common Lord!

3 And if so sweet this feast below,
What will it be to meet above,
Where all we see, and feel, and know,
Are fruits of everlasting love?

4 Soon shall we tune the heav'nly lyre,
While list'ning worlds the song approve,
Eternity itself expire
Ere we exhaust the theme of love.

MEANS OF GRACE—LORD'S SUPPER.

MEAR. C. M.

1. Ye men and an-gels, wit-ness now, Be-fore the Lord we speak;
To him we make our so-lemn vow, A vow we may not break.

702 *Vowing Allegiance to Christ.* **918**

YE men and angels, witness now,
  Before the Lord we speak;
To him we make our solemn vow,
  A vow we may not break,—

2 That long as life itself shall last,
  Ourselves to Christ we yield;
Nor from his cause will we depart,
  Or ever quit the field.

3 We trust not our unaided strength,
  But on his grace rely;
May he, with our returning wants,
  All needful wants supply.

4 Oh, guide our doubtful feet aright,
  And keep us in thy ways;
And while we turn our vows to pray'rs,
  Turn thou our pray'rs to praise.

703 *Remembering Christ at his Table.* **879**

IF human kindness meets return,
  And owns the grateful tie;
If tender thoughts within us burn,
  To feel a friend is nigh;—

2 Oh, shall not warmer accents tell
  The gratitude we owe
To him who died our fears to quell,
  And save from endless woe?

3 While yet his anguish'd soul survey'd
  Those pangs he would not flee,
What love his latest words display'd!—
  "Meet and remember me."

4 Remember thee! thy death, thy shame,
  The griefs which thou didst bear!
O mem'ry, leave no other name
  But his recorded there.

704 *Sealing the Covenant.*

THE promise of my Father's love
  Shall stand forever good:
HE said—and gave his soul to death,
  And seal'd the grace with blood.

2 To this dear covenant of thy word,
  I set my worthless name;
I seal th' engagement to my Lord,
  And make my humble claim.

3 I call that legacy my own,
  Which Jesus did bequeath;
'Twas purchas'd with a dying groan,
  And ratified in death.

4 The light & strength, the pard'ning grace,
  And glory shall be mine:
My life and soul, my heart and flesh,
  And all my pow'rs are thine.

MEANS OF GRACE—LORD'S SUPPER.

S. M. McEVERS.

705 *Christ our Passover.* 518

LET all who truly bear
  The bleeding Savior's name,
Their faithful hearts with us prepare,
  And eat the Paschal Lamb.

2 Our passover was slain,
  At Salem's hallow'd place,
Yet we who in our tents remain,
  Shall gain his largest grace.

3 This eucharistic feast
  Our ev'ry want supplies,
And still we by his death are blest,
  And share his sacrifice.

4 By faith his flesh we'll eat,
  Who here his passion show,
And God out of his holy seat
  Shall all his gifts bestow.

5 Who thus our faith employ
  His suff'rings to record,
E'en now we mournfully enjoy
  Communion with our Lord;

6 As though we ev'ry one
  Beneath his cross had stood,
And seen him heave, and heard him groan,
  And felt his gushing blood.

7 O God! 'tis finish'd now!
  The mortal pang is past!
By faith his head we see him bow,
  And hear him breathe his last.

8 We too with him are dead,
  And shall with him arise,
The cross on which he bows his head
  Shall lift us to the skies.

706 *Communion.* 516

JESUS invites his saints
  To meet around his board:
Here those he died to save may hold
  Communion with their Lord.

2 For food he gives his flesh,
  He bids us drink his blood;
Amazing favor! matchless grace
  Of our descending God!

3 This holy bread and wine
  Maintain our fainting breath,
By union with our living Lord,
  And interest in his death.

4 Our heav'nly Father calls
  Christ and his members one:
We are the children of his love,
  And he the first-born Son.

5 We are but sev'ral parts
  Of the same broken bread;
One body, with its sev'ral limbs,
  But Jesus is the head.

6 Let all our pow'rs be join'd
  His glorious name to raise;
Pleasure and love fill ev'ry mind,
  And ev'ry voice be praise!

MEANS OF GRACE—MINISTRY.

L. M. STERLING.

1. Thus spoke the Savior, when he sent His ministers to preach his word,— They thro' the world obedient went, And spread the gospel of their Lord.

707 *The Minister's Commission.* **565**

THUS spake the Savior, when he sent
His ministers to preach his word,—
They through the world obedient went,
And spread the gospel of their Lord:

2 "Go forth, ye heralds, in my name;
Bid the whole earth my grace receive;
The gospel jubilee proclaim,
And call them to repent and live.

3 "The joyful news to all impart,
And teach them where salvation lies;
Bind up the broken, bleeding heart,
And wipe the tear from weeping eyes.

4 "Be wise as serpents, where ye go,
But harmless as the peaceful dove;
And let your heav'n-taught conduct show
That you're commission'd from above.

5 "Freely from me ye have receiv'd;
Freely in love to others give;
Thus shall your doctrine be believ'd,
And by your labors, sinners live."

6 Happy those servants of the Lord,
Who thus their Master's will obey!
How rich, how full is their reward,
Reserv'd until the final day.

708 *Preaching of Christ.* **549**

GO thro' the gates, ('tis God commands;)
Workers with God, the charge obey,
Remove whate'er his work withstands,
Prepare, prepare his people's way.

2 Lift up for all mankind to see
The standard of their Savior God,
And point them to the shameful tree,
The cross all stain'd with hallow'd blood.

3 Sion, thy suff'ring Prince behold,
Thy Savior and Salvation too,
He comes, he comes, so long foretold,
Cloth'd in a vest of bloody hue.

4 Himself prepares his people's hearts,
Breaks and binds up, and wounds and heals;
A mystic death and life imparts;
Empties the full, the emptied fills.

5 He fills whom first he hath prepar'd,
With him all needful grace is giv'n,
Himself is here their great reward,
Their future and their present heav'n.

709 *Prayer for a Minister.* **574**

WITH heav'nly pow'r, O Lord, defend
Him whom we now to thee commend;
His person bless, his soul secure,
And make him to the end endure.

2 Gird him with all-sufficient grace;
Direct his feet in paths of peace;
Thy truth and faithfulness fulfill,
And help him to obey thy will.

3 Before him thy protection send,
Oh love him, save him to the end:
Nor let him, as thy pilgrim, rove
Without the convoy of thy love.

4 Enlarge, inflame, and fill his heart;
In him thy mighty pow'r exert;
That thousands yet unborn may praise
The wonders of redeeming grace.

MEANS OF GRACE—MINISTRY.

L. M. OLD HUNDREDTH.

1. Fa-ther of mercies, bow thine ear, At-ten-tive to our earnest pray'r;
We plead for those who plead for thee—Suc-cess-ful plead-ers may they be!

710 *Prayer for Ministers.* **569**

FATHER of mercies, bow thine ear,
 Attentive to our earnest pray'r;
We plead for those who plead for thee—
Successful pleaders may they be!

2 How great their work, how vast their
Do thou their anxious souls enlarge:[charge,
Their best endowments are our gain,
We share the blessings they obtain.

3 Clothe, then, with energy divine,
Their words, and let those words be thine:
To them thy sacred truth reveal,
Suppress their fear, inflame their zeal.

4 Teach them to sow the precious seed;
Teach them thy chosen flock to feed;
Teach them immortal souls to gain—
Souls that will well reward their pain.

5 Let thronging multitudes around
Hear from their lips the joyful sound,
In humble strains thy grace implore,
And feel thy new-creating pow'r.

711 *At the Ordination of a Minister.* **568**

BEFORE thy throne, Almighty pow'r,
 Thy servant bends in dust the knee,
And waits thy blessing on this hour
That binds his inmost soul to thee.

2 Thine are his thoughts and passions now,
To thee are all his labors giv'n;—
Oh, hear his prayer—accept his vow;
And seal this solemn deed in heav'n.

3 No human strength can e'er suffice
His load of pain and toil to bear;
To thine own breast his spirit flies,
And humbly leans his burden there.

4 Come to his soul:—through all his pow'rs
The warmth of holy love diffuse;
And bathe with mercy's gentlest show'rs
Each work of duty he pursues.

5 Come to thy church:—in glory come;
Oh, close her mourning, captive years;
Bring all thine exil'd people home,
And kindle gladness in their tears.

712 *The Solemn Charge.* **543**

GO, friends of Jesus, and proclaim
 The dear Redeemer you have found,
And speak his ever-precious name
To all the wond'ring nations round.

2 Go tell th' unletter'd, wretched slave,
Who groans beneath a tyrant's rod,
You bring a pardon bought with blood,
The blood of an incarnate God.

3 Go, tell the fierce, untutor'd chief
On Ethiopia's scorching sand,
You come with a refreshing stream,
To cheer and bless his thirsty land.

4 Go, tell the distant isles afar,
Tahiti and the poor Pelew,
That in the covenant of grace
Their unknown names are written too.

5 Go tell, on India's golden shores,
Of a rich treasure, more refin'd;
And tell them, tho' they'll scarce believe,
You come the friend of human kind.

MEANS OF GRACE—MINISTRY.

C. M. LANESBORO'.

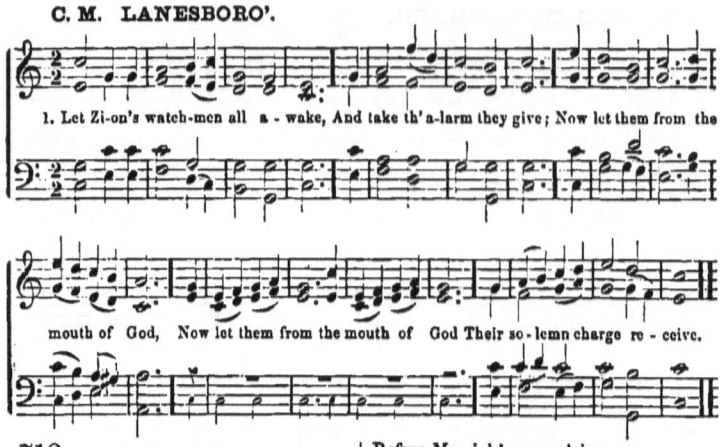

1. Let Zi-on's watch-men all a - wake, And take th' a-larm they give; Now let them from the mouth of God, Now let them from the mouth of God Their so-lemn charge re - ceive.

713 *Watching for Souls.* **567**

2 'Tis not a cause of small import
The pastor's care demands;
But what might fill an angel's heart,
And fill'd a Savior's hands.

3 They watch for souls, for which the Lord
Did heav'nly bliss forego;
For souls which must forever live
In raptures or in woe.

4 All to the great tribunal haste,
Th' account to render there;
And shouldst thou strictly mark our faults,
Lord, how shall we appear?

5 May they that Jesus, whom they preach,
Their own Redeemer see;
And watch thou daily o'er their souls,
That they may watch for thee.

714 *Ministers Encouraged.* **544**

GO, and the Savior's grace proclaim,
Ye messengers of God;
Go, publish, through Immanuel's name,
Salvation bought with blood.

2 What though your arduous track may lie
Through regions dark as death?
What though, your faith and zeal to try,
Perils beset your path?

3 Yet, with determin'd courage, go,
And arm'd with pow'r divine,
Your God will needful aid bestow,
And on your labors shine.

4 He who has call'd you to the war
Will recompense your pains;

Before Messiah's conqu'ring car,
Mountains shall sink to plains.

5 Shrink not, though earth and hell oppose,
But plead your Master's cause;
Nor doubt that e'en your mighty foes
Shall bow before his cross.

715 *Minister's Farewell.* **564**

WHEN Paul was parting from his friends,
It was a tearful day;
But Jesus made them all amends,
And wip'd their tears away.

2 In heav'n they meet again with joy,
Secure, no more to part;
Where praises ev'ry tongue employ,
And pleasure fills each heart.

3 Thus all the preachers of his grace
Their children soon shall meet;
Together see their Savior's face,
And worship at his feet.

716 *At the Death of a Pastor.* **578**

THOUGH earthly shepherds sink to dust,
The aged and the young;
The watchful eye in darkness clos'd,
And mute th' instructive tongue:

2 Th' eternal Shepherd still survives,
New comfort to impart;
His hand still guides us, and his voice
Still animates our heart.

3 The pow'rs of nature, Lord, are thine,
And thine the aids of grace:
Exert thy sacred influence here;
Thy mourning servants bless.

MEANS OF GRACE—MINISTRY.

8s, 7s. SICILIAN HYMN.

Men of God, go take your stations; Darkness reigns throughout the earth; Go proclaim among the nations Joyful news of heav'nly birth: Bear the tidings, Bear the tidings Of the Savior's matchless worth.

717 *Cry aloud, Spare Not.* **539**

MEN of God, go take your stations;
Darkness reigns throughout the earth;
Go proclaim among the nations
Joyful news of heav'nly birth:
  Bear the tidings
Of the Savior's matchless worth.

2 What though earth and hell, united,
Should oppose the Savior's plan?
Plead his cause, nor be affrighted:
Fear ye not the face of man:
  Vain their tumult;
Hurt his work they never can.

3 When expos'd to fearful dangers,
Jesus will his own defend,
Borne afar 'midst foes and strangers,
Jesus will appear your Friend:
  And his presence
Shall be with you to the end.

718 *At sending out of Missionaries.* **550**

GO, ye heralds of salvation,
Go proclaim redeeming blood;
Publish to each barb'rous nation
Peace and pardon from our God:
  Tell the heathen
None but Christ can do them good.

2 While the gospel trump you're sounding,
May the Spirit seal the word,
And, through plenteous grace abounding,
Heathen bow and own the Lord;
  Idols leaving,
God alone shall be ador'd.

3 Distant though our souls are blending
Still our hearts are warm and true;
In our pray'rs to heav'n ascending,
Brethren—we'll remember you:
  Heav'n preserve you
Safely all your journey through.

4 When your mission here is finish'd,
And your work on earth is done,
May your souls, by grace replenish'd,
Find acceptance through the Son;
  Thence admitted,
Dwell forever near his throne.

719 *For Ministerial Meetings.* **555**

BAND of brethren, who are given
To the Lamb of Calvary,
Call'd to preach the reign of heaven,
And the gospel jubilee,
  Jesus asks us—
"Simon Peter, lov'st thou me?"

2 Lord, thou knowest that we love thee;
Oh for grace to love thee more:
Let our notes of praise now move thee
Down upon our souls to pour
  Thy good Spirit,
Then we all shall love thee more.

3 When the sacred page we ponder,
Shine upon it from above,
When we gaze with deepest wonder
On the bleeding Savior's love,
  Holy Spirit,
Then our warm affections move.

4 Grant us heav'nly strength and blessing,
To be faithful to the end;
Let not one, thy love possessing,
Join at last th' Iscariot band!
  Oh, the traitor!
Save us, Jesus, from his end!

MEANS OF GRACE—MINISTRY.

L. M. FEDERAL STREET.

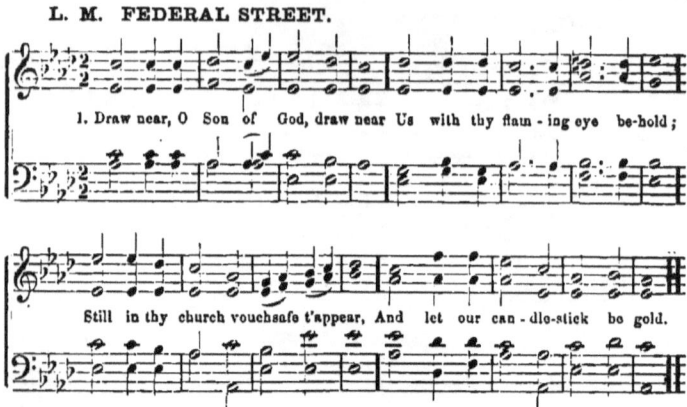

1. Draw near, O Son of God, draw near Us with thy flam-ing eye be-hold; Still in thy church vouchsafe t'appear, And let our can-dle-stick be gold.

720 *Prayer for Ministers.* **561**

DRAW near, O Son of God, draw near,
  Us with thy flaming eye behold ;
Still in thy church vouchsafe t' appear,
And let our candlestick be gold.

2 Still hold the stars in thy right hand,
And let them in thy lustre glow
The lights of a benighted land,
The angels of thy church below.

3 Make good their apostolic boast,
Their high commission let them prove,
Be temples of the Holy Ghost,
And fill'd with faith, and hope, and love.

4 Their hearts from things of earth remove,
Sprinkle them, Lord, from sin and fear;
Fix their affections all above,
And lay up all their treasures there.

5 Give them an ear to hear thy word ;
Thou speakest to the churches now ;
And let all tongues confess their Lord,
Let ev'ry knee to Jesus bow.

721 *The Ministry.* **566**

FATHER of mercies, in thy house
  Smile on our homage and our vows :
While with a grateful heart we share
These pledges of our Savior's care.

2 The Savior, when to heav'n he rose
In glorious triumph o'er his foes,
Scatter'd his gifts on men below,
And wide his royal bounties flow.

3 Hence sprung th' apostle's honor'd name,
Sacred beyond heroic fame ;

In lovelier form to bless our eyes,
Our pastors hence, and teachers, rise.

4 From Christ their varied gifts derive,
And fed by Christ their graces live ;
While guarded by his potent hand,
Against the rage of hell they stand.

5 So shall the bright succession run
Through the last courses of the sun ;
While unborn churches by their care
Shall rise and flourish large and fair.

6 Jesus our Lord their hearts shall know,
The spring whence all these blessings flow ;
Pastors and people sing his praise
Through the long round of endless days.

722 *Prayer for Ministers.* **900**

OH, pour thy Spirit from on high !
  Lord, thine appointed servants bless;
Thy promis'd power to each supply,
And clothe thy priests with righteousness.

2 Wisdom, and zeal, and faith impart,
Firmness and meekness from above,
To bear thy people on their heart,
And love the souls whom thou dost love.

3 To watch, and pray, and never faint;
By day and night their guard to keep;
To warn the sinner, cheer the saint,
Protect thy lambs, and feed thy sheep.

4 And, when their work is finish'd here,
Let them in hope their charge resign ;
Before the throne with joy appear,
And there with endless glory shine.

MEANS OF GRACE—MINISTRY.

L. M. OBERLIN.

1. Shep-herd of Is-rael, bend thine ear, Thy ser-vants' groans in-dul-gent hear; Per-plex'd, distress'd, to thee we cry, And seek the gui-dance of thine eye.

723 *A Church seeking a Minister.* **570**

SHEPHERD of Israel, bend thine ear,
Thy servants' groans indulgent hear;
Perplex'd, distress'd, to thee we cry,
And seek the guidance of thine eye.

2 Thy comprehensive view surveys
Our wand'ring paths, our trackless ways;
Send forth, O Lord, thy truth and light,
To guide our doubtful footsteps right.

3 With longing eyes, behold, we wait,
In suppliant crowds, at mercy's gate;
Our drooping hearts, O God, sustain:
Shall Israel seek thy face in vain?

4 O Lord, in ways of peace return,
Nor let thy flock neglected mourn;
May our blest eyes a shepherd see
Dear to our souls, and dear to thee!

5 Fed by his care, our tongues shall raise
A cheerful tribute to thy praise,
Our children learn the grateful song,
And theirs the cheerful notes prolong.

724 *Destitution of Ministers.* **556**

JESUS, thy wand'ring sheep behold!
See, Lord, in tender mercy, see
Poor souls that cannot find the fold
Till sought and gather'd in by thee.

2 Lost are they now, and scatter'd wide,
In pain and weariness and want;
With no kind shepherd near, to guide
The sick and spiritless and faint.

3 Thou, only thou, the kind and good,
The sheep-redeeming Shepherd art;

Collect thy flock, and give them food
And pastors after thine own heart.

4 In ev'ry messenger reveal
The grace they preach divinely free;
That each may by thy Spirit tell,
"He died for all who died for me."

5 A double portion from above
Of thine all-quick'ning grace impart:
Shed forth thy universal love
In ev'ry faithful pastor's heart.

725 *Prayer for a Sick Minister.* **575**

O THOU, before whose gracious throne
We bow our suppliant spirits down:
Thou know'st the anxious cares we feel,
And all our trembling lips would tell.

2 Avert thy swift-descending stroke,
Nor smite the shepherd of the flock,
Lest o'er the barren waste we stray,
To prowling wolves an easy prey.

3 Restore him sinking to the grave,
Stretch out thine arm, make haste to save;
Back to our hope and wishes give,
And bid our friend and father live.

4 Yet, if our supplications fail,
And pray'rs and tears can naught prevail,
Be thou his strength, be thou his stay;
Support him through the gloomy way.

5 Around him may thine angels wait,
Deck'd with their robes of heav'nly state,
To teach his happy soul to rise,
And waft him to his native skies.

MEANS OF GRACE—MINISTRY.

L. M. ALL-SAINTS.

1. We bid thee wel-come in the name Of Je-sus, our ex-al-ted Head;
Come as a ser-vant—so He came, And we re-ceive thee in his stead.

726 *Welcome to a Minister.* **571**

WE bid thee welcome in the name
Of Jesus, our exalted Head;
Come as a *servant*—so He came,
And we receive thee in his stead.

2 Come as a *shepherd;* guard and keep
This fold from hell, and earth, and sin;
Nourish the lambs and feed the sheep;
The wounded heal, the lost bring in.

3 Come as a *watchman;* take thy stand
Upon thy tow'r amidst the sky,
And when the sword comes on the land,
Call us to fight, or warn to fly.

4 Come as an *angel,* hence to guide
A band of pilgrims on their way,
That, safely walking at thy side,
We faint not, fail not, turn, nor stray.

5 Come as a *teacher,* sent from God,
Charg'd his whole counsel to declare;
Lift o'er our ranks the prophet's rod,
While we uphold thy hands with pray'r.

6 Come as a *messenger* of peace,
Fill'd with the Spirit, fir'd with love;
Live to behold our large increase,
And die to meet us all above.

727 *Installation of a Minister.* **572**

SHEPHERD of Israel, thou dost keep
With constant care thy humble sheep;
By thee our faithful pastors rise
To feed our souls and bless our eyes.

2 Pastors, to all thy church impart,
Model'd by thine own gracious heart,
Whose courage, watchfulness, and love,
Men may attest and God approve.

3 Fed by their active, tender care,
Healthful may all thy sheep appear,
And, by their fair example led,
The way to Zion's pasture tread!

4 Here hast thou listen'd to our vows,
And scatter'd blessings on thy house:
Thy saints are succor'd, and no more
As sheep without a guide, deplore.

728 *Meeting of Ministers.*

POUR out thy Spirit from on high;
Lord! thine assembled servants bless;
Graces and gifts to each supply,
And clothe thy priests with righteousness.

2 Within thy temple where we stand,
To teach the truth as taught by thee,
Savior! like stars, in thy right hand,
The angels of the churches be!

3 Wisdom, and zeal, and faith impart,
Firmness with meekness from above,
To bear thy people on our heart,
And love the souls whom thou dost love:—

4 To watch, and pray, and never faint;
By day and night strict guard to keep:
To warn the sinner, cheer the saint,
Nourish thy lambs, and feed thy sheep.

5 Then, when our work is finish'd here,
In humble hope, our charge resign:
When the chief Shepherd shall appear,
O God! may they and we be thine.

MEANS OF GRACE—MINISTRY.

S. M. GERAR.

1. How beauteous are their feet Who stand on Zi-on's hill! Who bring salvation on their tongues, And words of peace reveal.

729 *The Gospel Ministry.* **351**

HOW beauteous are their feet
 Who stand on Zion's hill!
Who bring salvation on their tongues,
 And words of peace reveal.

2 How charming is their voice!
 How sweet the tidings are!
"Zion, behold thy Savior King;
 He reigns and triumphs here."

3 How happy are our ears
 That hear this joyful sound,
Which kings and prophets waited for,
 And sought, but never found!

4 How blessed are our eyes
 That see this heav'nly light!
Prophets and kings desir'd it long,
 But died without the sight.

5 The watchmen join their voice,
 And tuneful notes employ;
Jerusalem breaks forth in songs,
 And deserts learn the joy.

6 The Lord makes bare his arm
 Through all the earth abroad;
Let all the nations now behold
 Their Savior and their God.

730 *Commissioning of Ministers.* **552**

YE messengers of Christ,
 His sov'reign voice obey:
Arise! and follow where he leads,
 And peace attend your way.

2 The Master, whom you serve,
 Will needful strength bestow
Depending on his promis'd aid,
 With sacred courage go.

3 Mountains shall sink to plains,
 And hell in vain oppose:
The cause is God's, and must prevail
 In spite of all his foes.

4 Go, spread a Savior's fame,
 And tell his matchless grace
To the most guilty and deprav'd
 Of Adam's num'rous race.

5 We wish you, in his name,
 The most divine success;
Assur'd that he who sends you forth
 Will your endeavors bless.

731 *Death of an Aged Minister.* **905**

"SERVANT of God, well done:
 Rest from thy lov'd employ;
The battle fought, the vict'ry won,
 Enter thy Master's joy."

2 The voice at midnight came;
 He started up to hear;
A mortal arrow pierc'd his frame—
 He fell, but felt no fear.

3 Tranquil amid alarms,
 It found him on the field,
A vet'ran slumb'ring on his arms,
 Beneath his red-cross shield.

4 The pains of death are past;
 Labor and sorrow cease;
And, life's long warfare clos'd at last,
 His soul is found in peace.

5 Soldier of Christ, well done;
 Praise be thy new employ;
And, while eternal ages run,
 Rest in thy Savior's joy.

MEANS OF GRACE—MINISTRY.

C. M. P. MERIBAH.

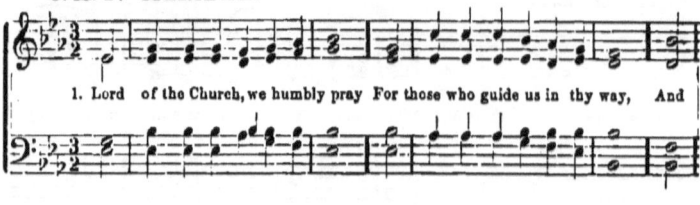

1. Lord of the Church, we humbly pray For those who guide us in thy way, And speak thy holy word; { With love divine their hearts inspire, And touch their lips with hallow'd fire, } And needful grace afford.

732 *Prayer for Ministers.* **576**

LORD of the Church, we humbly pray
  For those who guide us in thy way,
  And speak thy holy word;
With love divine their hearts inspire,
And touch their lips with hallow'd fire,
  And needful grace afford.

2 Help them to preach the truth of God;
Redemption through the Savior's blood;
  Nor let the Spirit cease
On all the Church his gifts to show'r;
To them, a messenger of pow'r;
  To us, of life and peace.

3 So may they live to thee alone;
Then hear the welcome word, "Well done!"
  And take their crown above:
Enter into their Master's joy,
And all eternity employ
  In praise, and bliss, and love.

733 *Minister's Prayer.* **559**

SHEPHERD of souls, if thou indeed
  Hast rais'd me up thy flock to feed,
  (Thy meanest servant I,)
Oh, may I all thy burdens share,
And gently in my bosom bear
  The lambs redeem'd by thee.

2 Thy Spirit send me from above,
Spirit of meek, long-suff'ring love,
  Of all-sufficient grace

Endue me with thy constant mind,
So good, so obstinately kind
  To our rebellious race

3 A faithful steward of my Lord,
Oh, may I minister thy word,
  And in thy footsteps tread:
By ev'ry sore temptation tried,
By suff'rings fully qualified
  Thine ailing flock to lead.

734* *For Missionaries.* **886**

ROLL on, thou mighty ocean;
  And, as thy billows flow,
Bear messengers of mercy
  To ev'ry land below.

2 Arise, ye gales, and waft them
  Safe to the destin'd shore,
That man may sit in darkness
  And death's deep shade no more.

3 O thou eternal Ruler,
  Who holdest in thine arm
The tempests of the ocean,
  Protect them from all harm.

4 Oh, be thy presence with them,
  Wherever they may be;
Though far from us who love them,
  Still let them be with thee.

* *To be sung to the tune on next page.*

MEANS OF GRACE—MINISTRY. 253

7s & 6s. MISSIONARY HYMN.

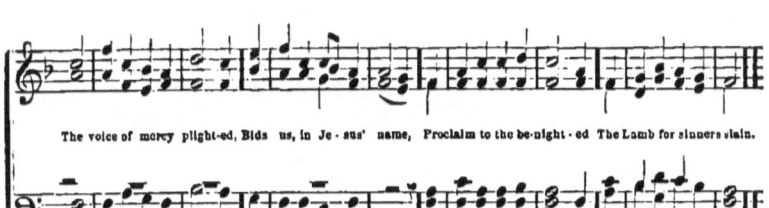

735 *For Ministerial Meetings.* **898**

FROM Calv'ry's sacred mountain,
 Where hung the Son of God,
Whilst from his heart's deep fountain
 Gush'd forth the crimson flood,
The voice of mercy plighted,
 Bids us, in Jesus' name,
Proclaim to the benighted
 The Lamb for sinners slain.

2 Come, brethren, whom, anointed
 With unction from on high,
The Master has appointed
 To preach his kingdom nigh;
We'll haste o'er mount and river,
 Through city, town, and plain,
The ruin'd to deliver
 From death and Satan's chain.

3 For us the great Creator,
 Forsook his heav'nly throne,
Array'd in human nature,
 For rebels to atone:
And shall we flee privation,
 Or dread his cross to bear,
Withholding his salvation
 From souls to Jesus dear?

4 We'll raise our Master's banner,
 We'll cry aloud to all,
Ho! heavy-laden sinner!
 Attend the Savior's call:

Come, thirsty! drink salvation;
 Come, blind! your sight receive;
Deaf! hear the invitation!
 Ye dead! arise and live!

5 Soon will our race be ended,
 Our journey soon be o'er,
By Jesus' arm defended,
 We'll reach fair Canaan's shore,
Where grateful plaudits greet us,
 Throughout the heav'nly dome,
And blessed spirits meet us,
 To shout us welcome home.

6 There may this congregation
 Unite to swell the theme
Of blood-bought, free salvation
 Through faith in Jesus' name:
O Jesus! Rock of ages!
 The God we all adore,
Through earth's bewild'ring stages
 Guide us to Canaan's shore!

Doxology.

ALL ye who grace inherit,
 The God of grace adore!
To Father, Son and Spirit
 Give praise for evermore!
Of mercies here, the treasure
 Demands our praise and love:
And praise shall be our pleasure
 Before his throne above.

254   MEANS OF GRACE—CHURCH AND KINGDOM.

S. M. WATCHMAN.

1. I love thy Zi-on, Lord, The house of thine a-bode; The church, O blest Re-deem-er, sav'd With thine own pre-cious blood.

736   *Love to the Church.*   **499**

I LOVE thy Zion, Lord,
   The house of thine abode;
The church, O blest Redeemer, sav'd
   With thine own precious blood.

2 I love thy church, O God!
   Her walls before thee stand,
Dear as the apple of thine eye,
   And graven on thy hand.

3 If e'er to bless thy sons
   My voice or hands deny,
These hands let useful skill forsake,
   This voice in silence die.

4 If e'er my heart forget
   Her welfare or her woe,
Let ev'ry joy this heart forsake,
   And ev'ry grief o'erflow.

5 For her my tears shall fall;
   For her my pray'rs ascend;
To her my cares and toils be giv'n,
   Till toils and cares shall end.

6 Beyond my highest joy
   I prize her heav'nly ways,
Her sweet communion, solemn vows,
   Her hymns of love and praise.

737   *Security of the Church.*   **963**

GREAT is the Lord our God,
   And let his praise be great;
He makes the church his own abode,
   His most delightful seat.

2 In Zion God is known,
   A refuge in distress:

How bright has his salvation shone
   Through all her palaces!

3 When kings against her join'd,
   And saw the Lord was there,
In wild confusion of the mind,
   They fled with hasty fear.

4 Oft have our fathers told,
   Our eyes have often seen,
How well our God secures the fold
   Where his own sheep have been.

5 In ev'ry new distress
   We'll to his house repair;
We'll call to mind his wondrous grace,
   And seek deliv'rance there

738   *Delight in God's House.*

OUR willing feet shall stand
   Within the temple-door,
While young and old, in many a band,
   Shall throng the sacred floor.

2 Thither the tribes repair,
   Where all are wont to meet,
And, joyful in the house of pray'r,
   Bend at thy mercy-seat.

3 Within these walls may peace
   And harmony be found;
Zion, in all thy palaces,
   Prosperity abound!

4 For friends and brethren dear,
   Our pray'r shall never cease;
Oft as they meet for worship here,
   God send his people peace!

MEANS OF GRACE—CHURCH AND KINGDOM.

7s. Double. TELEMAN.

1. Lord of hosts, to thee we raise Here a house of pray'r and praise;
Thou thy peo-ple's hearts pre-pare Here to meet for praise and pray'r.

2. Let the liv-ing here be fed With thy word, the heav'n-ly bread;
Here, in hope of glo-ry blest, May the dead be laid to rest.

739 *Dedication of a Church.* 929

LORD of hosts, to thee we raise
  Here a house of prayer and praise;
Thou thy people's hearts prepare
  Here to meet for praise and prayer.
2 Let the living here be fed
  With thy word, the heavenly bread;
Here, in hope of glory blest,
  May the dead be laid to rest.
3 Here to thee a temple stand,
  While the sea shall gird the land;
Here reveal thy mercy sure,
  While the sun and moon endure.
4 Hallelujah!—earth and sky
  To the joyful sound reply;
Hallelujah!—hence ascend
  Prayer and praise till time shall end.

740 *Messiah's Reign.* 530

HARK! the song of jubilee,
  Loud as mighty thunders' roar,
Or the fullness of the sea
  When it breaks upon the shore:
Hallelujah! for the Lord
  God omnipotent shall reign;
Hallelujah! let the word
  Echo round the earth and main.

2 Hallelujah! hark! the sound,
  From the depth unto the skies,
Wakes above, beneath, around,
  All creation's harmonies:—
See Jehovah's banner furl'd,
  Sheath'd his sword; he speaks—'tis done;
And the kingdoms of this world
  Are the kingdoms of his Son.
3 He shall reign from pole to pole
  With inimitable sway:
He shall reign when, like a scroll,
  Yonder heav'ns have pass'd away:—
Then the end—beneath his rod
  Man's last enemy shall fall;
Hallelujah! Christ is God,
  God in Christ is all in all.

741 *Messiah's Reign.*

HASTEN, Lord, the glorious time,
  When, beneath Messiah's sway,
Every nation, every clime,
  Shall the gospel call obey.
2 Then shall wars and tumults cease;
  Then be banish'd grief and pain;
Righteousness, and joy, and peace,
  Undisturb'd, shall ever reign.

MEANS OF GRACE—CHURCH AND KINGDOM.

H. M. LISCHER.

1. Rejoice, the Sa-vior reigns A-mong the sons of men; He breaks the pris'ners' chains, And makes them free a-gain: Let hell op-pose God's on - ly Son, In spite of foes His cause goes on, In spite of foes His cause goes on.

742 *Kingdom of Christ.* **534**

REJOICE, the Savior reigns
  Among the sons of men;
He breaks the pris'ners' chains,
  And makes them free again:
Let hell oppose God's only Son,
In spite of foes His cause goes on.

2 He died, but soon arose
  Triumphant o'er the grave;
And now himself he shows
  Omnipotent to save:
Let rebels bow Before his feet;
Eternal bliss His subjects meet.

3 All pow'r is in his hand,
  His people to defend;
To his most high command
  Shall millions more attend;
All heav'n with smiles Approve his cause;
And distant isles Receive his laws.

4 This little seed from heav'n
  Shall soon become a tree;
The ever-blessed leav'n
  Diffused abroad must be;
Till God the Son Shall come again,
It must go on. Amen; Amen!

743 *God's Promises to the Church.* **31**

THE promises I sing,
  Which love supreme once spoke;
Nor will th' eternal King
  His words of grace revoke.
They stand secure And steadfast still:
Not Sion's hill Abides so sure.

2 The mountains melt away
  When once the Judge appears;
And sun and moon decay,
  That measure mortal years:
But still the same, In radiant lines,
His promise shines Through all the flame.

3 Their harmony shall sound
  Through my attentive ears,
When thunders cleave the ground
  And dissipate the spheres.
'Midst all the shock Of that dread scene,
I'll stand serene, Thy word my rock.

744 *Joy in God's House.* **500**

LORD of the worlds above,
  How pleasant and how fair
The dwellings of thy love,
  Thine earthly temples are!
To thine abode My heart aspires,
With warm desires To see my God.

2 O happy souls that pray
  Where God appoints to hear!
O happy men that pay
  Their constant service there!
They praise thee still; And happy they
Who love the way To Zion's hill.

3 They go from strength to strength,
  Through this dark vale of tears,
Till each arrives at length,
  Till each in heav'n appears:
O glorious seat, When God our King
Shall thither bring Our willing feet!

MEANS OF GRACE—CHURCH AND KINGDOM.

H. M. ZEBULON.

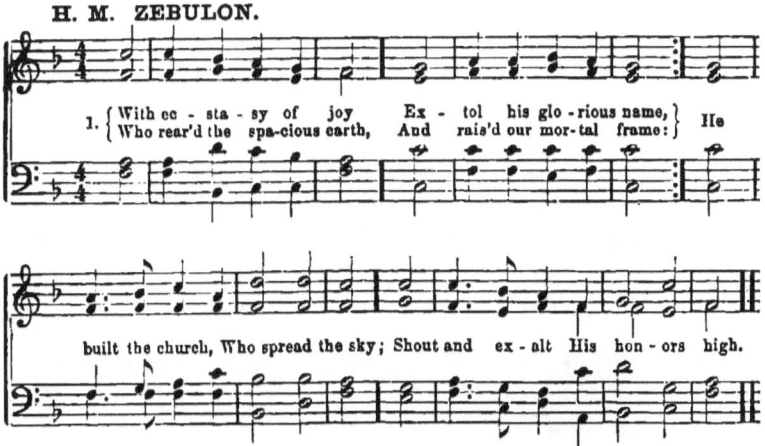

1. With ecstasy of joy   Extol his glorious name,
   Who rear'd the spacious earth,   And rais'd our mortal frame:
   He built the church, Who spread the sky; Shout and exalt His honors high.

745 *God the Church's Founder.* **128**

WITH ecstasy of joy
  Extol his glorious name,
Who rear'd the spacious earth,
  And rais'd our mortal frame:
He built the church, Who spread the sky;
Shout and exalt His honors high.

2 See the foundation laid
  By pow'r and love divine,
Jesus, his first-born Son,
  How bright his glories shine!
Low he descends, In dust he lies,
That from his tomb A church might rise.

3 But he forever lives,
  Nor for himself alone;
Each saint new life derives
  From him, the living stone.
His influence spreads Through ev'ry soul,
And in one house Unites the whole.

4 To him with joy we move;
  In him cemented stand;
The living temple grows,
  And owns the founder's hand.
That structure, Lord, Still higher raise,
Louder to sound Its builder's praise.

746 *The Kingdom of Christ.*

REJOICE—the Lord is King!
  Your God and King adore;
Mortals, give thanks and sing,
  And triumph evermore;
Lift up the heart, Lift up the voice,
Rejoice aloud, Ye saints, rejoice.

2 His kingdom cannot fail;
  He rules o'er earth and heav'n;
The keys of death and hell
  Are to our Jesus giv'n:
Lift up the heart, Lift up the voice,
Rejoice aloud, Ye saints, rejoice.

3 Rejoice, in glorious hope;
  Jesus the Judge shall come—
And take his servants up
  To their eternal home:
We soon shall hear Th' archangel's voice:
The trump of God Shall sound—rejoice!

747 *The Church Blessed.*

O ZION! tune thy voice,
  And raise thy hands on high;
Tell all the earth thy joys,
  And boast salvation nigh;
Cheerful in God, Arise and shine,
While rays divine Stream all abroad.

2 He gilds thy mourning face
  With beams that cannot fade;
His all-resplendent grace
  He pours around thy head;
The nations round Thy form shall view,
With lustre new, Divinely crown'd.

3 In honor to his name,
  Reflect that sacred light;
And loud that grace proclaim,
  Which makes thy darkness bright;
Pursue his praise, Till sovereign love,
In worlds above, The glory raise.

258 MEANS OF GRACE—CHURCH AND KINGDOM.

C. M. LANESBORO'.

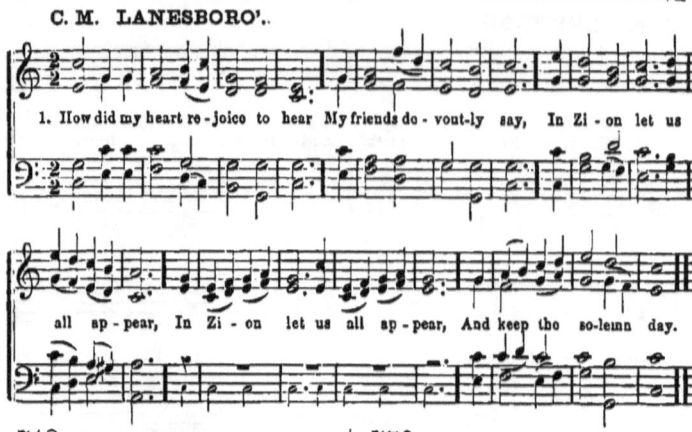

1. How did my heart re-joice to hear My friends de-vout-ly say, In Zi-on let us all ap-pear, In Zi-on let us all ap-pear, And keep the so-lemn day.

748 *Joy in God's House.* **769**

H OW did my heart rejoice to hear
My friends devoutly say,
"In Zion let us all appear,
And keep the solemn day!"

2 I love her gates, I love the road;
The church, adorn'd with grace,
Stands like a palace built for God,
To show his milder face.

3 Peace be within this sacred place,
And joy a constant guest;
With holy gifts and heav'nly grace
Be her attendants blest.

4 My soul shall pray for Zion still,
While life or breath remains;
There my best friends, my kindred, dwell,
There God, my Savior, reigns.

749 *Joy in God's House.* **504**

E ARLY, my God, without delay,
I haste to seek thy face;
My thirsty spirit faints away,
Without thy cheering grace.

2 I've seen thy glory and thy pow'r
Through all thy temple shine:
My God, repeat that heav'nly hour,
That vision so divine.

3 Not all the blessings of a feast
Can please my soul so well,
As when thy richer grace I taste,
And in thy presence dwell.

4 Not life itself, with all its joys,
Can my best passions move,
Or raise so high my cheerful voice,
As thy forgiving love.

750 *God's House.* **501**

T HE Lord in Zion plac'd his name;
His ark was settled there;
To Zion the whole nation came
To worship thrice a year.

2 But we have no such lengths to go,
Nor wander far abroad;
Where'er thy saints assemble now,
There is a house for God.

3 Arise, O King of grace, arise;
And enter this thy rest!
Lo! thy church waits, with longing eyes,
Thus to be crown'd and blest.

4 Here, mighty God! accept our vows;
Here let thy praise be spread:
Bless the provisions of thy house,
And fill thy poor with bread.

751 *The Christian Communion.* **744**

N OT to the terrors of the Lord,
The tempest, fire, and smoke;
Not to the thunder of that word
Which God on Sinai spoke;

2 But we are come to Zion's hill,
The city of our God,
Where milder words declare his will
And spread his love abroad.

3 The saints on earth, and holy dead,
But one communion make;
All join in Christ, their living head,
And of his grace partake.

4 In such society as this
My weary soul would rest!
The man that dwells where Jesus is,
Must be forever blest.

MEANS OF GRACE—CHURCH AND KINGDOM.

C. M. COWPER.

1. Behold, the mountain of the Lord In latter days shall rise Above the mountains and the hills, And draw the wond'ring eyes, And draw the wond'ring eyes.

752 *The Joyous Triumph.* **892**

BEHOLD, the mountain of the Lord
 In latter days shall rise
Above the mountains and the hills,
 And draw the wond'ring eyes.

2 To this, the joyful nations round,
 All tribes and tongues, shall flow :
"Up to the hill of God," they say,
 "And to his house, we'll go."

3 The beam that shines on Zion's hill
 Shall lighten ev'ry land :
The King who reigns on Zion's tow'rs
 Shall all the world command.

4 No strife shall vex Messiah's reign,
 Or mar the peaceful years ;
To plowshares men shall beat their swords,
 To pruning-hooks their spears.

5 Come, then, oh, come from ev'ry land,
 To worship at his shrine ;
And, walking in the light of God,
 With holy beauty shine.

753 *Consecration of a Church.* **931**

TO thee this temple we devote,
 Our Father and our God ;
Accept it thine, and seal it now
 Thy Spirit's blest abode.

2 Here may the pray'r of faith ascend,
 The voice of praise arise ;
Oh, may each lowly service prove
 Accepted sacrifice.

3 Here may the sinner learn his guilt,
 And weep before his Lord ;
Here, pardon'd, sing a Savior's love,
 And here his vows record.

4 Here may affliction dry the tear,
 And learn to trust in God,
Convinc'd it is a Father smites,
 And love that guides the rod.

5 Peace be within these sacred walls ;
 Prosperity be here ;
Still smile upon thy people, Lord,
 And evermore be near.

754 *Zion's Resurrection.* **891**

DAUGHTER of Zion, from the dust
 Exalt thy fallen head ;
Again in thy Redeemer trust ;
 He calls thee from the dead.

2 Awake, awake ; put on thy strength,
 Thy beautiful array ;
The day of freedom dawns at length,
 The Lord's appointed day.

3 Rebuild thy walls, thy bounds enlarge,
 And send thy heralds forth ;
Say to the south, "Give up thy charge,"
 And, "Keep not back, O north."

4 They come! they come! thine exil'd bands
 Where'er they rest or roam,
Have heard thy voice in distant lands,
 And hasten to their home.

5 Thus, though the universe should burn,
 And God his works destroy,
With songs thy ransom'd shall return,
 And everlasting joy.

MEANS OF GRACE—CHURCH AND KINGDOM.

L. M. ALWAY.

1. A-way from ev'-ry mor-tal care, A-way from earth, our souls retreat; We leave this worthless world a-far, And wait and wor-ship near thy seat.

755 *Meeting in the Temple.* **503**

AWAY from ev'ry mortal care,
Away from earth, our souls retreat;
We leave this worthless world afar,
And wait and worship near thy seat.

2 Lord, in the temple of thy grace,
We bow before thee and adore ;
We view the glories of thy face,
And learn the wonders of thy pow'r.

3 Whilst here our various wants we mourn,
United pray'rs ascend on high ;
And faith expects a sure return
From him who hears our feeble cry.

4 Father, my soul would here abide ;
But, if my feet must hence depart.
Still keep me, Father, near thy side,
Still keep thy dwelling in my heart.

756 *Blessedness of Church Privileges.* **502**

LORD, 'tis a pleasant thing to stand
In gardens planted by thy hand,
Let me within thy courts be seen,
Like a young cedar, fresh and green.

2 There grow thy saints in faith and love,
Blest with thine influence from above :
Not Lebanon with all its trees,
Yields such a comely sight as these.

3 The plants of grace shall ever live ;
Nature decays, but grace must thrive;
Time, that doth all things else impair,
Still makes them flourish strong and fair.

4 Laden with fruits of age, they show
The Lord is holy, just, and true :
None that attend his courts shall find
A God unfaithful or unkind.

757 *Meeting for Worship.*

HOW sweet to leave the world a while,
And seek the presence of our Lord!
Dear Savior, on thy people smile,
And come, according to thy word.

2 From busy scenes we now retreat,
That we may here converse with thee :
Ah, Lord, behold us at thy feet ;—
Let this the "gate of heaven" be.

3 " Chief of ten thousand!" now appear,
That we by faith may see thy face:
Oh, speak, that we thy voice may hear,
And let thy presence fill this place.

MEANS OF GRACE—CHURCH AND KINGDOM. 261

L. M. LITCHFIELD.

1. Je-sus shall reign where'er the sun Does his suc-cess-ive jour-neys run; His king-dom stretch from shore to shore, Till moons shall wax and wane no more.

758 *The Savior's Reign.* **529**

JESUS shall reign where'er the sun
  Does his successive journeys run;
His kingdom stretch from shore to shore,
Till moons shall wax and wane no more.

2 For him shall endless prayer be made,
And endless praises crown his head;
His name, like sweet perfume, shall rise
With every morning sacrifice.

3 People and realms of ev'ry tongue
Dwell on his love with grateful song;
And infant voices shall proclaim
Their early blessings on his name.

4 Blessings abound where'er he reigns;
The pris'ner leaps to loose his chains,
The weary find eternal rest,
And all the sons of want are blest.

5 Let every creature rise and bring
Peculiar honors to our King;
Angels descend with songs again,
And earth repeat the long Amen.

759 *For Zion's Increase.* **893**

ARM of the Lord, awake, awake!
  Put on thy strength—the nations shake,
And let the world, adoring, see
Triumphs of mercy wrought by thee.

2 Say to the heathen from thy throne,
"I am Jehovah!—God alone!"
Thy voice their idols shall confound,
And cast their altars to the ground.

3 No more let human blood be spilt—
Vain sacrifice for human guilt!

But to each conscience be applied
The blood that flow'd from Jesus' side.

4 Let Zion's time of favor come;
Oh, bring the tribes of Israel home;
And let our wond'ring eyes behold
Gentiles and Jews in Christ's one fold!

760 *The Kingdom Come.* **548**

BRIGHT as the sun's meridian blaze,
  Vast as the blessings he conveys,
Wide as his reign from pole to pole,
And permanent as his control—

2 So, Jesus, let thy kingdom come,
Then sin and hell's terrific gloom
Shall, at thy brightness, flee away,
The dawn of an eternal day.

3 Then shall the heathen, fill'd with awe,
Learn the blest knowledge of thy law;
And antichrist on ev'ry shore
Fall from his throne to rise no more.

4 Then shall thy lofty praise resound
On Afric's shores—thro' India's ground,
And islands of the southern sea
Shall stretch their eager arms to thee.

5 Then shall the Jew and Gentile meet
In pure devotion at thy feet:
And earth shall yield thee, as thy due,
Her fullness and her glory too.

6 Oh, that from Zion now might shine
This heav'nly light, this truth divine:
Till the whole universe shall be
But one great temple, Lord, to thee.

MEANS OF GRACE—CHURCH AND KINGDOM.

L. M. PARK STREET.

1. Hark! what triumphant strains are these Which echo thro' the vault of heav'n, "To Jesus once on Calv'ry slain, The kingdoms of the earth are giv'n, The kingdoms of the earth are giv'n."

761   *Triumph of the Church.*   531

HARK! what triumphant strains are these
Which echo thro' the vault of heav'n !
"To Jesus, once on Calv'ry slain,
The kingdoms of the earth are giv'n."

2 Hark ! the new song before the throne,
Which only the redeem'd can raise ;
Angels may tune their golden harps
But cannot reach these notes of praise.

3 They worship our exalted Lord,
And hail him universal King ;
But saints—the purchase of his blood,
Can strike a sweeter, nobler string.

4 The wonders of his dying love,
Their hallelujahs loud proclaim,
While with ecstatic joy they shout
New honors to his sacred name.

5 From ev'ry kindred, ev'ry tongue,
From barb'rous nations long unknown,
From polish'd Greeks and Scythians rude,
A countless host surround the throne.

6 In robes of spotless white array'd,
And palms of vict'ry in their hand,
With holy wonder and delight,
The trophies of his grace they stand.

762   *Founding a Church.*   928

WITH humble faith and fervent zeal,
We would address thy throne, O God ;
Oh, may our breathings reach thy hill,
The city of thy blest abode !

2 Oft hast thou, Lord, been pleas'd to bow
Thine ear, and listen to our cry ;

Encourag'd thus, we now presume,
Oh, let us feel thy presence nigh.

3 We come not, Lord, to plead for wealth,
Nor ask this world's vain, empty fame ;
But this we ask, (deny it not,)
"To build a house to thy great name."

4 We trust thy pow'r, and not our own,
The superstructure here to raise ;
May love divine our efforts crown,
And thy blest name have all the praise.

5 And while we're privileg'd to rear
A place in which t' approach thy throne,
Oh, may we know our souls are built
On Christ the true foundation-stone.

763   *The Millennial Reign.*   918

LOOK up, ye saints, with sweet surprise;
Behold the joyful coming day,
When Jesus shall descend the skies,
In noble form and bright array.

2 Nations shall in a day be born,
And swift, like doves, to Jesus fly ;
The church shall know no cloud's return,
Nor sorrows mixing with her joy.

3 The lion and the lamb shall feed
Together, in his peaceful reign ;
And Zion, blest with heav'nly bread,
Of poverty no more complain.

4 The Jew, the Greek, the bond, the free
Shall boast their sep'rate rights no more,
But join in sweetest harmony.
Their Lord, their Savior to adore.

MEANS OF GRACE—CHURCH AND KINGDOM.

L. M. LOUVAN.

1. O Sion's King, we suppliant bow, And hail the grace thy church enjoys; Her holy officers are thine, With all the gifts thy love employs.

764   *Church Officers.*   593

O SION'S King, we suppliant bow,
   And hail the grace thy church enjoys;
Her holy officers are thine,
With all the gifts thy love employs.

2 Up to thy throne we lift our eyes,
For blessings to attend our choice,
Of such whose gen'rous, prudent zeal
Shall make thy favor'd ways rejoice.

3 When pastor, saints, and poor they serve,
May their own hearts with grace be crown'd;
While patience, sympathy, and joy
Adorn, and through their lives abound.

4 By purest love to Christ and truth,
Oh, may they win a good degree
Of boldness in the Christian faith,
And meet the smile of thine and thee.

5 And when the work to them assign'd,
The work of love, is fully done,
Call them from serving tables here,
To sit around thy glorious throne.

765   *The Church blest in her Officers.*   902

L ORD, cause thy face on us to shine;
   Give us thy peace, and seal us thine;
Teach us to prize the means of grace,
And love thine earthly dwelling-place.

2 One is our faith, and one our Lord;
One body, spirit, hope, reward;
May we in one communion be,
One with each other, one with thee!

3 Bless all whose voice salvation brings,
Who minister in holy things;
Our pastors, elders, deacons, bless;
Cloth them with zeal and righteousness.

4 Let many in the judgment-day,
Turn'd from the error of their way,
Their hope, their joy, their crown, appear:—
Save those who preach, and those who hear.

766   *The World's Conversion.*   546

E XERT thy pow'r, thy rights maintain,
   Insulted, everlasting King!
The influence of thy crown increase,
And strangers to thy footstool bring.

2 We long to see that happy time,
That dear, expected, blissful day,
When countless myriads of our race
The second Adam shall obey.

3 The prophecies must be fulfill'd,
Though earth and hell should dare oppose;
The stone cut from the mountain's side,
Though unobserv'd, to empire grows.

4 Soon shall the blended image fall,
Brass, silver, iron, gold, and clay,
And superstition's gloomy reign
To light and liberty give way.

5 In one sweet symphony of praise,
Gentile and Jew shall then unite;
And infidelity, asham'd,
Sink in th' abyss of endless night.

6 From east to west, from north to south,
Immanuel's kingdom shall extend;
And ev'ry man, in ev'ry face,
Shall meet a brother, and a friend.

ZION. 8s, 7s, 4s.

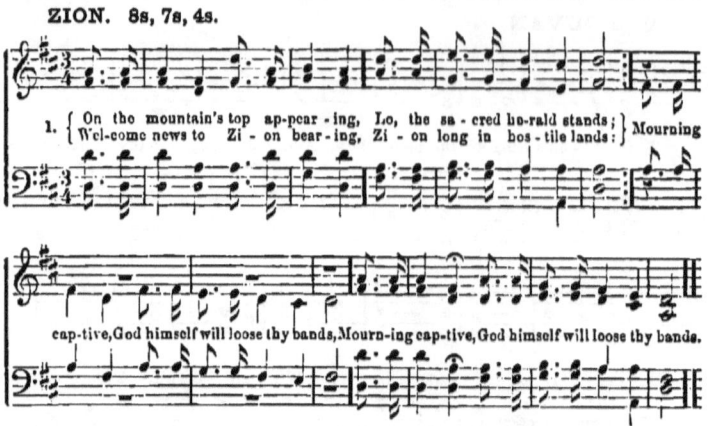

On the mountain's top ap-pear-ing, Lo, the sa-cred he-rald stands; Wel-come news to Zi-on bear-ing, Zi-on long in hos-tile lands; Mourning cap-tive, God himself will loose thy bands, Mourn-ing cap-tive, God himself will loose thy bands.

767 *Glad Tidings for Zion.* **585**

ON the mountain's top appearing,
  Lo, the sacred herald stands;
Welcome news to Zion bearing,
  Zion long in hostile lands:
    Mourning captive,
  God himself will loose thy bands.

2 Has thy night been long and mournful,
  All thy friends unfaithful prov'd?
Have thy foes been proud and scornful,
  By thy sighs and tears unmov'd?
    Cease thy mourning,
  Zion still is well belov'd.

3 God, thy God, will now restore thee!
  He himself appears thy Friend:
All thy foes shall flee before thee;
  Here their boasts and triumphs end.
    Great deliv'rance
  Zion's King vouchsafes to send.

4 Peace and joy shall now attend thee,
  All thy warfare now is past,
God, thy Savior, shall defend thee,
  Peace and joy are come at last;
    All thy conflicts
  End in everlasting rest.

768 *Dawning Glory.* **587**

YES! we trust the day is breaking:
  Joyful times are near at hand:
God, the mighty God, is speaking
  By his word in ev'ry land:
    When he chooses,
  Darkness flies at his command.

2 Let us hail the joyful season:
  Let us hail the dawning ray:
When the Lord appears, there's reason
  To expect a glorious day:
    At his presence
  Gloom and darkness flee away.

3 While the foe becomes more daring,
  While he enters like a flood,
God, the Savior, is preparing
  Means to spread his truth abroad;
    Ev'ry language
  Soon shall tell the love of God.

4 God of Jacob, high and glorious,
  Let thy people see thy hand,
Let the gospel be victorious
  Through the world in ev'ry land,
    And the idols
  Perish, Lord, at thy command.

769 *The Savior's Kingdom.* **586**

NOW we hail the happy dawning
  Of the gospel's glorious light:
May it take the wings of morning
  And dispel the shades of night;
    Blessed Savior,
  Let our eyes behold the sight.

2 Where, amid the desert dreary,
  Plant, nor shrub, nor flow'ret grows,
There refresh the wand'rer weary
  With the sight of Sharon's Rose,
    And its beauties
  To the longing eye disclose.

3 Oh, let all the world adore thee—
  Universal be thy fame;
Kings and subjects fall before thee,
  And extol thy matchless name;
    All ascribing
  Endless praises to the Lamb.

MEANS OF GRACE—CHURCH AND KINGDOM.

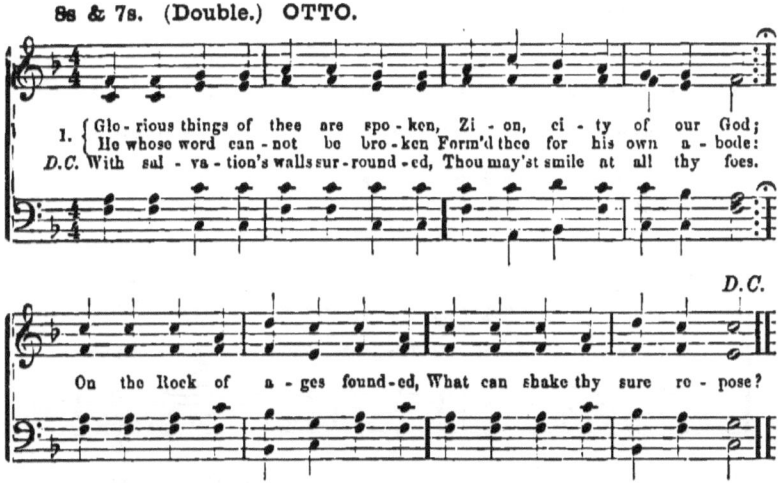

8s & 7s. (Double.) OTTO.

1. Glo-rious things of thee are spo-ken, Zi-on, ci-ty of our God;
He whose word can-not be bro-ken Form'd thee for his own a-bode:
D.C. With sal-va-tion's walls sur-round-ed, Thou may'st smile at all thy foes.

On the Rock of a-ges found-ed, What can shake thy sure re-pose?

770   *The City of God.*   533

GLORIOUS things of thee are spoken,
  Zion, city of our God;
He whose word cannot be broken
  Form'd thee for his own abode:
On the Rock of ages founded,
  What can shake thy sure repose?
With salvation's walls surrounded,
  Thou may'st smile at all thy foes.

2 See, the streams of living waters,
  Springing from eternal love,
Well supply thy sons and daughters,
  And all fear of want remove:
Who can faint while such a river
  Ever flows thy thirst t'assuage?
Grace which, like the Lord, the giver,
  Never fails from age to age.

3 Round each habitation hov'ring,
  See the cloud and fire appear!
For a glory and a cov'ring,
  Showing that the Lord is near:
Thus deriving from their banner
  Light by night and shade by day,
Safe they feed upon the manna
  Which he gives them when they pray.

771   *God, Zion's Defense.*   967

ZION stands with hills surrounded—
  Zion, kept by pow'r divine;
All her foes shall be confounded,
  Though the world in arms combine:

Happy Zion,
  What a favor'd lot is thine!

2 Every human tie may perish;
  Friend to friend unfaithful prove;
Mothers cease their own to cherish;
  Heaven and earth at last remove;
    But no changes
  Can attend Jehovah's love.

3 In the furnace God may prove thee,
  Thence to bring thee forth more bright,
But can never cease to love thee:
  Thou art precious in his sight:
    God is with thee—
  God, thine everlasting light.

772   *Sowing and Reaping.*

HE that goeth forth with weeping,
  Bearing precious seed in love,
Never tiring, never sleeping,
  Findeth mercy from above:
Soft descend the dews of heaven,
  Bright the rays celestial shine;
Precious fruits will thus be given,
  Through an influence all divine.

2 Sow thy seed; be never weary;
  Let no fears thy soul annoy;
Be the prospect ne'er so dreary,
  Thou shalt reap the fruits of joy:
Lo, the scene of verdure bright'ning!
  See the rising grain appear;
Look again! the fields are whit'ning,
  For the harvest-time is near.

MEANS OF GRACE—CHURCH—LORD'S DAY.

C. M. ATHENS.

1. Church of the ev-er-last-ing God, The Fa-ther's gra-cious choice, A-mid the voi-ces of this earth, How fee-ble is thy voice!

773 *The Church and the World.*

CHURCH of the everlasting God,
 The Father's gracious choice ;
Amid the voices of this earth,
 How feeble is thy voice !

2 Thy words amid the words of earth,
 How noiseless and how low !
Amid the hurrying crowds of time,
 Thy steps how calm and slow !

3 But 'mid the wrinkled brows of earth,
 Thy brow how free from care !
'Mid the flush'd cheeks of riot here,
 Thy cheek how white and fair !

4 Amid the restless eyes of earth,
 How steadfast is thine eye,
Fix'd on th' eternal loveliness
 Of scenes beyond the sky !

774 *God present in his Churches.*

MY soul, how lovely is the place
 To which thy God resorts !
'Tis heav'n to see his smiling face,
 Though in his earthly courts.

2 With his rich gifts the heav'nly Dove
 Descends, and fills the place ;
While Christ reveals his wondrous love,
 And sheds abroad his grace.

3 My heart and flesh cry out for Thee
 While far from thine abode ;
When shall I tread thy courts, and see
 My Savior and my God ?

4 To sit one day beneath thine eye,
 And hear thy gracious voice,
Exceeds a whole eternity
 Employ'd in carnal joys.

5 Lord ! at thy threshold I would wait,
 While Jesus is within,
Rather than fill a throne of state,
 Or live in tents of sin.

775 *Joy of Worship.*

WITH joy we hail the sacred day
 Which God has call'd his own ;
With joy the summons we obey,
 To worship at his throne.

2 Thy chosen temple, Lord, how fair !
 Where willing vot'ries throng
To breathe the humble, fervent pray'r,
 And pour the choral song.

3 Spirit of grace, oh, deign to dwell
 Within thy church below ;
Make her in holiness excel,
 With pure devotion glow.

4 Let peace within her walls be found ;
 Let all her sons unite
To spread, with grateful zeal, around,
 Her clear and shining light.

5 Great God ! we hail the sacred day
 Which thou hast call'd thine own ;
With joy the summons we obey,
 To worship at thy throne.

MEANS OF GRACE—LORD'S DAY.

7s. 6 lines. NUREMBURG.

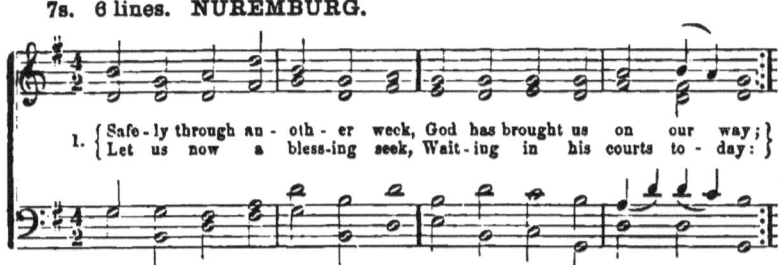

1. Safely through another week, God has brought us on our way;
Let us now a blessing seek, Waiting in his courts to-day:

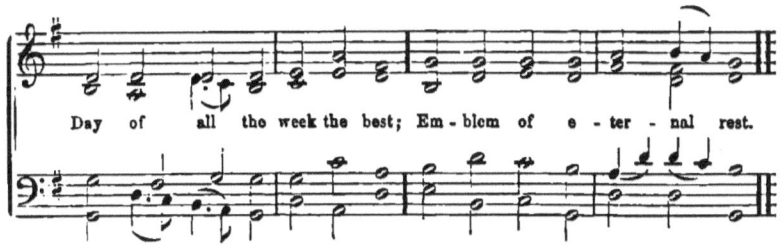

Day of all the week the best; Emblem of eternal rest.

776 *Sabbath Morn.*   **628**   **777** *Sabbath Eve.*

SAFELY through another week,
  God has brought us on our way;
Let us now a blessing seek,
  Waiting in his courts to-day:
Day of all the week the best;
Emblem of eternal rest.

2 While we seek supplies of grace,
  Through the dear Redeemer's name,
Show thy reconciled face—
  Take away our sins and shame:
From our worldly cares set free,
May we rest this day in thee!

3 Here we're come, thy name to praise;
  Let us feel thy presence near:
May thy glory meet our eyes,
  While we in thy house appear:
Here afford us, Lord, a taste
Of our everlasting feast.

4 May the gospel's joyful sound
  Conquer sinners, comfort saints;
Make the fruits of grace abound,
  Bring relief for all complaints:
Thus let all our Sabbaths prove,
Till we join the church above.

SOFTLY fades the twilight ray
  Of the holy Sabbath day;
Gently as life's setting sun,
When the Christian's course is run.

2 Night her solemn mantle spreads
O'er the earth as daylight fades;
All things tell of calm repose
At the holy Sabbath's close.

3 Peace is on the world abroad,
'Tis the holy peace of God—
Symbol of the peace within,
When the spirit rests from sin.

4 Still the Spirit lingers near,
Where the ev'ning worshipper
Seeks communion with the skies,
Pressing onward to the prize.

5 Savior, may our Sabbaths be
Days of peace and joy in thee,
Till in heav'n our souls repose,
Where the Sabbath ne'er shall close.

MEANS OF GRACE—LORD'S DAY.

C. M. ST. JOHN'S.

1. This is the day the Lord hath made; He calls the hours his own: Let heav'n rejoice, let earth be glad, And praise surround the throne.

778 *Sunday and the Resurrection.* **507**

THIS is the day the Lord hath made;
  He calls the hours his own:
Let heav'n rejoice, let earth be glad,
  And praise surround the throne.

2 To-day arose our glorious Head,
  And death's dread empire fell;
To-day, the saints his triumph spread,
  And all his wonders tell.

3 Hosannah to th' anointed King;
  To David's holy Son:
To God our grateful homage bring,
  And his Messiah own.

4 Blest be the Lord, who comes to men
  With messages of grace;
Who comes in God his Father's name
  To save our sinful race.

5 Hosannah in the highest strains
  The church on earth can raise!
The highest heav'ns in which he reigns
  Shall give him nobler praise.

779 *Sunday Morning.* **627**

COME, dearest Lord, and feed thy sheep
  On this sweet day of rest;
Oh, bless this flock, and make this fold
  Enjoy a heav'nly rest.

2 Welcome, and precious to my soul
  Are these sweet days of love;
But what a Sabbath shall I keep
  When I shall rest above!

3 I come, I wait, I hear, I pray,
  Thy footsteps, Lord, I trace;

Here, in thine own appointed way,
  I wait to see thy face.

4 These are the sweet and precious days
  On which my Lord I've seen;
And oft, when feasting on his word,
  In raptures I have been.

5 Oh, if my soul, when death appears,
  In this sweet frame be found,
I'll clasp my Savior in my arms,
  And leave this earthly ground.

780 *Sunday Morning.* **626**

ON this sweet morn my Lord arose
  Triumphant o'er the grave!
He dies to vanquish all my foes,
  And lives again to save.

2 This is the day for holy rest,
  Yet clouds will gather soon,
Except my Lord become my guest,
  And put my harp in tune.

3 No heav'nly fire my heart can raise,
  Without the Spirit's aid;
His breath must kindle pray'r and praise,
  Or I am cold and dead.

4 On all the flocks thy Spirit pour,
  And saving health convey;
A sweet, refreshing Sunday show'r
  Will make them sing and pray.

5 Direct thy Shepherds how to feed
  The flocks of thine own choice;
Give savor to the heav'nly bread,
  And bid the folds rejoice.

781   *Sunday Evening.*   938

FREQUENT the day of God returns,
  To shed its quick'ning beams;
And yet how slow devotion burns,
  How languid are its flames!

2 Accept our faint attempts to love;
  Our frailties, Lord, forgive:
We would be like thy saints above,
  And praise thee while we live.

3 Increase, O Lord, our faith and hope,
  And fit us to ascend
Where the assembly ne'er breaks up,
  The Sabbath ne'er shall end;

4 Where we shall breathe in heav'nly air,
  With heav'nly lustre shine,
Before the throne of God appear,
  And feast on love divine.

782   *Sunday Morning.*   935

AGAIN the Lord of life and light
  Awakes the kindling ray,
Dispels the darkness of the night,
  And pours increasing day.

2 Oh, what a night was that which wrapp'd
  A sinful world in gloom!
Oh, what a sun that broke this day
  Triumphant from the tomb!

3 This day be grateful homage paid,
  And loud hosannas sung:
Let gladness dwell in ev'ry heart,
  And praise on ev'ry tongue.

4 Ten thousand, thousand lips shall join
  To hail this welcome morn,
Which scatters blessings from its wings
  To nations yet unborn.

783   *Children's Sunday Song.*   670

ONCE more we keep the sacred day
  That saw the Savior rise;
Once more we tune our feeble song
  To him that rules the skies.

2 What numbers vainly spend these hours
  That are to Jesus due!
Children and parents, how they live!
  And how they perish too!

3 But we, a happier few, are taught
  The ways of heav'nly truth:
We hail once more the plan of love
  That pities wand'ring youth.

4 Our foolish hearts are prone to err;
  Too oft we find it so;
Oh, may the God of grace forgive,
  And better hearts bestow.

5 Teach us the way, while here we learn
  To read thy holy word;
Bless all the kind instructions giv'n,
  And make us thine, O Lord.

6 Praise to our God, and thanks to those
  Who thus our souls befriend;
While the rich benefit we reap,
  On them thy blessing send.

784   *Whitsunday.*   793

SPIRIT of truth, on this thy day
  To thee for help we cry,
To guide us through the weary way
  Of dark mortality.

2 We ask not, Lord, the cloven flame,
  Or tongues of various tone;
But long thy praises to proclaim,
  With fervor in our own.

3 We mourn not that prophetic skill
  Is found on earth no more:
Enough for us to trace thy will
  In scripture's sacred lore.

4 When tongues shall cease, & pow'r decay,
  And knowledge empty prove,
Do thou thy trembling servants stay
  With faith, and hope, and love.

785   *Lord's Day Evening.*   638

WHEN, O dear Jesus, when shall I
  Behold thee all serene,
Blest in perpetual Sabbath-day,
  Without a veil between!

2 Assist me, while I wander here
  Amidst a world of cares;
Incline my heart to pray with love,
  And then accept my pray'rs.

3 Release my soul from ev'ry chain,
  No more hell's captive led;
And pardon thy repenting child,
  For whom the Savior bled.

4 Spare me, my God, oh, spare the soul
  That gives itself to thee;
Take all that I possess below,
  And give thyself to me.

5 Thy Spirit, O my Father, give,
  To be my guide and friend,
To light my path to ceaseless joys,
  To Sabbaths without end.

MEANS OF GRACE—LORD'S DAY.

L. M. MENDON.

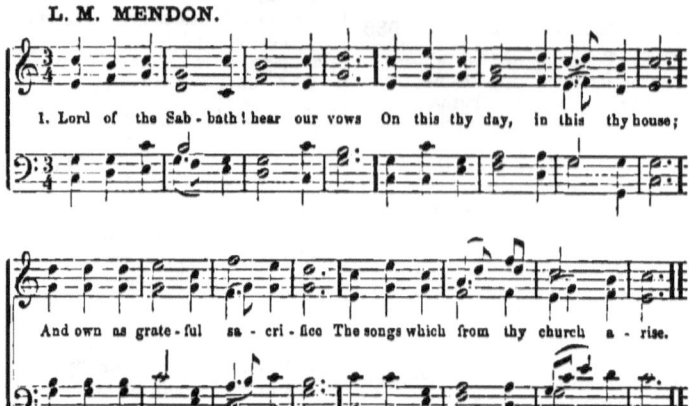

786 *The Sabbath and Heaven.* 505

LORD of the Sabbath! hear our vows
On this thy day, in this thy house;
And own as grateful sacrifice
The songs which from thy church arise.

2 Thine earthly sabbaths, Lord, we love;
But there's a nobler rest above:
Thy servants to that rest aspire
With ardent hope and strong desire.

3 There languor shall no more oppress;
The heart shall feel no more distress;
No groans shall mingle with the songs
That dwell upon immortal tongues.

4 No gloomy cares shall there annoy,
No conscious guilt disturb our joy;
But ev'ry doubt and fear shall cease,
And perfect love give perfect peace.

5 When shall that glorious day begin,
Beyond the reach of death or sin;
Whose sun shall never more decline,
But with unfading lustre shine!

787 *Comforts of Worship.* 491

HOW lovely, how divinely sweet,
O Lord, thy sacred courts appear!
Fain would my longing passions meet
The glories of thy presence there.

2 Oh, blest the men, blest their employ,
Whom thine indulgent favors raise
To dwell in those abodes of joy,
And sing thy never-ceasing praise.

3 One day within thy sacred gate
Affords more real joy to me
Than thousands in the tents of state:
The meanest place is bliss with thee.

4 God is a sun; our brightest day
From his reviving presence flows;
God is a shield through all the way,
To guard us from surrounding foes.

5 O Lord of hosts, thou God of grace,
How blest, divinely blest, is he
Who trusts thy love and seeks thy face,
And fixes all his hopes on thee!

788 *Delight in Worship.* 490

FAR from my tho'ts, vain world, begone,
Let my religious hours alone:
Fain would my eyes my Savior see;
I wait a visit, Lord, from thee.

2 My heart grows warm with holy fire,
And kindles with a pure desire;
Come, my dear Jesus, from above,
And feed my soul with heav'nly love.

3 Blest Jesus, what delicious fare!
How sweet thine entertainments are!
Never did angels taste above
Redeeming grace and dying love.

4 Hail, great Immanuel, all divine!
In thee thy Father's glories shine;
Thou brightest, sweetest, fairest one
That eyes have seen, or angels known!

MEANS OF GRACE—LORD'S DAY. 271

L. M. LURMAN.

1. Sweet is the work, my God, my King! To praise thy name, give thanks & sing; To show thy love by morn-ing light, And talk of all thy truth at night.

789 *Sweetness of the Sabbath.* 506

SWEET is the work, my God, my King!
To praise thy name, give thanks & sing;
To show thy love by morning light,
And talk of all thy truth at night.

2 Sweet is the day of sacred rest:
No mortal care shall fill my breast;
My heart shall triumph in the Lord,
And bless his works, and bless his word.

3 And I shall share a glorious part,
When grace has well refin'd my heart,
When doubts and fears no more remain
To break my inward peace again.

4 Then shall I see, and hear and know
All I desir'd or wish'd below;
And ev'ry pow'r find sweet employ
In that eternal world of joy.

790 *Lord's Day Evening.* 639

LORD, how delightful 'tis to see
A whole assembly worship thee;
At once they sing, at once they pray!
They hear of heav'n and learn the way.

2 I have been there, and still would go;
'Tis like a little heav'n below:
Not all that hell or sin can say
Shall tempt me to forget this day.

3 Oh, write upon my mem'ry, Lord,
The text and doctrine of thy word;

That I may break thy laws no more,
But love thee better than before.

4 With thoughts of Christ and things divine,
Fill up this foolish heart of mine;
That, hoping pardon through his blood,
I may lie down and wake with God.

791 *The Christian Sabbath.* 937

LORD of the Sabbath and its light,
I hail thy hallow'd day of rest;
It is my weary soul's delight,
The solace of my care-worn breast.

2 Its dewy morn, its glowing noon,
Its tranquil eve, its solemn night,
Pass sweetly; but they pass too soon,
And leave me sadden'd at this flight.

3 Yet, sweetly as they glide along,
And hallow'd though the calm they yield,
Transporting though their rapturous song,
And heav'nly visions seem reveal'd;

4 My soul is desolate and drear,
My silent harp untun'd remains,
Unless, my Savior, thou art near,
To heal my wounds and soothe my pains.

5 O Jesus, ever let me hail
Thy presence with thy day of rest;
Then will thy servant never fail
To deem thy Sabbath doubly blest.

MEANS OF GRACE—LORD'S DAY.

S. M. SHIRLAND.

1. Welcome, sweet day of rest, That saw the Lord a-rise; Welcome to this reviving breast And these rejoicing eyes.

792   *Day of Rest.*   **936**

WELCOME, sweet day of rest,
  That saw the Lord arise;
Welcome to this reviving breast
  And these rejoicing eyes.

2 The King himself comes near,
  And feasts his saints to-day;
Here we may sit, and see him here,
  And love and praise and pray.

3 One day, amid the place
  Where my dear Lord has been,
Is better than ten thousand days
  Of pleasure and of sin.

4 My willing soul would stay
  In such a frame as this,
And sit and sing herself away
  To everlasting bliss.

793   *Rest for the Soul.*   **698**

OH, where shall rest be found,
  Rest for the weary soul?
'Twere vain the ocean's depths to sound,
  Or pierce to either pole.

2 The world can never give
  The bliss for which we sigh:
'Tis not the whole of life to live,
  Nor all of death to die.

3 Beyond this vale of tears
  There is a life above,
Unmeasur'd by the flight of years—
  And all that life is love.

4 There is a death whose pang
  Outlasts the fleeting breath:
Oh, what eternal horrors hang
  Around the second death!

5 Lord God of truth and grace!
  Teach us that death to shun:
Lest we be driven from thy face,
  And evermore undone.

6 Here would we end our quest—
  Alone are found in thee
The life of perfect love—the rest
  Of immortality.

794   *The Eternal Sabbath.*

AND is there, Lord, a rest
  For weary souls design'd,
Where not a care shall stir the breast,
  Or sorrow entrance find?

2 Is there a blissful home,
  Where kindred minds shall meet,
And live and love, nor ever roam
  From that serene retreat?

3 Forever blessed they,
  Whose joyful feet shall stand,
While endless ages waste away,
  Amid that glorious land!

4 My soul would thither tend,
  While toilsome years are giv'n;
Then let me, gracious Lord, ascend
  To sweet repose in heaven!

MEANS OF GRACE—LORD'S DAY.

L. M. ELPARAN.

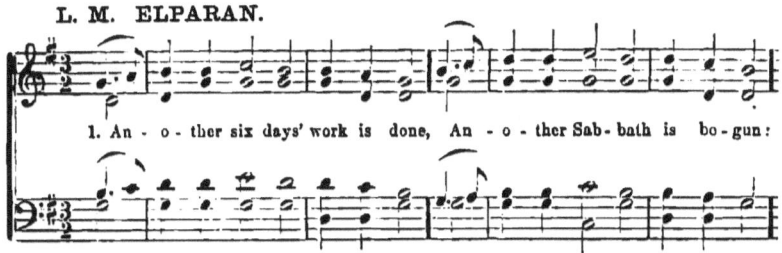

1. An-o-ther six days' work is done, An-o-ther Sab-bath is be-gun:

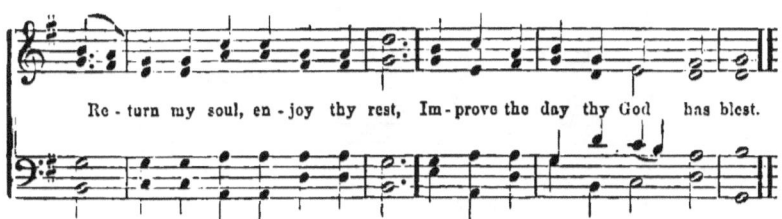

Re-turn my soul, en-joy thy rest, Im-prove the day thy God has blest.

795 *The Lord's Day.* **624**

ANOTHER six days' work is done,
Another Sabbath is begun:
Return, my soul, enjoy thy rest,
Improve the day thy God has blest.

2 Come, bless the Lord, whose love assigns
So sweet a rest to wearied minds;
Provides an antepast of heav'n,
And gives this day the food of sev'n.

3 Oh that our tho'ts and thanks may rise
As grateful incense to the skies;
And draw from heav'n that sweet repose
Which none, but he who feels it, knows.

4 With joy, great God! thy works we view
In various scenes, both old and new;
With praise we think of mercies past,
With hope we future pleasures taste.

5 In holy duties let the day,
In holy pleasures pass away:
How sweet a Sabbath thus to spend,
In hope of one that ne'er shall end!

796 *The Sabbath.* **625**

OUR Sabbaths come so welcome on,
We wish them to remain a while,
But soon, alas! their joys are gone,
And scarce "bequeath a parting smile."

2 Full many are the hours of grief,
Allotted to the sons of men,
Our Sabbaths bring a short relief,
Yet leave us but to mourn again.

3 Ye peaceful days! and thou, blest sun!
Why roll ye in such haste away?
Ye happy hours! why flow ye on
So fast towards eternity?

4 Oh, if ye bring an endless day,
Speed fast along, nor ever cease;
We'll gladly feel your joys decay,
In perfect and enduring bliss.

797 *Sabbath Eve.*

SWEET is the light of Sabbath eve,
And soft the sunbeams lingering there;
For these blest hours, the world I leave,
Wafted on wings of faith and prayer.

2 The time how lovely and how still!
Peace shines and smiles on all below—
The plain, the stream, the wood, the hill—
All fair with evening's setting glow.

3 Season of rest! the tranquil soul
Feels the sweet calm, and melts to love—
And while these sacred moments roll,
Faith sees the smiling heaven above.

4 Nor will our days of toil be long:
Our pilgrimage will soon be trod;
And we shall join the ceaseless song—
The endless Sabbath of our God.

MEANS OF GRACE—PRAYER.

L. M. DUKE STREET.

1. Our Father, thron'd a-bove the sky, To thee our emp-ty hands we spread; Thy children at thy foot-stool lie, And ask thy bless-ings on their head.

798 *Confidence in Prayer.* **394**

OUR Father, thron'd above the sky,
To thee our empty hands we spread;
Thy children at thy footstool lie,
And ask thy blessings on their head.

2 With cheerful hope and filial fear,
In that august and precious name
By thee ordain'd, we now draw near,
And would the promis'd blessing claim.

3 Does not an earthly parent hear
The cravings of his famish'd son?
Will he reject the filial prayer,
Or give for bread the flinty stone?

4 Our heav'nly Father, how much more
Will thy divine compassions rise,
And open thy unbounded store,
To satisfy thy children's cries!

5 Yes, we will ask, and seek, and press
For gracious audience at thy seat;
Still hoping, waiting for success,
If persevering to entreat.

6 For Jesus in his faithful word
The upright supplicant has bless'd;
And all thy saints with one accord
The prevalence of prayer attest.

799 *Christ's Assistance in Prayer.* **837**

WHERE is my God? does he retire
Beyond the reach of humble sighs?
Are these weak breathings of desire
Too languid to ascend the skies?

2 He hears the breathings of desire;
The weak petition, if sincere,
Is not forbidden to aspire
And hope to reach his gracious ear.

3 Look up, my soul, with cheerful eye;
See where the great Redeemer stands,
The glorious Advocate on high,
With precious incense in his hands.

4 He hears and soothes each humble groan;
He recommends each broken pray'r;
Recline thy hope on him alone
Whose pow'r and love forbid despair.

800 *Efficacy of Prayer.* **483**

PRAY'R was appointed to convey
The blessings God designs to give;
Long as they live, should Christians pray,
For only while they pray they live.

2 The Christian's heart his pray'r indites,
He speaks as prompted from within;
The Spirit his petition writes,
And Christ receives, and gives it in.

3 And shall we in dead silence lie,
When Christ stands waiting for our pray'r?
My soul, thou hast a friend on high;
Arise, and try thine int'rest there.

4 If pains afflict, or wrongs oppress—
If cares distract, or fears dismay—
If guilt deject—if sin distress,
The remedy's before thee—pray.

5 'Tis pray'r supports the soul that's weak;
Though thought be broken—language lame,
Pray, if thou canst, or canst not speak,
But pray with faith in Jesus' name.

L. M. GERHARD.

1. From ev'ry storm-y wind that blows, From ev'ry swell-ing tide of woes, There is a calm, a sure re-treat, 'Tis found be-neath the Mer-cy-seat.

801   *The Mercy-Seat.*   790

FROM ev'ry stormy wind that blows,
  From ev'ry swelling tide of woes,
There is a calm, a sure retreat,
'Tis found beneath the Mercy-seat.

2 There is a place where Jesus sheds
The oil of gladness on our heads,
A place than all besides more sweet—
It is the blood-bought Mercy-seat.

3 There is a scene where spirits blend,
Where friend holds fellowship with friend,
Though sunder'd far, by faith they meet
Around one common Mercy-seat.

4 Ah! whither could we flee for aid,
When tempted, desolate, dismay'd,
Or how the host of hell defeat,
Had suff'ring saints no Mercy-seat?

5 There, *there* on eagle wings we soar,
And sin and sense seem all no more;
And heav'n comes down our souls to greet,
And glory crowns the Mercy-seat.

6 Oh, let my hand forget her skill,
My tongue be silent, cold, and still,
This bounding heart forget to beat,
If I forget the Mercy-seat.

802   *Exhortation to Prayer.*   484

WHAT various hindrances we meet
  In coming to a mercy-seat!
Yet who that knows the worth of pray'r,
But wishes to be often there!

2 Pray'r makes the darken'd cloud withdraw,
Pray'r climbs the ladder Jacob saw—
Gives exercise to faith and love,—
Brings ev'ry blessing from above.

3 Restraining pray'r, we cease to fight;
Pray'r makes the Christian's armor bright,
And Satan trembles when he sees
The weakest saint upon his knees.

4 Have you no words? ah! think again:
Words flow apace when you complain,
And fill your fellow-creature's ear
With the sad tale of all your care.

5 Were half the breath thus vainly spent,
To heav'n in supplication sent—
Your cheerful songs should oft'ner be,
"Hear what the Lord has done for me!"

803   *The Hour of Prayer.*

HOW sweet the hour when man retires
  To hold communion with his God—
To send to heaven his warm desires,
And listen to the sacred word!

2 It is the hour when God draws nigh,
Well pleased his people's voice to hear;
To hush the penitential sigh,
And wipe away the mourner's tear.

3 It is the hour, supremely blest,
When largest grace to man is given;
The hour that yields his spirit rest,
That joins his anxious soul to heaven.

MEANS OF GRACE—PRAYER.

C. M. WOODSTOCK.

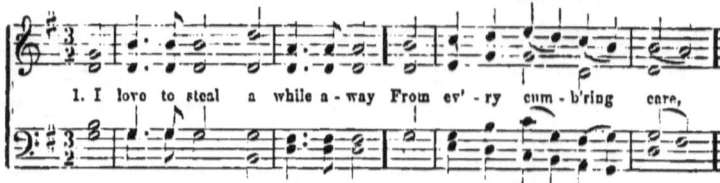

1. I love to steal a while a-way From ev'-ry cum-b'ring care,
And spend the hours of set-ting day In hum-ble, grate-ful pray'r.

804 *Prayer at Evening.* 376

I LOVE to steal a while away
 From ev'ry cum'bring care,
And spend the hours of setting day
 In humble, grateful pray'r.

2 I love in solitude to shed
 The penitential tear,
And all his promises to plead,
 Where none but God can hear.

3 I love to think on mercies past,
 And future good implore,
And all my cares and sorrows cast
 On him whom I adore.

4 I love by faith to take a view
 Of brighter scenes in heav'n;
The prospect doth my strength renew,
 While here by tempests driv'n.

5 Thus, when life's toilsome day is o'er,
 May its departing ray
Be calm as this impressive hour,
 And lead to endless day.

805 *Religious Retirement.* 375

FAR from the world, O Lord, I flee;
 From strife and tumult far;
From scenes where Satan wages still
 His most successful war.

2 The calm retreat, the silent shade,
 With pray'r and praise agree;
And seem by thy sweet bounty made
 For those who follow thee.

3 There if thy Spirit touch the soul,
 And grace her mean abode,

Oh, with what peace, and joy, and love,
 Does she commune with God!

4 Author and Guardian of my life,
 Sweet Source of light divine,—
And (all harmonious names in one)
 My *Savior*, thou art mine.

5 What thanks I owe thee, and what love!
 And praise, an endless store,
Shall echo through the realms above
 When time shall be no more.

806 *Nature of Prayer.* 487

PRAY'R is the soul's sincere desire,
 Utter'd or unexpress'd,
The motion of a hidden fire
 That trembles in the breast.

2 Pray'r is the burden of a sigh,
 The falling of a tear;
The upward glancing of an eye
 When none but God is near.

3 Pray'r is the simplest form of speech
 That infant lips can try;
Pray'r the sublimest strains that reach
 The Majesty on high.

4 Pray'r is the Christian's vital breath,
 The Christian's native air,
His watchword at the gate of death—
 He enters heav'n with pray'r.

5 Pray'r is the contrite sinner's voice
 Returning from his ways,
While angels in their songs rejoice,
 And say, "Behold, he prays."

MEANS OF GRACE—PRAYER.

C. M. (Double.) BRATTLE STREET.

1. While thee I seek, protecting Pow'r, Be my vain wishes still'd; And may this consecrated hour With better thoughts be fill'd. Thy love the pow'rs of thought bestow'd; To thee my thoughts would soar: Thy mercy o'er my life has flow'd; That mercy I a-dore.

807 *The Hour of Prayer.* **393**

WHILE thee I seek, protecting Pow'r,
  Be my vain wishes still'd;
And may this consecrated hour
  With better thoughts be fill'd.
Thy love the pow'rs of thought bestow'd,
  To thee my thoughts would soar:
Thy mercy o'er my life has flow'd;
  That mercy I adore.

2 In each event of life how clear
  Thy ruling hand I see!
Each blessing to my soul more dear,
  Because bestow'd by thee.
In ev'ry joy that crowns my days,
  In ev'ry pain I bear,
My heart shall find delight in praise,
  Or seek relief in pray'r.

3 When gladness wings my favor'd hour,
  Thy love my thoughts shall fill:
Resign'd, when storms of sorrow low'r,
  My soul shall meet thy will.
My lifted eye, without a tear,
  The low'ring storm shall see;
My steadfast heart shall know no fear:
  That heart will rest on thee.

808 *Secret Devotion.* **486**

FATHER Divine, thy piercing eye
  Sees through the darkest night:
In deep retirement thou art nigh,
  With heart-discerning sight.
There may that piercing eye survey
  My solemn homage paid,
With ev'ry morning's dawning ray,
  And ev'ry ev'ning's shade.

2 Oh, let thine own celestial fire
  The incense still inflame:
While my warm vows to thee aspire
  Through my Redeemer's name.
So shall the visits of thy love
  My soul in secret bless:
So shalt thou deign in worlds above,
  Thy suppliant to confess.

809 *The Sweetness of Prayer.*

SWEET is the pray'r whose holy stream
  In earnest pleading flows:
Devotion dwells upon the theme,
  And warm and warmer glows.
Faith grasps the blessing she desires
  Hope points the upward gaze;
And love, untrembling love, inspires
  The eloquence of praise.

MEANS OF GRACE—PRAYER.

S. M. ST. THOMAS.

1. The Lord, who tru-ly knows The heart of ev'-ry saint,
In-vites us by his ho-ly word To pray and nev-er faint.

810 *Importunate Prayer.* **485**

1 THE Lord, who truly knows
  The heart of ev'ry saint,
Invites us by his holy word
  To pray and never faint.

2 He bows his gracious ear;
  We never plead in vain:
Yet we must wait till he appear,
  And pray, and pray again.

3 Though unbelief suggest,
  Why should we longer wait?
He bids us never give him rest,
  But be importunate.

4 'Twas thus a widow poor,
  Without support or friend,
Beset the unjust judge's door,
  And gain'd at last her end.

5 And shall not Jesus hear
  His children when they cry?
Yes, though he may a while forbear,
  He'll not their suit deny.

6 Then let us earnest be,
  And never faint in pray'r;
He loves our importunity,
  And makes our cause his care.

811 *The Lord's Prayer.* **875**

1 OUR heav'nly Father, hear
  The pray'r we offer now;
Thy name be hallow'd far and near,
  To thee all nations bow.

2 Thy kingdom come; thy will
  On earth be done in love,
As saints and seraphim fulfill
  Thy perfect law above.

3 Our daily bread supply,
  While by thy word we live;
The guilt of our iniquity
  Forgive as we forgive.

4 From dark temptation's pow'r,
  From Satan's wiles, defend;
Deliver in the evil hour,
  And guide us to the end.

5 Thine shall forever be
  Glory and pow'r divine;
The sceptre, throne, and majesty
  Of heav'n and earth are thine.

812 *"Watch and Pray."*

1 A CHARGE to keep I have,
    A God to glorify,
A never-dying soul to save
  And fit it for the sky.

2 Arm me with jealous care,
  As in thy sight to live;
And, oh, thy servant, Lord, prepare
  The strict account to give.

3 Help me to watch and pray
  And on thyself rely,
Assured if I my trust betray
  I shall forever die.

ANGELS.

L. M. ORFORD.

1. Great God! what hosts of an-gels stand In shin-ing ranks at thy right hand, Ar-ray'd in robes of daz-zling light, With pinions stretch'd for dis-tant flight!

813 *The Ministry of Angels.* **63**

GREAT God! what hosts of angels stand
In shining ranks at thy right hand,
Array'd in robes of dazzling light,
With pinions stretch'd for distant flight!

2 Immortal fires! seraphic flames!
Who can recount their various names?
In strength and beauty they excel;
For near the throne of God they dwell.

3 How eagerly they wish to know
The duties he would have them do:
What joy their active spirits feel,
To execute their Sov'reign's will!

4 Hither, at his command, they fly
To guard the beds on which we lie;
To shield our persons night and day,
And scatter all our fears away.

5 Send, O my God, some angel down,
(Though to a mortal eye unknown,)
To guide and guard my doubtful way
Up to the realms of endless day.

814 *Christ the Lord of Angels.* **810**

GREAT God! to what a glorious height
Hast thou advanc'd the Lord, thy Son!
Angels, in all their robes of light,
Are made the servants of his throne.

2 Before his feet their armies wait,
And swift as flames of fire they move,
To manage his affairs of state,
In works of vengeance, or of love.

3 Now they are sent to guide our feet,
Up to the gates of thine abode,
Through all the dangers that we meet
In trav'ling o'er the heavenly road.

4 Lord! when we leave this mortal ground,
And thou shalt bid us rise and come,—
Send thy beloved angels down
Safe to conduct our spirits home.

815 *The Angels.*

HIGH on a hill of dazzling light,
The King of glory spreads his seat,
And troops of angels, stretch'd for flight,
Stand waiting round his awful feet.

2 Here a bright squadron leaves the skies,
And thick around Elisha stands;
Anon a heavenly soldier flies,
And breaks the chains from Peter's hands.

3 Thy winged troops, O God of hosts,
Wait on thy wandering church below;
Here we are sailing to thy coasts,
Let angels be our convoy too.

4 Are they not all thy servants, Lord?
At thy command they go and come,
With cheerful haste obey thy word,
And guide thy children to their home.

ANGELS.

C. M. SWANWICK.

1. Beyond the glitt'ring, star-ry skies Far as th' eter-nal hills, There, in the boundless worlds of light, Our dear Re-deem-er dwells, Our dear Re-deem-er dwells.

816 *Sympathy of Angels.* **808**

BEYOND the glitt'ring, starry skies
  Far as th' eternal hills,
There, in the boundless worlds of light,
  Our dear Redeemer dwells.

2 Legions of angels round his throne
  In countless armies shine;
And swell his praise with golden harps
  Attun'd to songs divine.

3 "Hail, glorious Prince of peace!" they cry,
  "Whose unexampled love
Mov'd thee to quit these glorious realms,
  And royalties above."

4 Through all his travels here below
  They did his steps attend,
Oft wond'ring how, or where, at last,
  The mystic scene would end.

5 They saw his heart transfix'd with wounds
  And view'd the crimson gore;
They saw him break the bars of death,
  Which none e'er broke before.

6 They brought his chariot from above,
  To bear him to his throne;
Clapp'd their triumphant wings, and cried,
  "The glorious work is done!"

817 *Angelic Ministrations.*

ANGELS, where'er we go, attend
  Our steps, whate'er betide,
With watchful care their charge defend,
  And evil turn aside.

2 Ten thousand offices unseen
  For us they gladly do,
Deliver in the furnace keen,
  And safe escort us through.

3 But thronging round, with busiest love
  They guard the dying breast,
And come in convoys from above
  To bear us to our rest.

4 They do the will of Christ our King,
  To him they all are giv'n;
They grace his throne, his praises sing,
  And waft his saints to heav'n.

11s. HINTON.

1. How cheer-ing the tho't that the spi-rits in bliss, Should bow their bright A.S. To breathe o'er our

DEPRESSIONS AND REVIVALS.

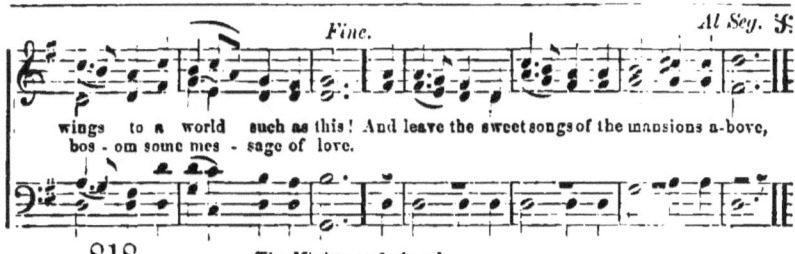

wings to a world such as this! And leave the sweet songs of the mansions a-bove,
bos - om some mes - sage of love.

818 *The Ministry of Angels.*

HOW cheering the thought that the spirits in bliss
Should bow their bright wings to a world such as this!
And leave the sweet songs of the mansions above,
To breathe o'er our bosom some message of love.

2 They come—on the wings of the morning they come,
To convoy the stranger in peace to his home;
The pilgrim to waft from this stormy abode,
And lay him to rest in the arms of his God.

3 They come when we wander, they come when we pray,
In mercy to guard us wherever we stray:
A glorious cloud their bright witness is given;
Encircling us here are these angels of heaven.

8s, 7s. BAVARIA.

1. Sa - vior, vis - it thy plan - ta - tion, Grant us, Lord, a gra - cious rain!
All will come to de - so - la - tion, Un - less thou re - turn a - gain:
D.C. Lord, re - vive us, Lord, re - vive us, All our help must come from thee.

Lord, re - vive us, Lord, re - vive us, All our help must come from thee.

819 *For Revival.* **580**

SAVIOR, visit thy plantation,
Grant us, Lord, a gracious rain!
All will come to desolation,
Unless thou return again: Lord, &c.

2 Surely, once thy garden flourish'd,
Ev'ry part look'd gay and green:
Then thy word our spirits nourish'd,—
Happy seasons we have seen. Lord, &c.

3 But a drought has since succeeded,
And a sad decline we see;
Lord, thy help is greatly needed,—
Help can only come from thee. Lord, &c.

4 Some in whom we once delighted,
We shall meet no more below:
Some, alas! we fear are blighted,
Scarce a single leaf they show.
Lord, &c.

5 Dearest Savior, hasten hither,
Thou canst make them bloom again!
Oh, permit them not to wither,
Let not all our hopes be vain. Lord, &c.

6 Break the tempter's fatal power;
Turn the stony heart to flesh;
And begin from this good hour
To revive thy work afresh. Lord, &c.

REVIVALS.

L. M. EFFINGHAM.

1. O God of Zi-on! from thy throne Look with an eye of pi-ty down; Thy church now humbly makes her pray'r—Thy church the ob-ject of thy care.

820 *Entreaty for Zion.* **579**

O GOD of Zion! from thy throne
  Look with an eye of pity down;
Thy church now humbly makes her pray'r—
Thy church the object of thy care.

2 We are a building thou hast rais'd;
How kind thy hand, that hand be prais'd:
Yet all to utter ruin falls
If thou forsake our tott'ring walls.

3 We call to mind the happier days
Of life and love, of pray'r and praise,—
When holy services gave birth
To joys resembling heav'n on earth.

4 But now the ways of Zion mourn,
Her gates neglected and forlorn:
Our life and liveliness are fled,
And many number'd with the dead.

5 We need defense from all our foes,
We need relief from all our woes;
Oh, pour thy Spirit from on high,
And all our num'rous wants supply.

821 *Entreaty for Zion.* **582**

INDULGENT Sov'reign of the skies,
  And wilt thou bow thy gracious ear?
While feeble mortals raise their cries,
Wilt thou, the great Jehovah, hear?

2 How shall thy servants give thee rest,
Till Zion's mould'ring walls thou raise?
Till thine own power shall stand confess'd,
And make Jerusalem a praise?

3 Look down, O God, with pitying eye,
And view the desolation round:
See what wide realms in darkness lie,
And hurl their idols to the ground.

4 Lord, let the gospel trumpet blow,
And call the nations from afar,
Let all the isles their Savior know
And earth's remotest ends draw near.

5 On ev'ry soul let grace descend,
Like heav'nly dew in copious show'rs,
That we may call our God our friend,
That we may hail salvation ours.

822 *For the Spirit's Return.* **911**

O LORD, and shall our fainting souls
  Thy just displeasure ever mourn?
Thy Spirit griev'd, and long withdrawn,
Will he no more to us return?

2 Great Source of light and peace, return,
Nor let us mourn and sigh in vain;
Come, repossess our longing hearts
With all the graces of thy train.

3 This temple, hallow'd by thy hand,
Once more be with thy presence blest;
Here be thy grace anew display'd;
Be this thine everlasting rest.

823 *For Revival.* **907**

GREAT Lord of all thy churches, hear
  Thy ministers' and people's prayer;
Perfum'd by thee, oh may it rise
Like fragrant incense to the skies.

2 May ev'ry pastor from above
Be new inspir'd with zeal and love,
To watch thy flock, thy flock to feed,
And sow with care the precious seed.

3 Revive the churches with thy grace,
Heal our divisions, grant us peace;
Rouse us from sloth, our hearts inflame
With ardent zeal for Jesus' name.

4 May young and old thy word receive,
Dead sinners hear thy voice and live,
The wounded conscience healing find,
And joy refresh each drooping mind.

824　　*For Revival.*　　**909**

COME, Sacred Spirit, from above,
And fill the coldest heart with love;
Soften to flesh the flinty stone,
And let thy God-like pow'r be known.

2 Speak thou, and from the haughtiest eyes
Shall floods of pious sorrow rise;
While all their glowing souls are borne
To seek that grace which now they scorn.

3 In answer to our fervent cries,
Oh, may we see thy church arise;
Or, if that blessing seem too great,
Teach us to mourn its low estate.

C. M. IRISH.

1. Blest Jesus, come thou gently down, And fill this hal-low'd place; Oh, make thy glo-rious go-ings known, Dif-fuse a-round thy grace.

825　　*For Revival.*　　**588**

BLEST Jesus, come thou gently down,
And fill this hallow'd place;
Oh, make thy glorious goings known,
Diffuse around thy grace.

2 Shine, dearest Lord, from realms of day,
Disperse the gloom of night;
Chase all our clouds and doubts away,
And turn the shades to light.

3 Behold, and pity from above,
Our cold and languid frame;
Oh, shed abroad thy quick'ning love,
And glorify thy name.

4 All-glorious Savior, source of grace,
To thee we raise our cry;
Unvail the beauties of thy face
To ev'ry waiting eye.

5 Revive, O God, desponding saints,
Who languish, droop, and sigh;
Refresh the soul that tires and faints,
Fill mourning hearts with joy.

6 Make known thy power, victorious King,
Subdue each stubborn will;
Then sov'reign grace we'll join to sing
On Zion's sacred hill.

826　　*Spiritual Winter.*　　**606**

STERN winter throws his icy chains,
Encircling nature round;
How bleak, how comfortless the plains,
So late with verdure crown'd!

2 My heart, when mental winter reigns,
In night's dark mantle clad,
Confin'd in cold, inactive chains,
How desolate and sad!

3 Return, O blissful Sun, and bring
The soul-reviving ray;
This mental winter change to spring,
This darkness into day.

4 Oh, happy state, divine abode,
Where spring eternal reigns,
And perfect day, the smile of God,
Fills all the heav'nly plains!

MISSIONS.

L. M. STONEFIELD.

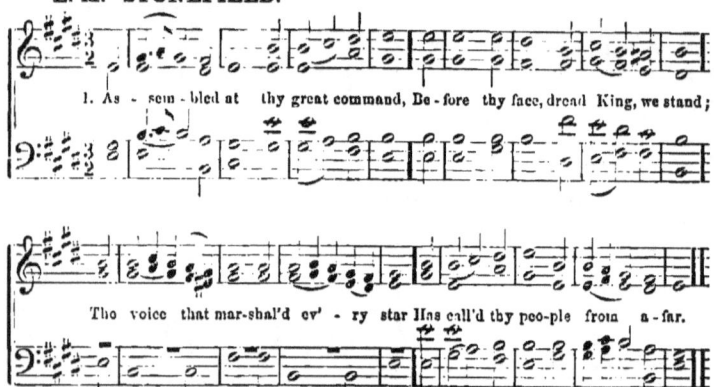

1. As-sem-bled at thy great command, Be-fore thy face, dread King, we stand; The voice that mar-shal'd ev'-ry star Has call'd thy peo-ple from a-far.

827 *Missionary Meeting.* **540**

ASSEMBLED at thy great command,
  Before thy face, dread King, we stand;
The voice that marshal'd ev'ry star
Has call'd thy people from afar.

2 We meet, through distant lands to spread
The truth for which the martyrs bled;
Along the line—to either pole—
The thunder of thy praise to roll.

3 First, bow our hearts beneath thy sway;
Then give thy growing empire way,
O'er wastes of sin, o'er fields of blood,
Till all mankind shall be subdu'd.

4 Our pray'rs assist; accept our praise;
Our hopes revive; our courage raise;
Our counsels aid; and, oh, impart
The single eye, the faithful heart!

5 Forth with thy chosen heralds come,
Recall the wand'ring spirit home:
From Zion's mount send forth the sound
To spread the spacious earth around.

828 *Signs of Promise.* **535**

BEHOLD th' expected time draw near,
  The shades disperse, the dawn appear;
The barren wilderness assume
The beauteous tints of Eden's bloom.

2 Events, with prophecies, conspire
To raise our faith, our zeal to fire;
The rip'ning fields, already white,
Present a harvest to our sight.

3 The untaught heathen waits to know
The joy the gospel will bestow;
The exil'd slave waits to receive
The freedom Jesus has to give.

4 Come, let us with a grateful heart
In this blest labor share a part,
Our pray'rs and off'rings gladly bring
To aid the triumphs of our King.

829 *For the Success of Missions.* **541**

INDULGENT God, to thee we pray
  Be with us on this solemn day;
Smile on our souls, our plans approve,
By which we seek to spread thy love.

2 Let party prejudice be gone,
And love unite our hearts in one;
Let all we have and are, combine
To aid this glorious work of thine.

3 Point us to men of upright mind,
Devoted, diligent, and kind;
With grace be all their hearts endow'd,
And light to guide them in the road.

4 With cheerful steps may they proceed,
Where'er thy providence shall lead;
Let heav'n and earth their work befriend,
And mercy all their paths attend.

5 Great let the bands of those be found
Who shall attend the gospel sound;
And let barbarians, bond and free
In suppliant throngs resort to thee.

6 Where pagan altars now are built,
And blood of beasts or men is spilt,
There be the bleeding cross high rear'd,
And God, our God, alone rever'd.

7 Where captives groan beneath their chain,
Let grace, and love, and concord reign;
The aged and the infant tongue
Unite in one harmonious song.

MISSIONS.

L. M. WARD.

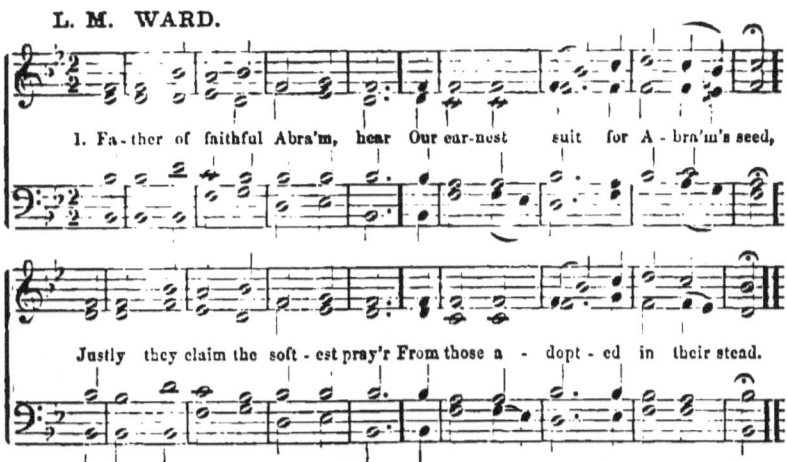

1. Fa-ther of faithful Abra'm, hear Our ear-nest suit for A-bra'm's seed, Justly they claim the soft-est pray'r From those a-dopt-ed in their stead.

830 *Prayer for Israel.* 553

FATHER of faithful Abra'm, hear
  Our earnest suit for Abra'm's seed,
Justly they claim the softest pray'r
From those adopted in their stead.

2 Outcast from thee, and scatter'd wide
Through ev'ry nation under heav'n,
Rejecting whom they crucified,
Unsav'd, unpitied, unforgiv'n.

3 Come then, thou great Deliv'rer, come,
The veil from Jacob's heart remove;
Receive thine ancient people home,
That they may sing redeeming love.

831 *For the Conversion of Israel.* 554

SHEPHERD of Israel, thou didst lead
  Thy chosen flock the desert through,
And from between the cherubim
Thy mercy and thy favor show.

2 And though their sins provoked thee oft,
To give them to their foes a prey,
Yet didst thou, for thy mercy's sake,
As often turn thy wrath away.

3 But now for ages they have been
Cast out and banish'd from thy sight,
Wand'ring through all the earth, as those
In whom thou hast no more delight.

4 Yet is thy word of promise sure,
That they shall be again restor'd,
And with the gentile church unite
To worship and to serve the Lord.

5 Our faith in expectation waits
To see that glorious morning rise:
Oh, bid the shadows flee away,
And satisfy our longing eyes.

832 *For more Laborers.* 542

LORD, when we cast our eyes abroad,
  And see on heathen altars slain
Poor helpless babes, for sacrifice,
T' efface their parents' guilty stain;

2 We cannot view such horrid deeds
Without a groan of ardent pray'r;
And while each heart in anguish bleeds,
We cry, Lord, send thy gospel there.

3 Oh, send out preachers, gracious Lord,
Among that dark, bewilder'd race;
Open their eyes, and bless thy word,
And call them by thy sov'reign grace.

4 Then shall they shout thine honor'd name,
And sound thy matchless praise abroad;
And we will join them in the theme,
Salvation to our risen God.

833 *For the Effusion of the Spirit.* 804

O SPIRIT of the living God,
  In all thy plenitude of grace,
Where'er the foot of man hath trod,
Descend on our apostate race.

2 Be darkness, at thy coming, light,
Confusion, order, in thy path;
Souls without strength inspire with might;
Bid mercy triumph over wrath.

3 Baptize the nations; far and nigh,
The triumphs of the cross record;
The name of Jesus glorify,
Till ev'ry kindred call him Lord.

4 God from eternity hath will'd
All flesh shall his salvation see;
So be the Father's love fulfill'd,
The Savior's suff'rings crown'd thro' thee.

MISSIONS.

C. M. DUNDEE.
With animation

1. Lord, send thy word, and let it fly, Arm'd with thy Spi-rit's pow'r,

Ten thou-sand shall con-fess its sway, And bless the sav-ing hour.

834 *For the Gospel's Success.* **536**

LORD, send thy word, and let it fly,
  Arm'd with thy Spirit's pow'r,
Ten thousand shall confess its sway,
  And bless the saving hour.

2 Beneath the influence of thy grace,
  The barren wastes shall rise,
With sudden greens and fruits array'd,
  A blooming paradise.

3 True holiness shall strike its root
  In each regenerate heart;
Shall in a growth divine arise,
  And heav'nly fruits impart.

4 Peace, with her olives crown'd, shall stretch
  Her wings from shore to shore;
No trump shall rouse the rage of war,
  Nor murd'rous cannon roar.

5 Lord, for those days we wait—those days
  Are in thy word foretold;
Fly swifter, sun and stars, and bring
  This promis'd age of gold!

6 Amen, with joy divine, let earth's
  Unnumber'd myriads cry;
Amen, with joy divine, let heav'n's
  Unnumber'd choirs reply.

835 *For the Gospel's Spread.* **532**

GREAT God! the nations of the earth
  Are by creation thine;
And in thy works, by all beheld,
  Thy radiant glories shine.

2 But, Lord, thy greater love has sent
  Thy gospel to mankind,
Unveiling what rich stores of grace
  Are treasur'd in thy mine.

3 Lord, when shall these glad tidings spread
  The spacious earth around,
Till ev'ry tribe and ev'ry soul
  Shall hear the joyful sound?

4 Oh, when shall Afric's sable sons
  Enjoy the heav'nly word,
And vassals, long enslav'd, become
  The freemen of the Lord?

5 When shall th' untutor'd heathen tribes,
  A dark, bewilder'd race,
Sit down at our Immanuel's feet,
  And learn and feel his grace?

6 Haste, sov'reign mercy, and transform
  Their cruelty to love;
Soften the tiger to a lamb,
  The vulture to a dove.

7 Smile, Lord, on each divine attempt
  To spread the gospel's rays;
And build on sin's demolish'd throne
  The temples of thy praise.

836 *Enlargement of the Church.* **885**

SHINE, mighty God, on Zion shine,
  With beams of heav'nly grace;
Reveal thy pow'r through ev'ry land,
  And show thy smiling face.

2 When shall thy name, from shore to shore,
  Sound through the earth abroad,
And distant nations know and love
  Their Savior and their God?

3 Sing to the Lord, ye distant lands;
  Sing loud, with joyful voice:
Let ev'ry tongue exalt his praise;
  And ev'ry heart rejoice.

MISSIONS.

C. M. P. ARIEL.

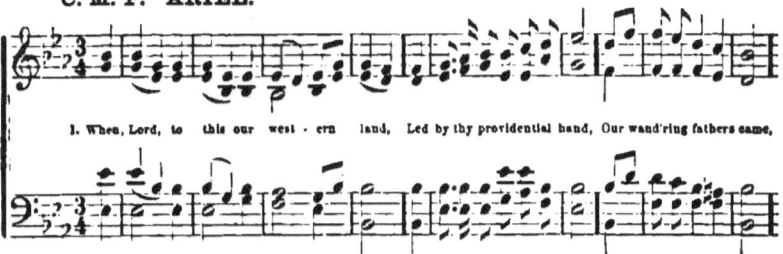

838 *Domestic Missions.* **894**

WHEN, Lord, to this our western land,
  Led by thy providential hand,
Our wand'ring fathers came,
Their ancient homes, their friends in youth,
Sent forth the heralds of thy truth,
  To keep them in thy name.

2 Throughout our solitary coast
The desert features soon were lost;
  Thy temples there arose;
Our shores, as culture made them fair,
Were hallow'd by thy rites, by pray'r,
  And blossom'd as the rose.

3 And, oh, may we repay this debt
To regions solitary yet
  Within our spreading land!
There, brethren, from our common home,
Still westward, like our fathers, roam,
  Still guided by thy hand.

4 Savior! we own this debt of love!
Oh, shed thy Spirit from above,
  To move each Christian breast;
Till heralds shall thy truth proclaim,
And temples rise to fix thy name
  Through all our desert West.

839 *Prayer for Missions.*

GOD of the nations, bow thine ear,
  And listen to our fervent prayer
    Through thy beloved Son;
Build up the kingdom of his grace
Amid the millions of our race,
  And make thy wonders known.

2 Send forth the heralds in his name;
Bid them a Savior's love proclaim
  With every fleeting breath;
Till distant lands shall hear the sound,
And send the joyful echoes round,
  Amid the shades of death.

3 Oh, let the nations rise and bring
Their offerings to th' Almighty King.
  And trust in him alone;
Renounce their idols, and adore
The God of gods for evermore,
  Upon his lofty throne.

4 The dying millions thus shall prove
The matchless power of bleeding love,
  And feel their sins forgiv'n;
Shall join the converts' joyful throng,
And raise on high redemption's song,
  Along the path to heav'n.

MISSIONS.

7s & 6s.   MISSIONARY HYMN.

1. From Greenland's icy mountains, From India's coral strand, Where Afric's sunny fountains Roll down their golden sand; From many an ancient river, From many a palmy plain, They call us to deliver Their land from error's chain.

840   *Missionary Field.*   537

FROM Greenland's icy mountains,
  From India's coral strand,
Where Afric's sunny fountains
  Roll down their golden sand;
From many an ancient river,
  From many a palmy plain,
They call us to deliver
  Their land from error's chain.

2 What though the spicy breezes
  Blow soft o'er Ceylon's isle;
Though ev'ry prospect pleases,
  And only man is vile?
In vain with lavish kindness
  The gifts of God are strewn;
The heathen, in his blindness,
  Bows down to wood and stone.

3 Can we, whose souls are lighted
  With wisdom from on high—
Can we to men benighted
  The lamp of life deny?
Salvation, oh, Salvation!
  The joyful sound proclaim,
Till earth's remotest nation
  Has learn'd Messiah's name,

4 Waft, waft, ye winds, his story,
  And you, ye waters roll,
Till, like a sea of glory,
  It spreads from pole to pole;
Till o'er our ransom'd nature
  The Lamb for sinners slain,
Redeemer, King, Creator,
  In bliss returns to reign.

841   *The Salvation of Israel.*   888

OH that the Lord's salvation
  Were out of Zion come,
To heal his ancient nation,
  To lead his outcasts home!

2 How long the holy city
  Shall heathen feet profane?
Return, O Lord, in pity,
  Rebuild her walls again.

3 Let fall thy rod of terror,
  Thy saving grace impart,
Roll back the vail of error,
  Release the fetter'd heart.

4 Let Israel, home returning,
  Her lost Messiah see;
Give oil of joy for mourning,
  And bind thy church to thee.

842   *Missionary Labors.*   882

ON Thibet's snow-capt mountains,
  O'er Afric's burning sand,
Where roll the fiery fountains
  Adown Hawaii's strand,—
In ev'ry distant nation
  The mighty globe around,
The heralds of salvation
  The gospel trumpet sound.

2 In golden armor blazing,
  They press their onward way,
And, high in air upraising,
  The glorious cross display:
Away their weapons hurling,
  The warring nations cease,
And hail with joy, unfurling,
  The banneret of peace.

3 Where sin hath fix'd her dwelling,
  Where death the tyrant reigns,
The heav'nly notes are swelling,
  In loudest, sweetest strains:
They breathe—the bones are shaken,
  And, cloth'd with flesh, arise;
They bid the dead awaken
  To glory in the skies.

4 What though hell's fiery regions
  Pour forth their dread array!
Look up!—angelic legions
  Attend you on your way.
March on, ye sons of heav'n,
  This precious promise sing:—
"The heathen shall be giv'n
  To Christ, our glorious King."

7s & 6s. PASSAIC.

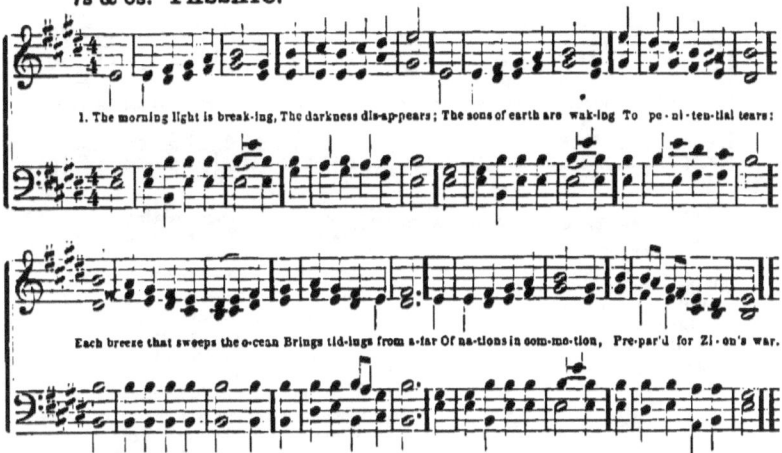

1. The morning light is break-ing, The darkness dis-ap-pears; The sons of earth are wak-ing To pe-ni-ten-tial tears:
Each breeze that sweeps the o-cean Brings tid-ings from a-far Of na-tions in com-mo-tion, Pre-par'd for Zi-on's war.

843 *Success of the Gospel.* **915**

THE morning light is breaking,
  The darkness disappears;
The sons of earth are waking
  To penitential tears:
Each breeze that sweeps the ocean
  Brings tidings from afar
Of nations in commotion,
  Prepar'd for Zion's war.

2 Rich dews of grace come o'er us
  In many a gentle shower,
And brighter scenes before us
  Are op'ning ev'ry hour:
Each cry to heaven going
  Abundant answers brings,
And heav'nly gales are blowing
  With peace upon their wings.

3 See heathen nations bending
  Before the God we love,
And thousand hearts ascending
  In gratitude above;
While sinners, now confessing,
  The gospel call obey,
And seek the Savior's blessing,—
  A nation in a day.

4 Blest river of salvation,
  Pursue thine onward way;
Flow thou to ev'ry nation;
  Nor in thy richness stay:
Stay not till all the lowly
  Triumphant reach their home;
Stay not till all the holy
  Proclaim, "The Lord is come."

844 *The Universal Halleluia.* **883**

WHEN shall the voice of singing
  Flow joyfully along?
When hill and valley, ringing
  With one triumphant song,
Proclaim the contest ended,
  And Him, who once was slain,
Again to earth descended,
  In righteousness to reign?

2 Then from the craggy mountains
  The sacred shout shall fly,
And shady vales and fountains
  Shall echo the reply;
High tower and lowly dwelling
  Shall send the chorus round,
The hallelujah swelling
  In one eternal sound.

MISSIONS.

ZION. 8s, 7s, 4s.

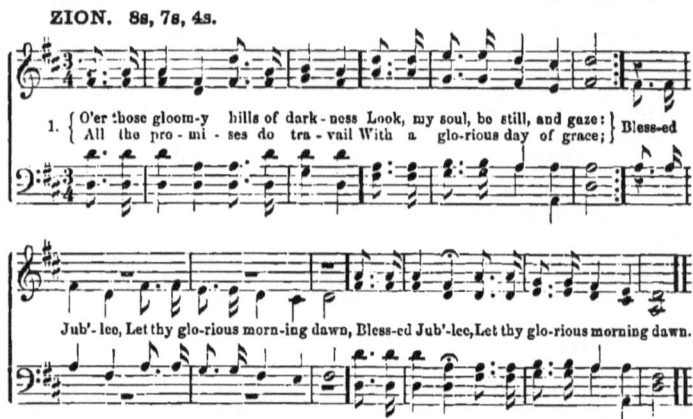

1. O'er those gloom-y hills of dark-ness Look, my soul, be still, and gaze: Bless-ed
All the pro-mi-ses do tra-vail With a glo-rious day of grace;

Jub'-lee, Let thy glo-rious morn-ing dawn, Bless-ed Jub'-lee, Let thy glo-rious morning dawn.

---

845 *For the Spread of the Gospel.* **538**

O'ER those gloomy hills of darkness
   Look, my soul, be still, and gaze;
All the promises do travail
   With a glorious day of grace:
     Blessed Jub'lee,
  Let thy glorious morning dawn.

2 Let the Indian, let the negro,
   Let the rude barbarian, see
That divine and glorious conquest
   Once obtain'd on Calvary;
     Let the gospel
  Soon resound from pole to pole.

3 Kingdoms wide, that sit in darkness,
   Grant them, Lord, the glorious light,
And from eastern coast to western
   May the morning chase the night;
     And redemption,
  Freely purchas'd, win the day.

4 May the glorious day approaching,
   Thine eternal love proclaim,
And the everlasting gospel
   Spread abroad thy holy name
     O'er the borders
  Of the great Immanuel's land.

5 Mighty Savior, spread thy gospe
   Win and conquer, never cease ;
May thy lasting, wide dominions
   Multiply and still increase ;
     Sway thy sceptre,
  Savior, all the world around.

846 *Idolatry Falling.* **889**

SEE how many, lately bowing
   To their idols, wood and stone,
Now, a blessed change avowing,
   Bow before the Savior's throne,
     And with gladness
  Praise the Savior's name alone.

2 This is cause of joy and wonder ;
   God has set the captives free,
He has burst their bonds asunder,
   Happy they and glorious he ;
     God our Savior !
  Who can be compar'd to thee ?

3 When thou workest, who shall stay thee?
   Who shall stay the work begun ?
Lord, go on, thy people pray thee,
   Till the glorious day is won,
     And the gospel
  Takes its circuit like the sun.

847 *Missionary's Farewell.* **887**

YES, my native land, I love thee;
   All thy scenes, I love them well ;
Friends, connections, happy country,
   Can I bid you all farewell ?
     Can I leave you,
  Far in distant lands to dwell ?

2 Yes, I hasten from you gladly,
   From the scenes I love so well,
Far away, ye billows, bear me ;
   Lovely native land, farewell !
     Pleas'd I leave thee—
  Far in heathen lands to dwell.

3 In the desert let me labor,
   On the mountain let me tell
How he died, the blessed Savior,
   To redeem a world from hell !
     Let me hasten—
  Native land, farewell ! farewell !

MISSIONS.

6s and 4s. AMERICA.

1. With thy pure dews and rains, Wash out, O God, the stains From Af-ric's shore; And while her palm-trees bud, Let not her children's blood With her broad Niger's flood Be mingled more!

848 *Prayer for Africa.*

WITH thy pure dews and rains,
　Wash out, O God, the stains
　　From Afric's shore;
And while her palm-trees bud,
Let not her children's blood
With her broad Niger's flood
　　Be mingled more!

2 Quench, righteous God, the thirst
That Congo's sons hath curs'd,
　　The thirst for gold.
Shall not thy thunders speak,
Where Mammon's altars reek,
Where maids and matrons shriek,
　　Bound, bleeding, sold!

3 Wilt thou not, Lord, at last
From thine own image cast
　　Away all cords
But that of love, which brings
Man from his wanderings
Back to the King of kings
　　And Lord of lords!

849 *General Prayer and Praise.*

COME, thou almighty King,
　Help all thy name to sing,
　　Help all to praise:
Father! all-glorious,
O'er all victorious,
Come, and reign over us,
　　Ancient of Days!

2 Come, thou incarnate Word!
Gird on thy mighty sword;
　　Our prayer attend:
Come, and thy people bless,
And give thy word success;
Spirit of holiness!
　　On us descend.

3 Come, holy Comforter!
Thy sacred witness bear,
　　In this, Earth's hour;
Thou, who almighty art,
Come rule in every heart,
And ne'er from us depart,
　　Spirit of power!

4 To the great One in Three,
The highest praises be,
　　Hence evermore!
His sovereign majesty
May we in glory see,
And to eternity
　　Love and adore.

850 *The Great Command.*

SOUND, sound the truth abroad!
　Bear ye the word of God
Through the wide world:
Tell what our Lord hath done;
Tell how the day was won,
And from his lofty throne
　　Satan is hurl'd.

2 Far over sea and land—
'Tis our Lord's own command—
　　Bear ye his name:
Bear it to ev'ry shore;
Regions unknown explore;
Enter at every door:—
　　Silence is shame.

3 Ye who, forsaking all
At your loved Master's call,
　　Comforts resign;
Soon will the work be done;
Soon will the prize be won:
Brighter than yonder sun
　　Then shall ye shine.

CHARITIES AND REFORMS.

C. M. GIVE.

1. Blest is the man whose heart ex-pands At melt-ing pi-ty's call,
And the rich bless-ings of whose hands Like heav'n-ly man-na fall.

851 *Care for Friendless Youth.* **666**

BLEST is the man whose heart expands
  At melting pity's call,
And the rich blessings of whose hands
  Like heav'nly manna fall.

2 Mercy, descending from above,
  In softest accents pleads;
Oh, may each tender bosom move
  When mercy intercedes.

3 Be ours the bliss in wisdom's way
  To guide untutor'd youth,
And lead the mind that went astray
  To virtue and to truth.

4 Children our kind protection claim,
  And God will well approve
When infants learn to lisp his name
  And their Creator love.

5 Delightful work! young souls to win,
  And turn the rising race
From the deceitful paths of sin,
  To seek redeeming grace.

6 Almighty God! thine influence shed
  To aid this good design:
The honors of thy name be spread,
  And all the glory thine.

852 *Christ in his Poor.* **665**

JESUS, my Lord, how rich thy grace!
  Thy bounties how complete!
How shall I count the matchless sum,
  How pay the mighty debt?

2 High on a throne of radiant light
  Dost thou exalted shine:
What can my poverty bestow,
  When all the worlds are thine?

3 But thou hast brethren here below,
  The partners of thy grace,
And wilt confess their humble names
  Before thy Father's face.

4 In them thou mayst be cloth'd and fed,
  And visited and cheer'd;
And in their accents of distress
  My Savior's voice is heard.

5 Thy face, with rev'rence and with love,
  We in thy poor would see;
Oh, let us rather beg our bread
  Than keep it back from thee.

853 *The Blessedness of Charity.*

BLEST is the man whose softening heart
  Feels all another's pain;
To whom the supplicating eye
  Was never rais'd in vain;

2 Whose breast expands with gen'rous warmth,
  A stranger's woes to feel;
And bleeds in pity o'er the wound
  He lacks the power to heal.

3 He spreads his kind, supporting arms
  To every child of grief;
His secret bounty largely flows,
  And brings unask'd relief.

4 To gentle offices of love
  His feet are never slow;
He views, through mercy's melting eye,
  A brother in a foe.

5 Peace from the bosom of his God
  The Savior's grace shall give;
And when he kneels before the throne,
  His trembling soul shall live.

CHARITIES AND REFORMS.

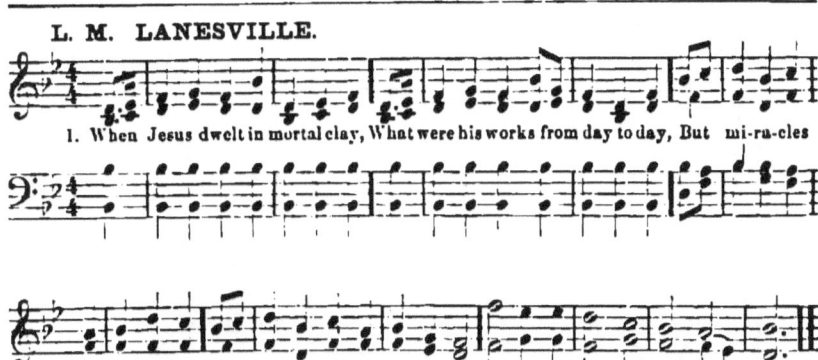

L. M. LANESVILLE.

1. When Jesus dwelt in mortal clay, What were his works from day to day, But mi-ra-cles of pow'r and grace, Which spread salvation thro' our race? Which spread salvation thro' our race?

854 *Christ's Example our Law.* **664**

WHEN Jesus dwelt in mortal clay,
 What were his works from day to day,
But miracles of pow'r and grace,
Which spread salvation through our race?

2 Teach us, O Lord, to keep in view
Thy pattern, and thy steps pursue:
Let alms bestow'd, let kindness done,
Be witness'd by each rolling sun.

3 That man may last, but never lives,
Who much receives, but nothing gives;
Whom none can love, whom none can thank,
Creation's blot, creation's blank.

4 But he who marks from day to day
In gen'rous acts his radiant way,
Treads the same path the Savior trod,
The path to glory and to God.

855 *Liberality.* **663**

THE gold and silver are the Lord's,
 And ev'ry blessing earth affords;
All come from his propitious hand,
And must return at his command.

2 The blessings which I now enjoy,
I must for Christ and souls employ;
For if I use them as mine own,
My Lord will soon call in his loan.

3 When I to him in want apply,
He never will my suit deny:
And shall I then refuse to give,
Since I so much from him receive?

4 Shall Jesus leave the realms of day,
And clothe himself in humble clay?
Shall he become despis'd and poor,
To make me rich for evermore?

5 And shall I wickedly withhold
To give my silver or my gold?
To aid a cause my soul approves,
And save the sinners Jesus loves?

856 *Charity.*

COME, let us sound her praise abroad,
 Sweet Charity—the child of God!
Hers, on whose kind maternal breast
The shelter'd babes of misery rest;

2 Who—when she sees the sufferer bleed—
Reckless of name, or sect, or creed,
Comes, with prompt hand and look benign,
To bathe his wounds in oil and wine;

3 Who in her robe the sinner hides,
And soothes and pities while she chides;
Who lends an ear to every cry,
And asks no plea but misery.

4 Her tender mercies freely fall,
Like heaven's refreshing dews, on all;
Encircling in their wide embrace
Her friends, her foes—the human race.

5 Nor bounded to the earth alone,
Her love expands to worlds unknown;
Wherever faith's rapt thought has soar'd,
Or hope her upward flight explor'd!

OCCASIONS, TIMES, AND SEASONS.

L. M. OLD HUNDREDTH.

1. Here, in thy name, e-ter-nal God, We build this earth-ly house for thee; Oh, choose it for thy fix'd a-bode, And guard it from all er-ror free.

857 *Dedication Hymn.* **594**

HERE, in thy name, eternal God,
  We build this earthly house for thee;
Oh, choose it for thy fix'd abode,
And guard it from all error free.

2 Here, when thy people seek thy face,
And dying sinners pray to live,
Hear thou in heav'n, thy dwelling-place,
And when thou hearest, Lord, forgive.

3 Here, when thy messengers proclaim
The blessed gospel of thy Son,
Still by the pow'r of his great name
Be mighty signs and wonders done.

4 When children's voices raise the song,
Hosanna to their heav'nly King,
Let heaven, with earth, the strain prolong;
Hosanna! let the angels sing.

5 Thy glory never hence depart;
Yet choose not, Lord, this house alone;
Thy kingdom come to ev'ry heart;
In ev'ry bosom fix thy throne.

858 *On Building a Church.* **595**

AND will the great eternal God
  On earth establish his abode?
And will he from his radiant throne
Regard our temples as his own?

2 We bring the tribute of our praise;
And sing that condescending grace,
Which to our notes will lend an ear,
And call us sinful mortals near.

3 Our Father's watchful care we bless,
Which guards our house of pray'r in peace,
That no tumultuous foes invade,
To fill the worshippers with dread.

4 These walls we to thy honor raise:
Long may they echo with thy praise;
And thou, descending, fill the place
With choicest tokens of thy grace.

5 And in the great decisive day,
When God the nations shall survey,
May it before the world appear
That crowds were born to glory here!

859 *New Year.* **607**

GREAT God! we sing that mighty hand
  By which supported still we stand;
The op'ning year thy mercy shows—
Let mercy crown it till it close.

2 By day, at night, at home, abroad,
Still we are guarded by our God;
By his incessant bounty fed,
By his unerring counsel led.

3 With grateful hearts the past we own;
The future, all to us unknown,
We to thy guardian care commit,
And, peaceful, leave before thy feet.

4 In scenes exalted or depress'd,
Be thou our joy, and thou our rest;
Thy goodness all our hopes shall raise,
Ador'd through all our changing days.

5 When death shall interrupt our songs,
And seal in silence mortal tongues,
Our helper, God, in whom we trust,
In better worlds our souls shall boast.

OCCASIONS, TIMES, AND SEASONS. 295

L. M. ELPARAN.

1. God of our lives! thy constant care With blessings crowns each op'ning year;
These lives, so frail, dost thou pro-long, And wake a-new our an-nual song.

860 *New Year.* 608

GOD of our lives! thy constant care
With blessings crowns each op'ning year;
These lives, so frail, dost thou prolong,
And wake anew our annual song.

2 How many precious souls are fled
To the dark regions of the dead,
Since, from this day, the changing sun
Through his last yearly course has run!

3 We yet survive: but who can say,
Or through the year, or month, or day,
I shall retain my vital breath,
Thus far at least in league with death?

4 That breath is thine, eternal God!
'Tis thine to fix the soul's abode:
We hold our lives from thee alone,
On earth, or in the world unknown.

5 To thee we all our pow'rs resign;
Make us and own us still as thine:
Then shall we smile, secure from fear,
Though death should blast the rising year.

6 Thy children, eager to be gone,
Bid time's impetuous tide roll on,
And land them on that blooming shore
Where years and death are known no more.

861 *Morning Ejaculations.* 613

GOD of the morning, at whose voice
The cheerful sun makes haste to rise,
And like a giant doth rejoice
To run his journey through the skies;

2 From the fair chambers of the east
The circuit of his race begins,
And without weariness or rest,
Round the whole earth he flies and shines.

3 Oh, like the sun may I fulfill
Th' appointed duties of the day,
With ready mind and active will
March on and keep my heav'nly way.

4 But I shall rove and lose the race,
If God my sun should disappear,
And leave me in this world's wild maze
To follow ev'ry wand'ring star.

5 Lord, thy commands are clean and pure,
Enlight'ning our beclouded eyes;
Thy threat'ning just, thy promise sure,
Thy gospel makes the simple wise.

862 *Evening Song.* 629

THUS far the Lord has led me on;
Thus far his pow'r prolongs my days:
And ev'ry ev'ning shall make known
Some fresh memorial of his grace.

2 Much of my time has run to waste,
And I, perhaps, am near my home;
But he forgives my follies past,
And strength supplies for days to come.

3 I lay my body down to sleep;
Peace is the pillow of my head:
While well-appointed angels keep
Their watchful stations round my bed.

4 Thus when the night of death shall come,
My flesh shall rest beneath the ground,
Waiting thy voice to pierce my tomb
With sweet salvation in its sound.

OCCASIONS, TIMES, SEASONS.

S. M. GERAR.

1. The day is past and gone, The ev'n-ing shades ap-pear, Oh, may I ev-er keep in mind The night of death draws near.

863 *Evening Song.* **635**

THE day is past and gone,
  The ev'ning shades appear,
Oh, may I ever keep in mind
  The night of death draws near.

2 I lay my garments by,
  Upon my bed to rest;
So death will soon remove me hence
  And leave my soul undrest.

3 Lord, keep me safe this night,
  Secure from all my fears;
May angels guard me while I sleep,
  Till morning light appears.

4 And when I early rise,
  To view th' unwearied sun,
May I set out to win the prize,
  And after glory run:

5 That when my days are past,
  And I from time remove,
Lord, I may in thy bosom rest,
  The bosom of thy love.

864 *Morning Song.* **618**

SEE how the rising sun
  Pursues his shining way,
And wide proclaims his Maker's praise,
  With ev'ry bright'ning ray.

2 Thus would my rising soul
  Its heav'nly parent sing,
And to its great original
  The humble tribute bring.

3 Serene I laid me down
  Beneath his guardian care;

I slept, and I awoke, and found
  My kind Preserver near!

4 Thus does thine arm support
  This weak, defenseless frame:
But whence these favors, Lord, to me,
  So worthless as I am?

5 Oh, how shall I repay
  The bounties of my God?
This feeble spirit pants beneath
  The pleasing, painful load.

6 Dear Savior, to thy cross
  I bring my sacrifice;
By thee perfum'd, it shall ascend
  With fragrance to the skies.

7 My life I would anew
  Devote, O Lord, to thee
And in thy blessed presence spend
  A long eternity.

865 *Evening Song.* **946**

ANOTHER day is past,
  The hours forever fled;
And time is bearing me away,
  To mingle with the dead.

2 My mind in perfect peace
  My Father's care shall keep;
I yield to gentle slumber now,
  For thou canst never sleep.

3 How blessed, Lord, are they
  On thee securely stay'd!
They shall not be in life alarm'd,
  Nor be in death dismay'd.

OCCASIONS, TIMES, SEASONS. 297

7s. BENEVENTO.

1. Om-ni-present God, whose aid No one ev-er ask'd in vain, Be this night a-bout my bed,
A. S. All mine en-e-mies con-trol,

Ev'-ry e-vil tho't re-strain. Lay thy hand up-on my soul, God of mine un-guarded hours!
Hell and earth, and nature's pow'rs!

866   *Evening Prayer.*   **632**

OMNIPRESENT God, whose aid
   No one ever ask'd in vain,
Be this night about my bed,
Ev'ry evil thought restrain.

2 Lay thy hand upon my soul,
God of mine unguarded hours!
All mine enemies control,
Hell and earth, and nature's pow'rs!

3 Loose me from the chains of sense,
Set me from the body free;
Draw with stronger influence
My unfetter'd soul to thee.

4 In me, Lord, thyself reveal,
Fill me with a sweet surprise;
Let me thee, when waking, feel;
Let me in thine image rise.

867   *At the New Year.*   **932**

WHILE with ceaseless course the sun
   Hasted through the former year,
Many souls their race have run,
Never more to meet us here;
Fix'd in an eternal state,
They have done with all below;
We a little longer wait,
But how little, none can know.

2 As the winged arrow flies
Speedily the mark to find;
As the lightning from the skies
Darts and leaves no trace behind;

Swiftly thus our fleeting days
Bear us down life's rapid stream;
Upward, Lord, our spirits raise,
All below is but a dream.

3 Thanks for mercies past receive,
Pardon of our sins renew;
Teach us henceforth how to live,
With eternity in view:
Bless thy word to young and old,
Fill us with a Savior's love;
And when life's short tale is told,
May we dwell with thee above.

868   *Morning Prayer.*   **623**

NOW the shades of night are gone,
   Now the morning light is come;
Lord, may I be thine to-day—
Drive the shades of sin away.

2 Fill my soul with heav'nly light,
Banish doubt and cleanse my sight,
In thy service, Lord, to-day,
Help me labor, help me pray.

3 Keep my haughty passions bound;
Save me from my foes around;
Going out and coming in,
Keep me safe from ev'ry sin.

4 When my work of life is past,
Oh, receive me then at last!
Night of sin will be no more,
When I reach the heav'nly shore.

L. M. TALLIS' EVENING HYMN.

1. Glo-ry to thee, my God, this night, For all the blessings of the light; Keep me, oh, keep me, King of kings, Un-der thine own al-migh-ty wings.

869   *Evening.*   631

GLORY to thee, my God, this night,
   For all the blessings of the light;
Keep me, oh, keep me, King of kings,
Under thine own almighty wings.

2 Forgive me, Lord, for thy dear Son,
The ills that I this day have done;
That with the world, myself, and thee,
I, ere I sleep, at peace may be.

3 Teach me to live, that I may dread
The grave as little as my bed;
Teach me to die, that so I may
With joy behold the judgment-day.

4 Lord, let my soul forever share
The bliss of thy paternal care;
'Tis heav'n on earth, 'tis heav'n above,
To see thy face and sing thy love.

870   *Morning Meditations.*   617

IN sleep's serene oblivion laid,
   I safely pass'd the silent night;
Again I see the breaking shade,
I drink again the morning light.

2 New-born, I bless the waking hour,
Once more, with awe, rejoice to be;
My conscious soul resumes her pow'r,
And springs, my guardian God! to thee.

3 Oh, guide me through the various maze
My doubtful feet are doom'd to tread;
And spread thy shield's protecting blaze
Where dangers press around my head.

4 A deeper shade shall soon impend,
A deeper sleep my eyes oppress;
Yet then thy strength shall still defend,
Thy goodness still delight to bless.

5 That deeper shade shall break away,
That deeper sleep shall leave mine eyes:
Thy light shall give eternal day;
Thy love, the raptures of the skies.

871   *Resolutions in the Morning.*   621

AWAKE, my soul! and with the sun
   Thy daily stage of duty run;
Shake off dull sloth, and joyful rise
To pay thy morning sacrifice.

2 Lord! I my vows to thee renew:
Disperse my sins as morning dew;
Guard my first springs of tho't and will,
And with thyself my spirit fill.

3 Direct, control, suggest, this day,
All I design to do or say;
That all my pow'rs, with all their might,
In thy sole glory may unite.

4 All praise to thee, who safe hast kept,
And hast refresh'd me, while I slept!
Grant, Lord, when I from death shall wake,
I may of endless light partake.

872   *Evening.*   630

ANOTHER fleeting day has gone,
   Slow o'er the west the shadows rise,
Swift the soft stealing hours have flown,
And night's dark mantle vails the skies.

2 Another fleeting day has gone,
Swept from the records of the year;

OCCASIONS, TIMES, SEASONS.   299

And still with each successive sun,
Life's fading visions disappear.

3 Another fleeting day has gone,
To join the fugitives before:
And I, when life's employ is done,
Shall sleep, to wake in time no more.

4 Another fleeting day has gone,
And soon a fairer day shall rise:
A day whose never-setting sun
Shall pour his light o'er cloudless skies.

5 Another fleeting day has gone,
In solemn silence rest, my soul ;
Bend—bend before his awful throne,
Who bids the morn and ev'ning roll.

873   *Morning.*   939

ARISE, my soul! with rapture rise!
 And, fill'd with love and fear, adore
The awful Sov'reign of the skies,
Whose mercy lends me one day more.

2 And may this day, indulgent Power!
Not id'ly pass, nor fruitless be ;
But may each swiftly flying hour
Still nearer bring my soul to thee !

3 I fain would serve thee all my days,
And may my zeal with years increase ;
For pleasant, Lord, are all thy ways,
And all thy paths are paths of peace.

L. M. ROSEDALE.

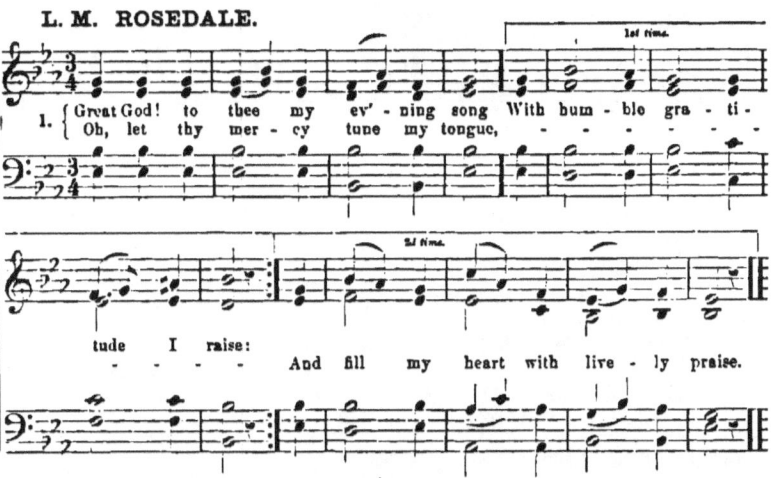

1. { Great God! to thee my ev'ning song With humble gratitude
     Oh, let thy mercy tune my tongue, }
I raise: And fill my heart with lively praise.

874   *Evening.*   945

GREAT God! to thee my ev'ning song
 With humble gratitude I raise:
Oh, let thy mercy tune my tongue,
And fill my heart with lively praise.

2 My days, unclouded as they pass,
And ev'ry onward rolling hour,
Are monuments of wondrous grace,
And witness to thy love and pow'r.

3 And yet this thoughtless, wretched heart,
Too oft regardless of thy love,
Ungrateful, can from thee depart,
And from the path of duty rove.

4 Seal my forgiveness in the blood
Of Christ, my Lord ; his name alone
I plead for pardon, gracious God,
And kind acceptance at thy throne.

5 With hope in him mine eyelids close,
With sleep refresh my feeble frame ;

Safe in thy care may I repose,
And wake with praises to thy name.

875   *Jesus Sought at Evening.*   947

THE busy scenes of day are fled,
 The ev'ning shades invite to rest ;
May I repose my weary head,
Reclining on my Savior's breast.

2 Jesus, to thee an ev'ning song
My soul in gratitude would raise ;
Oh, could I mount and join that throng,
I'd vie with angels in thy praise.

3 With tears of joy I'd sing the God
Who wept and groan'd and died for me ;
Then hide beneath that precious blood
Which freely flow'd on Calvary.

4 And when, at last, nor sun, nor moon,
Nor stars shall light the pilgrim's way,
Let angel bands convey me home
To realms of everlasting day.

L. M. MENDON.

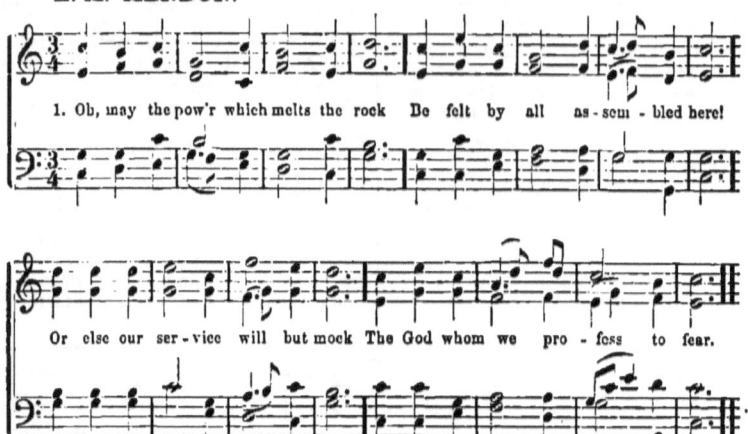

1. Oh, may the pow'r which melts the rock Be felt by all as-sem-bled here! Or else our ser-vice will but mock The God whom we pro-fess to fear.

876 *National Confession.* **692**

OH, may the pow'r which melts the rock
Be felt by all assembled here!
Or else our service will but mock
The God whom we profess to fear.

2 Lord, while thy judgments shake the land,
Thy people's eyes are fix'd on thee!
We own thy just, uplifted hand,
Which thousands cannot, will not see.

3 How long hast thou bestow'd thy care
On this indulg'd, ungrateful spot;
While other nations, far and near,
Have envied and admired our lot!

4 Here peace and liberty have dwelt,
The glorious gospel brightly shone;
And oft our enemies have felt
That God has made our cause his own.

5 But ah! both heav'n & earth have heard
Our vile requital of his love!
We, whom like children he has rear'd,
Against his goodness rebels prove.

6 His grace despis'd, his power defied,
And legions of the blackest crimes,
Profaneness, riot, lust, and pride,
Are signs that mark the present times.

7 Lord, hear thy people ev'rywhere,
Who meet to mourn, confess, and pray;
The nation and thy churches spare,
And let thy wrath be turn'd away.

877 *Prayer for National Piety.* **971**

LORD, let thy goodness lead our land,
Still saved by thine almighty hand,
The tribute of its love to bring
To thee, our Savior and our King.

2 Let ev'ry sacred temple raise
Triumphant songs of holy praise;
Let ev'ry peaceful, private home
A temple, Lord, to thee become.

3 Still be it our supreme delight
To walk as in thy glorious sight;
Still in thy precepts and thy fear,
Till life's last hour, to persevere.

878 *Public Humiliation.* **957**

GREAT Maker of unnumber'd worlds,
And whom unnumber'd worlds adore,
Whose goodness all thy creatures share,
While nature trembles at thy pow'r,—

2 Thine is the hand that moves the spheres,
That wakes the wind and lifts the sea;
And man, who moves the lord of earth,
Acts but the part assign'd by thee.

3 While suppliant crowds implore thine aid,
To thee we raise the humble cry:
Thine altar is the contrite heart,
Thine incense the repentant sigh.

4 Oh, may our land, in this her hour,
Confess thy hand and bless the rod,
By penitence make thee her Friend,
And find in thee a guardian God.

OCCASIONS, TIMES, SEASONS. 801

879 *Thanksgiving.* 685

PRAISE, happy land, Jehovah's name;
His goodness, and thy bliss, proclaim:
For thee each blessing largely flows
That freedom's lib'ral hand bestows.

2 Thy children are secure and blest;
Thy shores have peace, thy cities rest:
He feeds thy sons with finest wheat,
And adds his blessing to their meat.

3 Thy changing seasons he ordains,
Thine early and thy latter rains;
His flakes of snow like wool he sends,
And well the springing corn defends.

4 But he hath nobler works and ways,
To call his people to his praise:
To all our land his laws are shown;
His gospel's through the nation known.

8s. ST. HELEN'S.

880 *Praise for National Prosperity.* 968

SAY, should we search the globe around,
Where can such happiness be found
As dwells in this much favor'd land?
Here plenty reigns; here freedom sheds
Her choicest blessings on our heads:
By God supported, still we stand.

2 Here commerce spreads her ample store,
Which comes from ev'ry foreign shore;
Science and arts their charms display;
Religion teaches us to raise
Our voices in our Maker's praise,
As truth and conscience point the way.

3 These are thy gifts, almighty King:
From thee our matchless blessings spring;
Th' extended shade, the fruitful skies,
The comforts liberty bestows,
Th' eternal joys the gospel shows,
All from thy boundless goodness rise.

4 With grateful hearts, with cheerful tongues,
To God we raise united songs,
His pow'r and mercy we proclaim;
And still through ev'ry age shall own
Jehovah here has fix'd his throne;
And triumph in his mighty name.

5 Long as the moon her course shall run,
Or man behold the circling sun,
Do thou amidst our nation reign;
Still crown her counsels with success,
With peace and joy her borders bless,
And all her sacred rights maintain.

Doxology.

NOW to the great and sacred Three,
The Father, Son, and Spirit, be
Eternal praise and glory given—
Through all the worlds where God is known,
By all the angels near the throne
And all the saints in earth and heaven.

OCCASIONS, TIMES, SEASONS.

C. M. SILOAM.

1. In-dul-gent Fa-ther, by whose care I've pass'd an-o-ther day, Let me this night thy mer-cy share, And teach me how to pray.

881 *Evening.* **634**

INDULGENT Father, by whose care
  I've pass'd another day,
Let me this night thy mercy share,
  And teach me how to pray.

2 Show me my sins, and how to mourn
  My guilt before thy face;
Direct me, Lord, to Christ alone,
  And save me by thy grace.

3 Let each returning night declare
  The tokens of thy love;
And ev'ry hour thy grace prepare
  My soul for joys above.

4 And when on earth I close my eyes,
  To sleep in death's embrace,
Let me to heav'n and glory rise,
  T' enjoy thy smiling face.

882 *An Evening Hymn.* **944**

AND now another day is past,
  The sun has left our shore,
And weary lab'rers homeward haste—
  Their daily toil is o'er.

2 But, mighty God, thy wakeful eye
  Needs not sleep's balmy pow'r;
Oh, be thy watchful Spirit nigh,
  In night's unguarded hour.

3 For day and night, alike to thee,
  Are glorious and bright;
Thy dwelling-place is brilliancy,
  And thou thyself art light.

4 From Satan's sway—from sin's control,
  Do thou protect my heart;

Nor from thee let this wand'ring soul
  E'en in a dream depart.

5 From ev'ry light and vain desire
  This sinful bosom free;
My heart would burn with holy fire—
  An altar, Lord, for thee.

6 With confidence I'll take my rest,
  Relying on thy love;
Be ev'ry rising fear represt,
  Nor let thy grace remove.

7 But if this night should be my last,
  And end my transient days,
I'll live to thee when death is past,
  A sinless life of praise.

883 *Evening Prayer.* **633**

O LORD, another day is flown,
  And we, a lonely band,
Are met once more before thy throne,
  To bless thy fost'ring hand.

2 And wilt thou lend a list'ning ear
  To praises low as ours?
Thou wilt! for thou dost love to hear
  The song which meekness pours.

3 And, Jesus, thou thy smiles wilt deign,
  As we before thee pray;
For thou didst bless the infant train,
  And we are less than they.

4 Oh, let thy grace perform its part,
  And let contention cease;
And shed abroad in ev'ry heart
  Thine everlasting peace.

OCCASIONS, TIMES, SEASONS.

C. M. IRISH.

1. Dread Sov'-reign, let mine ev'-ning song Like ho-ly in-cense rise! As-sist the off'-rings of my tongue To reach the lof-ty skies.

884 *An Evening Song.* **640**

DREAD Sov'reign, let mine ev'ning song
 Like holy incense rise!
Assist the off'rings of my tongue
To reach the lofty skies.

2 Through all the dangers of the day
Thy hand was still my guard,
And still to drive my wants away
Thy mercies stood prepar'd.

3 Perpetual blessings from above
Encompass'd me around,
But oh, how few returns of love
Hath my Creator found!

4 What have I done for Him that died
To save my wretched soul?
How are my follies multiplied,
Fast as my minutes roll?

5 Lord, with this guilty heart of mine
To thy dear cross I flee,
And to thy grace my soul resign,
To be renew'd by thee.

6 Sprinkled afresh with pard'ning blood,
I lay me down to rest,
As in th' embraces of my God,
Or on my Savior's breast.

885 *Evening Prayer.* **642**

LORD! thou wilt hear me when I pray,
 I am forever thine:
I fear before thee all the day,
Nor would I dare to sin.

2 And while I rest my weary head,
From cares and bus'ness free,

'Tis sweet conversing on my bed
With my own heart and thee.

3 I pay this ev'ning sacrifice;
And, when my work is done,
Great God, my faith and hope relies
Upon thy grace alone.

4 Thus with my thoughts compos'd to peace,
I'll give mine eyes to sleep;
Thy hand in safety keeps my days,
And will my slumbers keep!

886 *Evening Hymn.* **637**

NOW from the altar of our hearts
 Let incense-flames arise;
Assist us, Lord, to offer up
Our ev'ning sacrifice.

2 Awake, our love, awake, our joy;
Awake, our hearts and tongue:
Sleep not when mercies loudly call,
Break forth into a song.

3 Minutes and mercies multiplied
Have made up all this day;
Minutes came quick, but mercies were
More fleet and free than they.

4 New time, new favors, and new joys
Do a new song require;
Till we shall praise thee as we would,
Accept our heart's desire.

5 Lord of our time, whose hand hath set
New time upon our score,
Thee may we praise for all our time,
When time shall be no more!

H. M. ZEBULON.

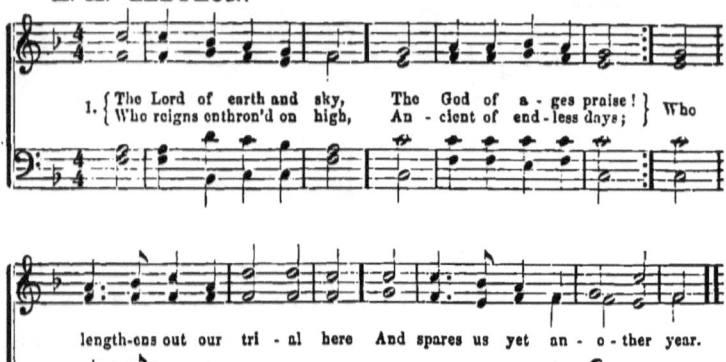

1. The Lord of earth and sky, The God of ages praise! Who reigns enthron'd on high, Ancient of endless days; Who lengthens out our trial here And spares us yet another year.

887 *New Year's Day.* **610**

THE Lord of earth and sky,
  The God of ages praise!
Who reigns enthron'd on high,
  Ancient of endless days;
Who lengthens out our trial here
And spares us yet another year.

2 Barren and wither'd trees,
  We cumber'd long the ground;
No fruit of holiness
  On our dead souls was found:
Yet doth he us in mercy spare
Another and another year.

3 When justice gave the word
  To cut the fig-tree down,
The pity of our Lord
  Cried, "Let it still alone:"
The Father mild inclines his ear,
And spares us yet another year.

4 Jesus, thy speaking blood
  From God obtain'd the grace,
Who therefore hath bestow'd
  On us a longer space:
Thou didst in our behalf appear,
And lo, we see another year!

5 Then dig about our root,
  Break up our fallow ground,
And let our gracious fruit
  To thy great praise abound;
Oh, let us all thy praise declare,
And fruit unto perfection bear.

888 *Church-Dedication Hymn.* **596**

IN sweet, exalted strains
  The King of glory praise:
O'er heav'n and earth he reigns,
  Through everlasting days.
He with a nod the world controls,
Sustains or sinks the distant poles.

2 Great King of glory! come,
  And with thy favor crown
This temple as thy dome,
  This people as thine own;
Within this house, oh, deign to show
How God can dwell with man below.

3 Here may thine ears attend
  Our interceding cries,
And grateful praise ascend
  All fragrant to the skies,
Here may thy word melodious sound,
And spread the joys of heav'n around.

4 Here may th' attentive throng
  Imbibe thy truth and love;
And converts join the song
  Of seraphim above;
And willing crowds surround thy board
With sacred joy and sweet accord.

5 In peace here may our sons
  And daughters sound thy praise,
And shine like polish'd stones,
  Through long succeeding days:
Here, Lord! display thy saving pow'r,
While churches stand and saints adore.

H. M. LENOX.

1. Blow ye the trumpet, blow The gladly solemn sound! Let all the nations know, To earth's remotest bound,

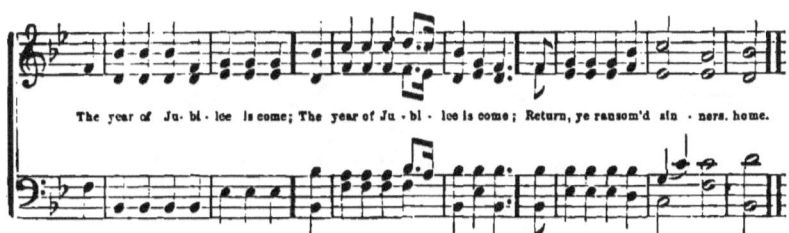

The year of Ju-bi-lee is come; The year of Ju-bi-lee is come; Return, ye ransom'd sin-ners, home.

889 *The Gospel Jubilee.* 186

BLOW ye the trumpet, blow
  The gladly solemn sound!
Let all the nations know,
  To earth's remotest bound,
The year of Jubilee is come;
Return, ye ransom'd sinners, home.

2 Exalt the Lamb of God,
  The sin-atoning Lamb;
Redemption by his blood
  Through all the lands proclaim:
The year of Jubilee is come;
Return, ye ransom'd sinners, home.

3 Ye slaves of sin and hell,
  Your liberty receive;
And safe in Jesus dwell,
  And blest in Jesus live.
The year of Jubilee is come;
Return, ye ransom'd sinners, home.

4 The gospel trumpet hear,
  The news of pard'ning grace;
Ye happy souls, draw near,
  Behold your Savior's face:
The year of Jubilee is come;
Return, ye ransom'd sinners, home.

5 Jesus, our great High-Priest,
  Has full atonement made;
Ye weary spirits, rest;
  Ye mournful souls, be glad!
The year of Jubilee is come;
Return, ye ransom'd sinners, home.

890 *The Year of Jubilee.* 811

FAIR shines the morning star!
  The silver trumpets sound—
Their notes re-echoing far,
  While dawns the day around!
Joy to the slave!—the slave is free!
It is the year of Jubilee.

2 Pris'ners of hope!—in gloom
  And silence left to die,
With Christ's unfolding tomb
  Your portals open fly;—
Rise with the Lord!—He sets you free:—
It is the year of Jubilee.

3 Ye, who have sold for naught
  The land your fathers won,
Behold how God has wrought
  Redemption through his Son!
Your heritage again is free,
It is the year of Jubilee.

4 Ye who yourselves have sold
  For debts to justice due,
Ransom'd, but not with gold,
  Christ gave himself for you;
His precious blood has made you free,
It is the year of Jubilee.

5 Captives of sin and shame,
  O'er earth and ocean, hear
An angel's voice proclaim
  The Lord's accepted year;—
Let Jacob rise, be Israel free,
It is the year of Jubilee.

OCCASIONS, TIMES, SEASONS.

C. M. HOWARD.

1. On thee each morn-ing, O my God, My wak-ing tho'ts at-tend; In whom are found-ed all my hopes, In whom my wish-es end.

891 *For Morning or Evening.* **940**

ON thee each morning, O my God,
My waking thoughts attend ;
In whom are founded all my hopes,
In whom my wishes end.

2 My soul, in pleasing wonder lost,
Thy boundless love surveys ;
And, fir'd with grateful zeal, prepares
The sacrifice of praise.

3 When ev'ning slumbers press mine eyes,
With thy protection blest,
In peace and safety I commit
My weary limbs to rest.

4 My spirit, in thy hands secure,
Fears no approaching ill ;
For whether waking or asleep,
Thou, Lord, art with me still.

5 Then will I daily to the world
Thy wondrous acts proclaim ;
Whilst all with me shall praise and sing,
And bless thy sacred Name.

892 *For a Public Fast.* **691**

SEE, gracious God, before thy throne
Thy mourning people bend !
'Tis on thy sov'reign grace alone
Our humble hopes depend.

2 Dark judgments from thy mighty hand
Thy dreadful power display ;
Yet mercy spares this guilty land,
And still we live to pray.

3 How chang'd, alas! are truths divine
For error, guilt, and shame!

What impious numbers, bold in sin,
Disgrace the Christian's name !

4 Regardless of thy smile or frown,
Their pleasures they require,
And sink with blind indiff'rence down
To everlasting fire.

5 Oh, turn us, turn us, mighty Lord,
By thine unbounded grace ;
Then shall our hearts obey thy word,
And humbly seek thy face.

893 *God's Love in Affliction.* **683**

WHEN languor and disease invade
This trembling house of clay,
'Tis sweet to look beyond my pains
And long to fly away ;

2 Sweet to look inward, and attend
The whispers of his love ;
Sweet to look upward to the place
Where Jesus pleads above ;

3 Sweet to look back, and see my name
In life's fair book set down ;
Sweet to look forward, and behold
Eternal joys my own ;

4 Sweet to reflect how grace divine
My sins on Jesus laid ;
Sweet to remember that his blood
My debt of suff'ring paid.

5 If such the sweetness of the streams,
What must the fountains be,
Where saints and angels draw their bliss
Immediately from thee !

SICKNESS, DEATH, JUDGMENT, ETERNITY.

C. M. ARLINGTON.

1. Stoop down, my thoughts, that used to rise, Converse a while with death; Think how a gasping mortal lies, And pants away with breath.

894 *Death and Eternity.* 247

1. STOOP down, my tho'ts, that us'd to rise,
Converse a while with death;
Think how a gasping mortal lies,
And pants away his breath.

2 His quiv'ring lip hangs feebly down,
His pulses faint and few,
Then, speechless, with a doleful groan
He bids the world adieu.

3 But, oh! the soul that never dies!
At once it leaves the clay!
Ye thoughts, pursue it where it flies,
And track its wondrous way.

4 Up to the courts where angels dwell,
It mounts triumphing there,
Or devils plunge it down to hell
In infinite despair.

5 And must my body faint and die?
And must this soul remove?
Oh for some guardian angel nigh
To bear it safe above!

6 Jesus, to thy dear faithful hand
My naked soul I trust,
And my flesh waits for thy command
To drop into my dust.

895 *God our Help in Trouble.* 677

1. MY soul, the awful hour will come,
Apace it passeth on,
To bear this body to the tomb,
And thee to scenes unknown.

2 My heart, long lab'ring with its woes,
Shall pant and sink away;
And you, my eyelids, soon shall close
On the last glimm'ring ray.

3 Whence in that hour shall I receive
A cordial for my pain,
When, if earth's monarchs were my friends,
Those friends would weep in vain?

4 Great King of nature and of grace,
To thee my spirit flies,
And opens all its deep distress
Before thy pitying eyes.

5 All its desires to thee are known,
And ev'ry secret fear;
The meaning of each broken groan
Well notic'd by thine ear.

6 Oh, fix me by that mighty pow'r,
Which to such love belongs,
Where darkness vails the eyes no more,
And groans are chang'd to songs.

896 *Comfort in Sickness and Death.* 681

1. WHEN sickness shakes the languid frame,
Each phantom pleasure flies;
Vain hopes of bliss no more obscure
Our long-deluded eyes.

2 The tott'ring frame of mortal life
Shall crumble into dust;
Nature shall faint; but learn, my soul,
On nature's God to trust.

3 The man whose pious heart is fix'd
Securely on his God,
In ev'ry frown may comfort find,
And kiss the chast'ning rod.

4 Nor him shall death itself alarm;
On heav'n his soul relies;
With joy he views his Maker's love,
And with composure dies.

C. M. FUNERAL THOUGHT.

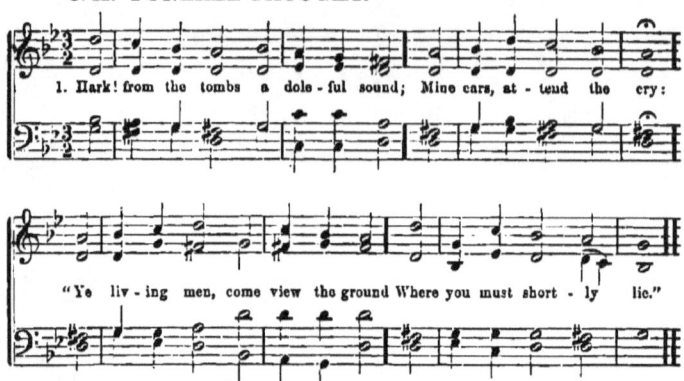

1. Hark! from the tombs a doleful sound; Mine ears, attend the cry: "Ye living men, come view the ground Where you must shortly lie."

897 *The Voice of the Tomb.* **701**

HARK! from the tombs a doleful sound;
 Mine ears, attend the cry:
"Ye living men, come view the ground
Where you must shortly lie.

2 "Princes, this clay must be your bed,
In spite of all your tow'rs!
The tall, the wise, the rev'rend head
Must lie as low as ours."

3 Great God! is this our certain doom?
And are we still secure?
Still walking downward to the tomb,
And yet prepare no more?

4 Grant us the pow'r of quick'ning grace
To fit our souls to fly;
Then, when we drop this dying flesh,
We'll rise above the sky.

898 *The Vanity of Man as Mortal.* **702**

TEACH me the measure of my days,
 Thou Maker of my frame!
I would survey life's narrow space,
And learn how frail I am.

2 A span is all that we can boast;
A fleeting hour of time:
Man is but vanity and dust,
In all his flow'r and prime.

3 See the vain race of mortals move,
Like shadows o'er the plain:
They rage and strive, desire and love,
But all the noise is vain.

4 Some walk in honor's gaudy show;
Some dig for golden ore;
They toil for heirs, they know not who,
And straight are seen no more.

5 What should I wish or wait for, then,
From creatures, earth and dust?
They make our expectations vain
And disappoint our trust.

6 Now I resign my earthly hope,
My fond desires recall;
I give my mortal int'rest up,
And make my God my all.

899 *Prayer for Support when Dying.* **696**

WHEN, bending o'er the brink of life,
 My trembling soul shall stand,
Waiting to pass death's awful flood,
Great God, at thy command;

2 When weeping friends surround my bed,
And close my sightless eyes;
When shatter'd by the weight of years
The broken body lies;

3 When ev'ry long-lov'd scene of life
Stands ready to depart;
When the last sigh that shakes the frame
Shall rend this bursting heart:

4 O thou great Source of joy supreme,
Whose arm alone can save,
Dispel the darkness that surrounds
The entrance to the grave.

5 Lay thy supporting, gentle hand
Beneath my sinking head;
And, with a ray of love divine,
Illume my dying bed.

6 Leaning on thy dear, faithful breast,
May I resign my breath!
And in thy fond embraces lose
"The bitterness of death!"

SICKNESS, DEATH, JUDGMENT, ETERNITY.

C. M. MEAR.

1. Thee we a-dore, e-ter-nal Name! And hum-bly own to thee How fee-ble is our mor-tal frame, What dy-ing worms are we.

900 *Death at Hand.* **703**

THEE we adore, eternal Name!
And humbly own to thee
How feeble is our mortal frame,
What dying worms are we.

2 Our wasting lives are short'ning still,
As months and days increase,
And ev'ry beating pulse we tell
Leaves but the number less.

3 Dangers stand thick thro' all the ground,
To push us to the tomb;
And fierce diseases wait around
To hurry mortals home.

4 Great God! on what a slender thread
Hang everlasting things!
Th' eternal states of all the dead
Upon life's feeble strings!

5 Infinite joy or endless woe
Attends on ev'ry breath,
And yet how unconcern'd we go
Upon the brink of death.

6 Waken, O Lord! our drowsy sense,
To walk this dang'rous road;
And if our souls are hurried hence,
May they be found with God!

901 *Death of Friends and Relatives.* **710**

MUST friends and kindred droop and die,
And helpers be withdrawn,
While sorrow, with a weeping eye,
Counts up our comforts gone?

2 Be thou our comfort, mighty God!
Our helper and our friend;
Nor leave us in this dang'rous road,
Till all our trials end.

3 Oh, may our feet pursue the way
Our pious fathers led;
While love and holy zeal obey
The counsels of the dead.

4 Let us be wean'd from earthly joys;
Let hope our grief dispel:
The dead in Jesus shall arise,
In endless bliss to dwell.

902 *Victory over Death.* **707**

WHEN Death appears before my sight,
In all his dire array,
Unequal to the dreadful fight,
My courage dies away.

2 But see my glorious Leader nigh!
Jesus, my Savior, lives:
Before him death's pale terrors fly
And my faint heart revives.

3 Lord, I commit my soul to thee;
Accept the sacred trust;
Receive this nobler part of me,
And watch my sleeping dust,

4 Till that illustrious morning come
When all thy saints shall rise,
And, cloth'd in full, immortal bloom,
Attend thee to the skies.

5 When thy triumphant armies sing
The honors of thy name,
And heaven's eternal arches ring
With glory to the Lamb;

6 Oh, let me join the raptur'd lays,
And, with the blissful throng,
Resound salvation, pow'r, and praise,
In everlasting song!

310　SICKNESS, DEATH, JUDGMENT, ETERNITY.

C. M. CHINA.

1. Why do we mourn de-part-ing friends, Or shake at death's a-larm? 'Tis but the voice that Jesus sends To call them to his arms.

903 *The Death and Burial of a Saint.* **718**

WHY do we mourn departing friends?
　Or shake at death's alarms?
'Tis but the voice that Jesus sends
　To call them to his arms.

2 Are we not tending upward too
　As fast as time can move?
Nor would we wish the hours more slow,
　To keep us from our love.

3 Why should we tremble to convey
　Their bodies to the tomb?
There the dear flesh of Jesus lay;
　And soften'd all its gloom.

4 The graves of all his saints he bless'd,
　And soften'd ev'ry bed;
Where should the dying members rest,
　But with the dying Head?

5 Thence he arose, ascending high,
　And show'd our feet the way;
Up to the Lord our flesh shall fly
　At the great rising-day.

6 Then let the last loud trumpet sound,
　And bid our kindred rise;
Awake, ye nations under ground,
　Ye saints, ascend the skies.

904　*Hope of Heaven.*　**712**

WHILE to the grave our friends are borne,
　Around their cold remains
How all the tender passions mourn,
　Each fond heart complains!

2 But down to earth, alas! in vain
　We bend our weeping eyes;
Ah! let us leave this place of pain,
　And upwards learn to rise.

3 Hope cheerful smiles amid the gloom,
　And beams a healing ray,
And guides us from the darksome tomb
　To realms of endless day.

4 To those bright courts when hope ascends,
　She calms the swelling woe;
In hope we meet our happy friends,
　And tears forget to flow.

5 Then let our hearts repine no more,
　That earthly comfort dies;
But lasting happiness explore,
　And ask it from the skies.

905　*On the Death of a Child.*　**714**

LIFE is a span, a fleeting hour;
　How soon the vapor flies!
Man is a tender, transient flow'r,
　That e'en in blooming dies.

2 The once-lov'd form, now cold and dead,
　Each mournful thought employs;
And nature weeps her comforts fled,
　And wither'd all her joys.

3 But wait the interposing gloom,
　And lo! stern winter flies;
And, drest in beauty's fairest bloom,
　The flow'ry tribes arise.

4 Hope looks beyond the bounds of time,
　When what we now deplore
Shall rise in full immortal prime
　And bloom to fade no more.

5 Then cease, fond nature! cease thy tears;
　The Savior dwells on high;
There everlasting spring appears,
　And joys shall never die.

SICKNESS, DEATH, JUDGMENT, ETERNITY.

C. M. DUNDEE.

1. Far from affliction, toil, and care, The happy soul is fled;
The breathless clay shall slumber here, Among the silent dead.

906 *Funeral of a Faithful Minister.* **577**

FAR from affliction, toil, and care,
  The happy soul is fled;
The breathless clay shall slumber here,
  Among the silent dead.

2 The gospel was his joy and song,
  E'en to his latest breath;
The truth he had proclaim'd so long
  Was his support in death.

3 Now he resides where Jesus is,
  Above his dusky sphere;
His soul was ripen'd for that bliss,
  While yet he sojourn'd here.

4 The Church's loss we all deplore,
  And shed the falling tear;
Since we shall see his face no more,
  Till Jesus shall appear.

5 But we are hasting to the tomb,
  Oh, may we ready stand;
Then, dearest Lord, receive us home,
  To dwell at thy right hand.

907 *At the Funeral of a Young Person.* **715**

WHEN blooming youth is snatch'd away
  By death's resistless hand,
Our hearts the mournful tribute pay
  Which pity must demand.

2 While pity prompts the rising sigh,
  Oh, may this truth, imprest
With awful power,—"I too must die!"
  Sink deep in ev'ry breast.

3 Let this vain world delude no more;
  Behold the gaping tomb!
It bids us seize the present hour,
  To-morrow death may come.

4 The voice of this alarming scene
  May ev'ry heart obey;
Nor be the heav'nly warning vain,
  Which calls to watch and pray.

5 Oh, let us fly—to Jesus fly,
  Whose pow'rful arm can save;
Then shall our hopes ascend on high,
  And triumph o'er the grave.

908 *The Blessed Dead.* **722**

HARK! from on high a solemn voice;
  Let all attentive hear!
'Twill make each pious heart rejoice,
  And vanquish ev'ry fear.

2 "Thrice blessed are the pious dead,
  Who in the Lord shall die;
Their weary flesh, as on a bed,
  Safe in the grave shall lie.

3 Their holy souls, at length releas'd,
  To heav'n shall take their flight;
There to enjoy eternal rest
  And infinite delight.

4 They drop each load as they ascend,
  And quit this world of woe;
Their labors with their life shall end,
  Their rest no period know.

5 Their conflicts with their busy foes
  For evermore shall cease;
None shall their happiness oppose,
  Nor interrupt their peace.

6 But bright rewards shall recompense
  Their faithful service here;
And perfect love shall banish thence
  Each gloomy doubt and fear."

SICKNESS, DEATH, JUDGMENT, ETERNITY.

L. M. GLASGOW.

1. My soul, the minutes haste away, A-pace comes on th' important day, When in the i-cy arms of death I must give up my vi-tal breath.

909 *Sickness and Death.* **233**

MY soul, the minutes haste away,
    Apace comes on th' important day,
When in the icy arms of death
I must give up my vital breath.

2 Look forward to the moving scene ;
How wilt thou be affected then ?
When from on high some sharp disease
Resistless shall my vitals seize.

3 When all the springs of life are low,
The spirits faint, the pulses slow ;
The eyes grow dim and short the breath,
Presages of approaching death ;

4 When all eternity's in sight,
The brightest day, or blackest night,
One shock will break the building down
And hurl thee into worlds unknown.

5 Oh, come, my soul, the matter weigh !
How wilt thou leave thy kindred clay !
And how those unknown regions try,
And launch into eternity !

910 *Improving Time.* **704**

THAT awful hour will soon appear,
    Swift on the wings of time it flies,
When all that pains or pleases here
Will vanish from my closing eyes.

2 Death calls my friends, my neighbors,
And none resist the fatal dart :   [hence,
Continual warnings strike my sense,
And shall they fail to strike my heart ?

3 Think, O my soul ! how much depends
On the short period of to-day :

Shall time, which heav'n in mercy lends,
Be negligently thrown away ?

4 Thy wasting minutes strive to use ;
Awake, rouse ev'ry active pow'r ;
And not in dreams and trifles lose
This little, this important hour !

5 Lord of my life, inspire my heart
With heav'nly ardor, grace divine ;
Nor let thy presence e'er depart,
For strength, and life, and death are thine.

911 *The Living know, &c.* **697**

WHERE are the dead ?—In heav'n or hell
    Their disembodied spirits dwell ;
Their faded forms in bonds of clay,
Reserv'd until the judgment-day.

2 Who are the dead ?—The sons of time
In ev'ry age, and state, and clime ;
Renown'd, dishonor'd, or forgot,
The place that knew them knows them not.

3 Where are the living ?—On the ground,
Where pray'r is heard and mercy found ;
Where, in the compass of a span,
The mortal makes th' immortal man.

4 Who are the living ?—They whose breath
Draws ev'ry moment nigh to death ;
Of endless bliss or woe the heirs ;
Oh, what an awful lot is theirs !

5 Then, timely warn'd, let us begin
To follow Christ and flee from sin ;
Daily grow up in him our Head,
Lord of the living and the dead.

SICKNESS, DEATH, JUDGMENT, ETERNITY. 313

L. M. HINGHAM.

1. God of e-ter-ni-ty! from thee Did in-fant time his be-ing draw; Moments and days, and months and years, Revolve by thine un-va-ried law, Re-volve by thine un-va-ried law.

912   *Numbering our Days.*   705

GOD of eternity! from thee
   Did infant time his being draw;
Moments and days, and months and years,
Revolve by thine unvaried law.

2 Silent and slow they glide away;
Steady and strong the current flows,
Lost in eternity's wide sea,
The boundless gulf from which it rose.

3 Thoughtless and vain, our mortal race
Along the mighty stream are borne
On to their everlasting home,—
That country whence there's no return.

4 Yet while the shore on either side
Presents a gaudy, flatt'ring show,
We gaze, in fond amazement lost,
Nor think to what a world we go.

5 Great Source of wisdom! teach my heart
To know the price of ev'ry hour;
That time may bear me on to joys
Beyond its measure and its pow'r.

913   *Man Fading and Reviving.*   706

THE morning flow'rs display their sweets,
   And gay their silken leaves unfold,
As careless of the noonday heats
And fearless of the ev'ning cold.

2 Nipt by the wind's untimely blast,
Parch'd by the sun's directer ray,
The momentary glories waste,
The short-liv'd beauties die away.

3 So blooms the human face divine,
When youth its pride and beauty shows;
Fairer than spring the colors shine,
And sweeter than the virgin rose.

4 Or worn by slowly rolling years,
Or broke by sickness in a day,
The fading glory disappears,
The short-liv'd beauties die away.

5 Yet these, new-rising from the tomb,
With lustre brighter far shall shine;
Revive with ever-during bloom,
Safe from diseases and decline.

6 Let sickness blast, and death devour,
If heav'n must recompense our pains;
Perish the grass, and fade the flow'r,
If firm the word of God remains.

914   *Death of an Infant.*   713

SO fades the lovely, blooming flow'r,
   Frail, smiling solace of an hour;
So soon our transient comforts fly,
And pleasure only blooms to die.

2 Is there no kind, no healing art
To soothe the anguish of the heart?
Spirit of grace, be ever nigh:
Thy comforts are not made to die.

3 Let gentle patience smile on pain,
Till dying hope revives again;
Hope wipes the tear from sorrow's eye,
And faith points upward to the sky.

SICKNESS, DEATH, JUDGMENT, ETERNITY.

L. M. OBERLIN.

1. Why should we start and fear to die? What tim'-rous worms we mor-tals are! Death is the gate of end-less joy, And yet we dread to en-ter there.

915 *Christ's Presence in Death Easy.* **708**

WHY should we start and fear to die?
What tim'rous worms we mortals are!
Death is the gate of endless joy,
And yet we dread to enter there.

2 The pains, the groans and dying strife,
Fright our approaching souls away;
Still we shrink back again to life,
Fond of our prison and our clay.

3 Oh, if my Lord would come and meet,
My soul should stretch her wings in haste,
Fly fearless through death's iron gate,
Nor feel the terrors as she pass'd.

4 Jesus can make a dying bed
Feel soft as downy pillows are,
While on his breast I lean my head,
And breathe my life out sweetly there.

916 *On the Death of a Parent.* **711**

THOUGH nature's voice you must obey,
Think, while your swelling griefs o'erflow,
That hand which takes your joys away,
That sov'reign hand can heal your woe.

2 And, while your mournful thoughts deplore
The parent gone, remov'd the friend,
With hearts resign'd, his grace adore,
On whom your nobler hopes depend.

3 Does he not bid his children come
Thro' death's dark shades to realms of light?

Yet, when he calls them to their home,
Shall fond survivors mourn their flight?

4 His word—here let your souls rely—
Immortal consolation gives:
Your heav'nly Father cannot die,
Th' eternal Friend forever lives.

5 Oh, be that best of friends your trust;
On his almighty arm recline;
He, when your comforts sink in dust,
Can give you comforts more divine.

917 *The Tolling Bell.* **699**

OFT as the bell, with solemn toll,
Speaks the departure of a soul,
Let each one ask himself, "Am I
Prepar'd, should I be call'd to die?"

2 Only this frail and fleeting breath
Preserves me from the jaws of death;
Soon as it fails, at once I'm gone,
And plung'd into a world unknown.

3 Then, leaving all I lov'd below,
To God's tribunal I must go,
Must hear the Judge pronounce my fate,
And fix my everlasting state.

4 Lord Jesus! help me now to flee
And seek my hope alone in thee;
Apply thy blood, thy Spirit give,
Subdue my sin, and let me live.

5 Then, when the solemn bell I hear,
If sav'd from guilt, I need not fear;
Nor would the thought alarming be—
"Perhaps it next may toll for me."

SICKNESS, DEATH, JUDGMENT, ETERNITY.

L. M. MUNICH.

1. Sweet is the scene where Christians die, Where ho-ly souls re-tire to rest;
How mild-ly beams the clo-sing eye! How gen-tly heaves th' expi-ring breast!

918 *Death Peaceful and Triumphant.* **724**

SWEET is the scene where Christians die,
  Where holy souls retire to rest;
How mildly beams the closing eye!
How gently heaves th' expiring breast!

2 So fades a summer cloud away;
So sinks the gale when storms are o'er;
So gently shuts the eye of day;
So dies a wave along the shore.

3 Triumphant smiles the victor's brow,
Fann'd by some guardian angel's wing;
O Grave, where is thy vict'ry now?
And where, O Death, is now thy sting?

919 *Death is Gain.* **717**

FROM his low bed of mortal dust,
  Escap'd the prison of his clay,
The new inheritant of bliss
To heav'n directs his upward way.

2 Ye fields, that witness'd once his tears,
Ye winds, that wafted oft his sighs,
Ye mountains, where he breath'd his pray'rs,
When sorrow's shadows veil'd his eyes;

3 No more the weary pilgrim mourns,
No more affliction wrings his heart,
Th' unfetter'd soul to God returns—
Forever he and anguish part!

4 Receive, O earth, his faded form,
In thy cold bosom let it lie;
Safe let it rest from ev'ry storm—
Soon must it rise, no more to die.

920 *Rest in the Grave.* **723**

THE grave is now a favor'd spot,—
  To saints who sleep, in Jesus bless'd,
For there the wicked trouble not,
And there the weary are at rest.

2 At rest in Jesus' faithful arms;
At rest as in a peaceful bed;
Secure from all the dreadful storms
Which round this sinful world are spread.

3 Thrice happy souls, who're gone before
To that inheritance divine!
They labor, sorrow, sigh no more,
But bright in endless glory shine.

4 Then let our mournful tears be dry,
Or in a gentle measure flow;
We hail them happy in the sky,
And joyful wait our call to go.

921 *Longing for the Resurrection.* **727**

NO, I'll repine at death no more,
  But, calm and cheerful, will resign
To the cold dungeon of the grave,
These dying, with'ring limbs of mine.

2 Let worms devour my wasting flesh,
And crumble all my bones to dust;
My God shall raise my frame anew
At the revival of the just.

3 Break, sacred morning, thro' the skies,
And usher in that glorious day:
Cut short the hours, dear Lord, and come:
Thy ling'ring wheels, how long they stay!

SICKNESS, DEATH, JUDGMENT, ETERNITY.

C. M. BALERMA.

1. Hear what the voice from heav'n pro-claims For all the pi-ous dead:
"Sweet is the sa-vor of their names, And soft their sleep-ing-bed.

---

922 *Those blessed who die in the Lord.* **725**

HEAR what the voice from heaven pro-
  For all the pious dead: [claims
"Sweet is the savor of their names,
  And soft their sleeping-bed.

2 "They die in Jesus, and are blest;
    How kind their slumbers are!
  From suff'ring and from sin releas'd,
    They're freed from ev'ry snare.

3 "Far from this world of toil and strife,
    They're present with the Lord;
  The labors of their mortal life
    End in a large reward."

923 *The Moment after Death.* **719**

IN vain our fancy strives to paint
    The moment after death;
  The glories that surround a saint,
    When yielding up his breath.

2 One gentle sigh his fetters breaks,
    We scarce can say, "He's gone!"
  Before the willing spirit takes
    Its mansions near the throne.

3 Faith strives, but all its efforts fail,
    To trace the spirit's flight;
  No eye can pierce within the veil
    Which hides the world of light.

4 Thus much (and this is all) we know,
    Saints are completely blest;
  Have done with sin, and care, and woe,
    And with their Savior rest.

5 On harps of gold they praise his name,
    His face they always view;
  Then let us foll'wers be of them,
    That we may praise him too.

924 *Mourning with Hope.*

WHY should our tears in sorrow flow,
    When God recalls his own;
  And bids them leave a world of woe,
    For an immortal crown?

2 Is not e'en death again to those
    Whose life to God was giv'n?
  Gladly to earth their eyes they close
    To open them in heaven.

3 Their toils are past—their work is done,
    And they are fully blest;
  They fought the fight, the vict'ry won,
    And enter'd into rest.

4 Then let our sorrows cease to flow—
    God has recall'd his own;
  But let our hearts in ev'ry woe,
    Still say, "Thy will be done!"

925 *Death and Immediate Glory.* **721**

THERE is a house not made with hands,
    Eternal and on high;
  And here my spirit waiting stands,
    Till God shall bid it fly.

2 Shortly this prison of my clay
    Must be dissolv'd and fall,
  Then, O my soul, with joy obey
    Thy heav'nly Father's call.

3 'Tis he, by his almighty grace,
    That forms thee fit for heav'n,
  And as an earnest of the place,
    Has his own Spirit giv'n.

4 We walk by faith of joys to come,
    Faith lives upon his word;
  But while the body is our home,
    We're absent from the Lord.

SICKNESS, DEATH, JUDGMENT, ETERNITY.

C. M. PHUVAH.

1. Soon in the grave my flesh shall rest, My soul from earth re-move, And, in the Sa-vior's glo-ry dress'd, Shall reach the home I love.

926 *Release by Death.* **983**

SOON in the grave my flesh shall rest,
  My soul from earth remove,
And, in the Savior's glory dress'd,
  Shall reach the home I love;—

2 My friends—the whole celestial choir;
  My ev'ry feeling—joy;
To honor God—my one desire;
  His praise—my one employ.

3 Nor would I wait till angel-host
  Shall teach their song to raise:
To Father, Son, and Holy Ghost
  I'll here begin my praise.

4 Now to our God, the Father, Son,
  And Holy Spirit, sing!
With praise to God, the Three in One,
  Let all creation ring!

927 *Hope in the Resurrection.* **729**

THRO' sorrow's night and danger's path,
  Amid the deep'ning gloom,
We soldiers of an injur'd King
  Are marching to the tomb.

2 There, when the turmoil is no more,
  And all our pow'rs decay,
Our cold remains in solitude
  Shall sleep the years away.

3 Our labors done, securely laid
  In this our last retreat,
Unheeded o'er our silent dust
  The storms of life shall beat.

4 Yet not thus lifeless, thus inane,
  The vital spark shall lie,

For o'er life's wreck that spark shall rise
  To seek its kindred sky.

5 These ashes, too, this little dust,
  Our Father's care shall keep,
Till the last angel rise, and break
  The long and dreary sleep.

6 Then Love's soft dew o'er ev'ry eye
  Shall shed its mildest rays,
And the long-silent dust shall burst
  With songs of endless praise.

928 *The Resurrection of the Just.* **730**

HOW long shall Death, the tyrant, reign,
  And triumph o'er the just,
While the rich blood of martyrs slain
  Lies mingled with the dust?

2 Lo! I behold the scatter'd shades!
  The dawn of heav'n appears:
The sweet, immortal morning spreads
  Its blushes round the spheres.

3 I hear the voice, "Ye dead, arise!"
  And lo! the graves obey;
And waking saints with joyful eyes
  Salute th' expected day.

4 They leave the dust, and on the wing
  Rise to the midway air:
In shining garments meet their King,
  And low adore him there.

5 Oh, may our humble spirits stand
  Among them cloth'd in white!
The meanest place at his right hand
  Is infinite delight.

SICKNESS, DEATH, JUDGMENT, ETERNITY.

L. M. LURMAN.

1. A-sleep in Je-sus! bless-ed sleep! From which none ev-er wake to weep; A calm and un-dis-turb'd re-pose, Un-bro-ken by the dread of foes.

929 *Asleep in Jesus.*

ASLEEP in Jesus! blessed sleep!
From which none ever wake to weep;
A calm and undisturb'd repose,
Unbroken by the dread of foes.

2 Asleep in Jesus! peaceful rest,
Whose waking is supremely blest;
No fear, no woes, shall dim that hour,
Which manifests the Savior's power.

3 Asleep in Jesus! oh, for me
May such a blissful refuge be;
Securely shall my ashes lie,
And wait the summons from on high.

4 Asleep in Jesus! far from thee
Thy kindred and their graves may be;
But thine is still a blessed sleep,
From which none ever wake to weep.

930 *Death of the Righteous.* 986

HOW blest the righteous when he dies!
When sinks a weary soul to rest!
How mildly beam the closing eyes!
How gently heaves th' expiring breast!

2 So fades a summer cloud away;
So sinks the gale when storms are o'er;
So gently shuts the eye of day;
So dies a wave along the shore.

3 A holy quiet reigns around,
A calm which life nor death destroys;
And naught disturbs that peace profound
Which his unfetter'd soul enjoys.

4 Farewell, conflicting hopes and fears,
Where lights and shades alternate dwell;
How bright th' unchanging morn appears!
Farewell, inconstant world, farewell.

5 Life's labor done, as sinks the clay,
Light from its load the spirit flies,
While heaven and earth combine to say,
"How blest the righteous when he dies!"

931 *Resurrection from the Grave.* 989

SHALL man, O God of light and life,
Forever moulder in the grave?
Canst thou forget thy glorious work,
Thy promise and thy pow'r to save?

2 Shall life revisit dying worms,
And spread the joyful insect's wing!
And oh, shall man awake no more
To see thy face, thy name to sing?

3 Cease, cease, ye vain desponding fears!
As Christ our Lord from darkness sprung,
Death, the last foe, was captive led,
And heav'n with praise and wonder rung.

4 Him, the first fruits, his chosen sons
Shall follow from the vanquish'd grave;
He mounts his throne, the King of kings,
His church to quicken and to save.

5 Faith sees the bright, eternal doors
Unfold to make his children way;
They shall be cloth'd with endless life,
And shine in everlasting day.

L. M. HAMBURG.

1. Ex-alt-ed high at God's right hand, Near-er the throne than cher-ubs stand; With glo-ry crown'd, in white ar-ray, My wond'-ring soul says, "Who are they?"

932 *Saints' Employ in Heaven.* **746**

EXALTED high at God's right hand,
Nearer the throne than cherubs stand;
With glory crown'd, in white array,
My wond'ring soul says, "Who are they?"

2 These are the saints, belov'd of God—
Wash'd are their robes in Jesus' blood;
More spotless than the purest white,
They shine in uncreated light.

3 Brighter than angels, lo! they shine;
Their glories great, and all divine;
Tell me their origin, and say
Their order what, and whence came they?

4 Through tribulation great they came,
They bore the cross and scorn'd the shame;
Within the living temple blest,
In God they dwell, and on him rest.

5 Unknown to mortal ears they sing
The sacred glories of their King;
Tell me the subject of their lays,
And whence their loud exalted praise?

6 Jesus, the Savior, is their theme;
They sing the wonders of his name;
To him ascribing pow'r and grace,
Dominion and eternal praise.

933 *Judgment.* **733**

HOW great, how terrible that God
Who shakes creation with his word!
He speaks, and earth's foundations shake,
And all the wheels of nature break.

2 Where now, oh, where shall sinners seek
For shelter in the gen'ral wreck?
Shall falling rocks be o'er them thrown?
See rocks, like snow, dissolving down!

3 But saints, undaunted and serene,
Your eyes shall view the dreadful scene
Your Savior lives, the worlds expire,
And earth and skies dissolve in fire.

4 Jesus, the helpless sinner's friend,
To thee my all I dare commend;
Thou canst preserve my feeble soul,
When lightnings blaze from pole to pole.

934 *Books opened.* **734**

METHINKS the last great day is come,
Methinks I hear the trumpet sound
That shakes the earth, rends ev'ry tomb,
And wakes the pris'ners under ground.

2 The mighty deep gives up her trust,
Aw'd by the Judge's high command:
Both small and great now quit their dust,
And round the dread tribunal stand.

3 Behold the awful books display'd,
Big with th' important fates of men;
Each word and deed now public made,
Written by heav'n's unerring pen.

4 To ev'ry soul the books assign
The joyous or the dread reward;
Sinners in vain lament and pine:
No pleas the Judge will here regard.

5 Lord, when these awful leaves unfold,
May life's fair book my soul approve;
There may I read my name enroll'd,
And triumph in redeeming love!

SICKNESS, DEATH, JUDGMENT, ETERNITY.

S. M. AYLESBURY.

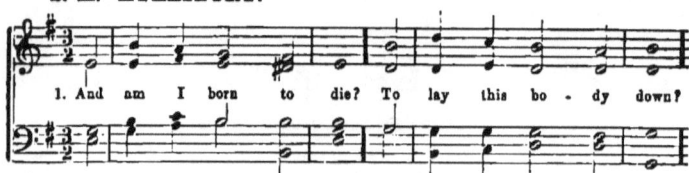

1. And am I born to die? To lay this bo-dy down?

And must my trem-bling spi-rit fly In-to a world un-known?

935 *Thoughts on the Future.* **231**

1 AND am I born to die?
  To lay this body down?
  And must my trembling spirit fly
  Into a world unknown?

2 Soon as from earth I go,
  What will become of me?
  Eternal happiness or woe
  Must then my portion be!

3 Wak'd by the trumpet's sound,
  I from my grave must rise,
  And see the Judge with glory crown'd,
  And see the flaming skies.

4 How shall I leave my tomb?
  With triumph or regret?
  A fearful or a joyful doom,
  A curse or blessing meet?

5 Will angel hands convey
  Their brother to the bar?
  Or devils drag my soul away
  To meet its sentence there?

6 Who can resolve the doubt
  That tears my anxious breast?
  Shall I be with the damn'd cast out,
  Or number'd with the blest?

7 I must from God be driv'n,
  Or with my Savior dwell;
  Must come at his command to heav'n,
  Or else depart to hell.

8 O thou that wouldst not have
  One wretched sinner die,
  Who diedst thyself, my soul to save
  From endless misery,

9 Show me the way to shun
  Thy dreadful wrath severe,
  That when thou comest on thy throne,
  I may with joy appear.

936 *Hope of the Resurrection.* **709**

1 AND must this body die?
  This mortal frame decay?
  And must these active limbs of mine
  Lie mould'ring in the clay?

2 Corruption, earth, and worms,
  Shall but refine this flesh,
  Till my triumphant spirit comes
  To put it on afresh.

3 God, my Redeemer, lives,
  And often, from the skies,
  Looks down, and watches all my dust,
  Till he shall bid it rise.

4 Array'd in glorious grace
  Shall these vile bodies shine,
  And ev'ry shape, and ev'ry face,
  Look heav'nly and divine.

5 These lively hopes we owe
  To Jesus' dying love;
  We would adore his grace below,
  And sing his pow'r above.

6 Dear Lord, accept the praise
  Of these our humble songs,
  Till tunes of nobler sounds we raise
  With our immortal tongues.

SICKNESS, DEATH, JUDGMENT, ETERNITY.

8s, 7s. HOLLAZ.

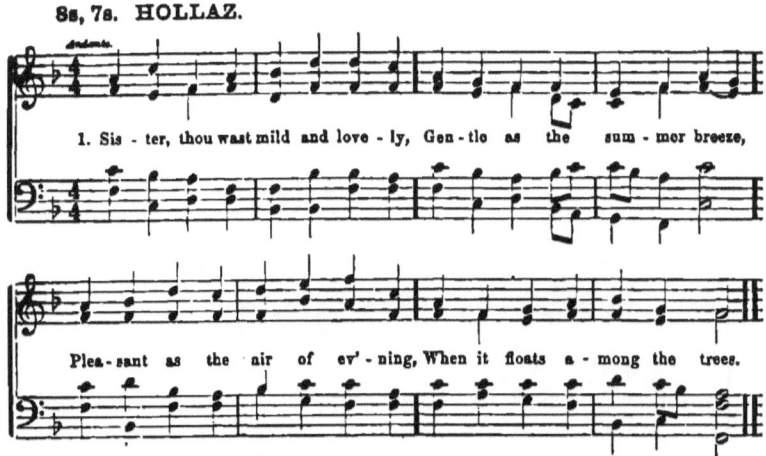

1. Sister, thou wast mild and lovely, Gentle as the summer breeze, Pleasant as the air of ev'ning, When it floats among the trees.

937 *Interment of a Sister.* **984**

SISTER, thou wast mild and lovely,
  Gentle as the summer breeze,
Pleasant as the air of ev'ning,
  When it floats among the trees.

2 Peaceful be thy silent slumber—
  Peaceful in the grave so low:
Thou no more wilt join our number;
  Thou no more our songs shalt know.

3 Dearest sister, thou hast left us;
  Here thy loss we deeply feel;
But 'tis God that hath bereft us:
  He can all our sorrows heal.

4 Yet again we hope to meet thee,
  When the day of life is fled,
Then in heaven with joy to greet thee
  Where no farewell tear is shed.

938 *Weep not for the Departed Saint.*

O YE mourners! cease to languish
  O'er the grave of those ye love!
Pain and death, and night and anguish,
  Enter not the world above.

2 While in darkness ye are straying,
  Lonely in the deepening shade,
Glory's brightest beams are playing
  Round th' immortal spirit's head.

3 O ye mourners! cease to languish
  O'er the grave of those ye love!
Far removed from pain and anguish,
  They are chanting hymns of love.

4 Light and peace at once deriving
  From the hand of God most high:

In his glorious presence living,
  They shall never, never die.

939 *The Dying Christian.*

PARTING soul! the flood awaits thee,
  And the billows round thee roar;
Yet rejoice—the holy city
  Stands on yon celestial shore.

2 There are crowns, and thrones of glory,
  There the living waters glide;
There the just, in shining raiment,
  Standing by Immanuel's side.

3 Linger not—the stream is narrow,
  Though its cold, dark waters rise:
He, who pass'd the flood before thee,
  Guides thy path to yonder skies.

940 *The Dying Saint Comforted.*

HAPPY soul! thy days are ending—
  All thy mourning days below:
Go, the angel guards attending—
  To the sight of Jesus go!

2 Waiting to receive thy spirit,
  Lo! the Savior stands above;
Shows the fullness of his merit—
  Reaches out the crown of love.

3 For the joy he sets before thee,
  Bear a momentary pain;
Die—to live a life of glory;
  Suffer—with the Lord to reign:

4 Struggle, through thy latest passion,
  To thy dear Redeemer's breast—
To his uttermost salvation,
  To his everlasting rest.

DEATH AND JUDGMENT.

C. M. P. AITHLONE.

1. And am I only born to die? And must I suddenly comply
   What after death for me remains? Celestial joys, or hellish pains,
   With nature's stern decree?
   To all Eternity.

941 *Life and Death.* **232**
(Stanza 1 in Music.)

2 HOW then ought I on earth to live,
While God prolongs the kind reprieve,
And props the house of clay?
My sole concern, my single care,
To watch, and tremble, and prepare
Against that fatal day!

3 No room for mirth or trifling here,
For worldly hope, or worldly fear,
If life so soon is gone;
If now the Judge is at the door,
And all mankind must stand before
Th' inexorable throne!

4 Nothing is worth a thought beneath,
But how I may escape the death
That never, never dies;
How make mine own election sure,
And, when I fail on earth, secure
A mansion in the skies.

5 Jesus, vouchsafe a pitying ray,
Be thou my guide, be thou my way
To glorious happiness!
Ah, write the pardon on my heart!
And whensoe'er I hence depart,
Let me depart in peace.

942 *A Peaceful Death.* **720**

WHEN life's tempestuous storms are o'er,
How calm he meets the friendly shore,
Who liv'd averse from sin!
Such peace on virtue's path attends,
That, where the sinner's pleasure ends,
The Christian's joys begin.

2 No sorrow drowns his lifted eyes;
No horror wrests the struggling sighs,
As from the sinner's breast:
His God, the God of peace and love,
Pours kindly solace from above,
And heals his soul with rest.

3 Oh grant, my Savior and my friend!
Such joys may gild my peaceful end,
So calm my ev'ning close,
While, loos'd from ev'ry earthly tie,
With steady confidence I fly
To thee from whom I rose!

943 *Preparation for Death.*

O THOU that hear'st the pray'r of faith!
Wilt thou not save a soul from death,
That casts itself on thee?
I have no refuge of my own,
But fly to what my Lord hath done
And suffer'd once for me.

2 Oh, save me from eternal death!
The Spirit of adoption breathe,
His consolations send;
By him some word of life impart,
And sweetly whisper to my heart,
"Thy Maker is thy Friend."

3 The king of terrors then would be
A welcome messenger to me,
To bid me come away:
Unclogg'd by earth, or earthly things,
I'd mount, I'd fly, with eager wings,
To everlasting day.

DEATH AND ETERNITY.

6s & 8s. DWIGHT.

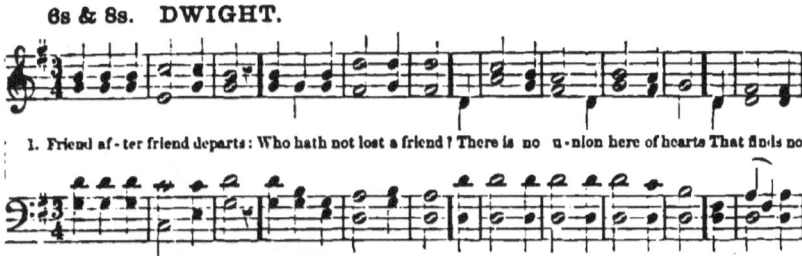

1. Friend af-ter friend departs: Who hath not lost a friend? There is no u-nion here of hearts That finds not

here an end: Were this frail world our fi-nal rest, Liv-ing or dy-ing, none were blest.

944 *Loss of a Friend.* **1001**

FRIEND after friend departs:
 Who hath not lost a friend?
There is no union here of hearts
 That finds not here an end:
Were this frail world our final rest,
Living or dying, none were blest.

2 Beyond the flight of time,
 Beyond the reign of death,
There surely is some blessed clime
 Where life is not a breath,
Nor life's affections transient fire,
Whose sparks fly upward and expire.

3 There is a world above,
 Where parting is unknown;
A long eternity of love,
 Form'd for the good alone;
And faith beholds the dying here
Translated to that glorious sphere.

4 Thus star by star declines,
 Till all are passed away;
As morning high and higher shines,
 To pure and perfect day;
Nor sink those stars in empty night,
But hide themselves in heaven's own light.

945 *The Death of the Righteous.* **981**

THIS place is holy ground:
 World! with thy cares away!
Silence and darkness reign around;
 But lo! the break of day!
What bright and sudden dawn appears,
To shine upon this scene of tears!

2 Behold the bed of death,—
 This pale and lovely clay!
Heard ye the sob of parting breath?
 Mark'd ye the eyes' last ray?—
No!—life so sweetly ceas'd to be,
It laps'd in immortality.

3 Bury the dead,—and weep,
 In stillness, o'er the loss;
Bury the dead,—in Christ they sleep,
 Who bore on earth his cross,
And, from the grave, their dust shall rise
In his own image to the skies.

946 *Rest in Jesus.*

JESUS, we rest in thee,
 In thee ourselves we hide;
Laden with guilt and misery,
 Where could we rest beside?
'Tis on thy meek and lowly breast
Our weary souls alone can rest.

2 Thou holy One of God!
 The Father rests in thee,
And in the favor of that blood
 Once shed on Calvary;
The curse is gone,—thro' thee we're blest;
God rests in thee—in thee we rest.

3 Soon the bright, glorious day—
 The rest of God shall come;
Sorrow and sin shall pass away,
 And we shall reach our home:
Then of the promis'd land possessed,
Our souls shall know eternal rest.

JUDGMENT.

ZION. 8s, 7s, 4s.

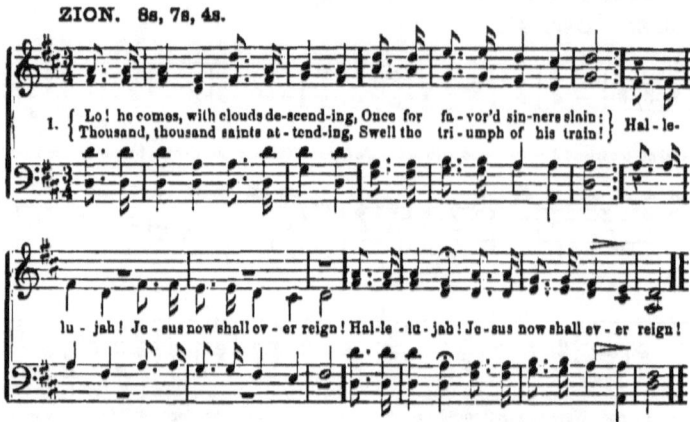

Lo! he comes, with clouds descending, Once for favor'd sinners slain: Thousand, thousand saints attending, Swell the triumph of his train! Hallelujah! Jesus now shall ever reign! Hallelujah! Jesus now shall ever reign!

947 *Judgment.* **731**

LO! he comes, with clouds descending,
  Once for favor'd sinners slain:
Thousand, thousand saints attending,
  Swell the triumph of his train:
    Hallelujah!
Jesus now shall ever reign!

2 Ev'ry eye shall now behold him
    Rob'd in dreadful majesty;
  Those who set at naught and sold him,
    Pierc'd and nail'd him to the tree,
      Deeply wailing,
  Shall the great Messiah see!

3 Ev'ry island, sea, and mountain,
    Heav'n and earth, shall flee away;
  All who hate him must, confounded,
    Hear the trump proclaim the day:
      Come to judgment!
  Come to judgment! come away!

4 Now redemption, long expected,
    See in solemn pomp appear!
  All his saints, by man rejected,
    Now shall meet him in the air!
      Hallelujah!
  See the day of God appear!

5 Yea! Amen! let all adore thee,
    High on thine exalted throne:
  Savior! take the pow'r and glory;
    Claim the kingdom for thine own!
      Oh, come quickly!
  Hallelujah! come, Lord, come!

948 *The Day of Judgment.* **732**

DAY of judgment,—day of wonders,
  Hark! the trumpet's awful sound,
Louder than a thousand thunders,
  Shakes the vast creation round!
    Now the summons
  Will the sinner's heart confound!

2 See the Judge our nature wearing,
    Cloth'd in majesty divine!
  Ye who long for his appearing,
    Then shall say, "This God is mine!"
      Gracious Saviour!
  Own me in that day for thine!

3 At his call the dead awaken,
    Rise to life from earth and sea;
  All the pow'rs of nature, shaken
    By his looks, prepare to flee:
      Careless sinner!
  What will then become of thee?

4 But to those who have confessed,
    Lov'd, and serv'd the Lord below,
  He will say, "Come near, ye blessed!
    See the kingdom I bestow!
      You forever
  Shall my love and glory know."

949 *The Judgment.* **737**

SEE th' eternal Judge descending!
  View him seated on his throne!
Now, poor sinner, now, lamenting,
  Stand and hear thine awful doom:—
    Trumpets call thee!
  Stand and hear thine awful doom.

2 Now, despisers, look and wonder!
    Hope and sinners here must part;
  Louder than the pealing thunder,
    Hear the dreadful sound, "Depart!"
      Lost forever,
  Hear the dreadful sound, "Depart!"

THE JUDGMENT AND END.

C. M. CRAVEN.

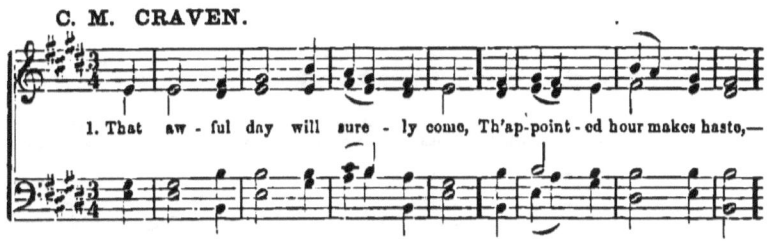

1. That awful day will surely come, Th'appointed hour makes haste,— When I must stand before my Judge, And pass the solemn test.

950 *The Awful Day.*

THAT awful day will surely come,
  Th' appointed hour makes haste,—
When I must stand before my Judge,
  And pass the solemn test.

2 Thou lovely Chief of all my joys!
  Thou Sovereign of my heart!
How could I bear to hear thy voice
  Pronounce the word—Depart!

3 Oh, wretched state of deep despair—
  To see my God remove,
And fix my doleful station where
  I must not taste his love!

4 Jesus! I throw my arms around,
  And hang upon thy breast;
Without some gracious smile from thee,
  My spirit cannot rest.

951 *The Final Day.*

THE day approaches, O my soul!
  The great decisive day,
Which from the verge of mortal life
  Shall bear thee far away.

2 Another day more awful dawns,
  And, lo, the Judge appears,
Ye heav'ns, retire before his face;
  And sink, ye darken'd stars.

3 Yet does one short preparing hour,
  One precious hour remain:
Rouse thee, my soul, with all thy pow'r,
  Nor let it pass in vain.

4 For this, thy temple, Lord! we throng;
  For this, thy board surround,
Here may our service be approv'd,
  And in thy presence crown'd.

952 *The End.*

"STAND still, refulgent orb of day!"
  The Jewish victor cries:
So shall, at last, an angel say,
  And tear it from the skies.

2 A flame, intenser than the sun,
  Shall melt his golden urn;
Time's empty glass no more shall run,
  Nor human years return.

3 Then, with immortal splendor bright
  That glorious orb shall rise,
Which through eternity shall light
  The new-created skies.

4 His moral triumphs then complete,
  Jesus, our Lord, shall place
Before his heav'nly Father's seat
  The heirs of life and grace.

5 Unceasing flows the mortal tide;
  Unceasing let it flow:
If thou, O Lord, our guard and guide,
  Wilt daily grace bestow.

6 Then, sun of nature! roll along
  And bear our years away:
The sooner shall we join the song
  Of everlasting day.

DISMISSION AND DOXOLOGIES.

8s, 7s. SICILIAN HYMN.

1. Lord, dismiss us with thy blessing— Fill our hearts with joy and peace;
Let us each, thy love possessing, Triumph in redeeming grace;
Oh, refresh us! Oh, refresh us! Trav'ling thro' this wilderness.

953 *Dismission.* **752**

LORD, dismiss us with thy blessing—
  Fill our hearts with joy and peace;
Let us each, thy love possessing,
  Triumph in redeeming grace;
    Oh, refresh us!
Trav'ling through this wilderness.

2 Thanks we give, and adoration,
  For thy gospel's joyful sound;
May the fruits of thy salvation
  In our hearts and lives abound:
    May thy presence
  With us evermore be found.

3 So, whene'er the signal's given,
  Us from earth to call away,
Borne on angels' wings to heav'n,
  Glad to leave our cumbrous clay,
    May we, ready,
  Rise and reign in endless day!

954 *Parting Prayer.* **757**

MAY the grace of Christ our Savior,
  And the Father's boundless love,
With the Holy Spirit's favor,
  Rest upon us from above.

2 Thus may we abide in union
  With each other and the Lord,
And possess, in sweet communion,
  Joys which earth cannot afford.

1 *Doxology.* **8s, 7s.**

GREAT Jehovah! we adore thee,
  God the Father—God the Son—
God the Spirit—join'd in glory,
  On the same eternal throne;
    Endless praises
  To Jehovah, Three in One.

2 *Doxology.* **8s, 7s.**

FATHER, Son, and Holy Spirit,
  Thou the God whom we adore,
May we all thy love inherit,
  To thine image us restore;
    Vast Eternal!
  Praises to thee evermore.

3 *Doxology.* **8s,7s, (double.)**

PRAISE the God of all creation;
  Praise the Father's boundless love:
Praise the Lamb, our expiation,—
  Priest and King enthron'd above:
Praise the Fountain of salvation,—
  Him by whom our Spirits live;
Undivided adoration
  To the one Jehovah give.

7s. PLEYEL'S HYMN.

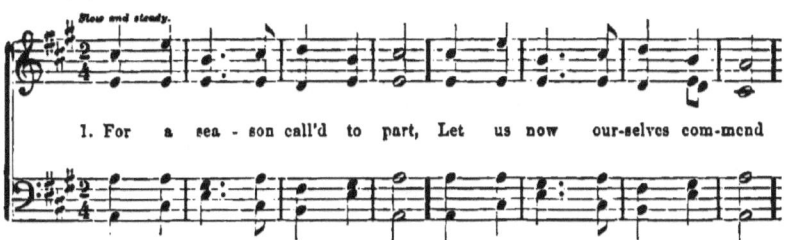

955 *Prayer at parting.* **657**

FOR a season call'd to part,
  Let us now ourselves commend
To the gracious eye and heart
  Of our ever-present Friend.

2 Jesus, hear our humble pray'r!
  Tender Shepherd of thy sheep!
Let thy mercy and thy care
  All our souls in safety keep.

3 In thy strength may we be strong;
  Sweeten ev'ry cross and pain:
Give us, if we live, ere long
  In thy peace to meet again.

4 Then, if thou thy help afford,
  Ebenezers shall be rear'd;
And our souls shall praise the Lord
  Who our poor petitions heard.

956 *Conclusion.* **758**

THANKS for mercies past receive;
  Pardon of our sins renew;
Teach us henceforth how to live
  With eternity in view.

2 Bless thy word to old and young;
  Grant us, Lord, thy peace and love;
And when life's short course is run,
  Take us to thy house above.

No. 1.   *Doxology.*   **7s.**

HOLY Father, holy Son,
  Holy Spirit, Three in One!
Glory, as of old, to thee,
Now and evermore shall be.

No. 2.   *Doxology.*   **7s.**

SING we to our God above
  Praise eternal as his love;
Praise him, all ye heav'nly host,
Father, Son, and Holy Ghost.

No. 3.   *Doxology.*   **7s.**

PRAISE the Father, earth and heaven,
  Praise the Son, the Spirit praise;
As it was and is, be given,
  Glory through eternal days.

7s. 6 lines. NUREMBURG.

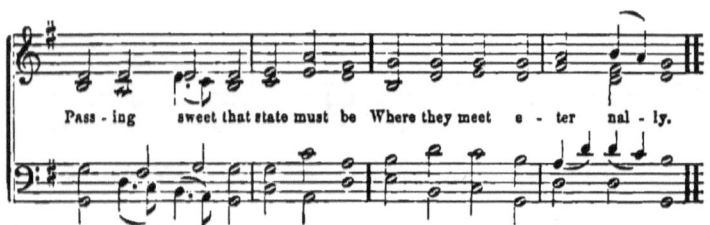

1. If 'tis sweet to mingle where Christians meet for social pray'r;
If 'tis sweet with them to raise Songs of holy joy and praise;
Passing sweet that state must be Where they meet eternally.

957 *The Meeting in Heaven.* **1005**

IF 'tis sweet to mingle where
Christians meet for social pray'r;
If 'tis sweet with them to raise
Songs of holy joy and praise;
Passing sweet that state must be
Where they meet eternally.

2 Savior, may these meetings prove
Preparations for above;
While we worship in this place,
May we grow from grace to grace,
Till we, each in his degree,
Fit for endless glory be.

958 *At Parting.* **871**

WHEN shall we all meet again?
When shall we all meet again?
Oft shall glowing hope expire;
Oft shall wearied love retire,
Oft shall death and sorrow reign,
Ere we all shall meet again.

2 When in distant lands we sigh,
Parch'd beneath a burning sky,
Though the deep between us rolls,
Friendship shall unite our souls;
And in fancy's wide domain
Oft shall we all meet again.

3 When the dreams of life are fled,
When its wasted lamp is dead,
When in cold oblivion's shade
Beauty, wealth, and fame are laid,—
Where immortal spirits reign,
There may we all meet again.

1   *Doxology.*   **7s. 6 lines.**

FATHER, Son, and Holy Ghost,
One in Three, and Three in One,
As by the celestial host,
Let thy will on earth be done;
Praise by all to thee be giv'n,
Glorious Lord of earth and heav'n.

2   *Doxology.*   **7s. 6 lines.**

PRAISE the name of God most high,
Praise him, all below the sky,
Praise him, all ye heav'nly host,
Father, Son, and Holy Ghost;
As through countless ages past,
Evermore his praise shall last.

DISMISSION AND DOXOLOGIES.

L. M. OLD HUNDREDTH.

1. Chris-tians and breth-ren! ere we part, Join ev'-ry voice and ev'-ry heart;
One so-lemn hymn to God we'll raise, One fi-nal song of grate-ful praise.

959 *Dismission, or a parting Hymn.* **753**

CHRISTIANS & brethren! ere we part,
  Join ev'ry voice and ev'ry heart;
One solemn hymn to God we'll raise,
One final song of grateful praise.

2 Christians! we here may meet no more,
But there is yet a happier shore;
And there, releas'd from toil and pain,
Dear brethren, we shall meet again.

3 Now to our God, the Three in One,
Be everlasting glory done;
Raise ye, his saints, the sound again,
Ye nations, join the loud Amen.

4 Give us, in thy beloved house,
Again to pay our grateful vows;
Or, if that joy no more be known,
Give us to meet around thy throne.

960 *Christian Farewell.* **759**

THY presence, everlasting God!
  Wide thro' all nature spreads abroad:
Thy watchful eyes, which never sleep,
In ev'ry place thy children keep.

2 While near each other we remain,
Thou dost our lives and pow'r sustain:
When sep'rate, we rejoice to share
Thy counsels and thy gracious care.

3 To thee we now commit our ways,
And still implore thy heav'nly grace;
Still cause thy face on us to shine,
And guard and guide us still as thine.

961 *The Peace of God, &c.* **754**

THE peace which God alone reveals,
  And by his word of grace imparts
Which only the believer feels,
Direct, and keep, and cheer our hearts.

2 And may the holy Three in One,
The Father, Word, and Comforter,
Pour an abundant blessing down
On ev'ry soul assembled here!

1 *Doxology.* **L. M.**

TO God the Father, God the Son,
  And God the Spirit, Three in One,
Be honor, praise, and glory giv'n,
By all on earth and all in heav'n.

2 *Doxology.* **L. M.**

PRAISE God, from whom all blessings flow,
  Praise him, all creatures here below;
Praise him above, ye heav'nly host;
Praise Father, Son, and Holy Ghost!

DISMISSION AND DOXOLOGIES.

C. M. HENRY. *Animated.*

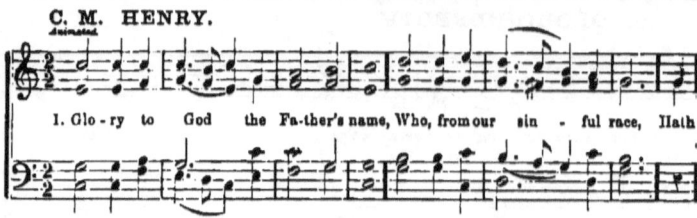

1. Glo-ry to God the Fa-ther's name, Who, from our sin - ful race, Hath

cho - sen myr - iads to pro-claim The hon - ors of his grace.

962 *Glory to God.* **806**

GLORY to God the Father's name,
  Who, from our sinful race,
Hath chosen myriads to proclaim
  The honors of his grace.

2 Glory to God the Son be paid,
  Who dwelt in humble clay,
And, to redeem us from the dead,
  Gave his own life away.

3 Glory to God the Spirit give,
  From whose almighty power
Our souls their heav'nly birth derive,
  And bless the happy hour.

4 Glory to God, that reigns above,
  The holy Three in One,
Who, by the wonders of his love,
  Has made his nature known.

1 *Doxology.* **C. M. (double.)**

THE God of mercy be adored,
  Who calls our souls from death,
Who saves by his redeeming word
  And new-creating breath;
To praise the Father and the Son
  And Spirit all-divine,—
The one in three, and three in one,—
  Let saints and angels join.

2 *Doxology.* **C. M.**

NOW let the Father and the Son
  And Spirit be ador'd,
Where there are works to make him known,
  Or saints to love the Lord.

3 *Doxology.* **C. M.**

ALL glory to th' Eternal Three,
  And undivided One;
To Father, Son, and Spirit, be
  Co-equal honors done.

4 *Doxology.* **C. M.**

TO Father, Son, and Holy Ghost,
  The God whom we adore,
Be everlasting honors paid,
  Henceforth, for evermore.

5 *Doxology.* **C. M.**

TO God the Father, God the Son,
  Your grateful voices raise;
And God the Spirit, Three in One,
  Give an immortal praise.

DISMISSIONS AND DOXOLOGIES.

S. M. SHIRLAND.

963   *Dismission.*   756

ONCE more, before we part,
   Great God, attend our pray'r,
And seal the gospel on the heart
   Of all assembled here.

2 And if we meet no more
   On Zion's holy ground,
Oh may we reach that blissful shore
   Whither thy saints are bound.

1   *Doxology.*   S. M.

YE angels round the throne,
   And saints that dwell below,
Worship the Father, praise the Son,
   And bless the Spirit too.

2   *Doxology.*   S. M.

TO God, the Father, Son,
   And Spirit, One in Three,
Be glory, as it was, is now,
   And shall forever be.

3   *Doxology.*   S. M. (double.)

LET God the Maker's name
   Have honor, love, and fear;
To God the Savior pay the same,
   And God the Comforter.
Father of lights above,
   Thy mercy we adore,
The Son of thine eternal love,
   And Spirit of thy power.

Doxology.   7s, 6s.

TO Father, Son, and Spirit,
   From earth let praise arise!
Ye angels, as ye hear it,
   Prolong it through the skies!

Doxology.   8s. 6 lines.

NOW to the great and sacred Three,
   The Father, Son, and Spirit, be
Eternal praise and glory given—
Through all the worlds where God is known,
   By all the angels near the throne,
And all the sients in earth and heaven.

Doxology.   6s, 4s.

TO God—the Father, Son,
   And Spirit—Three in One,
    All praise be given!
Crown him in ev'ry song:
To him your hearts belong;
Let all his praise prolong—
    On earth—in heaven.

Doxology.   8s. 6 lines.

TO God the Father, God the Son,
   And God the Spirit, Three in One,
Be glory in the highest given,
   By all on earth, and all in heaven,
As was through ages heretofore
Is now, and shall be evermore.

Doxology. **8s, 8s, 7s.**

COME, let us now our honors bring,
　To Father, Son, and Spirit sing,—
The song of angels raising!
Let all below, and all above,
Unite in holy joy and love,
　Our God Jehovah praising!

Doxology. **8, 6, 8, 8, 6.**

TO Father, Son, and Spirit bless'd,
　Supreme o'er earth and heaven,
Eternal Three in One confess'd,
Be highest glory given,
As was through ages heretofore,
Is now, and shall be evermore,
　By all in earth and heaven.

1 *Doxology.* **H. M.**

GLORY to God on high;
　Salvation to the Lamb;
Let earth, and sea, and sky,
　His wondrous love proclaim.
　　Upon his head
　　　Shall honors rest,
　　And every age
　　　Pronounce him bless'd.

2 *Doxology.* **H. M.**

TO God the Father's throne,
　Your highest honors raise;
Glory to God, the Son,—
　To God, the Spirit, praise:
　　With all our powers,
　　　Eternal King!
　　Thy name we sing,
　　　While faith adores.

Doxology. **C. M. P.**

TO Father, Son, and Holy Ghost,
　Be praise amid the heavenly host,
And in the church below;
From whom all creatures draw their breath,
By whom redemption bless'd the earth,
　From whom all comforts flow.

Doxology. **7s, 6s, (Double.)**

ALL ye who grace inherit,
　The God of grace adore!
To Father, Son, and Spirit
　Give praise for evermore!
Of mercies here, the treasure
　Demands our praise and love;
And praise shall be our pleasure
　Before his throne above.

Doxology. **8s, (Double.)**

THIS *God* is the *God* we adore,
　Our faithful, unchangeable Friend;
Whose love is as large as his pow'r,
　And knows neither measure nor end;
'Tis *Jesus*, the first and the last,
　Whose Spirit shall guide us safe home;
We'll praise him for all that is past,
　And trust him for all that's to come.

Doxology. **11s.**

O FATHER Almighty, to thee be addressed'd,
With Christ and the Spirit, one God ever bless'd,
All glory and worship from earth and from heaven,
As was, and is now, and shall ever be given.

CHANTS AND ANTHEMS.

CHANTS.

No. 1. DOUBLE.

VENITE EXULTEMUS DOMINO.   Psalm 95.

OH, come, let us sing un- | to the | Lord:
   Let us make a joyful noise to the | Rock of | our sal- | vation.

Let us come before his presence | with thanks- | giving,
   And make a joyful | noise .. unto | him with | psalms.

For the Lord is a | great— | God,
   And a great | King a- | bove all | gods.

In his hand are the deep places | of the | earth ;
   The strength of the | hills is | his— | also.

The sea is his, | and he | made it ;
   And his hands | formed the | dry— | land.

Oh, come, let us worship | and bow | down :
   Let us kneel be- | fore the | Lord our | Maker.

For he | is our | God ;
   And we are the people of his pasture, | and the | sheep of .. his | hand.

To-day, if ye will | hear his | voice,
Harden not your heart, as in the provocation,
And as in the day of temptation in the wilderness ;
   When your fathers tempted me, | proved .. me, and | saw my | work.

Forty years long was I grieved with this generation,
And said, It is a people that do | err .. in their | heart,
   And they | have not | known my | ways.

Unto whom I sware | in my | wrath,
   That they should | not .. enter | into .. my | rest.

No. 2. SINGLE.

No. 3. DOUBLE.

VENITE EXULTEMUS DOMINO. Ps. xcv.

OH, come, let us sing un- | to the ⸱ Lord:
   Let us make a joyful noise to the | Rock of | our sal- | vation.

Let us come before his presence | with thanks- | giving,
And make a joyful | noise..unto | him with | psalms.

For the Lord is a | great— | God,
And a great | King a- | bove all | gods.

In his hand are the deep places | of the | earth;
The strength of the | hills is | his— | also.

The sea is his, | and he | made it;
And his hands | formed the | dry— | land.

Oh, come, let us worship | and bow | down:
Let us kneel be- | fore the | Lord our | Maker.

For he | is our | God;
And we are the people of his pasture, | and the | sheep of..his | hand.

To-day, if ye will ⸱ hear his | voice,
Harden not your heart, as in the provocation,
And as in the day of temptation in the wilderness;
When your fathers tempted me, | proved..me, and | saw my | work.

Forty years long was I grieved with this generation,
And said, It is a people that do | err..in their | heart,
And they | have not | known my | ways.

Unto whom I sware | in my | wrath,
That they should | not..enter | into..my | rest.

No. 4. SINGLE.

GLORIA IN EXCELSIS.

1.

GLORY be to | God on | high ;
    And on earth, | peace, good | will towards | men.
We praise thee, we bless thee, we | worship | thee,
We glorify thee, we give thanks to | thee for | thy great | glory.

2.

O Lord God, | heavenly | King,
God the | Father | Al- — | mighty.
O Lord, the only-begotten Son, | Jesus | Christ ;
O Lord God Lamb of | God Son | of the | Father,

3.

That takest away the | sins .. of the | world, ‖ have mercy up- | on | us.
Thou that takest away the | sins .. of the | world, ‖ receive — | our | prayer.
Thou that sittest at the right hand of | God the | Father, ‖ have mercy up- | on | us.

D. C.

For thou | only art | Holy ; ‖ thou | only | art the | Lord.
Thou only, O Christ, with the | Holy | Ghost, ‖ art most high in the | glory of |
    God the | Father. ‖ Amen.

No. 6. DOUBLE.

GLORIA IN EXCELSIS.

GLORY be to | God on | high ;
  And on earth, | peace, good | will towards | men.

We praise thee, we bless thee, we | worship | thee,
We glorify thee, we give thanks to | thee for | thy great | glory.

Lord God, | heavenly | King,
God the | Father | Al- — | mighty.

Lord, the only-begotten Son, | Jesus | Christ ;
Lord God, Lamb of | God, Son | of the | Father

That takest away the | sins .. of the | world,
Have | mercy | upon | us.

Thou that takest away the | sins .. of the | world,
Have | mercy | upon | us.

Thou that takest away the | sins .. of the | world,
Re- | ceive — | our — | prayer.

Thou that sittest at the right hand of | God the | Father,
Have | mercy | upon | us.

For thou | only art | Holy ; || thou | only | art the | Lord.
Thou only, O Christ, with the | Holy | Ghost, || art most high in the glory of |
  God the | Father. A- | men.

No. 7. SINGLE.

CHANTS.

No. 8. Double.

TE DEUM LAUDAMUS.

WE praise | thee, O | God ; ‖ we acknowledge | thee to | be the | Lord.
  All the earth doth | worship | thee, ‖ the | Father | ever- | lasting.
To thee all Angels | cry a- | loud ; ‖ the Heavens, and | all the | Powers there- | in.
To thee Cherubim, and | Seraph- | im ‖ con | tinual- | ly do | cry,
Holy, Holy, Holy, Lord | God of | Sabaoth ; ‖ Heaven and earth are full of the | majesty | of thy | glory.
The glorious company of the Apostles | praise — | thee. ‖ The goodly fellowship of the | Prophets | praise — | thee.
The noble army of Martyrs | praise — | thee. ‖ The holy Church throughout all the world | doth ac- | knowledge | thee ;
The | Fa- — | ther ‖ of an | infinite | majes- | ty ;
Thine adorable, true, and | only | Son ; ‖ Also the | Holy | Ghost, the | Comforter.
Thou art the King of Glory, | O — | Christ ; ‖ Thou art the everlasting | Son — | of the | Father.
When thou tookest upon thee to de- | liver | man, ‖ thou didst humble thyself to be | born — | of a | virgin.
When thou hadst overcome the | sharpness of | death, ‖ thou didst open the kingdom of | heaven to | all be- | lievers.
Thou sittest at the right | hand of | God, ‖ in the | glory | of the | Father.
We believe that thou shalt come to | be our | Judge. ‖ We therefore pray thee, help thy servants, whom thou hast redeemed | with thy | precious | blood.
Make them to be numbered | with thy | saints, ‖ in glory | ever- | lasting.
O Lord, | save thy | people, | and | bless — | thine — | heritage.
Gov- | — ern | them, ‖ and | lift them | up for- | ever.
Day by day we | magnify | thee ; ‖ And we worship thy name ever, | world with- | out — | end.
Vouch- | safe, O | Lord, ‖ to keep us this | day with- | out — | sin.
O Lord, have | mercy up- | on us, ‖ have | mer- — | cy up- | on us.
O Lord, let thy mercy | be up- | on us, ‖ as our trust is | in — | thee.
O Lord, in thee | have I | trusted ; ‖ let me | never | be con- | founded.

No. 9. Double.

JUBILATE DEO. Psalm c.

MAKE a joyful noise unto the Lord, | all ye | lands,
Serve the Lord with gladness ;
Come before his | presence | with— | singing.

Know ye that the Lord, | he is | God :
It is he that hath made us, and not we ourselves.
We are his | people, .. and the | sheep .. of his | pasture.

Enter into his gates with thanksgiving,
And into his | courts with | praise :
Be thankful unto | him, and | bless his | name.

For the Lord is good, his mercy is | ever- | lasting.
And his truth endureth to | all— | gene- | rations.

No. 10. Double.

CHANTS.

No. 11. DOUBLE.

JUBILATE DEO. Psalm c.

MAKE a joyful noise unto the Lord, | all ye | lands,
  Serve the Lord with gladness;
Come before his | presence | with— | singing.

Know ye that the Lord, | he is | God :
It is he that hath made us, and not we ourselves.
We are his | people, .. and the | sheep .. of his | pasture.

Enter into his gates with thanksgiving,
And into his | courts with | praise :
Be thankful unto | him, and | bless his | name.

For the Lord is good, his mercy is | ever- | lasting.
And his truth endureth to | all— | gene- | rations.

GLORIA PATRI.

GLORY be to the Father, and | to the | Son,
  And | to the | Holy | Ghost ;

As it was in the beginning, is now, and | ever | shall be,
World | without | end. A- | men.

No. 12. SINGLE.

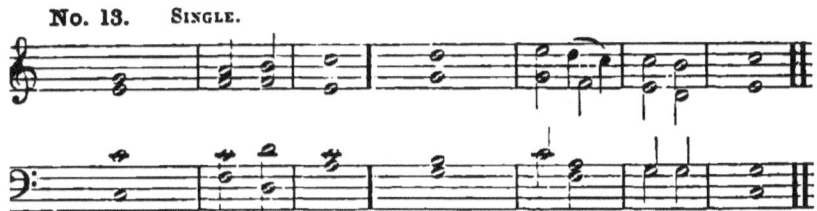

No. 13. SINGLE.

BENEDICTUS. St. Luke i. 68-75.

BLESSED be the Lord | God of | Israel;
    For he hath visited | and re- | deemed his | people;

And hath raised up a mighty sal- | vation | for us,
In the house | of his | servant | David;

As he spake by the mouth of his | holy | Prophets,
Which have been | since the | world be- | gan:

That we should be saved | from our | enemies,
And from the | hand of | all that | hate us.

GLORIA PATRI.

GLORY be to the Father, and | to the | Son, ||
    And | to the | Holy | Ghost.

As it was in the beginning, is now, and | ever | shall be ||
World without | end. A- | men. A- | men.

No. 14. DOUBLE.

No. 15.

Ho-ly, Ho-ly, Ho-ly, Lord God of Hosts; Heav'n and earth are full of thy glo-ry: Glo-ry be to thee, O Lord Most High. A - men, A - men.

TRISAGION.

HOLY, Holy, Holy, Lord God of Hosts;
    Heaven and earth are full of thy glory:
Glory be to thee, O Lord Most High.
    Amen, Amen.

No. 16.   Single.

SANCTUS DOMINUS DEUS.   From Rev. iv. and v.

HOLY, holy, holy, Lord | God al- | mighty,
    Which was, and | is, and | is to | come.

Thou art worthy, O Lord, to receive glory, and | honor .. and | power;
For thou hast created all things, and for thy pleasure they | are and | were cre- | ated.

Worthy is the Lamb | that was | slain,
    To receive power, and riches, and wisdom, and strength, and | honor, .. and | glory, .. and | blessing.

Blessing, and honor, and | glory, .. and | power,
Be unto him that sitteth upon the throne,
And unto the Lamb for | ever .. and | ever. A- | men.

CHANTS.

No. 17.

GLORIA TIBI DOMINE.

GLORY be to Thee,
Glory be to Thee,
Glory be to Thee,
To Thee, O Lord.

No. 18. SINGLE.

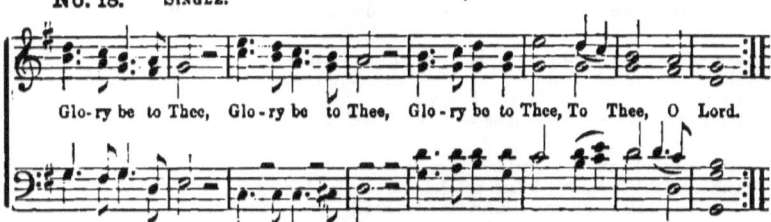

GLORIA PATRI.

GLORY be to the Father, and | to the | Son,
And | to the | Holy | Ghost;

As it was in the beginning, is now, and | ever | shall be,
World | without | end. A- | men.

No. 19. SINGLE.

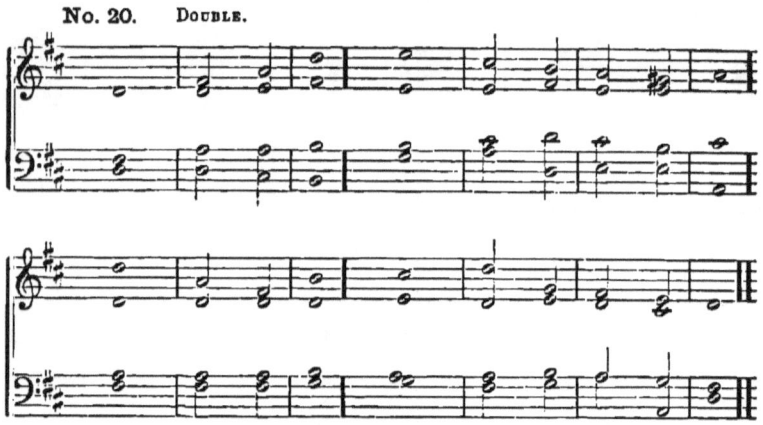

CANTATE DOMINO. Ps. xcviii.

O SING unto the | Lord..a new | song,
   For he | hath done | marvelous | things:
His right hand, and his | holy | arm,
Hath | gotten | him the | victory.

The Lord hath made known | his sal- | vation:
His righteousness hath he openly showed | in the | sight .. of the | heathen.
He hath remembered his mercy and his truth toward the | house of | Israel;
And all the ends of the earth have seen the sal- | vation | of our | God.

Make a joyful noise unto the Lord, | all the | earth;
Make a loud noise, and re- | joice — | and sing | praises.
Sing unto the Lord | with the | harp,
With the harp and the | voice — | of a | psalm.

With trumpets and | sound of | cornet,
Make a joyful noise be- | fore the | Lord the | King,
Let the sea roar, and the | fullness | thereof,
The world, and | they that | dwell there- | in.

Let the floods | clap their | hands;
Let the hills be joyful together | before | the — | Lord:
For he cometh to | judge the | world
And | — the | people..with | equity.

No. 22. DOUBLE.

BONUM EST CONFITERI. Ps. xcii.

IT is a good thing to give | thanks .. unto the | Lord :
And to sing praises unto thy | name, — | O Most | High;

To show forth thy loving-kindness | in the | morning,
And thy faithfulness | ev- — | ery— | night;

Upon an instrument of ten strings, and up- | on the | lute;
Upon the harp | with a | solemn | sound.

For thou, Lord, hast made me | glad .. through thy | work,
And I will triumph in the | works — | of thy | hands.

Glory be to the Father, and | to the | Son,
And | to the | Holy | Ghost;

As it was in the beginning, | is — | now,
And ever | shall be, | world .. without | end.
                                    Amen.

No. 23. SINGLE.

No. 24. Double.

BENEDIC ANIMA MEA. (First Part.) Ps. ciii.

BLESS the Lord, | O my | soul;
    And all that is within me, | bless his | holy | name.

Bless the Lord, | O my | soul,
And for- | get not | all his | benefits.

Who forgiveth all | thine in- | iquities;
Who | healeth | all thy .. dis- | eases.

Who redeemeth thy | life .. from de- | struction;
Who crowneth thee with loving- | kindness .. and | tender | mercies;

Who satisfieth thy mouth with | good — | things;
So that thy youth is re- | newed | like the | eagle's.

The Lord executeth righteousness and judgment for all that | are op- | pressed.
He made known his ways unto Moses,
His acts | unto the | children of | Israel.

The Lord is merciful and gracious,
Slow to anger, and | plenteous .. in | mercy.
He will not always chide; neither will he | keep his | anger .. for- | ever.

He hath not dealt with us | after .. our | sins,
Nor rewarded us ac- | cording | to our .. in- | iquities.

For as the heaven is high a- | bove the | earth,
So great is his | mercy .. toward | them that | fear him.

As far as the east is | from the | west,
So far hath he removed | our trans- | gressions | from us.

Glory be to the Father, and | to the | Son,
And | to the | Holy | Ghost &c.

No. 25. Double.

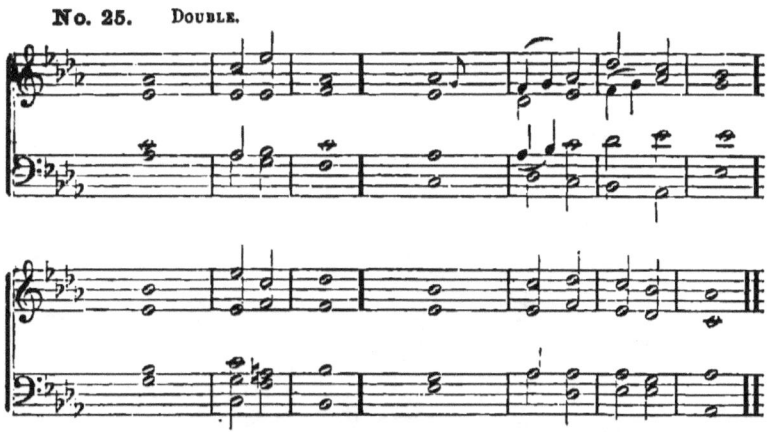

BENEDIC, ANIMA MEA. (Second Part.) Ps. ciii.

LIKE as a father pitieth his children,
  So the Lord pitieth ʾ| them that | fear him.
For he knoweth our frame; he | remembereth .. that | we are | dust.

As for man, his | days .. are as | grass;
As a flower of the field, | so he | flourish- | eth.

For the wind passeth over it, and | it is | gone;
And the place thereof | shall — | know it .. no | more.

But the mercy of the Lord is from everlasting to everlasting upon | them that | fear him,
And his righteousness | unto | children's | children;

To such as | keep his | covenant,
And to those that remember | his com- | mandments .. to | do them.

The Lord hath prepared his throne | in the | heavens;
And his kingdom | ruleth | over | all.

Bless the Lord, ye his angels, that ex- | cel in | strength,
That do his commandments, hearkening unto the | voice— | of his | word.

Bless ye the Lord, all | ye his | hosts:
Ye ministers of | his, that | do his ! pleasure.

Bless the Lord, all his works, in all places of | his do- | minion.
Bless the | Lord, — | O my | soul.

No. 26. Single.

No. 27. Double.

DEUS MISEREATUR. Ps. lxvii.

GOD be merciful unto | us, and | bless us,
And cause his | face to | shine up- | on us.

That thy way may be | known up- .. on | earth,
Thy saving | health a- | mong all | nations.

Let the people praise | thee, O | God:
Let all the | people | praise — | thee.

Oh, let the nations be glad, and | sing for | joy:
For thou shalt judge the people righteously, and govern the | na .. tions | upon | earth.

Let the people praise | thee, O | God;
Let | all the | people | praise thee.

Then shall the earth | yield her | increase,
And God, even | our own | God, shall | bless us.

God | shall — | bless us,
And all the ends of the | earth shall | fear — | him.

No. 28. Double.

No. 29. SINGLE.

TE DECET HYMNUS. Ps. lxv.

PRAISE waiteth for thee, O | God, in | Zion :
And unto | thee .. shall the | vow .. be per- | formed.

O thou that hearest prayer, unto thee shall | all flesh | come.
Iniquities prevail against me: as for our transgressions, | thou shalt | purge .. them a- | way.

Blessed is the man whom thou choosest, and causest to approach unto thee, that he may | dwell in .. thy | courts.
We shall be satisfied with the goodness of thy house, | even .. of thy | holy | temple.

By terrible things in righteousness wilt thou answer us, O God of | our sal- | vation.
Who art the confidence of all the ends of the earth, and of them that are afar | off up- | on the | sea.

Who by his strength setteth fast the mountains ; being | girded .. with | power :
Who stilleth the noise of the seas, the noise of their waves, and the | tumult | of the | people.

They also that dwell in the uttermost parts are | afraid .. at thy | tokens :
Thou makest the outgoings of the morning and | evening | to re- | joice.

Thou visitest the earth, and waterest it :
Thou greatly enrichest it with the river of God, which is | full of | water :
Thou preparest them corn, when thou hast | so pro- | vided | for it.

Thou waterest the ridges thereof abundantly : thou settlest the | furrows there- | of.
Thou makest it soft with showers; thou | blessest the | springing there- | of ;

Thou crownest the year with thy goodness ; and thy | paths drop | fatness.
They drop upon the pastures of the wilderness ; and the little hills re- | joice on | every | side.

The pastures are clothed with flocks; the valleys also are covered | over with | corn ;
They shout for | joy, they | also | sing.

No. 30. Double.

MAGNIFICAT. Luke i. 46-55.

MY soul doth magni- | fy the | Lord ; || and my spirit hath re- | joiced in | God my | Savior.

For he | hath re- | garded || the lowli- | ness of | his hand- | maiden ;

For behold, | from hence- | forth || all gene- | rations shall | call me | blessed.

For he that is mighty hath done to me great things, and holy | is his | name ; || and his mercy is on them that fear him, through- | out all | gene- | rations.

He hath showed strength | with his | arm ; || he hath scattered the proud in the imagi- | nation | of their | hearts.

He hath put down the mighty | from their | seats, || and exalted | them of | low de- | gree.

He hath filled the hungry | with good | things, || and the rich he | hath sent | empty a- | way.

He hath holpen his servant Israel in remembrance | of his | mercy ; As he spoke to our fathers, to Abraham, and | to his | seed, for- | ever.

No. 31. Single.

No. 32.   SINGLE.

LAETATUS SUM.   Ps. cxxii.

I WAS glad when they said unto me,
   Let us go into the | house .. of the | Lord.

Our feet shall stand within thy gates, O Jerusalem.
Jerusalem is builded as a city that | is com- | pact to- | gether.

Whither the tribes go up; the tribes of the Lord unto the testimony of Israel,
To give thanks unto the | name .. of the | Lord.

For there are set thrones of judgment,
The | thrones .. of the | house of | David.

Pray for the peace of Jerusalem,
They shall | prosper .. that | love thee.

Peace be within thy walls,
And pros- | perity with- | in thy | palaces.

For my brethren and companions' sake,
I will now say, | Peace .. be with- | in thee.

Because of the house of the Lord our God,
I will | seek thy | good.

BEATUS VIR.   Ps. i.

BLESSED is the man that walketh not in the counsel | of the .. un- | godly,
   Nor standeth in the way of sinners, nor sitteth in the | seat | of the | scornful.

But his delight is in the | law .. of the | Lord:
And in his law doth he | medi- .. tate | day and | night.

And he shall be like a tree planted by the | rivers .. of | water,
That bringeth forth his | fruit — | in his | season.

His leaf also | shall not | wither;
And whatso- | ever .. he | doeth .. shall | prosper.

THE UNGODLY | are not | so:
But are like the chaff which the | wind — | driveth .. a- | way.

Therefore the ungodly shall not | stand .. in the | judgment,
Nor sinners in the congre- | gation | of the | righteous:

For the Lord knoweth the | way .. of the | righteous:
But the way of the un- | godly | shall — | perish.

No. 33. SINGLE.

VOCE MEA AD DOMINUM. Psalm lxxvii.

FIRST PART.

I CRIED unto God with my voice, even unto God with my voice;
And he gave | ear .. unto | me.

In the day of my trouble I sought the Lord:
My sore ran in the night, and ceased not:
My soul re- | fused | to be | comforted.

I remembered God, and was troubled:
I complained, and my spirit was | over- | whelmed,
Thou holdest mine eyes waking: I am so troubled | that I | cannot | speak.

I have considered the days of old, the years of | ancient | times;
I call to remembrance my song in the night:
I commune with mine own heart; And my | spirit .. made | diligent | search

Will the Lord cast off forever?
And will he be favorable | no— | more?
Is his mercy clean gone forever?
Doth his promise | fail for | ever- | more?

Hath God forgotten to be gracious?
Hath he in anger shut up his | tender | mercies?
And I said, This is my infirmity,
But I will remember the years of the right | hand of | the Most | High.

I will remember the works of the Lord;
Surely I will remember thy | wonders .. of | old.
I will meditate also of all thy work, And | talk— | of thy | doings.

No. 34. DOUBLE.

CHANTS. 353

No. 35.   SINGLE.

VOCE MEA AD DOMINUM.   Psalm lxxvii.
SECOND PART.

THY way, O God, is in the sanctuary :
Who is so great a | God as | our God ?
Thou art the God that doest wonders :
Thou hast declared thy | strength a- | mong the | people.

Thou hast with thine arm redeemed thy people,
The sons of | Jacob .. and | Joseph.
The waters saw thee, O God, the waters saw thee ;
They were afraid : the | depths— | also .. were | troubled.

The clouds poured out water ; the skies sent out a sound :
Thine arrows also | went a- | broad.
The voice of thy thunder was in the heaven ;
The lightnings lightened the world :
The | earth— | trembled .. and | shook.

Thy way is in the sea, and thy path in the great waters,
And thy footsteps | are not | known.
Thou leddest thy people like a flock
By the | hand of | Moses .. and | Aaron.

CONFITEBOR TIBI.   Psalm cxxxviii.

I WILL praise thee with my | whole— | heart :
Before the gods will I sing | praise— | unto | thee.
I will worship toward thy holy temple, and praise thy name for thy loving-kindness and | for thy | truth ;
For thou hast magnified thy word a- | bove— | all thy | name.

In the day when I cried thou | answer- .. edst | me,
And strengthenedst me with | strength— | in my | soul.
All the kings of the earth shall praise | thee, O | Lord,
When they hear the | words of | thy— | mouth.

Yea, they shall sing in the | ways .. of the | Lord :
For great is the | glory | of the | Lord.
Though the Lord be high, yet hath he respect | unto .. the | lowly :
But the proud he | knoweth .. a- | far— | off.

Though I walk in the midst of trouble, thou | wilt re- | vive me :
Thou shalt stretch forth thine hand against the wrath of mine enemies, and | thy right | hand shall | save me.
The Lord will perfect that which con- | cerneth | me :
Thy mercy, O Lord, endureth forever : forsake not the | works of | thine own | hands.

No. 36. Single.

A - men.

LEVAVI OCULOS MEOS. Psalm cxxi.

I WILL lift up mine eyes | unto .. the | hills,
  From | whence— | cometh .. my | help.

My help cometh | from the | Lord,
  Which | made— | heaven .. and | earth.

He will not suffer thy | foot .. to be | moved:
  He that | keepeth .. thee | will not | slumber.

Behold, he that keepeth | Isra- | el
  Shall neither | slumber | nor— | sleep.

The Lord | is thy | keeper:
  The Lord is thy shade up- | on thy | right— | hand.

The sun shall not | smite thee .. by | day,
  Nor the | moon— | by— | night.

The Lord shall preserve thee from | all— | evil:
  He | shall pre- | serve thy | soul.

The Lord shall preserve thy going out and thy | coming | in
  From this time forth, and | even .. for | ever- | more.

THE LORD'S PRAYER. Matthew vi. 9-13.

OUR Father who | art in | heaven,
  Hallowed | be— | thy— | name.

Thy | kingdom | come,
  Thy will be done in earth | as it | is in | heaven.

Give us this day our | daily | bread:
  And forgive us our debts, as | we for- | give our | debtors;

And lead us not | into .. temp- | tation,
  But de- | liver | us from | evil.

For thine is the kingdom, and the | power, and the | glory,
  For- | ever | and — | ever.

No. 37. Single.

LEX DOMINI, ETC.   Psalm ix. 7-11.

THE law of the Lord is perfect, con- | verting .. the | soul:
  The testimony of the Lord is | sure, making | wise the | simple.

The statutes of the Lord are right, re- | joicing .. the | heart:
The commandment of the Lord is | pure, en- | lightening .. the | eyes.

The fear of the Lord is clean, en- | during .. for- | ever:
The judgments of the Lord are true and | righteous | alto- | gether.

More to be desired are they than gold, yea, than | much fine | gold:
Sweeter also than honey | and the | honey- | comb.

Moreover, by them is thy | servant | warned:
And in keeping of them | there is | great re- | ward.

No. 38. Single.

DOMINUS REGIT ME.   Psalm xxiii.

THE Lord is my Shepherd; I | shall not | want.
  He maketh me to lie down in green pastures;
He leadeth me be- | side the | still— | waters.

He re- | storeth .. my | soul;
He leadeth me in the paths of righteousness | for his | name's— | sake.

Yea, though I walk through the valley of the shadow of death,
I will | fear no | evil:
For thou art with me; thy rod and thy | staff they | comfort | me.

Thou preparest a table before me in the presence | of mine | enemies:
Thou anointest my head with oil; my | cup— | runneth | over.

Surely goodness and mercy shall follow me all the | days of .. my | life;
And I will dwell in the | house .. of the | Lord for- | ever.

CHANTS.

No. 39. Single.

DEUS NOSTER REFUGIUM. Psalm xlvi.

GOD is our | refuge .. and | strength,
   A very | present | help in | trouble.

Therefore we will not fear, though the | earth .. be re- | moved,
And though the mountains be carried into the | midst— | of the | sea;

Though the waters thereof | roar .. and be | troubled,
Though the mountains | shake .. with the | swelling .. there- | of.

There is a river, the streams whereof shall make glad the | city .. of | God;
The holy place of the tabernacles | of the | Most— | High.

God is in the midst of her, she shall | not be | mov-ed;
God shall help her, and | that— | right-- | early.

The heathen raged, the | kingdoms .. were | mov-ed,
He uttered his | voice, the | earth— | melted.

The Lord of | Hosts is | with us;
The God of | Jacob | is our | refuge.

Come, behold the | works .. of the | Lord;
What desolations | he hath | made .. in the | earth.

He maketh wars to cease unto the | end .. of the | earth;
He breaketh the bow, and cutteth the spear in sunder; he burneth the | chariot | in the | fire.

Be still, and know that | I am | God;
I will be exalted among the heathen, I will be ex- | alted | in the | earth.

The Lord of | Hosts is | with us;
The God of | Jacob | is our | refuge.

GLORIA PATRI.

GLORY be to the Father, and | to the | Son,
   And | to the | Holy | Ghost;

As it was in the beginning, is now, and | ever | shall be,
World | without | end. A- | men.

No. 40.

DOMINI EST TERRA. Psalm xxiv.

THE earth is the Lord's, and the | fullness..there- | of;
The world, and | they that | dwell there- | in.

For he hath founded it up- | on the | seas,
And established | it up- | on the | floods.

Who shall ascend unto the | hill..of the | Lord?
And who shall stand | in his | holy | place?

He that hath clean hands, and a | pure — | heart;
Who hath not lifted up his soul unto vanity, nor | sworn de- | ceitful- | ly.

He shall receive the blessing | from the | Lord,
And righteousness from the | God of | his sal- | vation.

This is the generation of them that | seek — | him;
That | seek thy | face, O | Jacob.

Lift up your heads, O ye gates, and be ye lifted up, ye ever- | lasting | doors;
And the King of | glory | shall come | in.

Who is this | King of | glory?
The Lord, strong and mighty, the Lord, | migh- — | ty in | battle.

Lift up your heads, O ye gates, even lift them up, ye ever- | lasting | doors;
And the King of | glory | shall come | in.

Who is this | King of | glory?
The Lord of hosts, | he..is the | King of | glory.

Glory be to the Father, and | to the | Son,
And | to the | Holy | Ghost;

As it was in the beginning, is now, and | ever | shall be
World | without | end. A- — | men.

No. 41.

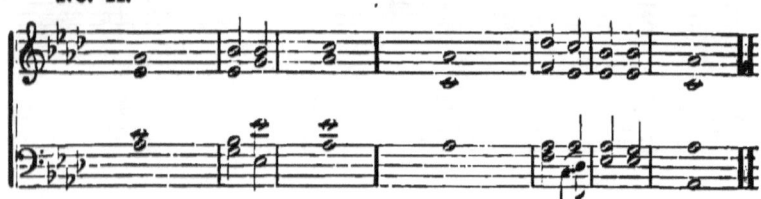

SURGE DOMINE.   Psalm cxxxi.

ARISE, O Lord, | into..thy | rest; ‖ Thou, and the | ark — | of thy | strength:
Let thy priests be clothed with | righteous- | ness, ‖
And thy saints | shout — | for — | joy.

The Lord hath | chosen | Zion: ‖ he hath desired it | for his | habi- | tation.
This is my | rest for- | ever: ‖ Here will I dwell; | for I | have de- | sired it.

I will abundantly bless | her pro- | vision: ‖
I will satisfy her | poor — | with — | bread.
I will also clothe her priests | with sal- | vation; ‖
and her saints shall | shout a- | loud for | joy.

No. 42.

LAUDATE DOMINI.   Psalm cl.

PRAISE ye the Lord. Praise God in his sanctuary.
Praise him in the firmament | of his | power.

Praise him for his mighty acts:
Praise him according | to his | excel-..lent | greatness.

Praise him with the sound of the trumpet;
Praise him with the | psaltery..and | harp.

Praise him with the timbrel and dance;
Praise him with | stringed..instru- | ments and | organs.

Praise him upon the loud cymbals:
Praise him upon the | high-sounding | cymbals.

Let every thing that hath breath praise the Lord.
| Praise— | ye the | Lord.

No. 43. Single.

GRATIAS AGIMUS.

WE give thee thanks, O Lord | God Al- | mighty,
    The King of kings and | Lord — | — of | Lords.

Salvation to our God which sitteth upon the throne,
And | unto .. the | Lamb.
A- | men: .. Halle- | luia! .. A- | men.

Blessing, and glory, and wisdom, and thanksgiving, and honor, and | power ..
    and | might,
Be unto our | God for | ever .. and | ever.

HALLELUIA.

GREAT and marvellous are thy works, | Lord .. God Al- | mighty!
    Just and true are thy | ways, thou | King of | saints.

Who shall not fear thee, O Lord, and | glorify .. thy | name!
For | thou — | only .. art | holy.

Salvation, and glory, and honor, and power, unto the | Lord our | God:
For true and | righteous | are his | judgments.

Praise ye our God, all ye his servants, and ye that fear him, both | small and |
    great: | A- | men: .. Halle- | luia! .. A- | men.

HALLELUIA.

AMEN: — | Halle- | luia!
    Amen: — | Hal- — | le- — | luia!

Praise our God, all | ye his | servants,
And ye that | fear him .. both | small and | great.

Halleluia! | Halle- | luia!
For the Lord | God Om- | nipo- .. tent | reigneth.

Let us be glad, and rejoice, and give | honor | to him:
Halle- | luia! — | A- — | men.

CHANTS—CHRISTMAS.

No. 44. DOUBLE.

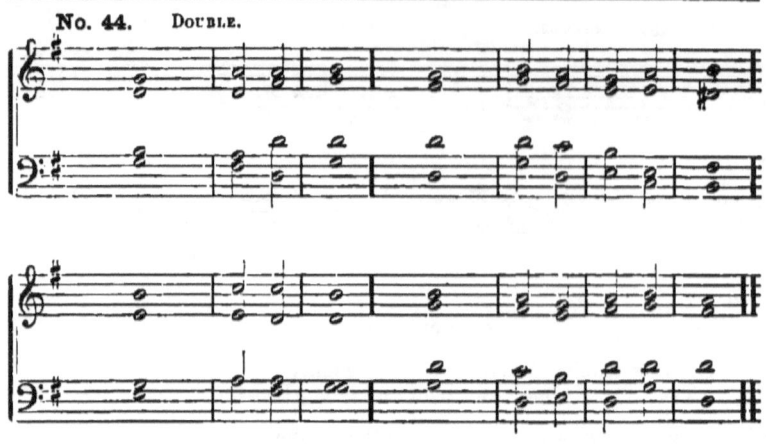

From St. John i.

IN the beginning | was the | Word ;
  And the Word was with God, | and the | Word was | God.
The same was in the be- | ginning with | God : ‖ all things were made by him ; and without him was not any thing | made — | that was | made.
In | him was | life ; ‖ and the life | was the | light of | men.
And the light | shineth in | darkness ; ‖ and the darkness | compre- | hended it | not ;
That was the | true — | Light, ‖ which lighteth every man that | cometh | into the | world.
He was in the world, and the world was | made by | him, ‖ and the | world — | knew him | not.
He came | unto his | own, ‖ and his | own re- | ceived him | not.
But as many | as re- | ceived him, ‖ to them gave he power to become the sons of God, even to them | that be- | lieve .. on his | name :
Which were born | not of | blood, ‖ nor of the will of the flesh, nor of the will of | man, — | but of | God.
And the Word was made flesh, and | dwelt a- | mong us ; ‖ and we beheld his glory, the glory as of the only-begotten of the Father, | full of | grace and | truth.
And of his fullness have all | we re- | ceived ; ‖ and | grace — | for — | grace.
For the law was | given by | Moses ; ‖ but grace and truth | came by | Jesus | Christ.

NUNC DIMITTIS. St. Luke ii.

LORD, now lettest thou thy servant de- | part in | peace,
  Ac- | cording | to thy | word ;
For | mine — | eyes ‖ have | seen — | thy sal- | vation,
Which thou | hast pre- | pared ‖ before the | face — | of all | people.
To be a light to | lighten the | Gentiles, ‖ and the glory | of thy | people | Israel.

CHANTS—CHRISTMAS.

No. 45. Single.

From Isa. ix. 6, 7.

FOR unto us a | child is | born ; || unto | us a | son is | given.
   And the government shall be up- | on his | shoulder, || and his | name — | shall be | called
Wonderful, Counsellor, the Mighty God, the Ever- | lasting | Father, || the | Prince — | of — | Peace.
Of the increase of his government and peace there shall | be no | end, || upon the throne of David | and up- | on his | kingdom:
To order it and to establish it with judgment | and with | justice, || from | henceforth, | even for- | ever.
The zeal of the | Lord of | Hosts || will | per- — | form — | this.
Glory be to the Father, and to the Son, &c.

No. 46. Single.

CHRISTMAS CANTATE.

O SING unto the Lord a | new — | song ;
   Let the congre- | gation .. of | saints — | praise him.
Let Israel rejoice in | Him that | made him ;
And let the children of Zion be | joyful | in their | King ;
In Him who is the First | and the | Last ;—
The same yesterday, to- | day, — | and for- | ever ;—
The | Son of | Mary ;—
The only-begotten of the Father, | full of | grace and | truth.
He is the Desire | of all | nations ;
The Glory | of his | people | Israel.
The Dayspring from on high hath | visited | us.
The Sun of Righteousness is risen with | healing | in his | wings.
Glory be to the Father, and | to the | Son,
And | to the | Holy | Ghost, &c.

No. 47. DOUBLE.

Slow, both in the recitatives and the cadence.

MISERERE MEI, DEUS. Psalm li.

HAVE mercy upon me, | O— | God, ‖ according to | thy— | loving- | kindness; According to the multitude of thy | tender | mercies ‖ blot | out— | my trans- | gressions.

Wash me thoroughly from | my in- | iquity, ‖ and | cleanse me | from my | sin.
For I acknowledge | my trans- | gressions; ‖ and my | sin is | ever be- | fore me.

Against thee, thee only, have I sinned, and done this evil | in thy | sight; ‖ that thou mightest be justified when thou speakest, and | be clear | when thou | judgest.
Behold, I was shapen | in in- | iquity; ‖ and in sin did my | mother con- | ceive me.

Hide thy face | from my | sins, ‖ and blot out | all— | mine in- | iquities.
Create in me a clean | heart, O | God; ‖ and renew a | right— | spirit with- | in me.

Cast me not away | from thy | presence; ‖ and take not thy | Holy | Spirit | from me.
Restore unto me the joy of | thy sal- | vation; ‖ and uphold me | with thy | free- | Spirit.

Thou desirest not sacrifice, else | would I | give it; ‖ thou delightest | not in | burnt- — | offering.
The sacrifices of God are a | broken | spirit: ‖ a broken and a contrite heart, O God, | thou wilt | not de- | spise.

No. 48. SINGLE.

CHANTS—GOOD FRIDAY.

No. 49. SINGLE.

From Isaiah liii.

HE was wounded for | our trans- | gressions,
  He was | bruised for | our in- | iquities:
The chastisement of our peace | was upon | him;
And with | his stripes | we are | healed.

All we like sheep have | gone a- | stray;
We have turned every | one to | his own | way:
And the Lord hath | laid on | him ‖ the in- | iquity | of us | all.

He was oppressed, and he | was afflicted, ‖ yet he | opened | not his | mouth.
He is brought as a lamb to the slaughter, and as a sheep before her | shearers is | dumb, ‖ so he [openeth | not his | mouth.

No. 50. DOUBLE.

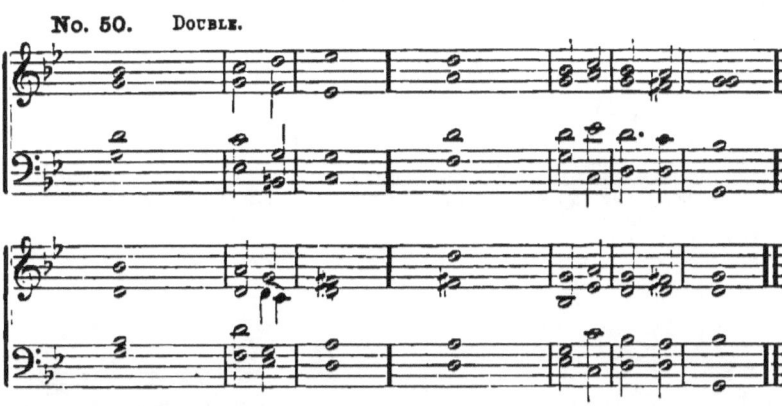

REPROACH hath broken | my— | heart; ‖ and | I am | full of | heaviness.
  I looked for some to take pity and for | comfort- | ers, ‖ but | there— | was— | none.

Then said I, | Lo, I | come; ‖ In the volume of the book it is | written | of— | me.
I delight to do thy will, | O my | God: ‖ yea, thy law | is with- | in my | heart.

They gave me gall | for my | meat, ‖ and in my thirst they gave me | vinegar | to— | drink.
They gaped upon me | with their | mouths; ‖ they pierced | my hands | and my | feet.

I am poured out | like— | water; ‖ and thou hast brought me in- | to the | dust of | death.
Make haste, O God, | to de- | liver me; ‖ make haste to | help— | me, O | Lord.

My God, my God, why hast | thou for- | saken me? ‖ why art thou so | far from | helping | me?
Be not thou far from me, | O— | Lord: ‖ O my Strength, | haste thee | to my | help.

No. 51.

BLESSED be the God and Father of our Lord | Jesus | Christ,
Who hath begotten us again unto a lively hope by the resurrection of | Jesus | Christ from the | dead,

To an inheritance incorruptible, and | unde- | filed,
And that fadeth not away, re- | served in | heaven for | us,

Who are kept by the power of God through faith un- | to sal- | vation,
Ready to be revealed | in the | last — | time.

For our conversation | is in | heaven;
From whence also we look for the Savior, the | Lord — | Jesus | Christ,

Who shall change our | vile — | body,
That it may be fashioned like unto his | own — | glorious | body,

According to the | mighty | working,
Whereby he is able even to subdue | all things | unto him- | self.

Blessing, glory, and honor, and power, unto him that liveth | and was | dead,
And is alive for evermore, and hath the | keys of | death and | hell;

Jesus Christ, the Resurrection | and the | Life;
The same yesterday, to-day, and forever. | Amen | and A- | men.

No. 52. DOUBLE.

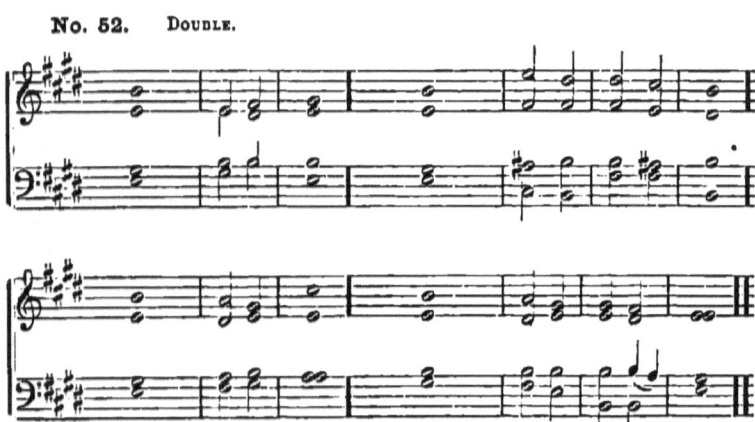

CHRIST, being raised from the dead, | dieth no | more;
　　Death hath no more do- | minion | over | him.

For in that he died, he died unto | sin — | once ;
But in that he liveth, he | liveth | unto | God.

Likewise reckon ye also yourselves to be dead indeed | unto | sin,
But alive unto God through | Jesus | Christ our | Lord.

CHRIST is risen | from the | dead,
　　And become the first- | fruits of | them that | slept.

For since by | man came | death,
By man came also the resur- | rection | of the | dead.

For as in Adam | all — | die,
Even so in Christ shall | all be | made a- | live.

Glory be to the Father, | and to the | Son,
And — | to the | Holy | Ghost ;

As it was in the beginning, is now, and | ever shall | be,
World without | end. — | A- — | men.

No. 53.　Single.

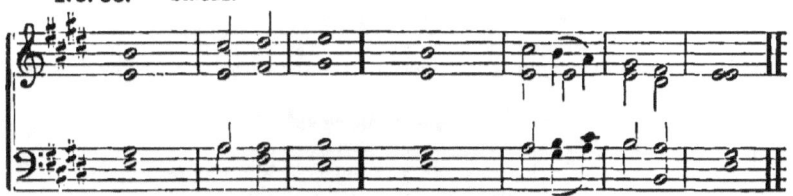

THIS is the day which the | Lord hath | made ;
　　We will rejoice | and be | glad in | it

The Lord is my strength | and my | song,
And is be- | come — | my sal- | vation.

The voice of rejoicing is in the tabernacles | of the | righteous ;
The right hand of the | Lord doeth | valiant- | ly.

The right hand of the Lord | is ex- | alted :
The right hand of the | Lord doeth | valiant- | ly.

I shall not | die, but | live,
And declare the | works — | of the | Lord.

The stone which the builders | re- — | fused
Is become the head- | stone — | of the | corner.

Glory be to the Father, and | to the | Son,
And | to the | Holy | Ghost ;

As it was in the beginning, is now, and | ever | shall be,
World without | end.— | A- — | men.

No. 54. Double.

LIFT up your heads, O ye gates; and be ye lifted up, ye ever- | lasting | doors;
   And the King of | glory | shall come | in.
Who is this | King of | glory?
The Lord, strong and mighty, the | Lord — | mighty .. in | battle.
Lift up your heads, O ye gates; even lift them up, ye ever- | lasting | doors;
And the King of | glory | shall come | in.
Who is this | King of | glory?
The Lord of hosts, | he .. is the | King of | glory.
Glory be to the Father, and | to the | Son, ‖ and | to the | Holy | Ghost;
As it was in the beginning, is now, and | ever | shall be, ‖ world without | end.
— | A- | men.

Romans viii. 31-35, 37-39.

IF | God be | for us, ‖ who | can— | be a- | gainst us?
   He that spared not his own Son, but delivered him up | for us | all,
How shall he not with him also | freely | give us | all things?
Who shall lay any thing to the charge of | God's e- | lect?
It is | God that | justi- | fieth.
Who is he that condemneth? It is Christ that died, yea, rather, that is | risen
   a- | gain, ‖ who is even at the right hand of God, who also maketh | inter- | cession | for us.
Who shall separate us from the | love of | Christ? ‖ Shall tribulation, or distress,
   or persecution, or famine, or nakedness, or | peril, | or — | sword?
Nay, in all these things we are | more than | conquerors
Through | him that | loved | us.
For I am persuaded that neither death, nor life, nor angels, nor | princi- | palities, ‖ nor powers, nor things present, | nor — | things to | come,
Nor height, nor depth, nor any | other | creature, ‖ shall be able to separate us
   from the love of God, which is in | Christ — | Jesus .. our | Lord.

No. 55. Single.

WHITSUNDAY OR PENTECOST. 367

Joel ii. 26-32.

PRAISE the name of the | Lord your | God,
That dealeth | wondrous- | ly — | with you.

I am the Lord your God, | and none | else:
And my people shall | never | be a- | shamed.

I will pour out my spirit | upon..all | flesh;
And your | sons and | daughters shall | prophesy.

And I will show wonders | in the | heavens;
And whosoever calleth on the name of the | Lord — | shall be | saved.

Glory be to the Father, and | to the | Son, ‖ and | to the | Holy | Ghost;

As it was in the beginning, is now, and | ever | shall be, ‖ world without | end.— | A— | men.

No. 56. Single.

Acts iv.

LORD, | thou art | God ‖ which hast made heaven, and earth, and the sea, and | all that | in them | is:

Who by the mouth of thy servant | David hast | said, ‖ Why did the heathen rage, and the people im- | agine | vain — | things?

The kings of the earth stood up, and the rulers were | gathered to- | gether ‖ against the Lord, | and a- | gainst his | Christ.

For of a truth against thy holy child Jesus, whom thou | hast a- | nointed,‖ both Herod and Pontius Pilate, with the Gentiles, and the people of Israel, | were — | gathered to- | gether.

For to do whatsoever thy hand | and thy | counsel ‖ determined be- | fore— | to be | done.

And now, Lord, be- | hold their | threatenings, ‖ and grant unto thy servants that with all boldness | they may | speak thy | word,

By stretching forth thy | hand to | heal, ‖ and that signs and wonders may be done by the name of thy | holy | child— | Jesus.

CHANTS—TRINITY SUNDAY.

No. 56. Single.*

TRINITAS.

HOLY, Holy, Holy, Lord | God Al- | mighty, ‖ who was, and | is, and | is to | come.

Thou art worthy, O Lord, to receive glory, and | honor, and | power, ‖ for thou hast created all things, and for thy pleasure they | are and | were cre- | ated.

And worihy is the Lamb that was slain to receive | power, and | riches, ‖ and wisdom, and strength, and | honor, and | glory, and | blessing.

And let every creature which is in heaven, and on the earth, and | under the | earth, ‖ and such as | are — | in them | say:

Blessing, and honor, and | glory, and | power, ‖ be unto Him that sitteth upon the throne, and un- | to the | Lamb for- | ever.

Holy, Holy, Holy, Lord | God Al- | mighty, ‖ who was, and | is, and | is to | come.

Glory be to the Father, and | to the | Son, &c.

No. 57. Single.*

THE CREED.

I BELIEVE in God the Father | Al- — | mighty, ‖ Maker of | heaven | and — | earth,

And in Jesus Christ, his only | Son our | Lord, ‖ who was conceived by the Holy Ghost, born of the Virgin Mary, suffered under Pontius Pilate, was cruci- | fied, — | dead, and | buried.

He descended | into | hell; ‖ the third day he | rose — | from the | dead.

He ascended into heaven, and sitteth at the right hand of God the | Father ..Al- | mighty; ‖ from thence he shall come to judge the | quick — | and the | dead.

I believe in the | Holy | Ghost; ‖ the holy catholic Church, the communion of saints, the resurrection of the body, and the | life — | ever- | lasting.

* *These may be used alternately the same as a double chant.*

CHANTS—FESTIVAL OF THE REFORMATION. 369

No. 58.   DOUBLE.

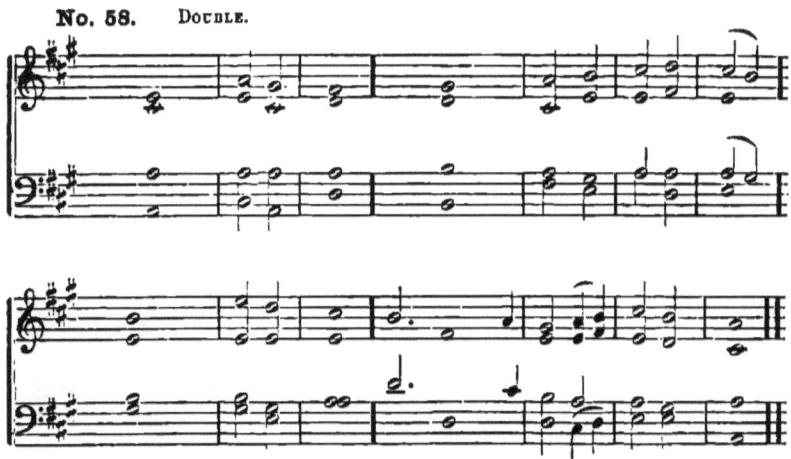

NISI QUIA DOMINUS. Ps. cxxiv.

IF it had not been the Lord who was on our side, now may | Is- .. rael | say ;
  If it had not been the Lord who was on our side, when | men rose | up
    a- | gainst us ;
Then they had swallowed | us up | quick,
When their | wrath was | kindled .. a- | gainst us.

Then the waters had | over- | whelmed us,
The stream had gone | over | our — | soul.
Blessed be the Lord, who hath not given us a prey | to their | teeth ;
Our help is in the name of the Lord who | made — | heaven and | earth.

Glory be to the Father, and | to the | Son,
And | to the | Holy | Ghost, &c.

IN CONVERTENDO. Ps. cxxvi.

WHEN the Lord turned again the captivity of Zion, we were like | them that |
    dream ;
Then was our mouth filled with laughter, | and our | tongue with | singing.
Then said they among the heathen, The Lord hath done | great things | for
    them.
The Lord hath done great things for | us, whereof | we are | glad.

Turn again our captivity, | O — | Lord ;
As the | streams — | in the | south.
They that sow in tears shall | reap in | joy.
He that goeth forth and weepeth, bearing precious seed, shall doubtless return
    again with rejoicing, | bringing | his sheaves | with him.

Glory be to the Father, and | to the | Son,
And | to the | Holy | Ghost ;
As it was, &c.

370 CHANTS—FESTIVAL OF THE REFORMATION.

No. 59. DOUBLE.

ALIUD FUNDAMENTUM.   1 Cor. iii. 11.

FOR other foundation can no man lay than | that is | laid,
  Which | is — | Jesus | Christ.
Now, if any man build upon | this foun- | dation,
Gold, silver, precious | stones, — | wood, hay, | stubble;

Every man's work | shall be .. made | manifest:
For the | day — | shall de- | clare it,
Because it shall be re- | vealed with | fire;
And the fire shall try every man's | work what | sort it | is.

Glory be to the Father, and | to the | Son,
And | to the | Holy | Ghost;
As it was in the be-ginning, is now, and | ever | shall be,
World without | end. — | A- — | men.

NISI DOMINUS.

EXCEPT the Lord build the house, they labor in | vain that | build it:
  Except the Lord keep the city, the | watchman | waketh in | vain.
They that trust in the Lord shall be | as Mount | Zion,
Which cannot be re- | moved, .. but a- | bideth .. for- | ever.

Glory be to the Father, and | to the | Son,
And | to the | Holy | Ghost;
As it was in the beginning, is now, and | ever | shall be,
World without | end. — | A- — | men.

CHANTS—THANKSGIVING.

No. 60. Single.*

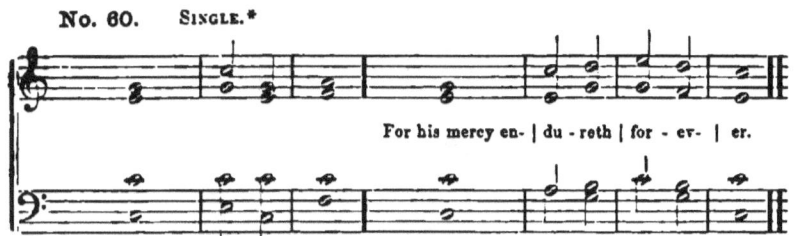

CONFITEMINI DOMINO. Ps. cxxxvi.

OH, give thanks unto the Lord, for | he is | good; || for his mercy, &c.

Oh, give thanks unto the | God of | gods; || for his, &c.

Oh, give thanks unto the | Lord of | lords; || for, &c.

To him who alone doeth | great — | wonders; || for, &c.

To him that by wisdom | made the | heavens; || for, &c.

To him that stretched out the earth a- | bove the | waters; || for, &c.

To him that made | great — | lights; || for, &c.

The sun to | rule by | day, || for, &c.

The moon and stars to | rule by | night; || for, &c.

Who remembered us in our | low es- | tate; || for, &c.

And hath redeemed us | from our | enemies; || for, &c.

Who giveth food to | all — | flesh; || for, &c.

Oh, give thanks unto the | God of | heaven; || for, &c.

No. 61. Single.*

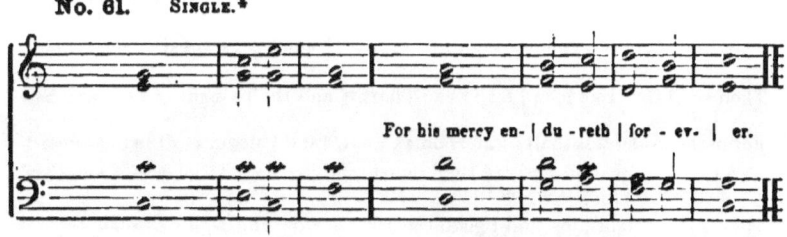

* *These two chants may be used alternately the same as a double chant.*

CHANTS—ORDINATION OR INSTALLATION.

No. 62. SINGLE.

QUAM PULCHRI. Isa. lii. 7-10.

HOW beautiful up- | on the | mountains ‖ are the feet of him that bringeth good tidings, | that — | publisheth | peace ;
That bringeth good tidings of good, that publisheth | sal- — | vation ; ‖ that saith unto Sion, | Thy — | God— | reigneth.
Thy watchmen shall lift | up the | voice ; ‖ with the voice to- | gether | shall they | sing :
For they shall see | eye t8 | eye, ‖ when the Lord shall | bring a- | gain — | Sion.
Break forth into joy, sing together, ye waste places | of Jer- | usalem ; ‖ for the Lord hath comforted his people, he | hath re- | deemed Jer- | usalem.
The Lord hath made bare his holy arm in the eyes of | all the | nations ; ‖ and all the ends of the world shall see the sal- | vation | of our | God.

No. 63. SINGLE.

LETABIT DESERTA. Isa. xxxv.

THE wilderness and the solitary place | shall be | glad for them, ‖ and the desert shall rejoice and | blossom | as the | rose.
It shall | blossom a- | bundantly ‖ and rejoice | even with | joy and | singing.
The glory of Lebanon shall be given unto it, the excellency of | Carmel and | Sharon : ‖ they shall see the glory of the Lord, and the | excellency | of our | God.
Then the eyes of the blind | shall be | opened, ‖ and the ears of the | deaf shall | be un- | stopped.
Then shall the lame man | leap as an | hart, ‖ and the | tongue of the | dumb — | sing.
For in the wilderness shall | waters break | out, ‖ and | streams — | in the | desert.
And the ransomed of the Lord shall return, and | come to | Zion ‖ with songs and everlasting | joy up- | on their | heads.
They shall obtain | joy and | gladness, ‖ and sorrow and sighing | shall — | flee a- | way.

CHANTS—CHURCH-CONSECRATION.

No. 64.   SINGLE.

QUAM DILECTA.   Ps. lxxxiv.

HOW amiable are thy tabernacles, O | Lord of | Hosts!
My soul longeth, yea, even fainteth for | the courts | of the | Lord.

Blessed are they that dwell | in thy | house:
They will be | still — | praising | thee.

A day in thy courts is better | than a | thousand.
I had rather be a doorkeeper in the house of my God, than to | dwell .. in the | tents of | wickedness.

The Lord God is a | sun and | shield:
The Lord will give grace and glory; no good thing will he withhold from | them that | walk — | uprightly.

O | Lord of | hosts,
Blessed is the | man that | trusteth | in thee.

No. 65.   SINGLE.

SUSCEPIMUS MISERECORDIAM.   Ps. xlviii. 9-14.

WE have thought of thy loving- | kindness, .. O | God, || in the | midst of | thy — | temple.
According to thy name, O God, so is thy praise unto the | ends .. of the | earth :||
Thy right hand is | full of | righteous- | ness.

Let Mount Zion rejoice, let the daughters of | Judah .. be | glad, || be- | cause of | thy — | judgments.

Walk about Zion, and go | round a- | bout her: || tell the | towers | there- — | of.

Mark ye well her bulwarks, con- — | sider .. her | palaces; || that ye may tell it to the | gener- | ation | following.

For this God is our God for | ever .. and | ever : || he will be our Guide | even | unto | death.

No. 66. Single.

DOMINE REFUGIUM. Ps. xc.

LORD, thou hast been our | dwelling- | place,
  In | all— | gene- | rations.

Before the mountains were brought forth, or even the earth | and the | world;
Even from everlasting to ever- | lasting, | Thou art | God.

Thou turnest man | to de- | struction:
And sayest, Return, ye | children | of— | men.

For a thousand years in thy sight are but as yesterday, when | it is | past,
And as a | watch— | in the | night.

Thou carriest them away as | with a | flood:
They | are— | as a | sleep.

In the morning they are like grass which | groweth | up:
In the morning it flourisheth, and groweth up;
In the evening it is cut | down, and | wither- | eth.

For we are consum-ed | by thine | anger;
And by thy | wrath— | are we | troubled.

Thou hast set our iniquities be- | fore— | thee;
Our secret sins in the | light of | thy— | countenance.

For all our days are passed away | in thy | wrath:
We spend our years as a | tale— | that is | told.

The days of our years are threescore years and ten;
And if by reason of strength they be | fourscore | years;

Yet is their strength labor and sorrow;
For it is soon cut off, | and we | fly a- | way.

No. 67. Single.

CHANTS—BURIAL OF THE DEAD.   375

No. 68.   Double.

BURIAL SERVICE.

M AN that is born of a woman hath but a short | time to | live, ‖
And is | full — | of — | trouble.

He cometh up like a flower and is | cut — | down ; ‖
He fleeth as it were a shadow, | and con- | tinueth | not.

In the midst of life we | are in | death. ‖ Of whom may we seek for succor but of
thee, O Lord, who for our | sins art | justly dis- | pleased?

Yet, O Lord God most mighty, O Lord most holy, O holy and most | merciful |
Savior, ‖ deliver us not into the bitter | pains of .. e- | ternal | death.

Thou knowest, Lord, the secrets | of our | hearts. ‖
Shut not thy merciful | ear — | to our | prayers.

But spare us, Lord most holy, O God most mighty, O holy and merciful Savior,
thou most worthy | Judge e- | ternal, ‖ suffer us not at our last hour for any
pains of | death to | fall from | thee.

No. 69.   Single.

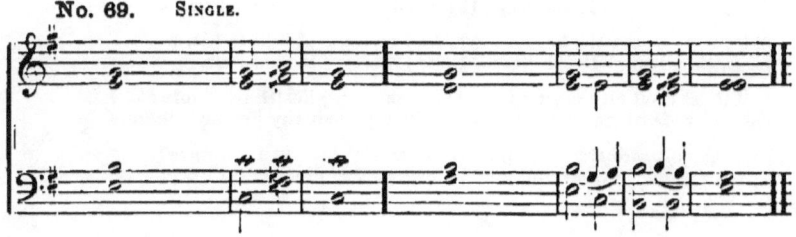

No. 70. Single.

"THY WILL BE DONE."

FATHER, I know thy ways are just, Although to | me un- | known;
  Oh, grant me grace thy love to trust, And | cry, " Thy | will be | done."

If thou shouldst hedge with thorns my path, Should wealth and | friends be | gone,
Still, with a firm and lively faith, I'll | cry, " Thy | will be | done."

Although thy steps I cannot trace, Thy sovereign | right I'll | own ;
And, as instructed by thy grace, I'll | cry, " Thy | will be | done."

'Tis sweet thus passively to lie Before thy | gracious | throne,
Concerning every thing to cry, " My | Father's | will·be | done."

No. 71. Single.

GOD OUR REFUGE.

DEAR Refuge of my weary soul, On thee, when | sorrows | rise;
  On thee, when waves of trouble roll, My | fainting | hope re- | lies.

To thee I tell each rising grief, For thou a- | lone canst | heal,
Thy word can bring a sweet relief For | ev'ry | pain I | feel.

Thy mercy-seat is open still,—Here let my | soul re- | treat;
With humble hope attend thy will, And | wait be- | neath thy | feet.

PLEADING FOR MERCY.

JESUS, and didst thou condescend, When vailed in | human | clay,
  To heal the sick, the lame, the blind, And | drive dis- | ease a- | way?

Didst thou regard the beggar's cry, And give the | blind to | see?
Jesus, thou Son of David, hear,—Have | mercy, | too, on | me.

And didst thou pity mortal woe, And sight and | health re- | store?
Then pity, Lord, and save my soul, Which | needs thy | mercy | more.

Didst thou regard thy servant's cry When sinking | in the | wave?
I perish, Lord! oh, save my soul! For | thou a- | lone canst | save.

No. 71. SINGLE.

RESIGNATION.

FRIEND after friend departs! Who hath not | lost a | friend?
  There is no union here of hearts, That finds not | here an | end:
Were this frail world our final rest, Living or | dying, | none were | blest.

Beyond the flight of time, Beyond the | reign of | death,
There surely is some blessed clime, Where life is | not a | breath;
Nor life's affections transient fire, Whose sparks fly | upward | and ex- | pire

There is a world above, Where parting | is un- | known;
A long eternity of love, Formed for the | good a- | lone;
And faith beholds the dying here, Translated | to that | glorious | sphere.

Thus star by star declines, Till all are | passed a- | way,
As morning high and higher shines To pure and | perfect | day:
Nor sink those stars in empty night, But lose them- | selves in | heaven's own | light.

No. 72. SINGLE.

DE PROFUNDIS. Ps. cxxx.

OUT of the depths have I cried unto | thee, O | Lord.
  Lord, hear my voice; let thine ears be attentive to the | voice .. of my | suppli- | — cations.

If thou, Lord, shouldst mark iniquities, O Lord, | who shall | stand?
But there is forgiveness with thee, that | thou — | mayest .. be | feared.

I wait for the Lord, my soul doth wait, and in his | word .. do I | hope.
My soul waiteth for the Lord more than they that watch for the morning, I say, | more than .. they that | watch .. for the | morning.

Let Israel hope in the Lord; for with the Lord there is mercy, and with him is | plenteous .. re- | demption.
And he shall redeem Israel from | all — | his in- | iquities.

No. 73. Double.

BENEDICITE, OMNIA OPERA DOMINI.

O ALL ye works of the Lord, | bless .. ye the | Lord ; ||
  Praise Him, and | magni- .. fy | Him .. for- | ever.
O ye Angels of the Lord, | bless .. ye the | Lord, ||
Praise Him, and | magni- .. fy | Him .. for- | ever.

O ye Heavens, | bless .. ye the | Lord ; ||
Praise Him, and | magni- .. fy | Him .. for- | ever.
O ye Waters that be above the firmament, | bless .. ye the | Lord ;
Praise Him, and | magni- .. fy | Him .. for- | ever.

O all ye Powers of the Lord, | bless .. ye the | Lord ; ||
Praise Him, and | magni- .. fy | Him .. for- | ever.
O ye Sun and Moon, | bless .. ye the | Lord ; ||
Praise Him, and | magni- .. fy | Him .. for- | ever.

O ye Stars of Heaven, | bless .. ye the | Lord ; ||
Praise Him, and | magni- .. fy | Him .. for- | ever.
O ye Showers and Dew, | bless .. ye the | Lord ; ||
Praise Him, and | magni- .. fy | Him .. for- | ever.

O ye Winds of God, | bless .. ye the | Lord ; ||
Praise Him, and | magni- .. fy | Him .. for- | ever.
O ye Fire and Heat, | bless .. ye the | Lord ; ||
Praise Him, and | magni- .. fy | Him .. for- | ever.
O ye Winter and Summer, | bless .. ye the | Lord ; ||
Praise Him and | magni- .. fy | Him .. for- | ever.
O ye Dews and Frosts, | bless .. ye the | Lord ; ||
Praise Him, and | magni- .. fy | Him .. for- | ever.
O ye Frost and Cold, | bless .. ye the | Lord ; ||
Praise Him, and | magni- .. fy | Him .. for- | ever.
O ye Ice and Snow, | bless .. ye the | Lord ; ||
Praise Him, and | magni- .. fy | Him .. for- | ever.
O ye Nights and Days, | bless .. ye the | Lord ; ||
Praise Him, and | magni- .. fy | Him .. for- | ever.
O ye Light and Darkness, | bless .. ye the | Lord ; ||
Praise Him, and magni- .. fy | Him .. for- | ever.
O ye Lightnings and Clouds, | bless .. ye the | Lord ; ||
Praise Him, and | magni- .. fy | Him .. for- | ever.

(Continued on next page.)

No. 74.   DOUBLE.

BENEDICITE.   (Continued from preceding page.)

OH, let the Earth | bless .. the | Lord ; ||
   Yea, let it praise Him, and | magni- .. fy | Him .. for- | ever.
O ye Mountains and Hills, | bless .. ye the | Lord; ||
Praise Him, and | magni- .. fy | Him .. for- | ever.
O all ye Green Things upon the earth, | bless .. ye the | Lord ; ||
Praise Him, and | magni- .. fy | Him .. for- | ever.

O ye Wells, | bless .. ye the | Lord ; ||
Praise Him and | magni- .. fy | Him .. for- | ever.
O ye Seas and Floods, | bless .. ye the | Lord ; ||
Praise Him, and | magni- .. fy | Him .. for- | ever.

O ye Whales, and all that move in the waters, | bless .. ye the | Lord ; ||
Praise Him, and | magni- .. fy | Him .. for- | ever.
O ye Fowls of the air, | bless .. ye the | Lord, ||
Praise Him, and | magni- .. fy | Him .. for- | ever.

O all ye Beasts and Cattle, | bless .. ye the | Lord ; ||
Praise Him, and magni- .. fy | Him .. for- | ever.
O ye Children of men, | bless .. ye the | Lord ; ||
Praise Him, and | magni- .. fy | Him .. for- | ever.

O let Israel | bless .. ye the | Lord ; ||
Praise Him, and | magni- .. fy | Him .. for- | ever.
O ye Priests of the Lord, | bless .. ye the | Lord ; ||
Praise Him, and | magni- .. fy | Him .. for- | ever.

O ye Servants of the Lord, | bless .. ye the | Lord ; ||
Praise Him, and | magni- .. fy | Him .. for- | ever.
O ye Spirits and Souls of the righteous, | bless .. ye the | Lord ; ||
Praise Him, and | magni- .. fy | Him .. for- | ever.

O ye Holy and Humble Men of Heart, | bless .. ye the | Lord ; ||
Praise Him, and | magni- .. fy | Him .. for- | ever.

Glory be to the Father, and | to the | Son, ||
And | to .. the | Holy | Ghost.
As it was in the beginning, is now, and | ever .. shall | be, ||
World with- | out .. end. | A- .. — | men.

380 ANTHEMS.

No. 1. PRAISE THE LORD.

No. 2. THANKSGIVING HYMN.

Con spirito.

Thy praise, O Lord, our thank-ful songs re-new, Thy mer-cies we with grate-ful hearts re-view; Thy glo-rious works of wis-dom, pow'r, and grace, Thy sov'-reign bless-ings to our fa-vor'd race; The ru-ling God our peace and free-dom prove, And the glad ti-dings of for-giv-ing love.

ANTHEMS.

No. 6. *CHRISTMAS NIGHT.

* Harmony of treble solo is after the style of A. Andre.

No. 7. PRAISE YE THE LORD.

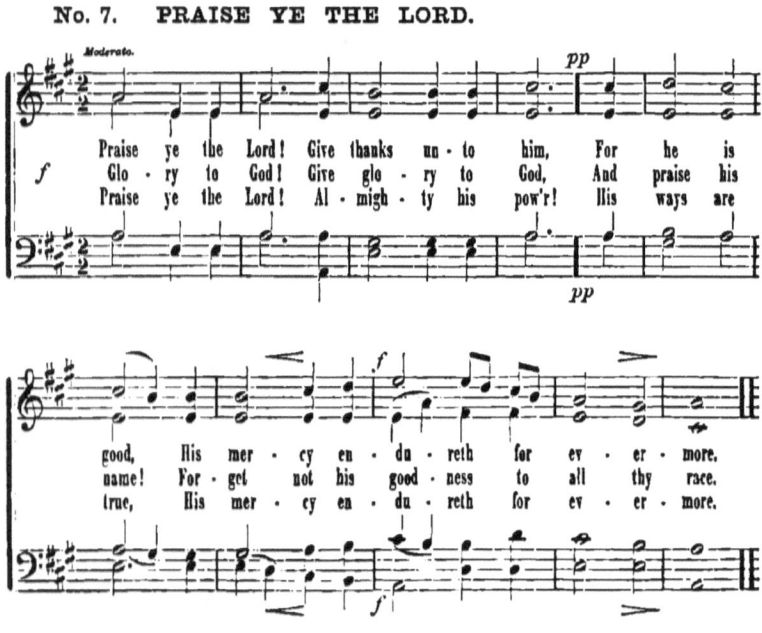

ANTHEMS.

No. 8. I WILL ARISE.

No. 11. HE SHALL COME DOWN LIKE RAIN.

No. 12. LAMENTATION.

ANTHEMS.

No. 13. DAUGHTER OF ZION.

No. 15. SANCTUS.

ANTHEMS.

No. 16. SANCTUS ET HOSANNA.

ANTHEMS.

No. 17. THE LORD THE UNIVERSAL KING.

ANTHEMS. 411

No. 20. SANCTUS ET GLORIA.

INDEX OF SUBJECTS.

THE FIGURES REFER TO THE NUMBERS OF THE HYMNS.

AFFLICTIONS, Blessings of, 507, 893.
 Faith under, 520, 521.
 From God, 118, 504.
 God a refuge in, 119, 504.
 Sanctified, 518.
ANGELS, Ministry of, 813, 814, 815, 817, 818.
 Songs of, 47, 146, 147, 149, 150.
 Sympathy of, 816.
ASPIRATIONS, Devout, 384, 543, 558, 559, 564, 570, 574, 575, 576, 577.
ASSURANCE, desired, 451, 554, 558.
AWAKENING, 282, 341, 359.

BACKSLIDERS admonished, 309, 536.
BACKSLIDING deplored, 435, 502, 534, 540, 541.
 Return from, 535.
BAPTISM, 673, 675, 676, 680, 684, 685, 702.
 of Infants, 670, 687, 688, 689.
BEATITUDES, 494.
BELIEVERS, Bearing the Cross, 524, 527.
 Blessedness of, 447, 452, 454, 455, 457, 458, 473, 495, 508, 661.
 Clinging to Christ, 444, 492.
 Death of, 903.
 Encouraged, 117, 447, 483, 497, 531, 772.
 Exhorted, 497, 498.
 Longing after God, 445, 512, 519, 546, 550.
 Peace of, 454, 455.
 Privileges of, 467.
 Rejoicing in God, 123, 124, 125, 128, 129, 420, 429, 453, 456, 457, 459, 461, 470, 474, 479, 485, 490, 491, 496, 500.
 Renouncing the World, 420, 426, 463, 579.
 Safety of, 107, 116, 119, 127, 130, 320, 513, 644, 895, 896.
 Union of, with Christ, 544.
 Unity of, 583, 586, 590.
BENEVOLENCE, 603, 854, 855.
BEREAVEMENT, 914.
BIBLE, 655, 656, 660.
 Inspiration of, 651, 653, 654, 659.

BIBLE, Love to, 7.
 Study of, 660.
 Value of, 162, 652, 658, 662, 663, 664.

CALVARY, 197.
CHARGE, the Christian's, 812.
CHARITY, 599, 851, 852, 853, 854, 855, 856.
CHEERFULNESS, 525.
CHILDREN, Baptism of, 667, 669, 670, 672.
 Christ's regard for, 683, 685.
 Exhorted, 289.
 Invited to Christ, 683, 685.
 Prayer for, 667, 670, 671, 672.
CHRIST, Advent of, 48, 143, 144, 145, 146, 147, 148, 149, 150, 151, 153, 154, 155, 228, 318.
 Advocate, our, 799.
 All-sufficiency of, 170, 195, 398, 537.
 Ascension of, 216, 699.
 Ashamed of, 423, 442.
 Coming to, 195, 342, 345, 346, 347, 351, 417, 418, 422, 425.
 Compassion of, 243.
 Condescension of, 178, 219, 243, 256, 304.
 Confessing, 423. See Confession.
 Conformity to. See Example of.
 Coronation of, 222, 223, 224.
 Cross of, 199, 265, 480, 484.
 Death of, 179, 181, 182, 189, 190, 192, 200, 201, 202.
 Deity of, 131, 132, 133, 134.
 Dependence on, 562.
 Exaltation of, 133, 216, 217, 218, 221, 222, 223, 224, 227, 814, 816.
 Example of, 157, 158, 159, 163, 164, 165, 854.
 Excellency of, 220, 249, 312, 463, 605.
 Following, 462.
 Forbearance of, 158.
 Fountain, 241.
 Fulfilled the law, 138.
 Glory of, 131, 132, 133, 136, 139, 141, 142, 222, 223, 224, 227.

419

INDEX OF SUBJECTS.

CHRIST, Hiding-place, our, 254.
  Honor to, 48, 133, 134, 137, 138.
  Humiliation of, 256.
  Impleaded, 196, 353, 379, 401, 405, 406.
  Incarnation of, 140.
  Intercessor, 225, 229, 230.
  Joy in, 177, 444, 460.
  Lamb, the, 705.
  Life, the, 253.
  Living for, 555.
  Longed for, 378
  Loveliness of, 170, 247, 248, 460.
  Love of, 160, 295, 563, 606.
  Love to, 448, 533, 538, 561, 602, 607, 604.
  Miracles of, 168.
  Mission of, 151, 152, 177, 243.
  Names of, 156, 160, 171, 172, 173, 174, 175, 176, 177, 235, 249, 253, 254, 398.
  Salvation through, 181, 189, 190, 191, 193, 195, 231, 232, 234, 236, 237, 240, 253, 254, 255, 295, 398, 399, 466, 486.
  Preciousness of, 226, 242, 247, 248, 250, 262, 405, 484, 486, 492, 608.
  Refuge, our, 398, 430, 440, 946.
  Reign of, 161, 740, 741, 742, 758, 763.
  Rejoicing in, 135, 262, 450, 476, 488, 489.
  Resurrection of, 203, 204, 205, 206, 207, 208, 209, 210, 211.
  Righteousness of, 468.
  Sacrifice of. *See Death of Christ and Redemption through Him.*
  Safety in, 262, 263, 405, 492.
  Second coming of, 282, 947, 948. *See Judgment.*
  Sufferings of, 178, 179, 180, 181, 182, 183, 184, 185, 186, 187, 188, 189, 190, 192, 193, 194, 199, 200, 201, 257, 700.
  Teachings of, 166.
  Transfiguration of, 167, 169.
  Trusting in, 428, 430, 441.
  Union with, 544.
CHRISTIAN Life, 516.
  Dangers of, 573.
  Difficulties of, 560.
CHRISTMAS. *See Christ, Advent of, and Angels, Songs of.*
CHURCH, Attendance at, 750, 755, 757.
  Beauty of, 773.
  Blessedness of, 747, 756, 770.
  Consecration of a, 739, 750, 753, 857, 858, 888.
  Delight in, 736, 738, 744, 748, 749, 774.
  Founding of a, 745, 762, 858.
  Officers, 764, 765.
  Prayer for, 759, 760, 819, 820, 821.
  Promises to, 743.
  Revival of, 745, 754, 819, 820, 821, 822.
  Safety of, 737, 743, 771.
  Seeking a minister, 723, 724.
  Uniting with, 587.

CHURCH, Unity of, 590, 751.
  Victory of, 761.
COMMUNION, 699.
  with God desired, 556, 557.
CONFESSION, 362, 374, 412, 876.
CONFIDENCE, 290, 609.
CONFIRMATION, 673, 674, 675, 677, 678, 679, 681, 682, 701, 702.
CONFLICT, Christian, 358, 505.
  Inward, 371.
CONSECRATION, 426, 668, 677, 678, 679.
CONTRITION, 365, 383.
CONVERSION, 684.
CONVICTION, 366.
COURAGE, Incitements to, 483, 514, 515.
CROSS, The, 524, 527.
  Glorying in, 246, 527, 531.
  of Christ, 185, 188, 200.
CRUCIFIXION, 183, 185, 199.

DARKNESS, Spiritual, 212, 499, 500, 502, 503, 508, 509, 510, 514, 515, 517, 525.
DEAD, The Pious, 908.
DEATH, Bed of, 909, 941.
  Disarmed, 902, 904, 915, 928.
  Gain of, 919, 924, 925.
  General, 900, 901, 917.
  of an Infant, 905, 914.
  of a Youth, 907.
  of a Parent, 916.
  of a Pastor, 716, 731, 906.
  of Friends, 916, 944.
  of Saints, 903, 918, 922, 923, 924, 929, 930, 937, 938, 939, 940, 942, 945.
  Preparation for, 899, 943.
  Thoughts on, 894, 895, 897, 926, 935, 936, 941.
DECLENSIONS, 502, 539, 540, 541, 819.
DEPRAVITY, 565.
DESPONDENCY, 515, 517.
DEVOTION, 804, 807, 808, 809.
DISMISSION, 953, 954, 959, 961, 963.

EARNESTNESS, 560.
EARTH, its Possessions, Vanity of, 330.
EASTER. *See Christ, Resurrection of.*
ETERNITY, 327, 344, 894, 911.
EVENING, 632, 862, 863, 865, 874, 875, 881, 882, 883, 884, 885, 886, 891.
EXAMINATION urged, 313, 553.
EXPOSTULATION, 287, 292, 293, 294, 299, 306, 308, 323, 324, 325, 337.

FAITH, 428, 430, 434, 437, 438, 439, 446, 595.
FAREWELL, 959, 960.
FASTING, Public, 892.
FEAST, Gospel, 297, 298.
FELLOWSHIP, 581, 582, 583, 586, 587, 588, 589, 590, 593, 958.
FORGIVENESS, Prayer for, 361, 376, 380, 416.
  Rejoicing in, 469, 493.

INDEX OF SUBJECTS. 421

GETHSEMANE, 178, 180, 201.
GOD, All in all, 27.
  All-sufficient, 419, 429, 529.
  Almighty, 84, 116.
  Compassion of, 105.
  Confidence in, 407, 609.
  Eternity of, 34.
  Glory of, 4, 9, 11, 23, 30, 88.
  Glory to, 962.
  Goodness of, 8, 81, 89, 91, 97, 98, 115, 126.
  Incomprehensible, 28, 39, 77, 104.
  Justice and Holiness of, 41.
  Light, our, 529.
  Love of, 83, 264.
  Majesty of, 22, 26, 31, 32, 42, 50, 87.
  Mercy of, 15, 17, 482.
  Omnipresence of, 38, 49, 80, 86.
  Omniscience of, 82, 86.
  Perfections of, 77, 78, 79, 93, 530.
  Spirituality of, 85.
  Sought, 43, 407, 512, 519.
  Trust in, 44, 53, 102, 106, 109, 111, 122, 129, 290, 322, 427, 431, 433, 435, 449, 477, 481, 492, 511, 526.
  Truth of, 530.
  Works of, 90, 94, 95, 745.
GOOD WORKS, 599.
GOSPEL, Excellency of, 272, 464.
  Feast, 297, 298.
  Invitations of, 280, 283, 284, 286, 291, 296, 297, 302, 315, 316, 317, 318, 319, 322, 343, 380.
  Spread of, 767, 768, 813, 844, 845, 846.
GRACE, 36, 243, 245, 251, 252, 258, 317, 475, 481, 489, 637.
GRATITUDE, 487.
GRAVE, The, 920.

HARDNESS lamented, 367.
HEATHEN, 832.
HEAVEN, Anticipations of, 338, 465, 617, 618, 620, 621, 622, 623, 625, 626, 627, 628, 629, 630, 631, 633, 634, 637, 638.
  Choosing, 424.
  Glory of, 56, 614, 616, 624, 615, 925, 957.
  Holiness of, 612.
  Home, there, 617, 630, 632, 636, 639, 647.
  Longed for, 613, 615, 617, 626, 631, 635, 642, 643.
  Nearness of, 446, 623, 637.
  Rest in, 627, 530, 639, 641, 648, 650.
  Saints in, 610, 611, 629, 640.
HOLY Spirit, The Comforter, 266, 269, 273.
  Grieving, 271, 305, 408.
  Praise for, 270.
  Prayer for, 13, 52, 54, 57, 68, 72, 268, 370, 408, 528, 552, 568, 676, 784, 822, 824, 833.
  Presence of, 273.
  Strivings of, 305.

HOLY Spirit, Witness of, 578.
  Work of, 267.
HOPE in Affliction, 520, 521.
  in Darkness, 508, 511, 512, 513.
HUMILIATION, Day of, 877, 878.
HUMILITY, 601.

INCONSTANCY, 540.
INSTALLATION, 727.
INVOCATIONS, 52, 54, 55, 56, 57, 58, 59, 61, 62, 63, 64, 65, 67, 68, 69, 70, 73, 75, 807.
ISRAEL, Prayer for, 830, 831, 841.

JOY, 471, 472, 478, 542, 649.
JUBILEE, 740, 752, 889, 890.
JUDGMENT, 307, 947, 948, 949.
  Christ coming to, 282, 947, 949.
  Final, 96, 282, 933, 934, 948, 950, 951, 952.
JUSTIFICATION. *See Forgiveness.*

KINGDOM of God, 746.
  Prayer for its coming, 741.
  Progress of, 768, 769, 828.
  Triumph of, 740, 752, 767.

LIFE, Brevity of, 334, 570, 632, 900, 910, 911, 912.
  Christian, 516.
  Uncertainty of, 913.
  Vanity of, 632, 633, 909, 912, 913, 941.
LORD'S DAY, 781, 783, 786, 789, 791, 795, 796.
  Delight in, 775, 787, 788, 792.
  Evening of, 777, 781, 785, 790, 797.
  Morning of, 776, 782.
LORD'S SUPPER, 690, 693, 694, 695, 697, 699, 700, 702, 703, 705, 706.
  Christ present in, 691.
  Christ remembered at, 692, 698.
  Institution of, 696.
LOVE, Brotherly, 580, 581, 583, 584, 585, 591, 592.
  demanded, 594, 596, 600.
  Redeeming, 244, 245.

MAN, Vanity of, as mortal, 898.
MEDITATION, 549.
MERCY Implored, 375, 389, 390, 391.
  Seat of, 331, 385, 443, 801.
MILLENNIUM, 740, 741, 763, 767.
MINISTERS, Commission to, 707, 708, 712, 713, 714, 717, 718, 730, 850.
  Death of, 716, 731, 906.
  Farewell, 715.
  Meetings of, 719, 728, 735.
  Ordination of, 711, 727.
  Prayer for, 709, 710, 720, 722, 732, 733.
  Scarcity of, 723, 724, 832.
  Sickness of, 725.
  Welcome to, 726.
MINISTRY, The, 721, 729.

MIRACLES, 168.
MISSIONARIES, Farewell of, 847.
   Prayer for, 738, 829, 839.
MISSIONS, 766, 827, 828, 832, 833, 834, 835, 836, 840, 841, 842, 844, 845, 848.
   Domestic, 838.
MORNING, 18, 37, 40, 114, 115, 861, 864, 870, 871, 873, 891.

NEW YEAR, 859, 860, 887.

PENITENCE, 345, 346, 347, 348, 349, 350, 352, 354, 355, 356, 357, 358, 359, 360, 361, 362, 363, 364, 368, 369, 371, 372, 373, 375, 377, 381, 382, 383, 384, 385, 386, 387, 388, 389, 390, 391, 392, 393, 394, 395, 396, 397, 398, 403, 404, 409, 410, 411, 413, 414, 415, 505, 534, 536, 545.
PERSEVERANCE desired, 539.
PRAISE, 21, 33, 46, 47, 143, 849.
   Call to, 1, 14, 19, 20, 35, 51.
   for Divine Blessings, 2, 110, 850.
   for Divine Glories, 3, 6, 7, 12.
   for Divine Goodness, 5, 10, 17, 24, 29, 113, 487.
   for Divine Mercies, 25, 112, 139.
PRAYER, 798, 799, 800, 801, 802, 803, 804, 806, 807, 810.
   Call to, 342.
   for Divine Grace, 55, 56, 74, 369, 375, 393, 413, 416, 439, 547, 548, 566, 567, 571, 572, 825.
   for National Prosperity, 877.
PROVIDENCE, 98, 99, 103, 104, 108, 118, 119, 120, 121, 129.

REDEMPTION, 295.
   Praise for, 239, 259.
   Wonders of, 238, 260.
RESIGNATION, 100, 921.
REST, 288, 648, 650, 720, 793, 946.
RESURRECTION, 927, 928, 931.
   longed for, 921.
RETIREMENT, 804, 805.
REVIVAL, Prayer for, 824, 825, 826.

SABBATH. *See Lord's Day.*
   The eternal, 794.

SAINTS, Example of, 619.
   in Heaven, 620, 932.
SALVATION, 252.
   for all, 226, 262.
SEASONS, 101, 126.
   Spring, 45.
   Winter, 826.
SOUL, The, 92.
   how to Win, 198.
SUPPLICATION, 52, 60, 63, 73, 75, 76.
   for Divine Presence, 66, 69, 70.
   for Grace in Trials, 71.
   for the Holy Spirit. *See Holy Spirit.*
SIN, Burden of, 872.
   Deceit of, 176, 311, 314, 551.
SINNERS, Admonished, 274, 278, 280, 294, 300, 312, 313, 321, 824, 825, 327, 328, 329, 335, 336, 337.
   Invitations to, 274, 275, 276, 277, 279, 284, 286, 291, 296, 297, 298, 302, 822, 831, 832.
   Warnings to, 281, 282, 285, 303, 305, 307, 309, 310, 311, 319, 321, 325, 333, 337, 340, 342.

THANKSGIVING, 879, 880.
TIME, Flight of, 339, 909, 910.
TRANSFIGURATION, 167, 169.
TRIALS, 371, 496, 499, 501, 502, 503, 504, 505, 506, 507, 508, 510, 514, 515, 518, 522, 523, 525, 527, 540, 541, 542.
TRUSTING in God, 427. *See Confidence.*

WARNING, 289, 306, 342.
WHITSUNTIDE, 266, 784.
WORD, The, 654, 655, 657.
   Light of, 657, 659, 666.
   Prayer for Success of, 663, 834, 835.
WORKS, 438, 595, 596, 597, 603, 604.
WORLD, renounced, 432, 436, 569.
WORSHIP, Meeting for, 755, 757.

YOUTH Called, 326.
   Exhorted, 289, 301.

ZEAL, 600.
ZION, Prayer for, 759, 820, 821, 836.
   Prospects of, 767, 768, 769.

INDEX OF FIRST LINES.

THE FIGURES HERE REFER TO THE NUMBERS OF THE HYMNS.

First Line	Author	Hymn
According to thy gracious	Montgomery	692
A charge to keep I have	C. Wesley	812
Acquaint thyself quickly, O sinner	Knox	336
Affliction is a stormy deep	Cotton	521
Again the Lord of life and	Barbauld	782
Again we sinners come to thee	Seiss	75
Ah, what can I, a sinner, do	Hyde	356
Ah, whither should I go	C. Wesley	372
Alas, alas, how blind I've been	Strong	359
Alas, and did my Savior bleed	Watts	190
Alas, what hourly dangers rise	Steele	522
All hail the power of Jesus'	Duncan	222
All-powerful, self-existent	Salisb. Coll.	84
All ye who laugh and sport with death		310
Almighty Father, gracious Lord	Steele	110
Almighty God, thy piercing	Beddome	82
Almighty God, thy word is	N. Y. Coll.	665
Almighty Sovereign of the skies		29
Amazing grace, how sweet the	Newton	481
Amazing sight, the Savior stands		299
Am I a soldier of the cross	Watts	501
Am I called, and can it be	C. Wesley	417
Amidst a world of hopes	Unit. Coll.	552
Am I the splendors of thy state	Steele	83
And am I born to die	C. Wesley	935
And am I only born to die?	C. Wesley	941
And are we yet alive	C. Wesley	585
And art thou with us	Doddridge	111
And didst thou, Jesus	Curtis's Coll.	406
And is the gospel peace and	Steele	165
And is there, Lord, a rest		794
And let our bodies part	C. Wesley	586
And let this feeble body fail	C. Wesley	627
And must this body die	Watts	936
And now another day is	From Herzog	882
And shall we still be	N. Y. Coll.	278
And will the great eternal	Doddridge	858
And will the Judge descen l	Doddridge	321
And will the Lord thus	Steele	402
And wilt thou yet be found	C. Wesley	371
Angels from the realms of	Montgomery	318
Angels, ro'l the rock away	Scott	207
Angels, where'er we go	C. Wesley, alt.	817
Another day is past	Curtis	865
Another fleeting day has gone		872
Another six days' work is	Stennett	795
Arise, my soul, arise	C. Wesley	225
Arise, my soul, my joyful	Watts	456
Arise, my soul, with	Montgomery	873
Arise, ye people, and adore	Lyte	223
Arm of the Lord, awake	C. Wesley	759
Around the Savior's lofty throne	Kelly	133
Asleep in Jesus, blessed	Mrs. Mackay	929
As on the cross the Savior	Stennett	404
As pants the hart for	Tate and Brady	512
Assembled at thy great	Collyer	827
As the eagle fondly hovers	Gerhardt	130
Astonished and distressed	Toplady	565
Author of life and bliss	N. Y. Coll.	231
Awake, and sing the song	Hammond	476
Awake, awake, O sluggish	Heginbotham	306
Awake, awake to prayer		812
Awake, our souls, away our	Watts	638
Awake, my soul, and with the	Ken	871
Awake, my soul, in joyful lays	Medley	264
Awake, my soul, stretch	Doddridge	618
Away from every mortal care	Watts	755
Backsliders, who your	Rippon's Coll.	309
Band of brethren, who are	Schmucker	719
Before Jehovah's awful	Watts, alt.	1
Before thy high and holy throne		364
Before thy throne, Almighty	Winchell	711
Behold a stranger at the door	Gregg	304
Behold the amazing sight	Doddridge	202
Behold, the blind their sight	Watts	168
Behold the expected time draw	Yoke	828
Behold, the mountain of the	Logan	752
Behold the Savior of	S. Wesley	189
Behold, what condescending	Fawcett	685
Behold, where in a mortal form	Enfield	157
Be merciful to me, O God	Ryle	523
Beneath our feet and o'er our	Heber	333
Beside the gospel pool	Newton	368
Be thou near us, blessed Savior		229
Be thou, O God, by night and day		73
Be thou, O Lord, my treasure here		569
Beyond the glitt'ring starry	Finch	816

INDEX OF FIRST LINES.

	HYMN
Bless'd be the Father and his....... *Watts*	33
Blest are the humble souls who.... *Watts*	494
Blest are the undefiled in heart.... *Watts*	458
Blest be the tie that binds......... *Fawcett*	583
Blest hour, when virtuous....... *Houghton*	629
Blest is the man, forever blest...... *Watts*	469
Blest is the man whose.......... *Barbauld*	853
Blest is the man whose heart.. *Strapham*	851
Blest Jesus, come now gently....... *Watts*	74
Blest Jesus, come thou gently down.....	825
Blest Jesus, when my........ *Heginbotham*	460
Blest Jesus, when thy....... *Heginbotham*	265
Blest morning, whose first.......... *Watts*	209
Blow ye the trumpet, blow........ *Toplady*	889
Bread of heav'n, on thee I feed.. *Conder*	175
Bright as the sun's............. *Vill. Hymns*	760
Bright King of glory, dreadful..... *Watts*	131
Bright source of everlasting....... *Boden*	595
Broad is the road that leads to..... *Watts*	328
Brother in Christ and well....... *C. Wesley*	673
By the thoughtless world.......... *Collyer*	162
By various maxims, forms, and.. *Newton*	255
Calm on the listening ear of night. *Sears*	149
Children of the heavenly King... *Cennick*	447
Christians and brethren, ere. ... *K. White*	959
Christ, the Lord, is ris'n........ *Cudworth*	205
Church of the everlasting God.... *Bonar*	773
Come, blessed Savior, from.. *Vest. Songs*	76
Come, blessed Spirit, source.... *Beddome*	59
Come, dearest Lord, and feed...... *Mason*	779
Come, every pious heart.......... *Stennett*	142
Come, gracious Spirit, heavenly. *Browne*	268
Come, guilty sinners, come and see......	184
Come hither, all ye weary souls... *Watts*	284
Come, Holy Ghost, come from on... *Reed*	676
Come, Holy Spirit, calm my....... *Burder*	57
Come, Holy Spirit, come............. *Hart*	370
Come, Holy Spirit, heavenly dove. *Watts*	54
Come, humble sinner, in whose..... *Jones*	332
Come in, thou blessed of the Lord. *Kelly*	582
Come, let our mournful songs...... *Watts*	183
Come, let us lift our voices... *Watts, alt.*	219
Come, let us join our.... *Montgomery, alt.*	681
Come, let us join our cheerful...... *Watts*	221
Come, let us sound her........ *Drummond*	856
Come, Lord, and warm each.. ...... *Steele*	56
Come, my soul, thy suit prepare..*Newton*	377
Come, O my soul, in sacred..... *Blacklock*	31
Come, O thou King of all thy....... *Steele*	43
Come, sacred Spirit, from.. ....*Doddridge*	824
Come, said Jesus' sacred........ *Barbauld*	291
Come, Savior Jesus, from above.. *Byrom*	444
Come, see on bloody.......... *Rippon's Col.*	700
Come, sinners, to the gospel.... *C. Wesley*	275
Come sound his praise abroad...... *Watts*	14
Come, thou almighty King... *Madan's Col.*	819
Come, thou fount of every....... *Robinson*	487
Come, thou Savior of our.. *From Luther*	48
Come, weary souls, with sins....... *Steele*	288
Come, ye disconsolate, where'er... *Moore*	831
Come, ye sinners, poor and......... *Hart*	315

	HYMN
Come, ye that love the Lord........ *Watts*	471
Come, ye weary sinners,.... *Vill. Hymns*	380
Commit thou all thy griefs..... *J. Wesley*	322
Courage, my soul, while God is... *Watts*	513
Daughter of Zion, from the. *Montgomery*	754
Day of judgment, day of.......... *Newton*	948
Dearest of all the names above.... *Watts*	242
Dear Father, to thy mercy-seat.... *Steele*	443
Dear Friend of friendless.......... *R. Hill*	414
Dear Jesus, let thy pitying.. *Vill. Hymns*	401
Dear Jesus, prostrate at thy..... *Stennett*	347
Dear Lord, my best desires........ *Cowper*	418
Dear Refuge of my weary soul..... *Steele*	407
Dear Savior, if these lambs .... *Hyde*	671
Dear Savior, when my thoughts.... *Steele*	405
Deep are the wounds which sin. ... *Steele*	173
Delay not, delay not, O sinner.. *Hastings*	335
Depth of mercy, can there be. . *C. Wesley*	399
Do not I love thee, O my...... *Doddridge*	561
Draw near, O Son of God....... *C. Wesley*	720
Dread Sov'reign, let mine evening.. *Watts*	884
Early, my God, without delay...... *Watts*	749
Earth has engrossed my love too. . *Watts*	613
Earthly joys no longer please us. . *Watts*	263
Earth's stormy night will soon.. *Hastings*	623
Eat, drink, in mem'ry of........ *N. Y. Col.*	698
Enslaved by sin, and bound in...... *Steele*	237
Equip me for the war............. *C. Wesley*	567
Ere the blue heav'ns were........... *Watts*	132
Eternal and immortal King.... *Doddridge*	22
Eternal God, almighty cause...... *Browne*	27
Eternal power, whose high abode. *Watts*	30
Eternal Source of every joy.. *Doddridge*	24
Eternal Spirit, Source of light.... *Davies*	13
Eternal Spirit, 'twas thy breath. ... *Scott*	651
Eternal Spirit, we confess......... *Watts*	267
Eternity is just at hand........... *Steele*	327
Eternity, terrific word .... *From Rist*	344
Every fallen soul by sinning..............	260
Exalted high at God's right...... *Duncan*	982
Exert thy power, thy rights .... *Yoke*	766
Fain would my soul with wonder. *Knight*	478
Fair shines the morning..... *Heginbotham*	890
Faith adds new charms to.......... *Turner*	437
Far from affliction, toil, and.. *Vill. Hymns*	906
Far from my tho'ts, vain world.... *Watts*	788
Far from these narrow scenes of... *Steele*	645
Far from the world, O Lord, I... *Cowper*	805
Far from thy fold, O God, my ... *Tatlock*	429
Father, at thy call I come....... *Stennett*	373
Father divine, the Savior...... *Doddridge*	164
Father divine, thy piercing ...... *Cowper*	808
Father, God, who seest in.. *Rippon's Col,*	416
Father, how wide thy glory shines.. *Watts*	4
Father, I bless thy gentle hand.... *Watts*	507
Father, in whom we live........ *C. Wesley*	16
Father of all our mercies, thou... *Urwick*	71
Father of faithful Abra'm, hear.. *Wesley*	830
Father of glory, to thy name ...... *Watts*	6

INDEX OF FIRST LINES. 425

	HYMN
Father of heaven, whose love. *Bickersteth*	58
Father of mercies, bow thine....*Beddome*	710
Father of mercies, God of love....*Raffles*	415
Father of mercies, in thy......*Doddridge*	721
Father of mercies, in thy word.....*Steele*	657
Father, Son, and Holy Ghost..*C. Wesley*	426
Father, thy paternal care.......*N. Y. Col.*	427
Friend after friend departs..*Montgomery*	944
Forever blessed be the Lord......... *Watts*	270
Forget thyself, Christ bade......*Hastings*	343
Fountain of mercy, God of love............	113
Frequent the day of God..........*Browne*	781
From all that dwell below the......*Watts*	20
From Calv'ry's sacred ...*S. S. Schmucker*	735
From ev'ry stormy wind that.....*Stowell*	801
From Greenland's icy mountains..*Heber*	840
From his low bed of mortal.......*Collyer*	919
From this world's joys and.......*Bowden*	639
Give me the wings of faith to rise..*Watts*	620
Give thanks to God most high......*Watts*	143
Give to the Lord immortal praise..*Watts*	25
Give to the Lord, ye sons of fame. *Watts*	35
Give to the winds thy fears.*From Gerhard*	122
Glorious things of thee are.......*Newton*	770
Glory be to God on high..........*N. Y. Col.*	46
Glory to God the Father's name....*Heber*	962
Glory to God, who reigns.........*Needham*	152
Glory to thee, my God, this night..*Kenn*	869
Go, and the Savior's grace ....*Morell*	714
God in the gospel of his Son....*Beddome*	654
God is a Spirit, just and wise....... *Watts*	78
God is love; his mercy brightens.*Bowring*	485
God is my light, never ......*Hengstenberg*	529
God is my strong salvation..*Montgomery*	290
God is the refuge of his saints.....*Watts*	102
God moves in a mysterious way. *Cowper*	104
God, my supporter and my hope... *Watts*	477
God of eternity, from thee....*Doddridge*	912
God of mercy, God of grace...*J. Taylor*	874
God of mercy, hear our prayer. *Campbell*	667
God of my life, to thee belong......*Scott*	98
God of my life, whose gracious power...	119
God of my mercy and my praise..*Watts*	158
God of our lives, thy constant..*Doddridge*	860
God of the morning, at whose..... *Watts*	861
God of the nations, bow thine...*Hastings*	839
Go, friends of Jesus, and proclaim... *Toke*	712
Go, holy Book, thou word divine	655
Go, labor on, spend and be spent. *Bonar*	604
Go to dark Gethsemane......*Montgomery*	201
Go thro' the gates, 'tis God commands..	708
Go watch and pray, thou canst not tell.	342
Go, ye heralds of salvation......*Baldwin*	718
Grace, 'tis a charming sound..*Doddridge*	475
Gracious Lord, incline......*Rippon's Col.*	378
Gracious Spirit, love divine. ......*Stocker*	67
Greatest of beings, Source of life..*Dyer*	26
Great God, and wilt thou... *Vestry Songs*	435
Great God, as seasons........*Camp's Col.*	101
Great God, at whose all-......*Gents. Mag.*	2
Great God, before thy mercy...*Beddome*	385

	HYMN
Great God, how infinite art thou... *Watts*	39
Great God, indulge my humble.... *Watts*	550
Great God, in vain man's narrow. *Kippis*	28
Great God, my early vows to.*Mrs. Rowe*	116
Great God, now condescend........*Fellows*	687
Great God of wonders, all thy..... *Watts*	493
Great God, to thee my evening.....*Steele*	874
Great God, to what a glorious..... *Watts*	814
Great God, the nations of..*Tate & Brady*	835
Great God, we sing that........*Doddridge*	859
Great God, what do I see and.....*Luther*	96
Great God, what hosts of angels.*Stennett*	813
Great is the Lord our God..........*Watts*	737
Great Maker of unnumbered........*Dyer*	878
Great was the day, the joy was.... *Watts*	266
Guide me, O thou great Jehovah..*Oliver*	526
Had I the tongues of Greeks and. *Watts*	599
Hail, boundless love, that first...*Brewer*	254
Hail, great Creator, wise.....*Gents. Mag.*	8
Hail, my ever-blessed Jesus....*Wingrove*	486
Hail, thou long-expected Jesus..*C. Wesley*	228
Hail, thou once-despised Jesus.*Bakewell*	227
Hail to the Lord's anointed..*Montgomery*	177
Happy is he whose early years...........	686
Happy soul, thy days are.......*C. Wesley*	940
Happy the heart where graces..... *Watts*	594
Happy the hours, the golden days. *Watts*	510
Happy the man whose wishes........*Steele*	455
Hark, from on high a solemn..*N. Y. Col.*	908
Hark, from the tombs a doleful.... *Watts*	897
Hark, my soul, it is the Lord.....*Cowper*	607
Hark, the glad sound, the ......*Doddridge*	145
Hark, the song of jubilee....*Montgomery*	740
Hark, the voice of love.....*Rippon's Col.*	193
Hark, 'tis our heav'nly ....*Doddridge*	483
Hark, 'tis the Savior's voice I......*Smith*	286
Hark, what celestial...*Salisb. Col., alt.*	144
Hark, what triumphant strains are these	761
Hasten, Lord, the glorious time.....*Lyte*	741
Hasten, O sinner, to be wise.........*Scott*	285
Hear, gracious Lord, my humble...*Steele*	593
Hear, O sinner, mercy hails you. ...*Reed*	319
Hearts of stone, relent, relent.*C. Wesley*	199
Hear what the voice from heaven. *Watts*	922
He dies, the friend of sinners. ... *Watts*	186
He lives, the great Redeemer lives.*Steele*	235
Here, at thy cross, my dying Lord. *Watts*	188
Here, at thy table, Lord, we....*Stennett*	695
Here, in thy name, eternal..*Montgomery*	857
He that goeth forth with..........*Hastings*	772
High in yonder realms of light...*Raffles*	610
High let us swell our tuneful..*N. Y. Col.*	146
High on a hill of dazzling light.... *Watts*	815
Holy and reverend is the..*Rippon's Col.*	41
Holy Ghost, with light divine........*Reed*	61
Hosanna to the royal Son.......... *Watts*	137
Hosanna to the Son................. *Watts*	233
Hosanna with a cheerful......*Watts, alt.*	125
How are thy servants blest, O....*Addison*	107
How beauteous are their feet....... *Watts*	729
How blest the righteous when.*Barbauld*	930

INDEX OF FIRST LINES.

	HYMN
How blest the sacred tie that..*Barbauld*	580
How calm and beautiful the......*Hastings*	211
How cheering the thought that the........	818
How condescending and how kind. *Watts*	244
How did my heart rejoice to hear. *Watts*	748
How do thy mercies close me..*C. Wesley*	636
How firm a foundation............*Kennedy*	644
How glorious is the land we seek..*Bonar*	624
How great, how terrible that God..*Davies*	933
How happy are the young who....*Logan*	661
How happy, gracious Lord, are..*C. Wesley*	491
How happy is the pilgrim's......*J. Wesley*	490
How long shall death the......*Watts, alt.*	928
How lovely, how divinely sweet....*Steele*	789
How lost was my condition.......*Newton*	176
How oft, alas, this wretched heart.*Steele*	535
How sad and awful is my state..*Cennick*	358
How shall the young secure their. *Watts*	660
How short and hasty is our life.... *Watts*	570
How sweet and heav'nly is the.....*Swain*	591
How sweetly flow'd the gospel..*Bowring*	166
How sweet the name of Jesus....*Newton*	247
How sweet to leave the world......*Kelly*	757
How sweet the hour when man retires	803
How tedious and tasteless the....*Newton*	537
How vain are all things here........ *Watts*	573
How various and how new.........*Stennett*	470
I asked the Lord that I might....*Newton*	509
If human kindness meets return....*Noel*	703
If 'tis sweet to mingle where..*Sel. Hymns*	957
I hear a voice that comes from far..*Kelly*	464
I know that my Redeemer lives..*Medley*	216
I'll praise my Maker whilst I've... *Watts*	12
I lay my sins on Jesus.................*Bonar*	195
I love the Lord, but ah, how far.........	506
I love thy Zion, Lord...............*Dwight*	736
I love to steal a while away........*Browne*	804
I'm not ashamed to own my Lord. *Watts*	442
Indulgent Father! by whose care.........	881
Indulgent Father! how ...... *Vill. Hymns*	9
Indulgent God, to thee I raise....*Francis*	466
Indulgent God, to thee we...*Griffin's Sel.*	829
Indulgent Sovereign of the ...*Doddridge*	821
In duties and in sufferings too..*Beddome*	159
Infinite grace, and can it be........*Tucker*	238
I now have found, for hope of......*Rothe*	492
In sleep's serene oblivion...*Hawkesworth*	870
In sweet, exalted strains....*B. Francis*	858
I saw beyond the tomb..............*Dwight*	282
I send the joys of earth away....... *Watts*	432
I thirst, but not as once I did......*Cowper*	541
I thirst, thou wounded Lamb...*J. Wesley*	544
In thy great name, O Lord, we..*Hoskins*	68
In vain our fancy strives to........*Newton*	923
In vain the world's alluring smile..*Steele*	554
In vain would boasting reason.*N. Y. Col.*	236
I was a grov'ling creature once...*Cowper*	450
I would, but cannot sing............*Newton*	367
I would not live alway..........*Muhlenberg*	643
Jehovah God! thy gracious...*Thompson*	38

	HYMN
Jehovah's grace, how full, how..*Hoskins*	251
Jerusalem, my happy home......*Unknown*	617
Jesus, and shall it ever be..........*Gregg*	423
Jesus, full of all compassion......*Turner*	396
Jesus, if still the same thou....*C. Wesley*	394
Jesus, if still thou art to-day...*C. Wesley*	353
Jesus, I my cross have taken.........*Lyte*	527
Jesus, in thy transporting name ...*Steele*	135
Jesus invites his saints............... *Watts*	706
Jesus is gone above the skies....... *Watts*	699
Jesus, lover of my soul .... *C. Wesley*	398
Jesus, my Lord, how rich......*Doddridge*	852
Jesus, my Lord, my life, my light.*Steele*	136
Jesus, my Savior and my God,...*Stennett*	589
Jesus, my Savior, Brother........*C. Wesley*	562
Jesus, my strength, my hope...*C. Wesley*	566
Jesus, our triumphant head,....*N. Y. Col.*	206
Jesus, save my dying soul....*Spir. Songs*	379
Jesus shall reign where'er the sun. *Watts*	758
Jesus, thou dear redeeming....*C. Wesley*	64
Jesus, thy blessings are not few... *Watts*	272
Jesus, thy blood and..............*J. Wesley*	468
Jesus, thy boundless love to....*C. Wesley*	563
Jesus, thy wandering sheep.....*C. Wesley*	724
Jesus, we rest in thee.........................	946
Jesus, where'er thy people meet.*Cowper*	65
Join all the glorious names .... *Watts*	141
Joy to the world, the Lord is ...... *Watts*	148
Just as I am, without ...*Charlotte Elliott*	425
Kindred in Christ, for his dear...*Newton*	581
Know, my soul, thy full salvation..*Grant*	575
Laden with guilt and full of fears. *Watts*	663
Lamb of God, for sinners slain............	422
Lamb of God, we fall before thee.........	262
Lamp of our feet, whereby we...*Barton*	664
Let all the heathen writers join..... *Watts*	658
Let all who truly bear............*C. Wesley*	705
Let av'rice, borne from shore to.*Stennett*	662
Let carnal minds the world.........*Newton*	436
Let earth and heaven agree.....*C. Wesley*	226
Let every ear attend................*Watts, alt.*	277
Let others boast how strong they. *Watts*	106
Let pharisees of high esteem .... *Watts*	596
Let the high heavens your......*N. Y. Col.*	89
Let the whole race of............*Watts, alt.*	44
Let thoughtless thousands..........*Hoskins*	535
Let Zion's watchmen all.........*Doddridge*	713
Life is a span, a fleeting hour........*Steele*	905
Life is the time to serve the Lord. *Watts*	303
Lo, he comes, with clouds...........*Oliver*	947
Long as I live I'll bless thy name. *Watts*	7
Look up, ye saints, with sweet surprise.	763
Lord, all I am is known to thee...*Watts*	80
Lord, at thy feet in dust I lie....*Browne*	381
Lord, at thy feet I prostrate fall.*Cennick*	361
Lord, at thy table I behold........*Stennett*	693
Lord, cause thy face to shine on us......	705
Lord, didst thou die, and not..*Cruttenden*	428
Lord, dismiss us with thy..........*Burder*	953
Lord, how delightful 'tis to see.... *Watts*	790

INDEX OF FIRST LINES. 427

	HYMN
Lord, I am thine, entirely thine...*Davies*	674
Lord, I am vile, conceived in sin..*Watts*	362
Lord, in the morning thou shalt...*Watts*	40
Lord, I would spread my sore......*Watts*	387
Lord, let thy goodness lead..*Pratt's Col.*	877
Lord of hosts, to thee we.....*Montgomery*	739
Lord of my life, oh, may thy.......*Steele*	112
Lord of the church, we humbly pray...	732
Lord of the Sabbath and its light........	791
Lord of the Sabbath, hear.....*Doddridge*	786
Lord of the sea! thy potent....*N. Y. Col.*	50
Lord of the worlds above............*Watts*	744
Lord, send thy word, and let it..*Gibbons*	834
Lord, thou hast searched and seen. *Watts*	86
Lord, thou wilt hear me when I...*Watts*	885
Lord, 'tis a pleasant thing to......*Watts*	756
Lord, we come before thee now.....*Hart*	62
Lord, we confess our numerous...*Watts*	101
Lord, what a thoughtless......*Watts, alt.*	329
Lord, what our ears have heard..........	689
Lord, what was man when made..*Watts*	256
Lord, when together here we meet......	589
Lord, when we cast our.....*Dobell's Col.*	832
Loud hallelujahs to the Lord.......*Watts*	155
Love divine, all love excelling.*C. Wesley*	574
Love divine, how sweet the...*Reed's Col.*	448
Lo, what an entertaining sight.....*Watts*	592
Lo, what a pleasing sight............*Watts*	584
Majestic sweetness sits.......*Stennett*	247
Maker of all things, mighty Lord........	116
Man has a soul of vast desires.....*Watts*	564
May the grace of Christ our......*Newton*	954
Men of God, go take your stations.*Kelly*	717
Mercy, O thou Son of......*Rippon's App.*	397
Methinks the last great day is..*Needham*	934
Mid scenes of confusion and creature...	647
Mistaken souls, that dream of.....*Watts*	438
Mortals, awake, with angels join.*Medley*	150
Must friends and kindred droop...*Watts*	901
Must Jesus bear the cross alone....*Allen*	524
My dear Redeemer, and my Lord. *Watts*	103
My drowsy powers, why sleep ye. *Watts*	560
My Father, cheering name............*Steele*	474
My former hopes are fled..........*Cowper*	366
My God, and is thy table.*Doddridge, alt.*	697
My God, how endless is thy love..*Watts*	120
My God, my portion, and my love. *Watts*	461
My God, permit me not to be......*Watts*	547
My God, the spring of all my......*Watts*	459
My God, thy boundless...*Doddridge, alt.*	10
My gracious, loving Lord....................	369
My hope, my all, my Savior thou.........	548
My hope, my portion, and my..*N. Y. Col.*	70
My rising soul, with strong.....*Beddome*	546
My Savior, whom absent I love..*Cowper*	538
My song shall bless the Lord of.*Cowper*	88
My soul, be on thy guard..........*Heath*	498
My soul doth magnify the...*Vill. Hymns*	453
My soul, how lovely is the place.*Watts*	774
My soul lies cleaving to the dust..*Watts*	571
My soul, repeat his praise..........*Watts*	15

	HYMN
My soul, the awful hour will..*N. Y. Col.*	895
My soul, the minutes haste away.*Brown*	909
My spirit looks to God alone........*Watts*	511
My spirit sinks within me, Lord...*Watts*	517
No, I'll repine at death no more...*Watts*	921
Nor eye hath seen, nor ear hath...*Watts*	616
Not all the blood of beasts..........*Watts*	232
Not all the nobles of the earth...*Stennett*	467
Not by the law of innocence.........*Watts*	434
Not from relentless fate's dark.*Brist. Col.*	118
Not from the dust affliction grows. *Watts*	504
Not to the terrors of the Lord......*Watts*	751
Now begin the heavenly theme...*Rippon*	295
Now be that sacrifice surveyed.*N. Y. Col.*	187
Now, Father, Son, and Holy Ghost......	672
Now from the altar of our........*Hoskins*	886
Now, in the heat of youthful. *Watts, alt.*	326
Now I resolve, with all my heart..*Steele*	678
Now is the accepted time............*Dobell*	280
Now is the day of grace......*Sel. Hymns*	283
Now is the time, the accepted.....*Cowper*	300
Now let us raise our cheerful.......*Steele*	218
Now the shades of night are. *Vill. Hymns*	868
Now we hail the happy......*Vill. Hymns*	709
O Christian, remember the blood that...	179
O come, thou great and gracious power	445
O'er those gloomy hills of.......*Williams*	845
Of all the joys we mortals know...*Watts*	602
Of him who did salvation.......*(German)*	240
Oft as the bell with solemn toll..*Newton*	917
Oft in danger, oft in woe.........*K. White*	582
O God of Jacob, by whose hand...*Logan*	421
O God of Zion, from thy...*Rippon's Col.*	820
O God, our help in ages past......*Monty.*	127
O happy day, that stays my...*Doddridge*	677
Oh, bless the Lord, my soul!......*Watts*	17
Oh, could I find, from day...*Vill. Hymns*	556
Oh, could I find some peaceful.*Harrison*	505
Oh, could I speak the matchless..*Medley*	605
O hear me, Lord, on thee I call..*Merrick*	60
Oh for a closer walk with God...*Cowper*	534
Oh for a faith that will not........*Bathurst*	489
Oh for a glance of heavenly day...*Hart*	357
Oh for a heart to praise my...*C. Wesley*	349
Oh for a sight, a blissful sight.....*Watts*	217
Oh for a thousand tongues......*C. Wesley*	250
Oh for that tenderness of......*C. Wesley*	348
Oh, happy soul, that lives on high........	454
Oh, how divine, how sweet.......*Needham*	684
Oh, if my soul were formed for...*Watts*	352
Oh, it is joy in one to......*Ancient Hymns*	593
Oh, let me now repent.............*C. Wesley*	411
Oh, let me now repent.............*C. Wesley*	365
Oh, let my trembling soul be...*Bowring*	212
Oh, let our thoughts and wishes....*Steele*	622
Oh, may the power which melts.*Newton*	876
O Holy Ghost, descend, we......*Schirmer*	528
Oh, pour thy Spirit from on high..........	722
Oh, say no more there's nothing true...	649
Oh, speak that gracious word....*Newton*	457

INDEX OF FIRST LINES.

	HYMN
Oh that I had a seraph's fire..........*Kent*	239
Oh that I knew the secret place....*Watts*	519
Oh that I were as heretofore....*C. Wesley*	502
Oh that my load of sin were....*C. Wesley*	545
Oh that the Comforter would come.......	576
Oh that the Lord's salvation..........*Lyte*	841
Oh that the Lord would......*Vill. Hymns*	391
Oh that the Lord would guide.*Watts, alt.*	559
Oh, the delights, the heav'nly.*Watts, alt.*	220
Oh, what amazing words of..........*Medley*	276
Oh, what stupendous mercy......*Rippon*	603
Oh, when wilt thou my Savior be..........	384
Oh, where shall rest be........*Montgomery*	793
O Lord, and shall our fainting......*Scott*	822
O Lord, another day is flown....*K. White*	883
O Lord, my God, in mercy turn.*K. White*	360
O Lord, our languid souls..........*Newton*	55
O Lord, thy heav'nly grace.......*Oberlin*	679
O Love divine, how sweet thou.*C. Wesley*	606
Omnipresent God, whose aid..............	866
O my soul, what means this......*Fawcett*	525
Once more, before we part.. *Griffin's Sel.*	963
Once more, my soul, thy rising....*Watts*	114
Once more we keep the......*Dobell's Col.*	783
Once more we meet to pray..................	412
One there is above all others.....*Newton*	160
On Jordan's stormy banks I......*Stennett*	446
On Tabor's top the Savior........*Collyer*	169
On the brink of fiery ruin...........*Swain*	489
On thee, each morning, O my God.*Kipp*	891
On the mountain's top appearing..*Kelly*	767
On Thibet's snow-capt mountains........	842
On this sweet morn my Lord....*Berridge*	780
O sacred head, once wounded...*Gerhardt*	194
O Sion's King, we suppliant bow.........	764
O Spirit of the living God...*Montgomery*	833
O thou, before whose.........*Rippon's Col.*	725
O thou from whom all goodness..*Haweis*	441
O thou God of my salvation....*C. Wesley*	259
O thou that dost in secret see..............	392
O thou that hearest prayer.....*Campbell*	52
O thou that hearest the prayer..*Toplady*	943
O thou that hearest when sinners.*Watts*	393
O thou, whose beams serenely....*Collyer*	171
O thou, whose tender mercy hears.*Steele*	383
O thou who this mysterious head.........	691
O turn, great Ruler of the skies.*Merrick*	409
Our country is Immanuel's.....*Barbauld*	462
Our days, alas, our mortal days...*Watts*	626
Our Father throned above the sky.*Scott*	798
Our God is true, then he will....*Liebich*	530
Our heav'nly Father, hear...*Montgomery*	811
Our Lord is risen from the......*C. Wesley*	215
Our Sabbaths come so welcome on.......	796
Our souls by love together knit.....*Miller*	588
Our souls with pleasing..*Doddridge, alt.*	91
Our willing feet shall stand.*Montgomery*	738
O ye mourners, cease to............*Collyer*	938
O Zion, tune thy voice..........*Doddridge*	747
O Zion, when I think of thee.......*Kelly*	631
Pardoned through redeeming grace.......	668

	HYMN
Parent of good! thy works of...*Fawcett*	11
Parting soul, the flood awaits.*Edmeston*	989
Peace, troubled soul, whose........*Watts*	641
People of the living God.....*Montgomery*	587
Plunged in a gulf of dark...........*Watts*	243
Poor, weak, and worthless........*Newton*	410
Pour out thy Spirit from on.*Montgomery*	728
Praise, happy land, Jehovah's.*N.Y.Col.*	879
Praise ye the Lord, who..........*N.Y.Col.*	109
Prayer is the soul's sincere.*Montgomery*	806
Prayer was appointed to convey....*Hart*	800
Prepare us, Lord, to view...*Pratt's Col.*	480
Proclaim, said Christ, my.*J.Newton, alt.*	680
Quench not the Spirit of the...*C. Wesley*	271
Raise, thoughtless sinner......*Doddridge*	307
Raise your triumphant songs.....*Watts*	130
Rejoice in God, the word............*Swain*	500
Rejoice, the Lord is King.......*C. Wesley*	746
Rejoice, the Savior reigns...*Bristol Col.*	742
Rejoice, ye shining worlds on......*Watts*	213
Religion is the chief concern....*Fawcett*	572
Remember thy Creator..........*S.F. Smith*	289
Retire, vain world.....................*Watts*	74
Return, my roving heart......*Doddridge*	549
Return, O wanderer, return......*Collyer*	302
Rise, O my soul, pursue the....*Needham*	619
Rise, my soul, and stretch thy...*Cennick*	338
Rock of ages, cleft for me........*Toplady*	174
Roll on, thou mighty ocean........ ...*Noel*	734
Safely thro' another week...*Newton, alt.*	776
Salvation, oh, the joyful sound....*Watts*	252
Savior, canst thou love a.*Aldridge's Col.*	395
Savior, Father, Brother........*Doddridge*	669
Savior, visit thy plantation........*Newton*	819
Savior, when in dust to thee........*Grant*	196
Say, should we search the.*Rippon's Col.*	880
Say, sinner, hath a voice within.....*Hyde*	305
Searcher of hearts! to thee.*Montgomery*	49
Search not in yonder........*Sternhold, alt.*	210
See from Zion's sacred mountain..*Kelly*	317
See, gracious God, before thy........*Steele*	892
See how many lately bowing..............	846
See how the rising sun................*Scott*	864
See Israel's gentle Shepherd..*Doddridge*	683
See th' eternal Judge descending.........	949
See what a living stone............*Watts*	203
Self-righteous souls on......*Dobell's Col.*	258
Servant of God, well done...*Montgomery*	731
Shall atheists dare insult the......*Watts*	246
Shall man, O God of light and...*Dwight*	931
Shepherd of Israel, bend......*Doddridge*	723
Shepherd of Israel, thou......*Vill. Hymns*	831
Shepherd of Israel, thou......*Doddridge*	727
Shepherd of souls, if thou indeed........	733
Shine, mighty God, on Zion shine.*Watts*	836
Shine on our souls, eternal....*Doddridge*	36
Show pity, Lord, O Lord......*Watts, alt.*	389
Sing to the Lord, who loud...*Doddridge*	433
Sin has a thousand treacherous...*Watts*	311

INDEX OF FIRST LINES. 429

	HYMN
Sinner, art thou still secure?.....*Newton*	239
Sinner, is thy heart at rest...............	293
Sinner, rouse thee from thy... *Epis. Col.*	324
Sinners, the voice of God.........*Fawcett*	308
Sinners, this solemn truth........*Hoskins*	312
Sinners, turn, why will ye...... *C. Wesley*	294
Sinners, will ye scorn the message.*Allen*	316
Sinner, what has earth to show... *Urwick*	823
Sister, thou wast mild and.....*S.F. Smith*	937
Smote by the law, I'm justly ......*Strong*	354
So fades the lovely blooming.........*Steele*	914
Softly fades the twilight ray...*S.F. Smith*	777
Soldiers of Christ, arise......... *C. Wesley*	497
So let our lips and lives express... *Watts*	599
Some seraph, lend your heav'nly.. *Watts*	77
Songs of immortal praise belong.. *Watts*	93
Songs of praise the angels sang.........	47
Soon in the grave my flesh shall.. *Knapp*	926
Sound, sound the truth abroad..*Sabb. Col.*	850
Source of eternal joys divine. ......*Steele*	351
Sovereign Ruler, Lord of all ......*Raffles*	376
Sovereign Ruler of the skies......*Ryland*	449
Spirit divine, attend our prayer.....*Reed*	72
Spirit of holiness, look down...*Bathurst*	568
Spirit of truth, on this thy.....*N.Y. Col.*	784
Stand still, refulgent orb of.....*N.Y. Col.*	952
Stand up, my soul, shake off thy. *Watts*	514
Stay, thou insulted Spirit....... *C. Wesley*	408
Stern winter throws his icy ....*Steele*	826
Stoop down, my thoughts, that.... *Watts*	894
Stop, poor sinner, stop and.......*Newton*	337
Stretched on the cross, the. ....*Steele*	182
Stricken, smitten, and afflicted.....*Kelly*	192
Strive first of all thyself to know.........	313
Supreme High-priest, the pilgrim's	558
Sure the blest Comforter is nigh ...*Steele*	269
Sweet is the light of Sabbath..*Edmeston*	797
Sweet is the mem'ry of thy......... *Watts*	81
Sweet is the prayer whose holy stream..	809
Sweet is the scene where........*Barbauld*	918
Sweet is the thought, the promise.......	640
Sweet is the work, my God, my... *Watts*	789
Sweet the moments, rich in........*Beatty*	484
Sweet was the time when first I..*Newton*	499
Teach me the measure of my...... *Watts*	898
That awful day will surely come.. *Watts*	950
That awful hour will soon appear..*Steele*	910
That warning voice, O sinner...*Hastings*	380
The busy scenes of day are fled............	875
The Christian navigates a sea..............	516
The darkened sky, how thick.*Doddridge*	508
The day approaches, O my......*N.Y.Col.*	951
The day is past and gone. ......*N.Y. Col.*	863
The earth, where'er I turn mine..*Gellert*	95
Thee we adore, eternal......*Rippon's Col.*	134
Thee we adore, eternal Name ...... *Watts*	900
The gold and silver are the.*Griffin's Sel.*	855
The grave is now a favored.. *Vill. Hymns*	920
The Holy Comforter has come.............	273
The King of heav'n his table. *Doddridge*	298
The Lord, how fearful is his	42

	HYMN
The Lord in Zion placed his......... *Watts*	750
The Lord is ris'n indeed. ....*Kelly*	204
The Lord my pasture shall.......*Addison*	129
The Lord my Shepherd is.......... *Watts*	123
The Lord of earth and sky.....*C. Wesley*	887
The Lord of life with glory...*N.Y. Col.*	224
The Lord our God is full of......*K. White*	84
The Lord will happiness divine..*Cowper*	346
The Lord, who truly knows........*Newton*	810
The man is ever blest................ *Watts*	320
The mind was formed to mount. ...*Steele*	579
The morning flowers display...*S. Wesley*	913
The morning light is..............*S.F. Smith*	843
The new-born child of gospel....*Cowper*	518
The peace which God alone........*Newton*	961
The prodigal with streaming ...... *Watts*	403
The promise of my Father's love. *Watts*	704
The promises I sing....... ......*Doddridge*	743
There is a fountain filled with.....*Cowper*	241
There is a glorious world on high..*Steele*	465
There is a house not made with ... *Watts*	925
There is a land of pure delight.... *Watts*	614
There is an hour of hallowed.*Union Col.*	650
There is an hour of peaceful......*Tappan*	648
There is a place of sacred rest.*Turnbull*	630
There is a pure and peaceful wave.........	637
There is a voice of sov'reign....... *Watts*	345
The saints on earth and those.*Doddridge*	590
The Savior calls, let ev'ry ear...... *Steele*	296
The spacious firmament on.......*Addison*	90
The Spirit breathes upon the.....*Cowper*	659
The Spirit in our hearts...*Epis. Col., alt.*	279
The swift declining day........*Doddridge*	281
The time is short, the season....*Hoskins*	334
The wandering star and..........*Beddome*	540
This is the day the Lord hath...... *Watts*	778
This is the feast of heav'nly...*Cowper*	690
This place is holy ground ...*Montgomery*	945
This world that we so highly prize.......	656
Thou art my portion, O my God... *Watts*	420
Thou art, O God, a Spirit..*Rippon's Col.*	85
Thou art the way, to thee alone...*Doane*	249
Though earthly shepherds.....*Doddridge*	716
Though nature's voice you......*N.Y. Col.*	916
Thou God of glorious majesty.*C. Wesley*	341
Thou God of sovereign grace...*Campbell*	688
Thou great, mysterious God ...*C. Wesley*	578
Thou hidden God, for whom I..*C. Wesley*	355
Thou Lord of all above.........*Beddome*	413
Thou Lord of all the worlds...*Doddridge*	451
Thou man of griefs, remember me.......	390
Thou only Sovereign of my heart..*Steele*	430
Thou Shepherd of Israel.........*C. Wesley*	513
Thou sweet gliding Kedron....*De Fleury*	178
Thrice holy Lord, I love thy truth.......	551
Thro' sorrow's night and.........*K. White*	927
Through all the various....*Rippon's Col.*	97
Through shades and............*Montgomery*	495
Thus far on life's perplexing...*N.Y. Col.*	128
Thus far the Lord hath led me on. *Watts*	862
Thus spake the Savior, when..*N.Y. Col.*	707
Thy ceaseless, unexhausted....*C. Wesley*	245

INDEX OF FIRST LINES.

HYMN	
Thy presence, everlasting......*Doddridge*	960
Thy presence, gracious God......*Fawcett*	65
Thy way, O God, is in the sea...*Fawcett*	108
Thy ways, O Lord, with wise.. .....*Seele*	99
Time is winging us away. ....*Burton*	339
'Tis a point I long to know........*Newton*	533
'Tis by the faith of joys to come., *Watts*	446
"'Tis finished !" so the Savior..*Stennett*	181
'Tis midnight, and on Olive's...*K. White*	180
'Tis my happiness below............*Cowper*	531
'Tis sweet to rest in lively hope. *Toplady*	628
'Tis wisdom, mercy, love divine....*Steele*	100
To calm the sorrows of the mind...*Jervis*	105
To God the only wise................*Watts*	19
To God, the universal King......*Stennett*	21
To languish for his native air..............	642
To our Redeemer's glorious..........*Steele*	138
To praise the ever-bounteous.....*Rippon*	126
To thee let my first off'rings rise.*Rippon*	37
To thee, O God, my prayer....*N. Y. Col.*	557
To thee this temple we devote......*Scott*	753
To thy pastures fair and large...*Merrick*	609
To thy temple we repair......*Montgomery*	63
To your Creator God...................*Steele*	51
'Twas by an order from the..........*Watts*	658
'Twas for our sake, eternal... *Watts, alt.*	257
'Twas God who hurled the. ....*Mart. Col.*	94
'Twas on that dreadful, doleful.... *Watts*	696
United prayers ascend to thee.............	670
Upward I lift mine eyes.. ....*Newton*	53
Wake, O my soul, and hail. *Vestry Songs*	153
Walk in the light, so shalt thou..*Barton*	666
Weary sinner, keep thine eyes......*Anon*	200
We bid thee welcome in the...*Montgomery*	726
Welcome, sweet day of rest........ *Watts*	792
Welcome the hope of Israel's......*Merrick*	154
Welcome, thou well-beloved of... *Godwin*	675
Welcome, welcome, dear...... *Vill. Hymns*	488
Welcome, ye hopeful heirs.. *Vill. Hymns*	701
We lift our hearts to thee.........*Stennett*	18
Well, the Redeemer's gone.......... *Watts*	230
We sing th' almighty power of...*Minstrel*	3
We sing the wise, the......*N. Y. Col.*	234
We've no abiding city here..........*Kelly*	632
What are possessions, fame...*Blackmore*	380
What cheering words are these......*Kent*	473
What could your Redeemer. ...*C. Wesley*	292
What equal honors shall we raise. *Watts*	214
What is our God, or what his...... *Watts*	32
What is the thing of greatest.....*Montg.*	92
What language now salutes the.*Hoskins*	274
What mean these jealousies and.*Stogden*	431
What shall I render to my God?... *Watts*	682
What sinners value I resign.. ...... *Watts*	633
What strange perplexities arise...*Davies*	553
What thousands never knew the.*Cowper*	424
What various hindrances we......*Cowper*	802
What various, lovely characters............	170
When all thy mercies, O my......*Addison*	482
When any turn from Zion's way..*Newton*	536
When at a distance, Lord......*Doddridge*	167
When bending o'er the brink of..*Collyer*	899
When blooming youth is snatched..*Steele*	907
When darkness long has veiled...*Cowper*	542
When death appears before my.....*Steele*	902
When earthly joys glide swift away......	109
When faith beholds the.. ...*Dobell's Col.*	634
When gloomy thoughts and......*N. Y. Col.*	472
When God revealed his gracious... *Watts*	452
When God's own people stand....*Fawcett*	103
When I can read my title clear. ... *Watts*	625
When in the light of faith divine.. *Watts*	419
When Israel forth from Egypt went........	87
When Israel thro' the desert....*Beddome*	652
When I survey thy wondrous ...... *Watts*	185
When Jesus dwelt in mortal. ...*Gibbons*	854
When languor and disease........*Toplady*	893
When life's tempestuous.........*N. Y. Col.*	942
When, Lord, to this our.........*N. Y. Col.*	888
When marshalled on the..........*K. White*	156
When mortal man resigns his breath....	121
When musing sorrow weeps the......*Noel*	615
When, O dear Jesus, when shall.*Cennick*	785
When on Sinai's top I see.....*Montgomery*	197
When overwhelmed with grief...... *Watts*	406
When Paul was parted from his.*Newton*	715
When rising from the bed of......*Addison*	382
When shall the voice of......*Pratt's Col.*	844
When shall we all meet........*Sel. Hymns*	958
When sickness shakes the..*Enfield's Col.*	896
When streaming from the..*Lord Glenelg*	577
When the poor leper's case I read........	314
When verdure clothes the fertile...*Steele*	45
Where are the dead ?—In....*Montgomery*	911
Wherefore should man, frail.......*Enfield*	601
Where is my God? does he retire..*Steele*	799
Where shall the tribes of Adam... *Watts*	253
Where shall we sinners hide our... *Watts*	440
Where two or three, with sweet.*Stennett*	66
While my Redeemer's near. ....*Steele*	124
While on the verge of life I...*Doddridge*	635
While shepherds watched their...... *Tate*	147
While thee I seek............*Mrs. Williams*	807
While to the grave our friends........*Steele*	904
While with ceaseless course the..*Newton*	867
Who are these in bright......*Montgomery*	611
Who is this that comes from...*N. Y. Col.*	161
Why do we mourn departing. ...... *Watts*	903
Why should a living man. ....*Stennett*	520
Why sinks my weak, desponding...*Steele*	515
Why should our tears in sorrow flow. ...	924
Why should the children of a...... *Watts*	479
Why should this earth delight us.. *Watts*	621
Why should we start and fear to... *Watts*	915
Why will ye lavish out your...*Doddridge*	287
Wide, ye heavenly gates, unfold.....*Lyte*	612
Will the pard'ning God despise.............	375
With ecstasy of joy...............*Doddridge*	745
With eye impartial, heaven's...*Needham*	79
With guilt oppressed, bowed down with	386
With heav'nly power, O...*Radford's Col.*	709
With humble faith and......*Dobell's Col.*	762

	HYMN		HYMN
With joy we hail the sacred day....*Lyte*	775	Ye messengers of Christ............*Voke*	730
With melting heart and weeping.*Fawcett*	363	Ye saints, proclaim abroad........*Ryland*	140
With tears of anguish I lament..*Stennett*	350	Yes, my native land, I love...*S.F. Smith*	847
With thy pure dews and rains..*Pierpont*	848	Ye sons of men, in sacred....*Pope's Col.*	23
Would you win a soul to God.*Hammond*	198	Yes, there are joys that...*Ch. Psalmody*	597
		Yes, we trust the day is breaking.*Kelly*	768
Ye followers of the......*Birmingham Col.*	694	Ye trembling souls, dismiss.....*Beddome*	117
Ye glittering toys of earth, adieu..*Steele*	463	Ye worlds of light that roll so..*Beddome*	172
Ye hearts with youthful vigor.*Doddridge*	301	Ye wretched, hungry, starving.....*Steele*	297
Ye humble souls, approach your...*Steele*	5		
Ye humble souls that seek.....*Doddridge*	208	Zeal is that pure and heavenly...*Newton*	600
Ye men and angels, witness......*Beddome*	702	Zion stands with hills surrounded.*Kelly*	771

CHANTS AND ANTHEMS.

	PAGE		PAGE
Amen, Hallelniu........................	359	I was glad when they said...........	351
Arise, O Lord, into thy rest........	358	I will arise........................	375
Blessed be the God and Father..........	362	I will lift up mine eyes.............	354
Blessed be the Lord God of Israel.......	341	I will praise thee...................	353
Blessed is the man................	351	Lift up your heads, O ye gates........	364
Bless the Lord, O my soul...........	346	Like as a father pitieth his children......	347
Calm was the night.................	390	Lord, now lettest thou thy servant......	360
Christ, being raised from the dead.......	363	Lord of heaven, and earth, and ocean...	416
Christ the Lord is risen to-day.........	412	Lord, thou art God...............	365
Daughter of Zion, awake............	402	Lord, thou hast been our dwelling-place	372
Dear Refuge of my weary soul...........	376	Man that is born of woman............	373
Except the Lord build the house	370	Make a joyful noise. &c...........	339, 340
Father, I know thy ways are just........	376	My soul doth magnify the Lord...........	350
For other foundation can no may lay....	370	O all ye works of the Lord..............	378
For unto us a child is born.............	359	Oh, come, let us sing unto the Lord	334, 335
Friend after friend departs................	377	Oh, give thanks unto the Lord......	371
Glory be to God on high...............	336, 337	Oh, how lovely is Zion..............	384
Glory be to thee......................	344	Oh, sing unto the Lord................	344
Glory be to the Father and to the Son...	340, 341, 344, 356	Oh, sing unto the Lord a new song......	359
		Our Father, who art in heaven........	354
Glory to God in the highest...........	387	Out of the depths have I cried...........	377
God be merciful unto us................	348	Praise God, from whom all blessings flow	388
God is our refuge and strength.........	356	Praise the Lord, praise the Lord........	380
Great and marvelous are thy works.....	359	Praise the name of the Lord...........	365
Great is the Lord, and greatly to be.....	396	Praise waiteth for thee, O God...........	349
Hark! the herald angels sing...........	414	Praise ye the Lord...................	358
Have mercy upon me. O God........	362	Praise ye the Lord, give thanks........	394
He shall come down like rain...........	299	Reproach hath broken my heart.	363
He was wounded for our transgressions..	363	Sing unto God......................	406
Holy, Holy, Holy, Lord God Almighty	342, 368	The earth is the Lord's.............	357
" " " of hosts...	312, 398	The law of the Lord is perfect.........	355
" " " of Sabaoth..	407, 408, 418.	The Lord is my Shepherd..............	355
		The Lord, the universal King...........	410
How amiable are thy tabernacles.........	373	The wilderness and the solitary place...	372
How beautiful upon the mountains......	372	This is the day which the Lord hath.....	363
I believe in God......................	368	Thy praise. O Lord, our thankful songs	383
I cried unto God with my voice.........	352	Thy way, O God, is in the sanctuary....	353
If God be for us, who can be against us	364	We give thee thanks, O Lord God.......	359
If it had not been the Lord............	369	We have thought of thy loving-kindness	373
In the beginning was the Word........	360	We praise thee, O God.............	338
It is a good thing to give thanks.........	345	When the Lord turned again the........	369

INDEX OF TUNES—ALPHABETICAL.

		PAGE
Aithlone	German	121, 322
All-Saints	Knapp	176, 250
Alway	Woodbury	260, 191
America	Handel	291
Amsterdam	Nares	120
Ariel	Mason	168, 209, 287
Arlington	Arne	125, 165, 307
Athens	Giardini	46, 266
Avon	Scottish	118, 173
Averno	Hayes	136, 188
Aylesbury	Green	320
Balerma	Wilson	178, 316
Barby	Tansur	26, 158
Bavaria	German	70, 281
Benevento	Webbe	105, 297
Blendon	Giardini	148, 219
Brattle Street	Pleyel	216, 277
Brighton	English	144, 199
Brower	Bethune	170, 227
Calvary	Jenks	78
Cana		65
Chemnitz	German	49, 234
Chestnut Street	Oliver	127, 206
China	Swan	310
Christmas	Handel	55, 214
Clarendon	Tucker	32, 111, 193
Come, ye Discons.	Webbe	117
Communion		60, 207, 241
Coronation	Holden	81
Coventry	Howard	192, 215
Cowper	Mason	88, 259
Craven		205, 325
Creation	Haydn	56, 96
Crucifix	Greek	71
Devizes	Tucker	20, 164, 228
Dorchester	Stanley	58, 212
Dover	English	45, 130
Duke Street	Hatton	16, 78, 274
Dundee	Scottish	238, 286, 311
Dwight		323
Eastburn	Meineke	32, 110, 172
Edyfield	Latrobe	115, 203
Effingham	English	189, 282
Elias	Mozart	24, 47, 169
Elparan	Shultz	66, 273, 295
Endor	Marsh	147
Eshtamoa	T. B. Mason	104, 211
Eternity	Seiss	123
Federal Street	Oliver	87, 208, 248
Funeral Thought	Smith	308
Gerar		251, 296
Gerhard	German	68, 275
Give	Griggs	42, 292

		PAGE
Glasgow	English	174, 312
Greenfields		185
Hamburg	Gregorian	34, 100, 319
Heath		124, 197
Heber	Kingsley	106, 220
Hendon	Malan	23, 75, 155
Henry	Pond	54, 99, 330
Heyl	L. Heyl	182
Hingham		93, 313
Hinton	German	119, 222, 280
Hollaz	German	59, 138, 321
Home		224
Hotham	Madan	63, 139
Howard	Mrs. Cuthbert	196, 306
How Calm	Hastings	77, 122
Illa		154, 233
Inverness	Mason	101, 202
Iosco	John Huss	62, 161
Irish	Williams	283, 303
Jerusalem	Arranged by Seiss	213
Laban	Mason	84, 162
Lanesboro'	English	21, 246, 258
Lanesville	Osgood	186, 293
Lenox	Edson	53, 82, 305
Lischer	German	52, 256
Litchfield		201
Louvan	Taylor	27, 97, 263
Lurman	Meineke	160, 271, 318
Luther's Hymn	Luther	37
Luton	Burder	29, 190
Martin	Marsh	72, 183
McEvers	Meineke	143, 171, 243
Mear	Luther	242, 309
Melancthon	Seiss	48
Mendon	German	38, 270, 300
Meribah	Mason	12, 200, 252
Migdol	Mason	79, 232
Missionary Hymn	Mason	64, 253, 288
Munich	German	67, 315
Naomi	Mason	69, 239
Newcourt	Bond	13, 85
Nuremburg	Bach	145, 267, 328
Oberlin	Neukomm	240, 314
Old Hundredth	Luther	1, 240, 245, 294, 329
Oliphant		94, 106
Orford		128, 279
Orland	Arnold	30, 137
Ortonville	Hastings	90, 184, 235
Osgood	Ritter	113, 180
Otto	Oliver	83, 166, 265
Palestrina	Mazzinghi	221

INDEX OF TUNES—ALPHABETICAL—CHANTS AND ANTHEMS. 433

	PAGE		PAGE
Parker.........Jackson.........	98, 236	St. Martin's......Tansur......	140, 223
Park Street......Venua......	35, 57, 262	Stonefield......Stanley......	92, 284, 218
Passaic......	103, 289	St. Thomas......Williams......	51, 278
Phuvah......Vulpius......	76, 134, 317	Swanwick......Lucas......	156, 280
Pleyel's Hymn....Pleyel......	28, 231		
Portland......Oakley......	187	Tallis' Hymn......Tallis......	298
		Teleman......Teleman......	149, 255
Ripley......Gregorian......	95, 198	Thatcher......Handel......	114, 195
Rosedale......Root......	299, 175	Trias......	126, 152
Rosefield......Malan......	132, 210		
Rothwell......Tansur......	86, 220	Uxbridge......Mason......	108, 150
Schirmer......German......	181	Ward......Scottish...	18, 44, 116, 285
Schneider......Bradbury......	15	Warwick......Stanley......	80, 36
Shirland......Stanley......	100, 272, 331	Watchman......Leach......	74, 254
Sicilian Hymn...Sicilian......	167, 326, 247	Wells......Holdroyd......	102, 201
Siloam......Woodbury...	89, 204, 302	Windham......Read......	142
Silver Street......I. Smith......	14, 237	Woodland......Gould......	225
St. Ann's......Croft......	50, 159	Woodstock......Dutton......	91, 276, 146
Sterling......Harrison......	194, 244		
Stephen's......Jones......	40, 107, 179	Zanesville......	22, 230
St. Helen's......Jennings......	301	Zebulon......Mason......	25, 257, 304
St. John's......English......	10, 268	Zion......Hastings......	290, 324, 264

CHANTS AND ANTHEMS.

	PAGE		PAGE
Aliud Fundamentum......	370	Lamentation......Old German.	400
Beatus vir......	351	Levavi oculos meos......	354
Burial Service......	373	Letabit deserta......	372
Benedic, anima mea......	346, 347	Lex Domini......	355
Benedicite, omnia......	378, 379	Lovely Zion......Romberg......	38½
Benedictus......	341	Lord of Heaven......Mendelsohn..	418
Bonum est confiteri......	345	Lord's Prayer......	354
Cantate Domino......	344, 359	Magnificat......	350
Christmas......Mozart......	414	Miserere Mei Deus......	362
Christmas Night......Kochersperger.	390	Nisi Dominus......	370
Confitemini Domino......	371	Nisi quia Dominus......	369
Confitebor tibi......	353	Nunc Dimittis......	360
Daughter of Zion......From Mason.	402	Pleading for mercy......	376
De Profundis......	377	Praise God......Sharp......	388
Deus Misereatur......	348	Praise the Lord......De Monti...	380
Deus noster Refugium......	356	Praise ye the Lord......Schultz......	394
Domini est terra......	357	Pentecost......	365
Domino Refulgium......	372	Quam dilecta......	373
Easter......Mozart......	412	Resignation......	377
Gloria in Excelsis......	326	Sanctus......Haydn......	407
Gloria Patri......	340, 341, 343, 356, 357	Sanctus et Gloria......Atwood.	398, 418
Gloria tibi Domine......	343	Sanctus et Hosanna......	408
Glory to God......Kreutzer......	387	Sanctus Dominus Deus......	342
Gratias Agimus......	359	Sing unto God......	406
Great is the Lord......Calcott......	396	Surge, Domine......	358
God our Refuge......	376	Suscepimus Misericordiam......	373
Halleluias......	359	Te Deum......	338
He shall come down......Portogallo...	399	Thanksgiving Hymn......Kochersperger.	383
In Convertendo......	369	The Lord, the Universal...Hummel......	410
I will arise......Cecil......	395	The Creed......	368
Jubilate Deo......	339, 340	Thy will be done......	376
Lætatus sum......	351	Trinitas......	368
Laudate Domini......	358	Venite, Exultimus Domino......	335

28

INDEX OF TUNES—METRICAL.

L.M.

	PAGE
All-Saints	176, 250
Alway	191, 260
Averno	136, 188
Blendon	148, 219
Brower	170, 227
Chemnitz	49, 234
Communion	60, 207, 241
Creation	56, 96
Duke Street	16, 78, 274
Effingham	189, 282
Elparan	66, 273, 295
Federal Street	87, 248, 208
Gerhard	68, 296
Glasgow	174, 312
Hamburg	34, 109, 319
Hingham	93, 313
Illa	154, 233
Iosco	62, 161
Lanesville	186, 293
Litchfield	261
Louvan	27, 97, 263
Lurman	160, 271, 318
Luton	29, 190
Mendon	38, 270, 300
Migdol	79, 232
Munich	67, 315
Oberlin	249, 314
Old Hundred	1, 235, 240, 294, 329
Orford	128, 279
Orland	39, 137
Park Street	35, 57, 262
Rosedale	175, 299
Rothwell	86, 220
Sterling	194, 244
Stonefield	218, 92, 284
Tallis' Hymn	298
Uxbridge	108, 150
Ward	44, 18, 116, 285
Wells	102, 201
Windham	142

C.M.

	PAGE
Arlington	125, 165, 307
Athens	46, 266
Avon	118, 173
Balerma	178, 316
Barby	26, 158
Brattle Street (double)	216, 277
Chestnut Street	127, 206
China	310
Christmas	55, 214
Clarendon	111, 32, 193
Coronation	81
Coventry	192, 215
Cowper	88, 259
Craven	205, 325
Devizes	20, 164, 228
Dorchester	58, 212
Dundee	286, 238, 311
Eastburn	32, 110, 172
Funeral Thought	308
Give	42, 292
Heath	124, 197
Heber	106, 229
Henry	54, 99, 330
Howard	196, 306
Irish	283, 303
Jerusalem	213
Lanesboro	21, 258
Mear	242, 309
Naomi	69, 239
Ortonville	184, 90, 235
Parker	98, 236
Phuvah	76, 134, 317
Siloam	89, 204, 302
St. Ann's	50, 159
Stephens	40, 107, 179
St. John's	10, 268
St. Martin's	140, 223
Swanwick	156, 280
Trias	126, 152
Warwick	36, 80
Woodland	225
Woodstock	276, 91, 146
Zanesville	22, 230

S.M.

	PAGE
Aylesbury	320
Dover	45, 130
Gerar	251, 296
Inverness	101, 202
Laban	84, 162
McEvers	143, 171, 243

INDEX OF TUNES—METRICAL.

	PAGE
Schneider	15
Shirland	100, 272, 331
Silver Street	14, 237
St. Thomas	51, 278
Thatcher	114, 195
Watchman	74, 254

C.M.P.

Aithlone	121, 322
Ariel	168, 287, 209
How Calm	77, 122
Meribah	12, 200, 252

L.M. 6 LINES.

Brighton	144, 199
Elias	24, 47, 169
Newcourt	13, 85
Palestrina	221
St. Helen's	303

L.M. (DOUBLE.)

Greenfields	185
Portland	187

H.M.

Lenox	53, 82, 305
Lischer	52, 256
Zebulon	25, 257, 304

11s.

Cana	65
Hinton	119, 222, 280
Home	224

10s AND 11s.

Come, ye Disconsolate	117

8s AND 7s.

Bavaria (6 lines)	70, 281
Hollaz	59, 138, 321
Oliphant (6 lines)	94, 106

	PAGE
Osgood	113, 180
Otto	86, 166, 265
Ripley (double)	95, 198
Sicilian Hymn	167, 326, 247
Zion (6 lines)	264, 290, 324

SEVENS.

Benevento (double)	105, 297
Calvary (6 lines)	73
Edyfield	115, 203
Eshtamoa	104, 211
Hendon	23, 155, 75
Hotham (double)	63, 139
Martin (double)	72, 183
Nuremburg (6 lines)	145, 267, 328
Pleyel's Hymn	28, 231
Rosefield	132, 210
Teleman (double)	149, 255

7s AND 6s.

Amsterdam (double)	120
Crucifix (double)	71
Missionary Hymn (double)	64, 288, 253
Passaic (double)	103, 289

7s, 6s, AND 8s.

Endor	147

6s AND 4s.

America	291

6s AND 8s.

Dwight	323

PECULIAR.

Eternity	123
Heyl	182
Luther's Hymn	37
Melancthon	48
Schirmer	181

INDEX OF NUMBERS TO HYMNS.

AS CHANGED FROM THE OLD ARRANGEMENT TO THE NEW.

To find a Hymn in this book when it is announced from the ordinary hymn book, refer in the first column to the number given, and the figures opposite will give the number of the Hymn in this book.

OLD.	NEW.	OLD.	NEW.	OLD.	NEW.	OLD.	NEW.	OLD.	NEW.
1	651	50	14	100	131	148	203	199	301
2	653	51	9	101	134	150	204	200	299
3	657	52	7	102	152	151	213	201	272
4	662	53	17	104	144	152	206	202	402
5	658	56	4	105	145	153	224	203	302
7	162	57	11	106	139	154	214	204	304
8	652	58	8	107	148	155	215	205	408
9	660	59	90	108	146	156	230	206	404
10	659	60	3	109	151	157	225	207	314
11	663	61	89	110	143	158	216	208	396
12	246	62	95	111	88	159	218	209	494
13	30	63	813	112	140	161	156	210	458
14	85	64	92	114	163	162	171	211	495
15	77	65	44	115	157	163	172	212	320
16	32	66	42	116	158	164	174	213	565
18	27	67	26	117	164	165	160	214	405
19	28	68	97	118	167	166	410	215	812
20	39	69	104	119	168	167	398	216	332
21	34	71	102	120	165	168	173	217	303
22	35	72	122	121	249	169	176	218	285
23	94	73	118	122	180	172	267	221	291
25	86	74	105	123	183	173	268	222	573
26	80	75	106	124	189	174	54	223	626
27	93	76	53	125	182	175	70	224	570
28	41	78	111	126	192	176	270	225	564
29	78	79	129	127	257	177	269	226	279
30	79	80	36	128	745	178	552	227	334
31	743	81	107	129	185	179	559	228	408
32	245	82	108	130	278	181	13	229	305
33	10	83	103	131	244	182	280	230	300
34	81	84	99	132	188	183	315	231	935
35	91	85	130	133	190	184	275	232	941
36	15	86	100	135	233	185	292	233	909
37	23	87	110	136	221	186	880	234	306
38	83	88	117	137	231	187	316	235	307
39	21	90	387	138	181	188	277	236	310
40	22	91	311	139	193	189	251	237	282
41	6	92	256	140	219	190	274	239	325
42	33	93	554	141	202	191	276	240	337
44	1	94	329	142	187	192	286	241	345
45	5	95	419	143	483	193	284	242	327
46	25	96	621	144	186	194	296	243	308
47	12	97	330	145	207	195	298	244	287
48	51	98	323	146	208	196	317	245	344
49	46	99	132	147	205	198	207	247	894

INDEX OF NUMBERS TO HYMNS. 437

OLD.	NEW.	OLD.	NEW.	OLD.	NEW.	OLD.	NEW.	OLD.	NEW.
248	341	311	265	376	804	444	531	516	706
249	365	312	433	377	543	445	509	517	690
250	348	313	437	378	519	446	599	518	705
251	349	314	446	379	556	447	632	519	691
252	411	315	236	380	537	448	631	520	698
253	357	316	475	381	563	450	424	522	694
254	362	317	258	382	491	451	490	523	700
255	346	318	484	383	546	452	487	524	693
256	373	320	232	384	544	453	447	525	695
257	347	321	260	385	561	454	462	526	697
258	374	322	237	386	460	455	526	528	266
259	350	323	438	387	607	457	516	529	758
260	358	324	606	388	555	458	504	530	740
261	359	325	486	389	650	459	507	531	761
262	356	326	605	390	602	460	508	532	835
263	409	327	241	391	448	461	521	533	770
264	366	328	264	392	420	462	501	534	742
265	377	329	226	393	807	463	498	535	828
266	360	330	135	394	798	464	520	536	834
267	352	331	548	395	510	466	625	537	840
268	854	332	141	396	499	467	636	538	845
269	463	333	238	397	533	468	478	539	717
270	395	334	254	398	500	469	119	540	827
271	361	335	253	399	525	470	627	541	829
272	363	336	262	401	505	471	513	542	832
273	390	337	250	402	558	472	459	543	712
274	389	338	191	403	515	473	511	544	714
275	393	339	243	404	542	474	628	546	766
276	394	340	289	405	536	475	261	548	760
277	353	342	444	407	309	476	446	549	708
278	369	343	562	408	506	477	642	550	718
279	422	344	259	409	540	479	635	552	730
280	396	345	240	410	560	483	800	553	880
281	351	346	227	411	514	484	802	554	831
282	415	347	137	412	413	485	810	555	719
283	376	348	242	413	399	486	808	556	724
284	392	349	248	414	535	487	806	558	198
285	557	350	295	415	497	489	478	559	733
286	461	351	729	416	534	490	788	560	665
287	477	352	530	417	401	491	787	561	720
288	355	353	188	418	502	492	66	562	567
289	566	354	695	419	539	493	55	564	715
290	381	355	450	420	541	494	64	565	707
291	367	356	451	421	551	495	69	566	721
292	368	357	492	422	512	496	68	567	713
293	578	358	489	423	574	497	62	568	711
294	375	359	464	424	545	499	736	569	710
295	19	360	452	425	456	500	744	570	723
296	414	361	470	426	547	501	750	571	726
297	416	362	252	427	549	502	756	572	627
298	382	363	453	428	474	503	755	574	709
299	383	364	469	429	449	504	749	575	725
300	558	365	466	430	601	505	786	576	732
301	384	366	518	431	596	506	789	577	906
302	391	367	471	432	583	507	778	578	716
303	428	368	467	433	580	508	689	579	820
304	429	369	454	434	584	509	683	580	819
305	488	370	472	435	418	510	685	582	821
306	430	371	465	436	600	511	680	583	684
307	436	372	455	437	421	512	668	585	767
308	407	373	248	438	504	513	692	586	769
309	431	374	484	441	426	514	696	587	768
310	432	375	805	442	423	515	690	588	825

INDEX OF NUMBERS TO HYMNS.

OLD.	NEW.	OLD.	NEW.	OLD.	NEW.	OLD.	NEW.	OLD.	NEW.
589	673	670	783	757	954	837	799	916	763
590	674	673	121	759	960	838	871	917	678
591	675	677	895	767	43	839	386	918	702
592	701	681	896	768	63	840	880	919	587
593	764	683	893	769	748	841	199	920	582
594	857	685	879	770	47	845	222	921	682
595	858	691	892	771	31	846	184	922	677
596	888	692	876	772	87	848	481	923	442
597	55	696	899	773	38	849	441	924	532
598	2	697	911	774	82	851	482	925	527
599	24	698	793	775	48	852	322	926	681
601	45	699	917	777	177	854	338	927	679
603	126	701	897	778	318	855	123	928	762
605	101	702	898	780	166	856	290	929	739
606	826	703	900	781	406	857	618	930	30
607	859	704	910	782	170	858	529	931	753
608	860	705	912	783	124	859	638	932	867
609	98	706	913	784	169	860	201	933	113
610	887	707	902	785	178	861	197	935	782
612	120	708	915	788	194	863	598	936	792
613	861	709	936	789	235	864	313	937	791
614	114	710	901	790	801	865	445	938	781
615	125	711	916	791	247	866	439	939	873
616	112	712	904	792	196	867	468	940	891
617	870	713	914	793	784	869	620	941	577
618	864	714	905	794	528	870	619	942	40
619	115	715	907	795	61	871	958	944	882
620	37	717	919	796	370	872	040	945	874
621	871	718	903	797	57	873	643	946	865
622	18	719	923	798	67	874	644	947	875
623	808	720	942	799	479	875	811	949	667
624	795	721	925	800	568	876	669	950	661
625	796	722	908	801	271	877	670	954	289
626	780	723	920	802	52	878	676	957	878
627	779	724	918	803	576	879	703	958	496
628	776	725	922	804	833	880	175	959	127
629	862	726	333	805	58	882	842	961	116
630	872	727	921	806	962	883	844	963	737
631	869	728	633	807	16	885	836	967	771
632	866	729	927	808	816	886	734	968	880
633	883	730	928	810	814	887	847	969	29
634	881	731	947	811	890	888	841	971	877
635	863	732	948	813	572	889	846	973	571
637	886	733	933	814	331	891	754	974	71
638	785	734	934	815	342	892	752	975	522
639	790	735	96	816	212	893	759	978	655
640	884	737	940	817	328	894	838	980	656
642	885	738	614	820	293	895	20	981	945
647	581	739	613	822	200	896	590	983	926
649	586	740	220	823	336	897	588	984	937
650	589	741	634	824	294	898	735	986	930
652	686	742	616	825	335	899	585	989	931
653	326	744	751	826	283	900	722	993	622
654	671	745	56	827	281	902	765	994	648
657	688	746	932	828	324	905	731	995	650
658	687	747	639	829	569	907	823	997	647
659	672	748	610	830	340	908	412	998	687
661	603	749	617	831	385	909	824	999	645
662	597	751	321	832	417	910	74	1000	630
663	855	752	953	833	265	911	822	1001	944
664	854	753	959	834	440	912	288	1002	611
665	852	754	961	835	379	914	476	1003	629
666	851	756	963	836	372	915	843	1005	957

www.ingramcontent.com/pod-product-compliance
Lightning Source LLC
Chambersburg PA
CBHW020532300426
44111CB00008B/638